THE CONSTRUCTION LAW LIBRARY FROM ASPEN LAW & BUSINESS

SOFTWARE PATENTS

SUBSCRIPTION NOTICE

This Aspen Law & Business product is updated on a periodic basis with supplements to reflect important changes in the subject matter. If you purchased this product directly from Aspen Law & Business, we have already recorded your subscription for the update service.

If, however, you purchased this product from a bookstore and wish to receive future updates and revised or related volumes billed separately with a 30-day examination review, please contact our Customer Service Department at 1-800-234-1660, or send your name, company name (if applicable), address, and the title of the product to:

ASPEN LAW & BUSINESS
A Division of Aspen Publishers, Inc.
7201 McKinney Circle
Frederick, MD 21701

SOFTWARE PATENTS

GREGORY A. STOBBS

Harness, Dickey & Pierce, P.L.C.
Troy, Michigan

ASPEN LAW & BUSINESS

This publication is designed to provide accurate and
authoritative information in regard to the subject
matter covered. It is sold with the understanding that
the publisher is not engaged in rendering legal, accounting,
or other professional services. If legal advice or other
expert assistance is required, the services of a competent
professional person should be sought.

Library of Congress Cataloging-in-Publication Data

Stobbs, Gregory A.
    Software patents / Gregory A. Stobbs.
        p.   cm.
    Includes bibliographical references.
    ISBN 0-471-06324-X (cloth : acid-free paper)
    1. Computer programs—Patents. 2. Patent laws and legislation-
-United States. 3. Software protection—Law and legislation—United
States. I. Title
KF3133.C65S76 1995
346.7304'86—dc20
[347.306486]   94-41806
                                                                         CIP

Printed in the United States of America

10 9 8 7 6 5 4

 Published by Aspen Law & Business
Formerly published by John Wiley & Sons, Inc.

To Beth and my parents.

FOREWORD

It is indeed the right time for a book that spells out, for the legal practitioner and others, what is behind current patent law as it relates to software, how to draft patent applications, how to work with the U.S. Patent & Trademark Office (PTO) to carry them through to approval, and all the other aspects of law and procedure that are so necessary to participate in the rapidly growing software industry.

The real history of the software industry started in 1969, with the unbundling of software by IBM and others. Consumers had previously regarded application and utility programs as cost-free because they were bundled in with the hardware. With unbundling, competing software products could be put on the market because such programs were no longer included in the price of the hardware. Almost immediately, the software industry was born. On the other hand, it was quickly evident that some type of protection would be needed for this new form of intellectual property.

Unfortunately, neither copyright law nor patent law seemed ready to take on this curious hybrid of creative expression and functional utility. During the 1970s, there was total confusion as to how to protect software from piracy. A few copyrights were issued by the Copyright Office, but most were rejected. A few software patents were granted by the PTO, but most patent applications for software-related inventions were rejected. The worst effect for the new industry was the uncertainty as to how this asset could be protected.

Finally, in 1980, after an extensive review by the National Commission on New Technological Uses of Copyrighted Works (CONTU), Congress amended the Copyright Act of 1976 to cover software. It took a number of important cases to resolve most of the remaining issues in the copyright law, and there are still some issues being litigated, such as the so-called "look and feel," but it appears that this area of the law is quite well understood now.

For patents, it took a 1981 Supreme Court decision, *Diamond v. Diehr,* to bring software into the mainstream of patent law. This decision ruled that the presence of software in an otherwise patentable invention did not make that invention unpatentable. *Diamond v. Diehr* opened the door for a flood of software-related patent applications. Unfortunately, the PTO was not prepared for this new development, and in the intervening years they have issued thousands of patents that appear to be questionable to the software industry.

It took a few years after 1981 for the flow of software-related applications to increase, and then there was some delay because of the processing of those applications. Now, the number of infringement cases is on the rise. It is very important for the legal community to understand this development so that lawyers can properly write software patent applications and work with the PTO in the most effective way.

Greg Stobbs is the ideal person to write this book. His interests in software go far beyond the functional aspects that are most relevant to patents. He is genuinely interested in and knowledgeable about both copyright and patent law, and the philosophical issues in both. Given his long experience in intellectual property protection litigation, he is in a unique position to write this in-depth guide to patent law as it applies to software.

BERNARD A. GALLER
President, Software Patent Institute

PREFACE

In cosmological terms the software industry has gone supernova—the industry has exploded. If you look, and you don't have to look too closely, you will find that software has permeated our consumer products, our business systems, and our society. Software is no longer confined to the hulking mainframe computer tended by technicians in white coats, nor is it confined to the desktop computer that has all but replaced the typewriter. Software has broken free of its containment vessels and has leaked into everything: your VCR, the transmission of your car, the typesetting equipment that printed this book, and even the air traffic control system guiding your next landing.

No one can deny the importance of software. Yet there is a controversy raging. Who shall be permitted to own this important technology? Is the Patent Office equipped to decide? There are those who argue that software is so fundamental that our society should not allow anyone to own it to the exclusion of anyone else. Some are content to treat software as copyrightable literature, affording protection only to its expressive, but not its functional, aspects. Some argue strenuously that the patent system that has existed since 1790 is not equipped to handle this new technology, and that some different, *sui generis,* form of protection should be created for software. Others argue, just as strenuously, that the current patent system is working fine, and that it will adapt to this new technology, just as it has adapted to new technology many times before.

This book explores software patents in depth. It is a how-to manual, explaining how the software patent application should be drafted to maximize the likelihood of being granted a patent; exposing who holds software patents today and for what inventions; and discussing what can be done to protect software inventions in the worldwide marketplace. This book also explores the software patent controversy—what should be protected and what should not—and exposes the common thread running through all of the patentable subject matter cases. I hope you will enjoy and use this book. The following is a brief synopsis of its chapters.

Chapter 1 takes you on a journey through history of patents, computers, and software. You will discover that the arguments for and against software patents are not new arguments. They have been echoing for centuries. The next time you confront the issue of who owns an idea, find out in **Chapter 1** how Thomas Jefferson handled the question.

Chapter 2 is a software primer for lawyers. Use it to fill in the gaps in your knowledge of how software is created, what object-oriented programming is about, how client-server techniques are applied in software systems, what the Internet protocol involves, how Microsoft Windows™ works, and more.

Chapter 3 is for the software professional. It explains some of the basics about the legal system and the courts and familiarizes the layperson with the concepts that lawyers take for granted. **Chapter 3** places special emphasis on property law, explaining important concepts underlying all intellectual property law and its keystone, patent law. For the layperson and the general practitioner, the chapter ends with a concise treatment of patent law, a discussion of the patent office, and an explanation of how to read and understand patents,

Chapter 4 is about prior art. One of the principal objections to the current software patent system is that it is difficult to find the most pertinent prior art. This chapter explains how to find software prior art. It explains how the Patent Office Classification System works and how to use on-line database services such as DIALOG and LEXIS and the CASSIS CD-ROM database to find that "needle in a haystack" prior art reference. If you do not use these services often, it is easy to forget the search technique details. This chapter summarizes what you need to know in a handy quick-reference format. Were you aware that the IBM Technical Disclosure Bulletins covering software prior art are now available on-line? This chapter tells you how to access this information.

Chapter 5 explains how to draft a software patent specification that meets all of the requirements of 35 U.S.C. § 112. The chapter discusses each of the leading cases concerning adequacy of the disclosure in software patent applications. You will learn how to avoid having your application rejected by the Patent Office and how to immunize your patents from being invalidated by the courts. The chapter includes a handy checklist of topics to cover with the inventor when meeting prior to drafting and filing the application.

Chapter 6 is about patent drawings. In this chapter you will learn about a number of different ways to illustrate software inventions through drawings. You will improve your patent applications by selecting drawings that clearly explain abstract software concepts. In addition to all the different international standard ISO 5807 flow charts discussed in this chapter, you will also learn about the new object-oriented notations of Booch, Gane/Sarson, and Yourdon/DeMarco.

Chapter 7 discusses the mechanics and strategy of claim drafting. You will learn what patent examiners are looking for when they examine your claims. For the beginning patent attorney struggling to master this difficult subject, this chapter provides a step-by-step analysis technique to help find the invention and draft claims of proper scope.

Chapter 8 deals with the patent application examination. It takes you from the Patent Office mail room to the examiner's desk, describing what happens to your patent application as it is examined. You will find this chapter a convenient reference for questions often asked during patent prosecution, such as how to get the application on file more quickly by taking advantage of "missing parts" practice, and how to expedite prosecution through a petition to make special. This chapter places special emphasis on the duty of disclosure and on how to cite prior art in software patent applications.

Chapter 9 addresses the important 35 U.S.C. § 101, patentable subject matter, issue that is often critical to the patentability of a software invention. Many attorneys fear the § 101 patent application rejection because this is one of the most confusing issues in patent law today. This chapter seeks to clear away the confusion by tracing the origins of the § 101 rejection through the last century of Supreme Court decisions. Included in this chapter is a convenient gazette of reported decisions ruling for and against patentability. The cases are arranged by inventive subject matter, so you can easily find the reported decision on point. The chapter includes a full discussion of the important en banc decision of the Federal Circuit Court of Appeals in *In re Alappat* and concludes by exposing the common thread to all § 101 decisions.

Chapter 10 discusses the software patent worldwide. Principal emphasis is on practice in the European Patent Office (EPO) and the Japanese Patent Office (JPO). The chapter gives the salient features of the European and Japanese patent systems and includes a full discussion of what kinds of software may be patentable in these important jurisdictions.

Chapter 11 is a software patent sampler, giving summaries of each of the software patents owned by some of the software industry leaders, including Microsoft, WordPerfect, Borland International, and Lotus Development Corporation. The patent sampler also summarizes several software patents on various "pure software" components such as the data structure, the algorithm, the user interface, the business method, and more.

I certainly welcome your comments, suggestions, and criticisms. You may address them to me at Harness, Dickey & Pierce, P.L.C., 5445 Corporate Drive, Troy, Michigan 48098; phone 810-641-1600.

Troy, Michigan   GREGORY STOBBS
November 1994

ACKNOWLEDGMENTS

My sincere thanks go out to:

Harness, Dickey & Pierce, P.L.C. for its support and its excellent patent law library;

Bernard Galler who inspired me to write this book;

Gerald Goldberg, U.S. Patent and Trademark Office Director Group 2300, who welcomed me into Group 2300 and provided me with much valuable information;

Gareth Shaw, U.S. Patent and Trademark Office Supervisory Patent Examiner, for sharing with me his experienced perspective of software patents;

Jim Gallo, U.S. Patent and Trademark Office Chief Classification and Employment Division 2, for explaining the intricacies of software prior art classification;

Martyn L.S. Ayers of J.A. Kemp & Co. for his insight into European practice;

Kristine Potter, for her artistry in drawing the many figures in this book; and

John Biernacki, my law clerk, for his energy, his enthusiasm, and his entity relationship diagrams.

ABOUT THE AUTHOR

Gregory A. Stobbs is a principal in the patent firm of Harness, Dickey & Pierce, P.L.C., where he specializes in computers and software. He holds B.S.E.E summa cum laude (electrical engineering) and J.D. degrees from the Ohio State University. Before joining Harness, Dickey & Pierce, he practiced as a patent attorney for Sperry Corporation (UNIVAC) and as a prosecuting attorney in Ohio, conducting first chair civil and criminal trials.

SUMMARY CONTENTS

DETAILED CONTENTS

Chapter 8   Examination of the Application by the Patent Office

PATENT OFFICE ORGANIZATION AND APPLICATION
PROCESS FROM PATENT OFFICE'S PERSPECTIVE

APPLICATION PROCESS FROM PATENT APPLICANT'S
PERSPECTIVE

CHAPTER 1

HISTORY OF
SOFTWARE PATENTS

HISTORY OF PATENTS

§ 1.1   Why Study History?

The history of software patents begins in the Middle Ages. Why go back that far, you may ask. After all, computers were not developed until the twentieth century. There is little chance of finding much software to patent before the twentieth century. All of that is true, for the most part. If you look deeply enough, however, you may find examples of software that predate the computer—harbingers of the software age.

However, that is not the reason to begin the history of software patents in the Middle Ages. The reason to begin in the Middle Ages is that modern day patents have their roots in the Middle Ages.[1] Long ago a debate raged over where to draw the line between patentable creations and unpatentable thoughts and ideas. Software patents have rekindled the debate.

Why software patents have rekindled the historical debate has a lot to do with the computer. The computer empowers a programmer to capture a creative thought in software, and then watch as the computer makes the creation come alive. Essentially all of the human effort is mental, and the end result may be completely intangible. In this sense, software is very close to pure thought, which has long been regarded as something to which no one can own an exclusive right.

Some argue that the entire legal system should be discarded and rewritten. Others argue that an exception should be made for software. Arguments like these make little sense, coming from persons who do not understand what they are proposing to throw out, or from persons who believe themselves to possess more wisdom than 600 years of humanity.

§ 1.2   Ancient History of Patents

Patents can be traced far back into history. The research may be difficult, but you can find patents in use as far back as the third century B.C. In that century,

---

[1] There is evidence that the ancient Greeks were the first to employ patents. However, very few details have survived.

Greek historian Phylarchos tells us that the Greek City of Sybaris granted a patent for an article of cuisine, presumably a recipe.[2] In this early context, the patent was a form of monopoly, the word monopoly being derived from the Greek words ΜΟΝΟΣ and ΠΩΛΕΙΝ, meaning "alone" and "to sell."

The idea that a city-state or sovereignty had the power to grant such a monopoly carried over into the Middle Ages. In the tenth century, commerce and industry standards in England were lower than elsewhere on the continent, no doubt due to England's comparative isolation. To raise England's standard of living, the Crown established a reward to encourage subjects to travel outside the realm and bring back goods that England did not have. Travel abroad in those days was costly and dangerous. To anyone who made three trading voyages abroad, the Crown granted the title of "thane."[3] A thane ranked somewhere between an earl and an ordinary freeman. Notwithstanding the dangers, many adventurers, seeking the title of thane, did travel abroad and bring back goods and technology that England would not otherwise have had.

By the 1300s trading abroad became big business in England. Powerful trading guilds and craft guilds rose to power, largely fed by the profits derived through trading abroad. Originally these merchant guilds were private associations, formed voluntarily by merchants of a town. Gaining political power, these merchant guilds eventually worked their way into town government, and were rewarded by a most important privilege: the exclusive right to trade within the town. Seeing the value of the exclusive trading right, craftsmen and artisans soon formed similar craft guilds. Similar forces are still at work today. Observe the trade unions' rise to power in the United States, some 600 years later.

Whereas the guild primarily served its membership, the power of the monopoly was also exploited to further larger goals. Technology and commerce in England still lagged behind much of the rest of Europe even into the 1300s, and the English Crown still had a legitimate interest in raising the standard of living by luring new technology and commerce into England. Granting the title of thane may have worked in the 1100s, but in the more sophisticated 1300s, a better incentive was needed.

In 1326, the Crown established a new policy to encourage importation of new arts into England. It began granting monopolies to the first individuals or guilds willing to undertake importing new products. When the Crown granted such monopolies, it was a public event. The Crown publicized the grant by issuing proclamations or "open letters," the term open referring to the fact that the official seal was applied with the letter left open. In those days, another term for open letters was "letters patent." The term patent simply means open.

---

[2] E.B. Lipscomb, 1 Lipscomb's Walker on Patents § 1.1 at 7 (3d ed. 1984).

[3] P.J. Federico, *Origin and Early History of Patents,* 18 J. of Patent Off. Soc'y No. 7, at 19, at 20 (July 1936).

Powerful monopolies were granted in virtually every trade and branch of business. England's textile industry today can trace its roots to this 1326 policy of granting letters patent monopolies.

For the first hundred years, or so, the Crown granted monopolies to importers of goods, for example, articles grown or manufactured abroad. Gradually, however, the Crown also began granting monopolies to importers of inventions, for example, processes and methods of manufacture. For example, in 1440 the Crown granted John of Shiedame a monopoly on a process for manufacturing salt. John of Shiedame did not actually invent the process; he simply imported it from abroad—learning the process while on a journey and bringing the knowledge back to England.

Imagine how John of Shiedame must have convinced the Crown to grant him a monopoly for the process of making salt. He must have argued the benefits of the process: lower production cost, purer quality, more plentiful supply. Salt was important. It was a potent flavoring agent and would prevent food from spoiling. John of Shiedame must have also argued how difficult was his journey and how unlikely another with his ability to understand and explain the salt-making process would soon make the same journey. Maybe he even demonstrated the process to the Crown, like a magician, obscuring some of the critical details, just to whet the royal curiosity. The argument was irresistible. "How can John Shiedame be denied this monopoly?" the Crown must have reasoned. After all, England would benefit greatly; and it would not be fair to John of Shiedame that everyone should benefit at his expense; and John of Shiedame could pay the Crown a "royalty," just to square things with the Crown for exercising its "royal prerogative."

The trend of granting letters patent monopolies continued until 1485, when the Crown changed head. Under Tudor control, the sovereign curtailed the practice of granting letters patent, instead favoring private deals in which skilled artisans worked directly for the sovereign (for the sovereign's private benefit). The Tudor plan lasted one hundred years.

In 1558 Queen Elizabeth gained the Crown and changed things back to the way it was before the Tudors. Emphasis was, once again, on promoting commerce—or so it would be argued. Granting Letters Patent in 1562 on a dredging machine introduced into England, the Queen stated that the grant was to be a reward for "diligent travail" and to "give courage to others to study and seke for the knowledge of like good devyses."[4] Within the first 10 years of Queen Elizabeth's reign, at least 20 major Letters Patent monopolies were granted in important technologies of the day: production of soap, saltpeter, alum, sulfur, oil, salt, glass, cloth and leather treatment, dredging, draining, grinding machines, ovens, furnaces, and mining.

According to the practice of the day, these letters patent were granted primarily to those who found technology or goods abroad and brought them

---

[4] *Id.* at 25.

back to England. The patent grantee did not have to be the actual inventor, but only the first importer.

The first application for letters patent for something actually invented by the applicant was by an Italian, Giacopo Acontio. Giacopo Acontio had invented a new kind of furnace and wheel machine. He petitioned the Queen in 1559 to be granted letters patent. In his petition, Giacopo Acontio urged:

> nothing is more honest than that those who by searching have found out things useful to the public should have some fruits of their rights and labors, as meanwhile they abandon all other modes of gain, are at much expense in experiments, and often sustain much loss.[5]

It took six years, but the Queen was eventually convinced, and in 1565, she granted Giacopo Acontio the first letters patent for his invention.

It is interesting that the first letters patent granted to reward an actual inventor was applied for by a noncitizen. Actually, before Giacopo Acontio received his patent grant, he was made a naturalized citizen of England. Whether this was done to legitimize the patent grant, or simply because Giacopo Acontio wanted to be an English citizen is not important. What is important is the effect of England's letters patent system. By having this system of rewards in place, England drew technology to it, inducing citizens and noncitizens, like Giacopo Acontio, to disclose inventions, which England might not otherwise enjoy. This benefit remains one of the principal arguments in favor of the patent system.

There was a dark side to England's letters patent system, however. With people owning monopolies on basic necessities of life, many of the monopolies got out of control and became the subject of much public protest for good reason. For instance, after the patent on salt was granted, the price of salt rose from 16 pence a bushel to 14 or 15 shillings (there are 12 pence in a shilling, hence the increase was more than tenfold). Hume describes the unfortunate state of affairs:

> It is astonishing to consider the number and importance of those commodities which were thus assigned over to patentees. Currants, salt, iron, powder, cards, calf-skins, fells, pouldavies, ox shin-bones, train oil, list of cloth, potashes, anise-seeds, vinegar, seacoals, steel, acquavitae, brushes, pots, bottles, saltpetre, lead, accidences, oil, calamine stone, oil of blubber, glasses, paper, starch, tin, sulphur, new drapery, dried pilchards, transportation of iron ordnance, of beer, of horn, of leather, importation of Spanish wool, of Irish yarn; these are but a part of the commodities which had been appropriated to monopolists. When this list was read in the House, a member cried, "Is not bread in the number?" "Bread," said every one in astonishment. "Yes, I assure you,"

---

[5] *Id.*

replied he, "if affairs go on at this rate, we shall have bread reduced to a monopoly before next parliament."[6]

To make matters worse, Queen Elizabeth was also in the habit of granting the best monopolies to her friends. This must have enraged those who were not similarly blessed. The story of Queen Elizabeth and Sir Walter Raleigh makes illustrative reading.

Queen Elizabeth was nearing 50 when she met Walter Raleigh. How Walter Raleigh managed to get Queen Elizabeth's attention is not clear. One popular version is that Walter Raleigh, in the Queen's proximity after a rain, seized the moment, and threw down his expensive cloak over a mud puddle, so the Queen would not have to step in the puddle. Walter Raleigh may have seized other advantages as well. He was apparently well connected. Raleigh's mother was a relation of Elizabeth's old governess, and some believe Raleigh used that connection to gain access to the Queen.[7]

At any rate, once the two were introduced, the Queen took quite a liking to Raleigh, who was at that time a "'tall, handsome and bold man' in his late twenties, with a beard that 'turned up naturally'".[8] Anne Somerset, author and historian, reports that from the Queen's point of view, Raleigh was not only handsome, but also a freethinker, a poet, and extremely stimulating company.[9] Within two years of their meeting, the Queen granted Raleigh a monopoly license to export woolen broadcloths (worth £3,500 a year) and the right to charge every tavern in the country a £1 a year license fee.[10] Shortly thereafter, Raleigh was knighted, hence the title Sir Walter Raleigh by which he is known today.

Public protest, in those days, was not easy or safe. Public protest could get a subject exiled or beheaded. It was considered a grave lack of respect for anyone to question the royal prerogative. Nevertheless, the House of Commons grew increasingly bold and began openly contesting these monopolies of the royal prerogative. The protests lasted more than 50 years.

The first protest by the House of Commons was mounted in 1571. The Queen sternly responded, directing the House to "meddle with no matters of state but such as should be propounded to them." The House of Commons was persistent, and 1597 it proposed a bill intended to deal with the abusive monopolies, a bill "touching sundry enormities growing by patents or privilege and monopolies." The Queen responded, this time more softly, that she "hoped that her dutiful and loving subjects would not take away her prerogative, which is the chiefest flower of her garden and the principal and head

---

6 D. Hume, 3 The History of England 541 (1776).

7 Anne Somerset, Elizabeth I 336 (1991).

8 *Id.*

9 *Id.*

10 *Id.* at 337.

pearl of her crown and diadem." She promised to discontinue the abusive monopolies and the House of Commons backed down.

The Queen broke her promise. In 1601 the House of Commons responded with another bill designed to deal with the abusive monopolies, described as "an exposition of the common law touching those kinds of patents commonly called monopolies." The debate was fiery. The Queen had many friends in Parliament.

Francis Bacon, whom some believe to be William Shakespeare, spoke out against the bill. Whether Bacon influenced many votes is debatable. Bacon was not a man to be trusted. Francis Bacon, son of Elizabeth's first Lord Keeper of the Great Seal, since 1593 had been trying to get appointed by the Queen as Attorney General. Robert, Earl of Essex, a friend of Francis Bacon, recommended him, but the Queen did not consider Bacon fit for the job. Later (in 1601) Essex was tried for treason. Francis Bacon, his old friend, prosecuted him on behalf of the Crown.

Sir Walter Raleigh also spoke out against the bill, defending the validity of the royal prerogative and the monopolies the Queen had granted, including, of course, his own. His credibility was also therefore rather lacking.

Appreciating the gravity of the situation, this time the Queen personally addressed Parliament. In her address she apologetically begged, "that my grants should be grievous to my people, and oppressions to be privileged under colour of our patents, our kingly dignity shall not suffer it, yea, when I heard it, I could give no rest to my thoughts till I had reformed it." The bill was withdrawn, but this time the Queen had been backed into a corner.

The Queen revoked the most offensive monopolies. More importantly, she allowed the common law courts to try the remaining monopolies, to test whether they were valid or void. This opened the floodgates for what might now be called patent litigation.

§ 1.3   The Case of Monopolies

The first monopoly suit to be tried in the common law courts was Edward Darcy's patent on playing cards, tried in 1602. So famous was this first suit, it was called "The Case of Monopolies."[11] The case was argued on behalf of the patentee by law officers of the Queen. Her officers argued that playing cards were not a necessity, but merely a vanity, and that the Queen had the power "to suppress entirely or tolerate vain amusements," hence the patent was valid. The defense saw it differently, drawing the line between valid and invalid monopolies as follows.

---

[11] Darcy v. Allein, 11 Coke, R. 84b (1 Abbott Patent Cases 1602).

When any man by his own charge and industry, or by his own wit and invention, doth bring any new trade into the realm, or any engine tending to the furtherance of a trade that never was used before; and that for the good of the realm;—in such cases the King may grant to him a monopoly-patent for some reasonable time, until the subjects may learn the same, in consideration of the good that he doth bring by his invention to the commonwealth, otherwise not.[12]

According to the line drawn by the defense, there is still room for monopoly-patents, provided the subject matter is new, that it was the patentee's efforts which brought it into the realm and that the monopoly is reasonably limited in time. Note that the defense also sees the patent monopoly in contractual terms. The patent-monopoly is granted *in consideration* for the good that he doth bring by his invention to the commonwealth. The case was argued on three separate occasions and was not decided until after Queen Elizabeth's death in 1603. The Court ruled for the defense, finding the playing card monopoly was invalid as "against common law on four grounds." First, the court found, the monopoly causes unemployment:

All trades, mechanical as well as others, which prevent idleness (the bane of the commonwealth), and exercise men and youth in labor, for the maintenance of themselves and their families, and for the increase of their substance, to serve the queen when occasion shall require, are profitable for the commonwealth; and therefore the grant to the plaintiff, to have the sole making of them, is against the common law . . . .

Second, the monopoly raises prices and lowers quality:

[T]here are three inseparable incidents to every monopoly against the commonwealth: that the price of the same commodity will be raised, for he who has the sole selling of any commodity may and will make the price as he pleases; that after the monopoly granted the commodity is not so good and merchantable as it was before, for the patentee, having the sole trade, regards only his private benefit and not the commonwealth; and that it tends to the impoverishment of divers artificers, and others, who before by the labor of their hands in their art or trade, had maintained themselves and their families, who now will of necessity be restrained to live in idleness and beggary.

Third, the Queen was deceived:

The queen was deceived in her grant; for the queen, as by the preamble appears, intended it to be for the weal public, whereas it will be employed for the private gain of the patentee, and for the prejudice of the weal public.

---

[12] P.J. Federico, *Origin and Early History of Patents* 18 J. of Patent Off. Soc'y No. 7, at 19, 30 (July 1936).

Fourth, the act of playing cards is not patentable subject matter:

> This grant is *primae impressionis,* ['case of first impression'] for no such was ever seen to pass by letters patent under the great seal before these days; and therefore it is a dangerous innovation as well without any precedent or example as authority of law or reason. And as to what has been said that to play cards is a vanity, this is true if it is abused; but the making of them is neither a vanity nor a pleasure, but labor and pains. And it is true that none can make a park, chase or warren, without the king's license; for that is *quodam nodo* ['requires a certain grant'] to appropriate those which are *ferae naturae et jullius in bonis* ['wild animals or those in the possession of another'], and to restrain them of their natural liberty, which he cannot do without the king's license; but for hawking, hunting, etc., which are matters of pastime, pleasure and recreation, there needs no license, but every man may, in his own land, use them at his pleasure, without any restraint to be made, unless by parliament.

The fourth point of the court is worth consideration. The court distinguishes between the cards themselves and the act of playing cards. The court categorizes the act of playing cards, along with hawking and hunting, as a natural liberty that needs no license. In other words, the act of playing cards is not subject matter to which the patent-monopoly can extend. Recall the Queen's officers argued that the Queen had the power to suppress the act of playing cards, hence she had the power to grant a monopoly on the making, importing, and selling of the cards themselves. The defense countered, arguing that the Queen had no right to take as much as a penny from a subject without an act of Parliament, therefore, she could not take any moderate recreation from her subjects without similar authority.[13] The argument went something like this:

Queen: The practice of playing cards is unimportant; I could outlaw it. Since I could outlaw the practice, I can grant a monopoly on the cards.

Defense: Playing cards is a recreation. It is no different from hunting, and you cannot restrain that. If you had the right to grant a monopoly on the cards, then you are in effect restraining the playing of cards, which you cannot do. Therefore the monopoly on cards is invalid.

At the heart of the argument lies the notion that some things are a "natural liberty." Some things are beyond the sovereign's power to grant monopolies; some things, like hunting and playing cards, are not patentable subject matter. This is an important notion, for it is still being argued today. Those who oppose software patents on the basis that software is not patentable subject matter, in effect, argue that software is like hunting and playing cards.

The decision in the Case of Monopolies did not have much impact on the deeds of Queen Elizabeth's successor, King James I. When James I ascended the throne in 1603 he gave lip service to opposing monopolies and issued a

---

[13] *Id.*

proclamation condemning existing monopolies. He ordered all monopolies suspended, pending an investigation. He assigned the investigation to a Privy Council, including none other than Sir Francis Bacon. Recall that, during Queen Elizabeth's reign, Bacon had argued in favor of monopolies, no doubt trying to gain the Queen's favor, like Sir Walter Raleigh had done. Now Sir Francis Bacon found himself in charge of reviewing the existing monopolies. It was his job to determine which monopolies were valid and which were invalid. Bacon did not reduce the number of monopolies at all, but rather increased the number in scores. Petitions of grievance were presented in 1606 and again in 1610.

In 1610 the King issued a proclamation, known as the Book of Bounty, in which the King condemned monopolies and promised that he would only grant patents for "projects of new invention so that they be not contrary to the law, nor mischievous to the State, by raising prices of commodities at home, or hurt of trade, or generally inconvenient." The King's promises were not fulfilled.

Things got quite divisive, even within the King's court. In 1616, the King removed his Lord Keeper of the Great Seal from office for refusing to apply the seal to some patents the King had granted. In his place, the King appointed Sir Francis Bacon. Now Bacon was in charge of enforcing the Book of Bounty.

Perhaps Bacon had a vision of what a well-run patent system could provide, for he wrote in his *Treatise on Interpreting Nature:*

> Now among all the benefits that could be conferred upon mankind, I discovered none so great as the discovery of new arts for the bettering of human life. For I saw that among the rude people of early times, inventors and discoverers were reconed as gods. It was seen that the works of founders of States, lawgivers, tyrant-destroyers, and heroes cover but narrow spaces, and endure but for a time; while the work of the inventor, though of less pomp, is felt everywhere, and lasts forever.[14]

Notwithstanding these noble words, under Bacon's watch, the King issued numerous "illegal" patents, often to the King's personal friends. Whether Bacon was corrupt, or simply that his enemies made it appear so, a new Parliament assembled in the House of Commons in 1621. Many of the monopolies were invalidated and Bacon was impeached for taking bribes. With Bacon branded a crook and with public protest mounting, both Houses of Parliament finally acted in 1623, passing the Statute of Monopolies. The Statute of Monopolies was approved in final form May 25, 1624 and assented to by King James, to become the first patent statute. This statute remained on the books as the patent statute of Great Britain until well into the nineteenth century.[15]

---

[14] E.B. Lipscomb, 1 Lipscomb's Walker on Patents § 1.6 at 48 (3d ed. 1984).

[15] P.J. Federico, *Origin and Early History of Patents,* 18 J. of Patent Off. Soc'y No. 7, at 19, at 34 (July 1936).

§ 1.4   Statute of Monopolies

The Statute of Monopolies of 1624 began by sweeping away all existing monopolies, with certain exceptions. Among the exceptions were patents for new inventions granted for not more than 21 years, and certain patents on warlike manufactures and materials.[16] What makes the Statute of Monopolies historically important is the sixth section, which authorizes patents for new inventions:

> [A]ny declaration [outlawing monopolies] before mentioned shall not extend to any letters patents and grants of privileges for the term of fourteen years or under, hereafter to be made of the sole working or making of any manner of new manufactures within this realm, to the true and first inventor and inventors of such manufactures, which others at the time of making such letters patents and grants shall not use, so as also they be not contrary to the law nor mischievous to the state, by raising prices of commodities at home, or hurt of trade, or generally inconvenient, the said fourteen years to be accounted from the date of the first letters patents or grants of such privilege hereafter to be made, but that the same shall be of such force as they should be if this act had never been made and of none other.[17]

The Statute of Monopolies codified the common law. The concepts expressed in the Statute are essentially those expressed by the defense in the playing card case, The Case of Monopolies.[18] The Statute did not fundamentally change the way patents were granted. Inventors still had to petition the Crown; there was no statutory right to a patent—that was left entirely to the king's grace.

§ 1.5   Evolution of Written Description Requirement

In the early days under the Statute of Monopolies, the patent contained no written description or drawing to teach the invention.[19] The patent was granted simply as a reward for creating a new industry. The patentee's knowledge was simply given to the public by actual establishment of the industry or by teaching apprentices. It was not until the end of the eighteenth century that a written specification was required as consideration for the patent grant. The Statute was not amended to require a written teaching. This

---

[16] *Id.* at 32; 1 Lipscomb's Walker on Patents § 1.3 at 16 (3d ed. 1984).

[17] P.J. Federico, *Origin and Early History of Patents,* 18 J. of Patent Off. Soc'y No. 7, at 19, at 32 (July 1936).

[18] Darcy v. Allein, 11 Coke, R. 84b (1 Abbott Patent Cases).

[19] P.J. Federico, *Origin and Early History of Patents,* 18 J. of Patent Off. Soc'y No. 7, at 19, at 33 (July 1936).

requirement simply evolved through many court decisions over the period of about two hundred years. Federico describes the beginnings and endings of this evolution this way:

> In the early period, the consideration for the grant was the introduction and establishment of a new industry, no formal written disclosure was required, patents for improvements were of doubtful validity, and the patent was invalid if a prior use could be shown. In the later period, the consideration for the grant was a written description which disclosed the invention to the public, actual establishment of the industry or working of the invention was not necessary, patents for improvements were good at law and the patent was invalid if it was not novel.[20]

HISTORY OF PATENT LAW IN THE UNITED STATES

§ 1.6   Patent Act of 1790

The United States government began operation under the Constitution on March 4, 1789. The Constitution gave Congress the power to promote science and the useful arts. At first, Congress took this literally. Patent and copyright petitions were handled by Congress itself, on an ad hoc basis; each time a person petitioned for a patent or copyright an individual bill was introduced in Congress. Most of the petitions were for patents. It did not take long before Congress realized it would be inundated with petitions for patents, unless something was done to delegate the responsibility.

On June 23, 1789, Benjamin Huntington of Connecticut introduced a bill designed to take the load off of Congress, providing new institutions for both patents and copyrights. Congress could not act on the bill that session; however, when the second session of the First Congress convened in January 1790, President George Washington set the tone in his address to the joint session, delivered in New York, January 8, 1790:

> The advancement of agriculture, commerce, and manufactures, by all proper means, will not, I trust, need recommendation, but I cannot forbear intimating to you the expediency of giving effectual encouragement, as well to the introduction of new and useful inventions from abroad, as to the exertions of skill and genius in producing them at home, and of facilitating the intercourse between the distant parts by a due attention to post office and post roads. Nor am I less persuaded that there is nothing which can better deserve your patronage than the promotion of science and literature.

---

[20] *Id.* at 34.

This First Congress was inspired, and it immediately took up Huntington's bill, which had been tabled at the close of the previous session. Believing the copyright law would be easier to draft than the patent law, Congress decided that separate copyright and patent bills should be drafted. Congress knew that there was likely to be little debate over literary property and how it should be protected. Inventive property was another matter; hence separate copyright and patent bills were drafted. It is interesting that the two bodies of law, copyright law and patent law, remain separate today. It is also significant that over two hundred years after the First Congress, computer software is the first technology to be protected by both bodies of law.

The first patent bill was introduced February 16, 1790, debated, and quickly passed by both House and Senate. President Washington signed the act into law on April 10, 1790. Interestingly, Congress tackled first what it perceived the more difficult task. It passed the patent act before it passed the copyright act. The copyright act was enacted May 31, 1790.

In the first patent act, known as the Patent Act of 1790, Congress created a patent agency in the Department of State, headed by a board comprising the Secretary of State, the Secretary of the Department of War, and the Attorney General. This board, whose members administered the patent system along with their other public duties, was known by its own designation as "Commissioners for the Promotion of Useful Arts."[21] Any two of the board members could issue a patent, for a period not exceeding 14 years, to any petitioner that "hath . . . invented or discovered any useful art, manufacture, . . . or device, or any improvement therein not before known or used," if the board found that "the invention or discovery [was] sufficiently useful and important . . . ."[22] To apply for a patent under this act, the applicant had to submit a written specification, a drawing, and, if possible, a model. The application fee varied between four and five dollars.

The first board consisted of Thomas Jefferson, Secretary of State, Henry Knox, Secretary of War, and Edmund Randolph, Attorney General. Jefferson, in particular, took the job of patent commissioner quite seriously. He personally examined all applications. As the United States' first patent examiner, Jefferson was extremely tight-fisted, issuing only 57 patents during the three years in which the Patent Act of 1790 was in force.[23]

---

[21] Graham v. John Deere Co., 383 U.S. 1, 7 (1966).

[22] 1 Stat. 110 (1790).

[23] P.J. Federico, *Origin and Early History of Patents,* 18 J. of Patent Off. Soc'y No. 7, at 19, at 71 (July 1936).

§ 1.7   Thomas Jefferson

Thomas Jefferson was a deep thinker and he held very strong views concerning invention, patents, and monopolies. An inventor himself, Jefferson had every reason to favor patents. While Jefferson was in France shortly after the Constitutional Convention, he worked out the mathematics for a new moldboard plow, which was a far superior plow to those he had watched the French farmers using in the fields. While Jefferson was vice president, he disclosed his moldboard to farmers and it quickly replaced existing plow technology on two continents. So significant was his invention that in 1806 the Agricultural Society of Paris awarded Jefferson's moldboard plow a gold medal. Jefferson never thought of patenting his moldboard plow, for he opposed the monopoly of any useful idea.[24] Justice Clark, writing for the Supreme Court in *Graham v. John Deere Co.,* wrote that "Jefferson, like other Americans, had an instinctive aversion to monopolies. It was a monopoly on tea that sparked the Revolution and Jefferson certainly did not favor an equivalent form of monopoly under the new government."[25]

Jefferson wanted a bill of rights, as a guarantee that the Constitutional government could not lapse into despotism. Jefferson did not want all 13 colonies to adopt the Constitution until a bill of rights was in place. James Madison was initially opposed to a federal bill of rights and saw danger in tacking on additional bill of rights provisions that might prevent ratification of the Constitution. The two corresponded at length on this subject.

Writing from France in July 1788, Jefferson urged Madison that there should be a Bill of Rights provision restricting monopolies. Jefferson countered the argument that a limited monopoly might incite ingenuity, with the argument that "the benefit even of limited monopolies is too doubtful to be opposed to that of their general suppression."[26] Later, in another letter to Madison (August 1789) after drafting the Bill of Rights, Jefferson stated that he would have been pleased by an express provision in this form:

> Art. 9. Monopolies may be allowed to persons for their own productions in literature & their own inventions in the arts, for a term not exceeding—years but for no longer term & no other purpose.[27]

---

[24] Merrill D. Peterson, Thomas Jefferson and the New Nation 589–90 (1970).

[25] 383 U.S. 1, 7 (1966).

[26] Letter from Thomas Jefferson to James Madison (July 1788) *in* 5 Writings of Thomas Jefferson 47 (Paul L. Ford, ed., 1895), *cited by* U.S. Supreme Court in Graham v. John Deere Co., 383 U.S. 1, 8 (1966).

[27] Letter from Thomas Jefferson to James Madison (July 1788) *in* 5 Writings of Thomas Jefferson 113 (Paul L. Ford, ed., 1895), *cited by* U.S. Supreme Court in Graham v. John Deere Co., 383 U.S. 1, 8 (1966).

Later he wrote:

> Certainly an inventor ought to be allowed a right to the benefit of his invention for some certain time.

*   *   *

> Nobody wishes more than I do that ingenuity should receive a liberal encouragement.[28]

Ultimately Jefferson and Madison reached an understanding, for the Constitution was ratified and Madison, almost single-handedly, carried through the First Congress the first ten amendments (the Bill of Rights) to the Constitution.[29]

§ 1.8   —Jefferson, First Patent Examiner

As a patent examiner there was none tougher. Only 57 patents were issued during Jefferson's watch as America's first patent examiner.[30] Jefferson made it a point to personally examine each application, ever vigilant lest an onerous monopoly should be granted. Being patent examiner for the entire country was hard, time-consuming work. It troubled Jefferson that he could not find the time required to examine each patent application as fully and carefully as he thought necessary.

Thus, Jefferson drafted a bill, introduced it in Congress on February 7, 1791, which reflected the sentiment that if you cannot do a proper job of examining, then do not do it all. The bill was not passed, although many provisions of it are found in the bill introduced on December 10, 1792, passed on February 4, 1793, and signed into law on February 21, 1793, to be known as the Patent Act of 1793.[31]

The Patent Act of 1793 significantly changed the requirements for obtaining a patent. The 1793 Act removed the requirement of the 1790 Act that the invention be deemed "sufficiently useful and important" and the 1793 Act eliminated examination of the application, making the grant of a patent a purely clerical matter.[32] In short, the 1793 Act relieved Jefferson and the other two board members of the responsibility of reviewing each application. The 1793 Act simply shifted this responsibility to the courts.

---

[28] Letter from Thomas Jefferson to Oliver Evans (May 1807) *in* 5 Writings of Thomas Jefferson 75–76 (A.A. Lipscomb & A.E. Berg, eds., 1903), *cited by* United States Supreme Court in Graham v. John Deere Co., 383 U.S. 1, 8 (1966).

[29] Merrill D. Peterson, Thomas Jefferson and the New Nation 361 (1970).

[30] P.J. Federico, *Origin and Early History of Patents,* 18 J. of Patent Off. Soc'y No. 7, at 19, at 71 (July 1936).

[31] *Id.* at 77–78.

[32] *Id.* at 81.

With the passage of the 1793 Act, Jefferson would appear to have softened his views regarding the evils of monopolies. This is not the case. Federico reports:

> One object, expressed by Jefferson, in eliminating the examination system, was to give the courts an opportunity to develop a system of jurisprudence with respect to patentability, but after a number of years experience with a registration system, Jefferson become convinced that preliminary examination of applications and a refusal of a patent when the patent was not warranted, would better safeguard the public.[33]

Jefferson also expressed his views, by letter, in a famous patent infringement suit, brought on an invention for which he had granted a patent under the 1790 Act. It may be that Jefferson was the first expert witness in a patent trial.

§ 1.9 —Jefferson, First Patent Expert Witness

The suit involved Oliver Evans's patent (U.S. Patent number three), granted December 18, 1790, on the use of a bucket conveyor and Archimedean screw for conveying grain. The device, called a hopper-boy, was used in a flour mill. Jefferson had a flour mill, himself, and employed Oliver Evans's hopper-boy, paying Evans's agent $89.90 for the use of the invention. Peterson reports, "He paid willingly, as a tribute to a man whose talents were so useful to mankind, but at the same time denied he was under legal obligation to pay."[34]

Oliver Evans took full advantage of the patent laws available to him. Not only did he seek and obtain a United States Letters Patent for his hopper-boy, he also held a wide assortment of pre-1790 Act state patents:

Maryland:

1787 "Elevator" (14 year term)

1787 "Hopper-boy" (14 year term)

1787 "Steam Carriage" (14 year term)

New Hampshire:

1788 "Elevator for Flour Mills" (14 year term)

1788 "Hopper Boy for Flour Mills" (14 year term)

1788 "Steam Carriages" (14 year term)

---

[33] *Id.* at 78–79.

[34] Merrill D. Peterson, Thomas Jefferson and the New Nation 937 (1970).

1789 "Elevator" (7 year term)

1789 "Hopper Boy" (7 year term)[35]

In 1813 Evans brought suit for patent infringement in Baltimore. Isaac McPherson, of that city, wrote to Jefferson, asking for his expert opinion of the case. Jefferson's reply, a letter to McPherson dated August 13, 1813, rebukes Evans's position that his patent covers all forms of elevators and screws used in manufacturing flour. Jefferson finds the hopper-boy itself to be original to Evans, but shows that elevators and screws date back to ancient Egypt and to Archimedes. Moreover Jefferson's letter is a remarkable essay on Jefferson's philosophy on the nature and purpose of the patent monopoly.

> If nature has made any one thing less susceptible than all others of exclusive property, it is the action of the thinking power called an idea, which an individual may exclusively possess as long as he keeps it to himself; but the moment it is divulged, it forces itself into the possession of every one, and the receiver cannot dispossess himself of it. Its peculiar character, too, is that no one possesses the less, because every other possesses the whole of it. He who receives an idea from me, receives instruction himself without lessening mine; as he who lights his taper at mine, receives light without darkening me. That ideas should freely spread from one to another over the globe, for the moral and mutual instruction of man, and improvement of his condition, seems to have been peculiarly and benevolently designed by nature, when she made them, like fire, expansible over all space, without lessening their density in any point, and like the air in which we breathe, move, and have our physical being, incapable of confinement or exclusive appropriation. Inventions then cannot, in nature, be a subject of property. Society may give an exclusive right to the profits arising from them, as an encouragement to men to pursue ideas which may produce utility, but this may or may not be done, according to the will and convenience of the society, without claim or complaint from any body.[36]

This language is quoted by the United States Supreme Court in the seminal patent law decision in *Graham v. John Deere Co.,* when that Court examines the conditions for patentability.[37]

§ 1.10   Patent Act of 1793

The Patent Act of 1793 changed the patent system from an examination system to a registration system. Similar to our copyright system today,

---

[35] E.B. Lipscomb, 1 Lipscomb's Walker on Patents § 1.7 at 52–53 (3d ed. 1984).

[36] Letter from Thomas Jefferson to Isaac McPherson (Aug. 13, 1813) *in* VI Writings of Thomas Jefferson 180–81. (H.A. Washington, ed. 1854) The full text of Jefferson's Letter to McPherson is reproduced in **App. C.**

[37] 383 U.S. 1, 8 n 2. (1966).

applications for patent under the 1793 Act were not examined for novelty. Our copyright system today is a registration system, in which submissions for which copyright registration is sought are not examined for originality. Under the 1793 Act, the Secretary of State received the patent application and kept records. A patent was issued on the application as a simple clerical act, although the issued patent had the appearance of great importance, each patent being signed by the President of the United States. The application fee was changed to thirty dollars—a rather stiff increase over the four dollar fee under the 1790 Act, considering that the four dollar fee entitled the applicant to examination by Thomas Jefferson. Perhaps the increased fee was designed to deter all but the most serious inventors.

The registration system did not work and was replaced in 1836 with an examination system. However, there are several vestiges of the 1793 Act in our patent law today. The 1793 Act clarified a confusing point, which is still widely misunderstood, that the inventor of an improvement in something previously patented by another cannot make, use, or sell the original discovery of the first patentee, and neither can the first patentee use the improvement of the later. The Act also provided that mere changes in form or proportions (for example, changes in size or shape) are not patentable. The Act further required the inventor to swear or affirm that he or she believed himself or herself to be the true inventor, and to provide a full, clear, and exact description of the invention, and also a drawing if the application admitted drawings, and a model, if deemed necessary.[38]

The 1793 Act also contained provisions for administering interferences between two or more applications claiming the same invention. This possibility had been overlooked in the 1790 Act. Interferences were resolved by three arbitrators, one chosen by each applicant and one chosen by the Secretary of State. In an interference between more than two applicants, the Secretary of State chose all three arbitrators.[39]

Roughly 10,000 patents were granted under the 1793 Act, which was replaced in 1836. See **Figures 1–1** and **1–2.** Although it would still be many years before the invention of the programmable digital computer, there is evidence even back then that the software patent was about to emerge. In 1837 Samuel Morse applied for a patent on the telegraph. Morse's patent, Number 1,647, was granted in 1840. In that and his subsequent reissue patents Morse made sweeping claims, some of which the United States Supreme Court declared to be invalid in *O'Reilly v. Morse*.[40] Struck down, for example, was Morse's claim 8 that read:

---

[38] P.J. Federico, *Origin and Early History of Patents,* 18 J. of Patent Off. Soc'y No. 7, at 19, at 81–82 (July 1936).

[39] *Id.* at 82.

[40] 56 U.S. 62 (1853).

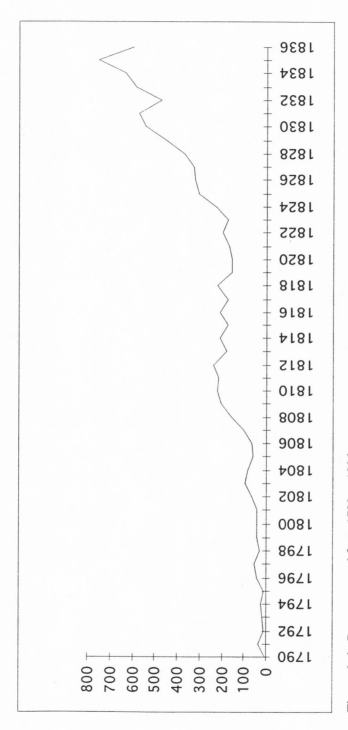

Figure 1–1. Patents granted from 1790 to 1836.

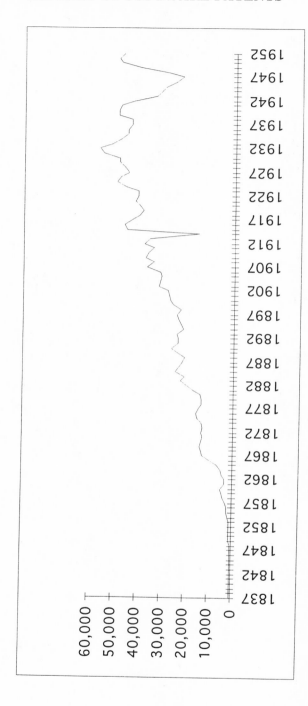

Figure 1–2. Patents granted from 1837 to 1952.

I do not propose to limit myself to the specific machinery, or parts of machinery, described in the foregoing specifications and claims; the essence of my invention being, the use of the motive power of the electric or galvanic current, which I call electro-magnetism, however developed, for making or printing intelligible characters, letters or signs, at any distances, being a new application of that power of which I claim to be the first inventor or discoverer.[41]

More interesting from a software patent standpoint is Morse's claim 5, which was not struck down. There is little difference between Morse's claimed telegraphic code and modern computer "machine code":

I claim, as my invention, the system of signs, consisting of dots and spaces, and of dots, spaces, and horizontal lines, for numerals, letters, words or sentences, substantially as herein set forth and illustrated, for telegraphic purposes.[42]

§ 1.11 Patent Act of 1836

As Federico notes, the Act of 1793 gave trouble almost from the start.[43] Patents of dubious originality clogged the courts with litigation. Whatever incentive to innovation the Act of 1793 provided, it was largely offset, Federico notes, by the "mass of worthless and conflicting patents granted, by excessive litigation and many cases of fraud and extortion."[44] Maine Senator, John Ruggles, only recently elected, moved that a committee be formed to study the state of the patent system. Ruggles got what he asked for. He was elected chairman of a committee newly formed to investigate the patent system and prepare a report to the Senate. Four months later, on April 28, 1836, Ruggles completed his investigation and reported this to the Senate:

[T]he Department of State has been going on for more than forty years, issuing patents on every application, without any examination into the merits or novelty of the invention . . .

A considerable portion of some of the patents granted are worthless and void, as conflicting and infringing upon one another, or upon public rights . . . a great many law suits arise from this condition . . .

The country becomes flooded with patent monopolies, embarrassing to *bona fide* patentees, whose rights are thus invaded from all sides . . .

---

[41] *Id.* at 112.

[42] *Id.*

[43] P.J. Federico, *Origin and Early History of Patents,* 18 J. of Patent Off. Soc'y No. 7, at 19, at 91 (July 1936).

[44] *Id.* at 91–92.

It opens the door to frauds, which have already become extensive and serious. . . . it is not uncommon for persons to copy patented machines in the model room; and, having made some slight immaterial alterations, they apply in the next room for patents.[45]

By Ruggles' account, patents had become of little value, and the object of the patent laws had been, in great measure, defeated.

The Senate acted, passing Ruggles' bill that accompanied the report. The bill became law on July 4, 1836, known as the Patent Act of 1836. The new law reverted to an examination system, established the Patent Office, and placed a chief to be known as the Commissioner of Patents in charge.

The Patent Act of 1836 provided a fourteen-year term, extendible for an additional seven years with the approval of the patent board. The fee for applying for a patent varied, depending on the nationality of the applicant. For a United States citizen the fee was $30; for an alien the fee was $300; for a British citizen the fee was $500. To be considered patentable an invention had to be novel, original, and useful. If the commissioner found an application did not meet these requirements, the patent was refused. The refusal could be appealed to a board of three disinterested persons appointed by the Secretary of State for each case. The fee for an appeal was $25.

The 1836 Act underwent several modifications over the years following its enactment. On August 29, 1842, designs were made patentable. The first design patent issued under this provision was to George Bruce for printing types.

On March 2, 1861, less than one month before the beginning of the American Civil War, Congress extended the patent term from 14 years to 17 years. Why 17 years? The 17-year term was enacted as a compromise to abolish the optional seven-year extension. In effect, Congress took the original 14-year term, plus the optional seven-year extension, and split the difference, arriving at seventeen years.

By the 1930s much research was being done in the field of botany. Being life forms, plants did not seem to fit the usual subject matter of patentable inventions. Wanting to give an incentive to developers of new varieties of plants, Congress amended the patent laws, adding a new type of patent called a plant patent.

§ 1.12   Patent Act of 1952

In 1926 Congress adopted the United States Code, which was a codification of the existing general and permanent laws of the United States, arranged in 50 titles according to subject matter. Congress declared that the United States

---

[45] *Id.* at 93.

Code would be *prima facie* evidence of the law. However, because of the large size of the Code, Congress did not enact the entire Code into positive law at once; it merely gave the Code *prima facie* status. Congress decided it would be better to separately enact each of the titles into positive law, one title at a time.

In 1949 Congress got around to reenacting the patent law under the codification program it began in 1926. It was at about this same time that Congress independently decided that it was time to revise the patent law. These projects were combined, and a preliminary draft of the Proposed Revision and Amendment of the Patent Laws was distributed in early February 1950.

In drafting the Proposed Revision, Congress collected all patent-related statutes passed from the Revised Statutes of 1874 to the current date. Much of the existing law was retained. In addition, Congress factored in many of the Supreme Court and Court of Customs and Patent Appeals decisions, codifying much of the accepted case law precedent. Numerous minor improvements in wording were adopted. One rather significant change was made. Section 103 was added to codify the "invention" requirement that a patent would only be granted for a nonobvious invention.

The newly adopted § 103 states:

> A patent may not be obtained though the invention is not identically disclosed or described as set forth in section 102 of this title, if the differences between the subject matter sought to be patented and the prior art are such that the subject matter as a whole would have been obvious at the time the invention was made to a person having ordinary skill in the art to which said subject matter pertains. Patentability shall not be negatived by the manner in which the invention was made.

This was not new law, per se. With reference to section 103 the Committee Report states:

> Section 103, for the first time in our statue, provides a condition which exists in the law and has existed for more than 100 years, but only by reason of decisions of courts.
>
> *   *   *
>
> That provision paraphrases language which has often been used in decisions of courts, and the section is added to the statute for uniformity and definiteness. This section should have a stabilizing effect and minimize great departures which have appeared in some cases.[46]

---

[46] P.J. Federico, Commentary on the New Patent Act, *reprinted in* U.S. Code Ann., Tit. 35, 20.

§ 1.13   1966 Presidential Commission on Patent System

In 1965 President Johnson by Executive Order commissioned a comprehensive study of the United States Patent System.[47] The President's Commission on the Patent System was comprised of 10 members of the public and representatives of four government agencies: Secretary of Commerce, Secretary of Defense, Small Business Administration, and National Science Foundation. Also present were official observers from the office of the Secretary of State and the Office of Science and Technology. Then Patent Commissioner, Edward J. Brenner, participated as designee of the Secretary of Commerce.

Commencing August 15, 1965, the Commission held 13 meetings, each meeting lasting from one to four days, for a total of 31 days. The Commission produced its final report to the President on November 17, 1966. The Commission recommended change.

In its Report, the Commission downplays the importance of the 1952 Patent Act, noting that the current patent law has seen no basic change in the 130 years since the Patent Act of 1836 (not even mentioning the 1952 Act by name):

> The Act of 1836 established the pattern for our present system by providing statutory criteria for the issuance of patents and requiring the Patent Office to examine applications for conformance thereto. Although the law has been amended on numerous occasions—and even rewritten twice since 1836—no basic changes have been made in its general character in the succeeding one hundred and thirty years.[48]

To justify the need for change, the Commission contrasts the agricultural economy of 1836 with the exploding technological economy of 1965, noting that in 1836 most innovation came from individuals, whereas now much innovation comes from organized research. The Commission also paints the current system as gridlocked, with an application backlog of over 200,000 applications and an average pendency period of two and one-half years, with a "substantial number" of applications having a pendency period of five to ten years or more. The Commission warns the President that a simple fix in a few areas would not work because:

> Many of the problems related to these objectives are intertwined. An attempt to solve or reduce a problem at one point of the system can expose or create a dislocation at another. Separate and uncoordinated solutions to individual

---

[47] Exec. Order No. 11,215, 30 Fed. Reg. 4661 (1965).

[48] 1966 Report of the President's Comm'n on the Patent Sys. 1.

problems would yield a gerrymandered patent system full of internal contradictions and less efficient than the one we now have.[49]

Instead of a few ad hoc solutions, the Commission recommends:

1. Implement a "first-to-file" system.
2. Issue no patents on designs, plants, or computer programs.
3. Allow application filing by assignee.
4. Require that a claim for priority date, if made at all, be made when application is filed.
5. Publish all applications after pending 18 months.
6. Require continuation applications to be filed before allowance of pending claims; require continuation-in-part applications to be filed before publication of its parent; require divisional applications be filed during the pendency of the application in which the restriction was first required.
7. Give applicant the option of deferred examination—examine an application only on request.
8. Place the burden on applicant to persuade Patent Office that a claim is patentable.
9. Allow the public to cite prior art after the 18-month publication.
10. Implement a Patent Office quality control program.
11. Make appeal of patent denial more difficult by giving the Patent Office decision a presumption of correctness, reversible only when clearly erroneous.
12. Make decisions of the CCPA reviewable by a Court of Appeals of general jurisdiction (that is, jurisdiction over infringement cases).
13. Adopt an ex parte administrative procedure for reexaminination.
14. Abolish broadening reissue applications.
15. Allow a patentee to recover damages for preissuance infringement.
16. Change the patent term to expire 20 years after filing.
17. Make terminal disclaimers unavailable to overcome double patenting rejections.
18. Make importing a product made abroad by a patented process an act of infringement.
19. Treat a claim, once held invalid, as canceled from the patent.
20. Establish an office of civil commissioner to sit in a quasi-judicial capacity in patent infringement litigation, to conduct pretrial hearings, supervise discovery, and preside at depositions of the parties.

---

[49] *Id.* at 4.

21. Give litigants the option of conducting infringement litigation by stipulation of facts or affidavit—defendant guaranteed no injunctive relief and damages limited to a reasonable royalty.

22. Establish a Statutory Advisory Council.

23. Allow the commissioner to set Patent Office fees based on the cost of providing the services and use tax funds to supplement (at the time of the report, the Patent Office was self-sustaining).

24. Allow applicants to amend applications following any new ground of rejection; make rejections final if applicant introduces new claim limitation not found in any of the original claims.

25. Form a study group to consider better ways for document storage and retrieval.

26. Develop a worldwide patent index for obtaining the status of any patent or application throughout the world.

27. Pursue international harmonization of patent practice, with ultimate goal being the establishment of an international patent, respected throughout the world.

The President's Commission recommended that patents on computer programs should not be permitted. Why? The stated reason is as follows:

> Uncertainty now exists as to whether the statute permits a valid patent to be granted on programs. Direct attempts to patent programs have been rejected on the ground of non-statutory subject matter. Indirect attempts to obtain patents and avoid the rejection, by drafting claims as a process, or a machine or components thereof programmed in a given manner, rather than as a program itself, have confused the issue further and should not be permitted.
>
> The Patent Office now cannot examine applications for programs because of the lack of a classification technique and the requisite search files. Even if these were available, reliable searches would not be feasible or economic because of the tremendous volume of prior art being generated. Without this search, the patenting of programs would be tantamount to mere registration and the presumption of validity would be all but nonexistent.
>
> It is noted that the creation of programs has undergone substantial and satisfactory growth in the absence of patent protection and that copyright protection for programs is presently available.[50]

The Report of the President's Commission is significant for what it does not do. The Commission's recommendations were published, debated, but, for the most part, rejected. On the issue of software patentability, the principal objection of the Commission—that the Patent Office cannot classify software effectively—is simply not true. The argument that patent protection is

---

[50] *Id.* at 14.

not necessary, because copyright protection is available for software, presumes that copyright protection is adequate. A fundamental flaw in this reasoning is that copyright has long been held not to protect utilitarian articles or functional features. Hence the utilitarian aspects of software cannot be adequately protected by copyright.

§ 1.14 National Commission on New Technological Uses of Copyrighted Works (CONTU)

On October 19, 1976, Congress enacted Public Law 94-553, the first major revision of the copyright law since 1909. The law took effect January 1, 1978 and remains in force as the copyright law of the United States. Prior to enacting this law, Congress formed a National Commission on New Technological Uses of Copyrighted Works (CONTU), created to evaluate the adequacy of copyright law regarding computer-based information systems and photocopying technology.[51]

One of the Software Subcommittee's mandates was to consider whether some hybrid form of protection should be created for protecting computer programs. Such hybrid proposals generally combine elements of patent and copyright.[52] Among the hybrid proposals considered were those presented to the World Intellectual Property Organization (WIPO) in Kolle.[53] The Subcommittee rejected hybrid forms of protection, stating that "[a]ny form of protection for computer programs other than copyright would restrict society's access to information to a greater extent than does copyright because such other forms afford proprietors far greater monopoly power over their wares."[54]

The Software Subcommittee articulated one key difference between copyright protection and patent protection:

Copyright law gives moderate protection to the original writings of authors for an extended period of time without regard to the quality of the work. Patent law, on the other hand, gives stronger protection to certain discoveries of inventors for a much shorter period of time if and only if the federal government is satisfied that the work is useful, novel and nonobvious to those familiar with the related technology. Very broadly, copyright is designed to protect the

---

[51] House Comm. on the Judiciary Hearings on Act of Dec. 31, 1974, 93rd Cong. 2d Sess. (Feb. 23, 1976).

[52] *See, e.g.,* Kindermann, *Special Protection Sys. for Computer Programs,* 7 I.I.C. Quarterly 301 (1976).

[53] *See* Kolle, *Computer Software Protection—Present Situation & Future Protection— Present Situation & Future Prospects* 13 Copyright 72 (1977).

[54] Software Subcomm. to the Nat'l Comm'n on New Technological Uses of Copyrighted Works 7–8. Report of the Software Subcomm. to the Nat'l Comm'n on New Technological Uses of Copyrighted Works (July 13, 1978).

expression of ideas while patent's purpose is to protect what are generally understood to be inventions—in a sense the ideas themselves.[55]

The above quote bears exploring, for computer software is protectable under both copyright and patent. Many software developers state that for software they prefer copyright protection to patent protection. Some of the advantages of copyright often expressed are that a copyright registration is easier and cheaper to obtain than a patent, that the software developer is often able to secure the copyright registration without hiring a lawyer, and that the copyright protection so obtained lasts roughly four times longer than patent protection.

All of this is true. However, proponents of copyright cannot escape the timeless adage, "You get what you pay for." Thus those who rely solely on software copyright protection may be setting themselves up to learn a painful lesson, of precisely what the CONTU Software Subcommittee meant in distinguishing "moderate" copyright protection from "stronger" patent protection.

The difference in the degree of protection stems from what is actually being protected. The difference resides in the "idea-expression" dichotomy. Although many subtleties are ignored in its statement, the Software Subcommittee, in the above quote, said it well, that copyright protects the expression of ideas; patent protects the ideas themselves.

When considering the CONTU Software Subcommittee's report, keep in mind that the Subcommittee's mission was to update the copyright law. This is evident in the way the Committee defines the term *computer program,* as a "writing." Writings are the subject matter of copyright, and the Committee uses this in its definition:

> A computer program is a writing which sets forth instructions which can direct the operation of an automatic system capable of storing, processing, retreiving [sic] or transferring information. It is an explanation of a process and not the process itself.[56]

The Subcommittee did not rule out patent protection for software; indeed the Subcommittee acknowledged that patent protection may also be possible for the underlying idea or software process itself:

> This distinction between the process and the writing which describes it is of critical importance to understanding how copyright applies to computer programs. With a computer program as with all forms of creative endeavor, there are three different phenomena:

---

[55] *Id.* at 2–3.

[56] *Id.* at 3.

(1)   A description of the activity (process)

(2)   The activity (process) itself; and

(3)   The results of the activity (process).

Descriptions of a process are protectable through copyright without regard to whether they are narrative descriptions or lists of instructions. Processes or principles of operation—indicated by the second category—are protectable, if at all, through patents or trade secrecy.[57]

However, the Subcommittee does express three "problems" with software patents:

In the first place, the availability of patent protection for programs is unclear . . .

In the second place, even if available, only software meeting the rigid standards of novelty and nonobviousness required by Title 35 of the United States Code could be patented . . .

[i]n the third place, unlike copyright, patents can be used to protect "processes," and under the patent system the independent development of the same work is an infringement.[58]

The first problem identified by the Software Subcommittee stems directly from then-existing uncertainties over what subject matter the courts considered patentable. Lower court interpretation of the Supreme Court decision in *Gottschalk v. Benson*[59] is the principal source of the problem. The Software Subcommittee explains their uncertainty in the following footnote:

Recent decisions in the Court of Customs and Patent Appeals ordered the award of patents to software (or softwarelike creations) over the strenuous objection of two judges who held that *Gottschalk v. Benson* . . . and *Dann v. Johnston* . . . , cases in which the Supreme Court found software to be ineligible for patent protection, precluded such protection. *In re Chatfield* . . . and *In re Noll* . . . . The precedential value of these cases in the face of possible Supreme Court review seems questionable, at best. In any event, the Patent and Trademark Office announced on December 14, 1976, that it would rely on *Benson* rather than *Noll* or *Chatfield* "since further review or clarification [of them] may be forthcoming." . . . The Solicitor General has asked the Supreme Court to review the decisions of *Noll* and *Chatfield*.[60]

---

[57] *Id.* at 3–4.

[58] *Id.*

[59] 409 U.S. 63 (1972).

[60] Final Report of the Nat'l Comm'n on New Tech. Uses of Copyrighted Works 8 n.13 (July 31, 1978) published in 954 *Official Gazette,* 312 *Patent, Trademark & Copyright J.* at A-12 (citations omitted).

Today, the uncertainties injected into patent law by *Benson* have been largely erased by the Supreme Court in the landmark decision in *Diamond v. Chakrabarty* that held that Congress in drafting the Patent Act of 1952 intended statutorily patentable subject matter to include "anything under the sun that is made by man."[61] Having crystallized the issue in *Chakrabarty,* finding that anything created by humanity is potentially patentable, the Supreme Court thereafter ruled in *Diamond v. Diehr* that software is patentable subject matter.[62]

See **Chapter 9** for a fuller consideration of *Benson, Chakrabarty, Diehr,* and the question of what is patentable subject matter under 35 U.S.C. § 101 of the Patent Act of 1952.

The remaining two problems the CONTU Software Subcommittee found in using patents to protect software are not criticisms of patent law at all. The second problem, for example, simply states that not all software is protectable by patent—only that software which is novel and nonobvious is eligible for patent under Title 35 of the United States Code. Thus, the Committee notes, much software would go wholly unprotected, if a patent-only approach were adopted. The third problem is simply a truism about the difference between copyright and patent. Unlike copyright, a patent will protect a utilitarian process, and a patent granted to the first to discover a new and nonobvious process can block those who independently, but later, discover the same process.

§ 1.15   1994 Software Patent Hearings

In the winter of 1994, the Patent Office held public hearings on software patents in San Jose, California and in Washington, D.C. Anyone interested in offering testimony was permitted to do so. Software developers, hardware developers, computer programmers, trade organizations, universities, and attorneys from all over the country participated in the hearings. The testimony given, when compared to the CONTU Software Subcommittee Report, provide interesting evidence that history repeats itself. The testimony is reproduced in the Appendix.

One sentiment expressed by several "anti-patent" witnesses was that patent protection is not needed in the software industry, for the software industry has done quite well for itself with only copyright to protect it. Others, of similar leaning, urged that patent protection is infeasible, due to the difficulties in determining what was covered by patent and what was not. These arguments amount to criticism that patent protection is neither needed nor workable in protecting software. Some of these arguments were well

---

[61] 447 U.S. 303, 309 (1980).

[62] 450 U.S. 175 (1981).

presented, and in San Jose, several witnesses expressing these views were cheered by members of the audience.[63]

These arguments against the patent system and favoring the copyright system lose considerable force when considering that the same arguments were levied against the copyright system, when the CONTU Software Subcommittee held similar hearings on the protection of software. The CONTU Software Subcommittee Report states:

> The Subcommittee, of course, is aware of some testimony received by the Commission to the effect that copyright may be neither needed nor useful in protecting programs. Two general contentions were made: first, that the software industry is burgeoning in a market where the availability and efficacy of legal protection is unclear and, second, that, since infringements of programs are difficult to detect, enforcement of any law is rendered difficult.[64]

The Software Patent Hearings produced much interesting testimony. With a few notable exceptions, most large corporate software developers and computer manufacturers favor software patents. Microsoft, for example, supports software patents, notwithstanding that, at that time, it was engaged in a software patent infringement action, *Stac Electronics v. Microsoft,*[65] that resulted in a jury verdict of $120 million against Microsoft. Many smaller, start-up companies testified that they also favor software patents as a means of obtaining investment dollars and as protection against competitors. As might be expected, the patent attorneys who testified also favor software patents. While this undoubtedly has the appearance of nest-feathering, keep in mind that nearly all patent attorneys also practice copyright law.

Two groups took a stand against software patents. Arguably the most vocal against software patents were the individual computer programmers. These persons express concern that writing software is next to impossible if every line of code must receive patent clearance. Also quite vocal were a handful of individual companies that have been accused of infringing a software patent. Many of these witnesses express outrage over what the Patent Office has been issuing.

The Software Patent Hearings also demonstrate that there is much confusion over software patents. One witness, believing himself to be testifying *for* software copyrights and *against* software patents, cites the *Apple v. Microsoft*[66] litigation over the Windows™ interface as an example of how wasteful and

---

[63] A transcript of the Software Patent Hearings in San Jose and in Washington, D.C. is found in **App. A.**

[64] 1978 Software Subcomm. to the Nat'l Comm'n on New Technological Uses of Copyrighted Works 11.

[65] Stac Electronics v. Microsoft Corp., No. 93-00413 (C.D. Cal. Jan 23, 1994).

[66] Apple Computer, Inc. v. Microsoft Corp., No. C88-20149 (N.D. Calif. filed Mar. 17, 1986).

expensive patent litigation is. Unfortunately, the witness fails to recognize that *Apple* was a copyright infringement case. No patent was involved.

HISTORY OF COMPUTERS

§ 1.16   First Computer

It is difficult to identify the very first computer, because the answer depends on how the term "computer" is defined. Writing about computers, or "mechanical brains," in 1949, Edmund Berkeley defined it this way:

> Essentially, a *mechanical brain* is a machine that handles information, transfers information automatically from one part of the machine to another, and has a flexible control over the sequence of its operations.[67]

Berkeley claims that much of the technology in the mechanical brain had existed for more than 2000 years. Only two properties were missing:

> No human being is needed around such a machine to pick up a physical piece of information produced in one part of the machine, personally move it to another part of the machine, and there put it in again. Nor is any human being needed to give the machine instructions from minute to minute. Instead we can write out the whole program to solve a problem, translate the program into machine language, and put the program into the machine.[68]

The written "program" Berkeley describes is software.

To fully understand Berkeley's "mechanical brain" definition, you can treat the definition like a patent claim and compare it with the prior art. James Burke gives a good account of the prior art in his book *Connections.*[69] By the early 1700s inventors developed a technology to give minute by minute instructions to a machine, in this case an automated organ. Using the pegged cylinder, of the now familiar music box, physical "machine language" instructions caused the water wheel driven organ to play a preprogrammed tune, without human intervention. The pegged wheel was hardly flexibly programmable, although it was constructed using software. The software involved placing pegs on the cylinder according to a series of holes cut in a piece of squared paper, which was fitted around the cylinder as a pattern.[70]

---

[67] Edmund C. Berkeley, Giant Brains or Machines that Think 5 (John Wiley & Sons 1949).

[68] *Id.*

[69] James Burke, Connections (1978).

[70] *Id.* at 110–11.

Burke reports that Basile Bouchon (son of an organ maker), working to improve weaving looms, saw a useful connection between the organ and the loom. Bouchon used a punched paper roll containing a "program" of the desired woven pattern. The roll was pressed against a series of rods that in turn raised and lowered the appropriate threads to produce the programmed woven pattern.[71] Bouchon's innovation was improved upon in 1741 by automata maker, Jacques de Vaucanson, who placed the punched paper roll program on a ratchet-driven cylinder, allowing the program to operate automatically. The silk weavers of the day rioted and Bouchon's innovation was imprisoned in a museum. Fifty years later, in 1800, Joseph Marie Jacquard rebuilt the Vaucanson loom, keeping the ratchet drive but replacing the paper roll cylinder with a series of punched cards.[72] Jacquard's punched cards made the system more flexibly programmable, because the weaver could easily modify or extend the woven pattern by exchanging or adding new cards.

From the weaving trade, the idea of using punched paper as a program spread to manufacturing, and ultimately to data processing. In 1847 Richard Roberts in England used the technique to control a riveting machine.[73] Herman Hollerith in the United States developed a system using punched cards for recording and tabulating census data. Hollerith's punched card system was used when the 1890 census was taken.

In designing his punch cards, Hollerith made them the size of dollar bills. He did so to be able to use the dollar bill holders already on the market.[74] There was genius in his decision, for standardizing his cards on an existing commercial size made the technology affordable and allowed the cards to proliferate well beyond the single census application.

§ 1.17 —Charles Babbage

Had Charles Babbage gotten funding, the history of the first computer would be written differently. Charles Babbage, born in 1791, had been exasperated by the numerous inaccuracies he found in published mathematical tables. These tables were important. Scientists, engineers, bankers, accountants, and everybody relied on them when calculating to an accuracy beyond a few figures. In 1822 Babbage built a prototype mechanical calculator called a "difference engine," named after the way multiplication and division were calculated as a series of "differences." Babbage convinced the British government to fund his difference engine project (Difference Engine No. 1), and Babbage worked on the device for ten years, without success. Later, in 1834,

---

[71] *Id.*

[72] *Id.* at 111.

[73] *Id.* at 112.

[74] *Id.*

he conceived of a more powerful "Analytical Engine." Another mechanical design, the Analytical Engine could perform all of the arithmetic operations, executing them in any sequence. It included a separate "store" and "mill," equivalent to the memory and CPU of today's computers. The Analytical Engine could be programmed using punched cards (à la the Jacquard loom) and it could control the sequence of its calculations, taking alternate courses of action depending on the result of a calculation.

Sadly, the Analytical Engine was never built. The British government refused Babbage a grant to build it, which is not surprising given the experience with Difference Engine No. 1. Whether Babbage could have built his Analytical Engine no one knows. Perhaps, someday, someone will build Babbage's Analytical Engine to prove that his design was correct. This has already happened with the Difference Engine. In November 1991, Doron D. Swade and colleagues built a later, more elegant version of Babbage's Difference Engine (Difference Engine No. 2), and it worked—on November 29, 1991, less than a month before Babbage's 200th birthday, the machine completed its first full-scale calculation successfully.[75]

§ 1.18   —Founding of IBM

Following his success in automating the 1890 census, Hollerith formed the Tabulating Machine Company in 1896, which he later sold in 1911 to the Computing-Tabulating-Recording Company (CTR). Hollerith personally received over $1 million for his shares of the Tabulating Machine Company. Three years later, in 1914, CTR hired Thomas J. Watson to be its general manager. When Watson joined, CTR was an uncoordinated conglomeration. It sold meat and cheese slicers, commercial scales, industrial time clocks, and tabulators. It took Watson ten years to restyle the company, but in 1924 Watson finally managed to focus the company on one business, calling the new company the International Business Machines Corporation (IBM).[76] It was not long before punch card products became the primary business of this newly restructured IBM.

With the business genius of Watson behind it, the Hollerith punched-card technology proliferated. The first punched-card machines were simple tabulators, capable of counting but not much else. The tabulator was a machine roughly the size of a small spinet piano. It had clock face counter dials on which the tabulated "count" was displayed. Punched cards were read by spring loaded pins that the operator lowered onto the card by pulling a handle.

---

[75] *See* Doron D. Swade, *Redeeming Charles Babbage's Mechanical Computer* 268 Scientific Am. 86 (Feb. 1993).

[76] Charles J. Bashe, Lyle R. Johnson, John H. Palmer & Emerson W. Pugh, IBM's Early Computers (1986).

Where pins encountered punched holes in the card, the pins descended through the holes to make electrical contact with little pools of mercury retained in cups below the card. Each time electrical contact was made, the "count" stored in an "accumulator" was increased, and the new count was shown on the counter dial so the operator could write it down if desired. A separate sorting box, mounted on the far right of the operator, was electrically connected to the pools of mercury, such that metal lids of the appropriate sorting bin opened upon contact of the pins with the mercury, allowing the operator to place the card in the open bin, manually close the lid, and proceed with the next card. The tabulator could be "programmed" by suitably wiring selected pools of mercury to the counting dials and sorting bins.

During the early 1900s engineers added many features to the basic punched-card tabulator. For example, they added an electrically powered accumulator reset in 1917. In 1925 IBM engineers modified the sorter so it would automatically sort cards by designated column. In 1927 accumulators were improved to record subtotals within subtotals. In 1928 IBM replaced Hollerith's dollar bill-sized card of 45 round holes with the 80-column, rectangular hole card, which became the industry standard IBM 80-column card. Also in 1928 IBM modified its tabulators to handle negative numbers. This was done by adding an eleventh row on the card. The row was punched to "flag" negative numbers, so that the tabulator could properly "add" the negative number by first forming its complement (digits which when added result in subtraction). Multiplication was made possible in 1931; so was the ability to represent alphabetical characters.

In 1937 a significant computer milestone was reached. IBM introduced the Type 77 collator, a machine that could make comparisons. The collator had two hoppers for input decks and four card stackers for output decks. It could compare two numbers (or alphabetical characters) and reach a three-way decision: whether number a is less than number b, whether a is greater than b, or whether a is equal to b. This ability to compare one condition with another condition is essential to perform branching, if-then-else logic.

Punched-card machines were still not flexibly programmable, however. Programming via plugwires was simply too slow. It was not IBM, but one of IBM's customers who conceived of a way to make these machines flexible programmable. Wallace J. Eckert, a Columbia University astronomer, wanted to use Columbia University's IBM Difference Tabulator to solve differential equations of planetary motion. Eckert's planetary motion problem was considerably more difficult than balancing a business account ledger, a task for which the IBM machine was designed.

The planetary motion differential equation problem has many computational steps involving integral calculus (integration). To solve differential equations on the Columbia machine meant many labor intensive steps of changing plugwire control panels needed to perform integration. Eckert envisioned a better way, a "calculation control switch." In Eckert's own words:

The calculation control switch contains a row of electric contacts each of which is operated by a rotating cam. The cam is a circular fiber disk which is notched at various points around the circumference. A series of about twenty of these disks are attached to a common shaft to form a sort of player piano roll. When this roll is rotated from one position to the next the various contacts open and close according to the notches in the disks. The circuits from the contacts are used to operate the various control switches on the tabulator and multiplier, and also a number of multicontact relays which effectively change the wiring of the plugboards. Each step in the integration consists of a certain number of distinct machine operations which always come in the same order. Hence in order to have the machines ready for each operation it is only necessary to rotate the roll from one position to the next, one complete revolution corresponding to a complete step in the integration. One roll serves for all equations of a given form, and a new one could be prepared in a few hours.[77]

Eckert's idea caught on. With Watson's support, Eckert got his control switch. Built at IBM's facility at Endicott, the control switch could step through a dozen different operating modes, making it highly useful for scientific calculations. In 1937, IBM offered Eckert's control switch to other astronomers. It was enthusiastically received. Still, most scientists and engineers did not have access to punched-card machines. Thus, while historically quite important, Eckert's invention did not add much to the bottom line at IBM.

§ 1.19   —ENIAC, First Electronic Computer

It was not until World War II that computers entered the electronic age. Prior to and during the war, electronic engineers made great strides improving and using vacuum tubes. Vacuum tubes will amplify tiny signals, making devices such as radar and television possible. Vacuum tubes can also be made to switch on and off, just like a mechanical relay.

In 1941, a physicist, Dr. John W. Mauchly, was contemplating how he could better handle the great mass of numerical information involved in his work. It struck Mauchly that someone should substitute vacuum tubes for the mechanical relays in conventional computers. Numerical computations could then be done at high speeds. That someone turned out to be him.

Mauchly joined the Moore School of Electrical Engineering in 1941, hoping to find some way of developing electronic computing. With the war imminent, Mauchly was able to convince the Ordnance Department of the United States Army to fund a project to build a computer using vacuum tubes. With the aid of a young electrical engineering student, J. Presper Eckert, Jr., Mauchly designed and build the first electronic computer. It took

---

[77] W.J. Eckert, Punched Card Methods in Scientific Computation 77 (1940).

about four years and 18,000 vacuum tubes, but the computer worked. Named ENIAC, for Electronic Numerical Integrator and Calculator, it could perform 5,000 additions per second. That was lightning fast, compared to mechanical relay computers, which could only perform about 10 additions per second.[78]

ENIAC was an enormous device. Its main part comprised 42 panels, each nine feet high, two feet wide and one foot deep. Counting all of the parts, including the 18,000 vacuum tubes, ENIAC had nearly a half a million parts. ENIAC required about 150 kilowatts of power to operate (equivalent to 1,500 100-watt light bulbs). The cost to develop ENIAC was over a half a million dollars.

Eckert and Mauchly left the University and formed the Eckert-Mauchly Computer Corporation to build a vacuum tube computer for the United States Bureau of Census. Delivered to the Census Bureau in 1951, the new computer was called UNIVAC, which stands for Universal Automatic Computer. Eckert and Mauchly applied for and were granted a patent on their vacuum tube computer invention. Unfortunately for them, the application for patent was not filed in time and the patent was declared to be invalid.[79]

The controversy over the Eckert and Mauchly patent application did not stop there, however. During patent infringement litigation which resulted in the patent being declared invalid, Dr. John Vincent Atanasoff testified as a key witness for the defense. Atanasoff testified that he and his graduate student assistant, Clifford Berry, were the first to develop the all-electronic digital computer and that Mauchly derived the idea from them. Judge Earl R. Larson was persuaded by Atanasoff's testimony and found that Mauchly had indeed derived certain concepts from Atanasoff.

Judge Larson's decision divided the sea of controversy into two bodies, those who credit Eckert and Mauchly and those who credit Atanasoff and Berry with the discovery of the first electronic digital computer. No matter who is correct, one thing is clear. The electronic digital computer has changed humanity.

§ 1.20 Software Soul of Computer Self-Control

Before moving ahead to the history of software, take another look at Berkeley's definition of a "mechanical brain," noting what parts of the brain were developed when. Berkeley defines a mechanical brain as "a machine that handles information, transfers information automatically from one part

---

[78] Edmund C. Berkeley, Giant Brains or Machines That Think 113 (John Wiley & Sons 1949).

[79] Honeywell, Inc. v. Sperry Rand Corp., 180 U.S.P.Q. (BNA) 673 (D. Minn. 1973).

of the machine to another, and has a flexible control over the sequence of its operations."[80]

Digital control based on binary numbers existed with the very first pegged cylinder automated organ, and with the very first Bouchon loom. Eighteenth century organ makers and loom makers probably did not know or care that they were using binary numbers, but by constructing machines that responded to on-off signals encoded in pegged wheels and in punched paper rolls and cards, they were using digital control and binary numbers to handle and transfer information from one part of the machine to another. These machines were not computers, however.

Getting back to Berkeley's definition of the "mechanical brain," the missing link appears to be the ability to exert flexible control over its operations. This is what distinguishes the UNIVAC computer from the Jacquard loom. Both handle and transfer information, but the loom cannot flexibly control its own operations. True, the weave patterns are programmable by exchanging punched cards for other punched cards. However, the UNIVAC computer can itself control the sequence of operations; the Jacquard loom cannot. The UNIVAC computer can perform conditional "if-then" logic; the Jacquard loom cannot. The UNIVAC computer can add two binary numbers, and make a decision based on the result; the Jacquard loom cannot. Thus, flexible self-control, it would seem, is the essential ingredient that distinguishes a computer from other automated machines, and software is the soul of this self-control.

HISTORY OF SOFTWARE

§ 1.21   Unbundling of Software

From the day the first UNIVAC was delivered to the United States Bureau of Census in 1951, until the mid 1960s, software was not thought of as a product that could be bought and sold apart from the computer. Software was "bundled" with the computer, meaning that the software was furnished "free" with the purchase of a computer. Of course, the software was not really "free." The customer paid for the software as part of the computer system, and the software could not be purchased separately. All of the major computer manufacturers of that era, IBM, Univac, Honeywell, RCA, Burroughs, and NCR, bundled software with hardware.

There was good reason for this. Computers, in those days, were massive mainframes and software was mostly esoteric operating system software, low

---

[80] Edmund C. Berkeley, Giant Brains or Machines That Think 5 (John Wiley & Sons, New York 1949).

level system utilities, and language compilers. In fact, before 1955 computers were coded entirely in machine language.[81] There were no consumer-oriented software packages even remotely resembling the software now available for personal computers. Software was largely unique to each computer, because each computer had to be programmed locally. Except for universities and large corporate and government institutions, most computer owners simply did not have the expertise to program their computers, hence they relied heavily on the computer manufacturer to provide them with software and support.

As computers proliferated, providing this software and support became increasingly costly for computer manufacturers. During the IBM antitrust litigation IBM presented testimony that "[d]uring the early and mid 1960s persons within IBM observed that programming expenditures were 'skyrocketing' and 'increasing dramatically'."[82]

Between 1955 until roughly 1962 computer owners started learning how to program their computers for themselves. This placed even greater pressure on the computer manufacturers, because these educated computer owners now knew what software they wanted, and they wanted more. Computer owners formed users groups to help each other and to provide the additional level of support which the computer manufacturers were not able to provide. One notable users group was SHARE. SHARE was formed by IBM computer users to share programming information and software. Wisely, IBM worked cooperatively with SHARE, and between 1962 and 1970 SHARE made systematic attempts to select and distribute the most useful software. Among the software distributed were manufacturer's libraries of subroutines, algorithms published in technical journals, computer code published in textbooks, and in some instances, programs written to solve problems in specific areas.[83] While SHARE members were busy distributing software for free, by the mid 1960s, software houses also entered the marketplace and began selling software products that competed with IBM's unpriced offerings.[84]

IBM faced a dilemma. Should it continue to bundle software and support with its computers; or should it unbundle software and price it as a separate product like the software houses were doing? To continue to bundle software meant to lose revenue; to unbundle software meant to lose control. IBM could remain bundled and keep its software proprietary, as it had been doing.

---

[81] Computer Science & Engineering Research Study (COSARS), *What Can Be Automated?* 110 (Bruce W. Arden, ed. 1980).

[82] Historical narrative statement of Richard B. Mancke, Franklin M. Fisher & James W. McKie, United States v. IBM, Exhibit 14,971, p. 464.

[83] Computer Science & Engineering Research Study (COSARS), *What Can Be Automated?* 110 (Bruce W. Arden, ed. 1980).

[84] Historical narrative statement of Richard B. Mancke, Franklin M. Fisher & James W. McKie, Exhibit 14,971, at 464, *cited in* U.S. v. IBM.

This meant IBM would continue to bear the skyrocketing expense of programming without cost recovery, and to watch while users groups freely traded and while software houses got rich. Alternatively, IBM could unbundle and face the question of how to protect its software from being freely copied and from having its value thereby destroyed.

During the IBM antitrust litigation IBM presented testimony that, in 1965, it was stated within IBM that "an overriding factor against unbundling [certain programming] is our present inability to protect the proprietary use of our programming systems."[85] R.H. Bullen, then an IBM Vice President and Group Executive, saw this as the critical issue, writing in 1965, "We must settle on whether or not, and to what degree, we can protect programs before we can deal adequately with the question of selling them."[86]

Market pressures ultimately won out, and IBM decided it must unbundle. However, IBM did not jump into the unbundling waters without careful testing. In 1966 IBM made attempts to quantify the return to IBM on its programming expenditures.[87] On December 6, 1968, with the return looking favorable, IBM publicly announced its plans "to make changes in the way it charges for and supports its data processing equipment."[88] IBM gave details of the unbundling plan on June 23, 1969, but the actual unbundling plan did not take effect until January 1, 1970.

§ 1.22   Recognition of Software Patent Law by Supreme Court

Justice Jackson once stated in a dissent, "The only patent that is valid is one this Court hasn't been able to get its hands on."[89] At the turn of the twentieth century, and indeed until the 1970s, the Supreme Court favored free market competition and disfavored legal monopolies.[90] Many patents were struck down. Ever wary, the Supreme Court feared that Congress would, like the sovereign in England had, remove existing knowledge from the public domain, or might restrict free access to materials already available. Thus even though the Patent Act of 1952 had codified the nonobviousness requirement of patentability,[91] the Supreme Court made it clear in *Graham v. John Deere Co.* that Congress did not have the power to take away:

---

[85] *Id.*

[86] *Id.*

[87] *Id.*

[88] *Id.*

[89] Jungersen v. Ostby & Barton Co., 335 U.S. 560, 572 (1949).

[90] Oxford Companion to the Supreme Court of the United States 623 (Kermit L. Hall, ed. 1992).

[91] 35 U.S.C. § 103 (1952).

The Congress in the exercise of the patent power may not overreach the restraints imposed by the stated constitutional purpose. Nor may it enlarge the patent monopoly without regard to the innovation, advancement or social benefit gained thereby. Moreover, Congress man not authorize the issuance of patents whose effects are to remove existent knowledge from the public domain, or to restrict free access to materials already available.[92]

These are strong words, expressed in the negative, stating what Congress may not do. The Constitution, to which the Supreme Court is bound, states in positive terms, Congress shall have the power "to promote the Progress of Science and the useful Arts."[93] The Supreme Court, in *Graham v. John Deere Co.,* interprets what the Constitution means to promote progress:

Innovation, advancement, and things which add to the sum of useful knowledge are inherent requisites in a patent system which by constitutional command must "promote the Progress of . . . useful Arts." This is the *standard* expressed in the Constitution and it may not be ignored.[94]

The Court in *Graham* quoted at length from the writings of Thomas Jefferson in weighing precisely how to measure innovation and advancement. "The inherent problem," the Court stated, "was to develop some means of weeding out those inventions which would not be disclosed or devised but for the inducement of a patent."[95] The answer, the Court found, was in the statutorily codified requirement of nonobviousness.

Why all the fuss? Why go back to the writings of Thomas Jefferson? After all, the 1952 Act includes a nonobviousness provision. The reason was that some of the parties, and several "friends of the court" in gratuitously submitted amicus briefs, contended that the nonobviousness provision of the 1952 Act was intended to sweep away the judicial precedent of the last one hundred years, and to *lower* the standard of patentability. The Supreme Court disagreed with this contention and ruled that the nonobviousness provision, 35 U.S.C. § 103, merely codified judicial precedent first embraced in 1851 in *Hotchkiss v. Greenwood.*[96]

---

[92] 383 U.S. 1, 5–6 (1966).

[93] U.S. Const. art. I, § 8, cl. 8.

[94] Graham v. John Deere Co., 383 U.S. 1, 6 (1966).

[95] *Id.* at 11.

[96] 11 How. 248, 13 L. Ed 683 (1851); *cited in* Graham v. John Deere Co., 383 U.S. 1, 16–17 (1966).

§ 1.23   —*Gottschalk v. Benson*

Although the family tree of software patent decisions traces its roots back to the 1840s,[97] the Supreme Court first ruled on a modern day software patent in the 1972 decision in *Gottschalk v. Benson*.[98] This is an extremely important case in the law of software patents, for it is largely the reason most did not even consider filing software patent applications until the 1980s.

At issue in *Benson* was a claimed invention for converting binary-coded decimal (BCD) numerals into pure binary numbers. The claims required a series of bit manipulations which, when performed, converted the number from BCD form to binary form. Claim 8 could be entirely performed by a person with pencil and paper. Claim 1 recited use of a "re-entrant shift register," but could otherwise be performed by a person with pencil and paper.

The Supreme Court struck down the claims as being nonstatutory subject matter, holding:

> It is conceded that one may not patent an idea. But in practical effect that would be the result if the formula for converting BCD numerals to pure binary numerals were patented in this case. The mathematical formula involved here has no substantial practical application except in connection with a digital computer, which means that if the judgment below is affirmed, the patent would wholly pre-empt the mathematical formula and in practical effect would be a patent on the algorithm itself.[99]

The decision in *Benson* was correct. The problem with the *Benson* decision was that people read *Benson* to be a prohibition of software patents, notwithstanding that the Court expressly states that the decision is not a prohibition, "It is said that the decision precludes a patent for any program servicing a computer. We do not so hold."[100]

The root of the confusion lies in the way the Court expresses its holding. In his decision, Justice Douglas ties together three concepts: the idea, the formula, and the algorithm. These concepts are not synonymous.

A naked idea, not reduced to practice, is not patentable (for example, we should mine the moon for minerals and use those minerals to build spaceships is a naked idea, without current reduction to practice). A formula can be patentable (for example, the formula for making polystyrene). An *algorithm,* defined as "a predetermined set of instructions for solving a problem in a limited number of steps"[101] can also be patentable (See, for example,

---

[97] See **Ch. 9.**

[98] 409 U.S. 63 (1972).

[99] *Id.* at 71–72.

[100] *Id.* at 71.

[101] Webster's New World Dictionary of Am. English 34 (3d ed. 1994).

the Karmarkar patent on efficient resource allocation, discussed in **Chapter 11.**)[102]

The difficulty lies in the word "mathematical." The dictionary defines *mathematics* as the group of sciences dealing with quantities, magnitudes, and forms, and their relationships, attributes, and so forth by the use of numbers and symbols.[103] Mathematics therefore encompasses quite a vast intellectual territory. Certainly the Court did not intend to exclude this vast territory from the protection of the patent system. Nevertheless, although the decision simply holds that one may not patent an idea, and that Benson's claimed invention was just an idea, some read Justice Douglas to be equating algorithm with mathematical formula and mathematical formula with idea. Thus, despite the express statement that this was not a prohibition on patents for computer programs, some concluded that computer programs were not patentable.

§ 1.24   —*Parker v. Flook*

The fate of software patents took a temporary turn for the worse in 1978, when *Parker v. Flook*[104] was decided. At issue in that case was a claimed method for updating the alarm limit (a number) used in the catalytic chemical conversion of hydrocarbons. The patent examiner and the Board of Appeals of the Patent Office had rejected Flook's claims because the "point of novelty" in the claimed method was a mathematical algorithm or formula, citing *Gottschalk v. Benson*.[105] Flook appealed, and the Court of Customs and Patent Appeals reversed, holding that, because the claims were limited to updating alarm limits in catalytic conversion processes, the claims did not wholly preempt the mathematical algorithm or formula. This time acting Commissioner of Patents, Lutrelle F. Parker, appealed by filing a petition for a writ of certiorari, urging that "the decision of the Court of Customs and Patent Appeals will have a debilitating effect on the rapidly expanding computer software industry, and will require him to process thousands of additional applications."[106]

The Court's opinion, written by Justice Stevens, states that the case turns entirely on the proper construction of § 101 of the Patent Act, which describes the subject matter that is eligible for patent protection.[107] "It does

---

[102] Karmarkar, "Method and Apparatus for Efficient Resource Allocation," U.S. Patent No. 4,744,028 (May 10, 1988), assigned to AT&T Bell Lab.

[103] Webster's New World Dictionary of Am. English 835 (3d ed. 1994).

[104] 437 U.S. 584 (1978).

[105] 409 U.S. 63, 71 (1972).

[106] Parker v. Flook, 437 U.S. 584, 587–88 (1978).

[107] *Id.* at 588 (1978); 35 U.S.C. § 101.

not involve," Stevens writes, "the familiar issues of novelty and obviousness that routinely arise under §§ 102 and 103 when the validity of a patent is challenged."[108] This statement is significant, because in the analysis which follows, Justice Stevens appears to apply issues of novelty and obviousness in the Court's § 101 analysis:

> Respondent's process is unpatentable under § 101, not because it contains a mathematical algorithm as one component, but because once that algorithm is assumed to be within the prior art, the application, considered as a whole, contains no patentable invention.[109]

Justice Stewart, joined by Chief Justice Burger and Justice Rehnquist, points out this inconsistency in the dissent:

> The Court today . . . strikes what seems to me an equally damaging blow at basic principles of patent law by importing into its inquiry under 35 USC § 101 [35 USCS § 101] the criteria of novelty and inventiveness.[110]

Regardless of the analysis used, the Court saw its holding as follows: "Very simply, our holding today is that a claim for an improved method of calculation, even when tied to a specific end use, is unpatentable subject matter under § 101."[111]

§ 1.25   —*Diamond v. Chakrabarty*

Beginning in the 1970s, the executive and legislative branches reassessed the role of intellectual property, as the United States continued to lose market share in the international markets. The Supreme Court similarly responded in the 1980s with a series of decisions demonstrating that the judicial pendulum had changed direction and had began to swing in a pro-patent direction.[112]

Without a doubt, the most significant decision of the 1980s in the pro-patent direction is *Diamond v. Chakrabarty,* the decision, written by Justice Burger, which held biogenetically engineered life forms are patentable.[113] The invention was a human-made, genetically engineered bacterium that was capable of breaking down multiple components of crude oil—the invention is therefore of potentially significant value in treating oil spills. Chakrabarty

---

[108] Parker v. Flook, 437 U.S. 584, 588 (1978); 35 U.S.C. §§ 102, 103.

[109] 437 U.S. 584, 594 (1978).

[110] *Id.* at 600.

[111] *Id.* at 595 n.18.

[112] Oxford Companion to the Supreme Court of the United States 623 (Kermit L. Hall, ed. 1992).

[113] 447 U.S. 303 (1980).

and Chakrabarty's assignee, General Electric Company, must be credited with the patience of Job, if not visionary genius, for the Chakrabarty patent application was filed in 1972—eight years before the Supreme Court ruling.

To answer the question of whether human-made life forms are patentable subject matter, Justice Burger turns to the words of Thomas Jefferson and to the Patent Act of 1793, which defined statutory subject matter as "any new and useful art, machine, manufacture, or any new or useful improvement [thereof]."[114] The Act, Justice Burger notes, embodied Jefferson's philosophy that "ingenuity should receive a liberal encouragement."[115] Subsequent patent statutes in 1836, 1870, and 1874, Burger observes, employed this broad language. The 1952 Patent Act replaced the word "art" with the word "process," but otherwise left Jefferson's language intact. Perhaps the most forceful evidence relied upon by Burger, and certainly the most frequently quoted, was the legislative history accompanying the 1952 Patent Act. The Committee Reports leading up to that act inform us that Congress intended statutory subject matter to "include anything under the sun that is made by man."[116]

Justice Burger makes it clear that § 101 has its limits. Not every discovery qualifies as patentable subject matter. The laws of nature, physical phenomena, and abstract ideas, for example, are not patentable.[117] Burger considers the inventions in *Parker v. Flook*[118] and *Gottschalk v. Benson*[119] to fall within this category, for he cites those cases for the proposition that laws of nature, physical phenomena, and abstract ideas are not patentable.[120] Burger has no difficulty finding that these microorganisms fall into the category of patentable subject matter:

> [R]espondent's micro-organism plainly qualifies as patentable subject matter. His claim is not to a hitherto unknown natural phenomenon, but to a non-naturally occurring manufacture or composition of matter—a product of human ingenuity "having a distinctive name, character [and] use."[121]

Why a decision on patentability of human-made, genetically engineered life forms has any applicability to the patentability of computer software was made clear one year later in *Diamond v. Diehr.*[122]

---

[114] § 1, 1 Stat. 319 (1793).

[115] Diamond v. Chakrabarty, 447 U.S. 303, 308–09 (1980), quoting Letter to Oliver Evans (May 1807), 5 Writings of Thomas Jefferson, at 75–76 (Washington, ed. 1871).

[116] *Id.* at 309, *citing* S. 1979, 82d Cong., 2d Sess. (1952); H.R. 1923, 82d Cong., 2d Sess. (1952).

[117] Diamond v. Chakrabarty, 447 U.S. 303, 309 (1980).

[118] 437 U.S. 584 (1978).

[119] 409 U.S. 63 (1972).

[120] Diamond v. Chakrabarty, 447 U.S. 303, 309 (1980).

[121] *Id.* at 309–10, *citing* Hartranft v. Wiegmann, 121 U.S. 609, 615 (1887).

[122] Diamond v. Diehr, 450 U.S. 175 (1981).

§ 1.26   —*Diamond v. Diehr*

The rationale in *Diamond v. Chakrabarty,*[123] that Congress intended statutory subject matter to "include anything under the sun that is made by man,"[124] is powerful. If, under this rationale, biogenetically engineered life forms are patentable subject matter, then computer software must also be patentable subject matter. This was the holding in *Diamond v. Diehr,*[125] which was decided nine months after *Diamond v. Chakrabarty.*

At issue in *Diamond v. Diehr* was a claimed process for molding raw, uncured synthetic rubber into cured precision products. One step in the process involved performing a mathematical computation of Arrhenius' equation for calculating the cure time, in order to determine when to automatically open the mold. The Patent Examiner and the Board of Appeals had both found Diehr's claim, like the claim in *Parker,* to be directed to unpatentable subject matter. The Court of Customs and Patent Appeals, reviewing the decision of the Examiner and the Board of Appeals, reversed. The Court of Customs and Patent Appeals found that a claim drawn to subject matter otherwise statutory does not become nonstatutory because a computer is involved.[126] Again, as had been done in *Parker,* the Commissioner of the Patent Office sought certiorari.

Justice Rehnquist, writing the opinion of the Court, agreed with the Court of Customs and Patent Appeals.

> Arrhenius' equation is not patentable in isolation, but when a process for curing rubber is devised which incorporates in it a more efficient solution of the equation, that process is at the very least not barred at the threshold by § 101.[127]

The error the Patent Examiner and the Board of Appeals had made was to dissect the claim into old and new elements, and then to ignore the presence of the old elements in the § 101 analysis. The Court denounces this approach, stating that the claim as a whole must be considered. Considering Diehr's claim as a whole, the Court states:

> We view respondents' claims as nothing more than a process for molding rubber products and not as an attempt to patent a mathematical formula. We recognize, of course, that when a claim recites a mathematical formula (or scientific principle or phenomenon of nature), an inquiry must be made into

---

[123] 44 U.S. 303 (1980).

[124] S. 1979, 82d Cong., 2d Sess. (1952); H.R. 1923, 82d Cong., 2d Sess. (1952).

[125] Diamond v. Diehr, 450 U.S. 175 (1981).

[126] *In re* Diehr, 602 F.2d 982 (C.C.P.A. 1979).

[127] Diamond v. Diehr, 450 U.S. 175, 188 (1981).

whether the claim is seeking patent protection for that formula in the abstract. A mathematical formula as such is not accorded the protection of our patent laws.[128]

The history of software patents is not through being written. *Diamond v. Diehr* has shined the sunlight of *Chakrabarty* on software patents, and software patents will no doubt flourish. Yet decisions like *Parker v. Flook* remain, to hold this growth in check, just as the Case of Monopolies did nearly 400 years ago. (See § **1.3.**)

---

[128] *Id.* at 191.

CHAPTER 2

SOFTWARE TECHNOLOGY PRIMER FOR THE ATTORNEY

§ 2.1   Software Primer

This chapter is a primer on software technology for the attorney. The focus is on software, not hardware. This chapter assumes a basic knowledge of how a computer works.

With a basic understanding of software technology, you can communicate with an inventor, or with a client, or with an expert witness. In reviewing a software patent, you want to understand the technology, in order to understand the scope of the claimed invention. In drafting a software patent application, you want to ferret out what the invention is, so you can claim it. You want to be able to recognize an enabling disclosure, and how to write an enabling disclosure that will minimize the chances of criticism that the disclosure leaves too much to "undue experimentation."

§ 2.2   Nature of Computers and Software

Software is that which empowers a computer to handle information and to control information flow. One scholar takes the essence of software even farther:

What is a program? At first glance, programs have two different sorts of manifestations. On the one hand, they are documents of some kind that give a series of instructions to be executed by a computer. But these passive documents can be turned into active physical processes: when a program is executed, the instructions in the document are carried out. The program text is passive, but the *executing* program is an event in real time. Does "program" refer to the passive text, or the active event? The answer is *both,* because from our point of view . . . , *a program is a machine.* The program text represents the machine before it has been turned on. The executing program represents the powered-up machine in active operation. There is no fundamental distinction between the passive program text and the active executing program, just as there is none between a machine before and after it is turned on.[1]

---

[1] David Gelernter & Suresh Jagannathan, Programming Linguistics 1 (1990).

The modern day computer traces its beginnings to the "mechanical brains" of the 1940s. MIT's "differential analyzer," Harvard's IBM "automatic sequence-controlled calculator," Bell Laboratories' "general-purpose relay calculator," and Moore School's ENIAC (Electronic Numerical Integrator and Calculator) are all examples of such mechanical brains.

Edmund Berkeley, publishing in 1949, gives a fascinating account of each of these mechanical brains, predicting that "someday" we will have machines to automatically address envelopes using an address list; we will have an information library allowing us to dial in "making biscuits" and see a movie of how to do it together with printed recipe; we will have automatic translators turning English into Swedish; we will have automatic typists capable of scanning printed text and controlling a typewriter to reproduce that text; and we will have an automatic stenographer that will listen to our spoken sounds and write them down in properly spelled English words.

It is intriguing to compare Berkeley's predictions with what has already come true. Today, nearly all word processor software has a mail merge feature for automatically addressing envelopes. Our mailboxes are stuffed with bulk mailings generated by such programs. There are currently several recipe programs and current multimedia technology makes the computer-controlled movies a reality. We also have programs that can translate text from one language to another, although presently the translations are not as artful as a human translator can do. Berkeley's automatic typist is no doubt met by today's text scanning and optical character recognition software. As to Berkeley's automatic stenographer, that technology is on the verge of becoming reality. Continuous speech recognizers have already been introduced that allow computers to be operated using spoken commands. Presently these recognizers are not good enough to take dictation, but someday they will be.

Some of these early mechanical brains were comprised of gears, screws, and shafts. Others were comprised of electromagnetic relays. Perhaps the most advanced, ENIAC, used 18,000 vacuum tubes, capable of performing 5000 additions a second (when all of the tubes worked).[2]

When these mechanical brains were first developed, Berkeley reports, much of the information processing essence of software was already known. What made these machines and their software different was that, for the first time, information could be transferred automatically and the sequence of computing operations could be controlled flexibly. As Edmund Berkeley explains it:

> Essentially, a *mechanical brain* is a machine that handles information, transfers information automatically from one part of the machine to another, and has a flexible control over the sequence of its operations.

*   *   *

---

[2] Edmund Callis Berkeley, Giant Brains or Machines that Think (John Wiley & Sons 1949).

Machines that handle information have existed for more than 2000 years. These two properties [transferring information automatically and controlling sequence of operations] are new, however, and make a deep break with the past.[3]

It is a bit unfortunate that Berkeley, and others, chose to describe the first computers as "mechanical brains" because that description may be, in part, responsible for the historic difficulty the legal system has had with software patents—although certainly through no fault of Berkeley.

In the 1800s, many years before mechanical brains were invented, the courts established a doctrine that mental steps were not patentable. When the mental steps doctrine was established, certainly no judge was thinking about mechanical brains. Similarly, when Berkeley used the term mechanical brains, he could not have foreseen, and probably would not have agreed with, the argument that computer processes are unpatentable mental steps. Patent attorneys spent much of the 1980s arguing this point, and they will probably spend some future decade arguing the point again—when "mechanical brains" actually do evolve into conscious, thinking entities.

Berkeley's mechanical brains of the 1940s were quite primitive, yet they had all components needed to handle and transfer information automatically from one part of the machine to another, and to exert flexible control over the sequence of its operations.

Essential to the function of these early computers, Berkeley explains, are *input* and *output,* where numbers or other information go in and come out, respectively; *storage,* where information can be stored; a *computer* (processor), where numbers and processing instructions are loaded and the processing instructions are performed on the numbers to produce new numbers; and *control,* which coordinates operations, telling input, output, storage, and computer when to exchange information. Modern day computers still employ these essentials, shown in **Figure 2–1.**

Where does software fit in? In Berkeley's simple model, software is information, fed into the input, placed in storage, then delivered from storage to the computer to be used as processing instructions, at a rate dictated by the control. That is essentially the process taking place in computers today. However, as you might suspect, software has become much more sophisticated.

§ 2.3 Computer Science, a Science of Complexity

After mechanical brains, it did not take long for software to evolve from simple processing instructions into higher and higher forms of abstraction. Driving this evolution, computers keep getting faster, storage capacity keeps

---

[3] *Id.* at 5.

getting larger, and the problems to be solved keep getting more complex. Complexity, as it turns out, is the mother of software invention.

Facing complexity, computer scientists devised a "divide and conquer" strategy. In software development today, the divide and conquer strategy is everywhere. The strategy is quite simple. Take a large, unmanageable problem and break it into smaller, more manageable parts. Build the parts; test them. Assemble them into the whole, then test the whole. Conceptually, this is no different than the way a machine of nuts and bolts is built.

§ 2.4   —Layers of Abstraction

Having a mathematical bent, computer scientists went further than simple divide and conquer, however. Computer scientists started looking closely at the problems they were being asked to solve and started seeing those problems as layers of abstraction, like layers of an onion.

For example, consider the problem faced in writing a computer program to print an alphabetically sorted, newspaper column-formatted, *Who's Who in American Literature,* using a computer file containing names stored as lists or strings of letters. At the core of the problem is the simple problem of how to store a string of letters as words of text. Surrounding the core is the next problem layer, how to sort those stored words alphabetically. Surrounding that layer is a yet another layer, how to obtain the sorted list, one name at a time, for printing. Surrounding that layer is a further layer, how to format that list into newspaper columns on a printed page. The layers continue to grow outwardly, like this, until you have conceptually, everything needed to print *Who's Who In American Literature.*

What makes layers of abstraction so powerful is its inherent ability to hide the details. After all, it is all the details that can distract and overwhelm. If

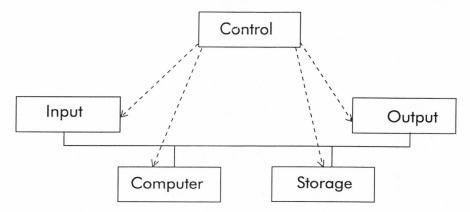

Figure 2–1. Essential components of a computer.

you are trying to print a list of names in newspaper columns, for example, you don't want to be worried, at that stage, about certain letters being accidentally dropped randomly from certain names. Clearly, you want the details properly handled, but you don't want to have to worry about them at every layer of the program. Seeing layers of abstraction in a problem and using this to intelligently hide the details in the appropriate layers is how computer scientists manage complexity.

Layering and detail hiding also does more. A detail hidden at a lower level is invisible from higher levels. Hidden at a lower level, the detail is safe from being inadvertently corrupted by program operations performed at higher levels. Being safe from higher levels makes debugging and maintaining the computer program easier. If data is found corrupted at one level, you know it had to be due to something in that level, or perhaps in some level below, but not in the levels above.

Although the layering concept is still plainly there, there is another way to look at layers. If you wish, you can treat each layer as a separate software entity or module. The modules are linked together like a chain. This linked modules model can be useful, because software is often written as linked modules. **Figures 2–2** and **2–3** compare the layered and linked modules as ways of representing abstractions. Both are used extensively by software developers.

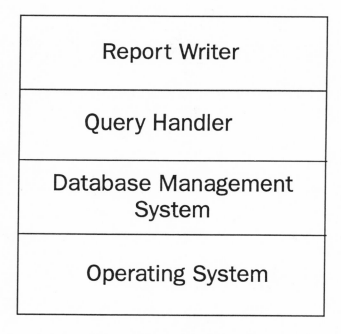

Figure 2–2. Software—layered representation.

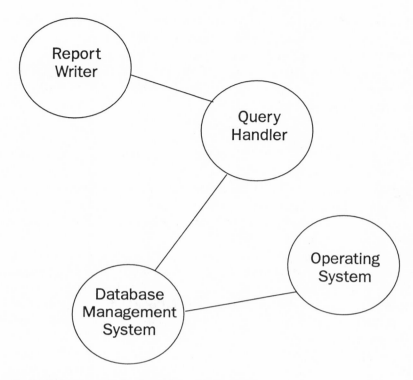

Figure 2–3. Software—linked module representation.

§ 2.5   —Software Interface

There is another important concept lurking between the layers of abstraction. It is the software interface. You may not have seen it at first, but the act of layering implies that information at one layer must communicate with the layers adjacent. Otherwise the layers cannot work as a whole. The linked modules way of representing software shows the interfaces more clearly, as lines connecting the modules.

Whether you prefer to think of software as layers of abstraction or as linked modules, the interface is still there, where the parts are joined, or where the layers meet. The interface serves an important function. It forms a working connection between two software entities. Keep in mind, you are dealing with abstractions and relationships between abstract entities. These abstractions and relationships do not necessarily involve a physical joinder or physical boundary.

Interface is a very powerful concept. It makes division of labor possible. Programmers use division of labor to great advantage. Why write the same information sorting routine ten times, just because information needs to be sorted for ten different purposes? Instead, why not write one, general purpose sorting entity and allow other parts of the program to ask it for sorting help when needed. To do this, programmers simply design the individual entity they need and design an interface to connect them. In this way, each individual entity specializes in only one part of the problem. The interface connects the entities together, allowing them to work in concert while still retaining their individual specialties.

§ 2.6   Building Software

Building software is like building a bridge. You make a survey of what is needed, engineer a proposed solution, write code to implement that solution, test the code, and thereafter maintain the code by adding features, expanding capabilities, and fixing bugs.

The initial survey may involve asking users what the software is to do, where it will be installed, and what type of use it will receive. The engineering work involves designing a model to describe the problem and your proposed solution. At first the model is a mental one, later a written one. Most likely you will discuss the written model with the users, to make sure it will suit their needs.

The written model, like architectural blueprints, may serve as a legal document, becoming part of the contract describing what the programmer has agreed to build and what the user has agreed to pay for. The contract may describe what "deliverables" must be produced and delivered to the user by certain dates.

After the written model has been agreed upon, you begin coding, that is, writing the actual computer program code, or at least the parts of it that are not obtained from other sources.

The above is a very general description of the overall software development process. There are many variations. Today there is even a branch of engineering, called software engineering, devoted to software development. As Roger Pressman describes it:

> Software engineering is an outgrowth of hardware and systems engineering. It encompasses a set of three key elements—methods, tools, and procedures— that enable the manager to control the process of software development and provide the practitioner with a foundation for building high-quality software in a productive manner.[4]

The next section describes two popular approaches for controlling the software engineering process.

---

[4] Roger S. Pressman, Software Engineering: A Practitioner's Approach 19 (2d ed. 1987).

§ 2.7   —Software Engineering

Software engineers view the software engineering process as software development life cycle. Software engineers have several life cycle models, sometimes called life cycle paradigms, that represent different ways of building software. You will learn about two here. There are, no doubt, many more.

§ 2.8   —Waterfall Model

The classic life cycle model is the "waterfall model." Shown in **Figure 2–4,** the waterfall model sequentially cascades from determining requirements, to analysis, to design, to coding, to testing, and finally to maintenance. Each stage depends on completion of the stage before it. The waterfall model is in widespread use today, yet it is also criticized as inflexible, because users are rarely able to state all requirements explicitly at the outset of the requirements stage. Unforeseen requirements always seem to come up. Also, because code is not tested until late in the life cycle, logic errors made in early stages may not get detected until it is too late to fix them without major, costly delays. Nevertheless, the waterfall model lends itself well to target completion date management. Thus, many software project managers and those responsible for keeping the project on schedule use the waterfall model.

§ 2.9   —Rapid Prototyping Model

In response to shortcomings in the waterfall model, the rapid prototyping model was developed. Shown in **Figure 2–5,** the rapid prototyping model proceeds from requirements gathering, to quick design, to prototype building. Then, instead of proceeding immediately to the final product, the prototype is evaluated and this evaluation is used to refine the original requirements. This can result in throwing away the original prototype and building a new one, or several new ones, through a series of iterations. Finally, when the prototype is deemed successful, the final product is engineered.

With its emphasis on iterative refinement, the rapid prototyping model fits many software development projects well, particularly those using object-oriented technology.[5] Logic errors made in early stages are caught and corrected early, before they spread throughout the program. The rapid prototyping model is also more flexible, in that users are encouraged to

---

[5] For more on software engineering and life cycle models, *see* Roger S. Pressman, Software Engineering: A Practitioner's Approach (2d ed.) and Grady Booch, Object-Oriented Design with Applications 267 (1991).

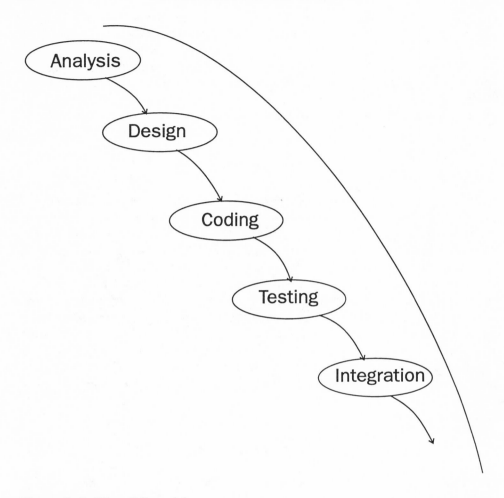

Figure 2–4. Waterfall model.

examine early prototypes and make suggestions for additional features that
may have been originally overlooked.

The disadvantage of the rapid prototyping model is that it is hard to tell
when the program is really finished. A prototype may look like a finished
program, and yet there may be many software quality issues left unad-
dressed. Users, and sometimes software development management, may not
appreciate this and may demand delivery of the prototype as the final product. Programmers dislike being put into this position, knowing the prototype
is being considered as finished when it is not, and knowing they are likely to
be blamed if the prototype fails.

Also, because the prototyping model encourages producing quick prototypes, programmers may use inefficient algorithms or ill-chosen data structures

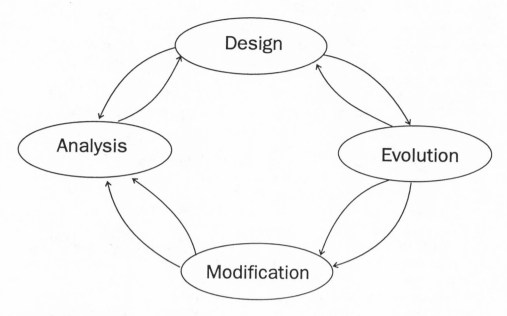

Figure 2–5. Rapid prototyping model.

and operating environments, just to get the prototype working. These poor choices can get overlooked and become a permanent part of the final product.

§ 2.10   —Software Design and Problem Modeling

Regardless of the life cycle model used to manage the development process, at some stage a software design must be developed. Pressman explains what this entails:

> Software design is actually a multistep process that focuses on three distinct attributes of the program: data structure, software architecture, and procedural detail. The design process translates requirements [requirements analysis stage] into a representation of the software that can be assessed for quality before coding begins.[6]

Data structures are very important. Data structures describe what data will be input and output, what data will be stored, and importantly, *how* the data will be stored. A well chosen data structure makes the program easier to write. A well chosen data structure can also make the program run more quickly.

The software design architecture depends on how you model the problem to be solved. You will learn about two different architectural models here, the

---

[6] Roger S. Pressman, Software Engineering: A Practitioner's Approach 21 (2d ed.).

procedural model and the object-oriented model. Software architecture is highly dependent on the capabilities and features of the programming language chosen. Software architectures, and the programming languages used to express them, have been constantly evolving since the first "mechanical brain" was programmed.

Procedural details usually involve algorithms. *Algorithms* are simply a series of steps or systematic procedures for accomplishing a given task.

§ 2.11 —Procedural, Structured Programming Models

Most programmers are first trained to use "top-down" structured design. This involves breaking a problem down first into major steps in the overall process, and then further breaking down each major step into smaller steps, and so forth. The focus is on the process, hence the model is called the procedural model.

Seemingly obvious today, top-down structured design was not always derigueur. In fact, there is good evidence the value of structured programming was not widely recognized before 1968. We can thank Edsger Dijkstra for the enlightenment.

Before about 1963, computer programs simply processed instructions in a single, sequential manner, one step after another. The steps each represented the logical next step of the step that preceded it. That was fine. However, there was one pesky little statement, the GOTO statement, which gave programmers the power to introduce chaos.

The GOTO statement allows programs to leap from one step in the middle of one process, into the middle of another process, skipping any intervening steps and processes. Fans of the television series *Star Trek* are familiar with the "beam me up Scotty" transporter, which occupants of the starship use to instantly transport themselves from the starship a planetary location of their choosing. That is the effect of the GOTO statement. The GOTO statement gives programmers the power of the Star Trek transporter, by allowing program control to vanish from one program space and materialize in another. The problem with this power is that, as a program grows more complex, overuse of the GOTO statement makes the program virtually impossible to read and understand. Programmers call the result "spaghetti code."

In 1968 Edsger Dijkstra wrote a letter to the editor of the *Communications of the ACM* (ACM is the Association for Computing Machinery, formed in 1948. *Communications* is its technical publication responding to rapidly changing subject matter needing shorter submission-to-publication time).

---

7 E.W. Dijkstra, *GOTO Statements Considered Harmful,* Comm. Ass'n for Computing Mach. 11 at 147–48 (Mar. 1968).

Dijkstra's letter, "GOTO Statements Considered Harmful"[7] touched off quite a controversy, but today there is little doubt Dijkstra was right.[8]

Whether the GOTO statement is considered evil and should be banished, or whether the GOTO statement has its place is beside the point. The point of Dijkstra's revelation is that programmers should stay in control and should avoid spaghetti code in favor of structured code. By revealing how the GOTO statement introduces chaos, Dijkstra challenged programmers to think about how to better structure a program to introduce order. Dijkstra's disciples learned quickly and began practicing what is now known as "structured programming."

§ 2.12   —Structured Programming

Structured programming is a disciplined approach to programming in which functional units of program code, such as subroutines or modules, are written as self-contained units that other portions of the program can call upon. Whatever you call these units—subroutines, modules, functions, or procedures—you place them in well-organized, highly structured locations in the program listing. In this way, reading the code months or years later, a programmer knows where to look for the particular code of interest.

§ 2.13   Object-Oriented Model

While the procedural model, using structured programming, is still in high regard, recently another model has risen to prominence. Called the object-oriented model, it involves breaking down a problem in terms of the individual physical entities that exist in the problem domain. For example, instead of concentrating on computer details, such as files, records, sorting algorithms, as a procedural programmer would do, the object-oriented programmer concentrates on problem domain details, such as company departments, products, and employees. These problem domain entities are called objects.

Objects store data representing attributes of the physical objects. They also store *procedures* representing actions the physical object is capable of carrying out. The idea of storing both data and procedures together is key to the object-oriented model.

Object-oriented programming represents a fundamental shift in the way programmers build software. Programmers nearly always write software to solve a problem by modeling the problem. How that model is designed can greatly affect how the software is written and how it performs.

---

[8] For an in-depth account of how software methodology has evolved, *see What Can Be Automated? The Computer Science and Engineering Research Study (COSERS)* 789–820 (Bruce W. Arden, ed., 1980).

§ 2.14 —Comparing Procedural and Object-Oriented Programming

In classic structured programming, using a procedural model, you model a problem in terms of what data is used to start with, what data is desired to end with, and what processes are performed on the starting data to yield the ending data. Procedural programming thus places much emphasis on the data and also on the processes that will be performed on that data. The viewpoint is clearly one of data processing.

In object-oriented programming, you model a problem by building software entities, called objects, which represent the actual physical entities they model. Although there are still data and data processing, they are often hidden within the objects.

Objects may be assembled into larger objects, just as gears, rods, solenoids, and flywheels are assembled into the transmission of your car. For example, assume the problem you are solving is one of managing a regional sales staff handling different product lines, A and B.

Using a procedural model, you might define database records to include "Product Name," "Product Code," "Cost," "Selling Price," "Sales Person," "Sales Volume," and so forth. You would then separately write a procedural program, comprising a series of subroutines, to tell the computer how to process these database records.

Using an object-oriented model, you might construct a "Sale Person" object, a "Product A" object, a "Product B" object, a "Warehouse" object, and maybe even a "Management" object and a "Customer" object. As in real life, each of these objects has certain properties or attributes and each is responsible for performing certain tasks. As in real life, one of these objects may dictate what happens to other objects. Thus the Customer object might contain the program code needed to print the address shipping label. The Product objects might contain the program code needed to update the Warehouse object.

One powerful advantage of object-oriented technology is how internal working details exist without being seen. This ability to hide details without losing them is one reason object-oriented programming is good for modeling large problems. Programmers call this detail hiding *encapsulation.* Details are hidden in a very clever way. They are stored inside the object that uses them. This is quite unlike subroutines of classic structured programming, in which subroutines are stored in a separate place.

In the above example, the Sales Person object, for example, may perform certain hidden functions needed to do its job but otherwise unimportant to the other objects. These are like bodily functions of a person, such as breathing, maintaining a heartbeat, and thinking. Vitally important to the person, these bodily functions of one person are generally not of concern to another person, unless they stop.

Why hide the details? Simply, hiding details helps manage the complexity of a problem; it helps not to lose sight of the forest for the trees. By hiding internal details of individual objects, you can concentrate on the overall system, without getting lost in the details. Because the internal details are stored with each object itself, you know precisely where to look if you need a particular detail.

§ 2.15 Programming Languages

The purpose of a programming language is communication. Fischer and Grodzinsky describe the nature of language this way:

> A set of symbols, understood by both sender and receiver, is combined according to a set of rules, its grammar or syntax. The semantics of the language defines how each grammatically correct sentence is to be interpreted.[9]

The computer does not have a language as much as it has a set of instructions or commands that it can understand. These instructions relate directly to the internal hardware components of the computer itself.

For example, the computer may be built using a microprocessor having an internal data storage cell called a register. The microprocessor comes equipped with the ability to perform certain functions with respect to that register, for example, store a value in the register, read a value from the register, add a value to the contents of the register, and so forth. Preassigned binary numbers are used to designate or name the register and to designate or name each of the possible instructions or commands.

The computer typically also includes additional random access memory (RAM) where data can be stored and retrieved. Each storage cell of this memory is also assigned a unique binary number, called the *memory address,* which is used when it is necessary to read or write data to that memory cell.

To communicate with the computer, that is, with its microprocessor and its memory, you must somehow give the computer instructions, using the binary number machine language it physically understands. To say that the computer actually "understands" is anthropomorphic. At this microscopic level the computer is nothing but a collection of transistorized on/off switches that are selectively turned on and off to match the binary number codes. Therefore, at least with current technology, you should not attribute too much artificial intelligence to the computer at this level.

Computer languages make it easier to give the binary number machine language instructions to the computer. You write instructions using a higher level

---

[9] Alice E. Fischer & Frances S. Grodzinsky, The Anatomy of Programming Languages 1 (1993).

computer language, such as C or FORTRAN or BASIC, and then use a program called a compiler to translate your instructions into machine language.

There have been hundreds of languages developed over the years, representing the evolution in how programmers reason. Computer scientists see this evolution as comprising four generations. Each generation builds on the strengths of prior generations, adding strengths where prior generations were deficient. Below is a list of the four generations, with examples of languages from each generation.

First Generation
   1. FORTRAN I
   2. ALGOL 58
   3. Flowmatic
   4. IPL V
Second Generation
   1. FORTRAN II
   2. ALGOL 60
   3. COBOL
   4. Lisp
Third Generation
   1. PL/1
   2. ALGOL 68
   3. Pascal
   4. C
   5. Simula
Fourth Generation
   1. Smalltalk
   2. Object Pascal
   3. C++
   4. CLOS
   5. Ada

Programs written in first and early second generation languages comprise multiple subroutines all accessing global data. This means that all subroutines have equal access to the data, and hence equal ability to change the data, creating situations in which an error in one subroutine can catastrophically affect all other subroutines by corrupting the data.

Late second generation and early third generation languages solve this problem through parameter passing and controlled data visibility. Where first generation languages rely solely on global data, these later languages also used local data, not visible outside the subroutine or module which owns it. Using local data, an error is less apt to propagate throughout an entire program. These languages also support structured programming. Sequential control or program flow operations such as IF-A-THEN-B-ELSE-C; and WHILE-A-DO-B are included, making it possible to rigorously impose structured programming. Finally these late second generation and early third generation languages add the ability to nest subroutines, allowing subroutines to be treated as physical building blocks.

Late third generation languages further improve modularity by allowing program building blocks or modules to be written as separately compiled entities, to be used at a later time by linking them with other modules. Programmers can thus write much larger programs and can begin to collect modules in organized libraries for later reuse.

Fourth generation languages do for object-oriented programming what the late second and early third generation languages do for structured programming. Fourth generation languages provide constructs for uniting data and program operations into logical building blocks called objects. These objects, called "packages" in Ada, called "classes" in C++ and called "objects" in Smalltalk, are powerful entities, combining properties of procedures and data, fully capable of performing computations and of storing local state.[10]

Computer programming languages are interesting in their own right, as they represent humanity's attempts to communicate our ideas to our machines. In April 1993 the Association of Computing Machines (ACM) held an internationally attended conference on the History of Computing Languages (HOPL-II). It was the second such conference. The first such conference (HOPL-I) was 15 years ago. The HOPL-II committee had the difficult task of selecting, from among hundreds of languages, the most important ones. The HOPL-II committee maintained a strict historian's perspective. No programming language was eligible unless it had been in use for at least 10 years. Of the languages for which papers were submitted, here is the list of the HOPL-II committee's 12 most important languages.

Ada

Algol 68

C

C++

CLU

FORMAC

Forth

---

[10] For more on evolution of languages and the programming topologies they enable, *see* Grady Booch, Object-Oriented Design with Applications 25–32 (1991).

Icon

Lisp

Pascal

Prolog

Smalltalk

Obviously, several important languages (for example, FORTRAN and COBOL) are missing from this list. This is simply because publishable papers on these languages were not submitted. These languages were featured in the first conference, HOPL-I: ALGOL, APL, APT, BASIC, COBOL, FORTRAN, GPSS, JOSS, JOVIAL, LISP, PL/1, SIMULA, and SNOBOL.

§ 2.16 —Language Selection

Once the programmer has the basic system design worked out, he or she starts building the actual computer code that will make up the components of the system. Some special purpose components, such as graphical components, may need to be built using special purpose graphics tools. Aside from these special purpose components, the remainder of the program will probably be written as what is called "source code," using one or more programming languages. As noted above, there are many different programming languages to choose from, each with its own strengths and weaknesses.

Sometimes a programmer will choose a certain programming language because it is better than other languages for expressing the abstractions of how the finished software system is to function. For example, the programming language LISP may be chosen if the finished software needs to understand complex English sentences. (That is not to say that other programming languages could not also be used for this purpose, however.)

The C programming language might be selected if the finished software needs to closely control the internal workings of a computer or microprocessor, especially where processing speed is important or where timing of events is critical.

FORTRAN might be chosen if the program needs to perform a great deal of scientific calculations, such as fast Fourier transforms (FFT's), and the programmer wants to use existing FORTRAN subroutines to do these calculations.

Sometimes a programmer will choose a certain programming language because the company, or the customer, has dictated that a particular language be used. It may be that the program being developed is part of a larger system being developed by different teams of programmers. In this case, a common programming language may be dictated at the outset, to simplify integrating the individual programs into the larger system.

If the system is being developed for the military or some other branch of the federal government, use of the programming language ADA may be a contractual requirement. The ADA programming language was developed under federal contract, to provide a full featured programming language for all military and federal government applications. The idea behind this is to require all government contract programmers to use the same language, so there would be no need to rely on one or two program gurus to maintain critical software systems.

Finally, programmers may select a given language simply because they are most familiar with it. Even for experienced computer programmers, it can take several weeks or more to become reasonably fluent in a programming language. Sometimes the subtleties of a given language, those that give it unique advantages, take years to learn. Therefore unless there is some special reason to select one particular language, many programmers stick to the one they are most familiar with.

As a patent attorney, it is impossible to become fluent in all the different programming languages available to programmers. There are hundreds of different languages and language dialects. Today, having some familiarity with the C programming language will certainly be helpful. Many programs are written in C. However, that was not always the case, and that may not continue to be the case. Nevertheless if you want to learn one programming language, C would be a good choice. There are many good introductory texts on learning C. While learning C, you may also want to learn C++, a close cousin to C. The C++ programming language adds object-oriented programming capabilities to the basic C language. If you want to own the seminal text on C, get *The C Programming Language*[11] by Kernighan and Ritchie. Kernighan and Ritchie developed the C language and describe it in their book.

§ 2.17   —Creating Source Code

Source code is created in much the same way as text is typed using a word processor. In fact, it is possible to use a word processor to create source code. Most programmers do not use general purpose word processors to create source code, but instead favor specialized source code development programs ranging from simple text editors to full-fledged program development systems. Source code development programs, like word processors, typically include text manipulating features such as copy and paste and display features, like multiple windows for viewing different portions of code (text) at the same time.

Unlike word processors, source code development programs also include syntax checkers that check the source code for typing mistakes and other

---

[11] Brian W. Kernighan & Dennis M. Ritchie, The C Programing Language (1978).

violations of the programming language's syntax rules. Often these syntax rules include many punctuation rules that can be quite complex. If the rules are not explicitly followed, the program will not run. A missing semicolon or extra parentheses could be very difficult to spot without the aid of a syntax checker.

§ 2.18 —Compiling Source Code

Once the source code is written, you feed it into a program, called a compiler, which processes the source code, changing it into a form that a computer can understand. This extra step seems curious. Since the programmer has presumably conformed to the computer's requirements by writing the source code in a programming language adapted to the computer's way of thinking, why is it necessary to go through this next step? You might think the computer should be smart enough to understand the source code directly. The answer is that the programming language is really not the language of the computer, but rather it is a language for describing a solution to a class of problems.

In any event, the compiler is the tool that reads the programmer's source code and builds a sequence or collection of binary number instructions to tell the computer precisely what to do. This sequence or collection of binary numbers is sometimes called *object code*. The object code may be a complete set of instructions necessary to operate the computer, or it may be an incomplete set of instructions, requiring that it be linked with additional object code in order operate the computer.

The term executable code is sometimes used to distinguish binary code that will actually run on the computer, as is, from binary code (object code) that needs further processing before it will run. Typically this extra processing involves a process called linking, using another tool called a linker. Large programs, and even moderate-sized programs may be written as several individual components or modules which need to be hooked together, or linked before they will run. Also, to enable a program to run under control of a particular operating system, it may be necessary to link the object code of that program to a stub of standardized object code, which provides an umbilical connection between the program and the operating system.

There are at least as many compilers as there are programming languages. With a few exceptions, most compilers work with source code in only one programming language and create object code for only one type of microprocessor. Thus a software developer writing a product in the C programming language for three platforms, for example, for the Sunn Workstation, the IBM-PC compatible, and the Apple Macintosh, would probably need three C compilers. If part of the program is written in FORTRAN, then three FORTRAN compilers are also required.

§ 2.19   —Computer Aided Software Engineering (CASE) Tools

Archimedes said, "Give me a lever long enough and I will move the world." Programming languages and compilers comprise a huge lever for computer programmers. Without programming languages and compilers, programmers would still be writing programs one computer instruction at a time, writing in native binary code (practically impossible), or writing in easier to remember pneumonic called assembler code or assembly language code (possible, but extremely hard to do).

CASE tools represent an even more powerful lever. CASE stands for Computer Aided Software Engineering. Although CASE tools can mean different things to different programmers, generally they are programs which actually write source code for the programmer. Using a CASE tool, the programmer may simply need to make various selections, by checking boxes or drawing diagrams, to represent the desired result. The CASE tool does the rest, responding to the programmer's selections and writing the source code needed to carry out the programmer's wishes. By producing source code, the programmer is then free to make further modifications directly to the source code if desired.

Actually the CASE tool is to software engineers and systems engineers what the computer-aided design (CAD) tool is to automotive engineers, aerospace engineers, and architects. Both rely heavily on producing computer-aided graphics, to which textual and numeric specifications are attached. The graphics and attached specifications are stored in a design database, where the design is tested for completeness and consistency. It is then printed out, as a series of system specifications and drawings, which comprise the blueprint from which the system is built. As noted above, some CASE tools will even generate actual program source code as one of the printed system specifications.

The ability to build a design database distinguishes CASE tools from other software engineering tools, such as compilers, assemblers, debuggers, project management tools, and reverse engineering tools. CASE tools are still very expensive. Many software developers simply cannot afford them, and therefore must rely on less sophisticated software engineering tools.

Of these other software engineering tools, compilers and assemblers are certainly standard issue to any computer programmer or software engineer. Compilers and assemblers are both forms of translators, taking human-readable code and converting it into machine-readable code. Debuggers are also standard issue. Debuggers are programs that allow you to run a program under controlled conditions, so you can stop the program in mid-cycle and look inside to see if everything is operating as expected. Most compilers today come with built-in debuggers. Project management tools are also quite common. These are simply scheduling tools, to help management keep track of the progress being made on a project.

Somewhat controversial are the reverse engineering tools. These include decompilers and disassemblers, which allow executable code to be converted back into human-readable source code. Some tools even watch as a program runs, and report which sections of the code are used and which are not. Reverse engineering tools are controversial because they enable one to copy another's code and then to disguise the deed. Were reverse engineering tools only useful for this purpose, they would probably be outlawed. However, there are legitimate reasons for reverse engineering.

One example where the legitimate use of reverse engineering tools can hardly be disputed is this. A software developer loses all copies of its source code in a fire. The source code was developed entirely by the software developer, but now only copies of the executable code remain. Can the software developer use reverse engineering tools to recover its source code? Certainly. Of course, real life legal issues are never this simple.

§ 2.20   Large Scale System Design

Some software systems have already become so large, they hardly resemble a computer program any longer. These are large, complex systems, far more intricate than the program that the United States Census Bureau used on its UNIVAC computer in the 1950s to automate the taking of the census. Yet even the largest, most complex systems of today pale in comparison to the biological system of a single living cell.

Large software systems exist today, thanks to the insights of people such as Dijkstra, who recognized that the ancient technique of mastering complexity: *Divide et impera* (Divide and rule), could be applied to build software.[12] In building software, *Divide et impera* translates into structured programming, in which a complex problem is broken down into smaller, but related components. At first, structured programming was used simply to organize source code.[13] Later, structured programming was enhanced by Wirth to include the strategy of successive refinement (or top-down design).[14] The successive refinement strategy starts with the big problem and breaks it down into a small number of tasks that can be combined to solve the big problem. Each of these tasks is, in turn, broken down into smaller subtasks, and the process

---

[12] E.W. Dijkstra, *Programming Considered as Human Activity,* Proceedings of 1965 IFIP Cong. 213–17 (1965).

[13] C. Böhm & G. Jacopini, *Flow Diagrams, Turning Machines and Languages with Only Two Formation Rules,* 9 Communications of the ACM 366–71 (May 1966).

[14] N. Wirth, *Program Development by Stepwise Refinement,* 14 Communications of the ACM 2221–227 (Apr. 1971).

is repeated, until each subtask is so simple that it can be coded with little chance of error.

After top-down, structured programming, the next big insight was the concept of layering, which can be traced to a paper by Dijkstra presented in 1967.[15] The paper describes an operating system, called THE, which had been built using an architecture of successive layers. Building in successive layers is a powerful technique. It allows the lower layers to hide details from the upper layers. This technique, called information hiding, was recognized by Parnas in 1972.[16]

Layering pervades all aspects of large scale systems, even how computers communicate with each other. Controlling how computers communicate with each other is key to building large scale systems, because the data stored in large scale systems and the functions performed by large scale systems are often distributed among a multitude of computers. To work, the computers in a large scale system must communicate, if they are to share data and functions. Computer networks in popular use today all employ some form of sharing data and functions. It is the natural outgrowth of *Divide et impera*.

Do not be misled. Layering, information hiding, distributed data, and distributed functions are not limited to organizing how multiple computers communicate. All of these concepts apply fully to organizing how software is decomposed into multiple modules and how those multiple modules communicate. Microsoft Windows and IBM OS/2 operating systems are each examples of complex software systems that can readily be described by all of these concepts.

There are a number of different layering schemes in use today. Some are proprietary, meaning that their descriptions are not published. Proprietary systems are sometimes called closed systems. Without a published description of the layers involved and how one communicates with them, it is difficult to build software that can communicate with the closed system. Some companies use a closed system architecture precisely for this reason. Making it difficult for others to communicate with the system keeps out competition.

On the opposite side of the fence are the open systems advocates. An open system is one in which a description of the system is published. The trend today is heading away from closed systems to open systems. Consumers are demanding systems that will connect and communicate with other systems. Several efforts have been made to fully document and standardize open systems. The following sections describe two such attempts, the ISO/OSI open systems interconnection standard, and the TCP/IP standard. The later standard is used by computers communicating over the Internet.

---

[15] E.W. Dijkstra, *Structure of the THE—Multiprogramming System,* 11 Comm. of the Ass'n for Computing Mach., 341–46 (May 1968).

[16] D.L. Parnas, On the Criteria to Be Used in Decomposing Systems into Modules, 5 *Comm. of the Ass'n of Computing Mach.* No. 12, at 1053–58 (Dec. 1972).

§ 2.21 —International Organization for Standardization/Open Systems Interconnection (ISO/OSI)

ISO/OSI stands for International Organization for Standardization/Open Systems Interconnection. It is a layered architectural model or plan for how computers communicate with each other over a communications network. The plan divides computer to computer communication into seven layers, each layer building on the one below it. **Figure 2–6** shows the seven layers for each of two computer applications communicating with each other over a physical communication medium. The medium can be anything from twisted pairs of wire, to fiber optic cable, to coaxial cable, to radio link. The objective is to enable application A to communicate with application B over the physical medium. The OSI model describes how this is done.

At the top layer is the OSI *application layer.* It is here that applications A and B are connected. The application layer is designed to insure that the two

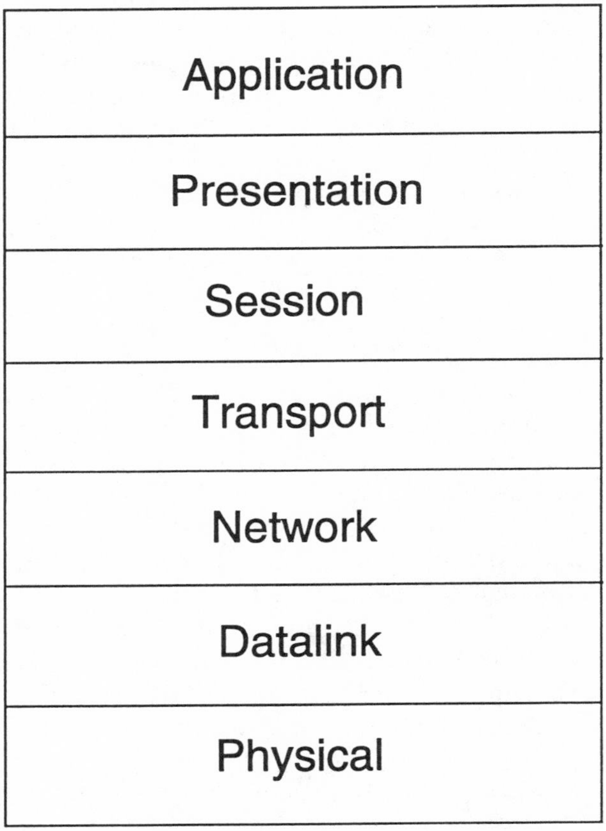

Application
Presentation
Session
Transport
Network
Datalink
Physical

Figure 2–6. ISO/OSI model.

applications understand each other while they each carry on their respective processing tasks. By analogy to a human to human conversation, the application layer is responsible to insure that both understand the semantic meaning of the words they are speaking.

§ 2.22   —Transmission Control Protocol/Internet Protocol (TCP/IP)

TCP/IP stands for Transmission Control Protocol/Internet Protocol. Its purpose is to permit different manufacturer's computing architectures to communicate and operate together. TCP/IP evolved in the United States at around the same time the International Organization for Standardization developed the OSI standard. Whereas, the OSI standard was developed with the rigorously enforced aim to remain completely implementation independent, TCP/IP adopted a more pragmatic approach. TCP/IP standards were based on requests of users. Instead of defining the standards as abstract, implementation independent, rules, TCP/IP was defined using familiar computer languages, usually C. The TCP/IP standards were freely disseminated, on line, and disciples of the standard used it in great numbers. Among the disciples was the United States government, which demanded TCP/IP for all government systems. **Figure 2–7** shows the TCP/IP layers. Note there are fewer layers than ISO/OSI.

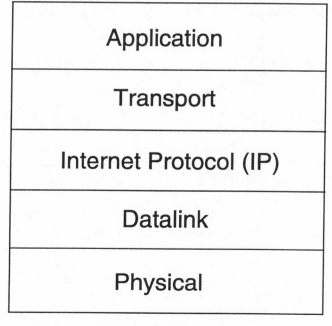

Figure 2–7. TCP/IP model.

§ 2.23 —Client-Server Technology

Client-server technology involves division of labor. More specifically, client-server technology involves a cooperative data processing effort between certain computer programs, called servers, and other computer programs, called clients. Servers provide data processing services to clients. Clients use the services of servers, so clients do not have to perform those processing services for themselves.

There are many ways to structure a client-server system. One very common way is to place the server program on a shared or centralized computer and to place the client programs on one or more desktop computers. You may be familiar with a networked office system that has a centralized file server to which many desktop computers are connected. The desktop computers each run their own copy of an application program, such as word processing. The application programs run independently of the centralized file server and independently of the other desktop computers—turning off one desktop computer does not affect operation of the central computer or of the other desktop computers.

Referring to the centralized computer as the file server is somewhat misleading, because it makes us think the term file server describes the computer. In some contexts that use of the term may be correct, but in the client-server context, the file server is the computer program that stores, organizes, and serves up files that the client programs need to use. These files can be data files, like a letter typed using a word processor; or these files can be application program files, like the word processor program itself.

§ 2.24 —Comparing Client-Server and
Conventional Programming

What's the big deal about client-server architecture? Many commonplace structured programs are constructed of modules or subroutines that call on other modules or subroutines to perform certain data processing tasks. However, client-server technology involves more than mere structured programming. It involves bundling of data with data processing, so that a given software entity can not only hold data, but can also process that data. In classic structured programming, a module or subroutine would rarely do both.

To illuminate, in a classic structured program there may be a subroutine for sorting a list of names alphabetically. Another part of the program responsible for storing a list of names might use the alphabetical sorting subroutine by sending it the list of names and asking that they be returned alphabetically sorted. Alternatively, the list storing part of the program might simply tell the alphabetical sorting subroutine where the list of names may be found, and then ask the alphabetical sorting subroutine to go find the list and sort it. In either case, the alphabetical sorting subroutine has no responsibility for storing the list. It simply operates on the list it is given.

Contrast this with the client-server approach. Assume that the list of names, once sorted, is to be used to generate a telephone book with headings at the top of the page, giving the first name on that page and the last name on that page. Let us say that there are 50 names on a page.

Using a client-server approach, a "Names" server is constructed that has the ability to maintain a database of all names and also has the ability to alphabetically sort those names. A "Page Layout" client is also constructed. The Page Layout client can ask the Names server for the next 50 names and can assume that the names have already been alphabetically sorted by the Names server.

The Page Layout client needs to know nothing about how names are stored or where they are stored. It only needs to know how to ask the Names server and to specify that the next 50 names should be delivered alphabetically sorted.

Similarly, the Names server needs to know nothing about how its names are used. Aside from knowing how to store and alphabetize names, it only needs to know how to receive and respond to requests from servers, such as the Page Layout server.

The client-server approach offers greater versatility still. Perhaps a CD-ROM generating program needs the alphabetized list of names, but it wants all names at once, not parceled out 50 names at a time. In this case, the "CD-ROM Generator" client can ask the Names server to send it all names in its database, at once. The Names server complies, with the same ease as it did to supply the next 50 names to the Page Layout client.

Consider the difference between the (client-server) Names server and the (structured programming) alphabetical sorting subroutine. Both are able to sort a list of names alphabetically. The Names server, however, is also responsible for storing and maintaining the data. It can therefore do far more than simply sort. The Names server can be a full-featured database management program.

Key to this client-server technology is an operating system that permits multiple software entities, that is, clients and servers, to communicate with one another through some form of messages. Client-server technology works best where the operating system permits multiple software entities to run concurrently.

Running concurrently allows the entities to hold a live conversation with one another, the client asking the server for information and the server providing it. This ability to permit multiple software entities to run concurrently is called *multitasking*. UNIX, OS/2 and Windows NT are fully multitasking operating systems, MS-DOS and Windows 3.1 currently are not. Thus expect to see one of the former group of operating systems used as the platform for a client-server system.

§ 2.25 —Client-Server Patent and Trademark Docketing System

What is client-server technology good for? It is good for building complex systems centered around one or more databases. It is good for building systems for which many users need access to data for different reasons, but have no need or desire to learn how to operate the database program that stores that data. Client-server architecture can be put to good use in constructing a patent and trademark docketing system—something with which patent attorneys are familiar. A patent and trademark database is constructed, containing all due dates for a firm or company's patent and trademark matters. The database is probably constructed using commercially available database management program. In the past, anyone wanting to enter new matters into the database, anyone wanting to update records when a due date has been met, anyone wanting to print a monthly report of pending due dates, or anyone simply wanting to check the status of a single matter would have to know how to log onto the database program and enter the required series of commands for that task. That may be fine for clerical users who operate the database program every day. However, occasional users may not remember how to operate the database program.

The client-server approach simplifies use, particularly for occasional users. Under the client-server approach, the database is made a server. Separate client applications are provided for each class of user, the data entry clerical person, the docket administrator, the attorney, and so forth. Each client application can be custom tailored to provide just what that user wants to do.

Being custom tailored, each client application is easy to remember how to use, and there is less chance for the user to get lost in some complex maze of menu selections. Thus one client application might be a Docket Clerk client, custom tailored for the docket clerk to log incoming mail which may trigger new due dates. Another client application might be an Attorney client, custom tailored for the attorney to obtain key information about a particular docket or a particular matter at a glance. Still another client application might be a Reports client, designed to print monthly reminder reports for each attorney in the firm or company.

Client-server can do even more than merely simplifying menu screens. In our docketing system example, it may be necessary to revise due dates each time a law affecting a due date changes. This is common in international patent and trademark docketing systems, where the law can change somewhere in the world on a fairly regular basis.

To handle this, a separate Country Law server is provided. The Country Law server contains the latest rules by which due dates are calculated. The Docketing server asks the Country Law server for this information, which it then uses to update its records of all due dates. This example shows that the names "client" and "server" are functional labels and that a given entity can function as a server in some instances and as a client in other instances. The Docketing server functions as a client when it asks for the latest rules from the Country Law server. The Docketing server functions as a server when client applications ask it for due date information.

Client-server technology is likely to appear in numerous software inventions, particularly as multitasking operating systems become more widespread. Be on the lookout for client-server technology in networked systems, particularly those involving databases. The client-server approach is not limited to databases, but that is where the technology is often found.

§ 2.26 Microsoft Windows

At present there are several different flavors of Microsoft Windows™ in existence, and more are on the way. This description will give an overview of some Windows basics. Windows programming can be quite demanding. The details are beyond the scope of this book.[17]

Windows provides a multitasking graphical environment that runs programs specially designed for Windows. Windows also runs programs written for MS-DOS, although without many of Window's more powerful features. Several features make Windows different from MS-DOS. They include the graphical user interface, device-independent graphics, a consistent user interface, multitasking, memory management, queued input, and data interchange between applications.

The graphical user interface (GUI, pronounced gooey) is what most users think of when they think of Windows, because it is the part they see and use. A *user interface* is simply the connection between the computer and the human user. It is the means by which the computer supplies information to the user and the means by which the user supplies information to the computer. Today everyone is familiar with the computer monitor (computer screen), the keyboard, and the mouse. These define the user interface.

A *graphical user interface* is simply a user interface that can display pictures to represent worldly objects and concepts. Of course, humans also like to communicate through the printed word, and hence a graphical user interface can also display text. You may find it interesting that a graphical user interface displays text as pictures of the text. That is how the size and appearance of text can be readily changed in a system having a graphical user interface. Representing text as pictures of text gives a very powerful advantage over older, fixed size text terminals. That advantage is WYSIWYG. Pronounced "wye-see-wig," this rather clumsy acronym stands for "What you see is what

---

[17] For a good introduction to Windows programming, *see* Charles Petzold, Programming Windows (2d ed. 1990).

you get," referring to the desired result that what you see on the computer screen is what it will look like on paper when printed.

The graphical user interface is more than just displaying pictures. It is using those pictures to represent abstract concepts, such as desired actions to be performed. Integral to today's graphical user interface is the pointing device, typically a trackball or mouse. The pointing device is the part of the user interface that the user interacts with the pictures displayed. You are probably familiar with operating a mouse to position a cursor on an icon or menu selection, and then clicking the mouse button to initiate the action represented by the icon or menu selection.

§ 2.27 —Device Independent Graphics

Windows provides a rich set of device-independent graphics operations, which an application program can use to draw pictures (including text, cursors, bitmaps, and so forth). Whether the pictures are to be drawn on the monitor screen or on a printer does not matter. Windows graphics operations are device-independent.

Windows does this with *device drivers* that convert the results of graphics operations into suitable format for the particular output device. Rather than have the application program send its output directly to the output device, Windows handles this for the application program.

Windows creates a *device context* that represents the device driver, the display device, and perhaps the communications port to which the display device is attached. The application carries out graphics operations within the context of that display device. When you see reference in a Windows program to the device context handle (sometimes abbreviated hdc) you know this refers to a particular display device.

Windows' graphical user interface is pleasing to look at, and perhaps more intuitive than MS-DOS to use. However, one of Windows' main strengths is its ability to provide a consistent user interface. This means that you can learn how to operate one program and that learning carries over to the next program. Not all application programs necessarily have the same user interface. However, because Windows provides a consistent graphical user interface environment, complete with device-independent graphics, Windows application programs quite naturally appear to the user to operate in a similar fashion.

§ 2.28 —Multitasking

Multitasking, another Windows feature, allows more than one application program to run at the same time, or at least to appear to do so. There are several ways to provide multitasking. In serial multitasking or context switched multitasking, two or more application programs are loaded at the same time, but only one application program is given processor time. This one program is said to be in the foreground. To give processor time to the one in the background, the user must request it, by bringing that application to the foreground and sending the other application to the background.

One step above context switched multitasking is cooperative multitasking. Background programs are automatically given processor time whenever the foreground application is idle. This can naturally happen when the foreground application is waiting for the user to enter the next keystroke. With cooperative multitasking the user does not have to request that the background application be given processor time.

More powerful yet is time-slice multitasking, sometimes called full multitasking or preemptive multitasking. Slices of processor time are automatically allocated to each application program. While some applications can be given a larger slice than others, no application can monopolize the system.

§ 2.29   —DOS 640K Boundary

In 1982, when the IBM PC was introduced with 64K of RAM on the motherboard, the maximum program size of 640K seemed enormous. Few users were concerned that the MS-DOS operating system itself, any memory resident device drivers, and the application program all had to fit within a 640K memory space. At that time there were not many application programs available, and for the most part they each fit easily into 64K. Today, of course, programs have grown enormous, DOS has gotten bigger, and there are all sorts of memory resident device drivers to add features that now seem essential. The bottom line is 640K is not enough. Windows is one attempt to fix this.

Although IBM and Microsoft established the 640K boundary, the Intel 8088 architecture is largely responsible. The original IBM-PC contained an Intel 8088 microprocessor. There are only so many metal leads you can have coming out of one package, and that number dictates how much memory the microprocessor can access. The Intel 8088 has 40 leads (20 for accessing memory), enough to access 1000K of memory. Designing the IBM PC, the engineers needed some of the 1000K so the computer could work with a computer monitor. An additional portion of the 1000K was used for basic system variables, needed to make the computer work. The engineers also reserved some of the 1000K for future use. What was left was our 640K.

In 1982 Intel improved upon the 8088 and introduced the 80286, which could address 16 megabytes of memory. Today, we often refer the 80286 by its short name the 286. Not wishing to lose its existing customer base, Intel made the 286 backwardly compatible with the 8088, meaning that the 286 can run all existing application programs written for the 8088.

The reverse was not true, however. The 286 can access memory that the 8088 cannot. To access this extra memory, the 286 slips into what Intel calls the "protected mode." Application programs must be specially written for this protected mode. In the early days of the 286 few programs were. One notable exception was Lotus 123®.

Spreadsheets have a ravenous appetite for memory, and Lotus wanted to be able to use the extra memory available to the 286. Therefore, Lotus, Intel, and Microsoft jointly developed a way for these more powerful 286's to access this *expanded memory,* while retaining compatibility with older 8088 computers. They did this by adding to the operating system the ability for a 286 to slip into protected mode to access the expanded memory and to slip back, without the program knowing what has happened. The slip into and out of protected mode allows much larger spreadsheets to be built, since spreadsheet data can now be put outside the 640K boundary.

A more significant improvement occurred in 1985 when Intel released the 80386, commonly called the 386. The 386 could address 4,000 megabytes (4 gigabytes) of memory. It retains backward compatibility with both the 8088 and the 286, and adds a third form of memory addressing by which the processor can subdivide its memory space into separate 640K partitions and can treat each partition as a separate machine. Called the *extended memory* model, the 386 can run multiple DOS applications in different 640K units, by fooling each DOS application into believing it is the only application running in a 640K memory space. A significant breakthrough, it is unfortunate the chosen term extended memory is not more different from the term expanded memory describing the more limited Lotus-Intel-Microsoft memory management technique of the 286.

Windows can use either expanded memory (such as 286) and extended memory (like 386). In this way Windows goes a long way toward overcoming the DOS 640K limitation. Currently, many versions of Windows still require DOS to run. In these versions, a vestige of the 640K limitation remains. Computers equipped with 386 processors or higher (for example, 486 or Pentium) can use Windows "386 Enhanced" mode causing 386 extended memory addressing to be used. In the 386 Enhanced mode, Windows can run multiple DOS applications concurrently, each in its own 640K memory space.

§ 2.30 —Windows Internals

From a programmer's point of view Windows handles input and output very differently from the way DOS does. Windows is a form of client-server architecture in which Windows applications are clients of Windows, with Windows providing all services that the application needs to be a well-behaved Windows application (for example, work with a pointing device or mouse, use device independent graphics, the Windows GUI, and so forth). There are several key components that make this client-server architecture possible. One is the Windows message loop. Another is the Windows Application Program Interface (API).

Shown in **Figure 2–8,** when the user presses a key on the keyboard, for example, that keystroke is taken into the Windows system queue. There the keystroke is copied to the Windows application queue. The message loop within the application program retrieves the keystroke from the application queue and translates it into an ANSI character message. The message loop exists within the application program by inheriting it from its WinMain function (all Windows applications must have this). Then the message loop dispatches the ANSI character message, as well as the keyboard message, to the appropriate window function to be acted upon. In this case the Windows TextOut function is used to display the typed keystroke in the client area of the window.

Windows can receive and dispatch input messages for several applications at once. By establishing one application queue for each Windows application, the system queue routes input messages to the appropriate application queue, where the message loop of the appropriate application retrieves it.

Some interaction between the user and a Windows application does not involve retrieving messages from the message queue. A mouse click to select Exit from a menu is an example. Windows handles these interactions more directly. Shown in **Figure 2–9,** when the user selects "Exit" Windows sends the window management message directly to the appropriate Window function, in this case the function WM_DESTROY. Windows bypasses the application queue. The Windows function then signals WinMain that the window is destroyed and that the application should terminate. The Windows function does this by copying a WM_QUIT message into the application queue, using yet another Windows function, PostQuitMessage. When the message loop of the application program receives the WM_QUIT message, the loop terminates and the WinMain function exits.

Data interchange between applications, another Windows feature, is made possible by the clipboard. The clipboard is a collection of Windows functions, found in Windows' USER module, which can be called to exchange information contained in blocks of memory. These clipboard functions are called when the user selects Cut, Copy, or Paste options from most Windows applications.

Do not confuse the clipboard, a collection of functions, with the Clipboard Viewer, a program that comes with many versions of Windows. The Clipboard Viewer program is a small Windows application (some versions of Windows call it the ClipBook Viewer) usually accessed as an icon under the Main group. This Viewer allows you to inspect the current contents of the blocks of memory controlled by the clipboard functions. In other words, after a Cut or Copy operation, you can use the Viewer to see exactly what was cut or copied. Similarly, you can use the Viewer before a Paste operation, to see what you are about to paste into the target window.

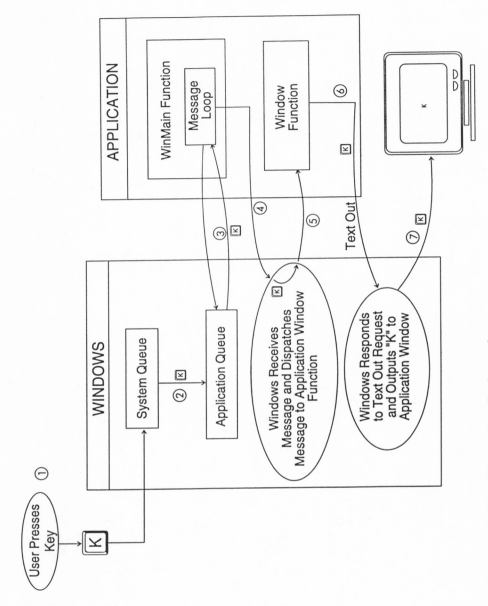

Figure 2–8. How Windows handles keystrokes.

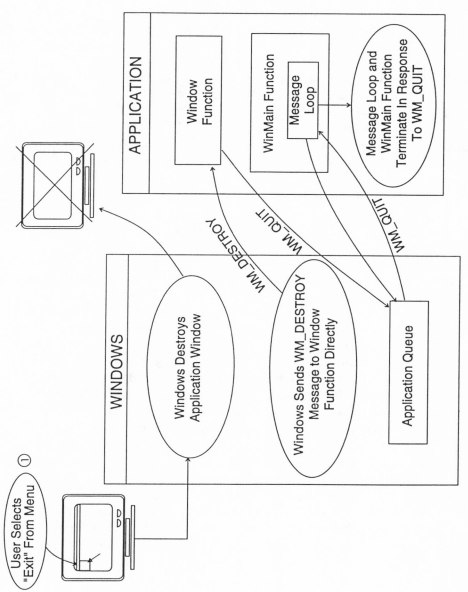

Figure 2-9. How Windows exits.

Windows provides many functions that control virtually every aspect of an application program's appearance. You can think of Windows as functional layers, much the same as the OSI model treats communication as functional layers. At the bottom layer are the lower level operating system functions Windows uses to access system resources, such as the disk drive, or the communications port, or the random access memory (RAM). At the top layer are the higher level functions Windows uses to manage how application programs may present information on the screen. This top layer is sometimes referred to as the presentation manager, although some reserve that term for the top layer of IBM's OS/2 operating system. A more widely used term for this top layer is the Application Program Interface or API.

§ 2.31   —Windows API

The *Windows API* may be thought of as a collection of tools (functions, messages, data structures, data types, statements, and files) that application programmers use to create Windows applications. By last count, there are over 500 functions in the Windows API collection. Some of these functions manage the appearance of a window itself, the basic element in every Windows application. Such functions, referred to collectively as the Windows Manager Interface, regulate how messages are passed, how windows are moved and sized, how the clipboard works, how menus are displayed, how scrolling is performed, how the screen is painted, and so forth. Other functions, collectively called the Graphics Device Interface (GDI), perform device-independent graphic operations within a Windows application. These GDI functions include functions to draw lines, text, bitmap images on a number of different display devices, including monitors and printers. Selection of different fonts for text and different pens and brushes for lines and drawings are made possible by GDI functions. Still other functions, collectively called the System Services Interface functions, handle lower level details such as how memory is managed, how communication is carried out through the system's I/O ports, how files are created, opened, and closed, how sounds are generated, and so forth.

§ 2.32   —Late Binding

Software starts out as a purely abstract entity, but ultimately it must be connected to a computer to run. For example, in the abstract state, mathematical variables represent values or the results of calculations, but there is yet no identified physical place for these values or results to be stored. Before there can be a physical place for these values or results to be stored, the software must be loaded in the computer and the variables must be assigned physical memory locations. This assigning of physical memory locations is called binding.

When to bind software to hardware involves tradeoffs. Once a variable is bound to a specific memory location, the program gains efficiency, because the computer is built to be very good at accessing specific memory locations. The tradeoff is loss of flexibility. Until binding takes place the program is free to alter how data may be represented and arranged.

For example, if you want to store 30 ordered pairs of numbers you might use a 2x30 array. Binding this array to computer memory, it might occupy 60 contiguous memory locations. However, if you later change your mind and desire a 3x30 array, or a totally different data structure such as a linked list or a stack, your bound 2x30 array becomes useless. You might even want the program to select the size and configuration of the data structure automatically. To do this, you may want the computer system to delay binding until after the program has made a decision of what size and configuration of data structure is best. Thus you might, in this case, want late binding.

The concept of binding is not restricted to data structures and variables. Executable program code is also bound to the computer through a process called linking. Most modern computer languages allow programs to be built using collections of pre-written functions stored in libraries. For example, a programmer might purchase a library of math functions for performing trigonometric calculations. Having this library available, the programmer can use these library functions as if they were provided by the programming language. The library might contain hundreds of functions, many of which the programmer may not want to use. This is no problem. There is a software building tool, called a linker, which automatically scans the programmer's compiled program searching for use of any functions that are not part of the programming language. When the linker finds such a function, it searches through the specified library or libraries, extracts any modules containing the missing functions, and copies them into the code at the appropriate place. In this way, the appropriate functions are bound to the rest of the program.

As with the binding of data structures and variables, executable program functions can also be bound early or late, depending on the capabilities of the computer operating system. Executable programs written to run under MS-DOS are bound early, that is, all executable object modules must be linked together before the program will run. This is called static linking. Static linking is performed when the executable file is created. The executable file is static and remains unchanged when it is loaded into the computer and run.

More sophisticated operating systems, such as Windows, allow executable object modules to be linked to the program while the program is running. This is called dynamic linking. The operating system contains a dynamic linker that detects calls to functions not already embedded in the program, searches through the specified library or libraries, extracts any modules containing the missing functions, and passes control to those functions at the appropriate time. Typically libraries must be constructed in a special way in order to work with dynamic linking. Such libraries are called dynamic link libraries.

Windows makes extensive use of dynamic link libraries. Windows programmers often refer to these *dynamic link libraries* as "dll's." Dll's contain groups of executable routines or functions that are loaded and executed by Windows on an as-needed basis.

Dll's offer at least two advantages. First, they allow large, complex programs to be run in a smaller memory space, because the entire program does not need to be loaded all at once. Second, dll's allow executable routines and functions to be shared by many application programs. For example, the object linking and embedding (OLE) functions of OLE2.DLL can be invoked by any Windows application that has been written to call those functions.

CHAPTER 3

A REVIEW OF
LEGAL CONCEPTS FOR THE
SOFTWARE PROFESSIONAL

§ 3.1   Introduction

This chapter is for the software professional. It explains some basic legal concepts that need to be understood before tackling software patent law. This chapter explains a little about the nature of law, where the law comes from, what the law is generally designed to do, and where the law is written. It also focuses on patent law, the United States Patent Office, and the patent court system. The chapter ends with a brief introduction to the patent itself.

§ 3.2   Nature of Law

If one really wanted to dig into the topic, our law can be traced back to biblical times and before. Supreme Court Justice, Oliver Wendell Holmes, Jr. (1841-1935), who served on the Supreme Court until three years before his death, left behind an invaluable treasure, a book entitled *The Common Law,* which chronicles, through a series of lectures, where our law comes from and what it is about.

Holmes describes our law, the direct offspring of the English common law, as the grandchild of two grandparents: Roman law and German law. It is interesting that both Roman law and German law are grounded in vengeance. Roman law and German law both evolved as a replacement for the earlier barbarian practice of the blood feud. Reduced to its essence, law is a mechanism for people to settle disputes without resorting to violence.

Of course, not every dispute involves vengeance. Vengeance is more fitting the response to an intentional wrongdoing. Some wrongdoings are accidental. As Holmes explains:

> Vengeance imports a feeling of blame, and an opinion, however distorted by passion, that a wrong has been done. It can hardly go very far beyond the case of a harm intentionally inflicted: even a dog distinguishes between being stumbled over and being kicked.[1]

Today, the law redresses not only intentionally inflicted harm, but also accidentally inflicted harm, under a theory called negligence. Negligence is the failure to use a reasonable degree of care. Most traffic accidents involve allegations of negligence. Thus, accidentally stumbling over Holmes' dog may be treated as negligence, for which the law may provide a remedy.

The law may have eliminated the blood feud; but the law has not eliminated adversity. To the contrary, the legal system is by definition adversarial. Litigants enter the courtroom like gladiators, facing off with opposite points of view. As in the blood feud, which our legal system replaces, the size of the

---

[1] Oliver Wendell Holmes, Jr., The Common Law & Other Writings 3 (1881).

legal battle and its eventual outcome, depends on the size and strength of the litigants and the will power of each.

Laypersons are sometimes surprised by this, for they assume that the law alone will dictate the outcome of every dispute. This assumption ignores that courts are impartial and that there are always two sides to every dispute. The degree to which one side or the other side advocates or fights for a given cause depends on willpower, on determination, and ultimately on what the dispute is worth.

§ 3.3   —Law Is Not Absolute

In day to day life, many view law as a set of black and white rules. Traffic laws are this way. Red light, stop; green light, go—a rule-based system. As a software professional, you are familiar with rule-based systems, in which the answer to any question is described with mathematical precision. Unfortunately, the rule-based system is too simple a model for our legal system. Holmes writes:

> The law embodies the story of a nation's development through many centuries, and it cannot be dealt with as if it contained only the axioms and corollaries of a book of mathematics. In order to know what it is, we must know what it has been, and what it tends to become.[2]

Thus, while you could write a rule-based computer program to model simple traffic laws, for example, you would need a far more sophisticated program to model the entire legal system. For starters, you would need an extensive history database, a language parser capable of reading old English as well as modern English, fuzzy logic, and a context-sensitive human reasoning system. Even with all of this, the model would lack wisdom and could not be relied upon to know when to change laws of the past to keep pace with the future.

§ 3.4   —Pyramidal Structure of the Court System

The legal system in the United States employs a system of courts in a pyramidal arrangement. At the base of the pyramid is the trial court. This is where a case is tried, that is, where witnesses testify and present evidence. The right to trial by jury exists only in the trial court.

In the trial court a single judge presides over a given case, typically from start to finish. The judge controls how the case is presented, what witnesses

---

[2] *Id.* at 1.

are permitted to testify, and what evidence is presented. The judge makes all rulings on matters of law, including instructing the jury on what law must be applied to the case. The jury hears all witnesses testify, examines all evidence presented, and applies the law, as instructed by the judge, to reach a verdict or judgment. Where there is a dispute of fact, as there often is, the jury decides which side's version of the facts is the more probable. If both parties agree they do not want a jury, then the judge decides the issues of fact, as well as the issues of law.

Above the trial court is the appellate court. The appellate court is composed entirely of judges. There is no right to trial by jury in the appellate court; no witnesses are permitted to testify; no new evidence is presented. The appellate court hears a case strictly to review whether the trial court conducted the trial properly. Thus arguments in the appellate court typically center on whether the trial judge applied the correct principles of law. The jury's determination of fact (which side's version was more probable) and the jury's ultimate verdict are not subject to review by the appellate court.

Finally, at the top of the pyramid is a single Supreme Court. The Supreme Court is the final court in the appeal process, although the vast majority of cases never reach this final stage. The Supreme Court makes major judicial policy decisions. There is no right to appeal to the Supreme Court, except in a few certain circumstances. To have an appeal heard by the Supreme Court, the appellant must be granted permission by obtaining what is called a writ of certiorari. The Supreme Court rarely grants writs of certiorari, only in cases that present a unique issue that, in the Court's view, is important and needs to be decided.

The United States Constitution establishes separate state and federal powers. Because of this there are separate state and federal court systems in the United States. The pyramidal structure of each system is essentially the same.

§ 3.5   Common Law and Statutory Law

There are two fundamentally different sources of law that represent the two pillars upon which our legal system rests. One pillar is common law; the other is statutory law. Common law began in 12th century England as unwritten law, reflecting "common" customs. Statutory law is even more ancient, dating back to the Romans. Statutory law is written law, a set of rules worked out in advance.

By about the 17th century, common law came to be written down, thus the distinction no longer applies that common law is unwritten and statutory law is written. A better distinction is this. Common law comes from judges, deciding actual cases, based on decisions of the past. Statutory law comes from the legislature, stating rules for governing future actions. Common law looks to the past, evolving new rules by adapting old ones. Statutory law looks to the future, fashioning new rules on the way things ought to be.

The law in the United States rests on both pillars. That is why the study of patent law involves the study of court decisions (common law) and federal patent statutes (statutory law). Both of these pillars are examined further below.

§ 3.6   Common Law

Describing where common law comes from, Oliver Wendell Holmes, Jr. wrote:

> A very common phenomenon, and one very familiar to the student of history, is this. The customs, beliefs, or needs of a primitive time establish a rule or a formula. In the course of centuries the custom, belief, or necessity disappears, but the rule remains.[3]

Lawyers use the term "common law" to refer to those rules of law that have evolved as Holmes describes above. These are rules of law, organically grown, as if following Darwin's principle of natural selection. Useful laws are used again and become part of the common law, to serve as the foundation for further refinements; useless laws are forgotten.

Common law is judge-made law. Each time a case is decided, it is added to the folklore that is the common law. Most decisions, and certainly the important ones, are written down. In this way, lawyers and judges can rely on them again. Written decisions become precedent that are used to decide future cases.

§ 3.7   —Written Decisions

The common law is not written in any one place where you can read all of it, start to finish. Rather, the common law is strewn throughout the hundreds of thousands of written decisions spanning centuries. Individually each of these written decisions represents somebody's particular lawsuit. Like people, no two lawsuits are exactly alike. Each lawsuit has its own unique facts and circumstances surrounding a controversy that the judge has resolved. To find the common law you must seek out prior written court decisions through library research and often read between the lines or interpret those decisions to extract the principles of common law.

---

[3] *Id.* at 5.

The task of the judge is a difficult one. Both parties must be treated fairly and (this is important) both parties must feel that they have been treated fairly. The judge's written decision instills fairness by explaining the basis for the judge's resolution of the controversy. The written decision explains why the winner won and the loser lost, an important ingredient in instilling the feeling of fairness. More important, the written decision makes the judge accountable. The written decision documents the judge's reasoning, so that a higher court may review it.

§ 3.8   —Precedent

Knowing that both parties, and possibly a higher court, will be reviewing the written decision, the judge works hard to ensure his or her reasoning is beyond attack, usually by basing the decision on earlier decisions that have already been reviewed and use accepted reasoning. This is the concept of precedent. Applying the concept of precedent, a judge reasons, "The present case of Alpha v. Beta is much like the earlier case of Doe v. Roe, where the judge, sitting as I do now, decided Doe wins and Roe loses for reasons A, B, and C. Doe v. Roe was reviewed by a higher court and the judge's reasoning was found to be sound. Therefore, I here adopt the reasoning of Doe v. Roe. Applying the reasoning of Doe v. Roe, I find that Alpha wins and Beta loses."

Although Beta is undoubtedly unhappy with the result, the judge's ruling is largely beyond attack. To attack the judge's ruling, Beta must show that the precedential analogy drawn between Alpha v. Beta and Doe v. Roe was not warranted by the facts; or that Doe v. Roe was wrongly decided and does not deserve to be treated as precedent. These are both difficult attacks. On interpretation of factual questions, higher courts, reviewing the judge below, assume that the judge below, who heard the facts firsthand, was in the better position to decide what is right. Higher courts are reluctant to reverse the judge below where it is argued that the facts have been wrongly decided. Higher courts are similarly reluctant to overrule the accepted precedent of an earlier decided case, since to do so would require that court to revisit the facts. Higher courts will reverse a judge's decision if they are convinced that the judge's reasoning was incorrect, or that the accepted precedent needs to be changed.

The concept of precedent has a number of practical advantages. It eliminates the need to solve the same legal issue twice, saving judicial time and energy. It makes our legal system less arbitrary, with the social benefit of making laws more predictable. Finally, it makes the system seem more fair, since all persons are treated alike under like circumstances.

A disadvantage of the concept of precedent is that the law is slow to change with changing times. It can take decades before the right circumstances are presented so that precedent can be changed. Another disadvantage is that precedent is not always easily located. To find the common law precedent lawyers and judges must read legal decision after legal decision, sifting through the facts in each case, to find those decisions which are most on point. Precedent is the soul of common law. It exists as a folklore, passed on from written decision to written decision, much the same way as our tribal ancestors passed on knowledge by word of mouth.

§ 3.9   Statutory Law

Statutory law is law that is enacted by the elected legislature. Federal statutory laws are laws enacted by the United States Congress and state statutory laws are laws enacted by the state legislature. Whereas common law is a disembodied folklore, extracted from past court decisions, statutory law is a concrete rule book, written in advance by the legislature to dictate future actions, or to restate or codify the precedent of past court decisions. Because statutory law begins as a preconceived set of rules, it can be written in one place, where you could read it, start to finish, if you wanted to.

Statutory laws do not always start out well-organized and collected in one place. The organization occurs later. The typical statutory law begins life as a bill, introduced into Congress or the legislature, stating someone's proposal of what the law should be. The bill is debated, amended, voted on, and passed. Once passed by both houses of Congress or the legislature, the bill is signed by the President or state governor, and the bill becomes a statute, part of the statutory law.

Patent law is federal statutory law, passed by Congress and signed by the President. The current patent law was passed by Congress and signed by the President in 1952.

The next few sections describe how federal laws are written and organized, and how patent statutory law is structured.

§ 3.10   —Organization of Federal Laws

Once Congress enacts a statute, the official text of a statute is first published as a *slip law,* as a single sheet, if it is short, or as a pamphlet with separate pagination, if it is longer. Slip laws of the United States Congress are available shortly after enactment. United States Congressional slip laws are printed by the United States Government Printing Office and can usually be obtained by asking your Congressperson. Slip laws are identified by Public Law number, and sometimes also by popular name. For example, On November 8, 1984, a new form of protection for semiconductor chip products was enacted. Popularly called the "Semiconductor Chip Protection Act," this act is identified as Public Law 98-620, sometimes abbreviated as Pub. L.

98-620. You can write your congressional representative to request a copy of this law (or any law), by simply giving the Public Law number.

If you wish to follow the enactments of Congress on a particular topic, you may wish to consult commercially published sources, such as the *United States Code Congressional and Administrative News,* which publishes every two weeks during the congressional session and monthly when Congress is not in session.

Slip laws are further organized into chronological collections, called *session laws,* published as bound volumes, usually with an index at the end. The session laws of the United States Congress are called *Statutes at Large.* To find a law in *Statutes at Large* you need to convert the Public Law number into the corresponding volume and page number, using the look-up table provided. For example, the Semiconductor Chip Protection Act, referenced above, may be found in *Statutes at Large* at 98 Stat. 3347, 3356. Both the Public Law number and the *Statutes at Large* citation tell you, by the number 98, that it was the 98th Congress that enacted the Semiconductor Chip Protection Act.

Having to look up laws chronologically is not very convenient if you are interested in all law on a particular topic. Although each *Statutes at Large* volume has an index, the indexes are not cumulative from volume to volume. To make matters worse, the political "give and take" process of enacting statutes often produces a hodgepodge of laws with "something for everybody." Thus, unless you happen to know that a certain session law includes a provision in your area of interest, you may overlook it.

For example, shortly after World War II, Congress passed the Atomic Energy Act of 1946 to regulate atomic energy. It is doubtful that many patent attorneys were aware of the bill's passage. However, that bill changed the patent law. It contained a provision that prohibited patents for inventions involving production of fissionable material.[4] Unless you had been following the atomic energy issue closely, you might be unaware of this patent provision in the Atomic Energy Act.

Fortunately statutory law is also organized and compiled by subject matter, through a process called codification, into a collection of volumes known as the *United States Code.* The United States Code, abbreviated U.S.C., is arranged by title and section, rather than by volume and page. Thus, for example, the United States Code citation to the Semiconductor Chip Protection Act is 17 U.S.C. §§ 901–914, that is, Title 17, Sections 901–914. This immediately follows the Copyright Law (17 U.S.C. §§ 101–810), its closest relative. Codification makes it much easier to find the current law, by putting all laws on a given topic in one place.

---

[4] This exclusion was later withdrawn by the Atomic Energy Act of 1954, 68 Stat. 919, codified at 42 U.S.C 2011.

§ 3.11 United States Code

The United States Code groups statutes into topical units called Titles. The Titles are in turn grouped into chapters and the chapters into sections. **Table 3–1** lists all of the current Titles in our United States Code. Note, Title 35 is devoted to Patent Law (the primary focus of this book). Title 17 is devoted to Copyright Law (another form of protection for software). In **§ 3.15, Table 3–2** breaks down the patent law, Title 35, into finer detail of Chapters and Sections.

Table 3–1

Titles of the United States Code By Title

1	General Provisions	26	Internal Revenue Code
2	The Congress	27	Intoxicating Liquors
3	The President	28	Judiciary and Judicial Procedure
4	Flag and Seal, Seat of Government, and the States	29	Labor
5	Executive Departments and General Officers and Employees	30	Mineral Lands and Mining
6	Official and Penal Bonds	31	Money and Finance
7	Agriculture	32	National Guard
8	Aliens and Nationality	33	Navigation and Navigable Waters
9	Arbitration	34	Navy
10	Armed Forces	35	Patents
11	Bankruptcy	36	Patriotic Societies and Observances
12	Banks and Banking	37	Pay and Allowances
13	Census	38	Veterans' Benefits
14	Coast Guard	39	The Postal Service
15	Commerce and Trade	40	Public Buildings, Property, and Works
16	Conservation	41	Public Contracts
17	Copyrights	42	The Public Health and Welfare
18	Crimes and Criminal Procedure	43	Public Lands
19	Customs and Duties	44	Public Printing and Documents
20	Education	45	Railroads
21	Food and Drugs	46	Shipping
22	Foreign Relations and Intercourse	47	Telegraphs, Telephones, and Radiotelegraphs
23	Highways	48	Territories and Insular Possessions
24	Hospitals, Asylums, and Cemeteries	49	Transportation
25	Indians	50	War and National Defense

Codification is so important an organizational tool that Congress often reenacts titles of the *United States Code* to be the authoritative text of the law. For the reenacted portions, the *United States Code* replaces the *Statutes at Large* as the official text. At least one-third of the United States Code has been reenacted in this fashion.

§ 3.12   Property Law and the Foundations of Patent Law

To most people, the topic of property law dredges up notions of real estate. What does property law have to do with software patents? The answer is simple. A patent is property. However, knowing that a patent is property really does not help much, without knowing what property is and how patents and real estate came to be cousins.

Property law has ancient roots. At one time property was quite simply things owned by persons. To own property meant to have exclusive control over the thing, including the right to sell it, give it away, destroy it, or just do nothing with it. Property law was then, largely, "rights of ownership" or "rights in things." The emphasis was on ownership and things.

Ownership of things is fairly easy to understand. The principal ingredient of ownership is having possession. One can, for example, possess a horse or a cow, and these are treated as property. Wild animals are another matter. Unless captured, wild animals belong to no one. Land can be possessed, by occupying it or by building a fence around it to prevent others from entering. Of course, many famous wars have been fought over land, demonstrating that it is not always easy to remain in possession.

To prevent private wars between citizens over land possession, the legal system employs specific rules for staking a claim to land and for enforcing that claim in the courts. The *deed* is the written legal instrument which the legal system uses to prove a person has lawful possession. The deed contains a precise description of the property and states the owner's name and how that owner came into possession of the property (typically bearing the signature of the previous owner who conveyed possession). The deed amounts to proof of ownership, serving to eliminate many disputes over possession.

While someone may unlawfully encroach on the property of another, the owner of that property can bring the deed to court, proving ownership, and then invoke the power of the court (that is, the power of the government) to have the encroaching party evicted. Being able to invoke governmental power to enforce properly documented (deeded) possession has eliminated the private war.

§ 3.13 Letters Patent

Long ago, in the Middle Ages, a legal right called a monopoly was devised to induce subjects of the Crown to travel abroad and bring back riches and knowledge from afar. The Crown granted a monopoly—the exclusive right to sell something—as a reward for enriching the kingdom. Often the grant was made subject to a certain payback or royalty to the Crown. In those days the Crown owned most of the land. Occasionally, the Crown would grant a parcel of land to a person, as a favor for being a loyal subject.

The concept of letters patent comes directly from these monopolies and land grants.

A grant of land in those days was made official through a written document known as letters patent. The term patent simply means open. Thus *letters patent* were open letters or public degrees. These letters were not sealed shut, like private letters or private grants were sealed. These letters were sealed open, as public proof of ownership.

The Crown also used letters patent to grant officially a monopoly to a subject, as a reward for bringing riches and knowledge into England. Gradually, over the centuries that followed, the term letters patent became associated with these monopoly grants. Gradually the focus of these monopolies shifted in purpose, from rewarding travelers bringing back riches, to rewarding inventors for bringing in new ideas and inventions.

Today patents for inventions are granted for much the same reason as they were granted in medieval England: to induce a person to disclose knowledge of new and useful inventions. The patent is, in effect, a deed, grant, or letters patent (in the medieval sense) from the sovereign authority (the government) to the inventor. It is a reward or inducement made in exchange for adding to the wealth of public knowledge.

Today, when real property (real estate) is bought and sold, the deed is simply one of the documents signed at the real estate closing. Few realize that today's real estate deed is a written instrument that has been around since the Middle Ages, and that a patent is a form of deed.

§ 3.14 Current Property Law

Today property law has evolved, placing less emphasis on ownership and things and more emphasis on rights. Today many legal scholars view property as a "bundle of rights." The property rights bundle can be broken up. Ownership of a thing can be split between two or more owners. An owner may sell one of the bundle of rights and retain the rest. The right sold can be divested permanently or divested for a limited time. Patent law follows directly in these footsteps. The owner of a patent can subdivide ownership among many, lease, sell, license, and so forth.

The bundle of rights is not absolute or all encompassing, however. There is a tension between private property and public property. The tendency since the early twentieth century has been the erosion of private property rights in favor of public rights or civil rights.

Private property rights no longer protect the owner from the regulatory power of the government, for example. This is true for patents as well. Although the owner of a patent can refuse to grant permission to others to use the invention, the owner is not empowered to refuse permission to the government. While the government must pay the patent owner a royalty for what it uses, the owner of the patent is powerless to stop the government from using it.

Anyone who has had the front yard taken by the county, when the street in front of the house is widened, understands the concept of *eminent domain.* For the good of the public, the government can take someone's land, provided a fair price is paid for it. The government's right to use patented inventions, paying a reasonable royalty but otherwise without permission, is a form of eminent domain.

The important point to remember is that a patent is intellectual property. It is granted by the government in exchange for sharing a new and useful invention with society. Being property, a patent can be owned, sold, traded, leased, licensed, regulated, or taken by the government, and even destroyed by its owner (by dedication to the public, for example).

§ 3.15 Current Patent Law,
Title 35 United States Code

The present patent statutory law was enacted in 1952. The Patent Act of 1952 represents the fourth time the patent statutory laws have been substantially revised since the United States began operating under the Constitution. The first was the Patent Act of 1790, written by Thomas Jefferson. That act was replaced by the Patent Act of 1793, and later by the Patent Act of 1836. Many of the features of the current act come directly from Thomas Jefferson, carried over verbatim from that first Act of 1790.

The Patent Act of 1952 is codified (that is, collectively printed) in the United States Code at Title 35. Characteristic of all statutory law found in the United States Code, Title 35 is broken down into Parts, Chapters, and Sections. The following **Table 3–2** shows the chapter breakdown. Although the table omits the law itself, it nevertheless shows the organizational structure and conveys a good idea of what the patent law is about.

Table 3–2

The United States Patent Laws By Chapter

1	Establishment, Officers, Functions	17	Secrecy of Certain Inventions and Filing Applications in Foreign Country
2	Proceedings in the Patent and Trademark Office	18	Patent Rights in Inventions Made with Federal Assistance
3	Practice Before Patent and Trademark Office	25	Amendment and Correction of Patents
4	Patent Fees; Funding; Search Systems	26	Ownership and Assignment
10	Patentability of Inventions	27	Government Interests in Patents
11	Application for Patent	28	Infringement of Patents
12	Examination of Application	29	Remedies for Infringement of Patent, and Other Actions
13	Review of Patent and Trademark Office Decisions	30	Prior Art Citations to Office and Reexamination of Patents
14	Issue of Patent	35	Patent Cooperation Treaty Definitions
15	Plant Patents	36	Patent Cooperation Treaty International Stage
16	Designs	37	Patent Cooperation Treaty National Stage

§ 3.16   Code of Federal Regulations (C.F.R.)

Over the years the Patent Office has promulgated a number of regulations. A regulation is a rule devised by the executive branch of government. Technically a regulation is not statutory law, as it is never passed by Congress and signed by the President. However, regulations are important because they set forth the working details not addressed by statutory law.

Patent Office regulations issue from the Patent Commissioner's Office, subject to the approval of the Secretary of Commerce. Like statutes, these regulations are collected, organized, and published as a set, called the Code of Federal Regulations, sometimes abbreviated C.F.R. The Code of Federal Regulations is arranged by Title, Part, and Section. Curiously, the Title, Part, and Section numbering system used for the Code of Federal Regulations does not match the numbering system used for the United States Code. Patent statutory law is found in Title 35 U.S.C. Patent regulations are found in Title 37 C.F.R. Do not let this confuse you.

Patent and Trademark regulations both fall under Title 37. The Copyright regulations fall under Title 37 as well, even though the Copyright Office is supervised and its regulations are made by a different person. The Copyright Office is run by an official known as the Register of Copyrights, who serves as the director of the Library of Congress. Even some attorneys are surprised to learn that the Patent Office and the Copyright Office are entirely separate, organized under separate executive branches of government, run by different officials, and even located in different places. The Patent Office is located in Crystal City, Virginia. The Copyright Office is located in Washington, D.C.

§ 3.17   *Manual of Patent Examining Procedure* (M.P.E.P.)

It would seem that all these statutes and regulations should be enough, but there is more. The Patent Office also has its own set of rules, specifically designed to guide the Patent Office employees and patent examiners in doing their jobs. This set of rules is known as the *Manual of Patent Examining Procedure,* abbreviated M.P.E.P. The M.P.E.P. is the patent examiner's authority. Technically, the M.P.E.P. is not statutory law or regulation, but rather it is the Patent Office's interpretation of the laws and regulations, written in a practical form that the examiners use on a daily basis. The foreward to the M.P.E.P. describes its purpose thus:

> This Manual is published to provide Patent and Trademark Office patent examiners, applicants, attorneys, agents, and representatives of applicants with a reference work on the practices and procedures relative to the prosecution of patent applications before the Patent and Trademark Office. It contains instructions to examiners, as well as other material in the nature of information and interpretation, and outlines the current procedures which the examiners are required or authorized to follow in appropriate cases in the normal examination of a patent application. The Manual does not have the force of law or the force of the Patent rules of Practice in Title 37, Code of Federal Regulations.

Table 3–3 lists the major chapter headings of the Manual of Patent Examining Procedure.

Table 3–3

Manual of Patent Examining Procedure by Chapters

100	Secrecy, Access, National Security and Foreign Filing	1300	Allowance and Issue
200	Types, Cross-Noting, and Status of Application	1400	Correction of Patents
300	Ownership and Assignment	1500	Design Patents

400	Representative of Inventor or Owner	1600	Plant Patents
500	Receipt and handling of Mail and Papers	1700	Miscellaneous
600	Parts, Form and Content of Application	1800	Patent Cooperation Treaty
700	Examination of Application	1900	Protest
800	Restriction in Applications; Double Patenting	2000	Duty of Disclosure; Rejecting and Striking of Applications
900	Prior Art, Classification, Search	2100	Patentability
1000	Maters Decided by Various Officials	2200	Citation of Prior Art and Reexamination of Patents
1100	Interference (old practice)	2300	Interference Proceedings (new practice)
1200	Appeal	2400	Biotechnology

§ 3.18   United States Patent Office

There is only one United States Patent Office. It is located outside Washington, D.C. in a group of government office buildings in Crystal City, Virginia. Not being located near the Capitol, the White House, or the other national monuments, the Patent Office is overlooked by most Washington tourists. The office buildings themselves are not much to look at. The true tourist attraction is what goes on inside.

The United States patent is one of the most sought legal documents in the world. Every patent issued by the United States Patent Office contains some bit of knowledge, preserved for humanity; the Patent Office houses every patent it has ever issued. Spending a little time at the Patent Office researching this vast collection of knowledge is a humbling experience. The next time you are in Washington, visit the Patent Office to see for yourself. Be prepared to be overwhelmed.

The easiest way to reach the Patent Office is by the Metro subway. The Metro is clean, safe, and well run. Take the Crystal City exit (near the National Airport exit) and then ask for directions. The Patent Office is within walking distance from the subway. There is an underground walkway system that will take you to the Patent Office. The underground walkway system includes a number of interesting shops, in case your traveling companions would prefer to shop rather than explore the Patent Office.

§ 3.19   Commissioner of Patents and Trademarks

When our current patent statute was enacted, Congress recognized that it would be impossible for it to spell out everything in sufficient detail to build a working patent office. Congress therefore established the Office of the Commissioner of Patents and Trademarks. The Commissioner runs the Patent Office and promulgates the necessary regulations to conduct proceedings in the Patent Office, subject to the approval of the Secretary of Commerce. Currently this same Commissioner also supervises the Trademark Office, hence the title, Commissioner of Patents and Trademarks.

As official figurehead of the Patent Office, the Commissioner of Patents is often a named party in court litigation involving patentability of an invention. The Commissioner of Patents has thus been a named party in some famous software patent decisions of the Supreme Court:

Gottschalk v. Benson[5] (Commissioner Robert Gottschalk)

Parker v. Flook[6] (Commissioner Lutrelle F. Parker)

Diamond v. Diehr[7] (Commissioner Sidney A. Diamond).

§ 3.20   Patent Court System

Patent law is federal law and therefore the federal court system has jurisdiction over most patent matters. State courts can become tangentially involved in patent matters, for example, when patent property is the subject of an ownership dispute that is otherwise decided under state law.

The federal court system decides all disputes involving substantive patent law issues. Most substantive patent law issues arise in one of three contexts:

1. Patentability of a new invention is in dispute
2. Two inventors each claim to be the first inventor of the same invention
3. Patent infringement.

In the first context, if the Patent Office has refused to grant a patent, the patent applicant may appeal through the federal court system to seek reversal of the Patent Office's refusal.

In the second context, two patent applicants, or a patent applicant and a patent owner, may each claim to be the first inventor of the same invention.

---

[5] 409 U.S. 63 (1972).

[6] 437 U.S. 584 (1978).

[7] 450 U.S. 175 (1981).

When this happens, the Patent Office initiates a tug-of-war proceeding, called an interference, to determine which of the two will be awarded the patent. Either applicant can appeal the Patent Office's determination through the federal court system.

Finally, in the third context, a patent owner may accuse another party of infringing a patent. The federal court system has exclusive jurisdiction to hear patent infringement actions or declaratory judgment actions questioning the validity or infringement of a patent. A declaratory judgment action is a patent infringement action in reverse. The party accused of infringement files a declaratory judgment action in federal court, seeking to be declared innocent, or seeking to have the patent declared invalid.

As previously described in § **3.4,** the federal court system is a three-tiered pyramid, with district courts at the entry level, circuit courts of appeals one level up, and the Supreme Court at the top.

§ 3.21   —Patent Office Quasi-court System

In addition to the federal court system, the Patent Office also has a quasi-court system. In the pyramidal scheme, the Patent Office's quasi-court system is positioned below the federal district courts. The Patent Office is an administrative agency of the executive branch, not the judicial branch. Hence the Patent Office court system, strictly speaking, does not have the power of a court. The Patent Office quasi-court system is more like a review board. The federal government has many administrative agencies (for example, Patent and Trademark Office, Bureau of Mines, the Peace Corps, the Small Business Administration, the Office of Workers' Compensation Programs, the Drug Enforcement Administration, the Environmental Protection Agency, Housing and Urban Development, the list goes on and on). Most of these agencies, have quasi-court review boards that handle special types of litigation.

The Patent Office Board of Patent Appeals and Interferences is such a review board. It reviews the examiners refusal to grant a patent. It also decides interferences in which two parties seek to be awarded a patent on the same invention.

Decisions of the Patent Office Board of Appeals may be reviewed by a United States District Court, the entry level court of our federal judicial system, or by the court of appeals for the Federal Circuit, one level above the district courts. The appealing party can elect whether a decision of the Board of Patent Appeals and Interferences is referred to a district court or to the court of appeals.[8]

---

[8] *See* 35 U.S.C. § 141–46.

§ 3.22   —Court of Appeals for the Federal Circuit

Since its formation on October 1, 1982, the Court of Appeals for the Federal Circuit, located in Washington, D.C., is the official Court of Appeals in all patent cases, including patent infringement cases, patent interferences, and appeals by a patent applicant seeking reversal of a Patent Office refusal to grant a patent. The Court of Appeals for the Federal Circuit also hears appeals in other areas of federal law, such as disputes over government contracts and appeals from the Court of Claims (actions against the federal government).

When the Court of Appeals was formed it was applauded by many patent attorneys, on the theory that having one court would make the patent laws more uniform. Prior to the formation of the Federal Circuit Court of Appeals, appeals in patent cases did not always go to the same court. Patent infringement cases were appealed to the circuit court of appeals in the physical jurisdiction where the district court was located. Appeals in interferences and patent grant refusals were appealed to a special court, known as the Court of Customs and Patent Appeals, sometimes abbreviated CCPA. The CCPA thus had jurisdiction over appeals from decisions of the Patent Office, but it did not have jurisdiction over appeals involving infringement lawsuits.

The prior arrangement was a natural division of labor. Appeals from the Patent Office in Washington go to the CCPA in Washington. Appeals from the district courts go to the court of appeals in the district where the trial was held, and, in many cases, where the litigants are located.

The prior arrangement has one advantage. The local courts of appeals have a constituency. The constituency of the Ninth Circuit (California, Washington, Oregon, Nevada, Idaho, Montana, and Arizona) include many in the computer industry. The constituency of the Sixth Circuit (Michigan, Ohio, Kentucky, and Tennessee) include many in the auto industry, for example. Thus naturally, the circuit court of appeals for a given geographic region tends to have more exposure to the technology of its constituency, and to have more opportunity to develop expertise in that technology.

There was a downside to the old setup, which ultimately caused Congress to amend the law, creating the Federal Circuit and redirecting all patent appeals to it. The local circuit courts of appeals were not always consistent in ruling on patent issues. The court of appeals in one circuit might rule one way, and the court of appeals in a different circuit might rule another way on the same issue. Attorneys had great difficulty advising clients on what is the law because the proper answer could depend on where the matter was raised.

In creating the Federal Circuit, Congress emphasized the need for greater uniformity in patent law. Congress also wanted to curtail the wasteful the process of *forum shopping,* in which litigants would file suit in the jurisdiction believed to have the more favorable law on a particular issue.

In its very first decision the Federal Circuit Court of Appeals determined that it would follow the precedent set by the Court of Customs and Patent Appeals (CCPA) and the Court of Claims.[9] Decisions from other circuits were ruled not to be binding. Thus right from the very beginning the newly formed court made it clear that it intended the earlier era of inconsistency to be at an end.

§ 3.23   State Court and Patent Ownership Issues

Up to now we have focused on the federal court system. There are times, however, when a state court may get into the act. Patent law is federal law, and the federal courts have exclusive jurisdiction in matters of patent law. Sometimes, however, other bodies of law may come into play when patents are involved.

Patents themselves are property, sometimes called intellectual property. Property is something that can be owned, as stocks and bonds, real estate, or an automobile can be owned. The ownership of property and the laws governing ownership are a matter of state law. Therefore, when disputes arise over who owns a patent, state law is applied and state courts may be called upon to make the decision.

This can be confusing. **Section 3.21** covered interferences, where two or more parties engage in a dispute over which one is entitled to be awarded a patent on an invention that all have invented. Would that be a dispute over patent ownership? The answer is no. Ownership of a patent should not be confused with entitlement to a patent. In an ownership dispute, the patent in question has already been awarded. It already exists. In the interference dispute, the patent in dispute is yet to be awarded. Depending on the outcome of the interference, it may not be awarded, although typically it will be awarded to one of the interference litigants.

§ 3.24   Particulars of a Patent

Figure 3–1 illustrates the front page of a United States patent. The Patent Number, 5,319,776 and the patent issue date, June 7, 1994, appear in the upper right-hand corner. The 17-year term of the patent is measured from the issue date.

In the upper right-hand corner is the last name of the inventor, Hile. This name is sometimes used when referring to a patent. Thus, this patent might be referred to as the "Hile" patent. In this case there are several inventors, hence the caption reads, "Hile et al."

---

[9] South Corp. v. United States, 690 F.2d 1368 (Fed. Cir. 1982).

United States Patent [19]

Hile et al.

[11] **Patent Number:**   **5,319,776**

[45] **Date of Patent:**   **Jun. 7, 1994**

US005319776A

[54] **IN TRANSIT DETECTION OF COMPUTER VIRUS WITH SAFEGUARD**

[75] Inventors: **John K. Hile; Matthew H. Gray,** both of Monroe; **Donald L. Wakelin,** Tecumseh, all of Mich.

[73] Assignee: **Hilgraeve Corporation,** Monroe, Mich.

[21] Appl. No.: **954,784**

[22] Filed: **Sep. 29, 1992**

Related U.S. Application Data

[63] Continuation of Ser. No. 511,218, Apr. 19, 1990, abandoned.

[51] Int. Cl.⁵ H04L 9/00
[52] U.S. Cl. 395/575; 380/4; 371/67.1
[58] Field of Search 364/200; 380/4, 25, 380/24; 371/67.1; 395/575

[56] **References Cited**

U.S. PATENT DOCUMENTS

4,384,325	5/1983	Slechta et al.	364/200
4,386,416	5/1983	Giltner et al.	364/900
4,864,573	9/1989	Horsten	371/5.1
4,975,950	12/1990	Lentz	380/4
4,979,210	12/1990	Nagata et al.	380/3
5,020,059	5/1991	Gorin et al.	371/11.3
5,051,886	9/1991	Kawaguchi et al.	364/200
5,144,659	9/1992	Jones	380/4
5,144,660	9/1992	Rose	380/4

OTHER PUBLICATIONS

Scientific American, "Cryptography and Computer Privacy", May 1973, vol. 228, No. 5, pp. 15–23.
Wiseman, Simon, "Preventing Viruses in Computer Systems", Elsevier Science Publishers Ltd., Computer & Security, Aug. 1989, pp. 427–432.
README file from the IBM Virus Scanning Program, Version 1.1, VIRSCAN.DOC from Version 1.2, IBM Virus Scanning Program's Version 1.2.
Simultaneous Search for Multiple Strings, Winter edition 1988 of the C Gazette, pp. 25–34, John Rex.

Primary Examiner—Charles E. Atkinson
Assistant Examiner—Ly V. Hua
Attorney, Agent, or Firm—Harness, Dickey & Pierce

[57]   **ABSTRACT**

Data is tested in transit between a source medium and a destination medium, such as between two computer communicating over a telecommunications link or network. Each character of the incoming data stream is tested using a finite state machine which is capable of testing against multiple search strings representing the signatures of multiple known computer viruses. When a virus is detected the incoming data is prevented from remaining on the destination storage medium. Both hardware and software implementations are envisioned.

20 Claims, 5 Drawing Sheets

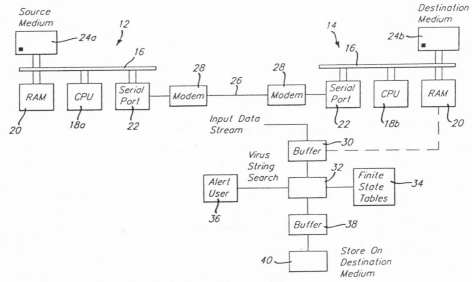

Figure 3–1. Sample front page of a United States patent.

The title of the invention appears immediately below the name Hile et al., in field [54] of the patent. The invention in this example is entitled, "In Transit Detection of Computer Virus with Safeguard." Below the title, is a listing of all inventors, in field [75]. The order that inventors names are listed does not denote that one inventor's contribution is more important than another. The listing order is simply the order in which the inventors' names appear in the patent declaration or oath that is signed by all inventors when the application is filed. The Patent Office automatically selects the first-named inventor as the name to print in bold at the top of the patent.

Below the list of inventors is the name of the assignee (field [73]), in this case, Hilgraeve Corporation. The assignee is the owner of the patent. In this case, the inventors assigned or transferred ownership of the patent to Hilgraeve Corporation. You cannot always rely on information in the assignee field. Patents can be assigned after they have been issued and this change of ownership is not reflected on the face of the printed patent. To find out the current owner of any patent, you can have an assignee search conducted, usually at nominal cost.

In field [21] below the assignee information is the application serial number. This is the serial number that the Patent Office uses to refer to the application while it is being examined. Field [22] below the serial number gives the application filing date. In this case the application was filed September 29, 1992. Keep in mind that the patent grant is measured from the issue date of the patent (June 7, 1994), not the application filing date.

Sometimes an application will be based on an earlier application, as in the case here. You can tell this by examining the field captioned, Related U.S. Application Data. In this case, the application is a continuation of Serial Number 511,218. That earlier application was filed April 19, 1990 and was abandoned in favor of later application Serial Number 954,784 (which issued as the patent).

Patents are organized by subject matter, so that they can be more readily located. The Patent Office assigns each patent to a class and subclass, and may also cross-reference the patent in other classes and subclasses. In field [52] the U.S. Patent Office classification for this patent appears in bold print as 395/575. This stands for class 395, subclass 575. The patent is also cross-referenced in classes 380/4 and 371/67.1.

A patent is not granted until the patent examiner conducts a prior art search and determines that the invention is patentable over the prior art. The examiner will often search several patent classes for prior art. You can tell in which classes the examiner searched for prior art before allowing this patent, by consulting the Field of Search entry in field [58]. Here, the examiner searched selected subclasses in classes 364, 380, 371, and 395. Field [56] References Cited lists all prior art that the examiner considered. In this case, the examiner considered several earlier United States patents and several other publications, including several journal articles and a README file from an IBM virus scanning program.

If you want to know who examined the patent and who represented the applicant, you will find this information on the face of the patent, in this case above the patent Abstract.

The Abstract, in field [57], gives a brief synopsis of the information disclosed in the patent. The primary purpose of the Abstract is to assist patent examiners when searching for prior art. Although the Abstract gives a flavor for what the patent is about, consult the patent claims to get the full picture of what the patent covers. In all U.S. patents, the claims appear at the end of the patent document. In this case, as indicated on the face of the patent, there are 20 claims.

CHAPTER 4

SEARCHING FOR PRIOR ART

§ 4.1   Prior Art

Prior art is important to all patents. It is axiomatic that no patent can cover the prior art, no matter how broadly drafted its claims are. Thus, you often look to the prior art when construing a patent claim to determine what the patent does not cover. This is certainly true for software patents.

During the 1970s and 1980s many attorneys believed software could not be patented, and counseled their clients accordingly. Few software applications were filed. Thus, in the 1990s, when more and more software patent applications were being filed, the Patent Office had scarcely any prior art software patents to which it could refer. Without an adequate collection of prior art, the Patent Office granted quite a number of software patents that software developers consider to be invalid. See the transcripts of the 1993–1994 Software Patent Hearings, reproduced in **Appendix A.**

Today the Patent Office is making great strides in improving its prior art collection. Much of this collection is the result of applications for software patents, and information disclosed to the Patent Office by patent applicants. It is in your interest to help the Patent Office, by submitting pertinent prior art of which you are aware. Aside from the fact that 37 C.F.R. § 1.56 requires such disclosure, by submitting prior art you help strengthen the patent system. It also strengthens a client's patent position, for a patent is presumed to be valid over all art considered by the Patent Office.

Finding the most pertinent prior art is another matter. Often a client will be aware of pertinent prior art, such as prior products, journal articles, textbooks, and the like. The remainder of this chapter concentrates on different ways of searching for prior art.

§ 4.2   Patent Classification System

Traditionally patent examiners have searched for prior art by hand. This entails combing through the vast collection of United States patents, foreign patents, and literature that is kept at the Patent Office. Copies of United States patents are kept in rooms with floor-to-ceiling compartment shelves, called *shoes.* There are millions of United States patents in these shoes. To a lesser extent, foreign patents and literature are also placed in these shoes. Today patent examiners also have computerized text searching tools to help search for prior art. The paper copy shoes are still maintained and frequently used.

Difficult as the hand searching task may be, it is not nearly so difficult as it would be without the Patent Classification System. All United States patents are assigned to one or more classes and subclasses, according to the invention claimed. Using this classification system the examiner can usually find pertinent prior art, by identifying the relevant classes and subclasses, and then by quickly leafing through each patent in the pertinent subclasses by hand.

Anyone can search for prior art in the same fashion. All that is required is an understanding of the Patent Classification System and a road map of the Patent Office—in order to find where the relevant classes and subclasses are physically located in the Patent Office. The following sections will give you an understanding of the Patent Classification System. For a road map of the Patent Office, you will have to wait until you get to the Patent Office and then ask. Patent Office employees are constantly moving things around to make room for the ever increasing patent collection.

§ 4.3   Patent Classification Procedures

When the Patent Office was established in 1790 there was little need for a patent classification system. Under the 1790 Patent Act only 57 patents were granted, hence it was feasible to search the entire body of issued patents by hand. Later, under the 1793 Patent Act, there was still little need for a classification system, for under that act Congress did away with patent examination altogether. Questions of novelty, utility, and scope of the patent grant were left to the courts. During that era, patents were not printed and were only available to the public in manuscript form in the files of the State Department.[1]

The need for a patent classification system arose in 1836, when Congress reinstituted an examination system and established the Patent Office to administer the system. Since its inception, the Patent Office has tried various classification systems, but finding one that works has proved quite difficult. One early system (1837) was a patent list divided into 21 classes.

Class 21, entitled Miscellaneous was the problem. It had no discernible order or basis and bore no relationship to the other classes. Every new technology (and many patents do involve new technology) ended up being classified under Miscellaneous. Later, in 1868, the Patent Office dropped the Miscellaneous category and adopted a class-subclass system. Problematically, the classes and subclasses were arranged alphabetically, so they still bore no relationship to one another.

Eventually the alphabetical arrangement was replaced by a outline arrangement, which shows relationships among classes and subclasses by hierarchical position. The current classification system uses such an arrangement. However, even the outline arrangement has problems with inconsistency and ambiguity arising from differences in subjective judgment. Deciding where a new subclass should be added in the positional hierarchy, the classifier must use subjective judgment. Naturally, different classifiers see classification relationships differently and therefore inconsistencies and ambiguities creep in.

To demonstrate, note the ambiguity in subclasses 2, 11, and 28 in the classification of Artificial Fuels, established in 1920. A subclass Apparatus appears in three different places:

1   ARTIFICIAL FUEL

2   Apparatus

---

[1] U.S. Dep't of Commerce, Development & Use of Patent Classification Sys., Libr. of Cong. Catalog No. 65-62235, at viii (1966).

10	Briquetting
11	Apparatus
27	Peat
28	Apparatus.

Today, there is a *Manual of Classification* that dictates how patents are assigned to a class and subclass. An example of the *Manual of Classification,* specifically classes 364 and 395, which are the principal classes for software patents, is reproduced at **Appendix C.** The *Manual of Classification* is structured according to formal principles of the United States Patent Classification System. These principles govern where a patent should be classified and when a new class or subclass should be created.

§ 4.4   —Principles of Patent Classification System

The present Patent Classification System is built on 24 principles or rules. Knowing these rules will help you decipher the *Manual of Classification.* After studying these rules, consult **Appendix C,** which reproduces the classification of classes 364 and 395 where many software patents are found. Here are the rules.

Utility as a Basis of Classification.   Patents are classified principally in terms of utility. Focus is upon the function, effect, or product of a process or apparatus. Specifically, it is the direct, proximate, or necessary function, effect, or product, and not some remote or accidental use or effect. By grouping together patents on the basis of function, effect, or product, the classification system tends to collect together similar processes or means that achieve similar results by the application of similar natural laws.[2]

This means that when searching for prior art, think about how the invention functions. Search subclasses that concentrate on those functions.

Proximate Function as a Basis of Classification.   Function is used as the basis of classification where a single causative characteristic can be identified and which requires essentially a single unitary act. Take a drilling machine, for example. It is designed to perform a single act, namely, to drill. Simple, single function inventions like this are classified according to the function they perform.[3]

---

[2] *Id.* at 3.

[3] *Id.*

Thus, if searching for prior art to an invention that has a well-defined, single causative characteristic, such as an elevator, look to find a subclass on point, for example, class 395, subclass 910, Elevators.

Proximate Effect or Product as a Basis of Classification.   The effect or product is used as the basis of classification where a single causative characteristic cannot be identified. In a complex system there may be many separate and diverse operations taking place. The result is not the utility of any one of the operations, but rather the contribution of each. For example, a shoemaking machine performs many diverse operations; it cuts, glues, and stitches to make the resulting shoe. Complex inventions like this are classified according to the product or effect produced.[4]

Often software systems involve many diverse operations. Thus you can expect many software system patents to be classified according to the effect produced, for example, class 364, subclass 148, Optimization or adaptive control.

Structure as a Basis of Classification.   The structural features (such as configuration or physical make-up) of the invention may be used when the subject matter is so simple that it has no clear functional characteristics. Tubular stock material is an example. Tubular stock can be used to make fence posts, plumbing pipes, or motorcycle engine cylinders. It has no single clear functional characteristic upon which it may be subdivided. Thus its configuration or physical make-up is the only characteristic that can be used to differentiate it, that is, round, hollow, made of steel, and so forth.[5]

Software (and humanity's thinking about software) has not yet evolved to the point where software may be considered simple. Thus this rule presently has little applicability. In the future, if object-oriented programming achieves the promised software reusability, it may very well be that software objects will be treated like tubular stock material. This rule may someday be useful.

Basis of Classification Applicable to Chemical Compounds and Mixtures or Compositions.   Chemical compounds are classified on the basis of chemical constitution regardless of utility. Mixtures or compositions are classified on the basis of disclosed utility for the particular material.[6]

Obviously, this rule has primarily to do with chemistry. It is included here for completeness, and in recognition that chemistry and software do often mix.

---

[4] *Id.*

[5] *Id.* at 4.

[6] *Id.*

Analysis as a Prerequisite to System Development.   The current classification system was created (and continues to evolve) to accommodate actual inventions, not hypothetical ones. This means that the claimed disclosure of a patent to be classified is first analyzed and then classes and subclasses are created to match, if they do not already exist. It is a pragmatic approach. Patent Office classifiers do not attempt to create theoretical classes and then try to fill them.[7]

Patents Grouped by Claimed Disclosure.   All patents are classified according to the subject matter defined by the claims. This is an important rule, and this may not be what you would expect. Because the primary purpose of the classification system is to help patent examiners find anticipatory subject matter, you might think that patents should be classified according to the subject matter disclosed in the specification. Such an approach does not work well, for it produces multiple classifications for identical subject matter.[8]

Using the disclosure to classify (as opposed to the claim), circuit boards, for example, might be classified under televisions, under garage door openers, under computers, and under room thermostats, simply because in each case the patentee happened to disclose that a conventional circuit board is used. This would not be a useful classification result.

By focusing instead on the claimed subject matter, the classification system places emphasis on what the inventor believes to be new. 35 U.S.C. § 112 of the patent law requires the applicant to fully teach how to make and use the claimed invention, thus the patent specification is usually most detailed surrounding the claimed subject matter. Classifying inventions based on claimed subject matter thus collects the most meaningful specification disclosure under one classification. As an important side benefit, the classification system is made a powerful tool in infringement investigations.

Patents Diagnosed by Most Comprehensive Claim.   Many times a patent will contain several claims, each of which covers the disclosed subject matter to different degrees. Under the current patent classification system, a patent is classified according to the claim that encompasses the largest amount of the disclosed subject matter. This is not the broadest claim—from a claim drafting standpoint—but rather, this is the most comprehensive claim, that is, the claim that includes the most disclosed elements. Simply put, a patent is assigned to the class that best fits the claim with the most disclosed elements.[9]

---

[7] U.S. Dep't of Commerce, Development & Use of Patent Classification Sys., Libr. of Cong. Catalog No. 65-62235, at 4 (1966).

[8] *Id.*

[9] *Id.*

To illustrate how classification based on disclosed claim elements works, consider the following example. Assume a software patent discloses a computer program having a graphical user interface, a joystick pointing device interface, a quicksort module, and a relational database, and presents the following two claims:

1.   A computer-implemented software apparatus comprising,

a quicksort module; and

at least one relational database coupled to said quicksort module.

10.   A computer-implemented software apparatus comprising,

a relational database having a joystick pointing device interface;

a graphical user interface coupled to said relational database; and

a quicksort module coupled to said relational database.

Claim 10 would probably be chosen for classification of this example patent, because claim 10 encompasses more of the claimed subject matter. Thus the original patent copy is placed with other patents containing elements comparable to claim 10. If the quicksort module happens to contain unusual features, or if the patent gives a particularly helpful disclosure of the quicksort module, the classifier may place a cross-reference copy of the patent in the class where other quicksort modules are classified.

Exception to Claimed Disclosure Principle for Assigning Patents to Specific Class.   Classification is not an exact science. There are always exceptions. There are four exceptions to the above rule that claimed disclosure is the basis of classification. These exceptions are:

1.   When the claimed disclosure is directed to an old or "exhausted" combination, a claimed subcombinational feature, rather than the claimed combination, may be used as the basis for classification.[10] (For example, a very large group of patents for an automobile all disclose a body (A), a motor (B), a transmission (C), wheels (D), and the most comprehensive claim in each patent is ABCD; the differences among most of the patents resides in variations of the individual elements A, B, C, and D. The classifier may place the original patent in a subclass covering subcombination ABC, if that is the salient combination.)

2.   When the claimed disclosure is directed to an article defined by the material from which it is made, the composition of materials may be used[11] (For example, a claim reciting "A razor comprising composition

---

[10] *Id.* at 4–5.

[11] *Id.* at 5.

r, s, and t" would not be classified under "razors" but rather under the composition r, s, and t);

3. When the claimed disclosure is directed to a process of using a composition, the composition may be used[12] (For example, a nominal mechanical process, such as refrigeration or coating, may be classified according to the composition of refrigerant or coating materials used); and

4. When the patent *claims* the subject matter of a subcombination subclass and *discloses* subject matter of a combination subclass, but when the disclosed combination subclass is classified subordinate to (indented under) the claimed subcombination subclass, the subordinate subclass is used.[13] This exception takes some explaining. To illustrate, assume the following hypothetical arrangement of subclasses:

> . . Data structure
> . . . with sorting means
> . . . with parameterized template means

In the above example, if the claim simply recites "data structure" but the disclosure includes the "sorting means" then the patent may be classified under the "with sorting means" subclass, because the "with sorting means" subclass already exists, indented under the subclass which would otherwise control.

Note that when conducting infringement investigations, consider subordinate subclasses of pertinent subclasses to avoid missing patents that have been classified according to this exception.

Exception to Claimed Disclosure Principle for Patent Assignment Between Subcombination Subclass and Indented Combination Subclass.

When a patent subclass has indented under it a combination subclass that includes as a subcombination thereof the subject matter of the parent subclass, a patent disclosing the subject matter of the combination subclass but claiming only the subject matter of the subcombination subclass is assigned to the indented combination subclass.[14]

The foregoing is essentially how the Patent Office explains the rule. Here is the translation. Assume the following classification exists:

> . . Subclass ABC
> . . . Combination ABCD

---

12 *Id.*

13 U.S. Dep't of Commerce, Development & Use of Patent Classification Sys., Libr. of Cong. Catalog No. 65-62235, at 5 (1966).

14 *Id.*

Even though the claim recites ABC, if the patent discloses ABCD, then the patent is classified under ABCD.

Exhaustive Division—Miscellaneous Subclass.   Despite the bad experience with Miscellaneous Class 21 in the 1830s, this rule provides that classes may have a miscellaneous subclass.[15] This is done to insure that the subdivisions or subclasses within every class are exhaustive. The miscellaneous subclass is provided to insure that the class may receive any future invention that falls within the scope of the class.[16]

The provision for a miscellaneous subclass does not mean that the problems experienced in the 1830s have been solved. By its very nature, a miscellaneous subclass is easy to fill up haphazardly because assigning a patent to a miscellaneous subclass requires less work than creating a new subclass. The work savings is only temporary, for eventually the miscellaneous subclass becomes bloated and must be reclassified.

This happened in the computer and software arts during the 1980s. The miscellaneous subclasses 200 and 900 of class 364 grew at such an exponential rate with the explosion of the computer industry, that searching these classes was a daunting task. In November 1991, both subclasses were abolished and new class 395 was created.[17]

Exhaustive Nature of Coordinate Subclasses: Combinations to Precede Subcombinations.   Coordinate subclasses are each exhaustive of the classification characteristic for which the subclass title and definition provides. Thus, in coordinate relationships, combinations including a detail should always precede subcombinations to the detail, per se.[18]

Coordinate subclasses refer to subclasses on the same hierarchical outline level. This requirement means that subclasses on the same level must be mutually exclusive.

Indentation of Subclasses.   As shown in the example reproduced below, the class schedule is arranged with certain subclasses appropriately indented. Hierarchy is further denoted by dots or periods preceding the subclass names.[19] The indenting format takes some getting used to, because the subclass numbers are not necessarily in numerical order.

---

[15] See § **4.3.**

[16] U.S. Dep't of Commerce, Development & Use of Patent Classification Sys., Libr. of Cong. Catalog No. 65-62235, at 5 (1966).

[17] Classification Order No. 1377 (U.S. Dep't of Commerce 1991).

[18] U.S. Dep't of Commerce, Development & Use of Patent Classification Sys., Libr. of Cong. Catalog No. 65-62235, at 5 (1966).

[19] *Id.* at 5–6.

ARTIFICIAL INTELLIGENCE

3   . Fuzzy logic hardware

10   . Knowledge processing

11   . . Plural processing systems

12   . . Graphical or natural language user interface

13   . . Genetic algorithms

20   . . Trainable (that is, adaptive) systems

21   . . . Neural networks

22   . . . . Connectionist expert system

For a complete listing of computer and software classes 364 and 395 see **Appendix C.**

Diverse Modes of Combining Similar Parts.   The classification system recognizes and provides for diverse modes of combining the same or similar parts or steps to obtain functionally (and possibly structurally) unrelated combinations.[20]

This rule essentially mirrors the rule that elements can be combined in different, nonobvious ways to result in different patentable combinations. The classification system should be expected to distinguish between these different inventions.

Relative Position of Subclasses.   The indented structure used by the current classification system follows four simple rules.

1. Characters deemed more important for purposes of search generally appear first.
2. Subclasses based upon effect or special use usually precede those based upon function or general use.
3. Subclasses that are directed to variants of a concept are usually indented under the subclass directed to such concept, or otherwise preceding the same.
4. Subclasses directed to combinations of the basic subject matter of the class, with means having function or utility unnecessary to the basic subject matter usually precede subclasses devoted to the basic subject matter.[21]

---

[20] *Id.* at 6.

[21] *Id.*

Each Class and Subclass Must Be Defined.   Each class and subclass is defined in a detailed statement setting forth the metes and bounds of the area of subject matter that each covers.[22] It is often helpful to read these descriptions, which can be found by consulting the CASSIS CD-ROM distributed at nominal cost by the Patent Office.[23]

Tentative Definition.   A tentative or preliminary definition of a class is written shortly after the class is created. It is understood that the tentative definition may be modified later, if necessary.[24] Thus, when reading a class or subclass definition of a newly formed class or subclass, recognize that it may be temporary. To find out if a class or subclass has been recently revised, you can consult the ASIST "Order" file of the CASSIS CD-ROM.[25]

Explanatory Notes for Class or Subclass Definition.   In many instances, explanatory notes relating to excluded subject matter, the explanation of some term or expression used in the definition, and clarifying statements may be appended to the definition.[26] These can be found by consulting the CASSIS CD-ROM.

Search Notes for Class or Subclass Definition.   To supplement or take the place of cross-referencing, search notes may be provided to indicate other classes or subclasses that are directed to analogous or related subject matter.[27] The Index to Classification is a useful guide in locating analogous or related subject matter. The Index to Classification is published in soft cover book form and also as part of the CASSIS CD-ROM.[28]

Cross-referencing.   Nearly every patent discloses subject matter that is classifiable in a different class or subclass than that which provides for the subject matter of the controlling claim. Sometimes the additional subject matter is separately claimed in some claim other than the controlling claim. Sometimes the additional subject matter is disclosed, but not claimed.[29] In either case, the patent may be assigned to one or more cross-reference classes or subclasses, as discussed below.

---

[22] *Id.*

[23] See §§ **4.6–4.12.**

[24] U.S. Dep't of Commerce, Development & Use of Patent Classification Sys., Libr. of Cong. Catalog No. 65-62235, at 6 (1966).

[25] See § **4.10.**

[26] U.S. Dep't of Commerce, Development & Use of Patent Classification Sys., Libr. of Cong. Catalog No. 65-62235, at 7 (1966).

[27] *Id.*

[28] See § **4.9.**

[29] U.S. Dep't of Commerce, Development & Use of Patent Classification Sys., Libr. of Cong. Catalog No. 65-62235, at 7(1966).

Cross-referencing Claimed Disclosure.   A patent may have several claims that would be assigned to different subclasses, if found separately in different patents, either in the same class or in different classes. In this instance the classifier is obligated to cross-reference the patent in those other subclasses, unless search notes are provided to lead a searcher to the other subclasses.[30] This means consider the search notes, for they could lead to art you may not otherwise uncover.

Cross-referencing Unclaimed Disclosure.   A patent may have disclosure of technology that is not claimed, and yet that patent may be cross-referenced in other subclasses (within the discretion of the classifier). Generally, the classifier will cross-reference a patent if the disclosure is novel (in the classifier's best judgment) and if the disclosure is of sufficient detail and clarity to be useful as a reference. The classifier will probably not make a cross-reference when an appropriate search note is appended to the subclass eligible to receive the cross-reference, instructing a searcher that the subclass containing the original copy of the patent must be searched.[31]

Superiority Among Classes.   When a patent has only one claimed disclosure, classification is straightforward. However, there are times when a patent includes disclosures to diverse inventions. In every case, a patent is assigned, as the "original" copy, to one and only one subclass. It may, of course, be cross-referenced elsewhere. Deciding which class and subclass to make the "original" patent assignment can be difficult. Here are the rules that the Patent Office classifier applies (in the order listed) to select the single disclosure that will control assignment.

1.   The most comprehensive claimed disclosure governs.
2.   Order of superiority of statutory subject matter categories is as follows:
    (a) Process of using a product;
    (b) Product of manufacture;
    (c) Process of making a product;
    (d) Apparatus;
    (e) Material used.
3.   When, and only when, the above two rules fail to solve the question of the controlling class, the relative superiority of types of subject matter is used, based on the following list:
    (a) Subject matter relating to maintenance or preservation of life is superior to subject matter itemized in (b)–(d) below.

---

[30] *Id.*

[31] *Id.*

(b) Chemical subject matter is superior to electrical or mechanical subject matter.

(c) Electrical subject matter is superior to mechanical subject matter.

(d) Dynamic subject matter (that is, relating to moving things or combination of relatively movable parts) is superior to static subject matter (that is, stationary things or of parts nonmovably related).[32]

Superiority Within a Class.   When different subclasses of the same class are involved, the patent is usually assigned to the one of several subclasses defined to receive the several claimed inventions that stands highest in the schedule of subclasses.[33]

§ 4.5   Classification of Software Patents

Software patents can be classified anywhere, although the majority are classified in class 364, Electrical Computers and Data Processing, and in class 395, Information Processing System Organization. The reason software can be classified anywhere is that software can be but one element in a larger system. Quite simply, anywhere there is a microprocessor there is software.

Prior to 1991, class 364 was the only software patent class. Some of class 364's subclasses, such as subclasses 100, and 400–800 were broken down into smaller subclasses. However, subclasses 200, 300, and 900 were not subdivided. In other words, under subclass 100 you would find subclasses 130, 131, 132 and so forth. In subclasses 200, 300, and 900 you would not see this type of breakdown.

Subclasses 200, 300, and 900 became quite full, making it impossible to find anything. Rather than subdivide these into smaller subclasses, the patent examiners devised a system of keywords to assist them in searching these subclasses. The examiners assigned a number to each keyword. These numbers resemble subclass numbers, although technically they are not. For example, you will find keywords such as, control systems (221), machine control (222), scientific (223), aeronautics/space (223.1), and so forth.

Because these keywords and numbers resemble subclass names and numbers, many people mistake these for official subclasses. The big difference between the keyword numbering system and the true subclass system is this. Patent copies are actually placed in shoes corresponding to the assigned subclass. Patents classified by keywords are not placed in separate shoes, but instead remain grouped together in one giant unsearchable subclass (for example, subclass 200). These keyword pseudo-subclasses are merely search

---

[32] *Id.* at 8.

[33] *Id.*

aids to help examiners find patents with particular features disclosed. Another similar search aid are the digest or art collections. These are unofficial collections of art on a particular topic, typically assigned pseudo-subclass numbers starting with 900.

Eventually, between subclasses 200, 300, and 900, there were 12,000 patents, filling an entire room. No one could search these by hand. Therefore, in 1991, examiners in Group 2300 and patent classifiers began a program to revise the classification of subclasses 200, 300, and 900. The first thing they did was create new class 395 and transfer subclasses 200, 300, and 900 (and a few other subclasses) from class 364 to it. Of course, there was no way the examiners could break up all 12,000 patents into useful subclasses all at once. Instead, they decided to do the job in phases.

Phase one, now complete, involved breaking down the artificial intelligence (AI) and display processing arts into subclasses. Examiners in these arts had already begun work on this while the art was still classified in class 364. Their work resulted in class 395, subclasses 200, and below. If you look at the subclass breakdown for class 395 in **Appendix C,** note that class 395 presently has numerous subclasses assigned numbers 200 and lower.

In addition, a dozen or so additional subclasses were created in class 395 to receive the remainder of the 12,000 patents. At this point, each of these subclasses contains roughly 1,000 patents, thus each is still too large to use. Examiners and classifiers are working on phase two, which they hope to have completed by January 1995. In phase two approximately half of the remaining subclasses will be broken down (for example, subclasses 275, 325, 400, 425, 725, and 750). Finally, with phase two completed, examiners will move on to phase three in which the remaining subclasses will be broken down. Realistically, phase three may never be completed. It is like painting the Golden Gate Bridge. Once you reach the end, it is time to repaint.

The upshot of this is that you cannot, and may never be able to, hand search in the software patent art. To search the software patent art you will need to use electronic searching tools, such as DIALOG, LEXIS, or the Patent Office APS system.

§ 4.6   Searching CASSIS

The Patent Office distributes a great deal of useful information on its CD-ROM collection, CASSIS. CASSIS is available on several computer terminals in the public search room of the Patent Office. You can also subscribe to CASSIS and periodically receive CD-ROMs containing the same information found on the Patent Office computer terminals. The subscription cost is nominal.

The information supplied on CASSIS has been continually growing. CASSIS currently comprises three CD-ROM disks, containing a variety of different "files" of patent information. Unfortunately present-day CD-ROM technology does not permit CASSIS to store all patents ever issued, let alone the full text and drawings of all patents ever issued. There is little doubt, however, that someday this will be possible. The April 1994 edition of CASSIS does include data on patents dating back to January 1969. The following data (and more) are included:

Patent Number

Inventor names and addresses

Title of Patent

Assignee

Patent Classification

Patent Abstract (only for patents issued after November 1991).

In addition to patent data, CASSIS also contains other information necessary in searching for prior art. For example, CASSIS contains a complete index to the U.S. patent classification manual. While there is a printed paper index to the classification manual, CASSIS is more useful than the paper index because the computer can search for you. CASSIS enables your computer to search for keywords in subject headings that refer to specific classes and subclasses of the classification system. For example, you could use CASSIS to find every class and subclass that refers to the term "fuzzy logic" or "artificial intelligence." You may or may not be able to do that using the paper index, depending on how much time you have and on whether the editor of the paper index has chosen to include those terms in the alphabetical listing.

One valuable piece of information only available on CASSIS (or in paper form at the Patent Office) is the dictionary of all patent classification definitions. These definitions are the official descriptions of what subject matter the various classes and subclasses cover. You need these descriptions to truly understand how one subclass differs from another, or to see the latest search notes directing you to other important areas to search a particular topic.

To further assist you in determining which classes and subclasses to search, CASSIS provides two views of the *Manual of Classification,* both in official outline form. It provides a wide view, called the Page view, which shows an entire *Manual of Classification* a chapter at a time. It also provides a narrow view, called the Title view, which shows a single section of a chapter at a time. You can easily select either view, depending on whether you want to see the big picture or focus on the details.

Because the classification system evolves, with old classes and subclasses being abolished, and new classes and subclasses being added, you need to have a way to stay current. If not, a subclass you have been monitoring for years may suddenly disappear or be reclassified so that it no longer covers the subject matter you are interested in. CASSIS provides an easy way to monitor subclass evolution through the Classification Order Index.

The Classification Order Index tracks Patent Office orders that change class and subclass coverage. All changes to the classification system are made through executive orders of the Commissioner of Patents. CASSIS provides an index of these orders, giving dates of each order and the classes and subclasses affected. To illustrate how useful this is, by entering class 364, subclass 200 into the CASSIS Classification Order Index, CASSIS will inform you that subclass 200 was abolished November 5, 1991 by order number 1377. Then, by entering order number 1377, you can learn that several other classes and subclasses were affected as well, specifically, class 364 subclass 900 was abolished and new class 395 was established.

This change was made in 1991, following a public meeting of examiners, classifiers, and public searchers in June 1990. At the meeting the Patent Office gathered comments and suggestions that it used to develop new class 395 to be administered by Group 2300 Art Units.[34]

§ 4.7   CASSIS Records

CASSIS is a multiple CD-ROM product comprising several different files that are accessed separately. With a CD-ROM system that has multiple CD-ROM drives or a CD-ROM jukebox, you can access the entire CASSIS library without loading a CD-ROM disk. If your CD-ROM system has only a single CD-ROM drive, such as the CD-ROM drive in a desktop multimedia system, you can still use CASSIS, although you will have to physically select and load the proper CD-ROM disk for the search you wish to perform. The April 1994 edition of CASSIS includes three disks, but that number is expected to grow as more information is added.

The CASSIS files are organized into the following major categories:

Bibliographic Information

Classification Information

General Information (called "ASIST")

The Bibliographic Information files give information about particular patents and groups of patents. The Classification Information files provide information identifying which patents are assigned to which classes and subclasses. The ASIST files contain information on a variety of topics, including the Patent Classification System, the *Manual of Patent Examining Procedure* (full text),

---

[34] 1133 Trademark Official Gazette 35 (Dec. 17, 1991).

and even a patent attorney roster. Each of these major categories is discussed in §§ **4.8** through **4.10.**

§ 4.8   —Bibliographic File

After entering the CASSIS Bibliographic File, you will see a menu screen similar to that of **Figure 4–1.** Use this screen to enter search terms into one or more menu screen fields, to which CASSIS responds by providing a list of all patents that meet the requirements of the search terms you have entered. For example, if you type the word "software" in the "Title or Abstract" field and then press the "Display" function key, CASSIS will respond by providing a list something like that of **Figure 4–2.** By pressing the "Full/List" function key, you can flip back and forth between the "List" view of **Figure 4–2** and an individual patent view or "Full" view of **Figure 4–3.** While you are in the Full view, you can page up and down, from patent to patent, by pressing the left and right cursor keys on your keyboard.

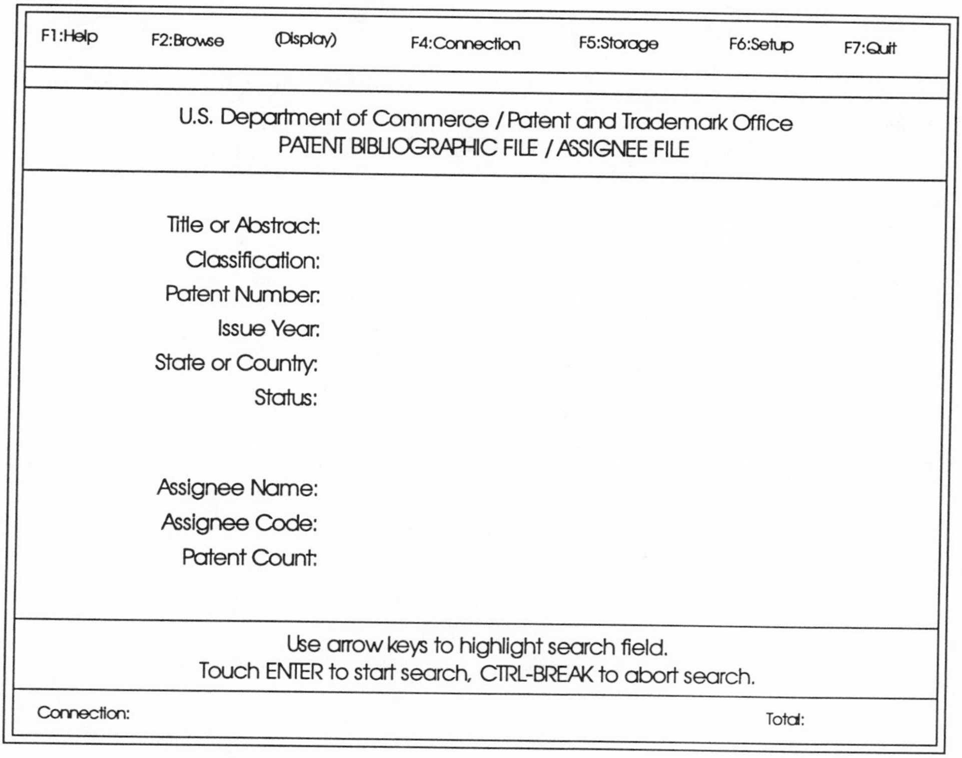

F1:Help	F2:Browse	(Display)	F4:Connection	F5:Storage	F6:Setup	F7:Quit

U.S. Department of Commerce / Patent and Trademark Office
PATENT BIBLIOGRAPHIC FILE / ASSIGNEE FILE

Title or Abstract:
Classification:
Patent Number:
Issue Year:
State or Country:
Status:

Assignee Name:
Assignee Code:
Patent Count:

Use arrow keys to highlight search field.
Touch ENTER to start search, CTRL-BREAK to abort search.

Connection: Total:

Figure 4–1.   CASSIS bibliographic file screen. Reprinted with permission of Dataware Technologies, Inc.

F1:Help F2:Full/List F3:Format (Sort) F5:Output F6:Jump (Image) F8:Done

Patent Classification List: 2 of 2

Patent ○ Classification
Number ○ Some classifications may be truncated, see Full Record.

○ * Assignee Name: HILGRAEVE CORPORATION

5310776 ○ 395/575 371/67.1 380/4

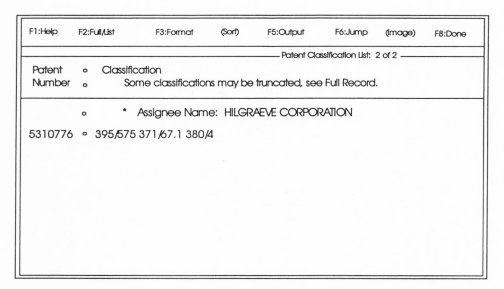

Figure 4–2. CASSIS list view. Reprinted with permission of Dataware Technologies, Inc.

F1:Help F2:Full/List F3:Format (Sort) F5:Output F6:Jump (Image) F8:Done

Full Record: 2 of 2

Patent Number	5319776
Issue Year	94
Assignee Code	702022
State/Country	MI
Classification	395/575 371/67.1 380/4
Title	In transit detection of computer virus with safeguard
Abstract	Data is tested in transit between a source medium and a destination medium, such as between two computer communicating over a telecommunications link or network. Each character of the incoming data stream is tested using a finite state machine which is capable of testing against multiple search strings representing the signatures of multiple known computer viruses. When a virus is detected the incoming data is prevented from remaining on the destination storage medium. Both hardware and software implementations are envisioned.

Figure 4–3. CASSIS full view. Reprinted with permission of Dataware Technologies, Inc.

You can obtain a lot of useful and interesting information from the CAS-SIS Bibliographic file. As in the previous example, you can search patent title and abstracts for key terms. This can be very useful when searching art with which you are unfamiliar. Starting with a key term search, you can discover a patent of possible interest and then see where that patent has been classified. This can help you find which classes and subclasses to search.

Currently CASSIS records do not cover all patents ever issued. For example, the April 1994 edition of CASSIS includes title and abstract information beginning with patents issued on the following dates:

Utility Patent Titles	January 1969
Utility Patent Abstracts	November 1991
Non-utility Patent Titles	January 1977
Non-utility Patent Abstracts	May 1992.

Because CASSIS records are not complete, you may wish to combine CAS-SIS key term searches with other search techniques.

You can also use the CASSIS Bibliographic file to find patents assigned to a particular assignee. This can be a very good way of finding pertinent classes and subclasses to search. There is a trick to finding patents assigned to a particular assignee. CASSIS organizes its assignee information using a numerical "Assignee Code." When you want to find all patents assigned to a given assignee, do so by searching that company's Assignee Code. The CASSIS documentation states that Assignee Codes remain the same from disc to disc. However, assignee names may be combined into a single code.

Fortunately, finding the Assignee Code is simple. Just type the company name (or as much of it as you know) into the "Assignee Name" field and press the "Display" function key. CASSIS responds, displaying a list of assignees having company names that match the words you entered. There may be several. For example, entering the name "Apple" in the April 1994 edition yields 9 assignee names, including Apple Computer, Inc. To find the Assignee Code simply move the cursor to the correct company and press enter. CASSIS will then switch to Full view, which gives the Assignee Code for the selected Assignee Name, as well as the "Patent Count," the number of patents currently assigned to that assignee. The April 1994 edition reports that Apple Computer, Inc. has Assignee Code 32940 and a Patent Count of 247.

Once you learn the Assignee Code, write it down and press the Escape key to return to the Bibliographic menu. Then enter the number you wrote into the Assignee Code field and erase (backspace over) the name you previously typed into the Assignee Name field and press enter. CASSIS will respond by looking up all patents assigned to the assignee you have designated. Press the

"Display" function key to see the list of patents; press the "Full/List" function key to flip between the list view and the individual patent view.

If you forget to erase the company name entered in the Assignee Name field, CASSIS will misunderstand your intentions. It will assume you want all records in that the Assignee Name and Assignee Code match. Quite logically, there is only one record that matches this constraint. In the above example, there is only one record that contains the Assignee Name "Apple" and the Assignee Code 32940. If you try it, you will see that CASSIS displays this one record, which contains only the Assignee Code, the Assignee Name, and the Patent Count—not the information about all patents that you are interested in.

There are still some other handy features of the CASSIS Bibliographic file that are worth mentioning. One is the "Status" field. You can use this field to find out about patents that have expired for nonpayment of maintenance fees, patents that have been reexamined, patents that have been corrected, and patents that have been withdrawn.

The "Status" field uses the following codes:

E   =   expired

W   =   withdrawn

B1   =   reexamined a first time

B2   =   reexamined a second time

B3   =   reexamined a third time

CC   =   certificate of correction.

For example, to obtain a list of IBM patents that are now expired, enter "e" in the Status field and enter the Assignee Code 280070 for IBM. The April 1994 edition of CASSIS returns a list of 315 patents. Similarly, to find software patents that have been reexamined, enter the following search

Classification: 364/* or 395/*

Status: B1 or B2 or B3

The April 1994 edition of CASSIS returns a list of 66 patents. Not all of these are pure software patents; some relate more to computer hardware. However, you could restrict this search further by selecting only certain subclasses within classes 364 and 395.

§ 4.9   —Classification File

When you enter the CASSIS Classification file, you will see a rather simple menu screen similar to that of **Figure 4–4.** Selecting classification "By Subclass" takes you eventually to a screen where you can enter a class and subclass by number. Separate the class and subclass numbers by a forward slash (/). For example, to designate class 364, subclass 130, enter: 364/130.

The CASSIS Classification file requires you to enter both a class and sub-class. To designate all subclasses within class, you can use the asterisk (*) truncation or "wildcard" character in place of a subclass designation. Thus, to designate all subclasses within class 364, enter: 364/*.

The Classification "By Subclass" file gives you a list of every patent classified in that subclass, as an "original" assignment or as a "cross-reference" assignment. You can use the Full/List function key to flip between an abridged display, showing only the number of patents originally assigned (Ors) and cross-referenced (Xrs) to the subclass, and a full display, showing each patent by patent number and marked with letters O for original or X for cross-referenced.

Taking the other menu option—By Patent Number—from the Classification file menu, takes you ultimately to a screen where you can enter a patent number and determine in what classes and subclasses that patent has been classified. From this screen you can also enter a class and subclass

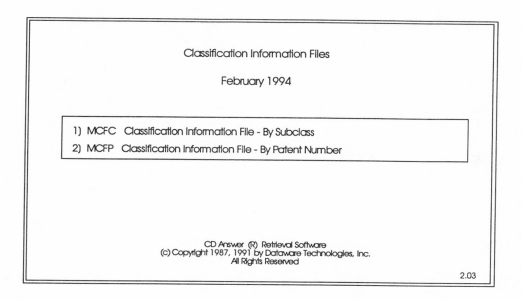

Classification Information Files

February 1994

1) MCFC   Classification Information File - By Subclass
2) MCFP   Classification Information File - By Patent Number

CD Answer (R) Retrieval Software
(c) Copyright 1987, 1991 by Dataware Technologies, Inc.
All Rights Reserved

2.03

Figure 4–4.   CASSIS classification file screen. Reprinted with permission of Dataware Technologies, Inc.

designation, to determine what patents are assigned to that subclass. This later option provides essentially the same information as the "By Subclass" menu option, although the information is presented on a patent-by-patent basis, rather than on a subclass-by-subclass basis.

§ 4.10   —ASIST Files

When you enter the ASIST files, you are presented with a multitude of different files to explore. Many of the menu options pertain to the Patent Classification System. The following is a brief description of each of the ASIST menu choices.

ATTY Attorney Roster File.   This option will allow you to look up the name, address, telephone number, and Patent Office registration number of every patent attorney and patent agent licensed to practice before the U.S. Patent Office. You can use the ATTY file, for example, to find all registered patent agents, by typing "ALL" in the Patent Agent field.

CNCD USPC to IPC Concordance.   This option will convert between U.S. Classification and International Patent Classification. This concordance is not a one-to-one translation between the two classification systems.

COIN Classification Order Index.   This option will allow you to look up Classification Orders by order number, date, and classes affected. The data include whether a class has been abolished or established.

DEFN Classification Definitions.   This option can be used to look up the class and subclass definitions. You can enter a search term in the "All Fields" field to search the class and subclass titles and definitions for any keywords of interest.

INDX Index to the U.S. Patent Classification.   This option is a substitute for the soft cover printed index to the Classification Manual. You can enter search terms in the "Index Term" field to find relevant classes and subclasses relating to those terms.

PAAS Patentee-Assignee File.   This option serves as the cross-reference between inventors and their assignees. Although you can get assignee information from the Bibliographic File, the Bibliographic File cross-references the assignee with a patent number. The PAAS File is a more detailed assignee cross-reference, giving you the ability to look up an inventor by name or address. By combining a partial name and a partial address, you can often find an assignee even if you are not sure of the inventor's full name (helpful in searching popular names such as Smith).

The PAAS File also classifies assignments by "Assignment Type." There are seven different assignment types, for example, assigned to a United States nongovernment organization, assigned to a United States federal government organization, and so forth. For a list of the seven different types and instructions on how to selectively search these types, place the cursor in the Assignment Type field and press the Help function key.

MPEP Manual of Patent Examining Procedure.   This option leads you to the full text of the *Manual of Patent Examining Procedure.* You can search by chapter, section, or text. The MPEP file can be quite useful, particularly if you are not intimately familiar with the organization of the *Manual of Patent Examining Procedure.* The text searching capability will allow you to find pertinent information that might not show up in the conventional table of contents or index. For example, if you enter the term "software*" in the Text field, the April 1994 edition of CASSIS returns 12 instances where the word software is used in the *Manual of Patent Examining Procedure.* Interestingly, several of these pertain to the field of biotechnology.

MPAG Manual of Classification-PAGE.   This option is one of two ways of searching and displaying the *Manual of Classification* in its official hierarchical outline format. You can enter search terms in the Class Title field and have CASSIS return all classes that contain that search term. This PAGE file is the more comprehensive of the two ways of displaying the *Manual of Classification.* When CASSIS returns a result, it returns the entire contents of one chapter of the Manual.

MTTL Manual of Classification-TITLE.   This option is the second of two ways of searching and displaying the *Manual of Classification.* It contains essentially the same information as MPAG PAGE file. This TITLE file differs from the PAGE file in that when CASSIS returns a result, it returns only one branch of the hierarchical outline at a time. Thus the TITLE file gives a more focused view than the all encompassing PAGE file.

§ 4.11   Conducting a CASSIS Keyword Search

CASSIS will allow you to search the Title and Abstract field for any word or group of words. To make most effective use of this feature, you need to use the CASSIS truncation characters and connectors. A truncation character is a wild-card character that replaces one or more characters in a search term. Truncation connectors allow you to search simultaneously for different variations of a search term; you can search for transistor, transistors, and transistorized at the same time, for example.

There are two CASSIS truncation characters, the asterisk (*) and the question mark (?). They are used as follows:

* Replaces any number of characters. May be placed anywhere in the search term.

? Replaces one character. May be placed anywhere in the search term.

Use the asterisk at the end of each search term as a matter of habit. Using the asterisk at the end of each search term will avoid missing a search term that happens to be followed by sentence punctuation, such as a comma or period. To illustrate, in the following sentence, CASSIS will find, or not find, the search term "data," depending on whether the asterisk truncation character is used.

> Example: "The microprocessor accesses live *data,* search methods and sorting processes, to determine if it is necessary to update the stored *data.*"
>
> Search for: data (no occurrences found)
>
> Search for: data* (two occurrences found).

In the above example the punctuation following the word "data" makes all the difference. If you ask CASSIS to search for "data" it will ignore "data," and "data." just as it would ignore "datalogical."

You can search for combinations of words and phrases, using the CASSIS search term connectors. Different connectors are provided to extract different results. For quick reference, here is the list of CASSIS connectors:

Connector	Alternate Symbol	What the Connector Does
AND	+	The terms must occur in the same field.
OR	,	Either one, or the other, or both of the search terms must occur in the same field.
NOT	#	Retrieve a document only if the search term does not appear in the search field.
WITHOUT		Equivalent to AND NOT.
NONE		Retrieve those documents for which this field is empty.

ALL	Retrieve those documents for which this field is not empty.
SAME	Terms must appear in the same field.
NEAR	Terms must appear in the same sentence.
ADJ	Terms must be immediately adjacent to each other, in the order they were typed.

CASSIS permits you to build complex search requests by using connectors and parentheses to make sure your instructions are not ambiguous. For example, to find all patents that contain both the terms "computer program" and "software" in the title or abstract, you could enter the following complex search:

(computer* adj program*) and software*

The April 1994 edition of CASSIS returns 19 patents that meet these search constraints.

§ 4.12 Searching for Prior Art with CASSIS

Not containing the full text and drawings of all patents, CASSIS is no substitute for a hand search in the Patent Office or for a full text database search (for example, LEXIS). However, CASSIS can help you refine your hand search or full text database search by eliminating many blind alleys and revealing areas to search that might have been overlooked. Because of its nominal cost, CASSIS is cheaper to use than a full text database search, and certainly worth experimenting with before going to the Patent Office in Washington.

There are several scenarios in which CASSIS search techniques work well. You will want to master these, and perhaps develop techniques of your own. Here are a few scenarios:

You have a name of a person or company doing work in a particular field. How can you find prior art patents in this field? For this, CASSIS is useful. First use CASSIS to locate all patents naming a particular inventor or naming a particular assignee. Then use CASSIS to determine what classes and subclasses those patents are assigned. Finally, use CASSIS again to look up the definitions of those classes and subclasses and to explore neighboring subclasses until you get a good picture of how the prior art is classified.

You have some key terms, but you do not know where to begin a prior art search.   Again, CASSIS comes to the rescue. First use CASSIS Class Definition database and search "All Fields" for all key terms you can think of. This will give you a list of classes and subclasses that contain the key terms and therefore may be worth considering. If a key term has different meanings in nonanalogous fields, many of the classes and subclasses CASSIS turns up may have nothing to do with your area of interest. Nevertheless, the nonanalogous fields can be readily ruled out by restricting a subsequent search to only the class or classes of possible interest.

Next use the CASSIS Bibliographic database and search "Title and Abstract" for the same key terms. This will give you a list of patents that use a key term or terms in the title or abstract. The Classification field will then give you the classes and subclasses to which each patent has been assigned.

You are conducting a thorough search through a particularly relevant subclass. How can you avoid overlooking patents that happen to be missing from the shoe when you do the search?   Here, you can use CASSIS to print out a list of every patent number assigned to the subclass of interest. To do this, simply enter the class and subclass in the "Classification" database. CASSIS provides a numerically sorted list of all patents assigned to that class and subclass, indicating with the letter "O" that the patent is an original assignment and with the letter "X" that the patent is a cross-reference assignment. You can select "Output" from the CASSIS menu and print a paper copy of the list to use as a checklist when hand searching.

§ 4.13   Searching for Prior Art with LEXIS

Most attorneys are familiar with using LEXIS to conduct legal research. LEXIS is also an excellent way to search for prior art patents, using the LEXPAT service. Currently LEXIS contains the full text of utility patents (excluding drawings, chemical symbols, and complex equations) dating from January 5, 1971, to the present. To check with LEXIS (currently at no charge) to see how far back its patent database goes, you can enter GUIDE from the LEXPAT library screen.

Searching for prior art patents using keywords can be difficult, because words often have completely different meanings, depending on the context. For example, the word "bus" means one thing to a public transportation commuter; it means something completely different to a computer hardware engineer.

A good way to make LEXIS work for you is to use segment searches. Segment searches allow you to restrict the keyword search to the relevant classes and subclasses, which you can first determine at no on-line charge using CASSIS. Although LEXIS will search the full text of an entire patent document, segment searches cause LEXIS to restrict its text search to a specific region, or segment, of the patent document. LEXIS has a number of segments from which to choose. You can search multiple segments at a time, or combine segment searches with other full text searching strategies. To illustrate combining a segment search with a full text search strategy, the following search looks for any occurrence of the term "data structure" in a patent classified in class 395 or class 364, subclass 443. Note the use of segment search restrictors CL and US-CL and the use of the pound sign "#" to separate class and subclass.

DATA PRE/1 STRUCTURE AND (CL (395) OR US-CL (364#443))

The following is a list of some useful LEXIS segment search restrictors, with examples in capital letters showing proper syntax for using them. You do not need to use capital letters to enter search terms in LEXIS. While using LEXIS on-line, you can press the Segments key to see a quick reminder list of the segments that are available for the particular library you are using.

Numbers
    Patent Number:
        PATNO=5,274,490
        PATNO(=(5,254,938 OR 4,598,387 OR 4,990,870))
    Application Serial Number:
        APPL-NO=456,976
    PCT Publication Number:
        PCT-PUB-NO=WO94/12345
Names
    Inventor:
        INVENTOR(SAMUEL W/2 MORSE)
    Assignee:
        ASSIGNEE(MICROSOFT)
    Examined By:
        EXMR(GARETH W/2 SHAW)
        PRIM-EXMR(GARETH W/2 SHAW)
        ASST-EXMR(KEVIN W/2 KRIESS)
    Legal Representative:
        LEGAL-REP(HARNESS DICKEY)
Related Cases
    Patent Application:
        PARCASE(4,736,308)

Div., Cont., CIP.:
   REL-US-DATA(5,105,220)

Dates
   Application Filing Date:
      FILED AFT 8-6-92
      FILED IS 8-6-88
      FILED BEF 1970
   Foreign Priority Date:
      FOR-PRIOR AFT 7-4-94
   Issue Date:
      DATE IS APR 14, 1992
      DATE BEF 1-1-90
      DATE AFT 1-1-90
   Expiration (fee not paid) Date:
      EXPIRATION-DATE BEF 8-30-95
   PCT Filing Date:
      PCT-FILED AFT 12-25-93
   PCT § 102(e) Date:
      § 102-DATE IS JUNE 12, 1990
   PCT § 371 Date:
      § 371-DATE AFT 6-12-90
   PCT Publication Date:
      PCT-PUB-DATE IS 4-1-94

Patent Disclosure
   Title:
      TITLE(OPERATOR W/5 SCREEN)
   Abstract:
      ABST(TOUCH SCREEN W/10 DISPLAY)
   Summary:
      SUM(DIALOG W/15 (OPERATOR OR USER))
   Detailed Description:
      DETDESC(ARRHENIUS OR RUBBER W/3 MOLD!)
   Specification (summary, detailed description and claims):
      SPEC(ARRHENIUS OR RUBBER W/3 MOLD!)

Patent Claims
   Claims:
      CLAIMS(ARTIFICIAL INTELLIGENCE OR NEURAL NET!)
   Representative Claim Number (as published in the Official Gazette):
      EXMPL-CLAIM=1
   Number of Claims:

NO-OF-CLAIMS=50
NO-OF-CLAIMS<25

Patent Drawings

Description of Drawings:
DRWDESC(BOOCH OR YOURDON W/5 DIAGRAM)

Number of Figures:
NO-OF-FIGURES>100

Number of Pages of Drawings:
NO-DRWNG-PP>50

Prior Art

References Cited:
REF-CITED(5,349,900)

Field of Search:
SEARCH-FLD(364#200 OR 364# PRE/10 200)

Classification

U.S. Class (entire class):
CL(364 OR 395)

U.S. Class and Subclass:
US-CL(364#200)

International Classification:
INT-CL(GO3G 15#00)   . . . note, replace slash (/) with pound (#)

Field of Search:
SEARCH-FLD(364#200 OR 364# PRE/10 200)

Litigation, Reexam., Reissue, Correction, Disclaimer

Certificate of Correction:
CERTCORR AFT JUNE 26, 1990

Disclaimer:
DISCLAIMER BEF 1993

Government Interest:
GOV-INT

Litigation/Reexamination:
LIT-REEX(CERTIFICATE)

Reexamination Certificate:
REEX-CERT (2nd)   Note that this retrieves the second reexamination certificate. You must first retrieve a patent with PATNO

Reissue:
REISSUE (29,834)

Another useful LEXIS search technique is to use the FOCUS feature. FOCUS allows you to do sub-searches within a larger search. It allows you to quickly look for specific details in a large body of patents, without having to discard your original search. LEXIS will permit you to FOCUS on any original search that has returned fewer than 1,000 documents. To illustrate how this might be used, say you have constructed a search which has retrieved 988 documents. This may be every patent in a relevant subclass, for example. Looking at each of the 988 documents is impractical. However, using FOCUS, you can work with these 988 documents, conducting a series of FOCUS sub-searches to find documents that have one or two relevant keywords. Because your original search (that yielded the 988 documents) is retained, you can try different FOCUS strategies, using all the key words you can think of, until you are satisfied that you have perused the 988 documents sufficiently.

You will want to master this FOCUS technique for one simple reason. It saves money. The LEXIS fee structure includes an on-line charge and a per-search charge. You can use FOCUS as much as you like, without incurring any additional per-search charges. Thus, if you can construct a comprehensive original search that yields a large collection of documents—but fewer than 1,000—you can browse through this collection all day long, incurring only the on-line charge. LEXIS currently offers a Zero Connect billing option in which the per-search charges are a little more, but the on-line charge is zero. If you use the Zero Connect billing option, you could theoretically browse through a large patent collection all day long at no on-line charge.[35]

If you are a corporate patent attorney with responsibility for a specific technology, or if you regularly search for prior art in a specific technology, you should experiment with LEXIS. Try to construct expansive search requests that will return slightly fewer than 1,000 documents. Your objective is to find one or more stock searches that you know will cover the subject. Then, using FOCUS, you can browse through the results of these stock searches for specific features of current interest.

For example, if you are a Motorola patent counsel responsible for cellular telephone technology, you may find it convenient to have a stock LEXIS search something like the following, just to keep track of what your own company is patenting. It may help you in preparing Information Disclosure Statements, for example.

ASSIGNEE(MOTOROLA) AND (CELLULAR OR WIRELESS) PRE/1 (PHONE OR TELEPHONE)

When you find a comprehensive stock search, write it down for later reference. You will probably want to use it again. Better yet, save the search in a

---

[35] Currently LEXIS offers several different billing options. To use them get separate login IDs from a LEXIS representative. The login ID used will determine how that LEXIS session will be billed.

file on your LEXIS computer, so that you can "copy and paste" the stored search request into an on-line LEXIS session.

§ 4.14   Basics of Internet

The Internet is a massive collection of computer systems, connected over the worldwide telecommunications system. Virtually any computer system can be part of the Internet, provided it can speak the TCP/IP protocol. The Internet began in the late 1960s as part of the United States Government sponsored project DARPA (Defense Advanced Research Projects Agency).

The TCP/IP protocol, and the other applicable standards on which Internet communication is based, are described in a collection of documents called requests for comments or RFCs. RFCs represent a growing collection of working notes, each RFC dealing with a different aspect of computer to computer communication. New protocols and proposed standards are typically published and discussed widely on the Internet, before they are adopted as standards. There are presently over 1,600 RFCs published to date.

The TCP/IP protocol is described in RFC 1310. You can log into the Internet and read RFC 1310 for yourself. The TCP/IP protocol is also discussed in **Chapter 2.**

Part of the Internet protocol is the Internet address system. An Internet address usually comprises at least two parts, the addressee's name and a domain name. These two parts are separated by the ampersand character "@". For example:

stobbs@hdp.com

You will note the domain name includes a suffix or "extension" that follows period or decimal point. These suffixes or extensions tell what type of organization with which you are dealing. Here is a list of domain name extensions that are in current use:

com	commercial organizations
edu	educational institutions
gov	governmental agencies (U.S.)
mil	military departments (U.S.)
net	network providers
org	other organizations

There are several different ways you can exchange information over the Internet. One way uses a guaranteed delivery protocol called TCP; another way uses a no-guaranteed delivery protocol, called UDP, which stands for User Datagram Protocol. Because of its guaranteed delivery, most Internet communications applications use TCP protocol.

If you explore the Internet, you are bound to discover NSFNet. NSFNet is one of the busiest networks in the Internet. NSFNet is the backbone that connects most of the education and research organizations today. Most Internet service providers provide a way to access the NSFNet, thereby giving you access to massive volumes of information.

In connecting to the Internet, you will probably want to exchange electronic mail, or e-mail, with others on the Internet. E-mail services are standard fare for all Internet service providers. You will need to check with an Internet service provider to learn how to exchange e-mail. Some systems, such as CompuServe and America OnLine, include the necessary e-mail software in the software package that you install on your desktop computer.

With other service providers, you must use a terminal emulation program. Most general purpose modem communication programs offer terminal emulation capabilities. When using a terminal emulation program, you are actually running the e-mail software that is installed on the service provider's host computer. Your desktop computer runs only the emulation software to allow it to act as a remote terminal connected to the host. Exchanging e-mail using the host's e-mail software is a bit more cryptic than using CompuServe or America OnLine. That is because you are running a UNIX application on the host, and these applications tend to be more spartan.

To get the full benefit of the Internet, you will want to do more than just exchange e-mail. You will want to explore obscure databases, download public domain software, and browse through gopherspace. All of this is possible, if you pick the right service provider. Therefore, when establishing an account with a service provider for yourself or for your company or firm, be sure to ask for these services. Even if you do not originally plan to use anything except e-mail, you will eventually want to use the Internet to do research. Therefore, it pays to be prepared.

After you have basic e-mail working, you will next want to acquire the ability to download a file. The file may be a public domain program or a lengthy document—perhaps from the Patent Office. To do this on the Internet, use the File Transfer Protocol, or FTP. Outside of e-mail, FTP is the most widely used TCP/IP application protocol. If you are familiar with transferring a file from one computer to another, using XMODEM protocol for example, FTP is essentially the same thing.[36] To use FTP, simply enter the command FTP.

---

36 For the definitive reference on FTP, *see* RFC 959 on the Internet.

§ 4.15   Software Patent Institute

A comparatively new source of software patent prior art is the on-line database of the Software Patent Institute. The Software Patent Institute is a non-profit organization with the following mission:

> The Software Patent Institute is dedicated to providing information to the public and assisting the United States Patent and Trademark Office and others by providing technical support in the form of educational and training programs and providing access to information and retrieval resources concerning software prior art.[37]

You can use the SPI software prior art database to find art that may not be available anywhere else. Case in point, the SPI database offers the only on-line access in the United States (outside of IBM) to the software-related items from IBM's *Technical Disclosure Bulletins.* IBM has been heavily involved in software development since the dawn of computer time. Its *Technical Disclosure Bulletins* comprise a vast warehouse of knowledge on software topics. The SPI database also provides access to many of the articles from *Dr. Dobb's Journal,* to sections of leading computer science reference works, to manuals and technical discussions from Apple, Digital Equipment Corporation, Hewlett-Packard, Microsoft, Xerox, and others that are not now available on-line elsewhere.

The Software Patent Institute has gone to considerable lengths to collect information that is not merely duplicative of that found on DIALOG, LEXIS, or the Patent Office APS databases. It proudly reports the following quote from Gerald Goldberg, Director of United States Patent and Trademark Office Group 2300 (Computer Systems and Computer Applications):

> Examiner [x] searched [the SPI database] for a specific multimedia feature he had been hunting for during the past week in conventional search areas. The hits on the SPI database were more relevant than any of his prior results.[38]

The Software Patent Institute encourages industry, academia, and the public to submit software prior art for inclusion in its database. Submissions should include the identity of the submitter, descriptive title, publication date (if known), references to other sources, if available, proposed keywords, and a free-form textual description of the software technique or process. Submissions should be in electronic form (e-mail, MS-DOS, or Macintosh disk). As an information submitter, you can request that your identity not be disclosed. There is no charge for submitting information.

---

[37] *Mission of the Software Patent Inst.*, SPI Reporter 12 (Fall 1993).

[38] Press release from Software Patent Inst., *Software Prior Art Research Made Easier* (Mar. 29, 1994).

If you wish to submit prior art information to the Software Patent Institute for defensive purposes (IBM publishes its *Technical Disclosure Bulletin* for defensive purposes), SPI offers a special one-day service. For a $200 per item fee the Software Patent Institute will, within one business day, add your disclosure to the SPI database and will place a printed version of the disclosure for public access in the University of Michigan Engineering Library. The SPI does not edit submissions published for defensive purposes.

Before the Software Patent Institute will place your prior art or defensive publication submission on its database, you will be asked to execute the following license:

> I grant to the Software Patent Institute (SPI) the following right to any submission from me to the SPI for its database, but not to any works referred to in the submission. I understand that I will receive no compensation from SPI for the submission.

> SPI may incorporate the submission into its database, and make it available on terms generally applicable to users of such databases. SPI may modify the submission as it deems necessary for use of the submission in the database, including conversion to and from machine readable form. If I request printed publication of any submission, SPI may print and make publicly accessible one to ten copies of that submission. To the extent necessary to do the above, SPI may reproduce, distribute, display, perform, and prepare derivative works based upon the submission. SPI may authorize others to do some or all of the above on its behalf.

> The rights I have granted to SPI are non-exclusive, irrevocable, and worldwide.

> I recognize that SPI cannot use the submission in its database without the legal right to do so. I certify that I did not copy the submission from other work, and that I have the right to grant SPI these rights. The submission contains no trade secrets of mine, and I did not obtain the information contained in the submission as trade secrets.

How can you access the SPI database or get more information about submitting information? Simply contact SPI and ask for instructions.[39] You will find using the SPI database similar to using LEXIS or DIALOG.

§ 4.16   DIALOG Information Services

DIALOG Information Services, Inc. maintains a database that contains nearly 500 unique subject files, ranging from business and industry to environment

---

[39] Software Patent Inst., 2901 Hubbard St., Ann Arbor, Mich. 48105-2467; tele. (313) 769-4606; fax (313) 769-4054; Internet e-mail: spi@spi.org.

and nutrition. DIALOG comprises one of the most extensive patent and trademark databases available today.

Using DIALOG Information Services, it is possible to search for specific U.S. patents as well as foreign patents and trademark information. For example, by typing a U.S. patent number, you may obtain front page patent information, including all cited U.S. and foreign references, inventor and assignee data, filing attorney or agent representative, statement of government interest, primary and assistant patent examiner(s), patent classification codes searched by examiner, related application data, and number and description of patent figures.

The U.S. patent database file spans from 1950 through the preceding six to eight weeks. Some files are updated weekly, others monthly. The coverage is slightly less for the design patent file, which spans from 1980 through the preceding six to eight weeks.

Each database file in DIALOG uses its own set of prefix codes for searching for specific information. You can consult the documentation for a listing of these codes. When using the patent database files, the common prefixes are:

PA=   assignee search

PN=   patent number search

AN=   application serial number search

CL=   patent classification search

For example, "PA=Monsanto Co" locates all patents assigned to Monsanto Co. "PN=5124325" locates patent number 5,124,325. In addition, you may wish to search U.S. classification codes to obtain relevant patents in a particular U.S. class. To do this, use the CL prefix.

Using the CL prefix to search for patents assigned to a particular patent class takes a bit of explaining. You must first convert the U.S. class code into one that contains at least nine digits, leaving out any intermediate punctuation. As an example, the class 219/10.55B would convert to CL=219010550B. The first three digits are the main class and are zero filled to the left (36 converts to 036); design classes use "D" in the first numeric position (D9 converts to D09). The next six digits are the subclass; the numbers to the left of the decimal point are zero filled to the left and the numbers to the right of the decimal point are zero filled to the right. Up to three letters may follow the nine-digit number. To further illustrate, the Patent Office classification number 310/75B is searched by entering CL=310075000B. Since there is nothing to the right of the decimal point, you must fill in with zeros, as illustrated.

Currently patent applications pending in the United States are not published until the patent issues. However, some U.S. patent applicants also file counterpart applications in one or more foreign countries that do publish the application prior to issuance. Therefore, it can be advantageous to search a particular applicant's foreign country applications first to gain advance information about any potential U.S. equivalents.

DIALOG maintains a database file entitled INPADOC for doing this. The INPADOC file contains information from 56 different publishing countries and patent issuing authorities. The INPADOC database file contains utility patent information dating back to 1968. If you need information prior to 1968, you can consult a different foreign patent database, entitled WORLD PATENTS INDEX (WPI), which spans 1963 to present. The WPI database contains fewer countries than INPADOC, but provides research and technology disclosures as well as English language abstracts.

You can use DIALOG to search international application serial numbers (AN=). However, to do so, you must understand the numbering system of the particular country. The United States uses a continuing series application numbering system. To search a U.S. application number, you first enter the two letter country code ("US") followed by one space and a one to eight digit serial number with no leading zeros. Example: "AN=US 34219" returns Serial Number 34,219.

Great Britain uses an annual numbering system. The application number is entered in the same way as the U.S. application number, except that the serial number in Great Britain contain one to six digits with no leading zeros.

Japan is by far the most complicated country to search for a patent document by serial number. The Japanese Patent Office (JPO) publishes five different kinds of patent documents. In the table below each type is listed along with the applicable database codes of the WPI and INPADOC files:

Document Type	WPI Kind Code	INPADOC Kind Code
Unexamined application (Koka)	A	A2
Examined application (Kokuku)	B	B4
Granted patent	not covered	not covered
PCT transfer to Japan	W,X,Y,Z	T2
Utility model	Y,Z	not covered unless a priority document for standard patent

Note that granted Japanese patents are not covered in DIALOG.

To make things more complex, the JPO uses three parallel serial numbering systems that restart at zero each year. Therefore a serial number and year alone will not uniquely identify a document.

To begin deciphering Japanese patent documents you need to understand the Japanese "year of the emperor" system. Unexamined applications use the Emperor's year. Examined patents use the Western year. In each case, the two least significant digits of the year form the prefix of a Japanese serial number.

Converting from Western year to Emperor's year depends on what Western year you start with. Dates before April 11, 1989 are treated one way, and dates after April 11, 1989 are treated a different way. If the date is before April 11, 1989, convert the Western year into the Emperor's year, by taking the Western year and subtracting 25. If the date is after April 11, 1989, you take the Western year and subtract 88. In either case, the two least significant digits of the Japanese year become the prefix of the Japanese serial number. Thus 1988 becomes 1963 (1988-25), and the serial number prefix is 63. Similarly 1993 becomes 1905 (1993-88), and the serial number prefix is 05.

Having deciphered the Japanese year to determine the proper two-digit prefix, next convert the serial number into eight digits. If the number does not comprise eight digits, you add zeros to the left (5435 becomes 00005435).

As an example, assume you have a Japanese serial number 8453344 that you want to look up in the WPI file. Assume further that this is an examined application (using Western year prefix). First, convert the number into the corresponding Emperor's year designation, by taking the prefix "84" (the Western year), and subtracting 25 to arrive at 59. Since there are only five digits—53344—following the two digit prefix, add zeros to the left—053344—so the resulting number is eight digits—59053344. Conduct the WPI search using this eight-digit number.

Had the first two digits been 89 or higher, then it is likely the document is dated after April 11, 1989. In that case, you subtract 88 (instead of 25) to obtain the Emperor's year prefix.

If, in the previous example, the document had been unexamined application, then the serial number is already in the Emperor's year format and the serial number is simply zero filled to the left to comprise eight digits (that is, 84053344).

Clearly, you may not always know whether the application is examined or unexamined, or whether the date is before or after April 11, 1989. The safest course of action is to search for all possible combinations—to each serial number prefix add 25, subtract 25, add 88, subtract 88.

DIALOG, like LEXIS and most other database information services, charges for connect time. The charges vary according to the display format selected. You should also be aware that different files have different on-line connect time charges.

§ 4.17   Searching CD-ROM Resources

There are thousands of pages of computer software prior art literature now available on CD-ROM. Finding these materials is another matter. It is usually not practical or cost effective to purchase a variety of different CD-ROMs, just to do one or two prior art patentability searches. Patent litigation is another matter, however. Where the stakes are high, you may well be justified in seeking out and purchasing CD-ROM titles containing potentially pertinent prior art.

How do you find CD-ROM titles in a particular field? The first place to start is to ask your client. CD-ROM titles of interest to a particular trade are usually advertised in the trade journals that your client probably reads. Other places to check are the on-line databases. Many of these have a section devoted to CD-ROM literature.

For software inventions, one good on-line service to check is the Software Patent Institute database. The Software Patent Institute (SPI), under the direction of Dr. Bernard Galler of the University of Michigan, has expended a considerable effort to collect software patent references. Where arrangements could not be made to make a commercially produced reference available on-line, the Software Patent Institute has nevertheless included a citation to the reference. Thus you may be able to locate CD-ROM titles of interest through SPI.

There are two CD-ROM titles, both at nominal cost, which you may want to own if you do a lot of software patent work. These are the *Dr. Dobb's Journal* on CD-ROM and the Microsoft Developer Network on CD-ROM.

§ 4.18   *—Dr. Dobb's Journal* on CD-ROM

General interest magazines for computer programmers have come and gone. One that has flourished is *Dr. Dobb's Journal,* a monthly publication for software professionals. *Dr. Dobb's Journal* is the place computer programmers check to read the latest reviews on new software development products, such as compilers, CASE tools, debuggers, and so forth. Each monthly issue contains several articles on computer programming techniques, computer languages, and solutions to computer programming problems. Often these articles will include a source code listing, to allow the reader to experiment. These articles tend to be at the cutting edge of software technology—but with a practical, everyday emphasis.

Dr. Dobb's Journal is an excellent source for learning the state of the software arts. The publishers of *Dr. Dobb's Journal* have produced a CD-ROM product that contains the full text and source code from the January 1988 through June 1993 editions. This CD-ROM is highly regarded and no doubt there will be more editions to follow. The CD-ROM allows you to search using either DOS or Windows operating systems.[40]

§ 4.19   —Microsoft Developer Network on CD-ROM

Microsoft is unquestionably a powerhouse in the software industry. With only a few "vertical market" exceptions, nearly every software developer builds its commercial products to run under a Microsoft operating system, such as DOS or Windows. In addition, many software developers also use Microsoft language products to build their products.

Therefore, as you might expect, the Microsoft technical documentation on its operating systems, and the Microsoft programming guides for its language products are the starting point for many software developers when they create new, inventive products. In other words, these Microsoft publications can often be an important source of prior art.

Microsoft periodically publishes a CD-ROM called the Microsoft Developer Network Development Library. The CD-ROM Library contains hundreds of in-depth technical articles, complete documentation sets, specifications, sample code, tools, utilities, certain Microsoft Press books, and the Microsoft Developer Knowledge Base. You can subscribe to the CD-ROM by paying the annual fee and joining the Microsoft Developer Network.[41]

---

[40] For more information about *Dr. Dobb's* CD-ROM call (800) 456-1215, or write to *Dr. Dobb's*/CD, Miller Freeman, Inc., 411 Borel Ave., Suite 100, San Mateo, CA 94402.

[41] For more information about the Microsoft Developer Network call (800) 759-5474, or write to Microsoft Developer Network, One Microsoft Way, Redmond, WA 98052-6399.

CHAPTER 5

SOFTWARE PATENT SPECIFICATION

LEGAL REQUIREMENTS OF THE SPECIFICATION

§ 5.1   Purpose of Specification

Chapter 1, History of Software Patents, explains the fundamental principle behind the patent system, that is, to promote science and the useful arts. It has been written that a patent is a contract between the government and the inventor. In exchange for a government grant of a patent monopoly, the inventor is required by this contract to disclose the invention, so that others may learn from it and thereby promote science and the useful arts. This contract between the government and the inventor becomes the guiding principle that dictates how the specification is to be drafted. Simply stated, the specification must disclose what the inventor claims the invention to be and what the inventor may later wish to claim the invention to be.

§ 5.2   Statutory Requirements of Specification

While it is the United States Constitution at Article I, Section 8, Clause 8, that creates the requirement that a patent application must include a specification, it is Title 35, United States Code, Section 112 that sets forth the actual legal standards that the specification must meet. 35 U.S.C. § 112 states:

> The specification shall contain a written description of the invention, and of the manner and process of making and using it, in such full, clear, concise, and exact terms as to enable any person skilled in the art to which it pertains, or with which it is most nearly connected, to make and use the same, and shall set forth the best mode contemplated by the inventor of carrying out his invention.

Dissecting the above statute, the written specification must meet three requirements.

1. It must contain a written description of the invention. This is sometimes called the written description requirement.

2. It must be sufficiently descriptive to enable one skilled in the art to practice the invention. This is sometimes called the enablement requirement.

3. It must disclose the best mode of practicing the invention contemplated by the inventor. This is sometimes called the best mode requirement.

Each of these requirements must be met for the specification to meet the terms of 35 U.S.C. § 112.

The price for failing to meet the terms of 35 U.S.C. § 112 is a high one. Since the patent grant is premised upon the full disclosure of an invention in exchange for the grant of a patent monopoly, the failure to provide a proper specification results in an invalid patent. It is for this reason that a great deal of care is given to drafting the specification.

§ 5.3   Regulations Governing Specification Content

It would be helpful to have more than one terse statutory sentence to guide in drafting the specification. Fortunately, there is more. The patent statute at 35 U.S.C. § 6(a) empowers the Commissioner of Patents and Trademarks to make regulations defining how the patent system shall work. These regulations are collected together or codified in the Code of Federal Regulations under Title 37—Patents, Trademarks, and Copyrights. Regulation 37 C.F.R. § 1.71, sometimes referred to by its shorthand name, Rule 71, tells more about what the specification should contain. This regulation states:

37 C.F.R. § 1.71

DETAILED DESCRIPTION AND SPECIFICATION OF THE INVENTION.

(a)   The specification must include a written description of the invention or discovery and of the manner and process of making and using the same, and is required to be in such full, clear, concise, and exact terms as to enable any person skilled in the art or science to which the invention or discovery appertains, or with which it is most nearly connected, to make and use the same.

(b)   The specification must set forth the precise invention for which a patent is solicited, in such manner as to distinguish it from other inventions and from what is old. It must describe completely a specific embodiment of the process, machine, manufacture, composition of matter or improvement invented, and must explain the mode of operation or principle whenever applicable. The best mode contemplated by the inventor of carrying out his invention must be set forth.

    (c)   In the case of an improvement, the specification must particularly point out the part or parts of the process, machine, manufacture, or composition of matter to which the improvement relates, and the description should be confined to the specific improvement and to such parts as necessarily cooperate with it or as may be necessary to a complete understanding or description of it.

The above regulation, to some extent, simply reiterates the language of the statute, 35 U.S.C. § 112. However, the regulation goes further than the statute, adding a bit more detail. Comparing the regulation with the statute, details added by Rule 71 include:

1.   The specification must set forth the precise invention claimed.

2.   The specification must distinguish the invention from the prior art.

3.   The specification must describe completely a specific embodiment of the invention. Frequently, since the specification must describe the best mode contemplated by the inventor, the specific embodiment described completely in the specification is the best mode embodiment. However, under certain circumstances, a patent applicant may also describe other specific embodiments, in addition to the best mode embodiment. This is sometimes done when the invention can be practiced in alternate ways. By including a description of such alternate ways, the patent applicant may improve the chances of having the claims expansively read under the doctrine of equivalents.

4.   The specification must explain the mode of operation or principle, where applicable.

5.   If the invention represents an improvement, the specification must particularly point out the part or parts of the process, machine, manufacture, or composition of matter to which the improvement relates. Arguably nearly every invention can be viewed as an improvement over the prior art. Therefore, this requirement needs to be considered together with the above requirements when the specification is drafted.

6.   Although not expressed as a requirement, when the invention is an improvement, the description should be confined to the specific improvement and to such parts as necessarily cooperate with it, or as may be necessary to a complete understanding or description of it. By way of example, if the invention is in an improved swivel head for a video camera tripod, a detailed description of the legs of the tripod, or of the standard threaded attachment to the camera would probably not be necessary for an understanding of the invention and probably should not be described in detail in the specification. Similarly, if a software

invention resides in an application program, which in turn runs on one or more existing operating system platforms, it should not be necessary to include a detailed description of the operating system or systems, unless the inventive application program interacts with the operating system in a nonstandard or inventive way.

§ 5.4 Case Law on Specification Content

Statutes and regulations often need court interpretation to come alive. Such is the case with 35 U.S.C. § 112 and its associated 37 C.F.R. § 1.71 regulations. While the statute and regulations are clear that the specification must contain a written description, must enable, and must disclose the best mode contemplated, what does this really mean? Every invention is different and therefore there can be no rigid rules or simple formulas.

Understand that courts do not meddle in scrutinizing patent specifications or give advisory opinions. Courts will only review the sufficiency of a patent specification if necessary to resolve an actual litigated dispute. Then, the sufficiency of that specification hinges on the facts of that case. Thus, the case law is more like clay than concrete. It provides guidelines and judicial reasoning, which help attorneys understand how to comply with the statutes and regulations.

§ 5.5 Written Description Requirement

The written description requirement ensures that the patent applicant is truly in possession of the claimed invention as of the application filing date. The written description requirement most often comes into play when claims not presented in the application when filed, are presented thereafter.[1] This happens frequently in interference proceedings when the one party copies the claims of another party to provoke the interference.

It may seem anomalous that 35 U.S.C. § 112 has been interpreted as requiring a separate written description requirement, when the invention is, necessarily, the subject matter defined in the claims. Why have this requirement when 35 U.S.C. § 112, second paragraph, requires "one or more claims particularly pointing out and distinctly claiming the invention?"

One explanation is historical. The written description requirement was a part of the patent statutes before claims were required. Back then, the specification served not only to teach or enable how to make and use the invention, but also to serve as a notice or warning of what not to infringe.[2]

---

[1] Vas-Cath, Inc. v. Mahurkar, 935 F.2d 1555 (Fed. Cir. 1991).

[2] *Id.*

Today, the continued existence of the written description requirement involves policy. Even though the second paragraph of 35 U.S.C. § 112 requires claims that particularly point out and distinctly claim the invention, that requirement provides the notice or warning of what not to infringe. The written description requirement guards against the inventor's overreaching, by insisting that the inventor recount the invention in such detail that the claims can be determined to be encompassed within the original creation.[3]

At first glance, it would also seem that the written description requirement and the enablement requirement are redundant. The enablement requirement, discussed at § **5.6,** involves providing a sufficient teaching to enable one of skill to make and use the invention. In contrast, the written description requirement involves providing proof in the specification that the applicant actually invented the thing claimed. In a case involving chemical subject matter, the Court of Customs and Patent Appeals expressly stated that "it is possible for a specification to *enable* the practice of an invention as broadly as it is claimed, and still not *describe* that invention."[4]

Whether the written description requirement has been met is a question of fact.[5]

§ 5.6   Enablement Requirement

The enablement requirement comes from the first paragraph of 35 U.S.C. § 112, which reads:

> The specification shall contain a written description of the invention, and of the manner and process of making and using it, in such full, clear, concise, and exact terms as to enable any person skilled in the art to which it pertains, or with which it is most nearly connected to make and use the same . . . .

§ 5.7   —Nature of Enablement Requirement

Enablement is a question of law, with underlying factual issues to be resolved.[6] It is the invention claimed which must be enabled.[7] The specification must enable at the time the application is filed. Thus, if a software invention needs a specific component to work, such as a specific operating system, that component must exist at the time of filing. That does not mean

---

[3] *Id.*

[4] *In re* DiLeone, 436 F.2d 1404, 1405 (C.C.P.A. 1971).

[5] *In re* Hayes Microcomputer Prods., Inc., 982 F.2d 1527 (Fed. Cir. 1992).

[6] Spectra-Physics, Inc. v. Coherent, Inc., 827 F.2d 1524 (Fed. Cir. 1987).

[7] *In re* Knowlton, 481 F.2d 1357 (C.C.P.A. 1973).

that the specification may later become nonenabling if the manufacturer of the component changes its design.[8]

The test for enablement is whether the specification teaches one skilled in the art to make and use the invention without undue experimentation. When the challenged subject matter is a computer program, enablement is determined from the viewpoint of a skilled programmer, using programming knowledge and skill. The amount of disclosure that will enable may vary according to the nature of the invention, the role of the program in carrying out the invention, and the complexity of the contemplated programming, all from the view point of the skilled programmer.[9]

Every detail need not appear for the specification to enable. Block diagrams and functional descriptions are permissible, provided they represent conventional structure and can be determined without undue experimentation. A minimum amount of experimentation is not fatal.[10]

§ 5.8   —Scope of Enablement Based on Predictability

The scope of the claims must bear a reasonable correlation to the scope of enablement provided by the specification. If the invention pertains to an art where the results are predictable, then a broad claim can be enabled by disclosure of a single embodiment.[11] In cases involving unpredictable factors, such as most chemical reactions and physiological activity, the scope of enablement varies inversely with the degree of unpredictability of the factors involved.[12] Many software inventions can be described with mathematical precision and thus arguably fall into the predictable category. However, this may not be true for all software inventions. For example, consider a software invention that mutates its behavior based on a genetic algorithm, or consider a software invention that predicts the weather. It may be that the results produced by these inventions are not predictable at all.

§ 5.9   —Undue Experimentation

The principal measuring stick for enablement is undue experimentation. The focus here is on the word undue, not on experimentation. Undue experimentation involves a standard of reasonableness, with due regard for the nature

---

[8] *In re* Comstock, 481 F.2d 905 (C.C.P.A. 1973).

[9] Northern Telecom, Inc. v. Datapoint Corp., 908 F.2d 931 (Fed. Cir. 1990).

[10] Hirschfeld v. Banner, 462 F. Supp. 135 (D.D.C. 1978).

[11] Spectra-Physics, Inc. v. Coherent, Inc., 827 F.2d 1524 (Fed. Cir. 1987).

[12] *In re* Fisher, 427 F.2d 833 (C.C.P.A. 1970).

of the invention and the state of the art.[13] Shedding light on the issue of undue experimentation, there is a line of cases that states eight factors to be considered. The Court of Appeals for the Federal Circuit, following this line of cases, has adopted these factors in at least one reported decision:

1. quantity of experimentation necessary
2. amount of direction or guidance presented
3. presence or absence of working examples
4. nature of the invention
5. state of the prior art
6. relative skill of those in the art
7. predictability or unpredictability of the art
8. breadth of the claims.[14]

This list is most often cited in cases involving unpredictable art, such as chemical or biological art. However, with the possible exception of the third factor (the presence or absence of working examples), the above factors apply equally well to inventions involving more predictable subject matter.

It is tempting to search for a rule that a certain length of experimentation time is per se undue experimentation. Certainly there have been cases where a certain length of experimentation time was found to be unreasonable. A case in point is *White Consolidated Industries v. Vega Servo-Control, Inc.*[15] This was a 1983 case involving a computer language translator needed to enable a numerical control system for machine tools. The Federal Circuit found the 1 1/2 to 2 person-years to develop a translator to be "clearly unreasonable."

However, to generalize that a certain experimentation time is, by definition, unreasonable, disregards the other factors recognized by the Federal Circuit. Thus *White Consolidated Industries* should not be taken as a quantitative rule of "per se" unreasonableness. The test is "not merely quantitative," as the Federal Circuit has noted, "since a considerable amount of experimentation is permissible, if it is merely routine, or if the specification in question provides a reasonable amount of guidance with respect to the direction in which the experimentation should proceed."[16]

In *The Mythical Man-Month*, Frederick Brooks, Jr. describes his rule of thumb for scheduling software tasks:

---

13 *In re* Wands, 858 F.2d 731 (Fed. Cir. 1988).

14 *Id.* at 737.

15 713 F.2d 788 (Fed. Cir. 1983).

16 *In re* Wands, 858 F.2d 731, 737 (Fed. Cir. 1988).

1/3 planning

1/6 coding

1/4 component test and early system test

1/4 system test, all components in hand[17]

Fred Brooks managed IBM's development of OS/360, so he ought to know.

Note that half of Brooks's estimate is devoted to debugging and that only one-sixth is devoted to actual coding. In evaluating undue experimentation, does debugging time count? At least one court has ruled that it does not. In *Hirschfeld v. Banner,*[18] Hirschfeld sued Commissioner Banner under 35 U.S.C. § 145, seeking a patent for a "Digitally Controlled Electro-Optical Imaging System." Hirschfeld's application described a technique to enhance the image of a television camera tube using a computer. The application described the computer application in words, but provided no source code listing and no flow chart.

To prove the specification enabling, Hirschfeld's attorneys gave the specification to witness Grey, who was skilled in the art of computer-controlled optical systems. Using only the specification (and knowledge of programming) Grey wrote a program within four hours. This evidence convinced the court that the specification was enabling. Interesting here is how the court treated debugging and the fact that the program did not run:

> The program contained certain routine programming errors of the type customarily expected and eliminated during a routine "debugging" operation. Such errors would quickly and easily be eliminated by one skilled in the art. Grey's program was not written for any specific computer and therefore contained some general portions written in English rather than the Fortran IV computer language used elsewhere throughout the program. The details for completing the program for a specific computer installation would require no undue experimentation on the part of one skilled in the art.[19]

§ 5.10   Best Mode Requirement

The best mode requirement also comes from the first paragraph of 35 U.S.C. § 112:

> The specification . . . shall set forth the best mode contemplated by the inventor of carrying out the invention.

---

[17] Frederick Brooks, Jr., The Mythical Man-Month 20 (2d ed. 1982).

[18] 462 F. Supp. 135 (D.D.C. 1978).

[19] *Id.* at 140.

Although from the same statutory section as the enablement requirement, the best mode requirement has a different purpose. Its purpose is to ensure that the public fully benefits from the patent grant. When the patent expires, it is the best mode taught by the patent that the public inherits.

§ 5.11   —Nature of Best Mode Requirement

The purpose of the best mode requirement is to restrain inventors from applying for patents while at the same time concealing from the public preferred embodiments of their inventions that they have, in fact, conceived.[20] It is the best mode *contemplated* by the inventor that counts, not some superior mode which may have existed, unknown to the inventor. In other words, there is no statutory requirement that the disclosed mode be the optimum one.[21]

The best mode requirement is different from the enablement requirement in its focus. As the court in *In re Glass* put it, "[t]he question of whether an inventor has or has not disclosed what he feels is his best mode is, however, a question separate and distinct from the question of the *sufficiency* of his disclosure to satisfy the [enablement] requirements."[22] Best mode is a question of fact.[23] It focuses on the state of mind of the inventor, whereas enablement focuses on the ability of the specification to teach an unidentified "one of skill in the art."

§ 5.12   —Concealment

For best mode, concealment is the issue. The case law has interpreted the best mode requirement to mean that there must be no concealment of a mode known by the inventor to be better than that which is disclosed.[24] The relevant time for the concealment inquiry is the time of filing the application. Best mode is determined by the knowledge of facts within the inventor's possession at the time of filing the application.[25] There is no objective standard for best mode; only evidence of concealment, whether accidental or intentional, is considered.[26] Whether best mode is met depends on the scope

---

[20] *In re* Gay, 309 F.2d 769 (C.C.P.A. 1962).

[21] *Id.*

[22] *In re* Glass, 492 F.2d 1228, 1223 (C.C.P.A. 1974).

[23] Amgen, Inc. v. Chugai Pharmaceutical Co., 927 F.2d 1200 (Fed. Cir. 1991) (citing DeGeorge v. Bernier, 768 F.2d 1318 (Fed. Cir. 1985)). *See also, In re* Hayes Microcomputer Prods., Inc., 982 F.2d 1527 (Fed. Cir. 1992).

[24] Amgen, Inc. v. Chugai Pharmaceutical Co., 927 F.2d 1200 (Fed. Cir. 1991).

[25] Spectra-Physics, Inc. v. Coherent, Inc., 827 F.2d 1524 (Fed. Cir. 1987).

[26] *Id.;* DeGeorge v. Bernier, 768 F.2d 1318 (Fed. Cir. 1985).

of the invention, the skill in the art, evidence of the inventor's belief and other surrounding circumstances.[27]

At the specification drafting stage, most best mode problems can be avoided by asking the inventor a few simple questions prior to filing. Has the inventor thought about the best way to practice the invention? If so, is that best way described in the application about to be filed? These questions may elicit information about a best mode that might otherwise be missed. This may seem obvious advice; yet consider how many applications are filed each year based on disclosure documents that are more than a year old. The older the disclosure, the more likely it is that the inventor has further perfected the invention, possibly contemplating a best mode not originally disclosed.

§ 5.13 —Accidental or Unintentional Concealment

While intentional concealment of the best mode is certainly fatal, the cases leave open the possibility that accidental concealment may also be fatal. Accidental concealment might apply to the case where the inventor improves the invention, after the initial disclosure, but before the application is filed, and does not disclose the improvements. Accidental or unintentional concealment can also occur if the disclosure is poor. Even though there may be a general reference to the best mode, the quality of the disclosure may be so poor as to effectively result in concealment.[28]

Whether the disclosure is so poor that it results in concealment may involve the same factors as are used to judge enablement (for example, whether only routine skill or undue experimentation is required to fill in the gaps). This was the view taken by the Court of Customs and Patent Appeals in *In re Sherwood*, where the court found "the specification in our view delineates the best mode in a manner sufficient to require only the *application of routine skill* to produce a workable digital computer program. Therefore, the quality of appellant's disclosure is not so poor as to result in the concealment of the best mode."[29]

The invention in *In re Sherwood* was an apparatus and method for producing cross-sectional seismic maps depicting the position and shape of subterranean geological formations. These maps are used to locate valuable oil and mineral deposits. To produce high quality maps, the invention used a computer to mathematically manipulate seismic data. The Patent Office rejected the application on best mode grounds, because the affidavit evidence showed the inventor had a working software program at the time the application was

---

[27] *In re* Hayes Microcomputer Prods., Inc. 982 F.2d 1527 (Fed. Cir. 1992).

[28] Spectra-Physics, Inc. v. Coherent, Inc., 827 F.2d 1524 (Fed. Cir. 1987); *In re* Sherwood, 613 F.2d 809 (C.C.P.A. 1980).

[29] 613 F.2d 809, 817 (C.C.P.A. 1980).

filed. A listing of the program was not disclosed. Reviewing the Patent Office rejection, the court did not agree that a program listing was required. Appreciating the wide spectrum onto which a programming task may fall, the court ruled,

> In general, writing a computer program may be a task requiring the most sublime of the inventive faculty or it may require only the droning use of a clerical skill. The difference between the two extremes lies in the creation of mathematical methodology to bridge the gap between the information one starts with (the input) and the information that is desired (the output). If these bridge-gapping tools are disclosed, there would seem to be no cogent reason to require disclosure of the menial tools known to all who practice this art.[30]

Having now reviewed the legal requirements of the specification, turn to the mechanics. **Sections 5.14** through **5.35** explore what the software patent specification actually looks like, who its readers are, and how to draft the specification, starting either from the top and working down, or starting from the bottom and working up. Most importantly, how to apply the written description, enablement, and best mode requirements and satisfy 35 U.S.C. § 112 will be discussed.

MECHANICS OF DRAFTING THE SPECIFICATION

§ 5.14   Form and Style of Specification

Different audiences read the patent specification: attorneys, judges, patent examiners, juries, business people, engineers, potential licensees, and venture capitalists, to name a few. These audiences all have different reasons for reading and they do so at different times.

For example, patent examiners read the specification to find out what the invention is and to check that the specification meets legal requirements. They do this while the application is pending, while the technology is still (in most cases) state-of-the-art.

Business people read the specification when considering spending money, for the right to make, use, or sell the invention. They may have engineers also read the specification, to help decide whether the technology is a good investment. Such business people and engineers may read the specification when the patent first issues, while the invention is still state-of-the-art, or they may not read it until years after the patent issues.

---

[30] *Id.* at 816–17.

§ 5.16 —Business Reader

The next reader of the specification may be a business person, potential licensee, or venture capitalist. These readers probably do not completely understand patents. They may not know that the patent claims define the scope of the patent monopoly, and they are therefore likely to think the patent covers whatever is described in the part they do understand, or have found time to read. Often, business people, potential licensees, and venture capitalists read only the title, abstract, and the first few paragraphs of the specification. Then, if they are interested in pursuing the patent further they will ask for a patent attorney's second opinion. Having reached this point and having committed to spend money for legal assistance, they are interested.

Therefore, the patent specification is a good place to sell the invention, particularly in the first few paragraphs. Put the features and benefits of the invention in the first few paragraphs, where you still have the reader's attention. Although the specification must enable one of skill in the art, there is no requirement that it must begin doing so in the first few paragraphs. Save the enablement for the description of the preferred embodiment. By that time, you have lost most of the business people, potential licensees, and venture capitalists, anyway.

It is best to refrain from such salesmanship in the abstract, even though this is one thing everyone reads, due to its brevity. The abstract is strictly a searching aid. Load the abstract with keywords and keep needless verbiage and claim language legalese to a minimum. The abstract's purpose is to make this one specification jump out when searching by hand or by keyword. Again, anyone who has searched patents will understand how the well-written abstract makes one patent get noticed, while a poorly written one glazes over the reader's eyes and is ignored.

§ 5.17 —Courts and Specification

Courts read patents because they have to. Federal judges are busy and reading patents is rarely considered a delight. Patent cases frequently take years to litigate, with countless discovery disputes, motions, protective orders, and requests for preliminary injunctions and motions for summary judgment. Federal judges are aware of this and no doubt many dread receiving a patent case, because it represents a truckload of papers they will be asked to read.

In a patent case, one document the judge is going to try to read is the patent. The patent, therefore, is the plaintiff's vehicle to victory. If the patent specification can convey the importance of the invention, how lacking the art would be without it, and why the patentee deserves a patent monopoly, then the specification has done its job. If the patent specification can explain, in layman's terms (not to one skilled in the art, but to the judge) what the invention is about, the patent claims will have meaning and the judge is far more apt to construe them in the patentee's favor.

§ 5.18   Mechanics of Specification

The Code of Federal Regulations gives basic guidelines for the elements of a patent application and the arrangement of those elements. These guidelines illustrate what form the specification should take. As set forth in 37 C.F.R. § 1.77, the elements of a patent application are and should appear in the following order:

1. Title of invention
2. Cross-reference to related applications, if any
3. Cross-reference to microfiche appendix, if any
4. Brief summary of the invention
5. Brief description of the drawings, if any
6. Detailed description
7. Claims
8. Abstract of the disclosure
9. Oath or declaration
10. Drawings, if any.

Consult the *Manual of Patent Examining Procedure* § 608 for additional details regarding the desired form and style of the specification.

§ 5.19   Defining the Software Invention

The first step in describing the software invention is to define what the invention is. Inventors usually have a pretty good idea of what they *think* the invention is. Inventors, however, often do not understand what it means to be an invention and they may have difficulty differentiating between the invention and their creation. Many inventors view their entire creation or product as the invention, even though the true invention may be in a specific improvement or discovery that makes that creation or product better than the competition. Thus, start by ferreting out the invention.

Experienced patent attorneys often draft claims before writing the specification. This is good practice as it forces you to find the invention. Having found the invention, you know better what must be disclosed in the specification and what is superfluous. Some may argue, "It helps me to understand the invention if I write the specification first." That may be so. Many people write to understand, and there is nothing wrong with sketching out thoughts in writing, as an aid to understanding the invention. If you do write the specification first, be aware that it may be necessary to go back and extensively revise the specification after the claims are written to insure that the specification supports the claims.

§ 5.20   —Collaboration Between Attorney and Inventor

To ferret out the invention and to draft a good specification, patent attorneys and inventors need to collaborate. Patent attorneys have the legal knowledge of what it takes to be a patentable invention; inventors have the technical knowledge of their development or discovery. It is only natural that both should be actively involved in drafting the document that will define the inventor's patent rights for the next 17 years and record the inventor's discovery for civilization.

This collaboration is not easy—patent attorneys and inventors speak different languages. Both must strive to communicate with the other, if an understanding of the invention is to be reached. Experienced patent attorneys are aware that many inventors find it frustrating to explain their invention to a patent attorney. Inventors live and breathe their inventions and they are used to discussing their inventions with peers who understand the technicalities of what they are doing. Patent attorneys may often start out knowing very little about an inventor's particular invention, but having been placed in a position of ignorance so often, are usually quite adept at learning the technology quickly.

Begin perhaps by explaining to the inventor what the legal objectives are. Explain how the patent grant will help the inventor or the inventor's company keep the competition in check, or how a patent will help attract investors. Also explain the importance of accurately describing the invention and of providing an enabling disclosure of the best mode. Explain that once issued the patent will be preserved forever as a part of the collective knowledge of humanity. That way you will get the inventor interested in collaborating with you. Make your inventor understand that this is not simply an explanation of the invention to you; the inventor is collaborating with you to draft an important document that neither could do alone.

Having communicated to the inventor your respective roles, the next step is to ferret out the invention.

§ 5.21   —Checklist of Specifics to Discuss with the Inventor

The following checklist of things to discuss with the inventor may be helpful.

_____ 1. What does the inventor think the invention is?

_____ 2. What was the objective in making the invention?

_____ 3. Component Parts of the invention

    _____ a) What component parts make up the invention?

    _____ b) What component parts, if any, are new?

    _____ c) How are the component parts connected? How do they work together?

    _____ d) Are any of the connections new or nonstandard?

    _____ e) What variations are possible?

    _____ f) What parts took longest to develop? Why?

_____ 4. Purpose and Function of the Invention

    _____ a) What does the invention do; what is it used for?

    _____ b) Are there other ways to do what the invention does?

_____ 5. Problems Solved by the Invention

    _____ a) What problems does the invention solve?

    _____ b) In solving those problems, what was the most difficult part?

    _____ c) Before the invention, how were those problems addressed?

_____ 6. Competition

    _____ a) What competes with the invention?

    _____ b) What are the advantages of the invention over the competition?

    _____ c) How are these advantages achieved?

    _____ d) What features will the competition want to copy?

    _____ e) How are these features achieved? How may the competition add them?

_____ 7. Commercialization of the Invention

    _____ a) Is the invention used in a commercial product?

    _____ b) Has the product been introduced? If so, when, and under what circumstances?

    _____ c) What advantages and features help sell the product?

    _____ d) How are these advantages and features achieved?

    _____ e) Does the invention improve upon a prior product? If so, what products and in what ways?

      ____   f) Provide a full description of prior product to cite as prior art.

____   8.   What is the skill in this art?

      ____   a) Who else works in this field? What is the general level of training and experience required?

      ____   b) What journals are published about this field?

____   9.   Best Mode Contemplated by the Inventor (This question should be asked or repeated just prior to filing.)

      ____   a) Has the inventor thought about a best mode of practicing the invention?

      ____   b) If a best mode has been contemplated, is it fully disclosed?

§ 5.22   Attorney-Client Privilege

Inventor-attorney communication is essential in finding and describing the invention. This raises a delicate subject, the attorney-client privilege. Attorneys are taught that communications between attorney and client are privileged. The privilege belongs to the client. The concept of privilege is deeply rooted in common law. The attorney-client privilege is designed to allow the client to freely communicate with the attorney, without fear that the attorney will later testify as a witness against the client. The attorney is also duty-bound to keep communications with the client confidential.

To qualify as an attorney-client privilege, the following criteria must be met:

1.   Asserted holder of the privilege is or sought to become a client

2.   Person to whom the communication was made is a member of the bar of a court and is acting as a lawyer in connection with the communication

3.   Communication relates to a fact of which the attorney was informed:

   (a) by attorney's client

   (b) without the presence of strangers

   (c) for the purpose of securing primarily either an opinion of law, or legal services, or assistance in some legal proceeding

   (d) not for the purpose of committing a crime or tort

4.   Privilege has been claimed, and not waived by the client.[33]

---

[33] United States v. United Shoe Mach. Corp., 89 F. Supp. 357, 358 (D. Mass. 1950).

Thus you might assume that the communications between inventor and patent attorney fall squarely into the realm of the attorney-client privilege. After all, the client is clearly seeking legal services, specifically assistance in drafting, and prosecuting a patent application.

The majority view is that the attorney-client privilege does apply to communications between patent attorney and client. See, for example, *Natta v. Zeltz*[34] (disclosure policies of the patent laws do not preclude the proper application of the attorney-client privilege); *Chubb Integrated Systems, Inc. v. National Bank of Washington*[35] (attorney-client privilege from discovery is not lost in a patent case merely because the communication contains technical data); *Knogo Corp. v. United States*[36] (accompaniment of a draft of an application to be submitted to the patent office with a letter from the client to his attorney does not destroy the attorney-client privilege).

There is, unfortunately, a minority view in which the attorney-client privilege does not apply. The minority view treats the patent attorney as a mere conduit between the inventor and the Patent Office.[37] Under this view, information given to the patent attorney to be submitted to the Patent Office is not protected. See for example, *W.R. Grace & Co. v. Viskase Corp.*[38] (information received solely for the purpose of conveying that information to the Patent Office is not protected by the attorney-client privilege).

The following lists demonstrate the types of things that are protected and that are not protected. Recognize, however, that courts have considerable latitude in deciding whether to apply the attorney-client privilege or not. Often the decision is made by a magistrate. As these lists demonstrate, there are numerous inconsistencies. The following examples illustrate when privilege has held:

1. Purely technical exposition of invention is privileged[39]

2. Technical explanation of general field of technology and technical comparison of the invention and other devices are privileged[40]

3. Letter accompanied by a draft of specification and claims from inventor to attorney is privileged[41]

4. Communications that contain opinion of the attorney regarding patentability and scope of the patent claims are privileged[42]

---

[34] 418 F.2d 633, 636 (7th Cir. 1969).

[35] 103 F.R.D. 52, 56 (D.D.C. 1984).

[36] 213 U.S.P.Q.2d (BNA) 936, 942 (N.D. Ill. 1991).

[37] Jack Winter, Inc. v. Koratron Co., 54 F.R.D. 44 (N.D. Cal. 1971); Duplan Corp. v. Deering Milliken, Inc., 397 F. Supp. 1146 (D.S.C. 1974).

[38] 21 U.S.P.Q.2d (BNA) 1121, 1122 (N.D. Ill. 1991).

[39] Knogo Corp. v. United States, 213 U.S.P.Q. (BNA) 936 (Ct. Cl. 1980).

[40] *Id.*

[41] *Id.*

[42] *Id.*

5.   Inventor's memo discussing prior relevant art is privileged[43]

6.   Invention Disclosure Forms are privileged[44]

7.   Interoffice memos with handwritten comments recounting legal opinion of counsel are privileged notwithstanding that an attorney did not prepare them[45]

8.   Testing and analysis of accused product is privileged[46]

9.   Infringement opinion by plaintiff's counsel relating to third party patent is privileged.[47]

The following examples illustrate when privilege did not hold:

1.   Cover letters accompanying a Patent Office communication are not privileged[48]

2.   Documents relating to foreign application filing are not privileged, when the documents are of public record and constitute information necessary to complete foreign filing[49]

3.   Information Disclosure Statement is not privileged[50]

4.   Factual information communicated in order that attorney could disclose it in a patent application is not privileged[51]

5.   Client authorization to file and prosecute application is not privileged[52]

6.   Papers submitted to Patent Office are not privileged[53]

7.   Technical information communicated to attorney but not calling for legal opinion or interpretation and meant primarily for aid in completing patent applications is not privileged.[54]

Since the conduit theory exists, be careful to avoid making a written record that could later be contrary to the inventor's interests. This caution does not prevent collaboration with the inventor. It simply means to use care

---

[43] F.M.C. Corp. v. Old Dominion Brush Co., 229 U.S.P.Q. (BNA) 150 (W.D. Mo. 1985).

[44] Illinois Tool Works, Inc. v. K.L. Spring & Stamping Corp., 207 U.S.P.Q. (BNA) 806 (N.D. Ill. 1980).

[45] *Id.*

[46] W.R. Grace & Co. v. Viskase Corp., 21 U.S.P.Q.2d (BNA) 1121 (N.D. Ill. 1991).

[47] *Id.*

[48] Knogo Corp. v. United States, 213 U.S.P.Q. (BNA) 936 (Ct. Cl. 1980).

[49] Illinois Tool Works, Inc. v. K.L. Spring & Stamping Corp., 207 U.S.P.Q. (BNA) 806 (N.D. Ill. 1980).

[50] W.R. Grace & Co. v. Viskase Corp., 21 U.S.P.Q.2d (BNA) 1121 (N.D. Ill. 1991).

[51] Hercules, Inc. v. Exxon Corp., 434 F. Supp. 136 (D. Del. 1977).

[52] Jack Winter, Inc. v. Koratron Co., 54 F.R.D. 44 (N.D. Cal. 1971).

[53] *Id.*

[54] *Id.*

when taking notes or when writing letters. This applies to letters written by the inventor to you, as well as letters from you to the inventor. A useful practice is to include a statement in the opening paragraph of letters that the client has requested specific legal advice, or that you are responding to a request for legal advice.

If there ever is an attempt to pierce the attorney-client privilege, it will probably be in the context of litigation discovery, when an accused defendant is trying to limit the patent coverage to the way the inventor originally explained the invention to the attorney when the application was being drafted. This could be disastrous, since, as noted, sometimes an inventor does not fully understand the true scope of the invention, particularly during the initial inventor-attorney collaboration.

§ 5.23   Describing Software Invention

A proper specification lies somewhere on a spectrum between a black box and full source code. A black box is descriptive concept engineers use when they want to simplify by hiding the details. The concept is simple. The black box is described simply as performing a given function, so that a given input, subjected to that function, produces a given output. The details of how the function is performed are not disclosed. Software can be described like this. For example, a spelling checker program can be described as a black box that takes a paragraph as input and produces a display of all misspelled words with suggestions on proper spelling as output. How the spelling checker does this is not revealed. If the spelling checker is the invention, then this description is not very useful, since it tells nothing but the end result and leaves everything to experimentation.

At the other end of the spectrum lies full source code, which arguably contains every detail one skilled in the art needs to make and use the invention. However, full source code may not provide a very good understanding of what the invention does.

The principal function of source code is to supply a rigorously complete description that the compiler processes to produce an executable computer program. Good programmers place comments in their source code to allow themselves and others to more quickly comprehend what the source code is about.

Even with well-documented comments, one person's source code can be difficult for another person to read and comprehend. Therefore, it is best not to rely entirely on source code in describing a software invention in the specification. In patent application practice, source code provides too much information and may not adequately identify what is new and inventive from what is old and commonplace.

There are many different ways to adequately describe a software invention. Almost certainly, the description of a software invention will fall somewhere between the above two ends of the spectrum. It is therefore possible to arrive at a fully enabling disclosure by starting from either end of the spectrum. We will consider both, using top-down and bottom-up techniques, which software professionals will recognize as techniques that they also use in developing software.

To a software professional, top-down programming starts with broad concepts and overall program structure and then iteratively refines those concepts and structures into subparts, sub-subparts, and so forth, until a complete, compilable source code has been created.

Bottom-up programming is the reverse process. The sub-subparts are written first and are then connected together and grouped into larger and larger parts, until the complete, compilable source code has been created.

The patent specification can be built in much the same way. Both the software professional and the patent practitioner need to understand this, since this similarity between software program writing and patent application writing can be a valuable common ground when the software professional and patent practitioner meet to discuss the invention.

§ 5.24   Functional Components of Software

A computer program is made up of building block components, just like any other machine. These components are data structures, data processors, and interfaces. These components are functional elements. Data structures are places to organize and store data. Data processors manipulate data by performing processes or algorithms upon the data. Interfaces connect data structures and data processors to the outside world, or to other data structures and data processors. You can use these three building block components to describe virtually any computer program.

Do not mistake these building block components for the source code files that may contain these components. Source code is really something different. Source code is a list of instructions, written in a selected computer language, and then converted into computer machine language, which the computer uses to build the software machine described by the instructions. The software machine is made up of the building block components; the source code is simply a detailed blueprint telling the computer how to assemble those components into the software machine.

Source code is often organized into separate files; files are organized into separate modules; modules are organized into separate functions or routines, and so forth. This organizational structure is largely for the benefit of the programmer. A program is easier to understand and to debug if it is well organized in this way.

If given source code as part of a disclosure, you can break it down fairly easily into files, modules, functions, and the like. Most programmers place file name and module description headers in the title block of each section of the source code that give the file, module, and function breakdown. Most programmers also record who authored the code, who modified it, and when and why in the title block. This can be a helpful indication of who may be a joint inventor of subject matter sought to be patented.

Finding the basic building blocks takes a little more work. The best approach is to have the inventor identify the basic building blocks for you. Whether you are working alone, with only the source code, or with the inventor's help, here is what to do. Keeping in mind what you are trying to patent, first identify what data is fed to the system as inputs. Similarly, identify what data is produced by the system as outputs. Then identify what data structures are required to build the preferred embodiment. Often these data structures will receive input data or supply output data. Be aware that there may also be additional data structures, used somewhere between input and output, but not necessarily directly involved with input and output.

Having identified the data structures, next identify the key data processors that manipulate the data in these data structures. The objective is to identify the processors responsible for making the claimed invention work.

In locating the key data processors, it is often helpful to use the process of elimination. Essentially all programs have some interface to a computer operating system, and some interface to the user. Often the claimed invention does not reside in either the operating system interface or the user interface. In other words, often the operating system interface and the user interface are conventional, or obvious variations of the conventional. If you know that these interfaces are conventional, locate the portions of the source code that implement these interfaces, and eliminate them from further detailed consideration. This will often eliminate huge sections of code, because a great deal of most computer programs involves the necessary, but strictly conventional handling of operating system and user interface details. This is especially true where graphical user interfaces (for example, Windows) are involved.

Once you have identified the data structures and key data processors, you are now ready to describe the preferred embodiment as a software machine. Show and describe how the data structures and processors are connected and how they work together to produce the claimed result. Use of one or more flow charts to illustrate how the key processors operate may be helpful.

Although the user interface may be conventional, you may also want to include examples of the user interface screens, if that will help give the reader an overview understanding of what the invention does.

Ordinarily, the way the source code has been organized into files, modules, and functions is a matter of design choice. Different programmers may structure their source code differently, and yet achieve the same overall result. Thus, providing a description of how the source code of the preferred embodiment has been structured is usually not necessary. Nevertheless, if the source code is particularly complex, you may want to show how it is organized and arranged, using an organizational chart (similar to a company organizational chart).

In drafting the specification in this fashion, do not lose sight of the claims. Be absolutely certain each claim element is fully supported by a building block component or process step in the preferred embodiment described. Also, be sure to include a full description of any necessary initialization variables or parameters. Courts often look to what is taught in the specification when deciding whether the subject matter is patentable under 35 U.S.C. § 101. The en banc decision in *In re Alappat* is a good example.[55]

Data structures and interfaces are described in greater detail in §§ **5.25** through **5.34.**

§ 5.25   —Data Structures

Data are simply organized information; data structure simply describes how the data are organized. In a spreadsheet program the data may be organized into cells identified by unique column and row numbers. In a word processing program the data may be organized into a single long chain, or "string" of letters, the letters forming words, the words forming sentences, the sentences forming paragraphs, and so forth.

These are examples of fairly specialized data structures. Software professionals have many different textbook data structures to choose from and when these do not quite fit, they make up their own. The textbook data structures include the array, the linked list, the stack, the queue, and the deque. The list goes on and on. In a fully developed computer program there may be many individual data structures.

Why worry about data structures? Part of the software professional's craft is choosing just the right data structures for the job. If the data structure is chosen wisely, the program becomes much easier to write. Chosen wisely, the data almost seems to process itself. Chosen poorly, the data resists. The practical implications of this phenomenon can be astounding, as AT&T learned in the early 1980s.

The local telephone operating companies needed a way to keep track of its cables and equipment in the field. Bell Labs developed a database to do this. The database was written using conventional CODASYL technology. The program comprised over 155,000 lines of COBOL code amounting to a printout four inches thick. The CODASYL database took 50 people five

---

[55] *In re* Alappat, No. 92-1381 (Fed. Cir. 1994).

years to develop. The program received many complaints. It was extremely slow and difficult to maintain; it rigidly resisted modification every time new telephone equipment was deployed. It required a maintenance staff of 50 people. The data structure did not fit the problem.

In the early 1980s Bell Labs took a fresh look at the problem. This time, instead of trying to force the problem to match an existing data structure, the programmers developed a new data structure, specifically to model this problem. They named the new data structure "a directed hypergraph." With the new data structure in place, a new database program was quickly written, in half the time, by half the number of programmers. The new program when printed out was less than one-half an inch thick. It was fast, easy to maintain, and easy to modify when new equipment was deployed. Now only five people are needed to maintain it. The data structure fit the problem.[56]

§ 5.26   —Common Data Structures

Data structures are important. When drafting a patent specification, how do you know if a data structure needs detailed explanation or if a data structure needs no explanation to one of ordinary skill in the art? Like so many questions about what is known in the art, it is possible to find the answer in books. The authority on data structures is Donald E. Knuth's *The Art of Computer Programming*.[57] Another well-organized and useful book on data structures is Robert L. Kruse's *Data Structures & Program Design*.[58] Consult these sources to help identify what is conventional and what is not. For quick reference, §§ **5.27** through **5.31** compare some common data structures you may encounter.

§ 5.27   —Array

Anyone who has taken a beginning course on computer programming has encountered the array. An array is simply a table of data values, all values of the same data type. Being of the same data type means that each of the data values is stored in the same way, using the same amount of memory space.

---

[56] For a complete account of how the directed hypergraph data structure solved AT&T's database problem, *see* A. Jay Goldstein *A Directed Hypergraph Database: A Model for the Local Loop Telephone Plant*, 61 Bell Sys. Tech. J. (Nov. 1982). See also Jon Bently, Programming Pearls 30 (1986).

[57] Donald E. Knuth, The Art of Computer Programming (1973); this is a multivolume work. Two other volumes have been published to date: Donald E. Knuth, Seminumerical Algorithms (2d ed. 1980); Donald E. Knuth, Sorting and Searching (1973).

[58] Robert L. Kruse, Data Structures & Program Design (2d ed. 1987).

Values of the same data type are computationally handled in the same way. For example, an array could comprise a table of integers, or a table of floating point numbers, or a table of alphanumeric characters, or even a table of five letter words. It makes no difference, as long as all data values are of the same type.

The array is not just any table, it is a look-up table in which each data value is assigned to its own indexed storage cell. These cells are sometimes called array elements. To look up the data value stored in a particular cell or array element, you simply refer to that cell or array element by index number. For example, consider the following a ten element array of five letter words, A[n], where n=10.

A[1]   =   alpha

A[2]   =   spock

A[3]   =   james

A[4]   =   mccoy

A[5]   =   earth

A[6]   =   venus

A[7]   =   pluto

A[8]   =   quark

A[9]   =   light

A[10] =   omega.

By specifying array element A[7] the computer looks up the data value stored at that data structure location and returns the value "venus." Due to the way arrays are stored in memory, all elements must be the same size (same data type). Here the array contains only five letter words. Each letter is, in turn, of the data type "character." Depending on the particular computer language implementation, the character data type may comprise a single byte, the smallest addressable unit of data. This is the case in ANSI C, where the *char* data type consists of one byte of storage.[59]

An array can be a simple, one-dimensional list, or it can be multi-dimensional. A two-dimensional array might appear as a spreadsheet-like table having horizontal and vertical indices. Both horizontal and vertical indices must be specified to address a given array element or data cell. The two-dimensional array is sometimes called a rectangular array.

Another important characteristic of the array is that, by definition, the array has a fixed size, that is, a fixed number of array elements or data cells.

---

[59] Mark Williams Company, ANSI C a Lexical Guide 95 (1988).

This can be quite a limitation, because you cannot, for example, stuff 11 data values into a 10 element array. The array is a "static" data structure. Once declared, or "bound" to specific memory locations, the size of the array cannot be increased. This limitation carries a hidden advantage, however. Because the array elements are each bound to a specific memory location, the computer can access the elements quite quickly. The array is therefore a good data structure to achieve speed.

§ 5.28 —List and Linked List

Sometimes a static data structure, such as an array, is too limiting. In some programming problems you simply do not know, in advance, how many data values you will have. In such cases, a better data structure is one that can vary in size as the program runs. Such a data structure is considered a dynamic data structure. The most generalized dynamic data structure is the list, or linked list. A *list* is simply a finite, ordered collection of elements that can vary in number. Lists can take many forms and arrangements, some of which are separately discussed at § 5.29 and § 5.30. The key difference between the list and the array is that the list is not a predefined size, whereas the array is a predefined size.

An important feature of a list is that you can insert an element between two existing elements, and all the existing elements automatically make room for the new element. Precisely how this is done depends on the type of list. Imagine a family of penguins lined up, single file, on the ice. A new penguin joins the family, squeezing in, between two penguins already in the line. All the penguins slide sideways on the ice, automatically making room for the new penguin. New element insertion may be thought of like this. The reverse process is also possible. With a list you can remove an element and the remaining elements automatically move in to fill the void.

For what kinds of things are lists practical? Grocery lists come to mind, of course. Yet there are uses for lists you might not consider. The words in this sentence, indeed the words in this entire book, may be stored as a list by a word processor. This is how a word can be so easily inserted in or deleted from a sentence.

Of course, computer data are not penguins. Data do not actually slip and slide around in memory, the way penguins might on the ice. To understand the way lists actually work, you need to know about the pointer. The pointer is a data type with a very special purpose. The pointer stores a value that points to a location in computer memory. Locations in computer memory are referred to by address number. To point to a given address, simply store the address number in the pointer. Having done so, the pointer now points to the given memory address. By comparison, the integer is a data type that stores a value representing a number. You can add +1 to the integer 10 and get 11. Similarly you can add +1 to memory address 65389 and get memory address 65390.

Understanding pointers, now envision the list composed of individual elements, each having a data cell to hold a data value, and each having at least one pointer to hold the memory address or addresses of that element's neighbor elements. To insert a new element into the list between two neighbor elements, simply change the neighbor elements' pointers to point to the new element and add the neighbor elements' addresses to the pointers of the new element. Now the new element is integrated into the list, just as if it had been present there in the first place. To remove the element, simply reverse the process. Unlike the penguins, which must physically slide sideways to make room for a new penguin, there is no need for the data to physically move. Although *logically* lined up in the list, the new element may physically occupy a memory address far removed from its adjacent neighbors. The computer does not care. It references different memory addresses with equal ease.

§ 5.29   —Stack

The *stack* is a special kind of list in which all insertions and deletions are made at one end, not in the middle. Called the "top" of the stack, this one end is where all data is "pushed" onto or "popped" from the stack. The analogy frequently given is that the stack works like the stack of lunchroom trays in the lunch room, or like the stack of salad plates at the salad bar.

The stack exhibits last-in, first-out (LIFO) behavior, making it an ideal scratchpad to temporarily store sequential information that needs to be popped off, in the reverse order it was pushed in. A program needs information fed to it in this way to be able to return where it left off when it executes procedures, which call other procedures (which may call still other procedures). Without the stack to guide it, the program is unable to retrace its steps and get hopelessly lost. MS-DOS uses a stack data structure to keep track of its place in much the same way.

§ 5.30   —Queue

Another variation on the basic list is the queue. The *queue* is a first-in, first-out (FIFO) structure in which all insertions to the list are made at one end, and all deletions to the list are made from the other end. The queue is used quite heavily, as it mimics many real world problems, such as standing in line at the ATM machine or waiting to take a ticket to gain entry to the parking garage.

A special queue worth knowing about is the deque, pronounced "D-Q" or "deck." The term *deque* is actually a contraction for "double ended queue." Being double-ended, insertions or deletions can be made from either end, but never from the middle.

§ 5.31   —Binary Tree

The *binary tree* is a linked data structure with a split personality. The lists discussed so far are linked in a sequential fashion. To get from one end of the list to the other, you must visit each element sequentially, like counting a string of pearls. The binary tree is different. Starting from the top you have two choices: either branch left or right. Having made your selection, you again have two choices: either branch left or right. The elements that make up the binary tree are sometimes called *nodes*. The node at the top is called the *root*. The two binary trees branching left and right from the root are called the *left subtree* and the *right subtree*. You sometimes see the outermost nodes referred to as *leaves,* in keeping with the tree metaphor. Actually, the way most binary trees are drawn, it would have been more accurate to call it the inverted binary tree, but nobody does that.

The term binary refers to the fact that there are two (and only two) subtrees branching from each node. Thus the number of nodes at every level increases as binary numbers increase with each placeholder digit: 1 . . 2 . . 4 . . 8 . . 16 . . 32, and so on.

The binary tree is an extremely useful data structure, which makes possible a very quick searching technique called binary search. In binary search you make a comparison at a given node of the tree and then traverse right or left, depending upon the outcome of the comparison. As it turns out, on average, the binary search technique is considerably faster than a linear search technique where you must make a comparison with every element of the list.

To demonstrate this, consider the guessing game in which you must guess the number I am thinking. The number may be from 1 to 10. Using a linear search technique you must ask: Is the number one? Is the number two? Is the number three? and so on, until I answer, Yes. If you are lucky, I was thinking of the number one, and you have the answer after only one guess. If you are unlucky, I was thinking of the number ten, and you have the answer after ten guesses.

Now change to a binary search technique. Start by picking a number in the middle and ask, "Is the number five?" I answer either "Higher," "Lower," or "Yes." Based on the answer, if the number is lower, pick again, selecting a number in the middle of the left branch of the tree. If the number is higher, pick a number in the middle of the higher branch of the tree. You will have the answer "Yes" after at least four questions.

Computers are blindingly fast at doing such comparisons. Therefore, why the big fuss over reducing the number of guesses from ten to four? Clearly if all you have is ten numbers, there is little computational difference between linear search and binary search. However, increase that number to one million and the point spread opens wide. Even taking into account that the linear search, on average, will find a match before reaching the end of the list, it will still take the linear search N/2 guesses, that is 500,000 guesses. The binary search will do it in twenty guesses, at most.

§ 5.32   —Interfaces

Software professionals use the term *interface* to refer to a working connection between two entities. Sometimes the connection is physical. Two software entities can be so integrally joined together that they simply merge into a new, larger software entity. More often, the connection is metaphysical—there is no physical connection. The two software entities retain their separate identities and simply communicate with one another.

Strictly speaking, the term interface describes the abstract concept of a working connection. In practice, the term interface is more often used to refer to the means or mechanism by which the working connection is made. Thus, the interface between two software entities will probably describe precisely how the entities exchange information and under what circumstances.

For example, software entity A may request software entity B to sort a list of numbers by supplying B with:

a.   Precise information about when the list may be found
b.   Size of the list
c.   What type of sorting is requested
d.   How B should notify A when finished, and so forth.

The interface would need to specify in what order this information must be passed from A to B, how the information must be expressed, and even how A is to notify B that this request is intended for you. Likewise the interface would also need to specify how B informs A when the sorting task is complete, how B informs A that an error has occurred, and what that error was. In a properly designed interface, nothing is left to chance. Every possible contingency is provided for with mathematical precision.

Interface is a very powerful concept. It makes division of labor possible. Programmers use division of labor to great advantage. Why write the same information sorting routine ten times, just because information needs to be sorted for ten different purposes? Instead, why not write one, general purpose sorting entity and allow other parts of the program to ask it for sorting help when needed? To do this, programmers simply design the individual entities they need and then design an interface to connect them. In this way, each individual entity specializes in only one part of the problem. The interface connects the entities together, allowing them to work in concert while still retaining their individual specialties.

§ 5.33 —Operating System Interface

Virtually every computer program has an interface. The operating system interface is the mechanism that connects the computer program to the operating system. The operating system interface may, for example, give a program access to the disk drive, so that information contained in a data structure can be stored on disk. It may also give a program access to a printer, for example. Practically every software program will have an operating system interface.

Rarely does the invention reside in the operating system interface, although it can happen. In those rare cases where the invention does modify the operating system, describe the operating system in detail. Usually, however, the operating system is not part of the invention and you should not need to include an extensive description of it.

§ 5.34 —User Interface

The user interface is one of the most interesting interfaces. It supplies the connection between the software program and the human user. Although admittedly dehumanizing, the user interface concept treats the software program as one entity and the user as another entity. As far as the software program is concerned, the two entities are equals. Today, the mention of user interface evokes notions of graphical screen displays, menus, button bars, function keys, point and click, and the ubiquitous mouse. These represent the user interface stone age, as far as what is possible.

In science fiction book *Neuromancer*,[60] William Gibson describes a future world where software programs are connected directly to the brain by inserting chips into medically implanted sockets behind the ear. The programs give the wearer instant knowledge of a selected subject. If your automatic transmission needs an overhaul, simply select the How to Repair Your Automatic Transmission chip, insert it behind the ear, and repair the transmission yourself, with complete confidence and expert knowledge of how to do the job. Gibson's vision is not farfetched. No doubt there will be many future biomedical inventions of great significance that will involve this very type of user interface. Although the socket behind the ear may not be cosmetically

---

[60] William Gibson, Neuromancer (1984).

appealing, it is no less appealing than a hearing aid inserted in the ear, and there are many other places to put the socket.

The user interface of the future need not involve implants at all. Spoken language may be used. Many will remember the dialogues between Dave Bowman and the HAL 9000 computer, in *2001, A Space Odyssey.* Through HAL's advanced technology, the user interface between HAL and Dave was all but invisible to us. HAL and Dave simply talked with one another, as two people do, using Dave's natural language, English. HAL understood more than English, however. HAL also understood how to hold a conversation with a human. This is undoubtedly a desirable goal for the user interface of the future.

§ 5.35   Checklist

The attorney who needs a quick answer to often-asked questions can use the following checklist. The cases cited in this checklist are good introductions to further research.

_____ Written Description Requirement[61]

    _____ Purpose: to show applicant was in possession of the invention.

    _____ Test: whether the specification reasonably conveys to the artisan that the inventor had possession of the invention on the filing date.[62]

    _____ Relevant time: application filing date[63]

    _____ Question of: fact[64]

    _____ Burden of Proof: clear and convincing evidence[65]

_____ Enablement Requirement

    _____ Purpose: to supply the *quid pro quo* for the patent monopoly by teaching how to make and use the invention.

    _____ Test: whether the specification teaches one skilled in the art to make and use the invention without undue experimentation.[66]

---

[61] Vas-Cath Inc. v. Mahurkar, 935 F.2d 1555 (Fed. Cir. 1991); *In re* Hayes Microcomputer Prods., Inc. Patent Litigation, 982 F.2d 1527 (Fed. Cir. 1992).

[62] *In re* Hayes Microcomputer Prods., Inc. Patent Litigation, 982 F.2d 1527 (Fed. Cir. 1992).

[63] Vas-Cath Inc. v. Mahurkar, 935 F.2d 1555 (Fed. Cir. 1991).

[64] *In re* Hayes Microcomputer Prods., Inc. Patent Litigation, 982 F.2d 1527, 1533 (Fed. Cir. 1992).

[65] DeGeorge v. Bernier, 768 F.2d 1318 (Fed. Cir. 1985).

[66] Northern Telecom, Inc. v. Datapoint Corp., 908 F.2d 931 (Fed. Cir. 1990).

_____ Relevant time: application filing date[67]

_____ Question of: law[68]

_____ Burden of Proof: thoroughly convincing evidence[69]

_____ Best Mode Requirement

_____ Purpose: To restrain inventors from concealing the preferred embodiments actually conceived.[70]

_____ Test: There is no objective standard for best mode; only evidence of concealment, whether accidental or intentional, is considered.[71] Whether best mode is met depends on the scope of the invention, the skill in the art, evidence of the inventor's belief and other surrounding circumstances.[72]

_____ Relevant time: Application filing date[73]

_____ Question of: Fact[74]

---

[67] *In re* Comstock, 481 F.2d 905 (C.C.P.A. 1973).

[68] Spectra-Physics, Inc. v. Coherent, Inc., 827 F.2d 1524 (Fed. Cir. 1987).

[69] Hirschfield v. Banner, 462 F. Supp. 135 (D.D.C. 1978).

[70] *In re* Gay, 309 F.2d 769, (C.C.P.A. 1962).

[71] Spectra-Physics, Inc. v. Coherent, Inc., 827 F.2d 1524 (Fed. Cir. 1987); DeGeorge v. Bernier, 768 F.2d 1318 (Fed. Cir. 1985).

[72] *In re* Hayes Microcomputer Prods., Inc. Patent Litigation, 982 F.2d 1527 (Fed. Cir. 1992).

[73] Spectra-Physics, Inc. v. Coherent, Inc., 827 F.2d 1524 (Fed. Cir. 1987).

[74] *In re* Hayes Microcomputer Prods., Inc. Patent Litigation, 982 F.2d 1527 (Fed. Cir. 1992); Amgen, Inc. v. Chugai Pharmaceutical Co., 927 F.2d 1200 (Fed. Cir. 1991); DeGeorge v. Bernier, 768 F.2d 1318 (Fed. Cir. 1985).

CHAPTER 6

SOFTWARE PATENT DRAWINGS

§ 6.1   Drawings in a Patent Application

Why have drawings in a patent application? There are at least five good reasons. First, in many cases the law requires it. Second, drawings help explain the invention and make the patent come alive. Trial lawyers, judges, and juries appreciate this. Third, drawings make the patent easier to comprehend at a glance, and thus easier to find when searching for a particular technology or when studying the state of the art. Patent examiners appreciate this. Fourth, drawings help establish the structure, sequence, and organization of how information is presented in the patent specification. Patent attorneys use drawings as an outline for drafting the written specification. Fifth, drawings help extract the key elements of an invention from the complexity of implementation details. Patent attorneys use drawings to sketch out thoughts for drafting claims.

The first reason for having drawings, that the law requires it is discussed further in § 6.2 under Legal Requirements. The remaining reasons for having drawings are practical reasons. These are discussed further in § 6.3 under Practical Considerations.

§ 6.2   Legal Requirements for Drawings

The patent statute requires drawings where necessary for the understanding of the subject matter sought to be patented. In the words of the statute:

> The applicant shall furnish a drawing where necessary for the understanding of the subject matter sought to be patented. When the nature of such subject matter admits of illustration by a drawing and the applicant has not furnished such a drawing, the Commissioner may require its submission within a time period of not less than two months from the sending of a notice thereof. Drawings submitted after the filing date of the application may not be used (i) to overcome any insufficiency of the specification due to lack of an enabling disclosure or otherwise inadequate disclosure therein, or (ii) to supplement the original disclosure thereof for the purposes of interpretation of the scope of the claims.[1]

---

[1] 35 U.S.C. § 113.

The Code of Federal Regulations further describes the drawings requirement:

§ 1.81   Drawings Required In Patent Applications

(a)   The applicant for a patent is required to furnish a drawing of his or her invention where necessary for the understanding of the subject matter sought to be patented; this drawing, or a high quality copy thereof, must be filed with the application. Since corrections are the responsibility of the applicant, the original drawings(s) should be retained by the applicant for any necessary future correction.

(b)   Drawings may include illustrations which facilitate an understanding of the invention (for example, flowsheets in cases of processes, and diagrammatic views).

(c)   Whenever the nature of the subject matter sought to be patented admits of illustration by a drawing without its being necessary for the understanding of the subject matter and the applicant has not furnished such a drawing, the examiner will require its submission within a time period of not less than two months from the date of the sending of a notice thereof.

(d)   Drawings submitted after the filing date of the application may not be used to overcome any insufficiency of the specification due to lack of an enabling disclosure or otherwise inadequate disclosure therein, or to supplement the original disclosure thereof for the purposes of interpretation of the scope of any claim.[2]

§ 6.3   —Necessity of Drawings

The statute and regulations do not explain the meaning of the statutory language "when necessary for the understanding." The Federal Circuit Court of Appeals has answered that question in *In re Hayes Microcomputer Products, Inc. Patent Litigation.*[3]

In *In re Hayes* one of the issues the court addresses is whether the patent adequately describes the invention and whether the drawings are adequate to meet the requirements of 35 U.S.C. § 113. The patent-in-suit comprises only 27 lines to describe the heart of the invention and only a single block, identified as microprocessor 55, to represent that heart. Finding both specification and drawing adequate, the court applies essentially the same rationale: that the specification and drawings are sufficient for one skilled in the art to understand. With regard to the drawing, the court states:

---

[2] 37 C.F.R. § 1.81.

[3] 982 F.2d 1527, 1536 (Fed. Cir. 1992).

According to section 113, "[t]he applicant shall furnish a drawing where necessary for the understanding of the subject matter sought to be patented."
Sufficient evidence exists to support the conclusion that, to the extent it was
necessary, the drawings were sufficient for a skilled artisan to understand the
subject matter of the claimed invention. The microprocessor is identified as
element 55 in Figure 1B of the specification. On the facts of this case, no more
needed to be included in the drawings to satisfy the description requirement.[4]

Recognize that the court relies on expert testimony evidence to conclude
that the drawing requirement of 35 U.S.C. § 113 has been met. The patentee
in that case wisely offered expert testimony to prove that the claimed functions were attributed to the microprocessor. Without this evidence the court
might not have concluded that § 113 had been satisfied, and the patent might
have been held invalid.

You should not mistake arguments of counsel for evidence. Therefore,
when confronted with a drawing requirements issue, proceed as the patentee
in *In re Hayes* did. Place evidence in the record to support the conclusion
that a skilled artisan will understand the subject matter of the claimed invention, without drawings of that subject matter.

Admittedly, the *Hayes* patent-in-suit is not a patent that is completely
devoid of drawings. Nevertheless, by applying and construing the applicable
statute, 35 U.S.C. § 113, the Federal Circuit Court of Appeals shows what
the statutory language "necessary for the understanding of the subject matter" must mean. It follows that, in some cases, a patent application requires
no drawings. This is the current practice in chemical patent applications.

That some applications may not require drawings implies the converse,
that some applications do require drawings. When drawings are required, the
Patent Office will not give an application a filing date if the drawings are
omitted. In order to receive a filing date, an application must meet the all of
the basic requirements stated in 35 U.S.C. § 111. Those requirements are:

Application for patent shall be made, or authorized to be made, by the inventor, except as otherwise provided in this rule, in writing to the Commissioner.
Such application shall include (1) a specification as prescribed by section 112
of this title; (2) a drawing as prescribed by section 113 of this title; and (3) an
oath by the applicant as prescribed by section 115 of this title.

* * *

The filing date of an application shall be the date on which the specification
and any required drawings are received in the Patent and Trademark Office.[5]

---

[4] *Id.*
[5] 35 U.S.C. § 111.

Receiving the earliest possible filing date can be important. An early filing date may make an otherwise key patent or a key publication unavailable as prior art. An early filing date may similarly avoid a public use or on sale bar under 35 U.S.C. § 102(b). An early filing date may give the applicant the tactical advantages of the "senior party" in an interference proceeding under 35 U.S.C. § 135, as prescribed by 37 C.F.R. §§ 1.601–.690.

The kind of problems that can arise when drawings are omitted is shown by *Jack Winter, Inc. v. Koratron Co.*[6] *Jack Winter* was a giant litigation involving 17 separate patent infringement actions consolidated by order of the Judicial Panel on Multidistrict Litigation.[7] The suit revolved around the Koratron patent for permanent press fabric. Accused of infringement were a veritable who's who of the garment industry, including Levi Strauss, Haggar, Deering Milliken, and others. The garment industry "adversaries," as the court referred to them, raised many issues, ranging from patent invalidity through public use bar, to fraud on the patent office, to patent misuse, to Sherman Act antitrust violations.

During the litigation, Koratron argued that certain public use activity did not operate as a bar under 35 U.S.C. § 102(b) because the patent application was "filed" within one year of the public use activity. True, an application had been filed; however, the Patent Office determined that drawings would be required and that the application could not be given a filing date until a drawing was filed with it. Koratron complied and filed drawings, but not until more than one year after the public use activity.

During litigation, Koratron argued that the Patent Office erroneously ruled that a drawing was required. The court rejected the argument out of hand, stating that whether an application required a drawing was a question solely within the discretion of the Patent Office.

On reflection, Koratron's argument is not substantively farfetched. The claimed subject matter deals primarily with chemical treatment of the fabric, whereas the drawings requested by the Patent Office simply show trousers hanging in an oven and various cross sectional views of the trousers' stitching. However, Koratron's argument is procedurally defective. Koratron made no attempt to correct the filing date problem when the application was pending.

Today it is unlikely that Koratron's dilemma will occur. The *Manual of Patent Examining Procedure* (M.P.E.P.) instructs examiners to carefully distinguish between applications filed without all figures of drawings and applications in which figures are subsequently required.[8] Applications filed without all figures of drawings are treated as *prima facie* incomplete and are not given a filing date. Usually this is detected by the Application Branch before the application ever gets assigned to an examiner in an Art Unit. On

---

[6] 375 F. Supp. 1 (N.D. Cal. 1974).

[7] 28 U.S.C. § 1407.

[8] U.S. Dep't of Commerce, Manual of Pat. Examining Proc. § 608.02 (Mar. 1994).

the other hand, acceptance by the Application Branch of an application without a drawing does not preclude the examiner from requiring one. In such a case, however, the filing date is not lost. On this point, the *Manual of Patent Examining Procedure* provides:

> The acceptance of an application without a drawing does not preclude the examiner from requiring an illustration in the form of a drawing under 37 CFR 1.81(c) or 37 CFR 1.83(c). In requiring such a drawing, the examiner should clearly indicate that the requirement is made under 37 CFR 1.81(c) or 37 CFR 1.83(c) and be careful not to state that he or she is doing so "because it is necessary for the understanding of the invention," as that might give rise to an erroneous impression as to the completeness of the application as filed.[9]

There may be times, however, when the examiner believes that the application should not have been given a filing date, because the application does not contain drawings. The procedure followed in this instance is spelled out in the *Manual of Patent Examining Procedure* as follows:

> If an examiner feels that a filing date should not have been granted in an application because it does not contain drawings, the matter should be brought to the attention of the supervisory primary examiner (SPE) for review. If the SPE decides that drawings are required to understand the subject matter of the invention, the SPE should return the application to the Application Branch with a typed, signed and dated memorandum requesting cancellation of the filing date and identifying the subject matter required to be illustrated.[10]

The Patent Office thus considers the first sentence of 35 U.S.C. § 113 to address the situation when the application is incomplete and cannot be given a filing date due to lack of drawings. The Patent Office considers the second sentence of 35 U.S.C. § 113 to address the situation when a drawing is not necessary for the understanding of the invention, but nevertheless desired by the examiner. In this latter case, the application is given a filing date.

§ 6.4 —Content of Drawings

As to what must be shown in the drawings, the Code of Federal Regulations offer some fundamental guidance:

§ 1.83 Content of Drawing

(a) The drawing must show every feature of the invention specified in the claims. However, conventional features disclosed in the description and

---

[9] *Id.*

[10] *Id.*

claims, where their detailed illustration is not essential for a proper understanding of the invention, should be illustrated in the drawing in the form of a graphical drawing symbol or a labeled representation (e.g. a labeled rectangular box).

(b)   When the invention consists of an improvement on an old machine the drawing must when possible exhibit, in one or more views, the improved portion itself, disconnected from the old structure, and also in another view, so much only of the old structure as will suffice to show the connection of the invention therewith.

(c)   Where the drawings do not comply with the requirements of paragraph (a) and (b) of this section, the examiner shall require such additional illustration within a time period of not less than two months from the date of the sending of notice thereof. Such corrections are subject to the requirements of § 1.81(d).[11]

The regulations make it clear that you are not required to show conventional features in great detail. "[C]onventional features disclosed in the description and claims, where their detailed illustration is not essential for a proper understanding of the invention, should be illustrated in the drawings in the form of a graphical drawing symbol or a labeled representation (e.g. a labeled rectangular box)."[12] On the other hand, the Patent Office will sometimes require structural details that are of sufficient importance to be described in the specification.[13] The reason for this is expressed in the 1911 Commissioner's Decision, *Ex parte Good:*

> This detail (a flange) is not found in the claims, and the only question is, therefore, whether the added illustration is necessary to make the described structure fairly clear and intelligible from the drawings.
>
> *   *   *
>
> The question is not whether one skilled in the art can decipher the invention, but whether the drawing is so clearly and artistically executed as to facilitate a ready understanding of the invention both at the time of examination and in searches afterward in which reference to the patent must be made.[14]

§ 6.5   Practical Considerations Prior to Litigation

Even if drawings are not required, there are still many good reasons to include them. Drawings help explain the invention and make the patent come alive. When drafting a patent application, it is easy to lose sight of the many

---

[11] 37 C.F.R. § 1.83.

[12] *Id.* § 1.83(a).

[13] U.S. Dep't of Commerce, Manual of Pat. Examining Proc. § 608.02(d) (Mar. 1994).

[14] *Ex parte* Good, 1911 C.D. 43, 164 O.G. 739 (1911).

purposes the patent may serve. Certainly it is possible that the patent will be involved in litigation. If so, it is a pretty safe bet that at least one of the patent drawings will be blown up to poster size for presentation to the judge or jury. Often the patent owner will call the inventor to the witness stand to explain the invention. For the patent owner, this testimony is great opportunity to sell the importance of the invention and the merits of the patentee's case to the judge or jury. Do not waste this opportunity by having poor drawings. Rather, use the drawings, presented clearly and arranged logically, so they tell the story.

§ 6.6   —Selecting Drawings

How do you structure the patent drawings so they tell a story? Begin by picturing yourself asking the inventor to show what he or she had been working on when the invention was conceived. Perhaps there are drawings that help to show this. Next, imagine asking the inventor to explain what problem he or she was trying to solve. There may well be drawings that show this. Finally, imagine asking the inventor how the problem was solved, what makes the invention work. Certainly you will want drawings of this.

Collect all of the drawings possible. It may be that you will choose not to use all of them, but the exercise of collecting them is valuable in two respects. First, collecting these drawings helps bring the invention into focus and helps put the invention in proper context with the prior art. Second, building this collection of drawings may prove immensely valuable if the application is ever involved in an interference.

§ 6.7   —Preserving Drawings for Interference Evidence

The rules of practice in interference proceedings require each party, in its preliminary statement, to state the date that drawings of the invention were first made, or first introduced into the United States (for inventions made abroad).[15] Copies of these first drawings are required to be submitted with the preliminary statement in a sealed envelope.[16]

In an interference, when the first party to conceive the invention is normally awarded the patent, submitting dated drawings can be critical. Without the drawings, the invention is treated as if conceived when the application was filed. 37 C.F.R. § 1.629(d) states this:

---

[15] 37 C.F.R. §§ 1.622–25.

[16] *Id.* §§ 1.623–26.

If a party files a preliminary statement which contains an allegation of a date of first drawing or first written description and the party does not file a copy of the first drawing or written description with the preliminary statement as required by § 1.623(c), § 1.624(c), or § 1.625(c), the party will be restricted to the earlier of the party's filing date or effective filing date as to the allegation unless the party complies with § 1.628(b).[17]

Thus every effort should be made to locate all drawings made by or under supervision of the inventor, as they may become critical interference proceeding evidence.

In some cases the inventor may have discarded the first sketches or drawings; or the inventor may have failed to date the drawings when made. This is not a desirable position. If an interference does arise, you will only be able to rely on corroborated, dated drawings and other physical evidence. Therefore, get in the habit of reminding inventors to sign and date their drawings and have them witnessed, to support later corroboration.

§ 6.8   —Organizing Drawings

Once you have gathered all existing drawings, mentally sketch out any additional drawings that may be needed, and start organizing the drawings in groups. Put drawings that show what the inventor had been working on when the invention was made in one group. These may represent the prior art, or the environment, or a field of use for the invention. When making this prior art and environment group, be alert to early drawings that may contain a glimmer of the invention in its formative stages. Such drawings should not be placed in the prior art group.

Put drawings that show the problem the inventor was trying to solve in another group. These may help show why the invention is important. Drawings that show why the invention is important are extremely valuable, because they can later become the icon for the invention itself. Few laypersons, judges and juries included, are able to understand the technical intricacies of how an invention works; yet most are able to understand that the invention solves a certain problem. Quite naturally, laypersons equate invention with a solution to that certain problem. The patentee wants the invention viewed in this way, because it allows the patent to cover equivalents more easily.

Litigation issues aside, good drawings also make the patent easier to comprehend at a glance. Not everyone needs to study a patent in detail. Searching for prior art or conducting research of a particular technology, a researcher needs to be able to quickly spot the feature the researcher is looking for.

---

[17] *Id.* § 1.629(d).

Similarly, a manager, managing a large patent portfolio, needs to be able to quickly distinguish the subject matter of one patent from another. Titles, abstracts, inventor names, and patent numbers do not convey the essence of the patent subject matter as well as drawings.

The Patent Office has long required applicants to provide drawings for quick comprehension. In *Ex Parte Sturtevant,* decided by the Patent Commissioner in 1904, this nugget appears:

> It is a great desideratum of Patent Office drawings that they should tell their story to the eye without making it necessary to go into the specification for explanation, which should be apparent upon inspection.

> * * *

> The suggestion by the applicants that the Examiner's objection should not be insisted upon, simply because one skilled in the art could make the invention from the present disclosure, does not overcome this necessity for such representation of the invention in the drawings as will make it intelligible for the purposes of search.[18]

§ 6.9 —Drawing for *Patent Office Gazette*

Finally, there is the *Official Gazette,* published every Tuesday, reporting each patent issued that day.[19] *The Official Gazette* includes, when applicable, one view taken from the patent drawings. Regarding this view, the regulations state that "[o]ne of the views should be suitable for publication in the Official Gazette as the illustration of the invention."[20]

With software inventions it is not always easy to pick one drawing that suitably represents the whole invention. Many software inventions are illustrated through flowcharts and flowcharts do not always show the big picture. At a certain level of detail, flowcharts tend to flow on and on, from page to page, with no single page representing the whole invention. To rectify this, consider adding an additional drawing that has been carefully crafted to be suitable for publication in the *Official Gazette.* This drawing may be a diagrammatic representation of a claim of broad or intermediate scope, for example. This drawing may otherwise be an object diagram or data flow diagram, showing the software components from which the invention is made.

---

[18] *Ex parte* Sturtevant, 108 O.G. 563 (1904).

[19] U.S. Dep't of Commerce, Manual of Pat. Examining Proc. § 1703 (Mar. 1994).

[20] 37 C.F.R. § 1.84(j).

§ 6.10 —Use of Drawings to Outline Specification

Not only do drawings help the reader, they also help in drafting the application. Drawings can establish the structure, sequence, and organization of how to present information in the patent specification. Drawings can serve as an outline for drafting the written specification and for constructing the claims.

Usually an invention is best explained using a top-down, general-to-specific approach. Explain the logical and physical structure first. Follow that with a description of how that structure operates. Properly selected drawings help orchestrate this explanation. In other words, start with drawings that show the big picture. Put the invention in context by showing where the invention fits in the environment. Next, show the invention broken down into major subcomponents. Some of these subcomponents may be old. For instance, some subcomponents may exist simply to connect the invention to the environment. Other subcomponents may be new and may form part of the claimed invention.

Finally, break the subcomponents that form part of the claimed invention into even smaller subcomponents, using additional views. You now have a series of drawings to use, as an outline, to draft the specification in a well-structured, top-down manner.

§ 6.11 —Use of Drawings to Develop Claims

Drawings can also help you extract the key elements of an invention from the complexity of implementation details. Use drawings to sketch out your thoughts for drafting claims. At first this may seem obvious, given the requirement of 37 C.F.R. § 1.83(a) that the drawings must show every feature of the invention specified in the claims. There is more here than meets the eye.

Claim drafting involves finding the key abstract concepts that comprise the essence of the invention. Complexity often complicates the task. One successful technique is to decompose the complex invention into more manageable parts. Break the invention into its essential components; examine those components; study how the components interact; identify which components or interactions are new and which are not. Then make drawings to capture your mental analysis to later draft claims at leisure. For further details regarding the claim drafting process, see **Chapter 7.**

Interestingly, software developers often work this way. Today, many software developers use computer-aided software engineering tools (CASE tools) to build software. Starting by drawing graphical symbols to represent the key abstractions of the software problem, programmers continue adding details of their design to these drawings until the drawings are so complete that the CASE tool can take over and write all the computer program source code needed. Patent attorneys do not yet have computer-aided claim drafting tools comparable to software developers' CASE tools, but that day is not far off. In the meantime, get ready for the patent application drafting tools of the future by making drawings to represent your main claims.

§ 6.12   Flowcharts

Most programmers today do not use them, yet flowcharts are currently the most used diagram in software patents. Why is this? To some extent the answer is simple inertia. Practically everyone who drafts his or her first software patent application will look at a sample patent first. Likely the sample patent contains a flowchart. Believing a flowchart to be necessary, one is included. Thus the flowchart tends to perpetuate itself.

That is not to say that flowcharts are not important. When software is viewed as a computer-implemented process, it is quite natural to resort to flowcharts. In fact, 37 C.F.R. § 1.81(b) specifically recognizes the propriety of flowcharts or "flowsheets." "Drawings may include illustrations that facilitate an understanding of the invention (for example, flowsheets in cases of processes, and diagrammatic views)."[21] Also, historically, computer programs were structured *procedurally,* as a set of step-by-step instructions for the computer to perform. Procedurally, structured programs and flowcharts are a natural fit.

Flowcharts have the imprimatur of the Code of Federal Regulations; why use anything else? One reason is that flowcharts do not always give a good overview of the big picture, particularly if many separate sheets are involved. If application preparation cost is a concern, lengthy flowcharts, paid for on a per-sheet basis, can get expensive.

Also, some nonprocedural programs simply do not fit the flowchart mold. Object-oriented or event-driven programs, for example, do not fit easily into flowcharts. To illustrate, whereas you can easily construct a flowchart to explain how to mail a letter; consider how difficult it is to construct a flowchart to explain how the post office functions. For the post office, an organizational chart, or some other object-oriented notation seems more appropriate.

The bottom line is not to abandon flowcharts. Flowcharts are excellent for many software inventions. However, do not, by habit, turn to flowcharts in every case. Consider the other possibilities. Several possibilities are described in this chapter. Also, ask the inventor for suggestions on what notation best suits the invention. You may learn of a new notation that you can use in other applications.

---

[21] *Id.* § 1.81(b).

§ 6.13 —ISO Flowchart Standards

There are international standards on flowchart symbols, known as ISO 5807. The standards describe several different kinds of flowcharts, including program flowcharts, data flowcharts, system flowcharts, program network charts, and system resource charts. The standards also describe a number of graphical symbols used to make these charts. Program flowcharts are most frequently used in patents to describe processes, including software processes. However, you may want to be familiar with the other kinds of flowcharts, as well.

All four kinds of ISO 5807 standard charts use basically two classes of symbols: process symbols and data symbols. The process symbols graphically represent process steps or method steps. The most commonly used process symbols are the rectangle, which represents any basic process, and the diamond, which represents a decision. The most commonly used data symbols are the slanted rectangle or parallelogram, which represents any basic data, and the cylinder or drum, which represents direct access storage, such as a file stored on a hard disk. **Figure 6–1** shows all of the ISO 5807 process symbols. **Figure 6–2** shows all of the ISO 5807 data symbols.

§ 6.14 —Program Flowcharts

Program flowcharts use process symbols, such as the familiar rectangular box and the diamond, to show processes or method steps. Lines interconnecting the process symbols show the flow of control. The emphasis is on showing the flow of control, that is, how one process leads to the next, or how one process passes control to the next. Therefore, use the program flowchart to explain or emphasize the sequence of procedures performed. An example of a program flowchart is shown in **Figure 6–3.**

§ 6.15 —Data Flowcharts

Data flowcharts use data symbols, such as the parallelogram, to represent data and data storage media, and use process symbols, such as the rectangular box and the diamond, to show processes performed on the data. Lines interconnecting these symbols show the flow of data between processes and data storage media. The emphasis is on the data and how it flows from process to process. Therefore, use the data flowchart to explain or emphasize how data is changed through a series of manipulating steps. Data may be anything from electrical signals received from a transmitter, to numerical data representing physical parameters (for example, from robot arm movements), to statistical

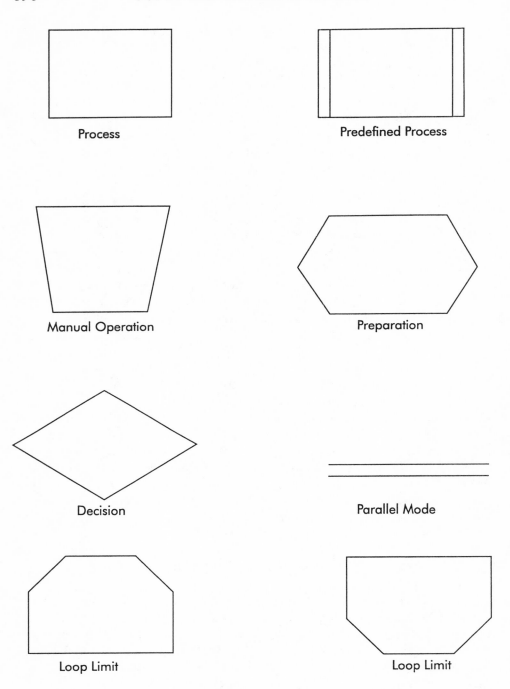

Figure 6–1.   Process symbols.

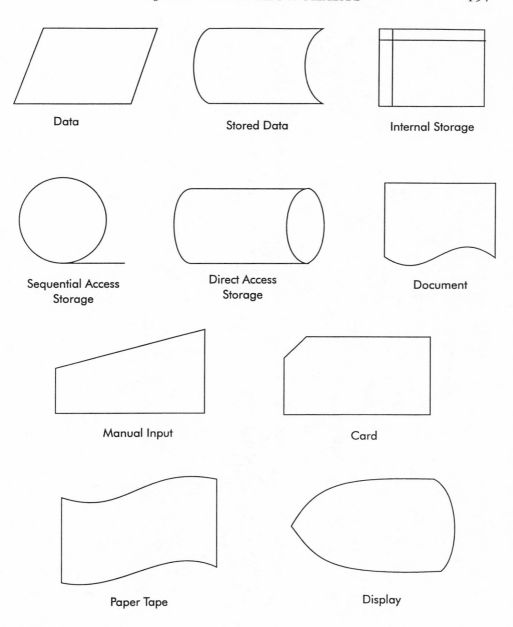

Figure 6–2. Data symbols.

Example of Program Flowchart

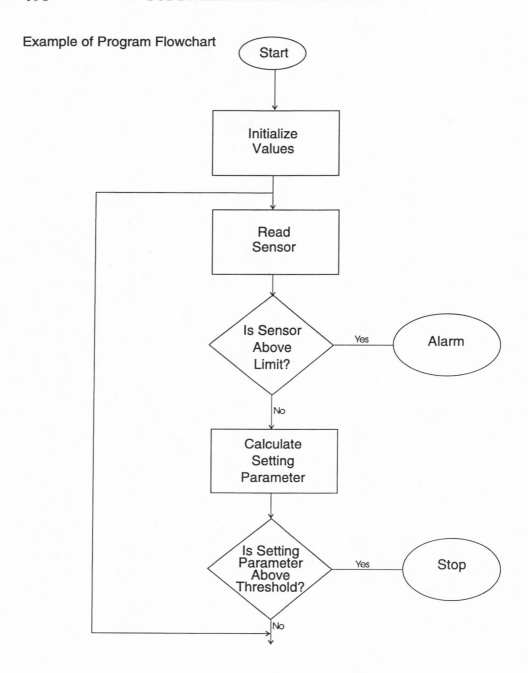

Figure 6–3.   Example of program flowchart.

data (for example, from a model of a gene pool) to computer data. Likewise, the processes may be anything from physical, chemical, and electrical processes, to computational processes. Of course, most software patents involve computational processes. Yet, recognize that these processes nevertheless usually involve data representing physical parameters. Therefore, even in software patents, data flowcharts focus on the problem solved by the software invention and not on how the computational processes are performed within the computer. An example of a data flowchart is given in **Figure 6–4.**

§ 6.16   —System Flowcharts

System flowcharts use data symbols to show the existence of data and process symbols to indicate the operations to be executed on data. Lines interconnecting the symbols show data flow between processes as well as control flow between processes. The emphasis is on the functional components of a system. Thus system flowcharts may frequently show databases or keyboard entry feeding processors with data, and further show processors feeding other processors with data. An example of a system flowchart is given in **Figure 6–5.**

§ 6.17   —Program Network Charts

Program network charts use data symbols and process symbols to show the existence of data and to show what operations are performed on that data. Lines show the relationship between processes and data, including the activation of processes and the flow of data to and from processes. The emphasis is on the relationships or interactions between data and processing elements. The program network chart is similar to the system flowchart, a principal difference being that the program network chart shows each data and processing element only once, whereas the system flowchart shows data devices and processors possibly more than once, as needed to describe the process flow. An example of a program network chart is given in **Figure 6–6.**

§ 6.18   —System Resources Charts

System resources charts use data symbols to show input, output, and storage devices and use process symbols to show processors, such as central processing units. Lines interconnecting these symbols represent data transfer between data devices and processors. Lines also show control transfer between processors. The emphasis is on how the system resources (data units and process units) are interrelated. Thus system flowcharts may

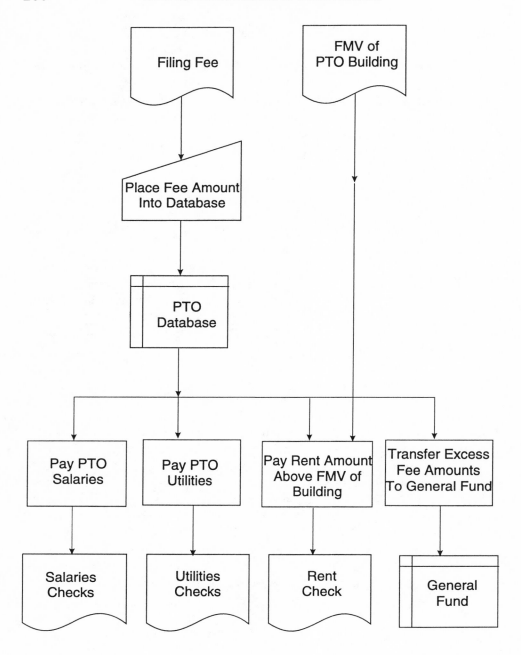

Figure 6–4.   Example of data flowchart.

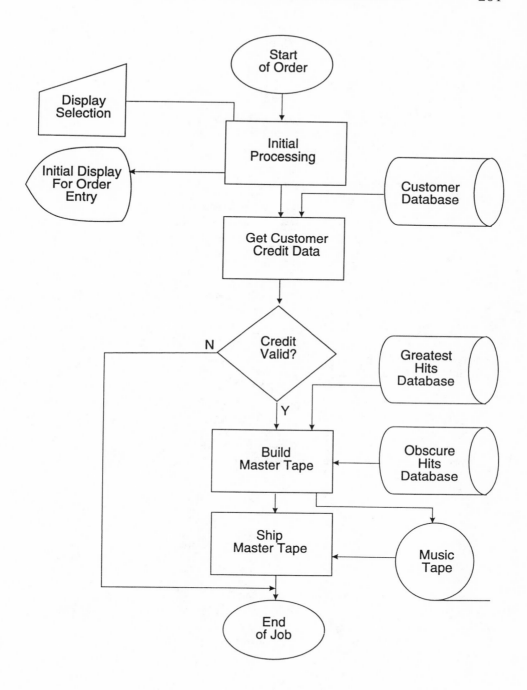

Figure 6–5. Example of system flowchart.

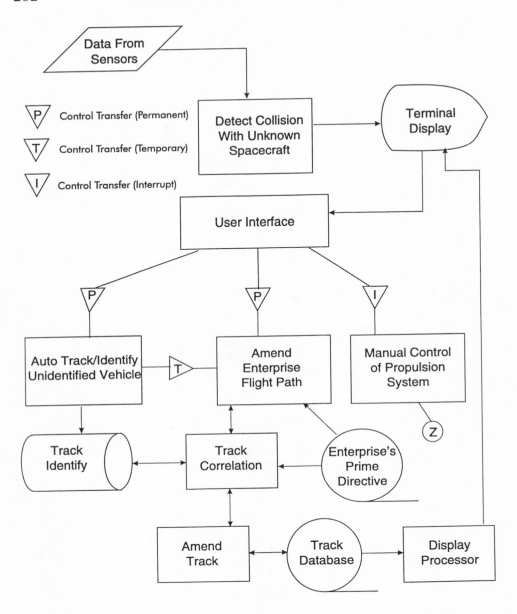

Figure 6–6.   Example of network chart.

frequently show databases connected to processing functions. An example of a system resources chart is given in **Figure 6–7.**

§ 6.19   Pseudocode

Pseudocode is one notation to consider if the process you are describing is long and involved. Pseudocode is simply source code, where the syntax rules are relaxed and where unimportant details are left out. Compared to flow-charts, pseudocode is quite compact. Because there are no boxes and dia-monds to draw, you can get the content of many pages of flowcharts onto a single page of pseudocode. Also, where appropriate, you can prepare pseudocode in the word processor and include it as an appendix to the appli-cation. That can save considerable patent drawing cost.

To demonstrate, U.S. Patent 5,016,009[22] contains a flowchart (Figure 5A). **Figure 6–8** shows the original flowchart as contained in the patent and how that flowchart might appear as pseudocode.

All these advantages are not without a price. Pseudocode is boring to look at and does work well at showing multiple layers of routines nested within other routines. Note how in **Figure 6–8** the nested routines, demarked by indentation and the terms BEGIN and END, are not easy to spot without drawing brackets or using a ruler. You are therefore better off using pseudocode only when concentrating on implementation details of a pre-ferred embodiment of the invention, or when you need to get an application on file quickly to meet a statutory deadline.

§ 6.20   —Pseudocode in the Application

If using pseudocode, determine where should it go—in the specification or as a drawing. You have a choice. The Code of Federal Regulations states that com-puter program listings of 10 printout pages or less may be submitted in the patent application either as part of the specification or as drawings.[23] There seems to be little reason not to treat pseudocode as a form of computer pro-gram listing. The regulation defines a computer program listing as "a print-out that lists in appropriate sequence the instructions, routines, and other contents of a program for a computer," a definition broad enough to cover pseudocode.[24]

---

[22] Whiting, "Data Compression Apparatus & Method," U.S. Pat. No. 5,016,009 (May 14, 1991). This is the patent-in-suit in Stac Elec. v. Microsoft Corp., No. 93-00413 (C.D. Cal. Jan. 23, 1994).

[23] 37 C.F.R § 1.96; *see also* U.S. Dep't of Commerce, Manual of Pat. Examining Proc. § 608.05 (Mar. 1994).

[24] 37 C.F.R § 1.96; *see also* U.S. Dep't of Commerce, Manual of Pat. Examining Proc. § 608.05 (Mar. 1994).

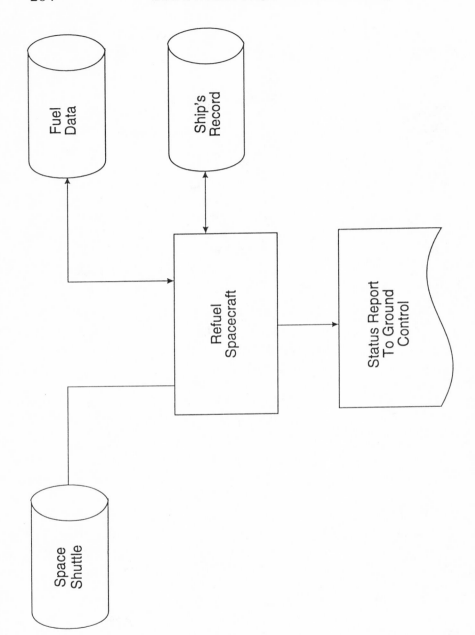

Figure 6-7. Example of system resources chart.

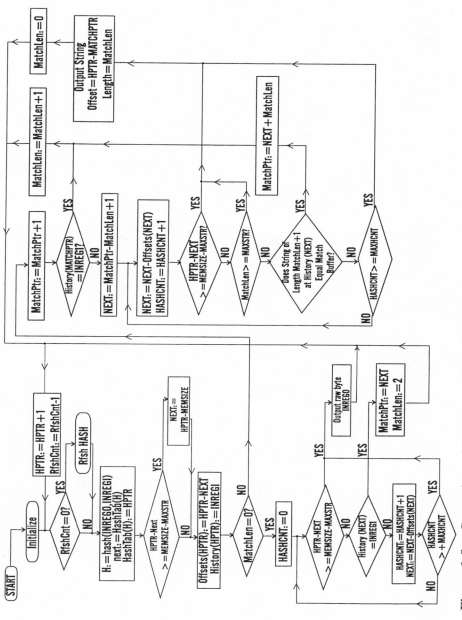

Figure 6–8. Comparison of flowchart and pseudocode listing.

```
        CALL  Initialize ( )

BEGIN:
        IF (flag = 0) THEN
                flag = 1
        ELSE
                /*  Bump Counters */
                HPTR = HPTR + 1
                RfshCnt = RfshCnt - 1
        END IF

        IF (RfshCnt = 0) THEN
                Call RefreshHash ( )
        END IF

        H = hash (INREG0, INREG1)
        Next = HashTab (H)
        HashTab(H) = HPTR

        IF ( (HPTR-Next) >= (MEMSIZE-MAXSTR) )  THEN
                Next = HPTR - MEMSIZE
        END IF
        Offsets(HPTR) = HPTR - Next
        History (HPTR) = INREG1

        IF (MatchLen = 0) THEN
                HASHCNT = 0
                REPEAT
                        IF ( (HPTR-Next) >= (MEMSIZE - MAXSTR))    THEN
                                CALL OutputRawByte (INREG0)
                                GOTO TOP
                        ELSE IF ((History(Next) = INREG1))  THEN
                                MatchPtr = Next
                                MatchLen = 2
                                GOTO TOP
                        ELSE
                                HashCnt = HashCnt + 1
                                Next = Next - Offsets (Next)
                        END IF
                UNTIL  (HashCnt >= MaxHCnt)

                CALL OutputRawByte (INREG0)
                GOTO TOP
```

Figure 6–8.   (*continued*)

```
        ELSE
                MatchPtr = MatchPtr + 1
                IF (History(MatchPtr) = INREG1)  THEN
                        MatchLen = MatchLen + 1
                        GOTO TOP
                ELSE
                        Next = MatchPtr - MatchLen + 1

                        REPEAT
                                Next = Next - Offsets (Next)
                                HashCnt = HashCnt + 1
                                IF ( ((HPTR-Next) >= (MEMSIZE - MAXSTR))     OR
                                        (MatchLen >= MAXSTR)              )
        THEN
                                        Call Output string
                                        Offset = HPTR - MatchPtr
                                        Length = MatchLen
                                        MatchLen = 0
                                        GOTO TOP
                                ELSE  IF  ( (String (1:MatchLen+1)) = MatchBuffer) THEN
                                        MatchPtr = Next + MatchLen
                                        MatchLen = MatchLen + 1
                                        GOTO TOP
                        UNTIL  (HashCnt >= MAXHCnt)

                        Call Output string
                        Offset = HPTR - MatchPtr
                        Length = MatchLen
                        MatchLen = 0
                        GOTO TOP


                END IF

        END IF
END
```

Figure 6–8.   (*continued*)

The regulations provide that if submitted as part of the specification, the listing should comply with 37 C.F.R. § 1.52, and should be placed at the end of the specification but before the claims. If submitted as a drawing, the listing should comply with 37 C.F.R. § 1.84, and should include at least one figure numeral per sheet.[25]

If the pseudocode is particularly short, in the nature of a table, consider placing the pseudocode in the body of the specification as a table. Tables, but not drawings or flowcharts, are permitted in the specification.[26] If placing pseudocode in the body of the specification as a table, keep in mind that the table should be limited to 5 inches (12.7 cm) width, so that it may appear as a single column in the printed patent.[27]

On the other hand, if your pseudocode is long, that is, more than ten pages, you have the option of submitting it on either paper or microfiche.[28] The Patent Office prefers microfiche, as it saves government printing costs.[29]

§ 6.21   Entity-Relationship Diagram

You may encounter a software invention that relies heavily on databases. In such cases, the entity-relationship diagram may be helpful. The entity-relationship diagram (or ERD as it is sometimes called) concentrates on the data model of a system, that is, it concentrates on what data entities exist and how they relate to one another. Data entities can be objects, which endure over time, or they can be events, which last only a moment.

To illustrate, if the software invention is a new kind of patent docketing system, a data entity object might be a patent database, containing information about each patent, or an assignee database, containing information about each patent owner. In this same example, a data entity event might be an "assigns" event whereby ownership of a certain patent by a certain assignee is noted.

Relationships between two data entity objects have a property called "cardinality." Cardinality denotes the number of entities that can exist on each side of a relationship. For example, there is a one-to-one relationship between a person and that person's physical location. Simply put, a person cannot be in two places at the same time. In the patent docketing system

---

25 37 C.F.R. § 1.96; *see also* U.S. Dep't of Commerce, Manual of Pat. Examining Proc. § 608.05 (Mar. 1994).

26 37 C.F.R. § 1.58.

27 *Id.; see also* U.S. Dep't of Commerce, Manual of Pat. Examining Proc. § 608.01 (Mar. 1994).

28 37 C.F.R. § 1.96; *see also* U.S. Dep't of Commerce, Manual of Pat. Examining Proc. § 608.05 (Mar. 1994).

29 U.S. Dep't of Commerce, Manual of Pat. Examining Proc. § 608.05 (Mar. 1994).

described above, there may be a one-to-many relationship between an assignee and the patents that assignee owns. Across a relationship there are basically three common kinds of cardinality: one-to-one, one-to-many, many-to-many.

In the entity-relationship diagram, data entities are represented by rectangular boxes containing the name of the data object or event. Relationships between data entities are represented by connecting lines, whose ends can be adorned to show cardinality. On each side of a relationship, if there is only one entity on a given side, the connecting line on that side is noted with a bar. If there are many entities on a given side, the connecting line on that side is noted with a crows-foot. To include the possibility that two entities may be related, but not in all instances, the connecting line is additionally marked with a small circle. **Figure 6–9** shows examples of each of these notations.

§ 6.22   Booch Notation

Grady Booch is one of the pioneers of object-oriented software design. He has developed a notation, called the Booch notation, to aid in designing object-oriented software. Not all object-oriented programmers use the Booch notation, although many use a notation similar to it. The Booch notation is quite expressive. Used properly, Booch devotees claim it can even help write object-oriented programs with fewer logical errors or oversights.

The Booch notation starts with the premise of an architectural model of a software system, or the need to design an architectural model of a software system. As in the physical world, there can be different ways of looking at the model, that is, different views of the model. No one view tells the whole story. For instance, it may be helpful to view a software architectural model in terms of its logical abstractions. In object-oriented terms, what classes exist and how are those classes related. It may also be helpful to view the model in terms of its physical components. What software and hardware components or modules must be assembled and in what manner. Further, it may be helpful to see how the assembled system functions, dynamically as opposed to how it is constructed statically.

The Booch notation provides diagram notation to express four different views of a software model. The four view concept is illustrated in **Figure 6–10.** Booch notation facilitates four views of a software model, using the following diagrams:

Class diagrams—indicating what classes (software abstractions) exist and how those classes are related

Object diagrams—indicating what mechanisms are used to regulate how objects collaborate

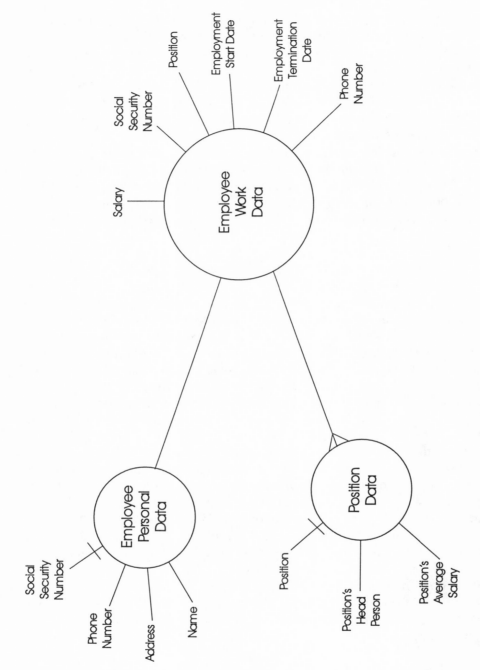

Figure 6–9. Example of entity relationship diagram.

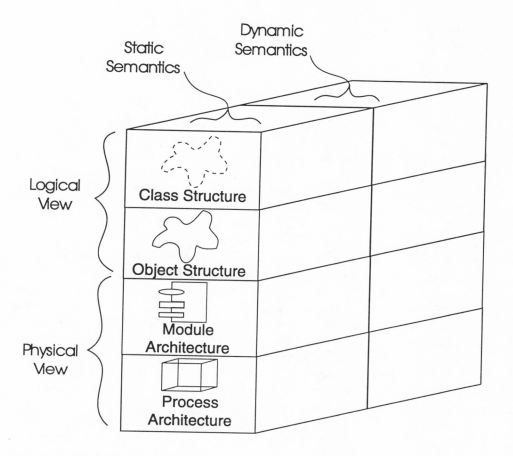

Figure 6–10.   Booch diagram notation.

Module diagrams—indicating where each class and object should be declared in the program

Process diagrams—indicating how multiple processes are scheduled and which processor is assigned which task.

In the above four views, class diagrams and object diagrams concentrate on the logical structure of the software model. Often the logical structure relates closely to the problem being solved by the software system. In contrast, module diagrams and process diagrams concentrate on the physical structure of the software model. Often the physical structure relates closely to code written to solve the problem in software.

Describing a software invention using Booch notation, it is not necessary to use all four types of diagrams in every application. Just as a golfer carries more clubs in the golf bag than may be needed in a given round, it is helpful to carry these four Booch diagrams in mind, to call upon as needed. The following describes the basics of the four Booch diagram notation. If you find the notation helpful, consult Booch's book for the details.[30]

§ 6.23   —Class Diagrams

The class diagram is used to show what classes exist in the software model and how these classes are related. The class diagram provides a logical view of the model. That is, it shows the key abstractions and mechanisms at work in the problem space. The logical view is distinguished from a physical view, which concentrates on the concrete software and hardware components that comprise the implementation space.

A class is an object-oriented programming concept that may be foreign to procedural programmers. If the whole notion of classes seems foreign, you are not alone. Many very fine programmers today still do not think this way, and consequently do not program this way. It takes time to become class conscious, particularly if you are used to considering software a series of procedural steps. Do not conclude that if the programmer did not use object-oriented programming, there is no need to worry about classes. You may not need classes to describe the preferred embodiment. But why be limited? If you have the ability to explain an invention in object-oriented terms, why not do so? It may someday help broaden the interpretation of the claims. Also, because identifying classes forces identification of the key abstractions, drawing class diagrams may help ferret out important elements of the patent claims.

A class is a group of things with common powers and attributes. In the Booch notation, a class is represented by a dotted-line cloud. Booch explains that the cloud is intended to suggest the boundaries of an abstraction or a concept, which may not have concrete boundaries.[31] For our purposes, there is no requirement that class diagrams comprise dotted-line clouds. Any shape will work, including ovals or rectangles, if you are not comfortable with clouds.

Viewing the software model as classes, you often find that classes interact with each other in a variety of ways. The Booch notation identifies four different relationships through which classes can interact with each other. Booch calls these four relationships:

1. "association"
2. "inheritance"
3. "has"
4. "using."

---

[30] Grady Booch, Object-Oriented Analysis and Design with Applications (2d ed. 1994).

[31] Grady Booch, Object-Oriented Analysis and Design with Applications 177 (2d ed. 1994).

An *association* between classes simply implies that there is a general relationship between the two, which Booch calls a semantic connection. The association relationship is thus the most general. It may be used if unsure or uncommitted as to the specific nature of the relationship between classes.

An *inheritance* relationship between classes is a more specific association relationship. It denotes a relationship from general to specific. For example, we can describe an inheritance relationship between the class "rowboat" and the class "watercraft." A rowboat *is a* form of watercraft. Thus, sometimes the inheritance relationship is referred to as the "is a" relationship.

The *has* relationship between classes is another, more specific association relationship, sometimes called an "aggregation" relationship. It denotes a relationship between the whole and its parts. For example, we can describe a has relationship between the class "Congress" and the class "Senate" or the class "House of Representatives."

Finally, the *using* relationship between classes is yet another more specific association relationship. The using relationship denotes a client-server relationship, in which the client is using services provided by the server. For example, the student-teacher relationship can be described as a using relationship, in the sense that the class "student" is *using* the teaching services of the class "teacher." Using relationships are also found in more abstract situations. For example, Booch gives an example of a hydroponic gardening system in which there is a using relationship between the class "temperature" and the class "actuator."[32] **Figure 6–11** gives an example of a Booch class diagram.

§ 6.24   —Object Diagrams

Like class diagrams, object diagrams give a logical (as opposed to physical) view of the software model. Whereas class diagrams concentrate on the key abstractions, object diagrams concentrate on the objects based on those abstractions. Object diagrams show prototypes or examples of a system based on the software model. Object diagrams are tied closely to class diagrams, because objects are treated as tangible embodiments of or instances of abstract states. For example, object Senator Edward Kennedy is an instance of the class Senator.

Like class diagrams, object diagrams also show relationships. Typically these are relationships by which objects communicate or interact. Objects interact with one another through messages. For example, object A may ask object B (via a message) to perform a service or to invoke an operation. This is the most common type of message. Object A's message may ask object B to invoke one of the operations defined by B's class. Thus object "Popeye's

---

[32] *Id.* at 181.

Remorse" of the class "rowboat" may ask object "boat" of the class "water-craft" to invoke the operation "float" on its behalf.

The Booch notation represents objects as solid line clouds, making them appear more tangible than the more abstract concept of classes. Messages are drawn as simple lines between linked objects. Customarily, the message lines are labeled to further describe the nature of the message. **Figure 6–12** shows an example of an object diagram with several message lines.

§ 6.25   Use of Object-oriented Notation

You now know more about object-oriented programming than many proce-dural language programmers. The question is why. Since one of the purposes of including drawings in a patent application is to explain how to make and use the invention, you may wonder why you would ever need to give a logi-cal view of the problem space. After all, it would seem that a physical view of the implementation should be more than adequate.

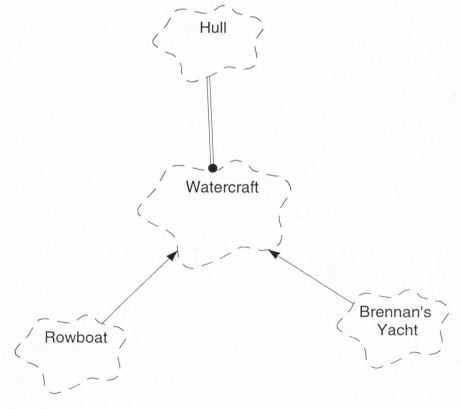

Figure 6–11.   Example of Booch class diagram.

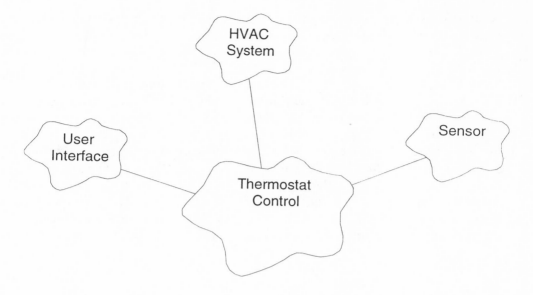

Figure 6–12.   Example of Booch object diagram.

The answer is quite simple. 35 U.S.C. § 112 has been interpreted to require the specification to teach in sufficient detail to avoid undue experimentation. The drawings help with this teaching. Thus by showing the logical structure of a software invention, you are teaching important principles of the invention, namely the architectural design of the system. In that way you are permitting a broader reading of the scope of the patent, while at the same time helping avoid undue experimentation.

In fact, today there are computer-aided software engineering tools (CASE tools) that can automatically generate program source code when fed sufficiently detailed design diagrams. Thus, in some cases, supplying sufficiently detailed design diagrams may be an excellent way of meeting the requirements of 35 U.S.C. § 112.

§ 6.26   Data Flow Diagram

The data flow diagram graphically models data and processes that operate on data. A form of data flow diagram, the ISO 5807 data flowchart, was described at § 6.13. Presented here are two other data flow diagrams, the Gane/Sarson data flow diagram[33] and the Yourdon/DeMarco data flow diagram.[34] Both are widely used to describe systems, including software systems.

---

[33] C. Gane & T. Sarson, Structured Systems Analysis: Tools and Techniques (1979).

[34] T. DeMarco, Structured Analysis and System Specification (1979).

Both also embody a system design philosophy of the respective authors. While the Gane/Sarson data flow diagram and the Yourdon/ DeMarco data flow diagram use similar symbols, the system design philosophies have a some substantive differences.

If you are devising data flow diagrams for a patent application from scratch, you probably do not need to worry about the philosophical differences between Gane/Sarson and Yourdon/DeMarco. In this case, simply use one notation or the other, to represent a system that is already designed. On the other hand, if you receive Gane/Sarson or Yourdon/DeMarco data flow diagrams from an inventor, it is helpful to know a little about the design philosophies of each. The design philosophy greatly affects the layout and content of the diagram. **Sections 6.27** and **6.28** describe the Gane/Sarson and the Yourdon/DeMarco data flow diagrams, the notation of each, and some of the underlying design philosophy of each.

§ 6.27   —Gane/Sarson and Yourdon/DeMarco Notations

Data flow diagrams, whether Gane/Sarson or Yourdon/DeMarco, use a collection of symbols to represent the data-related objects of a system. These objects include the "external entity," a generic entity representing any source of data flow into the system or any destination of data flow out of the system. These objects also include the "process," any process or function that transforms data in some way, and the "data store," a place where data is stored in the system. In addition, the data flow diagram uses an arrow symbol to represent data flow. Data flow is different from control flow. In a flowchart, connecting lines show the transfer of control from one process or method step to the next. In a data flow diagram, data flow arrows represent the path over which data are passed.

The respective Gane/Sarson and Yourdon/DeMarco object symbols are shown in **Figure 6–13.** Note that both Gane/Sarson and Yourdon/DeMarco use a square to represent the external entity. Both use an arrow to represent data flow. Gane/Sarson uses a rectangle with rounded corners to represent a process, whereas Yourdon/DeMarco uses a circle. The data store symbols are similar. Yourdon/DeMarco uses two parallel horizontal lines, whereas Gane/Sarson uses two parallel horizontal lines, closed at one end, to form an open-ended rectangle.

To compare the look of the Gane/Sarson data flow diagram with the look of the Yourdon/DeMarco data flow diagram, the same example system is illustrated using each in **Figures 6–14** and **6–15.**

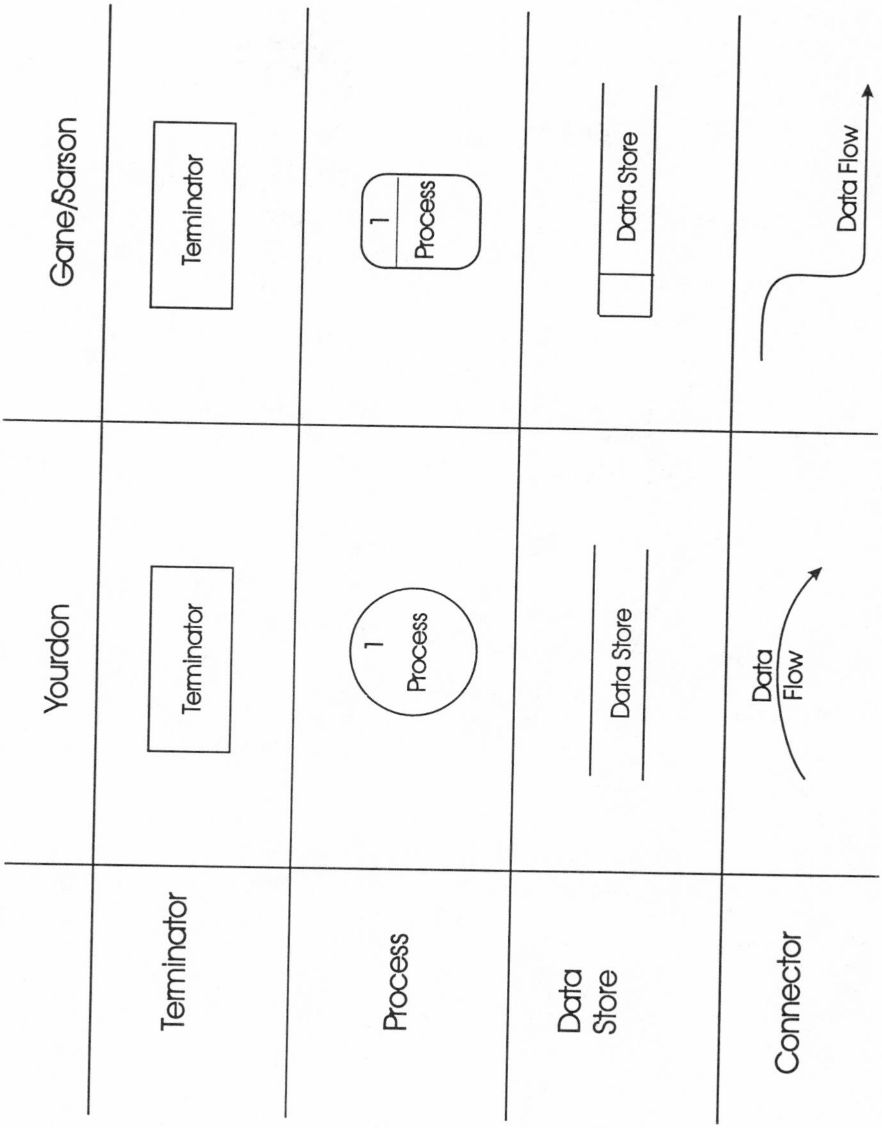

Figure 6–13.   Yourdon/DeMarco and Gane/Sarson diagrams.

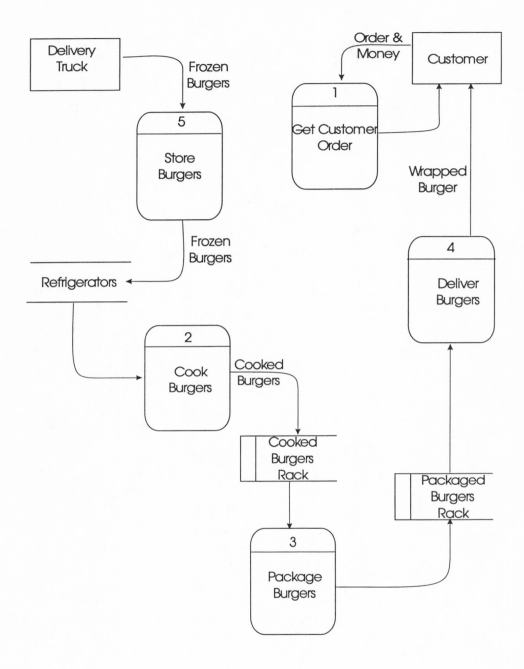

Figure 6–14.　Example of Gane/Sarson diagram.

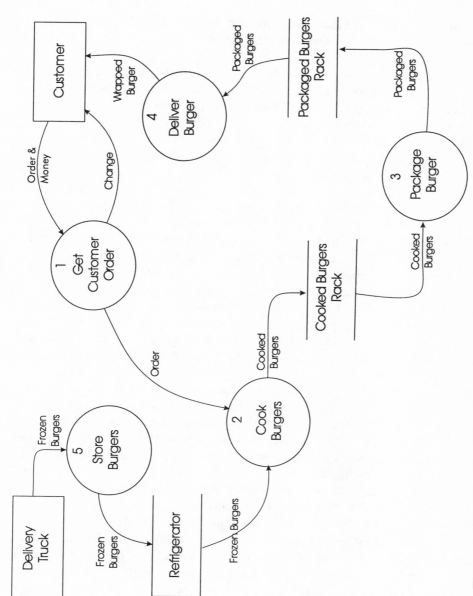

Figure 6–15.   Example of Yourdon/DeMarco diagram.

§ 6.28   —Gane/Sarson and Yourdon/DeMarco Design Philosophies

Although each has its own look, the substantive difference between Gane/Sarson and Yourdon/DeMarco lies in design philosophy. In designing a system, Gane/Sarson emphasizes focus on the whole, and recommends that the data flow diagram should include as many processes and data stores as you can fit on a page. Yourdon/DeMarco, on the other hand, emphasizes focus on the primitive processes, and recommends that the data flow diagram should include no more than about seven processes on it. When the number of processes rises much above seven, Yourdon/DeMarco recommends a layered approach in which elements on an overview diagram are decomposed into component parts through a series of exploded views.

The number seven is not arbitrary. Psychologists have determined that, most humans can only comprehend seven separate things at once, plus or minus two.[35] (Think about that next time you are cleaning off the top of your desk.) Given that a patent drawings are intended to help the reader understand the invention, there is good reason to adopt the Yourdon/DeMarco philosophy when laying out patent drawings. Although there is certainly nothing wrong with showing an entire data flow design on a single sheet of drawings, you may wish, in addition, to include a series of subdiagrams that concentrate on key parts of the system.

Another difference between Gane/Sarson and Yourdon/DeMarco is how the prior art is treated. Often, when a new software system is designed, it is to replace an existing system. The existing system may be computer implemented, or it may be manually implemented. Whether the existing system is used as the starting point for the new system, or whether the new system is developed from scratch, and not based on the prior system, can make a big difference. Yourdon/DeMarco recommends always using the prior system as the starting point. Gane/Sarson recommends always having the option of starting from scratch. Thus, Yourdon/DeMarco recommends a series of steps in which the existing system is analyzed and modeled; that model is then adapted to meet the needs of the new system. In the Yourdon/DeMarco approach, first model the existing system, then ask how this model needs to be changed to arrive at a proposed new model, which is then built into the new system. In contrast, Gane/Sarson recommends first building a logical model of the new system and then deciding whether it is more productive to modify the logical model of the existing system or whether it is more productive to start from scratch.

Because the Yourdon/DeMarco approach models the prior art system first, then identifies how that model must be changed, it is easy to spot the new

---

[35] G. Miller, *The Magical Number Seven, Plus or Minus Two: Some Limits on our Capacity for Processing Information,* 63 The Psychological Rev. 86 (1956).

and potentially patentable subject matter when the Yourdon/DeMarco approach has been used. If the inventor is a strict follower of the Yourdon/DeMarco approach, you may be able to get precise design documents showing how the new system differs from the prior art from the inventor. On the other hand, when the Gane/Sarson technique has been used, it may not be clear from the design documents how the new system differs from the prior art.

A final difference between Gane/Sarson and Yourdon/DeMarco is how the data flow diagram actually relates to the underlying data model. Each data flow arrow on the diagram is a path over which data travels; each data store on the diagram is a place where data are held when not traveling. However, the diagram gives no details about the data structures themselves. For example, a data flow diagram may indicate that "sales" data may flow from process A to data store B, but that diagram does not indicate that "sales" data comprises customer name, invoice number, item number, dollar amount, date, and so forth. Thus both Gane/Sarson and Yourdon/DeMarco recommend providing detailed data structure documentation, so it is clear what data structures are involved in the data flow diagram.

§ 6.29   Representing Data Structures

Gane/Sarson represent the data structure in "outline" form in which hierarchy is shown by indentation. Gane/Sarson might write a "Sales" data structure in this way:

Sales

    Customer-name

    Invoice-number

    Date

    Item

        Item-number

        Quantity

        Item-dollar-amount

    Total-sale-dollar-amount

Yourdon/DeMarco represents the data structure in "in-line," equation form. Yourdon/DeMarco might write the same "Sales" data structure:

Sales = Customer-name + Invoice-number + Date + [Item-number + Quantity + Item-dollar-amount] + Total-sale-dollar-amount

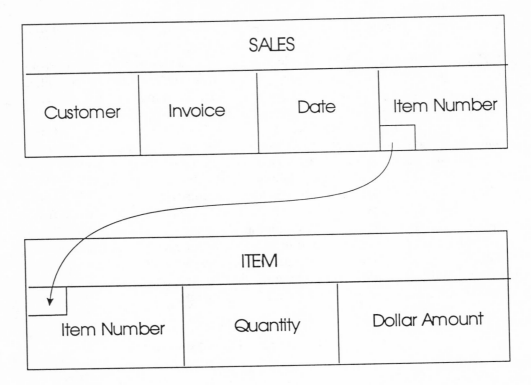

Figure 6–16.   Example data structure.

Clearly, either data structure notation is suitable for patent application purposes. If a particular data structure comprises a key part of the invention, you may wish to show the data structure as its own block diagram figure. See **Figure 6–16** as an example. This is especially true if the data structure happens to be an element of the claimed invention. The patent rules specifically require, "[T]he drawing must show every feature of the invention specified in the claims."[36]

§ 6.30   Checklist

_____ Prepare Drawings:
  _____ as future litigation exhibits
  _____ to organize before drafting the specification
  _____ to analyze what to claim

---

[36] 37 C.F.R. § 1.83.

____ Common Pitfalls:

    ____ Failure to retain dated, corroborated drawings. Without dated, corroborated (witnessed) drawings you may not be able to sustain your position in a patent interference

    ____ Failure to submit all necessary drawings in the application. The Patent Office will refuse to grant an application filing date if the written specification refers to a drawing (for example, in the Brief Description of the Drawings), but the drawing is inadvertently not submitted.

____ Types of Drawings Useful in Software Patents:

    ____ Flowcharts

    ____ Entity Relationship Diagrams

    ____ Pseudocode

    ____ Class/Object Diagrams

    ____ Data Structure Diagrams

____ Types of Flowcharts

    ____ Program Flow—illustrates flow of program control

    ____ Data Flow—illustrates flow of data from process to process

    ____ System Flow—illustrates functional components of system

    ____ Program Network—illustrates relationships between processes and data

    ____ System Resource—illustrates how system resources (process and data) are interrelated

    ____ Pseudocode Guidelines:

    ____ Insert specification as appendix or as drawings

    ____ If listing is short, pseudocode can be presented as a table, for reproduction in body of specification—must fit inside a single patent column when printed

CHAPTER 7

DRAFTING CLAIMS OF PROPER SCOPE

§ 7.1   Legal Requirements

Patent claims are the most focused upon part of the patent, because the patent claims define the metes and bounds of the patent grant. In both patent prosecution in the Patent Office and patent litigation in the courts, the claims are of paramount importance. Therefore, as a patent practitioner, give a great deal of thought to the drafting of claims.

Patent claims were not always this important. One hundred years ago the metes and bounds of the patent grant were defined by the specification. In those days, the patent claim might simply state omnibus claim language such as: "I claim the invention as substantially shown and described." Do not try to get an omnibus claim like the above allowed today. Patent examiners are trained to reject the omnibus claim as nonstatutory under 35 U.S.C. § 112.[1] The exception to this prohibition is design patents. Design patent claims are directed to the ornamental appearance of a design as shown in the patent drawings. Thus claims in design patents can and should state "The ornamental design, as shown and described."

§ 7.2   —Requirements of § 101

The statutory starting point for drafting any claim is 35 U.S.C § 101 that states what is patentable subject matter. Under § 101, there are four main categories of subject matter for which utility patents can be granted. They are a:

1. process
2. machine (apparatus)
3. article of manufacture
4. composition of matter.[2]

In addition to these categories, the patent laws contain separate statutory provisions for plants[3] and ornamental designs.[4]

These are the only statutory classes of patentable subject matter. No matter how novel, inventive, or clever a person's creation or discovery may be, if it does not fall within one of the statutory classes, the creation or discovery is not patentable. Examples include methods of doing business, scientific principles, laws of nature, naturally occurring articles, and printed matter.

---

[1] U.S. Dep't of Commerce, Manual of Pat. Examining Proc. § 706.03(h) (5th ed. Mar. 1994).

[2] 35 U.S.C. § 101.

[3] *Id.* § 161–64.

[4] *Id.* § 171–73.

Understanding what is statutory subject matter is particularly important for software patent attorneys because some (but not all) software involves nonstatutory subject matter. For example, in *Parker v. Flook* the Supreme Court held that "a claim for an improved method of calculation . . . is unpatentable subject matter under § 101."[5] The *Flook* decision created quite a stir, for many took the decision to mean that mathematical algorithms are unpatentable and that computer programs are therefore also unpatentable. (After all, what are computer programs, but mathematical algorithms?)

That analysis is imprecise. First, the term algorithm is largely synonymous with process or method, and a process or method is statutory subject matter. Second, the term mathematical is misleading, for it encompasses an open-ended universe of human analytical reasoning, presumably including Boolean logic: for example, "IF A AND B are TRUE, THEN Do C."

By saying mathematical algorithms are unpatentable, does this mean that all inventions involving Boolean decision-making logic are unpatentable? Certainly not, for such a restriction goes way too far. To illustrate, consider the following unquestionably patentable subject matter, expressed as a Boolean logic (mathematical?) algorithm: "IF the key fits the lock AND IF the doorknob is turned, THEN open the door." Clearly this is not the type of process the Supreme Court has declared non-statutory.

Do not be mistaken; some mathematical algorithms are nonstatutory. One cannot patent the formula for calculating how much energy can be released when matter is annihilated: $E = mc^2$.

However, rather than getting sidetracked over the question of which mathematical algorithms are statutory and which are not, a more helpful analysis is to treat mathematics simply as a descriptive language, and focus on which algorithms are simply an expression of the laws of nature. If the language of mathematics is used to describe a law of nature, then the subject matter is nonstatutory—not because mathematics is used in the description, but because it is a law of nature. However, if mathematics is used to describe an invention that falls into one of the statutory classes ("process, machine, [article of] manufacture, or composition of matter"), then the subject matter is patentable, notwithstanding the use of mathematics in the description.

Another example may be helpful. In *Gottschalk v. Benson* the Supreme Court held that a claimed process for converting a binary coded decimal number to a binary number is nonstatutory subject matter. In the words of the Court:

> It is conceded that one may not patent an idea. But in practical effect that would be the result if the formula for converting BCD numerals to pure binary numerals were patented in this case. The mathematical formula involved here has no substantial practical application except in connection with a digital

---

[5] 437 U.S. 584, 594–95 n.18 (1978).

computer, which means that if the judgment below is affirmed, the patent would wholly pre-empt the mathematical formula and in practical effect would be a patent on the algorithm itself.[6]

What Benson had "discovered" was an inherent property of numbers, a scientific principle or law of nature, not unlike the process of long division taught to children in grade school. This property of numbers has always existed. Benson simply discovered the property. Like any other scientific principle or law of nature, Benson has given us no ability to exert physical control over this property of numbers. We humans cannot, for example, cause Benson's discovery to cease to be true, as we can cause a table to cease to exist by removing its legs.

Benson sought by his claim to own *all* applications of this discovered property of numbers. That the patent laws do not allow. For an in-depth review of the statutory subject matter requirements under 35 U.S.C. § 101, see **Chapter 9.**

§ 7.3 —Nonart Rejections

Patent Examiners are trained to watch for a number of claiming errors, for which they issue nonart rejections under 35 U.S.C. § 112. Knowing these nonart rejections in advance will help you draft claims to avoid them.

The nonstatutory subject matter rejection has already been discussed in § 7.2. 35 U.S.C. § 101 treats everything as nonstatutory, except "process, machine, [article of] manufacture, or composition of matter."[7] From the examiner's perspective, it is often easier to identify a claim to nonstatutory subject matter by what it *is,* rather than by what it is *not.* Hence, the *Manual of Patent Examining Procedure* lists and briefly discusses the following four categories of nonstatutory subject matter:

1.   Printed matter
2.   Naturally occurring article
3.   Method of doing business
4.   Scientific principle.[8]

In addition, to these categories, the *Manual of Patent Examining Procedure* specifies that a claim should be rejected as nonstatutory if the claimed invention lacks utility.[9] This is a rejection under 35 U.S.C. § 101,

---

[6] 409 U.S. 63, 71–72 (1972).

[7] 35 U.S.C. § 101.

[8] U.S. Dep't of Commerce, Manual of Pat. Examining Proc. § 706.03(a) (Mar. 1994).

[9] *Id.* at Form Paragraph 7.04 and § 706.03(p).

because that section reads, "Whoever invents or discovers any new and *useful* process, machine, manufacture, or composition of matter . . . ." [emphasis added] The lack of utility rejection may be given if the invention, as disclosed, is inoperative. In this instance, the specification would presumably also be rejected under 35 U.S.C. § 112. Perpetual motion machines, for example, are rejected as lacking utility.[10]

§ 7.4 —Printed Matter Rejections

The printed matter rejection applies when the claim seeks to protect the mere arrangement of printed matter on a page.[11] Software patent examiners will sometimes use this rejection when the claim seeks to protect the arrangement of information displayed on a computer screen.

It is often possible to overcome the printed matter rejection by focusing on the apparatus or method responsible for generating the computer screen display alleged to be printed matter. Often you will find a combination of elements that is patentable subject matter. See *In re Miller* which held, "The fact that printed matter *by itself* is not patentable subject matter, because nonstatutory, is no reason for ignoring it when the claim is directed to a combination."[12] In some instances the printed matter may be responsible for producing physical results, as in an optical instrument for producing a diffraction grating or a semiconductor chip mask. If so, then the printed matter rejection can be overcome.[13]

§ 7.5 —Naturally Occurring Article Rejections

The naturally occurring article rejection applies when the claim seeks to protect a thing occurring in nature, which is substantially unaltered and hence not a "manufacture." A shrimp with the head and digestive tract removed is an example.[14]

It would seem unlikely that a software invention will ever be rejected as a naturally occurring article. The rejection is usually given when a naturally occurring article is treated in a particluar way, for example, soaking an orange in a borax solution to inhibit mold.[15] It is therefore conceivable that a

---

[10] U.S. Dep't of Commerce, Manual of Pat. Examining Proc. § 706.03(p) (5th ed. Mar. 1994).

[11] *In re* Miller, 164 U.S.P.Q. (BNA) 46 (C.C.P.A. 1969); *In re Jones,* 153 U.S.P.Q. (BNA) 77 (C.C.P.A. 1967); *Ex parte* Gwinn, 112 U.S.P.Q. (BNA) 439 (Bd. App. 1955).

[12] *In re* Miller, 418 F.2d 1392, 1396 (C.C.P.A. 1969) (emphasis in original).

[13] *See In re* Jones, 373 F.2d 1007 (C.C.P.A. 1967).

[14] *See* American Fruit Growers v. Brogdex, 283 U.S. 1 (1930).

[15] *Ex parte* Grayson, 51 U.S.P.Q. (BNA) 413 (Bd. App. 1941).

naturally occurring article may be treated using a software-controlled process. In such a case, if the claim is to the processed article, a naturally occurring article rejection may be given. To avoid such a rejection, focus the claim on the treatment process.

§ 7.6   —Method of Doing Business Rejections

The method of doing business has long been treated as nonstatutory subject matter.[16] The method of doing business rejection is an interesting one that has the potential to arise in software patent applications. In fact, the software patent may be a way to obtain patent protection for an otherwise nonstatutory method of doing business. The high water mark of this practice may be the Merrill Lynch Musmanno patent.

On August 24, 1982, Merrill Lynch obtained U.S. Patent No. 4,346,442 (the Musmanno patent)[17] on its cash management account (CMA) system. The CMA system combines three financial services commonly offered by financial institutions and brokerage houses, including a brokerage security account. So far, that system does not sound like patentable subject matter. The Musmanno patent further includes certain data processing methodology and apparatus to effect the CMA system. Merrill Lynch sued Paine, Webber[18] for infringing the Musmanno patent, and the Delaware District Court held that the claims recite statutory subject matter and not an unpatentable method of doing business. The following is an example of a Musmanno claim:

1. In combination in a system for processing and supervising a plurality of composite subscriber accounts each comprising

a margin brokerage account, a charge card and checks administered by a first institution, and participation in at least one short term investment, administered by a second institution,

said system including brokerage account data file means for storing current information characterizing each subscriber margin brokerage account of the second institution, manual entry means for entering short term investment orders in the second institution,

data receiving and verifying means for receiving and verifying charge card and check transactions from said first institution and short term investment orders from said manual entry means,

---

16 *See* Hotel Sec. Checking Co. v. Lorraine Co., 160 F. 467 (2d Cir. 1908); *In re* Wait, 24 U.S.P.Q. (BNA) 88 (C.C.P.A. 1934).

17 Musmanno, Securities Brokerage Cash Management Sys., U.S. Pat. No. 4,346,442 (Aug. 24, 1982), *assigned to* Merill Lynch, Pierce, Fenner & Smith, Inc.

18 Paine, Webber v. Merrill Lynch, 564 F. Supp. 1358 (D. Del. 1983).

means responsive to said brokerage account data file means and said data receiving and verifying means for generating an updated credit limit for each account,

short term investment updating means responsive to said brokerage account data file means and said data receiving and verifying means for selectively generating short term investment transactions as required to generate and invest proceeds for subscribers' accounts, wherein said system includes plural such short term investments,

said system further comprising means responsive to said short term updating means for allocating said short term investment transactions among said plural short term investments, communicating means to communicate said updated credit limit for each account to said first institution.[19]

§ 7.7   —Scientific Principle Rejections

The scientific principle rejection, the *Manual of Patent Examining Procedure* states, applies when a claim seeks to protect "[a] scientific principle, divorced from any tangible structure."[20] An example is Samuel Morse's claim 8 that covered:

. . . the use of the motive power of the electric or galvanic current, which I call electro-magnetism, however developed, for making or printing intelligible characters, letters, or signs, at any distances . . .[21]

The Supreme Court rejected that claim as trying to preempt all use of the scientific principle of electromagnetism.[22]

§ 7.8   —Omnibus and Single Means
Claim Rejections

Nonstatutory subject matter is not the only nonart rejection the patent examiner is trained to watch for and reject. There is the omnibus claim—"a device substantially as shown and described"—which examiners are trained to reject for failing to particularly point out and distinctly claim the invention as required in 35 U.S.C. § 112. The *Manual of Patent Examining Procedure* refers to the

---

[19] Musmanno, Securities Brokerage Cash Management Sys., U.S. Pat. No. 4,346,442 (Aug. 24, 1982), *assigned to* Merill Lynch, Pierce, Fenner & Smith, Inc.

[20] U.S. Dep't of Commerce, Manual of Pat. Examining Proc. § 706.03(a) (5th ed. Mar. 1994).

[21] O'Reilly v. Morse, 56 U.S. 62 (1853).

[22] *Id.* at 86.

omnibus claim as a nonstatutory claim, although this terminology should not be confused with nonstatutory subject matter (35 U.S.C. § 101).[23]

Related to the omnibus claim is the single means claim, which examiners are also trained to reject. The single means claim is one step removed from the omnibus claim. It recites the ultimate function of the invention in a single recitation. Example:

> A Fourier transform processor for generating Fourier transformed incremental output signals in response to incremental input signals, said Fourier transform processor comprising incremental means for incrementally generating the Fourier transformed incremental output signals in response to the incremental input signals.

This was the claim Gilbert P. Hyatt, prosecuting his application and appeal *pro se*, insisted he was entitled. The Federal Circuit Court of Appeals disagreed.[24]

The single means claim is an attempt to claim function or result, without being limited to any particular structure. This is impermissible, not because functional language is used, but because the claim has only functional recitation and is therefore too broad. Courts seem to have little difficulty finding some rationale for invalidating claims which are too broad by claiming only the desired result. See, for example, *O'Reilly* discussed at § **7.7,** which is a classic case of claiming too broadly.

§ 7.9   —Functional Language

Functional language, unsupported by structure, may get a claim rejected. This is not to say that functional language may never be used. 35 U.S.C. § 112 permits functional language to be used in a claim:

> An element in a claim for a combination may be expressed as a means or step for performing a specified function without the recital of structure, material, or acts in support thereof, and such claim shall be construed to cover the corresponding structure, material, or acts described in the specification and equivalents thereof.[25]

Thus, it is not functional language per se that is impermissible; it is using functional language to claim too broadly by claiming only the end result. Examiners are trained to watch for this. The *Manual of Patent Examining*

---

[23] U.S. Dep't of Commerce, Manual of Pat. Examining Proc. § 706.03(h) (5th ed. Mar. 1994).

[24] *In re* Hyatt, 708 F.2d 712 (Fed. Cir. 1983).

[25] 35 U.S.C. § 112.

Procedure instructs examiners to reject "[a] claim which contains functional language not supported by recitation in the claim of sufficient structure to warrant the presence of the functional language in the claim."[26] The example given of a claim of this character is the claim found in *In re Fuller.*[27] The claim reads: "A woolen cloth having a tendency to wear rough rather than smooth."

Many patent attorneys use functional language in "whereby" clauses. There is nothing wrong with using a whereby clause, provided you understand what it can and cannot do. Patent examiners are trained to treat the whereby clause as non-distinguishing recitation. The *Manual of Patent Examining Procedure* informs examiners of the holding in *In re Mason,* which held that the functional "whereby" statement does not define any structure and accordingly does not serve to distinguish.[28]

In litigation some courts also give the whereby clause no weight, if the clause expresses only a necessary result of the previously described structure or method.[29] Conversely, a whereby clause can sometimes help make the claim more understandable. Hence there are times when there may be good reason to use the whereby clause. Properly used, the whereby clause should not contain the only recitation of a patentably distinguishing feature of the invention; rather, it should sum up the function, operation, or result that necessarily follows from the previously recited structure or method.

§ 7.10   —Unduly Broad Claims

Whether a claim is unduly broad depends on the nature of the art and on what is disclosed in the specification. When the art produces predictable results, such as in much of the mechanical and electrical arts, broad claims may be properly supported by the disclosure of a single species.[30] However, when the art produces unpredictable results, such as in much of the chemical arts, broad claims may not be supported by the disclosure of a single species.[31] This is because in arts such as chemistry it is not obvious from the disclosure of one species that other species will work or what those other species might be.

---

[26] U.S. Dep't of Commerce, Manual of Pat. Examining Proc. § 706.03(c) (5th ed. Mar. 1994).

[27] 1929 C.D. 172, 388 O.G. 279 (1929).

[28] 114 U.S.P.Q. (BNA) 740 (C.C.P.A. 1957); U.S. Dep't of Commerce, Manual of Pat. Examining Proc. § 706.03(c) (5th ed. Mar. 1994).

[29] *In re* Certain Personal Computers, 224 U.S.P.Q. (BNA) 270 (Ct. Int'l Trade 1984).

[30] *In re* Cook & Merigold, 169 U.S.P.Q. (BNA) 298 (C.C.P.A. 1971); *In re* Vickers, 61 U.S.P.Q. (BNA) 122 (C.C.P.A. 1944); U.S. Dep't of Commerce, Manual of Pat. Examining Proc. § 706.03(z) (5th ed. Mar. 1994).

[31] *In re* Dreshfield, 1940 C.D. 351, 518 O.G. 255 (1940); *In re* Sol, 1938 C.D. 723, 497 O.G. 546 (1938); U.S. Dep't of Commerce, Manual of Pat. Examining Proc. § 706.03(z) (5th ed. Mar. 1994).

Software inventions usually produce results that are predictable, hence, broad claims may properly be supported by disclosure of a single preferred embodiment. This should be taken with a grain of salt, however, for there are classes of problems to which software may be applied that defy predictability.

Predicting the weather is an example. A supercomputer software invention that predicts the onset of hurricanes 24 hours in advance may not similarly predict the onset of hurricanes one year in advance. Likewise it may not predict drought. Hence a broad claim to weather prediction would not be supported by disclosure of a single 24 hour hurricane predictor. Why this is so is the subject of James Gleick's book, *Chaos Making A New Science*[32] that explains that some phenomena, like weather, are extremely "sensitive to initial conditions." A colorful way to state this sensitivity is that the flitting of a butterfly's wings in China will radically alter wind conditions halfway around the world.

§ 7.11   —Vague and Indefinite Claim Rejections

There are a number of other nonart rejections amounting to rejections of poor claim drafting style that examiners look for. These include rejections that the claim is vague and indefinite,[33] that the claim is incomplete,[34] that the claim is too wordy or prolix,[35] that the claim is a mere aggregation of elements because there is no claimed cooperation between elements.[36]

Usually the allegedly vague or ambiguous claim can be corrected by choosing different terms to describe the invention. Sometimes an examiner will assert that a claim is indefinite because the word "or" has been used. Use of the word "or" does not necessarily render a claim indefinite, although in some instances it can. If the word "or" separates two different elements, the *Manual of Patent Examining Procedure* instructs examiners to reject the claim as being indefinite. "Alternative expressions such as 'brake or locking device' may make a claim indefinite if the limitation covers two different elements."[37] However, the *Manual* also explains that if the word "or" separates alternate expressions of the same element, the claim should not be rejected as indefinite. "If two equivalent parts are referred to such as 'rods or bars,' the alternative expression may be considered proper."[38]

---

[32] James Glick, Chaos Making New Science (1987).

[33] U.S. Dep't of Commerce, Manual of Pat. Examining Proc. § 706.03(d) (5th ed. Mar. 1994).

[34] *Id.* § 706.03(f).

[35] *Id.* § 706.03(g).

[36] *Id.* § 706.03(i).

[37] *Id.* § 706.03(d).

[38] *Id.*

Software inventions may involve the word "or" as an operator in a Boolean logic expression, such as: If A OR B Then Do C. In this case, the patent examiner should recognize the word "or" as part of a single Boolean expression, that is, as alternate expressions of a single claim element. As such, the claim is quite precise and definite, and should not be rejected. Nevertheless, if an examiner cannot be persuaded to retract a rejection of the word "or" you may be able to get around the issue by restructuring the claim as follows: Do C if at least one of A AND B is met.

§ 7.12   —Incomplete Claim Rejections

When the examiner rejects a claim as being incomplete, this usually means that the claim omits essential elements or steps, or that the claim omits the necessary structural cooperative relationship of elements or steps.[39] Examiners are taught that this rejection should focus on the elements or steps that are essential to novelty or operability and that greater latitude should be given to elements or steps that are not essential.[40]

Aggregation is a related rejection, based on lack of cooperation between the elements of a claim. The example given in the *Manual of Patent Examining Procedure* is: A washing machine associated with a dial telephone.[41] As can be seen, here the term "associated with" fails to distinguish a dial telephone coupled to remotely control a washing machine, from a dial telephone temporarily placed upon a washing machine.

§ 7.13   —Duplicate Claims and Double Patenting

Examiners not only review individual claims for integrity, they also review the entire set of claims presented for integrity. If two or more claims are exact duplicates, or if they are so close in content that they cover the same thing, examiners are trained to give a duplicate claim or double patenting rejection.[42] Duplicate claims can occur by simple clerical or drafting error, often the result of inattentively using a word processor copy and paste function. Examiners may also find claims to be duplicates where the wording of the claims differ only in subject matter that is old in the art.[43]

---

[39] U.S. Dep't of Commerce, Manual of Pat. Examining Proc. § 706.03(f) (5th ed. Mar. 1994).

[40] *Id.*

[41] *Id.* § 706.03(i).

[42] U.S. Dep't of Commerce, Manual of Pat. Examining Proc. § 706.03(k) (5th ed. Mar. 1994).

[43] *Id., citing Ex parte* Whitelaw, 1915 C.D. 18, 219 O.G. 1237.

37 C.F.R. § 1.75(b) provides that "[m]ore than one claim may be presented, provided they differ substantially from each other and are not unduly multiplied." Undue multiplicity is thus a nonart rejection that the examiner can make when, in the examiner's judgment, the number of claims is "unreasonable in view of the nature and scope of applicant's invention and the state of the art."[44]

§ 7.14   Claim Drafting Process

Draft the claims first. That is what many experienced patent attorneys advise. There is good reason for this. The claims define the metes and bounds of the invention. The claims put the invention into perspective with the prior art. The claims are the words that the patent examiner spends most time reviewing, and the claims are the instrument construed by the court in litigation. The claims are important and should therefore be given primary attention. Starting with the claims helps you focus on the invention.

There are those who prefer to draft the specification first, and then draft the claims. They will tell you that writing the specification first helps them figure out what the invention is. There is nothing fundamentally wrong with this approach, but it can be considerably less efficient. Consider this analogy.

Before painting his famous mural on the ceiling of the Sistine Chapel, Michelangelo undoubtedly made sketches. Edgar Degas did this also, before he rendered his impressionistic pastels for which he is famous. Indeed, most artists make sketches and studies before undertaking a major work. (There are always exceptions, like artist Jackson Pollock, who exploited chaos and randomness in his swirling drip paintings. Pollock spread his canvas on the floor and spilled paint on it. He then selected and framed the good parts.)

Patent application drafting is an art form, more constrained than painting, but nevertheless an art form. It is quite natural to make sketches or studies of important inventive aspects before undertaking the patent application in earnest. Those who draft the specification first are actually making written sketches or studies in an effort to find the invention. Thus whether you draft the claims first, as advocated here, or draft the specification first, treat early efforts as sketches or studies, and be prepared to throw them away, just as the artist makes a sketch, learns from it, and then discards it. That is why it is more efficient to draft the claims first. Claims comprise fewer words; it is easy to draft a claim, study it, and discard it in favor of a better claim. It is much harder to draft a complete specification and then discard it, after learning that you missed the invention. So many pages of effort go into drafting the specification that many are strongly

---

[44] U.S. Dep't of Commerce, Manual of Pat. Examining Proc. § 706.03(l) (5th ed. Mar. 1994).

tempted to keep the specification that has been drafted, even though it may not focus precisely on the claimed invention.

There is no one proper way to express the metes and bounds of an invention. An invention is not one-dimensional. It is multidimensional—like sculpture. There is no one vantage point from which to look at an invention. There are many. Claims should be drafted to describe the invention from several different vantage points, thereby capturing a better image of the multidimensional nature of the invention.

§ 7.15   Finding the Invention

How do you go about finding the invention? Begin by assessing what are the commercially important features. What are the features that will motivate purchasers of a product to select the invention over the prior art? Having these features in mind while drafting will help keep the claim focused on what the inventor wants "to exclude others from making, using or selling . . . throughout the United States."[45]

Next, identify the essential claim elements that are required to make the invention. Often you can identify the essential claim elements by studying the component parts (or subassemblies of component parts) found in the inventor's preferred embodiment. Then identify those parts that are essential to the operation of the invention. In this endeavor, software inventions and hardware inventions are no different. Each can be broken down into component parts or modules or into subassemblies or submodules. The objective is to identify the essential component parts. Sifting through all the component parts, the essential ones are often those that make the commercially important features possible, or those that a competitor must employ to compete.

Having identified the essential component parts, devise claim element abstractions to represent the essential component parts. These abstractions are the essential claim elements that are required to make the invention, and that will ultimately become the elements of the claim you are drafting.

An essential component part and an essential claim element seem quite similar. Is there a difference? The answer is yes. The component part identifies part of the inventor's implementation or physical embodiment of the invention. The claim element more broadly identifies a class of component parts capable of making the invention.

Object-oriented software developers use a similar notion to write software. They model a solution to the problem to be solved, first by identifying classes of objects they believe are needed to solve the problem, and second by selecting specific objects from these classes to build the actual software

---

[45] 35 U.S.C. § 154.

embodiment. The specific objects selected are called "instances" of the class and the act of selecting such objects is called "instantiation." Knowing this terminology and the analogy between claim drafting and object-oriented software development may help if you are working with an inventor who is familiar with object-oriented programming. If you are fortunate, you may find that the software invention was developed using object-oriented techniques, in which case, there may be good design documentation that will virtually track the claim drafting process, step by step.

Having identified the essential claim elements, or at least those which at this stage you believe are essential, the next step is to identify the relationships between these elements. Often one element will be functionally "connected" to one or more other elements. The connection may be a direct or indirect physical attachment connection, for example, element A may be "coupled to" element B. The connection may be an information flow connection, such as, element A may "supply data (numbers, values, and so forth) to" element B; or element A may "supply a physical signal" to B. There are no doubt many other types of connections.

No element exists without some relationship to at least one other element. In your analysis, if an element floats alone, unconnected by any relationship with the other elements, chances are the floating element is not essential and should be discarded. If discarding the floating element destroys your perception of the essence of the invention, then put the element back in, and work harder at a deeper understanding of how that element is related to the other elements. A deeper understanding of the elusive relationship will often reward you with new insights and a new vantage point from which to see the invention.

§ 7.16 —Drawing Diagrams

In identifying the essential claim elements and the relationship between those elements, it is helpful to make diagrams. These diagrams are similar to the diagrams that patent examiners make from the claims in preparation for searching the prior art. System engineers use a diagram known as the entity relationship diagram or ERD, which can be employed to diagram claims. The diagramming technique is quite simple. Draw a circle (or any preferred shape) for each essential element. Label the inside of the circle with a broad or generic term that aptly describes that element. Next draw connecting lines between elements that are related in a way that is important to the invention. Place labels adjacent or on the lines to describe the nature of the particular relationship. That is essentially it, although there is a little extra detail that you may want to add to the diagram, if desired.

When appropriate, add arrowheads to the relationship lines, to show the direction of data flow or to show a dominant-subservient relationship. A claim element modifier (such as an adjective or a participle phrase), not important enough to be represented as an element itself, can be shown as an unterminated, cat whisker line originating from the element it modifies. **Figure 7–1** shows a sample claim diagram. The claim corresponding to this diagram is taken from claim 1 of U.S. Patent 5,233,685, assigned to WordPerfect Corporation. This patent is one of the patents featured in **Chapter 11.**

The diagram does several things. First, it serves as a shorthand notation for your thoughts. It is quicker to draw a diagram than it is to draft prototype claim language. The diagram allows you to think about claim elements and relationships, without worrying about what words to use. Second, the diagram helps identify nonessential elements and limitations, and elements that are floating— unrelated to the rest of the claim. Finally, the diagram is easy to comprehend at a glance, hence you can set it aside and forget about it, and then later pick it up and be instantly reminded of your claim drafting thoughts.

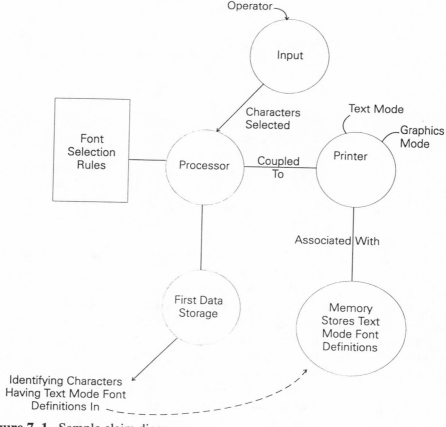

Figure 7–1. Sample claim diagram.

§ 7.17   —Working with Inventor's Drawings

Many times a claim diagram can be extracted from one of the inventor's drawings or from one of the patent drawings. This stands to reason—a drawing of a preferred embodiment of the invention would be expected to show all of the essential claim elements. However, drafting a claim to show every component of the preferred embodiment usually yields a narrow "picture claim." Thus the inventor's drawing or the patent drawing should not be thoughtlessly used as a claim diagram.

Rather, starting with the inventor's drawing or the patent drawing, try to group together certain component parts that provide a common function. Draw a box around these component parts and label the box to denote the common function. Do this for the other component parts as well. For example, if the software embodiment has several data structures and processes pertaining to data acquisition, group these data structures and processes together under the heading "data acquisition system," for example. Similarly, if there are several data structures and processes for supplying input and output to the user, these may be grouped together under the heading "user interface."

In grouping together functionally related component parts, keep in mind that not all groupings necessarily represent essential claim elements. In the above examples, it may well be that the "data acquisition mechanism" and the "user interface," while required for a working product, are not essential elements of the invention.

§ 7.18   —Working with Source Code

With software inventions, sometimes the inventor will have no drawings, only source code. When confronted with this situation, you may have to "reverse engineer" the source code to produce the claim diagram. Ideally you should do this with the inventor's help, because deciphering someone else's source code is a *very* time-consuming task.

In reverse engineering the source code, do essentially the same thing you would do if supplied with drawings. Identify the data structures, processes, subroutines, procedures, and modules that have a common purpose or function and then draw an appropriately labeled box to represent these component parts. Often it can be helpful to start by identifying all component parts that make up the user interface (that through which the user supplies input to the program and through which the program replies to the user), and by identifying all component parts that make up the operating system interface (that through which the program attaches to and invokes services of the operating system, for example, disk storage, file management, keyboard, and mouse support). These two interfaces are frequently not essential elements of the invention, yet they are nearly always present in a working software product.

By identifying and separating out these two interfaces, it is easier to examine what remains for elements that are essential to the invention.

§ 7.19   Testing Claims for Proper Scope

Having identified the essential elements, and having found the relationships between these elements, the next step is to test the model claim to see if it is of proper scope. Do this by testing the claim to determine if there are any undue limitations, and also to make sure the model claim does not read on the prior art. At this stage, it is not necessary to reduce the model claim to writing. The claim diagram alone will suffice.

Begin by identifying which claim elements are themselves new. Also identify if any of the relationships between elements are new. Often, none of the elements alone will be new, but the combination of elements and their relationship is new. By identifying which elements and relationships are new, you begin to focus on the essence of the invention. If you find that you have included several elements that are not new, then possibly these old elements should be lumped together under a collective or generic name. Doing this helps avoid unnecessary limitations.

What if none of the elements themselves are new, and none of the relationships are new either? This means you have not yet found the invention; it is hiding. In identifying the essential elements at the outset, you may have chosen element names that are now hiding the invention. Try to determine which element or elements contain the new or inventive matter. Then break these elements into two or more component elements, and define the relationships between them, so that the invention is no longer hidden.

The model testing process takes an iterative hierarchical approach. Combine multiple related old elements into a more generic single element; break apart new and inventive matter into more specific, separate elements. In the end you have a model claim, in diagram form, which shows quite clearly what is new.

§ 7.20   —Checking Claims Against Prior Art

It is usually a good idea to further test the model by attempting to read the model, as a whole, upon the known prior art. Take the known prior art, such as the inventor's own prior art product, or a competitor's prior art product, or the prior art patents developed during a patentability search, and see if each and every element of your model claim is found in a single prior art device or reference. If so, then an assumption made while preparing the model claim is incorrect. The elements identified as new are not new.

Do not despair. It is better to know that the claim is not of proper scope now, (before you file the application) while it can be corrected without a costly amendment responding to a Patent Office rejection. Try to identify how the invention differs from the prior art and add at least one claim element or limitation that will highlight the difference.

If it is not apparent what element to add, try to determine what makes the invention better than the prior art. For example, the invention may operate more efficiently than the prior art; the invention may have features that the prior art does not have; the invention may be easier and less expensive to manufacture; or the invention may be easier to use. Once you have determined how the invention differs from or improves upon the prior art, devise a claim element or combination of elements that are necessary to effect this difference or improvement.

§ 7.21   —Designing Around Claims

Claim drafting is an iterative art. Therefore, after adding the necessary claim elements to distinguish the invention from the prior art, go back and test the remaining elements to see if there are any that are unnecessary. One good way to test for unnecessary limitations is to pretend to be a competitor trying to design around the claim. Are there any elements that can be eliminated? If so, revise the claim model and eliminate those elements that a competitor can eliminate. Are there any elements that can be replaced with substantially nonequivalent elements? For these, try to devise different claim elements that are more generic and therefore cover both the originally contemplated element and the nonequivalent substitute. The objective is to make the claim devilishly difficult to design around.

§ 7.22   —Considering Fall Back Positions

Once you have constructed a claim model that highlights what is new about the invention, distinguishes the invention from all prior art of which you are aware, and is devilishly difficult to design around, there is one more thing to do. Think about your fall back position. How will you revise the claim if it is rejected by the Patent Office over art of which you are not aware?

Naturally, until you know about the prior art, you cannot possibly predict with certainty how to revise the claim to avoid the art. However, since most claims are rejected in the first office action, expect this one will be too. It is therefore wise to have some subject matter in the specification that can be later added to the independent claims.

§ 7.23   —Drafting and Refining Claims

There are several ways of drafting actual claim language, once you have the claim model worked out. If you are fairly skilled using a word processor, you may want to draft the claim language directly on the screen using your word processor. This can be a fairly efficient way to work, even if you are not a fluent typist, because drafting the claim language involves a great deal more thinking than it does typing.

Decide first on the form of the claim, for example, apparatus, method, Jepson. This will dictate how the claim preamble should be worded. However, do not consider initially what to put in the claim preamble. It is usually easiest to build the claim preamble after the claim element language has been drafted. Using the claim model diagram as a blueprint, start by drafting language to describe each of the elements and the relationships between elements. Be sure to organize the elements so that elements supplying an antecedent basis for other elements appear first in the claim. To illustrate, see **Figure 7–1** that shows a claim model diagram. A rough draft claim might be something like this:

A computer system for word-processing, comprising:

input means responsive to operator-input characters;

a printer capable of printing in text mode and in graphics mode;

a memory associated with said printer for storing text mode font definitions;

a data storage means for identifying characters having text mode font definitions in said memory;

a processing means coupled to said input means and to said data storage means and to said printer for comparing operator-input characters with said characters in said data storage means and for causing said printer to print the operator-input characters according to a predetermined set of font selection rules.

Note in the above rough draft example, the preamble is nothing more than a place holder. The antecedent basis details have not been added in the preamble at this point. Similarly, the individual claim elements are also lacking details. Integration of the claim elements is not yet tight, and the claim does not yet distinctly represent the invention.

Work with the rough draft claim language, tightening the phraseology and supplying missing antecedent bases, until the claim reads, start to finish, without ambiguity. Having done this, the finished claim might be something like this:

1. A computer system for performing wordprocessing operations, the computer system comprising:

(a) input means responsive to operator commands enabling an operator to specify any of a plurality of characters for inclusion in a document being created or edited;

(b) printing means having the capability of printing characters in either text or graphics mode;

(c) memory means associated with the printing means for storing a text mode definition for each of a subset of the plurality of characters that may be specified by the operator using the input means;

(d) a first data storage means identifying each character having a text mode definition in the memory means;

(e) processing means coupled to the input means, the first data storage means and the printing means for comparing each character selected by the operator with information stored in the first data storage means to determine whether, for each specified character, a text mode definition exits in the memory means and,

(i) if said definition exists, sending data to the printing means identifying the character; or

(ii) if said definition does not exist, taking alternative action comprising sending data identifying an alternative character to the printing means for printing in graphics mode or sending data identifying said alternative character in a substitute font to the printing means for printing in text mode.

§ 7.24   —Narrow Claims

There is more to claim drafting strategy than drafting a single independent claim. A utility patent with only one claim qualifies under the old adage as "putting all your eggs in one basket." While having at least one broad claim is certainly desirable, it is far better to cover the spectrum with broad, intermediate, and narrow claims. This may entail having different sets of independent claims, each of different scope. It may also entail having claims of different types, for example, apparatus claims, method claims, Jepson claims, Markush claims, means plus function claims, and so forth. Nearly without exception, this will entail having dependent claims.

Why have intermediate and narrow claims, and specifically, why have dependent claims? Simply, these claims serve as insurance against broad claim invalidity. All claims issued by the Patent Office are presumed valid over all prior art considered by the patent examiner. However, when there is a great deal of money at stake, defendants in patent infringement litigation go to great lengths to find closer prior art than the patent examiner considered—to prove that the claims in litigation should never have been granted.

Because broad claims cover more intellectual territory, they are easier to invalidate. To invalidate any claim under 35 U.S.C. § 102, you must show that the claim reads on (covers, element by element) a single prior art device or reference. Broader claims read on more, and they are therefore more vulnerable to being invalidated. Therefore, while most patent prosecution attorneys strive for the broadest claim allowable, most patent litigation attorneys prefer the narrowest claim that covers the accused. Litigation attorneys prefer a narrow claim, because a narrow claim is harder to invalidate and because a narrow claim, read on the accused, demonstrates how closely the accused has "copied" the invention.

§ 7.25   —Dependent Claims

A good way to a draft claim of narrower scope is to draft a dependent claim. A dependent claim is one that incorporates by reference or "depends" from an independent claim. Object-oriented computer programmers will recognize the dependent claim as a child claim that "inherits" all of the elements and limitations of the parent claim—just as rowboat inherits all properties of the class, watercraft. Incorporating all of the limitations of the independent claim parent, the dependent claim is, by definition, narrower than the independent claim parent. This narrowing inheritance relationship can cascade through several generations; hence one dependent claim can be based on another dependent claim, which in turn can be based on still another claim, perhaps an independent claim. The one dependent claim at the bottom of the cascade would be said to incorporate all of the elements and limitations of the independent base claim and any intervening claims.

There are typically two ways to draft dependent claims. You can amplify, by adding an additional limitation to an existing claim element of the parent claim; or you can augment, by adding a new claim element to the parent claim. The mechanics for each of these is quite simple. To amplify, use a "wherein" phrase:

2.   The invention of claim 1 wherein said balloon is blue.

To augment, use a "further comprising" phrase:

3.   The invention of claim 1 further comprising a second balloon.

It is also proper to cascade one dependent claim from another. Thus, you could add the following additional dependent claims, based on the ones presented above:

4.   The invention of claim 2 further comprising a second balloon.
5.   The invention of claim 3 wherein said second balloon is blue.

By the time you are done, you can have all permutations of one and two (blue and nonblue) balloon embodiments covered, as illustrated.

Dependent claims can get quite narrow quickly, when cascaded. This is usually not good practice. It is better practice to base most dependent claims directly upon an independent base claim. In that way each dependent claim can amplify or augment a single feature or aspect of the invention, in a narrower sense, without bringing in unnecessary limitations.

CHAPTER 8

EXAMINATION OF THE APPLICATION BY THE PATENT OFFICE

PATENT OFFICE ORGANIZATION AND APPLICATION PROCESS FROM PATENT OFFICE'S PERSPECTIVE

§ 8.1   Mail Room to Publication

Patent applicants always ask, "How long will it take to get my patent?" The answer often given includes an explanation that it takes about 12 to 18 months for the application to be examined. Patent issuance takes even longer. This is surprising news to many first time patent applicants. Usually after learning this, they want to know why it takes so long. The best answer is to explain how the application process physically works, that is, within the Patent Office, who does what to the application as it progresses through the stages of prosecution. Knowing all the steps involved helps put the 12 to 18 months in perspective.

§ 8.2   —Mail Room

All applications for a United States Patent enter the Patent Office through the same front door, the Patent Office Mail Room. Whether submitting an application by mail or by hand delivery, the application process starts in the Mail Room. In 1992, patent applicants submitted 185,446 applications.[1] All of these applications were first processed through the Mail Room.

With such a deluge of applications, it is easy to imagine the inside of the Mail Room as mountains of documents, waiting to be processed, pages of all shapes and sizes, files stacked everywhere, in no particular order, waiting to be routed to the examiners, and a staff of minimum wage government workers trying to keep this cattle drive moving.

Actually, the Mail Room is not like this at all. True, there is a mountain of paper. However, incoming applications are processed quite quickly and then passed on to the Classification and Routing Branch, where the first phases of examination are performed. It is in the Mail Room where the application serial number is assigned. Although a filing date is also documented in the Mail Room, the filing date does not become official until after the Classification and Routing Branch has verified that the application is complete enough to warrant a filing date.

Besides opening the mail, the Mail Room is responsible for putting the application into a file wrapper that resembles an 11" × 14" pocket envelope, open along the 11 inch top. Very little additional processing is performed by the Mail Room, other than to affix serial number and filing date information on the file wrapper.

---

1 Comm'r of Pat. & Trademarks, 1992 Annual Report Fiscal Year 57 (1993).

§ 8.3   —Application Branch, Classification and Routing

Once the contents of the application have been put into the file wrapper, the file is delivered to the Classification and Routing Branch upstairs where some important decisions are made. Each application is initially examined to determine which examining group will be assigned the application. This determination is made by a small group, expert in the Patent Office classification system. Applications are classified by what subject matter is claimed. Naturally, if the application is filed without claims (an error), the application cannot be classified. In such a case, the classification examiner tags the file and sends it to the Special Processing and Correspondence Branch, which has the responsibility of bringing this error to the applicant's attention.

Currently there are 11 classification examiners who work feverishly to classify on average 121 applications per day, each. That amounts to an average of 15.2 applications per hour. Although each classification examiner is skilled in the art of Patent Office classification, none of these examiners specialize in any particular technology. In other words, each classification examiner must be able to classify any application encountered.

Classification of the application includes not only assigning it to a Patent Class, but also to an examining Art Unit. The assignment process is further complicated in that some classes are shared by different Art Units, and the correlation between Patent Class and Art Unit is revised monthly.

The classification examiner's decision to assign an application to a particular Class and Art Unit is rarely challenged. If a classification error is made, it is usually corrected by the supervisory primary examiner in the Art Unit to which the application is originally assigned. The *Manual of Patent Examining Procedure* at § 903.08(d) states the procedure used by the supervisory primary examiner if the application needs to be transferred to a different examining group. Such transfer is administered by the examining groups involved. The applicant is not involved.

There is currently a voluntary procedure available to allow an applicant to designate the proposed class and subclass when the application is filed.[2] The stated purpose of the voluntary procedure is "for expediting newly filed application papers through pre-examination steps."[3] To use the procedure, determine what class and subclass seems proper and identify this in the upper right-hand corner of the letter of transmittal accompanying the application papers, for example, "Proposed class 364, subclass 402."

To determine what class and subclass a new application falls under, look to the most comprehensive claim, that is, the claim to the most extensive

---

[2] U.S. Dep't of Commerce, Manual of Pat. Examining Proc. § 601 (Mar. 1994).

[3] *Id.*

combination.[4] Select the class that encompasses this combination. Then select the subclass that best fits this combination.

In deciding between subclasses, the *Manual of Patent Examining Procedure* states, "[w]ithin a class, the first coordinate subclass that will take any claim controls classification."[5] This direction is admittedly a bit cryptic, and you may be reluctant to propose a subclass if unsure. A proposed subclass is not necessary because the pre-examination designation procedure is strictly voluntary. However, recognize that the Patent Office will correct a proposed classification if wrong. Also, although you are proposing class and subclass, you are actually only suggesting to which Art Unit the application should be assigned. Therefore, if you have the application narrowed down to one class, but cannot decide among several subclasses, and if the potential subclasses all fall under the same Art Unit, then pick one of the subclasses and rely on the supervisory primary examiner to assign it properly.

Another aid to choosing the right class and subclass is the prior art. If you have done a pre-application art search, look at how the most pertinent prior art is classified. If the art is close, chances are your application will go to the same Art Unit that prosecuted the prior art.

After classification, the application is passed to an Application Processing Team where the application is more thoroughly examined to see that it is complete. There are currently four such teams, each comprising essentially the same staffing and each performing the same functions. These teams have examiners who review each application to determine if the application is legally complete, and to determine if there are any (legally permissible) missing parts. If the application is filed without a filing fee or without a signed Inventor's Oath or Declaration, these "missing parts" are noted. An application with such legally permissible missing parts is given a filing date. If the application is filed without all specified drawings, the application is not given a filing date.

In addition to examining the application for completeness, the examiners of the Application Processing team also fill out a coding sheet, which data entry clerks use to enter pertinent application data into the Patent Office database. After entering the data, the data entry clerks print a gummed label and apply it to the file wrapper, after first being checked for accuracy by a team examiner. The data entry clerk also prints an Official Filing Receipt that is mailed to the applicant or the applicant's attorney.

This processing of the file is time-consuming. Currently the Patent Office goal is to process an application through an Application Processing Team in about 22–23 days. This suggests that Official Filing Receipts can be expected within about four weeks after filing, unless irregularities are encountered.

If the Processing Team finds any irregularities, such as missing parts or an incomplete application, the file is sent to the Special Processing and

---

[4] *Id.* § 903.08(e)(2).

[5] *Id.* § 903.08(e)(4).

Correspondence Branch. This Branch sends out a Notice of Missing Parts or other appropriate correspondence.

Assuming there is no need to refer the application to the Special Processing and Correspondence Branch, the application is next reviewed by an Official Draftsperson, who specifically examines the drawings, noting any informalities. If informalities are noted, the appropriate notice is placed in the file, where it can be sent out with the first office action.

Next, an important archival function is performed. The entire application is copied onto microfilm by the Microfilm Processing and Duplication Branch of the Micrographics Division. Ordinarily, this process takes an additional two to three days. Aside from the obvious archival benefit, microfilming also makes the application file history easier to copy. If you have ever ordered a certified copy of an application file history, it probably was made from these microfilmed records.

After microfilming, the application is finally hole-punched at the top, mounted in the file and then routed to the Art Unit to which the application has been assigned. At this point, the application has a serial number and filing date; it has been assigned to a patent Class and Art Unit; and it has been checked for completeness. The file wrapper has a printed label stating all pertinent information and a bar code representing the assigned series number and serial number. The file wrapper contains the application and drawings, and may contain any additional Patent Office notices, such as a Notice of Missing Parts or Notice of Drawing Objections.

Knowing the intricacies of the procedure, there are several things to do to help speed up the process. First, by avoiding Missing Parts practice (having the inventor sign the application before filing) there is no need to send the file to the Special Processing and Communications Branch. Second, by filing formal drawings, the Official Draftsperson does not have to spend as much time issuing a Notice of Drawing Objections.

§ 8.4   —Examining Groups

From the Application Branch, the application is carted to the Art Unit to which the application has been assigned. There the Supervisory Primary Examiner or SPE briefly reviews the application and assigns it to one of the examiners in the Art Unit. The assigned examiner, under the SPE's supervision, handles the bulk of the substantive examination of the application.

By regulation, each application is processed in the order received.[6] Thus, depending on the particular examiner's backlog of applications, further

---

[6] 37 C.F.R. § 1.102. However there is a procedure for prosecuting an application out of order. See § 8.12.

substantive examination of the application waits until the application reaches the top of the assigned examiner's stack.

The substantive prosecution begins when the assigned examiner picks up the application, reads it, and begins searching for prior art. The emphasis from the very beginning is on searching the prior art. The *Manual of Patent Examining Procedure* states, quite succinctly, "[a]fter reading the specification and claims, the examiner searches the prior art."[7]

Searching the prior art is difficult. It requires the examiner to think abstractly, to identify concepts in the claimed invention, and to find those concepts in the prior art. Prior art is a big ocean to fish in. There are millions of United States patents, millions of foreign patents, libraries full of technical journals and publications, countless copies of product literature, users manuals, and documentation. In theory, all of this must be searched before the examiner can truly know if the claimed invention already exists in the prior art.

§ 8.5   Examining Group Organization

Patents are classified under the U.S. Classification System, based on the subject matter claimed. In other words, it is the claims, not the specification, that dictate where a particular patent is classified. Under the U.S. Classification System patent claims fall broadly into three main categories:

I   Chemical and Related Arts

II   Communications, Designs, Radiant Energy, Weapons, Electrical and Related Arts

III   Body Treatment and Care, Heating and Cooling, Material Handling and Treatment, Mechanical Manufacturing, Mechanical Power, Static and Related Arts.[8]

If you have difficulty seeing an overall organizational structure to these three main categories, you are not alone. Fortunately, the *Manual of Classification* gives a hint. The Group Personnel Directory in that Manual lists telephone numbers of key personnel under three major headings: Chemical, Electrical, and Mechanical.[9] With this hint, the three main categories are seen to fall generally into these Chemical, Electrical and Mechanical categories, with a few rather odd exceptions.[10]

---

7 U.S. Dep't of Commerce, Manual of Pat. Examining Proc. § 704 (Mar. 1994).

8 U.S. Dep't of Commerce, Manual of Classification I-5 (June 1994).

9 *Id.* at II–1-5.

10 For a further explanation of the Classification System, see **Ch. 4,** which concentrates on searching for prior art and includes a description of the U.S. Classification System.

These broad Chemical, Electrical, and Mechanical categories serve not only to categorize prior art under the Patent Classification System, but also to organize the patent examining corps into groups. The Examining Branch is organized into groups, modeled directly after the art categories prescribed by the Patent Classification System. The Patent Office refers to these Groups by one of the following four digit numbers. Looking at the first digit of a group number tells you whether the group is Chemical, Electrical, or Mechanical.

CHEMICAL	ELECTRICAL	MECHANICAL
Group 1100	Group 2100	Group 3100
Group 1200	Group 2200	Group 3200
Group 1300	Group 2300	Group 3300
Group 1500	Group 2400	Group 3400
Group 1800	Group 2500	Group 3500
	Group 2600	
	Group 2900	

Software inventions, depending on the particular technology involved, can be assigned to any of these groups, although the majority are assigned to Group 2300. For example, if the claimed invention is primarily a chemical process involving software systems in the process, the application will likely be assigned to one of the Chemical Groups. Similarly, if the claimed invention is primarily a mechanical apparatus involving software systems, the application will likely be assigned to one of the Mechanical Groups. The vast majority of software inventions, however, are assigned to Group 2300.

The reason software-related inventions can be assigned to groups other than Group 2300 is that software can be embedded in many different technologies. For example, an automatic transmission for a car may use a software-implemented algorithm to determine at what rpm to shift. This would be an example of a primarily mechanical technology with an embedded software system.

Each group is headed by a Group Director, who is responsible for overseeing all administrative functions of the group. The patent examining groups are further subdivided into subgroups called Art Units. Art Units are formed along lines corresponding to the Class and Subclass structure of the Patent Classification System, although there is usually not a one-to-one correspondence. The Classes and Subclasses are divided up and assigned to Art Units, so that each Art Unit's assignment is unique. Each Art Unit is responsible for prosecuting all applications which fall into the Subclasses assigned to it. An Art Unit may have responsibility for technology classified in more than one Class. An Art Unit will almost always have responsibility for multiple Subclasses within a given Class.

Each Art Unit is headed up by a Supervisory Primary Examiner or SPE. Typically the SPE is an experienced examiner who came up through the ranks, often as an examiner in the same Art Unit. The remainder of the examiners in the Art Unit report directly to the SPE. The SPE assigns the application to one of the examiners. The assigned examiner performs the bulk of the actual patent examination, search, and prosecution. The SPE trains examiners when they are hired and thereafter reviews their work and answers their questions about the patent prosecution process. In addition, for the first year after an examiner's hire, the SPE must sign all prosecution actions prepared by the new examiner.

§ 8.6   Qualifications of a Patent Examiner

Patent examiners are required to have a science or technical degree. A law degree or legal education is not required. Many find it surprising that a legal education is not required, because the patent examiner job description certainly involves making a number of important legal decisions every day. One reason a law degree is not required is, of course, financial. Patent examiners are paid on a GS-05 through GS-11 salary base. See **Table 8–1** (effective 1994).

At this salary, the patent examiner position is probably competitive with entry level science and engineering positions. It is not competitive with patent law positions in corporate patent law departments and law firms. Therefore, requiring all examiners to have a law degree or legal education is simply not economically feasible. This is by no means a censure of the legal system, considering that the entry level requirement of a patent attorney is at least a bachelor's (four-year) degree in science or engineering plus a law (three-year) degree.

In practice, a law degree is not required anyway. The *Manual of Patent Examining Procedure* is an excellent guide through the legal principles in virtually every aspect of patent law that the examiner needs on a day-to-day basis. In fact, many patent attorneys study the *Manual of Patent Examining Procedure* in preparation for taking the patent bar examination.

Although a law degree is not required, many patent examiners are interested in law and simultaneously pursue law degrees. In fact, this is one of the attractions that draws many young persons into the patent examining profession. An individual can work in the Patent Office during the day to receive on-the-job-training in patent prosecution and attend law school after work. Although it takes a little longer to complete law school this way, the Patent Office experience is invaluable, and the paycheck isn't bad. George Washington University recognizes this demand and holds law school classes in facilities connected to the Patent Office via underground walkways. Examiners can attend law school without even venturing outside.

While the career opportunity for new examiners is great, staff attrition is a considerable downside for the Patent Office and the public. Many SPEs and Group Directors complain that they cannot seem to keep qualified examiners on staff. They work for a few years, while completing law degrees, and then

Table 8–1

Salary Table No. 576 from the United States Government

Grade	Step 1	Step 2	Step 3	Step 4	Step 5	Step 6	Step 7	Step 8	Step 9	Step10
5	23,839	24,450	25,061	25,672	26,283	26,894	27,505	28,116	28,727	29,338
7	29,530	30,287	31,044	31,801	32,558	33,315	34,072	34,829	35,586	36,343
9	32,419	33,345	34,271	35,197	36,123	37,049	37,975	38,901	39,827	40,753
11	35,865	36,986	38,107	39,228	40,349	41,470	42,591	43,712	44,833	45,954

leave for better paying careers as patent attorneys. The result of this is that the patent examining ranks need to be continually filled with new, untrained, and inexperienced examiners. This places a burden on the SPEs who must continually train new examiners.

Even this apparent downside has an upside, however. The continual influx of new examiners replenishes the Patent Office knowledge pool with current science and technology education. These new examiners come with new education. With that new education they are better equipped to understand the new patentable technology. Certainly this is the case in Group 2300, the group that examines software patents.

§ 8.7   Group 2300, Software Patent Examiners

Group 2300 concentrates on the technology found primarily in U.S. Patent Classes 364 and 395. These classes are the principal computer technology classes, Class 364 covering "Electrical Computers and Data Processing Systems" and Class 395 covering "Information Processing System Organization." Class 395 is a relatively new class, formed in 1991 when the overloaded subclasses 200 and 900 of Class 364 were reclassified.

Like all examining groups within the Patent Office, Group 2300 is organized into Art Units. Art Units are like teams, each specializing in a different technology. Group 2300 has 13 Art Units. Each Art Unit specializes in different subclasses of the Class 364 and Class 395 technologies. Here is the current breakdown:

Art Unit	Class	Subclasses
2301	395	100; 118–61
2302	395	800
2304	364	423–63; 480-512
2306	364	130–94; 468–79; 600-864
2307	364	221–86.6; 916–78.3
2307 (cont'd)	395	600
2308	381	29–53
2308 (cont'd)	395	1–99; 325; 725–50; 900–34
2311	364	400–22
2312	364	DIG 1; DIG 2
2312 (cont'd)	395	400–25
2313	371	All
2313 (cont'd)	395	575
2314	364	464.01–67; 514–82
2315	395	375; 500
2316	395	650–700
2317	395	101–17; 162–275; 550; 775

Consult the listing in **Appendix B** for a complete description of what subject matter each of the above subclasses cover. **Table 8–2** presents a thumbnail sketch of what each Art Unit does, greatly abridged.

Table 8–2

Art Unit Functions

Art Unit	Subject Matter
2301	Computer Graphics
2302	Processing Architecture
2304	Applications
	military; vehicle guidance, operation or indication; navigation; relative location; determining center of gravity (for example, load distribution); electrical and electronic engineering
2306	Computer Hardware
2307	Miscellaneous (old subclasses 200 and 900)
2308	Artificial Intelligence
2311	Applications
	business practice and management; government activities (that is, voting, law enforcement); games and amusements; life sciences; linguistics; word processing; document indexing or retrieval; measuring or testing human emotions or responses; earth sciences (for example, weather)
2312	Computer Hardware
2313	Reliability Testing
2314	Applications
	communication engineering (for example, pictorial and pulse communication); physics; measuring and evaluation (for example, performance); basic measurements; operations performed (for example, fast fourier transform)
2315	Simulations
2316	System Utilities and Task Management
2317	Computer Hardware

In **Table 8–2** software falls under the general subject matter "Applications." Note that certain Art Units within Group 2300 concentrate more on software than on hardware.

§ 8.8   Software Patent Statistics

Examiners in Group 2300 (the Patent Office group responsible for software patent technology) are sitting in a bunker at "ground zero" of the software patent explosion. Here are the statistics:

Fiscal Year	Class 364	Class 395	Total
1988	3,829	N/A	3,829
1989	5,444	N/A	5,444
1990	6,555	N/A	6,555
1991	4,105	2,495	6,600
1992	2,780	4,772	7,552
1993	2,628	6,033	8,661
1994 (estimated)	2,700	7,173	9,873[11]

In the above data, Class 395 was created in 1991 out of parts of class 364, because several subclasses in class 364 were overloaded.

Responding to the software patent explosion, the Patent Office hires, on average, 50 new examiners a year. Although it loses some examiners every year to attrition, the size of Group 2300 is steadily growing.

Fiscal Year	New Hires	Attrition
1989	14	21
1990	54	20
1991	39	21
1992	40	19
1993	48	18
1994	41	13 (through June)
1995 (estimated)	60	

Recognizing that, in most cases, patents issue approximately two to three years after filing, the data on patents issued in Group 2300 follows:

Year	Class 364	Class 395	Total
1987	1,774	N/A	1,774
1988	1,908	N/A	1,908
1989	2,858	N/A	2,858
1990	2,591	N/A	2,591
1991	1,524	1,123	2,647
1992	1,354	1,476	2,830
1993	1,673	1,940	3,613

§ 8.9   Qualifications for Examining Software Patents

Until as recently as 1994 the Director of Group 2300 was not permitted by Patent Office regulations to hire patent examiners with computer science

---

[11] All statistics in this section are courtesy of U.S. Patent & Trademark Office.

degrees. Surprisingly, computer science was not originally thought to be suitably technical to meet the Patent Office's hiring requirements. Perhaps this was due to a bias favoring computer hardware over computer software. Perhaps this was due to imprecise definition by universities of what computer science covers. Perhaps it was a combination of the two.

Today most agree that the refusal to hire examiners with computer science degrees was simply wrong, although not due to poor judgment as much as to history. The Patent Office does not exist in a vacuum. It has always been responsive to the needs of industry and to the attitudes of the courts. Thus, in earlier days when the computer industry sold hardware and gave away software, and when the courts pronounced software unpatentable unless disguised as hardware, the Patent Office naturally wanted computer hardware engineers, not computer software engineers.

All that has changed. Now computer hardware is often virtually given away to induce the purchase of software. According to Patent Office statistics, the software industry is today the fastest growing industry in the United States Economy. As the Patent Office reports:

> Over the past decade, the computer software industry has evolved into a critical component of the U.S. economy. It is presently the fastest growing industry in the United States, with 1992 sales in the three core elements of the software industry—programming services, prepackaged software and computer integrated design—accounting for over $36.7 billion of our domestic gross product. The software industry also has created jobs at a remarkable rate; since 1987, employment in the software industry has risen at an annual rate of 6.6 percent and today the industry employs about 4 percent of the American work force.[12]

Responding to this change, the Patent Office changed its hiring requirements to allow computer scientists to become patent examiners.

APPLICATION PROCESS FROM PATENT APPLICANT'S PERSPECTIVE

§ 8.10   Filing the Application

To receive a patent you must apply for it by filing an application. For an application to be entitled to a filing date, the following items must be present:

1. a specification, with all pages present
2. all drawings referred to in the specification

---

[12] 58 Fed. Reg. 66347, Issue No. 242 (Dec. 1993).

3. at least one claim

4. names of the actual inventors.[13]

There are several clerical mistakes to anticipate. Are all pages of the specification present? If submitting source code or pseudocode in an appendix, microfiche, or paper, have you included it? Word processors have been known to misnumber pages, and copy machines do occasionally skip a page.

Do the drawings correspond, number for number, to the drawings identified in the section of the specification, "Brief Description of the Drawings"? If not, there is a good chance the Applications Branch will refuse to give the application a filing date.

One way this error can inadvertently happen is when a draftsperson, making the patent drawings, has to break a large flowchart up into several sheets, so that what was Figure 1 in the application has now become three sheets of drawings labeled Figures 1A, 1B, and 1C, for example. Although Figure 1 is still unquestionably present in the application (as collective Figures 1A, 1B, and 1C), the Application Branch may refuse to give a filing date because Figure 1—literally—is not present. If this happens, petition the Office of the Assistant Commissioner to explain that the refusal to assign a filing date was erroneous. The refusal to assign a filing date is usually reversed, if the figures, on their face, show that Figures 1A, 1B, and 1C actually connect to comprise the allegedly missing Figure 1.

Another way the missing drawing error can appear is if, in a final revision of the application, a figure is deleted from the application as being unnecessary. If you delete a figure, *be sure* to delete all reference to that figure in the specification. If reference to the deleted figure remains, the Patent Office treats this as a missing drawing and will not give the application a filing date.

Because the drawing was deleted as unnecessary, the failure to remove reference to the drawing in the specification would seem to be a mere typographical error, and hardly grounds for refusing to grant a filing date. The error is more serious, however. The patent statute states, "[t]he applicant shall furnish a drawing where necessary for the understanding of the subject matter sought to be patented."[14] Understand that the Patent Office treats a reference to a certain drawing in the specification as an *admission* that the drawing is necessary for the understanding of the subject matter sought to be patented. Thus failure to supply a drawing referred to in the specification is treated as a statutorily incomplete application.[15]

---

[13] 37 C.F.R. § 1.53.

[14] 35 U.S.C. § 113.

[15] *Id.* § 111.

Another clerical error to be alert for is failure to give full names of all the inventors.[16] Although the inventors' signatures on the oath or declaration are not required to receive a filing date, all inventors must be identified by full name. It is therefore incorrect to refer to joint inventors collectively. Do not collectively identify joint inventors as "Mary Doe, et al." The Patent Office treats this as a missing inventor's name and the application is not given a filing date. Instead of "Mary Doe, et al.," list each inventor individually by full name, for example, "Mary Doe, Richard Keith Roe, and Francis Lynn Jones."

§ 8.11   Missing Parts Practice

Just as certain parts must be present for an application to receive a filing date, other parts can be omitted and the application will still receive a filing date. These parts include:

1. Statutory filing fee
2. Oath or declaration
3. Signature on the oath or declaration of the inventor or inventors
4. English language translation of an application filed in a language other than English.

When the Applications Branch of the Patent Office finds one or more of the above parts missing, it issues a Notice of Missing Parts, giving the applicant one month from the date of the Notice (or two months from the filing date) to submit the missing parts along with a surcharge.[17] The surcharge is currently $65 for applicants who qualify as a small entity and $130 for applicants who do not qualify as a small entity.[18]

Missing Parts practice under 37 C.F.R. § 1.53(d) makes it possible to get an application on file more quickly by allowing you to temporarily dispense with obtaining an inventor's signature. However, dispensing with the signature does not mean the application should be filed without the inventor reviewing it. In response to the Notice of Missing Parts, the inventor will be required to sign the oath or declaration and that oath or declaration must expressly refer to the application as filed. It can cause problems for the patentee during litigation if it is discovered that the application was filed without the inventor seeing it.

---

[16] Required by 37 C.F.R. § 1.41.

[17] 37 C.F.R. § 1.53(d).

[18] *Id.* § 1.16(e).

§ 8.12   Expediting the Process,
Petition to Make Special

Ordinarily, applicants for a patent must wait their turn. The Code of Federal Regulations states this: "[a]pplications will not be advanced out of turn for examination."[19] There are times when you simply cannot wait the normal pendency time for an application to be examined. The patent regulations recognize this and provide for expedited prosecution under certain conditions. Thus 37 C.F.R. § 1.102 provides:

> (a) Applications will not be advanced out of turn for examination or for further action except as provided by this part, or upon order of the Commissioner to expedite the business of the Office, or upon filing of a request under paragraph (b) of this section or upon filing a petition under paragraphs (c) or (d) of this section with a verified showing which, in the opinion of the Commissioner, will justify so advancing it.

> (b) Applications wherein the inventions are deemed of peculiar importance to some branch of the public service and the head of some department of the Government requests immediate action for that reason, may be advanced for examination.

> (c) A petition to make an application special may be filed without a fee if the basis for the petition is the applicant's age or health or that the invention will materially enhance the quality of the environment or materially contribute to the development or conservation of energy resources.

> (d) A petition to make special on grounds other than those referred to in paragraph (c) of this section must be accompanied by the petition fee set forth in § 1.17(I).[20] The fee for petition is $130.[21]

The above rule is clear that, unless some government department head happens to file a request to expedite on your behalf, the first step for having an application examined out of order is to ask for it by filing a Petition to Make Special. Of course, one of the reasons the pendency time is long is that there are many applications waiting to be prosecuted. It would quickly become a free-for-all if everyone requested special handling. Therefore, Petitions to Make Special are granted only on a showing of special conditions.

It is interesting that some petitions require a fee and some do not. If the applicant is 65 years of age (proved by birth certificate),[22] or if the applicant is in failing health and may be unable to assist in prosecuting the application

---

[19] 37 C.F.R. § 1.102.

[20] *Id.*

[21] *Id.* § 1.17(i).

[22] U.S. Dep't of Commerce, IV *Applicant's Age,* Manual of Pat. Examining Proc. § 708.02 (Mar. 1994).

(proved by doctor's certificate),[23] no fee is required. The remaining "no fee required" petitions all focus, not on the applicant, but on the importance of the invention to the public. It is expected that the list of important inventions may change over time. Here is the current list, not necessarily in order of importance:

Environmental Quality

Energy

Recombinant DNA

Superconductivity.

The Environmental Quality category refers to those inventions that "materially enhance the quality of the environment of mankind by contributing to the restoration or maintenance of the basic life-sustaining natural elements— air, water, and soil.[24]

The Energy category refers to those inventions that "materially contribute to (1) the discovery or development of energy resources, or (2) the more efficient utilization and conservation of energy resources."[25] The *Manual of Patent Examining Procedure* gives several examples of both categories, including in category (1) developments in fossil fuels, nuclear energy, and solar energy, and including in category (2) inventions in reducing energy consumption in combustion systems, industrial equipment, and household appliances.

The energy conservation category is one to keep in mind when applying for software patents, particularly if it is possible to demonstrate that the software invention is more energy efficient than its older mechanical counterpart.

The Recombinant DNA category refers to inventions "relating to the safety of research in the field of recombinant DNA."[26] This category is particularly interesting, because it deals not with DNA research itself, but with the possible hazards and safety practices in conducting DNA research.

The Superconductivity category refers to inventions involving superconductivity materials, including the materials themselves and their manufacture and application.[27]

---

[23] U.S. Dep't of Commerce, III *Applicant's Health,* Manual of Pat. Examining Proc. § 708.02 (Mar. 1994).

[24] U.S. Dep't of Commerce, V *Environmental Quality,* Manual of Pat. Examining Proc. § 708.02 (Mar. 1994).

[25] U.S. Dep't of Commerce, VI *Energy,* Manual of Pat. Office Examining Proc. § 708.02.

[26] U.S. Dep't of Commerce, VII *Inventions Relating to Recombinant DNA,* Manual of Pat. Office Examining Proc. § 708.02.

[27] U.S. Dep't of Commerce, *Special Status for Patent Applications Relating to Superconductivity,* Manual of Pat. Office Examining Proc. § 708.02.

Unfortunately, software is not on the above list. Does this mean that software inventions are not eligible for priority treatment? Not necessarily. There are still a few grounds left to discuss. These pertain to prospective manufacture and infringement, both seemingly related to financial hardship or opportunity lost if a patent is not granted quickly.

If an applicant is in a position to manufacture the invention, but needs a patent to convince the manufacturer to proceed, then the applicant may petition to make special based on "prospective manufacture." If the applicant believes someone is infringing the claimed invention, and has a solid basis for this belief, then the applicant may petition to make special based on this infringement.

§ 8.13 —Prospective Manufacture as a Basis for Expedited Prosecution

The prospective manufacture basis for expedited prosecution is interesting, for it appears to have great possibilities for expediting software patent applications. The *Manual of Patent Examining Procedure* states explicitly what is required. The applicant or the applicant's assignee must allege under oath or declaration:

1. The possession by the prospective manufacturer of sufficient presently available capital (stating approximately the amount) and facilities (stating briefly the nature thereof) to manufacture the invention in quantity or that sufficient capital and facilities will be made available if a patent is granted;

If the prospective manufacturer is an individual, there must be a corroborating affidavit from some responsible party, as for example, an officer of a bank, showing that said individual has the required available capital to manufacture.

2. That the prospective manufacturer will not manufacture, or will not increase present manufacture, unless certain that the patent will be granted;

3. That affiant obligates himself or herself or the prospective manufacturer, to manufacture the invention, in the United States or its possessions, in quantity immediately upon the allowance of claims or issuance of a patent which will protect the investment of capital and facilities.

The attorney or agent of record in the application (or applicant, if not represented by an attorney or agent) must file an affidavit or declaration to show:

1. That the applicant or assignee has made or caused to be made a careful and thorough search of the prior art, or has a good knowledge of the pertinent prior art; and

2. That the applicant or assignee believes all of the claims in the application are allowable.[28]

---

[28] U.S. Dep't of Commerce, I *Manufacture,* Manual of Patent Examining Proc. § 708.02.

Not every software invention fits the above criteria, but some may. If you have a manufacturer capable of manufacturing in quantity, if the manufacturer will not commit to manufacture in quantity unless a patent is granted, and if the applicant is willing to commit to begin manufacturing in quantity in the United States, then you have a candidate for a prospective manufacture Petition to Make Special.

Consider the following scenario. The applicant's assignee is a software development company that has developed a new software development tool. The development tool embodies an invention for which a patent is sought. The development tool was originally constructed for use in-house. However, recognizing great market potential for the development tool, the company has approached a software manufacturer, which has agreed to manufacture and market the development tool, *provided* a patent is granted on the invention and the manufacturer is given exclusive manufacturing and distributing rights under the patent. In this scenario, the software developer may file a Petition to Make Special based on prospective manufacture.

§ 8.14   —Infringement as a Basis for Expedited Prosecution

The Petition to Make Special based on infringement is also applicable to software inventions. The *Manual of Patent Examining Procedure* states explicitly what is required. The applicant or the applicant's assignee must allege *facts* under oath or declaration to show, or indicating why it is not possible to show:

(1) that there is an infringing device or product actually on the market or method in use,

(2) when the device, product or method alleged to infringe was first discovered to exist; supplemented by an affidavit or declaration of the applicant's attorney or agent to show,

(3) that a rigid comparison of the alleged infringing device, product, or method with the claims of the application has been made,

(4) that, in his or her opinion, some of the claims are unquestionably infringed,

(5) that he or she has made or caused to be made a careful and thorough search of the prior art or has a good knowledge of the pertinent prior art, and

(6) that he or she believes all of the claims in the application are allowable.[29]

Note that, unlike the case of prospective manufacture, here the *attorney* must declare by affidavit that a search has been conducted or caused to be conducted, not simply that the applicant has done so; or the *attorney* must

---

[29] U.S. Dep't of Commerce, II *Infringement,* Manual of Patent Examining Proc. § 708.02.

claim by affidavit to have a good knowledge of the pertinent prior art. Further, the *attorney* must declare by affidavit that the attorney believes all of the claims in the application are allowable. Thus, in a Petition to Make Special based on infringement, the attorney becomes a fact witness. The implication of this is that in litigation under the patent, it may give defense counsel an argument that the court should pierce the attorney-client privilege and allow the patent attorney's deposition to be taken.[30]

In the prospective manufacture Petition to Make Special, although the attorney must file an affidavit or declaration, that affidavit or declaration needs only to state on information and belief that the *applicant* conducted a search, or caused one to be conducted, or that *applicant* has a good knowledge of the pertinent prior art, and that *applicant* believes all claims are allowable.

§ 8.15   Duty of Disclosure

The examiner's search for prior art is a big job. It is the applicant's responsibility to help, by disclosing to the Patent Office all pertinent prior art the applicant is aware of. 37 C.F.R. § 1.56 states this:

§ 1.56 Duty of Disclosure—Information Material To Patentability

(a) A patent by its very nature is affected with a public interest. The public is best served, and the most effective patent examination occurs when, at the time an application is being examined, the Office is aware of and evaluates the teachings of all information material to patentability. Each individual associated with the filing and prosecution of a patent application has a duty of candor and good faith in dealing with the Office, which includes a duty to disclose to the Office all information known to that individual to be material to patentability as defined in this section. The duty to disclose information exists with respect to each pending claim until the claim is canceled or withdrawn from consideration, or the application becomes abandoned. Information material to the patentability of a claim that is canceled or withdrawn from consideration need not be submitted if the information is not material to the patentability of any claim remaining under consideration in the application. There is no duty to submit information which is not material to the patentability of any existing claim. The duty to disclose all information known to be material to patentability is deemed to be satisfied if all information known to be material to patentability of any claim issued in a patent was cited by the Office or submitted to the Office in the manner prescribed by §§ 1.97(b)–(d) and 1.98. However, no patent will be granted on an application in connection with which fraud on the Office was practiced or attempted or the duty of disclosure was violated through bad faith or intentional misconduct . . . .[31]

---

[30] For a discussion of attorney-client privilege, see **Ch. 5.**

[31] 37 C.F.R. § 1.56(a).

Aside from being required, it is to the applicant's advantage to disclose all pertinent prior art, because the resulting patent is presumed valid over all art the Patent Office considered.

Who has a duty of disclosure? As the rule language suggests, the duty of disclosure is now borne by more than just the patent applicant. The duty of disclosure now extends to any "individuals associated with the filing or prosecution" of the application. 37 C.F.R. § 1.56(c) makes it clear that this includes not only the applicant, but the applicant's patent attorney or patent agent, and may include the applicant's company supervisor, if the supervisor is substantively involved in the preparation or prosecution of the application:

(c) Individuals associated with the filing or prosecution of a patent application within the meaning of this section are:

(1) Each inventor named in the application;

(2) Each attorney or agent who prepares or prosecutes the application; and

(3) Every other person who is substantively involved in the preparation or prosecution of the application and who is associated with the inventor, with the assignee or with anyone to whom there is an obligation to assign the application.[32]

What information must be disclosed? 37 C.F.R. § 1.56 states that you must disclose information known to be "material to patentability." Material to patentability is defined as follows:

(b) Under this section, information is material to patentability when it is not cumulative to information already of record or being made of record in the application, and

(1) It establishes, by itself or in combination with other information, a *prima facie* case of unpatentability of a claim; or

(2) It refutes, or is inconsistent with, a position the applicant takes in:

  (i) Opposing an argument of unpatentability relied on the by Office, or

  (ii) Asserting an argument of patentability.[33]

In the above rule, an objective standard of materiality is used. The standard of materiality is whether a prima facie case of unpatentability is established. In practice under the rule prior to the current rule, a more subjective standard was used. Under the prior rule, materiality was judged by whether the information was such that there was "a substantial likelihood that a reasonable Examiner would consider it important in deciding whether to allow the application to issue as a patent."

---

[32] *Id.* § 1.56(c).

[33] *Id.* § 1.56(b).

The prior rule was criticized because it arguably allowed litigants to charge patentees with inequitable conduct based on allegedly withheld or misrepresented information not affecting patentability.[34] The current rule is intended to alleviate this problem. In its Notice of Final Rulemaking, the Patent Office stated its intentions regarding the new materiality standard:

> The amendment to § 1.56 was proposed to address criticism concerning a perceived lack of certainty in the materiality standard. The rule as promulgated will provide greater clarity and hopefully minimize the burden of litigation on the question of inequitable conduct before the Office, while providing the Office with the information necessary for effective and efficient examination of patent applications.[35]

Thus the current rule has replaced "reasonable examiner" materiality with "prima facie unpatentability" materiality. The current rule spells out what constitutes a prima facie case of unpatentability:

> A prima facie case of unpatentability is established when the information compels a conclusion that a claim is unpatentable under the preponderance of evidence, burden-of-proof standard, giving each term in the claim its broadest reasonable construction consistent with the specification, and before any consideration is given to evidence which may be submitted in an attempt to establish a contrary conclusion of patentability.[36]

Where are you likely to find information that should be disclosed? The Patent Office Rules make these suggestions:

> The Office encourages applicants to carefully examine:
>
> (1) prior art cited in search reports of a foreign patent office in a counterpart application, and
>
> (2) the closest information over which individuals associated with the filing or prosecution of a patent application believe any pending claim patentably defines, to make sure that any material information contained therein is disclosed to the Office.[37]

The first item suggested by the above rule is straightforward. If the present application has been foreign filed, or if a parent application of the present application has been foreign-filed, carefully consider disclosing to the U.S. Patent Office all art cited in the search reports of the foreign patent office or

---

[34] Rene D. Tegtmeyer, *Refocusing on Inequitable Conduct in New Rule 56,* 20 AIPLA Q. J. Nos. 3, 4 at 191, 194 (1992).

[35] 57 Fed. Reg. 2021 (1992).

[36] 37 C.F.R. § 1.56(b).

[37] *Id.* § 1.56(a).

offices. Although the rule says applicants are encouraged to "carefully examine" foreign-cited prior art, there is little reason not to simply disclose all foreign-cited art as a matter of course. If the art was considered pertinent enough for a foreign patent office to cite it, it is difficult to imagine how the art would not be pertinent in domestic prosecution.

The second item suggested by the above rule needs further explaining. Some patent attorneys used to believe, perhaps incorrectly, that if the claims patentably distinguish the applicant's invention from a prior art reference, then that reference can be ignored. The current rule dispels this belief by requiring the attorney to consider the art of which the attorney is aware, even if the pending claims patentability distinguish over that art. The current rule does not remove the patent attorney's dilemma, however.

> To disclose, or not to disclose, that is the question:
>
> Whether 'tis nobler in the mind to suffer
>
> The slings and arrows of outrageous prosecution,
>
> Or to take arms against a sea of troubles,
>
> During litigation.

§ 8.16   —Mechanics of Information Disclosure

To ensure that the pertinent prior art is disclosed in time for the examiner to consider it, 37 C.F.R. §§ 1.97 and 1.98 set forth guidelines:

§ 1.97 Filing of information disclosure statement.

(a) In order to have information considered by the Office during the pendency of a patent application, an information disclosure statement in compliance with § 1.98 should be filed in accordance with this section.

(b) An information disclosure statement shall be considered by the Office if filed:

(1) Within three months of the filing date of a national application;

(2) Within three months of the date of entry of the national stage as set forth in § 1.491 in an international application; or

(3) Before the mailing date of a first Office action on the merits, whichever event occurs last.

(c) an information disclosure statement shall be considered by the Office if filed after the period specified in paragraph (b) of this section, but before the mailing date of either:

(1) A final action under § 1.113 or

(2) A notice of allowance under § 1.311,

whichever occurs first, provided the statement is accompanied by either a certification as specified in paragraph (3) of this section or the fee set forth in § 1.17(p).

(d) An information disclosure statement shall be considered by the Office if filed after the mailing date of either:

(1) A final action under § 1.113 or

(2) A notice of allowance under § 1.311,

whichever occurs first, but before payment of the issue fee, provided the statement is accompanied by:

(i) A certification as specified in paragraph (e) of this section,

(ii) A petition requesting consideration of the information disclosure statement, and

(iii) The petition fee set forth in § 1.17(I)(1).

§ 8.17   Software Patent Hearings

In response to criticism by the software development community, the Commissioner of the Patent Office held hearings commencing in late 1993 to consider the public's view towards software patents. The software development community was up in arms over the issuance of number of patents that they believed to be invalid for obviousness and lack of novelty. The hearings were held in San Jose, California on January 26 and 27, 1994, to give the software community in Silicon Valley an opportunity to express their views. Further hearings were held in Washington, D.C. on February 10 and 11, 1994, to give the patent community an opportunity to express their views. Both sessions drew diverse crowds from all over the United States, and from around the world.[38]

One of the observations made by many at the hearings was that the Patent Office does not have an adequate collection of software prior art. This should come as no surprise. Throughout the 1970s and 1980s software was believed to be unpatentable subject matter, in large part due to the *Gottschalk v. Benson*[39] decision. Hence during those years, virtually no one submitted software patent applications and the Patent Office software prior art collection had no chance to stay current with the state-of-the-art. Today the Patent Office is still trying to recover.

Issued patents are the most convenient form of prior art for the Patent Office to search, since these are classified in a manner familiar to all patent examiners. However, given the current shortage of issued software patents, searching only the patent literature may not give an accurate picture of the state of the art. For a more accurate picture, the Patent Office may also need

---

[38] A transcript of the hearings appears in **App. A.**

[39] 409 U.S. 63 (1972).

to search technical journals, trade literature, software user documentation, and in some cases, even software source code.

Understand that searching these nonpatent sources is very difficult. There is currently no practical way for a patent examiner to search all of these nonpatent sources. This is why the duty of disclosure is particularly important in software patent applications. To the extent the applicant and applicant's counsel can supplement the examiner's search with nonpatent art, the stronger the issued patent will be and ultimately the more respected software patents in general will be.

§ 8.18   Disclosing Software Prior Art

What nonpatent information should be submitted? 37 C.F.R. § 1.56(a) suggests considering the closest information of which you and the applicant are aware, even if the claims patentably distinguish over that information. Of course, the rule requires submitting only art that is material to patentability (for example, that which makes a prima facie case of unpatentability).[40] However, given the current scrutiny software patents are given once issued, consider submitting all pertinent information, even though the claims clearly distinguish over that information. The information you submit will help the examiner, not only in your application, but in later applications of others.

Information to consider citing falls into several categories:

1. Prior versions of software that the present embodiment of the invention replaces. In other words, if the invention is embodied in software version 6.0, cite prior version 5.2.

2. Trade journal articles that address the subject matter of the invention, particularly those that discuss the problem the invention solves or related problems. Nearly every technical field has one or more trade journals. These are frequently a very good indicator of the state of the art because that is why readers subscribe.

3. Textbook algorithms and data structures used as key building blocks of the software embodying the invention. Citing this type of information may not be necessary to assist examiners who have a computer science education. However, keep in mind that many examiners do not have this background. The other advantage of citing this type of information is that it demonstrates to the examiner, and to others who may later read the file history, that you are not trying to claim well-known textbook algorithms or well-known textbook data structures.

---

[40] 37 C.F.R. § 1.56(a)–(b).

4. Beta testing and other experimental uses of the invention that took place more than one year before the application filing date. This category is not restricted to software inventions. Anytime there is a use of the invention more than one year before the application filing date, and you have determined an "experimental use" exception applies, bring this information to the attention of the Patent Office.[41] This issue arises frequently with software inventions because software is frequently beta tested. If you have the opportunity to counsel a software developer before beta testing has commenced, be sure all beta test sites receive the software under written agreement that supports the experimental use exception.

§ 8.19   —Citing Prior Software Versions

How do you cite prior versions of software to the Patent Office? The Patent Office is geared to accept information in printed form. Submitting a prior version on diskette will not do. This is not a case of the Patent Office being technologically antiquated. Rather, it is a case that the current diskette medium, whatever that may be, will eventually become outmoded. Plainly, to be useful to the Patent Office in the future, any prior art you submit must have greater longevity than the 8-inch floppy disk or the Hollerith card.

There are several options for submitting a prior version of software in printed form. One is to submit the source code; however for a number of reasons this may not be the best way. Source code is difficult to read. Even well-commented source code can be slow reading for one unfamiliar with the code. (Well-commented source code contains detailed marginal notes explaining what the code can do.) Moreover the examiner is usually interested in the functions and features of the prior version, not its implementation details. Source code can tend to hide functions or features. Finally, the applicant may wish to treat the source code of the prior version as confidential.

A better way to submit a prior version is to submit the user manual and related user documentation. If the documentation is relatively few pages, that is, less than 50, submit the entire manual. In this way the patent examiner can place the entire manual in one of the shoes in the examiners' search room for future reference. If the documentation is voluminous, you may wish to submit only the title page, showing publication date, table of contents, index, and pertinent sections of the manual germane to the functions and features sought to be patented.

If you believe the patentable difference lies in the presence of new functions or features not found in the prior version, then the user documentation

---

[41] If it is determined that the experimental use exception does not apply, the requirements of 35 U.S.C. § 102(b) are not met and the application should not be filed.

of the prior version should be sufficient to show the new functions or features are absent in the prior art version. However, if the patentable difference lies in the way a known function or feature has been constructed, then the user documentation may not be sufficient. In this case, you may wish to submit a technical description of the prior version, similar in detail to a patent specification. It may be necessary to draft this technical description yourself, based on information received from the prior version developers. The drafted technical description should be supported by affidavit of a person with knowledge that it fully and accurately describes the prior version.

This may seem like a lot of work, but consider the benefit. In litigation under the patent, defense counsel will raise the existence of the prior version as prior art to invalidate the patent. If you have disclosed the prior version, there is nothing for defense counsel to effectively challenge. Because the Patent Office considered the prior version, the patent is legally presumed valid over the prior version.

In citing the user manual to the Patent Office, recognize that the Patent Office will likely treat the user manual as a printed publication. In other words, you are actually disclosing the publication and not necessarily the prior software version itself. A printed publication can be a statutory bar under 35 U.S.C. §§ 102(a) or 102(b). Under 35 U.S.C. § 102(a) a person is not entitled to a patent if the invention was described in a printed publication before the invention date; similarly under 35 U.S.C. § 102(b) a person is not entitled to a patent if the invention was described in a printed publication more than one year prior to the patent application date.

As prior art, the Patent Office is likely to regard the software itself, not as a printed publication, but as evidence that the invention was known or used by others and hence lacks novelty under 35 U.S.C. §§ 102(a) or 102(b). Under 35 U.S.C. § 102(a) a person is not entitled to a patent if the invention was known or used by others in the United States before the invention date; similarly under 35 U.S.C. § 102(b) a person is not entitled to a patent if the invention was in public use or on sale in the United States before the application date.

Usually citing the publication instead of the software itself is not a problem, provided the user manual fully and accurately describes the functions and features that are germane to the issue of patentability. Where a problem can arise is if the function or feature in question is an undocumented function or feature. Software developers are familiar with the notion of the undocumented function or feature. Many software packages include a README file on disk, as a supplement to the printed user manual. These README files should therefore be checked, in the same way pocket parts in law books are checked. Also, be aware that some software packages provide complete documentation as online HELP files embedded in the program. To save cost, some software packages do not contain full documentation in the printed user manual. If you encounter this situation, you can usually use the online help system to print a hard copy of the topics of interest.

§ 8.20   Appeal Process

When the application has been twice rejected, the applicant may appeal to the Board of Patent Appeals and Interferences. The Board of Patent Appeals and Interferences is an administrative appeals board made up for the most part of former patent office examiners. Technically, the Board is not a court. It is part of the executive branch of government, whereas a court is part of the judicial branch of government.

Applicants dissatisfied with a decision of the Board of Patent Appeals and Interferences have two options for further review. One option is to appeal from the Board, directly to the Court of Appeals for the Federal Circuit. The other option is to sue the Commissioner in United States District Court. The first option, appeal, is governed by 35 U.S.C. § 141. The second option, civil action, is governed by 35 U.S.C § 145. If the second option is taken, the applicant can still ultimately appeal to the Court of Appeals for the Federal Circuit, since decisions of the United States District Court are reviewed by the Court of Appeals for the Federal Circuit.

If you decide to appeal, which option should you choose? By taking an appeal directly to the Federal Circuit, you bypass one opportunity to present testimony. In some cases such testimony can be helpful. In *Hirschfeld v. Banner,*[42] the applicant presented testimony to overcome the examiner's contention that the specification did not meet the enablement requirement.

Thus, in cases where the rejection turns on factual issues, consider seeking review in the United States District Court under 35 U.S.C § 145. On the other hand, where the rejection turns on a legal issue already well-framed by undisputed facts, you may prefer direct appeal to the Court of Appeals for the Federal Circuit under 35 U.S.C. § 141.

While the district court review and appeal remedies are available, in the vast majority of cases you should opt to simply file a continuation application and go back to the examiner for further consideration. There is a practical reason for this. Appeal and district court review both have a definite element of finality. If you convince the court to rule favorably, you get a patent. If you do not convince the court, you do not get a patent, and you lose the option of trying again in the Patent Office with a different tact. In other words, once the appeal strategy has been cast, there is no turning back.

In some cases you may have no choice but to appeal to the Court of Appeals for the Federal Circuit or to a United States District Court. The applicant may be satisfied with the scope of the claims and may be unwilling to narrow them further. Such a situation might occur, for example, where the invention is being infringed and the applicant cannot modify the claims further without jeopardizing the future suit for patent infringement.

---

[42] 462 F. Supp. 135 (D.D.C. 1978).

WHAT IS PATENTABLE SUBJECT MATTER

§ 9.1   Origins of § 101 Rejection

There are some things that simply cannot be patented. Breathing air and drinking water cannot be patented. A tennis serve and a golf swing cannot be patented. Solar flares and gravity cannot be patented. These examples appear intuitively obvious. Why is that? Laws of nature, methods of doing business, printed matter, and mathematical formulas are also not patentable. Why is that? **Chapter 9** explores these questions.

Chapter 1 presents a history of patents, dating far back into Middle Age England. As explained in that chapter, a patent is an inducement, an incentive, a reward. In medieval times a patent was an inducement designed to lure goods and technologies from foreign lands into England. Be the first to travel abroad and bring back new goods or technology, and get rewarded with letters patent—the exclusive right to sell the new goods or to profit by the new technology. That was the way it worked.

The medieval system of patents had a bright side. It lit the fires of ingenuity and helped lift the standard of living in England, which at that time was lagging far behind the rest of civilized Europe and Asia. The system had a dark side as well. Rooted in greed, the dark side cast the shadow of monopoly over many necessities of life (to the benefit of the crown and the crown's close friends).

There has always been a bright side and a dark side to the patent system. The sides are inseparable, just as two sides of the human personality are inseparable. The legal system of patents has this one simple goal: to allow the bright side to shine on innovation, and to keep the dark side in check.

In this regard, the United States patent system takes the following tack:

> Whoever invents or discovers any new and useful process, machine, manufacture, or composition of matter, or any new and useful improvement thereof, may obtain a patent therefor, subject to the conditions and requirements of this title.[1]

The above statutory language, commonly referred to as § 101, states, in positive terms, what subject matter is eligible to earn a patent. Looking on the bright side, the statutory language lists broad areas of technology: processes, machines, manufactured articles, compositions of matter, for which innovation is rewarded. To keep the dark side in check, only the enumerated subject matter is eligible to earn a patent. Elsewhere in the patent statute, the term of the patent is fixed to roughly two decades. The patent term is far shorter than the copyright term (currently 75 years for a corporation), for example.

It is instructive to compare 35 U.S.C. § 101 to the comparable statutory language in the European Patent Convention:

> (1) European patents shall be granted for any inventions which are susceptible of industrial application, which are new and which involve an inventive step.
>
> (2) The following in particular shall not be regarded as inventions within the meaning of paragraph 1:
>
> (a) discoveries, scientific theories and mathematical methods;
>
> (b) aesthetic creations;
>
> (c) schemes, rules and methods for performing mental acts, playing games or doing business, and programs for computers;
>
> (d) presentations of information.[2]

Note how the European law goes further than United States law by expressly listing certain things that are not patentable subject matter. Under European law, the list is not considered exhaustive, and software inventions may be patentable, despite the statutory exclusion of computer programs.

The issue of what is patentable subject matter is central to many software patents. Much can be learned about this issue by studying history, and in particular Supreme Court history. There are several important precomputer Supreme Court decisions that have shaped the law on this issue, and three Supreme Court decisions that have expressly ruled on software patentability. These decisions are discussed in the next sections.

---

[1] 35 U.S.C. § 101.

[2] Patentable Inventions, Art. 52(2), Eur. Pat. Convention (1973).

§ 9.2   Precomputer Software
Supreme Court Decisions

The Supreme Court interpretation of what is patentable subject matter dates back long before software patents. The Supreme Court first addressed software patents in 1972, in *Gottschalk v. Benson.*[3] This section reviews those pre-*Benson* Supreme Court decisions that developed the law on which *Benson* and the later cases rely. If you are primarily interested in what the Supreme Court's position has been on patentability of software, you may want to turn immediately to § **9.12.**

To many, the law in this area is confusing. What is patentable subject matter and what is not? Is computer software patentable subject matter or not? These are controversial issues. The primary objective of this chapter is to unify the diverse decisions in this area, and to uncover the common thread woven through the fabric of these decisions. Believe it or not, there is a common thread, discussed in § **9.41.**

§ 9.3   *—Neilson v. Harford*

Neilson v. Harford[4] is not a United States Supreme Court decision. It is an important 1841 decision of an English court. It is included here because several U.S. Supreme Court decisions cite it. The invention, the blast furnace, was described as follows: "a blast or current of air must be produced by bellows or other blowing apparatus, and is to be passed from the bellows, &c, into an air-vessel or receptacle, by means of a tube, pipe, or aperture, into the fire . . . ."[5]

The defendant asserted that the alleged invention is not patentable subject matter, because it claims a principle.

The English court upheld the patent, but not without admitting to being troubled by the issue of patentable subject matter. The problem the court faced was that the specification stated that the "size of the receptacle will depend on the blast necessary."[6] This description played to the defendant's argument that the invention was not a machine or apparatus, but sought to wholly preempt all use of the air blast principle. "The only question," the court stated, "is, whether on the whole the inventor has given sufficient information to the public by which the invention can, on the expiration of the term for which the patent is granted, be brought into public use without experiments or expense."[7]

---

[3] 409 U.S. 63 (1972).

[4] 151 Eng. Rep. 1266 (1841).

[5] *Id.* at 1266.

[6] *Id.* at 1274.

[7] *Id.* at 1272.

This case has been cited by the United States Supreme Court in several decisions. It is important because it shows that what you disclose (or fail to disclose) in the specification, will bear on whether the invention is patentable subject matter. In other words the concepts of § 112 and § 101 are intimately entwined. This case also demonstrates how overclaiming can get you into trouble. Here the patentee invented a blast furnace, but almost lost the patent by being accused of trying to patent the scientific facts that fire needs oxygen to burn and that hot air heats better than cold air.

Evidently *Neilson v. Harford*[8] created quite a stir among the United States patent bar of that era, for the U.S. Supreme Court analyzes this decision carefully in *O'Reilly v. Morse*[9] and *Tilghman v. Proctor*.[10] These cases are discussed in § 9.5 and § 9.8 respectively.

§ 9.4   —*Le Roy v. Tatham*

In *Le Roy v. Tatham*[11] the patent was for an improvement in the making of pipe. The patent disclosed an apparatus for making pipe, but the essential improvement was that these pipes were made of lead. The lead was formed under heat and pressure, so that it first melted and then cooled, resulting in a superior product. Simply, it was the melting property of lead that made the invention work.

The Supreme Court, with a lengthy dissent by Justice Nelson, held the invention did not constitute patentable subject matter. The majority emphasized the premise that a principle, in the abstract, is not patentable. According to the Court, "A principle, in the abstract, is a fundamental truth; an original cause; a motive."[12] Explaining the dividing line between patentable inventions and forbidden monopolies, the Court cited the example of a newly discovered form of energy or power:

Through the agency of machinery a new steam power may be said to have been generated. But no one can appropriate this power exclusively to himself, under the patent laws . . . . The same may be said of electricity, and of any other power in nature . . . . In all such cases, the processes used to extract, modify, and concentrate natural agencies, constitute the invention. The elements of the power exist; the invention is not in discovering them, but in applying them to useful objects.[13]

---

[8] *Id.*

[9] 56 U.S. 62 (1854).

[10] 102 U.S. 707 (1881).

[11] 55 U.S. 156 (1852).

[12] *Id.* at 173.

[13] *Id.*

Again, the Court looked to the patent specification, to see if the claimed invention was patentable subject matter:

A new property discovered in matter, when practically applied, in the construction of a useful article of commerce or manufacture, is patentable; but the process through which the new property is developed and applied, must be stated, with such precision as to enable an ordinary mechanic to construct and apply the necessary process.[14]

This case reveals an important concept. To be a patentable invention, there must be more than merely the discovery of a property existing in nature. The *disclosure* must show that the inventor is able to exert physical control over the discovered property. The invention must extract, modify, and concentrate a property of nature, not merely identify or name that property of nature.

§ 9.5   —*O'Reilly v. Morse*

O'Reilly v. Morse[15] involved a Copenhagen scientist named Oersted, who discovered electromagnetism in the winter of 1819–20. During the decade that followed, several prominent inventors saw Oersted's miraculous new form of energy as a possible way to communicate at a distance. Many tried, but Samuel Morse is credited as the one who first made it happen.[16] Morse's telegraph device solved the problem of how to put electromagnetic energy into one end of a long wire and receive the minuscule amount of energy remaining after the long journey to the other end so that it could be used to print intelligible characters. The U.S. Patent Office granted Morse a patent in 1840 and reissued it in 1948.

Morse brought suit on his patent, and the case rose to the Supreme Court, primarily because of patent claim 8, which read:

I do not propose to limit myself to the specific machinery or parts of machinery described in the foregoing specification and claims; the essence of my invention being the use of the motive power of the electric or galvanic current, which I call electromagnetism, however developed, for marking or printing intelligible characters, signs or letters, at any distances, being a new application of that power of which I claim to be the first inventor or discoverer.[17]

---

[14] *Id.*

[15] 56 U.S. 62 (1854).

[16] European readers may not agree that Morse was the first. Steinheil, Wheatstone, and Davy also lay claim to being first.

[17] O'Reilly v. Morse, 56 U.S. 62, 112 (1854).

The Supreme Court upheld the first seven claims of Morse's patent (including one that might be the first software patent); however, claim 8 was simply too broad, and the Supreme Court struck it down. The Court cited, with approval, the English case, *Neilson v. Harford*[18] (discussed in § 9.3) and questioned whether Morse had sought claim 8 because he had misconstrued that case.[19] The Supreme Court contrasted the Neilson's claim with Morse's:

> Undoubtedly, the principle that hot air will promote the ignition of fuel better than cold, was embodied in this machine [of Neilson]. But the patent was not supported because this principle was embodied in it . . . his [Neilson's] patent was supported because he had invented a mechanical apparatus, by which a current of hot air, instead of cold, could be thrown in.
>
> *   *   *
>
> But Professor Morse has not discovered that the electric or galvanic current will always print at a distance, no matter what may be the form of the machinery or mechanical contrivances through which it passes.[20]

In essence, the Supreme Court struck down Morse's claim 8 because it claimed more than Morse had truly invented. To make this point, the Court noted:

> If this claim can be maintained, it matters not by what process or machinery the result is accomplished. For ought that we now know some future inventor, in the onward march of science, may discover by means of the electric or galvanic current, without using any part of the process or combination set forth in the plaintiff's specification. His invention may be less complicated—less liable to get out of order—less expensive in construction, and in its operation. But yet if it is covered by this patent the inventor could not use it, nor the public have the benefit of it without the permission of this patentee.[21]

§ 9.6   —*Rubber Tip Pencil Co. v. Howard*

You are no doubt familiar with the rubber eraser that slips over the end of a pencil. James E. Blair got a patent on that in 1869. Blair had not discovered that rubber will erase pencil marks. That discovery had already been made. Blair's invention was claimed as "a new article of manufacture, an elastic, erasive pencil head, made substantially as in the manner described."[22]

---

[18] 151 Eng. Rep. 1266 (1841).

[19] O'Reilly v. Morse, 56 U.S. 62, 117 (1854).

[20] *Id.* at 117–18.

[21] *Id.* at 112–13.

[22] Rubber Tip Pencil Co. v. Howard, 87 U.S. 489 (1874).

The problem was that Blair's claim could only be interpreted in light of the teachings in his specification; and his specification left everything open to design choice. For instance, the eraser could be of rubber or rubber and some other material. Its shape could be any convenient external form. It could have a socket to receive one end of a pencil, and that socket could be of any shape. And so forth.

In the patent infringement litigation, the defense offered into evidence a rubber nipple, not designed to erase pencil marks, but a device which did fit onto the end of a pencil and that one witness testified he had used to erase pencil marks.

The Court took little time in ruling Blair's patent invalid, stating "[t]he idea of this patentee was a good one, but his device to give it effect, though useful, was not new. Consequently, he took nothing by his patent."[23]

Today the Patent Office will not allow omnibus claims, directed as Blair's claim was, to a device "made substantially as described."[24] Nevertheless, the error Blair made is still made today. Trying to cover every possible embodiment of his idea, he wrote his specification like a broad, open-ended claim. The result: "He took nothing by his patent."[25]

§ 9.7   —*Cochrane v. Deener*

In *Cochrane v. Deener*[26] the claimed invention was an improved process for making flour consisting of separating from the meal, first the superfine flour and then middlings meal. The middlings meal, when reground, was mixed with the superfine flour to produce a product of improved quality. During a patent infringement lawsuit, the defendants argued that the claimed invention was not patentable subject matter, because it was simply a process and was not limited to any arrangement of machinery.

The Supreme Court held that "a process may be patentable, irrespective of the particular form of the instrumentality's used."[27] This case is important because it decides that processes may be patentable subject matter. The law prior to this decision was not clear on that point. Many later cases build on this decision.

---

[23] *Id.* at 507.

[24] *Id.* Biotechnology claims are a possible exception.

[25] Rubber Tip Pencil Co. v. Howard, 87 U.S. 498, 507 (1874).

[26] 94 U.S. 780 (1877).

[27] *Id.* at 787.

§ 9.8 —*Tilghman v. Proctor*

In *Tilghman v. Proctor*[28] the invention was a treatment of fats and oils used in such products as margarine. The invention was a process of separating the fats and oils into their component parts using water action at high temperature and pressure. In the patent infringement litigation, the defendants argued that they were not using the apparatus or the high temperatures described in the patent. Defendant's process used heated water under pressure, but at a lower temperature and mixed with lime (lime was used in another prior art technique). Defendants argued that to construe the patent to cover them gave the plaintiff a patent on the principle of using heated water under pressure.

The Supreme Court addressed the issue head on, asking, "What did Tilghman discover?" The Court reasoned that "[h]ad the process been known and used before and not been Tilghman's invention, he could not then have claimed anything more than the particular apparatus described in his patent; but being the inventor of the process, as we are satisfied was the fact, he was entitled to claim it in the manner he did."[29] Thus, although in his patent Tilghman recommends a high degree of heat, the Court did not limit him to the temperature stated and defendants were found to infringe.

In reaching that decision, the Supreme Court had to decide whether Tilghman's discovery was a patentable process or an unpatentable principle. The Court resolved that question by looking at the scope of Tilghman's claim. The Court pointing out that Tilghman "only claims to have invented a particular mode of bringing about the desired chemical union between the fatty elements and water. He does not claim every mode of accomplishing this result."[30] To bolster its reasoning, the Court pointed out several other known ways of accomplishing the result of Tilghman's process, for example, lime saponification, and sulfuric acid distillation.

Tilghman contains a valuable practice tip for drafting software patents (or any patent involving a process). When drafting broad claims, keep the claim scope in context with other prior art techniques. Then you will be able to demonstrate, as Tilghman did, that the claim does not cover an unpatentable principle, because other prior technologies also employ the principle.

§ 9.9 —*Expanded Metal Co. v. Bradford*

If you frequent building supply stores you have probably seen expanded sheet metal screen or lath with diamond-shaped openings made from a single sheet of metal. If you have not, expanded sheet metal screen may be generally

---

[28] 102 U.S. 707 (1881).

[29] *Id.* at 721–22.

[30] *Id.* at 729.

described as metal openwork, held together by uncut portions of the metal, and constructed by making cuts or slashes in the metal and then opening or expanding the cuts to form a latticework. The claimed invention in *Expanded Metal Co. v. Bradford*[31] was a method of making expanded sheet metal screens.

The case rose to the Supreme Court on two conflicting writs of certiorari. The Third Circuit had ruled the patent invalid; the Sixth Circuit had ruled the patent valid. At issue was the fundamental question of whether mechanical processes are patentable subject matter. In prior decisions the patentable processes had involved chemical action. Unlike the patent statute today, the patent statute of that era did not include express language that a process was patentable subject matter.

The Supreme Court explained, "the word 'process' has been brought into the decisions because it is supposedly an equivalent form of expression, or included in the statutory designation of a new and useful art."[32] The Court had little difficulty holding that processes of all types, not just chemical processes, are patentable subject matter. As part if its rationale, the Court cited the following language from *Tilghman:*

> A machine is a thing. A process is an act, or a mode of acting. The one is visible to the eye,—an object of perpetual observation. The other is a conception of the mind,—seen only by its effects when being executed or performed. Either may be the means of producing a useful result.[33]

§ 9.10   —*MacKay Radio & Telegraph Co. v. Radio Corp. of America*

In *MacKay Radio & Telegraph Co. v. Radio Corp. of America*[34] the invention was a radio antenna. The antenna was shaped in the form of a V, at an angle described by a mathematical formula. The V-shape gave the antenna a desirable directional property. The patentee did not invent the formula. It had been discovered and published in a scientific journal thirty years before. The Court stated that the antenna was patentable subject matter, notwithstanding the mathematical language stating:

> While a scientific truth, or the mathematical expression of it, is not patentable invention, a novel and useful structure created with the aid of knowledge of scientific truth may be.[35]

---

[31] Expanded Metal Co. v. Bradford, 214 U.S. 366, 382 (1909).

[32] *Id.* at 384.

[33] *Id.* at 382 (citing Tilghman v. Proctor, 102 U.S. 707, 728 (1881)).

[34] MacKay Radio & Tel. Co. v. Radio Corp. of Am., 306 U.S. 86 (1939).

[35] *Id.* at 94.

The Court narrowly construed the claim and found that the patent was not infringed. This case is occasionally cited for the proposition that a mathematical expression is not patentable. More correctly, it is a scientific truth, or the mathematical expression of a scientific truth, that is not patentable. Keep in mind that mathematics is simply a very precise language or means of describing something. It can be used to describe scientific truths and features of patentable inventions alike. As this case demonstrates, if a mathematical expression is used to describe a useful structure created with the aid of knowledge of the scientific truth, the useful structure is patentable subject matter.

§ 9.11   —*Funk Bros. v. Kalo Co.*

In this case the Supreme Court declared the patent was invalid. The patentee had discovered that the nitrogen fixing ability of leguminous plants could be improved by mixing certain naturally occurring strains of different species of root-nodule bacteria and inoculating the plants with the mixture. The strains were selected because they could coexist, without inhibiting the effect of each other as other strains would do.

The Court held the patent invalid, stating:

> He who discovers a hitherto unknown phenomenon of nature has no claim to a monopoly of it which the law recognizes. If there is to be invention from such a discovery, it must come from the application of the law of nature to a new and useful end.[36]

Addressing whether this discovery qualified as an application of the law of nature, the Court ruled against the patentee:

> But however ingenious the discovery of that natural principle may have been, the application of it is hardly more than an advance in the packaging of the inoculates.

> *   *   *

> The combination of species produces no new bacteria, no change in the six species of bacteria, and no enlargement of the range of their utility. Each species has the same effect it always had.[37]

---

[36] Funk Bros. v. Kalo Co., 333 U.S. 127, 130 (1948).
[37] *Id.* at 131.

§ 9.12   *Gottschalk v. Benson*

Gottschalk v. Benson[38] is the first Supreme Court decision to address the software patent, and the patent was struck down as being unpatentable subject matter. Decided in 1972, during the reign of the IBM 360/375 mainframe computer, many viewed this decision as a condemnation of all software patents. It was not. The Supreme Court stated, "It is said that the decision precludes a patent for any program servicing a computer. We do not so hold."[39] However few took this statement to heart, for during the decade that followed *Gottschalk v. Benson* virtually no one sought software patents. No doubt the anti-software patent attitude within the Patent Office at the time contributed.

The *Benson* case found itself in the Supreme Court because Acting Commissioner of Patents, Robert Gottschalk, petitioned on behalf of the U.S. Patent Office for a writ of certiorari. The Patent Office had rejected claims 8 and 13 of Benson's application and the Court of Customs and Patent Appeals reversed.[40]

§ 9.13   —Numbering Systems in *Gottschalk v. Benson*

The invention in *Gottschalk v. Benson*[41] is a process for converting binary coded decimal numbers (BCD) into pure binary numbers. Why the big fight over this rather esoteric subject? One possible explanation is this. Computers use binary numbers. Many electronic devices use BCD. For example, most of the digital readouts found in calculators, digital clocks, microwave ovens, and VCRs internally use BCD numbers. Thus for a computer or microprocessor to read these devices, it needs to be able to convert BCD numbers into binary numbers. Here is what you need to know about these numbering systems in order to follow *Benson*.

People count in base ten. The Arabic numbering system that the entire world uses is a base ten numbering system. Why base ten? Probably because people have ten digits on their two hands and naturally learned to count using these digits.

Computers, on the other hand, count in base two. The binary numbering system is a base two numbering system. Why base two? Simply, computers do not have ten fingers. Computers have only electrical impulses, which can be either turned ON or turned OFF. It is as if computers have only two fingers—ON and OFF. Thus computers must count using only these two digits.

---

[38] 409 U.S. 63 (1972).

[39] *Id.* at 71.

[40] *In re* Benson, 441 F.2d 682 (C.C.P.A. 1971).

[41] 409 U.S. 63 (1972).

Binary numbers, while easy for computers, are difficult for people to read. The number 53 (in base ten) looks like 110101 (in base two). Imagine trying to balance your checkbook using the binary numbering system. It would be next to impossible. Thus, it is clear that you need a way to convert back and forth between decimal (base ten) numbers and binary (base two) numbers. That conversion, however, is not what *Benson* is about. *Benson* involves something more. It involves converting from "binary coded decimal" numbers to binary numbers. Thus you need to know about the binary coded decimal numbering system.

The binary coded decimal (or BCD) numbering system is a base ten system. Only it uses *binary digits* as replacements for the standard Arabic digits with which you are familiar. The best way to understand BCD is to see an example. The number 53 (in decimal numbers) is represented as 0101 0011 (in BCD). To understand what is going on here, note that in a decimal system the number 53 is made up of two side-by-side digits, a 5 and a 3. If you replace the Arabic digit 5 with its binary equivalent 0101, and if you replace the Arabic digit 3 with its binary equivalent 0011, and if you place those substituted digits side-by-side, you get 0101 0011, which is the BCD equivalent for the number 53.

§ 9.14   —Claims at Issue in *Gottschalk v. Benson*

At issue in *Gottschalk v. Benson*[42] were two claims, differently phrased, but covering essentially the same thing:

> 8.   The method of converting signals from binary coded decimal form into binary which comprises the steps of
> (1)   storing the binary coded decimal signals in a re-entrant shift register,
> (2)   shifting the signals to the right by at least three places, until there is a binary '1' in the second position of said register,
> (3)   masking out said binary '1' in said second position of said register,
> (4)   adding a binary '1' to the first position of said register,
> (5)   shifting the signals to the left by two positions,
> (6)   adding a '1' to said first position, and
> (7)   shifting the signals to the right by at least three positions in preparation for a succeeding binary '1' in the second position of said register.
> 13.   A data processing method for converting binary coded decimal number representations into binary number representations comprising the steps of
> (1)   testing each binary digit position '1,' beginning with the least significant binary digit position, of the most significant decimal digit representation for a binary '0' or a binary '1';

---

[42] 409 U.S. 63 (1972).

(2)   if a binary '0' is detected, repeating step (1) for the next least significant binary digit position of said most significant decimal digit representation;

(3)   if a binary '1' is detected, adding a binary '1' at the (i + 1)th and (i + 3)th least significant binary digit positions of the next lesser significant decimal digit representation, and repeating step (1) for the next least significant binary digit position of said most significant decimal digit representation;

(4)   upon exhausting the binary digit positions of said most significant decimal digit representation, repeating steps (1) through (3) for the next lesser significant decimal digit representation as modified by the previous execution of steps (1) through (3); and

(5)   repeating steps (1) through (4) until the second least significant decimal digit representation has been so processed.[43]

Although claim 8 recites use of a "re-entrant shift register" and claim 13 recites a "data processing" method, you can practice both methods with pencil and paper. Try it yourself. Try following claim 13 to convert BCD equivalent of 53 into pure binary:

0101 001; BCD for 53

0110 101; binary for 53

§ 9.15   —Holding in *Gottschalk v. Benson*

Justice Douglas wrote the opinion of the Court. He frames the issue as "whether the method described and claimed is a 'process' within the meaning of the Patent Act."[44] Previous Supreme Court decisions held that the discovery of a new and useful process was patentable subject matter; whereas the discovery of a new and useful principle was not.[45] For background on some of these decisions, see preceding §§ **9.2–9.11.**

In contrast the statutory backdrop to some of the earlier Supreme Court decisions on this issue, the Patent Act of 1952 contains an express definition of the term process. "The term 'process' means process, art or method, and includes a new use of a known process, machine, manufacture, composition of matter, or material."[46] Under prior patent acts, the term "process" was not defined, but was nevertheless treated as patentable subject matter as an equivalent form of expression, or included in the statutory designation of a new and useful art."[47]

---

[43] *Id.* at 73.

[44] Gottschalk v. Benson, 409 U.S. 63, 64 (1972).

[45] MacKay Radio & Tel. Co. v. Radio Corp. of Am., 306 U.S. 86 (1939); Rubber Tip Pencil Co. v. Howard, 87 U.S. 498 (1874); Le Roy v. Tatham, 55 U.S. 156 (1852).

[46] 35 U.S.C. § 100(b).

[47] Expanded Metal Co. v. Bradford, 214 U.S. 366, 382 (1909).

After reviewing several of the Supreme Court's prior decisions on the patentability issue, Justice Douglas, in a single paragraph, found the BCD conversion routine did not pass muster:

> It is conceded that one may not patent an idea. But in practical effect that would be the result if the formula for converting BCD numerals to pure binary numerals were patented in this case. The mathematical formula involved here has no substantial practical application except in connection with a digital computer, which means that if the judgment below is affirmed, the patent would wholly pre-empt the mathematical formula and in practical effect would be a patent on the algorithm itself.[48]

The Court thus concluded that the claimed invention was not a "process" within the meaning of the Patent Act. The claimed method was so abstract as to cover both known and unknown uses of the BCD to binary conversion.

The decision was read by many as a prohibition of software patents. Certainly the Court's decrying that this is an attempt to obtain "a patent on the algorithm itself"[49] promoted this reading. After all, reasoned many, the Court has in effect held that an algorithm is not patentable, and what is software but an algorithm? This reading was made further plausible by the Court's closing remarks:

> It may be that the patent laws should be extended to cover these programs, a policy matter to which we are not competent to speak. The President's Commission on the Patent System rejected the proposal that these programs be patentable.[50]

The President's Commission Report, to which the Court refers, is discussed in § 1.13. The President's Commission was appointed by President Johnson to study all aspects of the patent system. It makes interesting reading on a variety of patent law issues—recommending massive changes in numerous areas. The primary reason the President's Commission did not advocate patentability of software was that the Patent Office, in the Commission's view, could not examine applications because it lacked a reliable classification and searching technique.[51]

---

[48] Gottschalk v. Benson, 409 U.S. 63, 71–71 (1972).

[49] *Id.*

[50] *Id.* at 72 (citing *To Promote the Progress of . . . Useful Arts,* Report on the President's Comm'n on the Pat. Sys. (1966)).

[51] See **Ch. 4** for a discussion of how the Patent Office currently classifies and searches softwares prior art.

§ 9.16   —Analyzing *Gottschalk v. Benson*

Benson is often misunderstood. Many cite it for the proposition that a mathematical algorithm cannot be patented, and then jump to the erroneous conclusion that anything claimed in the language of mathematics is therefore unpatentable. *Benson* does not stand for this. Rather, *Benson* simply follows existing Supreme Court precedent that:

> Phenomena of nature, though just discovered, mental processes, and abstract intellectual concepts are not patentable, as they are the basic tools of scientific and technological work.[52]

If you will accept the notion that numbers and numbering systems have different properties (for example, commutative and distributive properties) and different innate characteristics (for example, rational, irrational, prime), then you are on your way to understanding *Gottschalk v. Benson*. These properties and characteristics of numbers and numbering systems exist, and have always existed, like any other law of nature. You can discover these properties and characteristics, and teach them to your children, but you are powerless to change them. (Try changing pi to a rational number and see if your circles still have 360 degrees.)

When properties and characteristics numbers and numbering systems are seen as phenomena of nature, *Benson* makes perfect sense. Nobody can claim a monopoly over all uses, now known or later discovered, of a phenomena of nature. Viewing the decision in this way demonstrates that *Benson* is consistent with later decisions upholding the patentability of software.

§ 9.17   *Parker v. Flook*

Parker v. Flook[53] is the second software patent decision of the Supreme Court. Decided in 1978, six years after *Benson*, *Parker v. Flook* represented, at the time, another blow to the viability of the software patent. However, as it had in *Benson* the Court made it clear that it was not condemning all software patents:

> Neither the dearth of precedent, nor this decision, should therefore be interpreted as reflecting a judgment that patent protection of certain novel and useful computer programs will not promote the progress of science and the useful arts, or that such protection is undesirable as a matter of policy.[54]

---

52 Gottschalk v. Benson, 409 U.S. 63, 67 (1972).

53 437 U.S. 584 (1978).

54 *Id.* at 595.

However, while the Court did not condemn all software patents, its decision in *Parker* did go quite far in that direction:

> Very simply, our holding today is that a claim for an improved method of calculation, even when tied to a specific end use, is unpatentable subject matter under § 101.[55]

If the "method of calculation" in the above language refers to a mathematical principle of nature, then *Parker* forbids patentability of no new territory. Mathematical principles of nature, like abstract ideas, cannot be patented. However, if the "method of calculation" refers more broadly to any data processing method, involving Boolean logic calculations for example, then the viability of the software patent is severely threatened. For example, what if the invention is a method of parallel processing, involving collections of calculating steps designed to allow multiple processors to work together as one? Is this method of facilitating multiple processors to act as one unpatentable because it is a mere "method of calculation"?

§ 9.18   —Technology in *Parker v. Flook*

The catalytic chemical conversion of hydrocarbons is a process widely used in the petrochemical industry. With the aid of acidic catalysts, the catalytic chemical conversion process decomposes large hydrocarbons, originally from crude oil, into smaller hydrocarbons for use as gasoline. During the conversion process a number of process variables (temperature, pressure, and flow rate) must be closely monitored. If these variables stray too far from proper values, an alarm must sound. Importantly, the alarm must sound if conditions are becoming dangerous (for example, pressure or temperature too high). The alarm must also sound if the process is operating far below acceptable efficiency (for example, pressure or temperature too low).

Monitoring the catalytic conversion process would seem a rather simple task of comparing the measured temperature, pressure, and flow rates with predetermined alarm limit values. If the measured parameters stray too far from the alarm limit values, the alarm is sounded. Naturally, there would be a set of upper alarm limits to signal danger, and a set of lower alarm limits to signal inefficiency.

However, the task is more complicated than this. Because petrochemical processes cannot be guaranteed to operate in a steady state, the value of the proper alarm limit itself may fluctuate. In other words, one fixed set of alarm limits, (predetermined in advance for use under all operating conditions) is not good enough. Rather, a range of alarm limits is needed, one set for steady

---

[55] *Id.* at n.19.

state operation, and another set for transient or start-up operation. To work this way, petrochemical engineers must update the alarm limits, in effect, choosing the proper set of alarm limits for the current mode of operation.

Flook's patent application described a method of updating the alarm limits, consisting essentially of three steps: an initial step which merely measures the present value of the process variable (for example, temperature), an intermediate step which uses an equation or algorithm to calculate an updated alarm-limit value, and a final step which adjusts the actual alarm limit to the updated value.

The Patent Examiner rejected Flook's application. He found that the mathematical formula was the only difference between Flook's claims and the prior art and therefore a patent on this method "would be in practical effect a patent on the formula or mathematics itself."[56] The Board of Appeals agreed with the Examiner and sustained the Examiner's rejection. The Court of Customs and Patent Appeals saw the matter differently and reversed.

Acting Commissioner of Patents, Lutrelle F. Parker, filed a petition for a writ of certiorari, urging that "the decision of the Court of Customs and Patent Appeals will have a debilitating effect on the rapidly expanding computer 'software' industry, and will require him to process thousands of additional patent applications."[57] The Supreme Court granted cert.

§ 9.19　—Claims at Issue in *Parker v. Flook*

At issue, claim 1 of the patent describes the method as follows:

1. A method for updating the value of at least one alarm limit on at least one process variable involved in a process comprising the catalytic chemical conversion of hydrocarbons wherein said alarm limit has a current value of

$$Bo + K$$

wherein Bo is the current alarm base and K is a predetermined alarm offset which comprises:

(1) Determining the present value of said process variable, said present value being defined as PVL;

(2) Determining a new alarm base B_1, using the following equation:

$$B_1 = Bo(1.0 - F) + PVL(F)$$

where F is a predetermined number greater than zero and less than 1.0;

(3) Determining an updated alarm limit which is defined as $B_1 + K$; and thereafter

(4) Adjusting said alarm limit to said updated alarm limit value.[58]

---

[56] Parker v. Flook, 437 U.S. 584, 587 (1978).

[57] *Id.* at 587–88.

[58] Parker v. Flook, 437 U.S. 584, 596–97 (1978).

Flook's method can be practiced using pencil and paper. In order to use Flook's method for computing a new limit, the operator must make four decisions. Based on individual knowledge of normal operating conditions, the operator first selects the original "alarm base" (Bo); if a temperature of 400 degrees is normal, that may be the alarm base. The operator must next decide on an appropriate margin of safety, perhaps 50 degrees; that is the "alarm offset" (K). The sum of the alarm base and the alarm offset equals the alarm limit.

Then the operator decides on the time interval that will elapse between each updating; that interval has no effect on the computation although it may, of course, be of great practical importance. Finally, the operator selects a weighting factor (F), which may be any number between 99 percent and 1 percent (a number greater than 0, but less than 1), and that is used in the updating calculation.

If the operator has decided in advance to use an original alarm base (Bo) of 400 degrees, a constant alarm offset (K) of 50 degrees, and a weighting factor (F) of 80 percent, the only additional information needed in order to compute an updated alarm limit (UAV), is the present value of the process variable (PVL). Flook's application does not explain how to select the appropriate margin of safety, the weighting factor, or any of the other variables.

The computation of the updated alarm limit according to Flook's method involves these three steps:

First, at the predetermined interval, the process variable is measured; assuming the temperature is then 425 degrees, PVL will then equal 425.

Second, the solution of Flook's formula will produce a new alarm base (B_1) that will be a weighted average of the preceding alarm base (Bo) of 400 degrees and the current temperature (PVL) of 425. It will be closer to one or the other depending on the value of the weighting factor (F) selected by the operator. If F is 80 percent, that percentage of 425 (340) plus 20 percent (1 - F) of 400 (80) will produce a new alarm base of 420 degrees.

Third, the alarm offset (K) of 50 degrees is then added to the new alarm base (B_1) of 420 to produce the updated alarm limit (UAV) of 470.

The process is repeated at the selected time intervals. In each updating computation, the most recently calculated alarm base and the current measurement of the process variable will be substituted for the corresponding numbers in the original calculation, but the alarm offset and the weighting factor will remain constant.

§ 9.20   —Holding of *Parker v. Flook*

In *Benson* the Supreme Court held a mathematical formula is like a law of nature; the patent law cannot allow anyone to wholly preempt a mathematical formula or law of nature. In ruling on Flook's application, the Court of Customs and Patent Appeals read *Benson* to apply only where *all* uses of a mathematical formula or law of nature are preempted. Only then is the subject matter nonstatutory. Flook's claim does not seek to preempt all uses of his mathematical formula—there are unclaimed uses of Flook's formula outside the petrochemical industry that remain in the public domain. Hence, the Court of Customs and Patent Appeals reasoned that Flook's claims did recite patentable subject matter. The Supreme Court did not agree.

Justice Stevens delivered the opinion of the Court. In his opinion, Justice Stevens quickly acknowledges that Flook does not seek to cover every conceivable application of the formula. However, that does not put an end to the matter, as the Court of Customs and Patent Appeals had assumed. The only novel feature of Flook's method, Justice Stevens notes, is the mathematical formula. Hence, the claim is still tantamount to a patent on the mathematical formula.

Flook had argued that the presence of specific "post solution" activity—the adjustment of the alarm limit—distinguishes the case from *Benson* and makes his process patentable. Justice Stevens rejects this argument, writing:

> The notion that post-solution activity, no matter how conventional or obvious in itself, can transform an unpatentable principle into a patentable process exalts form over substance.[59]

The analysis Justice Stevens uses is interesting, although somewhat confusing. He writes at the outset that the case turns entirely on the proper construction of § 101 of the Patent Act, which describes the subject matter that is eligible for patent protection. He writes that the case does not involve issues of novelty and obviousness that arise under §§ 102 and 103. He further writes that the Court's approach "is not at all inconsistent with the view that a patent claim must be considered as a whole."[60]

Justice Stevens proceeds to focus on Flook's mathematical formula (which he assumes to be novel) but nevertheless treats as though it were a familiar part of the prior art—hence incapable of imparting novelty to the claimed invention. Treating the formula as prior art, he disposes of the entire claim almost as if performing an obviousness analysis under 35 U.S.C. § 103.

> The question is whether the discovery of this feature [the mathematical formula] makes an otherwise conventional method eligible for patent protection.[61]

*   *   *

---

[59] Parker v. Flook, 437 U.S. 584, 590 (1978).

[60] *Id.* at 594.

[61] *Id.* at 588.

Respondent's process is unpatentable under § 101, not because it contains a mathematical algorithm as one component, but because once that algorithm is assumed to be within the prior art, the application, considered as a whole, contains no patentable invention.[62]

The analysis used by Justice Stevens—treating the mathematical formula as prior art—is not original to *Parker v. Flook*. The analysis is derived from the decision in *O'Reilly v. Morse*,[63] which is in turn borrowed from the English decision *Neilson v. Harford,* in which the court said, "we think the case must be considered as if, the principle being well known, the plaintiff had first invented a mode of applying it . . . ."[64]

§ 9.21   —Analyzing *Parker v. Flook*

Parker stands for three propositions.[65] First, the *Benson* rule of unpatentable subject matter is not limited to claims that *wholly* preempt a principle of nature, such as a principle of nature expressed as a mathematical formula. Form over substance distinctions, such as insignificant post-solution activity, will not save a claim, when the only novelty lies in the unpatentable principle. Second, an improved method of calculation, even when employed as part of a physical process, is not patentable subject matter under § 101. This proposition is best understood when you consider a method of calculation to be a mathematical calculation expressing a principle of nature. See § **9.16.** Care must be taken, however, not to equate the term calculation with the result of all operations performed by a computer. There are numerous computer operations that can result in solutions to problems that do not involve preempting a principle of nature. For example, a software air traffic control system may employ numerous computer operations. Simply characterizing the air traffic control system as a calculation does not render the subject matter unpatentable.

Third, a principle of nature or mathematical formula is treated for § 101 purposes as though it were a familiar part of the prior art; the claim is then examined to determine whether it discloses some other inventive concept. This is an analysis technique. It is a way of testing whether the claim as a whole recites a patentable invention. The technique originates from the 1841 English case *Neilson v. Harford.*[66] In that case the principle "that hot air will

---

62 *Id.* at 594.

63 56 U.S. 62, 115 (1854).

64 151 Eng. Rep. 1266 (1841)

65 According to J. Stevens in dissenting opinion in Diamond v. Diehr, 450 U.S. 175, 204 (1981).

66 151 Eng. Rep. 1266 (1841).

promote the ignition of fuel better than cold" was treated as well known. The court in that case found the invention was not this well-known principle, but rather a mechanical mode of applying the principle to furnaces.

In this context Flook's invention is different from Neilson's blast furnace. Flook teaches only the formula and suggests its possible application to the catalytic conversion process. He does not teach how to apply it to the catalytic conversion process, leaving to the human operator the problem of figuring out how to measure the variables, and how to select the appropriate margin of safety, the weighting factor, or any of the other variables.

Flook gives you an important practice tip. Make sure the specification contains a full disclosure, not only of the principle or formula involved, but of how to apply the formula or principle to a specific problem. When a mathematical formula is involved, be sure to disclose how to measure the variables and how to select appropriate values of any constants, multiplier factors, and so forth.

Another lesson of *Flook* is that, when possible, avoid claiming a software process or algorithm such that the result of the process is simply a number. In *Flook* the "alarm limit" is simply a number, which does not in any way alter or control a physical property, or transform or reduce an article to a different state or thing. Flook's attempt to render patentable the computation of this number, by restricting the claim to a field of use, did him no good. Had Flook tied the calculation of the alarm limit to a step that controls a petrochemical process, the claim would have recited statutory subject matter. See for example, *Diamond v. Diehr,*[67] discussed in § **9.27.**

§ 9.22   *Diamond v. Chakrabarty*

Decided by the Supreme Court on June 16, 1980, *Diamond v. Chakrabarty*[68] holds that a human-made microorganism is patentable subject matter, constituting a "manufacture" or "composition of matter." You may wonder, what this case has to do with patentability of software. Admittedly it does not have to do with software, but it does have everything to do with what is patentable subject matter. Chief Justice Burger, delivering the opinion of the Court, writes, "Congress intended statutory subject matter to 'include anything under the sun that is made by man.'"[69] Certainly, computer software, like human-made microorganisms, basks under the same sun.

---

[67] Diamond v. Diehr, 450 U.S. 175 (1981).

[68] Diamond v. Chakrabarty, 447 U.S. 303 (1980).

[69] *Id.* at 309.

§ 9.23   —Biotechnology in *Chakrabarty*

Chakrabarty, a microbiologist, discovered how to genetically alter the Pseudomonas bacterium with plasmids to digest oil spills. Plasmids are hereditary units physically separate from the chromosomes of the cell. In prior research, Chakrabarty and an associate discovered that plasmids control the oil degradation abilities of certain bacteria. In particular, the two researchers discovered plasmids capable of degrading camphor and octane, two components of crude oil. In the work represented by Chakrabarty's patent application, Chakrabarty discovered a process by which four different plasmids, capable of degrading four different oil components, could be transferred to and maintained stably in a single Pseudomonas bacterium, which itself has no capacity for degrading oil.

Prior to Chakrabarty's discovery, the biological control of oil spills required the use of a mixture of naturally occurring bacteria, each capable of degrading one component of the oil complex. In this way, oil is decomposed into simpler substances that can serve as food for aquatic life. However, for various reasons, only a portion of any such mixed culture survives to attract the oil spill. By breaking down multiple components of oil, Chakrabarty's genetically altered microorganism promises more efficient and rapid oil spill control.

§ 9.24   —Claims at Issue in *Chakrabarty*

Chakrabarty presented three types of claims: process claims for the method of producing the bacteria, claims for an inoculum comprised of a carrier material floating on water (such as straw) and the new bacteria, and claims to the bacteria themselves. The bacteria claims read:

> . . . a bacterium from the genus Pseudomonas containing therein at least two stable energy-generating plasmids, each of said plasmids providing a separate hydrocarbon degradative pathway.[70]

The patent examiner allowed the claims in the first two categories, but rejected the claims for the bacteria. The examiner reasoned that the bacteria are "products of nature" and "living things," and for both reasons they are not patentable subject matter. The Board of Appeals affirmed; the Court of Customs and Patent Appeals, by a divided vote, reversed; and acting Commissioner of Patents, Sidney A. Diamond, petitioned for certiorari.

---

[70] Diamond v. Chakrabarty, 447 U.S. 303, 305 (1980).

§ 9.25   —Holding in *Chakrabarty*

Chief Justice Burger delivered the opinion of the Court, which affirmed the Court of Customs and Patent Appeals, in a 5-to-4 decision. "The question before us in this case," Chief Justice Burger writes, "is a narrow one of statutory interpretation requiring us to construe 35 USC § 101."[71] He writes, "Specifically we must determine whether respondent's micro-organism constitutes a 'manufacture' or 'composition of matter' within the meaning of the statute."[72]

Chief Justice Burger draws on the legislative history of the patent law of the United States, referring to the Patent Act of 1793, authored by Thomas Jefferson. In that early statute, Burger notes, Jefferson defined statutory subject matter as "any new and useful art, machine, manufacture, or composition of matter, or any new or useful improvement [thereof]."[73] The Act embodied Jefferson's philosophy that "ingenuity should receive a liberal encouragement."[74]

When the patent laws were revised in 1836, in 1870, and in 1874, Jefferson's language remained intact. In 1952, when Congress enacted the present Patent Act, Jefferson's language was changed only slightly—the word "process" replaced the word "art." By citing Thomas Jefferson, the Court clearly adopts an expansive view of what is patentable subject matter. However, the quote most often attributed to *Diamond v. Chakrabarty* comes not from Jefferson, but from P.J. Federico, the principal draftsperson of the 1952 Act:

> [U]nder section 101 a person may have invented a machine or a manufacture, which may include anything under the sun that is made by man . . . . [75]

Chief Justice Burger notes that § 101 is not without its limits: "[t]he laws of nature, physical phenomena, and abstract ideas have been held not patentable."[76] However, Chakrabarty's genetically altered microorganism does not exist in nature. Hence Chakrabarty's claim, the Chief Justice reasoned, "is not to a hitherto unknown natural phenomenon, but to a non-naturally occurring manufacture or composition of matter—a product of human ingenuity."[77]

---

[71] Diamond v. Chakrabarty, 447 U.S. 303, 307 (1980).

[72] *Id.*

[73] Act of Feb. 21, 1793, § 1, 1 Stat. 319 (1793).

[74] 5 Writings of Thomas Jefferson 75–76 (1871).

[75] Hearings on H.R. 3760 before Subcomm. No. 3 of the House Comm. on the Judiciary, 82d Cong., 1st Sess. 37 (1951) (statement of P.J. Frederico).

[76] Diamond v. Chakrabarty, 447 U.S. 303, 309 (1980).

[77] *Id.*

§ 9.26   —*Chakrabarty* Impact on *Benson* and *Flook*

The decision in *Chakrabarty* does not overrule *Gottschalk v. Benson* or *Parker v. Flook.* To the contrary, *Chakrabarty* states that both of these prior precedents still stand, defining the limits of § 101. These prior cases both stand for the proposition that laws of nature, physical phenomena, and abstract ideas are not patentable. Nevertheless, the expansive view that "anything under the sun" that is made by woman or man is patentable subject matter, clearly removes the stigma implied by *Benson* and *Flook* that software may not be patentable.

Very little must be said to square the decision in *Chakrabarty* with that in *Gottschalk v. Benson,* which simply held that things existing in nature (even newly discovered things), including mathematical formulas, are not patentable.

Parker v. Flook requires more explaining, because in that decision Justice Stevens states that the judiciary "must proceed cautiously when . . . asked to extend patent rights into areas wholly unforeseen by Congress."[78] Chief Justice Burger, in the *Chakrabarty* decision, considers this cautionary statement, but does not read it to mean that inventions in areas not contemplated by Congress when the patent laws were enacted are unpatentable per se.[79] However, *Chakrabarty* was a 5-to-4 decision, and it is clear that the dissent (Justices Brennan, White, Marshall, and Powell) would have left the patentability of human-engineered lifeforms to Congress.

All in all, *Diamond v. Chakrabarty* breaks important new ground, for it opens the patent system to the cutting edge technology of the coming decade. Just as the English decision, *Neilson v. Harford*[80] first shocked the patent world and then spread throughout it, so too will *Diamond v. Chakrabarty.* As seen by the Supreme Court's decision in *Diamond v. Diehr,*[81] discussed in § 9.27, the software community has already felt *Chakrabarty*'s impact.

§ 9.27   *Diamond v. Diehr*

Diamond v. Diehr[82] is the first Supreme Court decision to clearly open the door for software patents, although prior Supreme Court decisions (*Benson* and *Flook*) did not expressly close that door. Also, by the time *Diamond v. Diehr* was decided in 1981, the Court of Customs and Patent Appeals had

---

[78] Parker v. Flook, 437 U.S. 584, 596 (1978).

[79] Diamond v. Chakrabarty, 447 U.S. 303, 315 (1980).

[80] 151 Eng. Rep. 1266 (1841), which held patentable the *applied* principle of using hot air to feed a blast furnace fire.

[81] 450 U.S. 175 (1981).

[82] 450 U.S. 175 (1981).

already made it clear that it was prepared to accept software patents. Nevertheless, *Diamond v. Diehr* is an important software patent case, following directly in the footsteps of *Diamond v. Chakrabarty* that "anything under the sun that is made by man" is patentable subject matter.

§ 9.28   —Technology in *Diamond v. Diehr*

The patent involves a process for curing synthetic rubber. When molding synthetic rubber into a precision product, raw, uncured synthetic rubber is placed in a mold, heat and pressure are applied, and the mold is then opened when the rubber has "cured" for the proper length of time. Once cured, the rubber retains the shape of the mold that produced it.

The cure is obtained by mixing curing agents into the uncured rubber polymer before molding and by then applying heat for the right length of time while the mixture is in the mold. The curing time must be neither too long nor too short. Curing time is a function of mold temperature, according to the relationship described by the well-known Arrhenius equation. Discovered by Svante Arrhenius, the relationship expresses the total cure time (v) as the following nonlinear function of activation constant (C), mold temperature (Z) and mold geometry-determined constant (x):

$$\ln v = CZ + x$$

The activation constant (C) is a unique figure for each batch of each compound being molded. It is determined by making viscosity measurements of the rubber mixture, using an instrument known as a rheometer. The geometry-dependent constant (x) takes into account the fact that the cure time will depend on the thickness and shape of the article to be molded.

Prior to Diehr and Lutton's invention the temperature variable (Z) was viewed as uncontrollable. This was because every time the mold press was opened to load the uncured rubber mixture, and again to remove the cured rubber product, the mold temperature cooled by an unknown amount. The industry practice was to calculate the cure time as the shortest time in which all parts of the product would definitely be cured, assuming a reasonable amount of mold-opening time during loading of the uncured rubber mixture and subsequent unloading of the cured rubber product.

Diehr and Lutton invention eliminates the need to make assumptions about how long the mold has been opened and how much it has cooled. Diehr and Lutton use temperature sensors to continuously read the temperature inside the mold cavity. These sensors automatically feed the mold cavity temperature information to a digital computer which constantly recalculates the cure time, based on the Arrhenius equation. The computer then signals precisely when to open the mold.

§ 9.29   —Claims at Issue in *Diamond v. Diehr*

Diehr and Lutton's application contains eleven different claims. Three examples are claims 1, 2, and 11 that are reproduced below:

1. A method of operating a rubber-molding press for precision molded compounds with the aid of a digital computer, comprising:

providing said computer with a data base for said press including at least,

natural logarithm conversion data (ln),

the activation energy constant (C) unique to each batch of said compound being molded, and

a constant (x) dependent upon the geometry of the particular mold of the press,

initiating an interval timer in said computer upon the closure of the press for monitoring the elapsed time of said closure,

constantly determining the temperature (Z) of the mold at a location closely adjacent to the mold cavity in the press during molding,

constantly providing the computer with the temperature (Z),

repetitively calculating in the computer, at frequent intervals during each cure, the Arrhenius equation for reaction time during the cure, which is

$$\ln v = CZ + x$$

where v is the total required cure time,

repetitively comparing in the computer at said frequent intervals during the cure each said calculation of the total required cure time calculated with the Arrhenius equation and said elapsed time, and

opening the press automatically when a said comparison indicates equivalence.

2.   The method of Claim 1 including measuring the activation energy constant for the compound being molded in the press with a rheometer and automatically updating said data base within the computer in the event of changes in the compound being molded in said press as measured by said rheometer.

11.   A method of manufacturing precision molded articles from selected synthetic rubber compounds in an openable rubber molding press having at least one heated precision mold, comprising:

(a)   heating said mold to a temperature range approximating a predetermined rubber curing temperature,

(b)   installing prepared unmolded synthetic rubber of a known compound in a molding cavity of predetermined geometry as defined by said mold,

(c)   closing said press to mold said rubber to occupy said cavity in conformance with the contour of said mold and to cure said rubber by transfer of heat thereto from said mold,

(d)   initiating an interval timer upon the closure of said press for monitoring the elapsed time of said closure,

(e)   heating said mold during said closure to maintain the temperature thereof within said range approximating said rubber curing temperature,

(f)   constantly determining the temperature of said mold at a location
closely adjacent said cavity thereof throughout closure of said press,

(g)   repetitively calculating at frequent periodic intervals throughout
closure of said press the Arrhenius equation for reaction time of said rubber to
determine total required cure time v as follows:

$$\ln v = cz + x$$

wherein c is an activation energy constant determined for said rubber being
molded and cured in said press, z is the temperature of said mold at the time of
each calculation of said Arrhenius equation, and x is a constant which is a
function of said predetermined geometry of said mold,

(h)   for each repetition of calculation of said Arrhenius equation
herein, comparing the resultant calculated total required cure time with the
monitored elapsed time measured by said interval timer,

(i)   opening said press when a said comparison of calculated total
required cure time and monitored elapsed time indicates equivalence, and

(j)   removing from said mold the resultant precision molded an
cured rubber article.[83]

The patent examiner rejected these claims on the sole ground that they
were drawn to nonstatutory subject matter under 35 U.S.C. § 101. The
examiner determined that those steps in the claims that are carried out by a
computer were nonstatutory subject matter under *Gottschalk v. Benson*.[84] The
remaining steps—installing rubber in the press and the subsequent closing of
the press—were, the examiner found, "conventional and necessary to the
process and cannot be the basis of patentability."[85]

The Patent and Trademark Office Board of Appeals agreed with the examiner. The Court of Customs and Patent Appeals disagreed and reversed.[86]
The Court of Customs and Patent Appeals noted that a claim drawn to subject matter otherwise statutory does not become nonstatutory because a computer is involved. The appeals court saw Diehr and Lutton's invention as an
improved process for molding rubber articles. In a now familiar pattern, the
Patent Office appealed. Commissioner, Sidney A. Diamond, filed a petition
for certiorari, arguing that the decision of the Court of Customs and Patent
Appeals was inconsistent with prior decisions of the Supreme Court.

---

83 *Id.* at 175 n.5.

84 409 U.S. 63 (1972).

85 Diamond v. Diehr, 450 U.S. 175, 181 (1981).

86 *In re* Diehr, 602 F.2d 982 (C.C.P.A. 1979).

§ 9.30 —Holding in *Diamond v. Diehr*

Justice Rehnquist delivered the opinion of the Court, which in a 5-to-4 decision sided with the Court of Customs and Patent Appeals and found the claimed invention was patentable subject matter. Justice Rehnquist begins his analysis with *Diamond v. Chakrabarty,*[87] reiterating the premise relied upon in that case that "anything under the sun that is made by man" is statutory subject matter under § 101.[88] Justice Rehnquist acknowledges, however, that § 101 does have its limits:

> This Court has undoubtedly recognized limits to § 101 and every discovery is not embraced within the statutory terms. Excluded from such patent protection are laws of nature, natural phenomena, and abstract ideas.[89]

As to the Court's prior computer-related cases, *Gottschalk v. Benson* and *Parker v. Flook,* Justice Rehnquist treats these as simply standing for the following "long-established principles."

1. Excluded from patent protection are laws of nature, natural phenomena, and abstract ideas.[90]
2. An idea of itself is not patentable.[91]
3. A principle, in the abstract, is a fundamental truth; an original cause; a motive; these cannot be patented.[92]
4. A law of nature, like a mineral discovered in the earth or a new plant found in the wild, is not patentable.[93]

Finally, distinguishing the Diehr and Litton invention from the invention in *Flook,* Justice Rehnquist finds that whereas in *Flook* the claims were drawn to a method for computing a number (an alarm limit), in Diehr and Lutton the claims seek protection for a process of curing synthetic rubber. Flook sought to foreclose all use of a mathematical formula in the petrochemical industry, but taught nothing of how the process variables are obtained; Diehr and Lutton, the majority found, "seek only to foreclose from

---

[87] Diamond v. Chakrabarty, 447 U.S. 303 (1980).

[88] Diamond v. Diehr, 450 U.S. 175, 182 (1981).

[89] *Id.* at 185.

[90] Parker v. Flook, 437 U.S. 584 (1978); Gottschalk v. Benson, 409 U.S. 63 (1970); Funk Bros. v. Kalo Co., 333 U.S. 127 (1948).

[91] Rubber Tip Pencil Co. v. Howard, 87 U.S. 498 (1874).

[92] Le Roy v. Tatham, 55 U.S. 156 (1852).

[93] Diamond v. Chakrabarty, 447 U.S. 303 (1980); Funk Bros. v. Kalo Co., 333 U.S. 127 (1948).

others the use of that equation [the Arrhenius equation] in conjunction with all of the other steps in their claimed process."[94]

§ 9.31 —Analyzing *Diamond v. Diehr*

It would seem that *Diamond v. Diehr* and *Parker v. Flook* lie, only inches away from one another, on opposite sides of the judicial line in the sand. Each includes a significant calculation step. The calculation step in each involves solving a mathematical formula. In each the mathematical formula represents some principle of nature. Each purports to include at least one additional method step, such that neither wholly preempts its mathematical formula. Yet, *Diehr* is patentable and *Flook* is not. Why?

One reason is that the invention in *Diehr* effects a change in state of a physical thing—a mold is opened. In *Flook* the invention effects a change in state of a nonphysical thing—a number is updated. Citing the 1877 decision in *Cochrane v. Deener*[95] and the Court's subsequent adoption of the principle in *Gottschalk v. Benson*,[96] Justice Rehnquist offers the following guidance on what distinguishes a patentable process:

> Transformation and reduction of an article 'to a different state or thing' is the clue to the patentability of a process claim that does not include particular machines.[97]

This clue is a helpful one because a computerized process running on a general purpose digital computer qualifies as a process that "does not include particular machines."

Another reason for the different outcome between *Diehr* and *Flook* may be a change in attitude of certain members of the Supreme Court. **Figure 9–1** shows how each Justice voted in *Benson, Flook, Chakrabarty,* and *Diehr.* Note how certain Justices have voted consistently for an expansive reading of § 101 whereas others have voted consistently for a restricted reading; note also how other Justices have changed their stance on this issue.

This is not to say that any of the Justices are pro-software patent or anti-software patent, per se. Rather, the difference of opinion seems to be whether the claim language alone should dictate whether an invention qualifies as statutory subject matter, or whether the claim language should be construed first in light of the prior art to determine what the applicant has actually discovered. *Diamond v. Diehr* best illustrates this difference of opinion.

---

[94] Diamond v. Diehr, 450 U.S. 175, 187 (1981).

[95] 94 U.S. 780 (1877).

[96] 409 U.S. 63, 70 (1972).

[97] Diamond v. Diehr, 450 U.S. 175, 184 (1981).

CASE/YEAR	MAJORITY	DISSENT	NO PART
Gottschalk v. Benson 1972	Douglas Burger Rehnquist Marshall Brennan White		Blackmun Stewart Powell
Parker v. Flook 1978	Stevens Marshall Brennan White Powell Blackmun	Burger Rehnquist Stewart	
Diamond v. Chakrabarty 1980	Burger Rehnquist Stewart Stevens Blackmun	Marshall Brennan White Powell	
Diamond v. Diehr 1981	Rehnquist Burger Stewart White Powell	Marshall Brennan Stevens Blackmun	

Figure 9–1.   How the justices voted.

Diamond v. Diehr is a 5-to-4 decision. The principal difference of opinion between the majority and the minority is not over the construction of § 101, but over the construction of the claims. The majority construes the claims to cover a method of constantly measuring the actual temperature in a rubber molding press and determining when to open the mold. The minority construes the claims to cover a method of calculating the time that the mold should remain closed during the curing process. In effect, the majority places more emphasis on the claim language—taking the applicant's word that this is the applicant's discovery; the minority looks throughout the claim language—in light of the prior art—to identify what the inventor claims to have discovered.

This can be a bit confusing, because ordinarily the prior art comes into play in determining novelty under § 102 and obviousness under § 103.

Here, however, the minority uses the prior art to assess what the applicant claims to have discovered. The justification for this discovery requirement comes from the language of § 101, itself: "Whoever invents or *discovers* any new and useful process . . . ."

If you are having difficulty understanding how the prior art has any bearing on what is patentable subject matter, you are not alone. Justice Stevens, writing for the minority in *Diehr,* accuses the majority of having the same difficulty:

> The Court . . . fails to understand or completely disregards the distinction between the subject matter of what the inventor *claims* to have discovered— the § 101 issue—and the question whether that claimed discovery is in fact novel—the § 102 issue.[98]

§ 9.32   Federal Circuit En Banc Decision
In re Alappat

The Federal Circuit Court of Appeals rarely decides a case en banc, and when it does you can be sure the case is an important one. Ordinarily the Federal Circuit sits as a three-judge panel. In *In re Alappat*[99] the court sat en banc to decide the fate of an invention that the patent examiner determined was an unpatentable mathematical algorithm. Eleven justices took part in the decision, resulting in a majority opinion and several dissenting and concurring opinions. You will need a score card to keep track of how each Judge ruled.

The case involves two issues, a jurisdictional issue of whether the Court of Appeals may review a reconsideration decision of the Board of Patent Appeals, and a 35 U.S.C. § 101 issue of whether a certain means-plus-function claim recites patentable subject matter. As the subject of this chapter is § 101, only the latter issue will be discussed in detail here.

Kuriappan Alappat, Edward Averill, and James Larsen (collectively Alappat) filed for a patent on a rasterizer for improving the quality of the display in a digital oscilloscope. The examiner rejected Alappat's claims as being directed to nonstatutory subject matter. The examiner read Alappat's means-plus-function claims as wholly preempting a mathematical algorithm. Alappat appealed and the Board of Patent Appeals, comprising a three-member panel, reversed the examiner's nonstatutory subject matter rejection. The examiner then requested reconsideration pursuant to § 1214.04 of the *Manual of Patent Examining Procedure,* stating that the panel's decision conflicted with Patent

---

[98] *Id.* at 211 (emphasis in original).

[99] *In re* Alappat, 33 F.3d 1526 (Fed. Cir. 1994).

Office policy. The examiner requested that reconsideration be carried out by an expanded panel.

An expanded, eight-member panel, acting as the Board, granted the examiner's request and affirmed the examiner's § 101 rejection. This time Alappat appealed, to the Court of Appeals for the Federal Circuit.

The Court of Appeals for the Federal Circuit found that it did have jurisdiction to hear the appeal, and then ruled that the claimed invention was patentable subject matter under § 101. Judge Rich wrote the majority opinion, with whom Judges Newman, Lourie, Michel, Plager, and Rader joined on the § 101 issue. Judge Archer wrote a dissenting opinion (on both jurisdiction and § 101 issues) with whom Judge Nies joined on the § 101 issue. Judges Mayer, Clevenger, and Schall took no position on the § 101 issue.

§ 9.33   —Technology in *In re Alappat*

Alappat's invention relates to a means for creating a smooth waveform display in a digital oscilloscope. The screen of an oscilloscope is the front of a cathode-ray tube (CRT). Like a television picture tube, the oscilloscope screen presents an array (or raster) of spots (or pixels) that glow when illuminated by an electron beam produced in the neck of the cathode-ray tube. To produce a display on the screen, the electron beam is scanned horizontally and vertically to successively illuminate selected pixels. The illuminated pixels glow to produce the waveform display.

A problem with digital oscilloscopes is that there are only a finite number of pixels on the screen. These pixels (spots) are arranged in a rectangular grid, and although quite close to one another, there is still space between them. On slowly rising and falling portions of a waveform, the eye ignores the fact that the waveform display is a series of dots and instead sees a continuous line. On rapidly rising and falling portions of a waveform, the eye does not infer smoothness and instead sees the waveform as discontinuous and jagged. The noticeability and appearance of these discontinuous and jagged effects is called aliasing.

To overcome the effects of aliasing, Alappat's invention employs a technique in which the illumination intensity of the electron beam is altered or "modulated" so that pixels that lie close to, but not quite on, the desired waveform to be displayed, glow less brightly than those which lie directly on the waveform to be displayed. This fools the eye into seeing a smooth appearing waveform.

Because the oscilloscope screen has a rectangular raster comprising a finite number of pixels, the amount of partial illumination to be given to in-between pixels can be worked out with mathematical precision.

§ 9.34   —Claims at Issue in *In re Alappat*

Claim 15, the only independent claim in issue, reads:

A rasterizer for converting vector list data representing sample magnitudes of an input waveform into anti-aliased pixel illumination intensity data to be displayed on a display means comprising:

(a)   means for determining the vertical distance between the endpoints of each of the vectors in the data list;

(b)   means for determining the elevation of a row of pixels that is spanned by the vector;

(c)   means for normalizing the vertical distance and elevation; and

(d)   means for outputting illumination intensity data as a predetermined function of the normalized vertical distance and elevation.[100]

§ 9.35   —Holding of the *In re Alappat* Majority

Writing for the majority, Judge Rich describes how the eight-member Board of Appeals erred. The Board took the position that during examination the Patent Office is exempt from the sixth paragraph of 35 U.S.C. § 112, which reads:

An element in a claim for a combination may be expressed as a means or step for performing a specified function without the recital of structure, material, or acts in support thereof, and such claim shall be construed to cover the corresponding structure, material, or acts described in the specification and equivalents thereof.[101]

The Board, in effect, converted the claim into a method claim, and then held the claim was nothing more that an attempt to wholly preempt a mathematical algorithm for computing pixel information.

That the Patent Office would be exempt from the law is not as farfetched as it might first appear. Patent examiners are trained to use the claims, not the specification, in searching for prior art. Examiners are taught this so they will not allow claims that read on the prior art, simply because the embodiment disclosed in the application and the embodiment disclosed in the prior art are different. In this light, it is understandable why the Board considered the Patent Office to be exempt from 35 U.S.C. § 112, paragraph 6.

The Federal Circuit majority, citing *In re Donaldson*[102] disagreed with the Board's approach:

---

[100] *In re* Alappat, 33 F.3d 1526, 1538–39 (Fed. Cir. 1994).

[101] 35 U.S.C. § 112.

[102] 16 F.3d 1189 (Fed. Cir. 1994).

Given Alappat's disclosure, it was error for the Board majority to interpret each of the means clauses in claim 15 so broadly as to "read on any and every means for performing the functions" recited, as it said it was doing, and then to conclude that claim 15 is nothing more than a process claim wherein each means clause represents a step in that process.[103]

The Federal Circuit majority was clearly moved by the nature of the disclosure in the Alappat application, because it went so far as to rewrite claim 15, for demonstration purposes, substituting the disclosed structure for each "means" element in the claim. The court then concluded that claim 15 "unquestionably recites a machine."[104]

The Board also took the position that the claim was nonstatutory because it falls within the "judicially created mathematical algorithm" exception to § 101. The Federal Circuit majority rejected this view as well, stating:

A close analysis of *Diehr, Flook,* and *Benson* reveals that the Supreme Court never intended to create an overly broad, fourth category of subject matter excluded from § 101.[105]

"[T]he proper inquiry in dealing with the so called mathematical subject matter exception," the Federal Circuit majority states, "is to see whether the claimed subject matter *as a whole* is a disembodied mathematical concept . . ."[106] The Federal Circuit majority equates this disembodied mathematical concept with a principle of nature:

. . . whether categorized as a mathematical formula, mathematical equation, mathematical algorithm or the like, which in essence represents nothing more than a "law of nature," "natural phenomenon," or "abstract idea."[107]

One thing that helps the Alappat claim considerably is that the preamble states the subject matter for which Alappat seeks a patent, and one of the elements in the body of the claim relates back to that preamble:

15.   A rasterizer for converting vector list data . . . into pixel *illumination intensity data* . . . comprising:

(a) means for . . . .

(b) means for . . . .

(c) means for . . . .

(d) means for outputting *illumination intensity data* . . . . (emphasis added)

---

[103] *In re* Alappat, 33 F.3d 1526, 1540 (Fed. Cir. 1994).

[104] *Id.* at 1541.

[105] *Id.* at 1543.

[106] *Id.* at 1544.

[107] *Id.*

Noting this about the claim, the court states:

> Indeed, the preamble specifically recites that the claimed rasterizer converts waveform data into output illumination data for a display, and the means elements recited in the body of the claim make reference not only to the inputted waveform data recited in the preamble but also to the output illumination data also recited in the preamble. Claim 15 thus defines a combination of elements constituting a machine for producing an anti-aliased waveform.[108]

The Federal Circuit majority also addresses the Board's concern that the claim reads on a general purpose computer. Alappat admits that this is true, and the Federal Circuit majority agrees. Nevertheless, the Federal Circuit majority does not see this as grounds for declaring the subject matter nonstatutory:

> We have held that such programming creates a new machine, because a general purpose computer in effect becomes a special purpose computer once it is programmed to perform particular functions pursuant to instructions from program software.[109]

§ 9.36   —Dissents in *In re Alappat*

Judge Archer writes a dissenting opinion, in which Judge Nies concurs. On the § 101 issue, Judge Archer disagrees with the majority that the claimed invention is a rasterizer. Judge Archer criticizes the majority's "simplistic approach of looking *only* to whether the claim reads on structure and *ignoring* the claimed invention or discovery for which a patent is sought."[110] The criticism is reminiscent of Justice Stevens's dissent in *Diamond v. Diehr* in which Stevens wrote that a § 101 analysis must address "what the inventor claims to have discovered."[111] Judge Archer writes:

> the dispositive issue is not whether the claim recites on its face something more physical than just abstract mathematics. If it were, *Benson* and *Flook* would have come out the other way and *Diehr* would have been a very short opinion. The dispositive issue is whether the invention or discovery *for* which an award of patent is sought is more than just a discovery in abstract mathematics.[112] (emphasis in original)

---

[108] *Id.*

[109] *In re* Alappat, 33 F.3d 1526, 1545 (Fed. Cir. 1994).

[110] *In re* Alappat, 33 F.3d 1526, 1554 (Fed. Cir. 1994) (emphasis in original).

[111] 450 U.S. 175, 205 (1981).

[112] *In re* Alappat, 33 F.3d 1526, 1557 (Fed. Cir. 1994).

Judge Archer and Judge Nies analyze the invention as a rasterizer that begins with vector data—two numbers, and that ends with other specific data—an array of numbers. This number to number conversion, in the opinion of Judges Archer and Nies, is not patentable subject matter.

Judge Archer makes his point, that simply finding physical structure in a claim is not enough, by using an example. He posits, what if an inventor discovers a new melody and records it on compact disc. Through the expedient of putting the melody on a known structure, is the inventor entitled to obtain a patent? The answer is clearly, no. Judge Archer's point is that the melody is an abstract idea, unpatentable, and that simply bottling it up in structure will not make it patentable. Instead of concentrating on structure, Judge Archer says that the majority should have concentrated on what the inventor claims to have discovered.

§ 9.37   —Analyzing *In re Alappat*

In re Alappat is an en banc decision and serves as binding precedent. On the basic premise of what is patentable subject matter, the *Alappat* decision follows *Benson, Flook,* and *Diehr,* as it should, these being Supreme Court decisions. The basic premise stated in these Supreme Court decisions is that a principle of nature (or an abstract idea) is not patentable subject matter. The *Alappat* decision extends judicial understanding of the software patent in two areas. First, the majority agrees that § 112, paragraph six applies during prosecution. In other words, the examiner must look to what is disclosed in the specification when deciding whether to give a § 101 rejection. Second, the majority rejects the notion that the § 101 includes a judicially created "mathematical algorithm" exception. That is not to say that mathematical algorithms per se are patentable under *Alappat.* Clearly some (such as the one in *Benson*) are not. Rather, the majority is saying that certain types of mathematical subject matter, standing alone, represent nothing more than abstract ideas until reduced to some type of practical application.

The dissenting view of Judge Archer, joined by Judge Nies, is also important to consider. On the facts in this case, they do not agree with the majority on the fundamental question: what did Alappat discover? (They see Alappat's discovery as an abstract idea; the majority see it as a machine.) It is not this difference of opinion that is important, rather it is Judge Archer's analysis as to why.

Judge Archer's analysis raises the good point that a § 101 analysis involves not merely determining whether the claim reads on structure, but whether the claim is to an invention or discovery that is patentable subject matter. Under the majority's ruling, in making a § 101 determination, the Patent Office must follow 35 U.S.C. § 112, paragraph six and consider the disclosed structure. Following the reasoning of Judge Archer's dissent, the Patent Office also needs to determine from the specification what the applicant claims to have discovered or invented. This will amount to using the specification as a litmus test, to determine whether the subject matter disclosed in the specification is statutory subject matter and whether the applicant's claim is commensurate in scope with what the applicant discloses.

§ 9.38   Patentable Subject Matter Case Digest

When evaluating the patentability of a new invention, it is sometimes helpful to see how others have claimed similar subject matter, and to see how courts have construed their claims. This is particularly true when there is some question regarding whether the invention is statutory subject matter or not. **Sections 9.39** and **9.40** contain a digest of cases where patentable subject matter under 35 U.S.C. § 101 is in issue. First presented are those cases where patentable subject matter is found. Second presented are those cases where patentable subject matter is not found.

Each case digest begins with an entry identifying the Technical Field to which the invention pertains. The chart below lists these technical fields and identifies the cases involved. Each case digest also includes a brief description of the invention or discovery, in most cases quoting the decision. Each case digest also recites the preamble of an example claim.

Use **Table 9–1** to find cases when the invention is similar to the one you are considering. In many instances you will find helpful ways to analyze the invention, and will be alerted to pitfalls others have discovered.

Table 9–1

Patent Case Digest

Technical Field	Case
Cat-scan & X-ray Diagnostics	*In re Abele*[113]
Computer Graphics	*In re Bernhart,*[114] *In re Noll*[115]
Computer Operating Systems	*In re Pardo,*[116] *In re Bradley,*[117] *In re Chatfield*[118]
Computer-aided Design — Architectural Specifications	*In re Phillips*[119]

[113] 684 F.2d 902 (C.C.P.A. 1982).
[114] 417 F.2d 1395 (C.C.P.A. 1969).
[115] 545 F.2d 141 (C.C.P.A. 1976).
[116] 584 F.2d 912 (C.C.P.A. 1982).
[117] 600 F.2d 807 (C.C.P.A. 1979).
[118] 545 F.2d 152 (C.C.P.A. 1976).
[119] 608 F.2d 879 (C.C.P.A. 1979).

Technical Field	Case
Computer-aided Design — Microwave Circuits	*In re Gelnovatch*[120]
Computer-controlled Oil Refineries	*In re Deutsch*[121]
Data Communication	*In re Mahony*[122]
Data Processing	*In re Waldbaum,*[123] *Gottschalk v. Benson*[124]
Digital Image Processing	*In re Alappat*[125]
Drafting & Milling Machines	*In re Castelet*[126]
Electrocardiograph Signal Analysis	*Arrhythmia Research Technology, Inc. v. Corazonix Corp.*[127]
Financial Recordkeeping	*In re Johnston*[128]
Information Processing	*In re McIlroy*[129]
Manufacturing — Molded Rubber	*Diamond v. Diehr*[130]
Medical Diagnostic Expert System	*In re Grams,*[131] *In re Meyer*[132]
Monitoring of Waterways	*In re Sarkar*[133]
Natural Language Translation	*In re Toma*[134]
Petrochemical Refining	*Parker v. Flook*[135]
Petroleum Engineering/Geology	*In re Christensen*[136]
Radar	*In re Richman*[137]

[120] 595 F.2d 32 (C.C.P.A. 1979).
[121] 553 F.2d 689 (C.C.P.A. 1977).
[122] 421 F.2d 742 (C.C.P.A. 1970).
[123] 457 F.2d 977 (C.C.P.A. 1972).
[124] 409 U.S. 63 (1972).
[125] 33 F.3d 1526 (Fed. Cir. 1994).
[126] 562 F.2d 1236 (C.C.P.A. 1977).
[127] 958 F.2d 1053 (Fed. Cir. 1992).
[128] 502 F.2d 765 (C.C.P.A. 1974).
[129] 442 F.2d 1397 (C.C.P.A. 1971).
[130] 450 U.S. 175 (1981).
[131] 888 F.2d 835 (Fed. Cir. 1989).
[132] 688 F.2d 789 (C.C.P.A. 1971).
[133] 588 F.2d 1330 (C.C.P.A. 1978).
[134] 575 F.2d 872 (C.C.P.A. 1978).
[135] 437 U.S. 584 (1978).
[136] 478 F.2d 1392 (C.C.P.A. 1973).
[137] 563 F.2d 1026 (C.C.P.A. 1977).

Table 9–1

(*continued*)

Technical Field	Case
Seismic Measurement	*In re Taner,*[138] *In re Johnson,*[139] *In re Walter,*[140] *In re Musgrave*[141]
Spectrographic Analysis	*In re Prater*[142]
Television Camera Tubes	*Hirschfeld v. Banner*[143]
Typesetting & Printing	*In re Freeman*[144]
Voice & Pattern Recognition	*In re Iwahashi*[145]

§ 9.39   Caselaw, Invention as Patentable Subject Matter

In re Prater[146]

Technical Field.   Spectrographic Analysis

Invention or Discovery.   "Applicants have discovered a way to identify one particular subset of equations, related to one optimum set of (spectrogram) peaks, which provides significantly more accurate values for the concentrations of the constituent gases than other subsets."[147]

Claim Preamble.   "The method of determining with minimum error from the spectra of spectral analysis the concentration of the components of a mixture where the components are known and the concentration-determining peaks of the spectral analysis are present in number exceeding the number of said components, which comprises . . . ."[148]

---

[138] 681 F.2d 787 (C.C.P.A. 1982).

[139] 589 F.2d 1070 (C.C.P.A. 1978).

[140] 618 F.2d 758 (C.C.P.A. 1980).

[141] 431 F.2d 882 (C.C.P.A. 1970).

[142] 415 F.2d 1378 (C.C.P.A. 1969).

[143] 462 F. Supp. 135 (D.D.C. 1978).

[144] 573 F.2d 872 (C.C.P.A. 1978).

[145] 888 F.2d 1370 (Fed. Cir. 1989).

[146] 415 F.2d 1378 (C.C.P.A. 1969).

[147] *Id.* at 1379.

[148] *Id.* at 1380.

In re Bernhart[149]

Technical Field.   Computer Graphics

Invention or Discovery.   "A method of an apparatus for automatically making a two-dimensional portrayal of a three-dimensional object from any desired angle and distance and on any desired plane of projection."[150]

Claim Preamble.   "A system for providing a planar illustration of a three-dimensional object as seen by an observer from a selected observation point in space comprising . . . ."[151]

In re Mahony[152]

Technical Field.   Data Communication

Invention or Discovery.   "Applicant has disclosed that one way of determining which bits in this (digital communication bit) stream are framing bits is to perform, by means of circuitry, a logical process of elimination."[153]

Claim Preamble.   "The method of establishing which bits in a bit stream are data bits and which are framing bits, where the framing bits appear in predetermined positions and have a predetermined sequence of values, comprising the steps of . . . ."[154]

In re Musgrave[155]

Technical Field.   Seismic Measurement

Invention or Discovery.   "Applicant has discovered that a family of seismograms obtained by using an *expanded*-spread of detectors can be most precisely corrected for the effect of the weathered layer by deriving the necessary time-correction from the time-occurrence of the first reflection on a corresponding family of seismograms obtained using a *split*-spread of detectors."[156]

---

[149] 417 F.2d 1395 (C.C.P.A. 1969).

[150] *Id.* at 1396.

[151] *Id.* at 1397.

[152] 421 F.2d 742 (C.C.P.A. 1970).

[153] *Id.* at 743.

[154] *Id.* at 744.

[155] 431 F.2d 882 (C.C.P.A. 1970).

[156] *Id.* at 884.

Claim Preamble. "In seismic exploration, the method of establishing weathering corrections in the form of individual static time-corrections for the signals from each of a plurality of seismic detecting stations spaced one from the other along a traverse which comprises . . . ."[157]

In re McIlroy[158]

Technical Field. Information Processing

Invention or Discovery: Little information is given, but the invention appears to be a form of indirect memory addressing.

Claim Preamble. "The method of processing information which comprises the steps of . . . ."[159]

In re Waldbaum[160]

Technical Field. Data Processing

Invention or Discovery. "a method of analyzing data words to determine the number of 1's they contain."[161]

Claim Preamble. A method for controlling the operation of a data processor to determine the number of 1's in a data word; said data processor including a memory . . . means for normally controlling the sequential execution . . . a plurality of registers; means for storing memory data words in said registers . . . means responsive to the execution of predetermined instruction . . . comprising the steps of . . ."[162]

In re Johnston[163]

Technical Field. Financial Recordkeeping

Invention or Discovery. "The checks and deposit slips are automatically processed by forming those items as machine-readable records; that is,

---

[157] *Id.* at 885.

[158] 442 F.2d 1397 (C.C.P.A. 1971).

[159] *Id.* at 1398.

[160] *In re* Waldbaum, 457 F.2d 997 (C.C.P.A. 1972).

[161] *Id.* at 998.

[162] *Id.* at 1000.

[163] 502 F.2d 765 (C.C.P.A. 1974).

magnetic ink characters are imprinted on the check, so that magnetic readers are enabled to process these checks and enter the data into a computer system in the form of coded electrical signals."[164]

Claim Preamble. "A record-keeping machine system for financial accounts, said system comprising . . . ."[165]

In re Noll[166]

Technical Field.   Computer Graphics

Invention or Discovery.   "A system and apparatus for the display of text or other graphical information on a device such as a cathode ray tube. The data to be displayed are supplied by a computer or similar source in 'point-plotting' format in which each element (point, line, character, etc.) is individually specified."[167]

Claim Preamble.   "A computer graphics system for displaying in a multi-line, multi-point-per-line format images corresponding to a sequence of input display commands comprising . . . ."[168]

In re Chatfield[169]

Technical Field.   Computer Operating Systems

Invention or Discovery.   "Chatfield's novel solution (to controlling multiple programs in a multi-programmed computer system) dynamically evaluates and reassigns program priorities as the program executes."[170]

Claim Preamble.   "A method of operating a computing system upon more than one processing program concurrently for improving total resource utilization, said computing system comprising . . . ."[171]

---

[164] *Id.* at 766.

[165] *Id.* at 767.

[166] 545 F.2d 141 (C.C.P.A. 1976).

[167] *Id.* at 142.

[168] *Id.* at 144.

[169] 545 F.2d 152 (C.C.P.A. 1976).

[170] *Id.* at 154.

[171] *Id.*

In re Deutsch[172]

Technical Field.   Computer-controlled Oil Refineries

Invention or Discovery.   "Deutsch controls and optimizes the operation of a system of multi-unit plants—e.g., oil refineries at different geographic locations."[173]

Claim Preamble.   "The method of operating a system of multi-plants which produce finished products from material derived from a plurality of sources at fluctuating costs for delivery to markets of variable prices, each of said plants having a different, unique, cost function in producing the products, said method comprising . . . ."[174]

In re Freeman[175]

Technical Field.   Typesetting & Printing

Invention or Discovery.   "Freeman's system is especially useful in printing mathematical formulae. Its particular advantage over prior computer-aided printing systems is its positioning of mathematical symbols in an expression in accordance with their appearance, while maintaining the mathematical integrity of the expression."[176]

Claim Preamble.   "In a computer display system . . . a data processor comprising . . . ."[177]

In re Toma[178]

Technical Field.   Natural Language Translation

Invention or Discovery.   "The invention involves a method of operating a digital computer to translate from a source natural language, e.g., Russian, to a target natural language, e.g., English. The method involves three phases.

---

172 553 F.2d 689 (C.C.P.A. 1977).
173 *Id.* at 690.
174 *Id.*
175 573 F.2d 1237 (C.C.P.A. 1978).
176 *Id.* at 1239.
177 *Id.* at 1242.
178 575 F.2d 872 (C.C.P.A. 1978).

The dictionary look-up phase . . . the syntactical analysis phase . . . the synthesis phase . . . ."[179]

Claim Preamble.   "A method for translation between source and target natural languages using a programmable digital computer system, the steps comprising . . . ."[180]

Hirschfeld v. Banner[181]

Technical Field.   Television Camera Tubes

Invention or Discovery.   "Plaintiffs' system increases the dynamic range of the vidicon by generating the electron beam at a repetition rate for each point in relation to the intensity of radiation falling on that point. Points exposed to low intensity radiation are thus read only when the illumination signal has been sufficiently integrated to yield an acceptable signal-to-noise ratio."[182]

Claim Preamble.   "In combination with an electro-optical imaging device having target means for receiving an image and means for generating an electron-beam for reading the image formed on said target means in said device . . . a digital control system comprising . . . ."[183]

In re Johnson[184]

Technical Field.   Seismic Measurement

Invention or Discovery.   "Methods for removing undesired components (noise) from seismic data . . . the invention makes use of the physical principle that, because of the manner in which the seismic data are gathered, closely adjacent detectors should receive reflections of essentially the same wave shape from a given layer."[185]

Claim Preamble.   "A machine implemented method for enhancing digital data in a seismic record, said data having a coherent signal component comprising a measure of the similarity between spatially related time series data,

---

[179] *Id.* at 874.

[180] *Id.* at 875.

[181] 462 F. Supp. 135 (D.D.C. 1978).

[182] *Id.* at 137.

[183] *Id.*

[184] 589 F.2d 1070 (C.C.P.A. 1978).

[185] *Id.* at 1070.

and a noise component, and for improving the signal to noise ratio thereof, comprising the steps of . . . ."[186]

In re Bradley[187]

Technical Field.   Computer Operating Systems

Invention or Discovery.   ". . . the internal operation of the computer and its ability to manage efficiently its operation in a multiprogrammed format. A multiprogrammed format is one in which the computer is capable of executing more than one program, and thus perform more than one application at the same time, without the need to reprogram the computer for each task it must perform. Specifically, the invention relates to altering or repositioning information in the computer's system base."[188]

Claim Preamble.   "In a multiprogramming computer system having a main memory, a central processing unit (CPU) coupled to said main memory, said (CPU) controlling the state of a plurality of groups of processes being in a running, ready, wait or suspended state, said computer system also having scratch pad registers . . . a data structure for storing coded signals for communicating between said processes and said operating system, and said scratch pad registers, said data structure comprising . . . ."[189] [Note that the claim is to a data structure.]

In re Phillips[190]

Technical Field.   Computer-aided Design of Architectural Specifications

Invention or Discovery.   "The invention relates to computer apparatus and process for preparing a complete set of printed architectural specifications, which describe the various materials and techniques used in constructing a building."[191]

Claim Preamble.   "A system for preparing a printed architectural specification comprising . . . ."[192]

---

[186] *Id.* at 1072.

[187] 600 F.2d 807 (C.C.P.A. 1979).

[188] *Id.* at 808.

[189] *Id.* at 809.

[190] 608 F.2d 879 (C.C.P.A. 1979).

[191] *Id.* at 879.

[192] *Id.* at 880.

Diamond v. Diehr[193]

Technical Field.   Manufacture of Molded Rubber

Invention or Discovery.   "According to the respondents, the continuous measuring of the temperature inside the mold cavity, the feeding of this information into a digital computer which constantly recalculates the cure time, and the signaling by the computer to open the press, are all new in the art."[194]

Claim Preamble.   "A method of operating a rubber-molding press for precision molded compounds with the aid of a digital computer, comprising . . . ."[195]

In re Taner[196]

Technical Field.   Seismic Exploration

Invention or Discovery.   "Appellants' invention relates to a method of seismic exploration by which substantially plane or substantially cylindrical seismic energy waves are simulated from substantially spherical seismic waves."[197]

Claim Preamble.   "A method of seismic exploration by simulating from substantially spherical seismic waves the reflection response of the earth to seismic energy having a substantially continuous wavefront over an extent of an area being explored having at least one dimension which is large relative to a seismic wavelength, comprising the steps of . . . ."[198]

In re Abele[199]

Technical Field.   Cat-scan and X-ray Diagnostics

Invention or Discovery.   "Appellants' invention is directed to an improvement in computed tomography whereby the exposure to X-ray is reduced while the reliability of the produced image is improved . . . When enough measurements have been taken, a computer is implemented to mathematically

---

[193] 450 U.S. 175 (1981).

[194] *Id.* at 179.

[195] *Id.* at n.4.

[196] 681 F.2d 787 (C.C.P.A. 1982).

[197] *Id.* at 787.

[198] *Id.* at 788.

[199] 684 F.2d 902 (C.C.P.A. 1982).

interpret the data, which is then displayed as a reconstruction of the slice on, *inter alia,* a television screen for diagnostic purposes."[200]

Claim Preamble. "A method of displaying data in a field comprising the steps of . . . ."[201]

In re Pardo[202]

Technical Field. Computer Operating Systems

Invention or Discovery. "A method for controlling the internal operation of a computer. The invention converts a computer from a sequential processor (which executes program instructions in the order in which they are presented) to a processor which is not dependent on the order in which it receives programmed steps."[203]

Claim Preamble. "A process of operating a general purpose data processor of known type to enable the data processor to execute formulas in an object program comprising a plurality of formulas, such that the same results will be produced when using the same given data, regardless of the sequence in which said formulas are presented in said object program, comprising the steps of . . . ."[204]

In re Iwahashi[205]

Technical Field. Voice Recognition and Pattern Recognition

Invention or Discovery. "The invention relates to an auto-correlation unit for use in pattern recognition to obtain auto-correlation coefficients as for stored signal samples."[206]

Claim Preamble. "An auto-correlation unit for providing auto-correlation coefficients for use as feature parameters in pattern recognition for N pieces of sampled input values X_n ($n = 0$ to $N - 1$), said unit comprising . . . ."[207]

---

[200] *Id.* at 903.

[201] *Id.* at 908.

[202] 684 F.2d 912 (C.C.P.A. 1982).

[203] *Id.* at 913.

[204] *Id.*

[205] 888 F.2d 1370 (Fed. Cir. 1989).

[206] *Id.* at 1371.

[207] *Id.* at 1372.

Arrhythmia Research Technology, Inc. v. Corazonix Corp.[208]

Technical Field.   Electrocardiograph Signal Analysis

Invention or Discovery.   "The invention claimed in the '459 patent is directed to the analysis of electrocardiographic signals in order to determine certain characteristics of the heart function."[209]

Claim Preamble.   "A method for analyzing electrocardiograph signals to determine the presence or absence of a predetermined level of high frequency energy in the late QRS signal, comprising the steps of . . . ."[210]

In re Alappat[211]

Technical Field.   Digital Image Processing (Digital Oscilloscope)

Invention or Discovery.   "To overcome these (discontinuous or jagged) effects, Alappat's invention employs an antialiasing system wherein each vector making up the waveform is represented by modulating the illumination intensity of pixels having centerpoints bounding the trajectory of the vector. The intensity at which each of pixels is illuminated depends upon the distance of the centerpoint of each pixel from the trajectory of the vector. Pixels lying squarely on the waveform trace receive maximum illumination, whereas pixels lying along an edge of the trace receive illumination decreasing in intensity proportional to the increase in the distance of the centerpoint of the pixel from the vector trajectory."[212]

Claim Preamble.   "A rasterizer for converting vector list data representing sample magnitudes of an input waveform into anti-aliased pixel illumination intensity data to be displayed on a display means comprising . . . ."[213]

---

[208] 958 F.2d 1053 (Fed. Cir. 1992).

[209] *Id.* at 1054.

[210] *Id.* at 1055.

[211] 33 F.3d 1526 (Fed. Cir. 1994).

[212] *Id.* at 1537.

[213] *Id.* at 1538.

§ 9.40 Caselaw, Invention as Unpatentable Subject Matter

Gottschalk v. Benson[214]

Technical Field.   Data Processing

Invention or Discovery.   An algorithm for converting binary coded decimal numerals into pure binary numerals.

Claim Preamble.   "The method of converting signals from binary coded decimal form into binary which comprises the steps of . . ."[215]

In re Christensen[216]

Technical Field.   Petroleum Engineering/Geology

Invention or Discovery.   "A method of determining the porosity of subsurface formations . . . to obtain a continuous plot of the porosity of the substances penetrated by a bore hole."[217]

Claim Preamble.   "The method of determining the porosity of a subsurface formation *in situ* comprising the steps of . . ."[218]

In re Richman[219]

Technical Field.   Radar

Invention or Discovery.   "The invention involves a method of calculating (according to a mathematical formula) an average boresight correction angle for an airborne, coherent pulse Doppler, synthetic aperture, signal processing radar, using actual terrain measurements, and a method of calculating (according to a mathematical formula) the average vertical velocity component of the aircraft carrying the radar, using these same measurements."[220]

---

214 409 U.S. 63 (1972).

215 *Id.* at 73.

216 478 F.2d 1392 (C.C.P.A. 1973).

217 *Id.* at 1392.

218 *Id.*

219 563 F.2d 1026 (C.C.P.A. 1977).

220 *Id.* at 1027.

Claim Preamble. "In an airborne coherent pulse Doppler synthetic aperture depression angle sensing processing radar, the method of calculating a correction factor δ, for measured values of depression angle, B, comprising . . . ."[221]

In re Castelet[222]

Technical Field. Drafting and Milling Machines

Invention or Discovery. "Inventor sought patent on method of generating a curve or family of curves, employing a computer in conjunction with drafting and milling machines."[223]

Claim Preamble. "A machine method of generating a curve from data supplied to a computer in the form of coordinates of points defining two given segments of tangents to the curve to be generated extending from the end of and substantially by said curve for controlling numerical control system type model forming means, wherein data, in the form of electrical signals representing a table of coordinates of points, of characteristics of a base curve inscribed on a unit-cube between two opposite vertices of said unit-cube is stored in a memory bank of said computer . . . said computer thereafter automatically performing the steps of . . . ."[224]

Parker v. Flook[225]

Technical Field. Petrochemical Refining

Invention or Discovery. "A method of updating alarm limits. In essence, the method consists of three steps: an initial step which merely measures the present value of the process variable (e.g. the temperature); an intermediate step which uses an algorithm to calculate an updated alarm-limit value; and a final step in which the actual alarm limit is adjusted to the updated value."[226]

Claim Preamble. "A method for updating the value of at least one alarm limit on at least one process variable involved in a process comprising the catalytic chemical conversion of hydrocarbons wherein said alarm limit has a current value of . . . which comprises . . . ."[227]

---

[221] *Id.* at 1028.

[222] 562 F.2d 1236 (C.C.P.A. 1977).

[223] *Id.* at 1236.

[224] *Id.* at 1238.

[225] 437 U.S. 584 (1978).

[226] *Id.* at 585.

[227] *Id.* at 596.

In re Sarkar[228]

Technical Field.   Monitoring of Waterways

Invention or Discovery.   "Sarkar's invention is a technique for mathematically modeling an open channel, e.g., a natural stream or artificial waterway. Sarkar says his method of constructing a mathematical model is capable of accurately providing the flow parameters of a river over a period of time . . . ."[229]

Claim Preamble.   "A method of constructing a mathematical model of at least a portion of an open channel segmented into at least one reach and in which there is a spatially varied unsteady flow and including the existence of at least one gravity wave during a given period of time comprising . . . ."[230]

In re Gelnovatch[231]

Technical Field.   Computer-aided Design—Microwave Circuits

Invention or Discovery.   "A process for determining a set of values for use in a mathematical model of a microwave circuit. The model comprises mathematical equations that describe both the functional characteristics, e.g., impedance, capacitance and inductance of the circuit components, and the manner in which the components interrelate to determine a circuit response. The purpose of the mathematical model is to select by arithmetical computations values for the functional characteristics of the circuit components so that the 'modeled' microwave circuit, if ever built, would exhibit a specified response."[232]

Claim Preamble.   "A computer method of automatically determining, from a set of initial reference parameters, a set of optimal microwave circuit element parameters for producing data defining a predetermined objective circuit response function of a given microwave circuit configuration comprising the steps of . . . ."[233]

---

[228] 558 F.2d 1330 (C.C.P.A. 1978).

[229] *Id.* at 1330.

[230] *Id.* at 1331.

[231] 595 F.2d 32 (C.C.P.A. 1979).

[232] *Id.* at 32–33.

[233] *Id.* at 33.

In re Walter[234]

Technical Field.   Seismic Measurement

Invention or Discovery.   "Applicant has invented a method and apparatus for performing the method of cross-correlating the returning jumbled signal with the original chirp signal which was transmitted into the earth. As a result, the returning signal is effectively unscrambled; each of the trains of waves received at each geophone station is converted to a form equivalent to the type of signal which would have been produced had an impulse-type signal been used in place of the chirp signal."[235]

Claim Preamble.   "In a method of seismic surveying in which a train of seismic source waves is transmitted downwardly into the earth and is there deflected by subsurface formations and in which corresponding trains of seismic waves deflected by such formation are received at geophone stations . . . the improved method of correlating said series of sampled signals for each geophone station with respect to said series of reference signals that comprises . . . ."[236]

In re Meyer[237]

Technical Field.   Medical Diagnostic Expert System

Invention or Discovery.   "The invention is a process and an apparatus for carrying out the process of testing a complex system and analyzing the results of these tests. The process proceeds by (1) dividing the complex system into a plurality of 'elements' and (2) associating a factor of *function or malfunction* with each of these elements. The factors, which are initialized at the outset, are updated or modified during the course of the process in dependence upon the responses of this system to a series of tests. When the tests have been completed, the resultant factors so produced indicate a measure of probability of function or malfunction of the elements with which they are associated. The patent uses as an example of a complex system, the human nervous system."[238]

Claim Preamble.   "A process for identifying locations of probable malfunction in a complex system, said process comprising the steps of . . . ."[239]

---

[234] 618 F.2d 758 (C.C.P.A. 1980).

[235] *Id.* at 761.

[236] *Id.*

[237] 688 F.2d 789 (C.C.P.A. 1982).

[238] *Id.* at 790.

[239] *Id.* at 792.

In re Grams[240]

Technical Field.   Medical Diagnostic Expert System

Invention or Discovery.   "The invention provides a method of testing a complex system to determine whether the system condition is normal or abnormal and, if abnormal, to determine the cause of the abnormality . . . the invention is applicable to any complex system, whether it be electrical, mechanical, chemical, biological, or combinations thereof."[241]

Claim Preamble.   "A method of diagnosing an abnormal condition in an individual, the individual being characterized by a plurality of correlated parameters of a set of such parameters that is representative of the individual's condition, the parameters comprising data resulting from a plurality of clinical laboratory tests which measure the levels of chemical and biological constituents of the individual and each parameter having a reference range of values, the method comprising . . . ."[242]

§ 9.41   Definition of Patentable Subject Matter, the Common Thread

Is there a common thread to all the § 101 patentable subject matter cases? What is the difference between a patentable invention and an unpatentable discovery?

This subject can divert you into hours of philosophical discussions. Many software professionals have pondered this subject and will jump at the chance to debate it. You may enjoy such debates, but ultimately you need a simple way to sift the patentable from the unpatentable, in order to advise clients, draft claims, argue motions, and get on with business.

So what is the common thread? What does the patentable invention have that the unpatentable discovery does not? The answer is human control. Human control is the common thread. *Diamond v. Chakrabarty*[243] maintains that "anything under the sun that is made by man," qualifies as patentable subject matter. To make something is to control its existence. Without control there is no possession and no ownership.

It is the old adage that possession is nine-tenths of the law. Case in point is the 1805 property law case of *Pierson v. Post.*[244] Post did not own the fox he

---

[240] 888 F.2d 835 (Fed. Cir. 1989).

[241] *Id.* at 836.

[242] *Id.*

[243] 447 U.S. 303 (1980).

[244] 3 Caines 175 (N.Y.S. Ct. 1805).

was chasing, because he did not have possession of it. Thus when Pierson jumped out of the bushes and shot the fox before Post could get to it, Post had no cause of action, even though he had been cheated out of his trophy (or perhaps his bounty). You cannot own a wild animal you cannot catch.

In translating *Pierson v. Post* to intellectual property law, what does it mean to have control? Some examples may help. You can draw a circle, but you cannot control pi. You can have control over how big the circle is, but you cannot change pi—the relationship between your circle and its diameter. Pi is a principle or law of nature. You can exploit a law of nature, but cannot change it. You can build and control a nuclear reactor, but cannot change nuclear energy or make nuclear energy cease to exist. A law of nature is a wild animal that can never be caught. Push an anvil off a cliff, and it falls, irreversibly. You control the push; gravity does the rest.

Think about what Newton and Einstein did. They each changed the way we understand nature. They did not change the way we think. Our thoughts are our own. No matter how brilliant their discoveries were, Newton and Einstein gave us understanding, but not control. Newton taught us calculus to explain why an apple falls from a tree. Calculus or no calculus, the apple always falls. Einstein taught us curved space-time, to explain why an apple falls from a tree. But the apple still always falls. Gravity remains a wild untamed animal, and we are powerless to change it.

Therefore, when confronted with the dilemma of patentable invention or unpatentable principle, ask yourself about the claimed invention, "Can humanity control this thing? Does humanity have the power to change this thing, or make this thing cease to be true or cease to exist?" If so, then this thing, if new, may be patented, for it qualifies as "anything under the sun that is made by man." If the answer is no, then you have discovered an untamable wild animal, beautiful to look at, perhaps, profoundly empowering, perhaps, but something that no one can own.

§ 9.42   *Freeman-Walter-Abele* Test

Although there is considerable evidence that the Federal Circuit Court of Appeals is moving away from this test, the *Freeman-Walter-Abele* two-step test for determining patentability of computer programs is still worth understanding. The test comes from the decisions of the Court of Customs and Patent Appeals in *In re Freeman, In re Walter,* and *In re Abele.*[245] The first step of the *Freeman-Walter-Abele* test is to determine whether a mathematical algorithm is recited directly or indirectly in the claim. If so, then the second step is to determine whether the claimed invention, as a whole, is no

---

[245] *In re* Freeman, 573 F.2d 1237 (CCPA 1978); *In re* Walter, 618 F.2d 758 (CCPA 1980); *In re* Abele, 684 F.2d 902 (CCPA 1982).

more than the algorithm itself. If so, then the claim recites nonstatutory subject matter.[246] The difficulty with the test, and the reason use of the test is waning, is that there is no clear agreement as to what is a "mathematical algorithm."

---

[246] *See In re* Schrader, 22 F.3d 290 (Fed. Cir. 1994).

CHAPTER 10

INTERNATIONAL PATENT PROTECTION FOR SOFTWARE

§ 10.1   Worldwide Software Patent Protection

The United States presently leads the world in software production. According to United States government figures, 1992 sales in the three core elements of the software industry—programming services, prepackaged software, and computer integrated design—accounts for over $36.7 billion of our domestic gross product. The software industry has created jobs at a remarkable rate; since 1987 employment in the software industry has risen at an annual rate of 6.6 percent; today the industry employs about 4 percent of the United States work force. United States firms hold about 75 percent of the world market for prepackaged software and approximately 60 percent of the world market for software and related services. In 1991 foreign sales of United States prepackaged software vendors totaled over 19.7 billion.[1] The United States also leads the world in providing legal protection for software. As a form of protection in

---

[1] U.S. Patent & Trademark Office, *PTO Notice of H'rgs on Software Patent Issues,* 58 Fed. Reg. 66347 (Dec. 1993).

the United States, software patent protection is reaching predominance, because patents can protect utilitarian aspects of software whereas copyright cannot.

The intellectual property laws in Europe and Asia recognize software as a protectable technology; however, the patent laws in Europe and Asia are not evolved to the extent of the United States. **Chapter 10** concentrates principally on the practices concerning software patents in the European Patent Office and in the Japanese Patent Office.

§ 10.2   European Patents

European patents are granted for any inventions that are susceptible of industrial application, that are new, and that involve an inventive step.[2] The patent term is 20 years from the filing date. Applications are published 18 months after the priority date. Absolute novelty is required. That is, the priority application must be filed before the invention is made available to the public, for example, by written or oral description or by use.[3]

The European Patent Convention or EPC has both a novelty requirement and a nonobviousness requirement, not unlike the law in the United States. The EPC novelty requirement simply provides that an invention shall be considered to be new if it does not form a part of the state of the art.[4] The nonobviousness requirement is expressed in terms of "inventive step." An invention shall be considered as involving an inventive step if, having regard to the state of the art, it is not obvious to a person skilled in the art.[5] To translate EPC requirements into U.S. Patent Law requirements, Article 54 EPC serves a purpose similar to 35 U.S.C. § 102, and Article 56 EPC serves a purpose similar to 35 U.S.C. § 103.

The EPC does not define the term invention. Thus there is no Article to serve the purpose, similar to 35 U.S.C. § 101, of defining what is patentable subject matter. Taking the opposite approach, Article 52(2) EPC gives a nonexhaustive list of what is *not* considered a patentable invention (that is, not patentable subject matter):

> The following in particular shall not be regarded as inventions within the meaning of paragraph 1:
>
> (a)   discoveries, scientific theories and mathematical methods;
>
> (b)   aesthetic creations;

---

[2] Art. 52(1) Eur. Pat. Convention (Oct. 5, 1973).

[3] *Id.* 54(2).

[4] *Id.* 54(1).

[5] *Id.* 56.

(c)   schemes, rules and methods for performing mental acts, playing games or doing business, and programs for computers;

(d)   presentations of information.[6]

Note that computer programs are explicitly excluded in Article 52(2)(c). However, this exclusion does not mean that software patents are forbidden under the EPC.

§ 10.3   History of Software Patents in Europe and the European Patent Convention

The 1962 and 1963 drafts of the European Patent Convention contained no exclusion of computer programs. That exclusion first appeared in the second preliminary draft of the European Patent Convention in 1971. When this exclusion was added, the drafters were no doubt mindful of the Patent Cooperation Treaty (PCT), which states that no International Searching Authority is required to search for prior art involving computer programs.[7]

However, the overriding reason computer programs were excluded as patentable subject matter is that when the exclusion was drafted, many European countries already had case law that frowned upon patentability of computer programs. Thus Article 52(2)(c) is, for the most part, a codification of existing European case law.[8] In fact, not all countries even felt this list of exceptions was necessary. Switzerland, for example, explicitly rejected the list of nonpatentable inventions when it adapted its national patent law to the EPC. To the Swiss, the exceptions were unnecessary, because the line between patentable and unpatentable subject matter was expected to evolve in any event.[9]

It is interesting to explore how software patent applications fared in various countries across Europe during the time the European Patent Convention was being worked out. In 1965 in the United Kingdom, for example, Slee and Harris's Application claimed a method of operating a computer to solve a linear programming problem by a new iterative algorithm. The method claims (method of operating a computer) were held to be unpatentable intellectual information that was not a "vendible product" and thus not "a matter of new manufacture"—in essence a "mental steps doctrine" rejection in United States patent law terms. More significant, however, the apparatus

---

[6] *Id.* 52(2).

[7] Rule 39.1(vi) Pat. Cooperation Treaty, Sept. 15, 1971.

[8] G. Gall, *1985 Eur. Pat. Office Guidelines on the Protection of Inventions Relating to Computer Programs,* 2 Computer L. & Prac., No. 1 at 2 (1985).

[9] *Id.*; (citing Explanatory n. on Art. 1(a) of Swiss Patents L. Amendment Bill 67 (a communication from the Fed. Council to the Fed. Assembly concerning three Pat. Conventions and amendment of the Pat. Law of 24 Mar. 1976).

claims (to the programming means and to the programmed computer) were held to be patentable subject matter, as a machine modified in a particular way.[10]

Slee and Harris's Application is interesting in several aspects. First, it was decided in 1965, three years before *In re Prater*[11] was decided in the United States, and seven years before the United States Supreme Court decision in *Gottschalk v. Benson.*[12] (In these famous cases the United States courts addressed whether mathematical calculations were patentable subject matter.) Second, the decision recognizes that there is something patentable when it comes to software. The decision did not see software as being patentable apart from the computer; it couched patentability in terms of the machine (computer) being programmed (modified) in a particular way. Although failing to recognize Slee and Harris's method claims, the court in the United Kingdom was nevertheless on the right track.

In Austria the software patent did not fare as well, although it must be remembered that each software patent test case involves different claims, some easier to find patentability than others. In 1968, an applicant sought an Austrian patent for an interest calculating program. The program was found not to comprise patentable subject matter. The Austrian court held that calculating rules, algorithms, and computer programs derived from such mental processes did not fall under the concept of "technical" invention—again a "mental steps doctrine" decision.[13]

The software patent suffered a similar fate in Switzerland (computer program held unpatentable in 1969),[14] and in the Netherlands (process for operating a software-controlled telecommunication apparatus held unpatentable).[15] France went a step further. In 1968 France included in its revised patent law a provision that excluded computer programs or sets of instructions covering the operation of a calculating machine.[16]

During the 1960s and 1970s the patent offices and the courts in Europe grappled with the concept of the software patent, just as the Patent Office and courts in the United States did. It is not an easy issue, particularly when many people during that era believed that computers were simply "thinking machines." Operating from that belief, it is easy to see how courts concluded that software was just a series of "mental steps."

---

[10] Slee & Harris's Application, [1966] RPC 194, [1966] FSR 51.

[11] 415 F.2d 1378 (1968), *aff'd in part & rev'd in part,* 415 F.2d 1393 (C.C.P.A. 1969).

[12] 409 U.S. 63 (1972).

[13] Interest Calculating Program, [1968] GRURInt. 211, Linear Programming Device III, [1968] GRURInt. 281.

[14] *Ex parte* Hufnagel [1969] GRURInt. 142, [1970] 1 IIC 148.

[15] Tel. Connecting Sys., [1971] BIE 54, [1971] 2 IIC 308.

[16] Art. 7, para. 2(3) French Pat. Act 1968; *see* [1968] Ind. Prop. 67.

A most remarkable demonstration of the difficulty this issue presents is this surprising turnabout. The German Federal Patent Court and the United States Supreme Court came down squarely on opposite sides of whether the Benson invention (for converting binary coded decimal numbers to binary numbers) was patentable subject matter. The United States Supreme Court struck down the Benson claims as being an attempt to preempt all use of a mathematical algorithm. The German Federal Patent Court saw it differently and deemed the claims to be patentable subject matter.

Benson developed an algorithm, discussed in **Chapter 9,** for manipulating the digits of a binary coded decimal number (then used to light glowing filament digital displays) into binary numbers (then used, and still used, as the lifeblood number system of digital computers). Although Benson's method claims recited the algorithm in a computer "shift register" environment, the method could be practiced by a human with pencil and paper.

The decision by the German Patent Court in *Benson* is, without a doubt, the high water mark for software patent protection in Germany, and indeed all of Europe. German courts later retracted fully from the *Benson* position and began uniformly rejecting applications where the invention was characterized as an algorithm, or a calculating or organizational rule to be applied or used in known data processing equipment.[17]

§ 10.4   Software Patents under the EPC, *Vicom* Decision

The EPC statutory language seems quite clear. Computer programs are expressly excluded by Article 52(2) EPC. Does this mean that software is simply unpatentable in Europe? Surprisingly, the answer is no, as *Vicom* held.[18]

Vicom involved a European patent application 79 300 903.6, filed May 22, 1979, (publication No. 0 005 954) claiming priority on a United States application filed May 26, 1978. Both method and apparatus claims were presented. The method claims recited a method of digitally processing images in the form of a two-dimensional data array by an operator matrix. The apparatus claims recited an apparatus for carrying out the claimed method. The applicant admitted that it was possible to implement the method and apparatus claims by a suitably programmed conventional computer. The Examining Division of the EPO rejected the application on the grounds that it was for a mathematical method and/or computer program as such. Thus, the EPO considered the application to fall squarely into the exclusionary language of Article 52(2) EPC.

---

[17] BCD Conversion, [1973] Mitt 171, [1974] 5 IIC 211.

[18] Vicom/Computer-related Invention, 2 Eur. Pat. Office Rep. 74 (1987).

Independent method claim 1 and independent apparatus claim 8 read as follows:

1. A method of digitally processing images in the form of a two-dimensional data array having elements arranged in rows and columns in which an operator matrix of a size substantially smaller than the size of the data array is convolved with the data array, including sequentially scanning the elements of the data array with the operator matrix, characterized in that the method includes repeated cycles of sequentially scanning the entire data array with a small generating kernel operator matrix to generate a convolved array and then replacing the data array as a new data array; the small generating kernel remaining the same for any single scan of the entire data array and although comprising at least a multiplicity of elements, nevertheless being of a size substantially smaller than is required of a conventional operator matrix in which the operator matrix is convolved with the data array only once, and the cycle being repeated for each previous new data array by selecting the small generating kernel operator matrices and the number of cycles according to conventional error minimization techniques until the last new data array generated is substantially the required convolution of the original data array with the conventional operator matrix.[19]

*   *   *

8. Apparatus for carrying out the method in Claim 1 including data input means (10) for receiving said data array, and said data array to generate an operator matrix for scanning said data array to generate the required convolution of the operator matrix and the data array, characterized in that there are provided feedback means (50) for transferring the output of the mask means (20) to the data input means, and control means (30) for causing the scanning and transferring of the output of the mask means (20) to the data input means to be repeated a predetermined number of times.

The Examining Division rejected the method claim as a mathematical method because the characterizing part of the claim ("characterized in that . . . .") "would only add a different mathematical concept and would not define new technical subject-matter in terms of technical features."[20] The Examining Division viewed the claim as concerning only a mathematical way of approximating the transfer function of a two-dimensional finite impulse response filter implemented by direct or conventional convolution. In effect, the Examining Division considered digital filtering to be a mathematical operation.

The Board of Appeal reversed. It recognized that "[t]here can be little doubt that any processing operation on an electric signal can be described in mathematical terms. The characteristic of a filter, for example, can be expressed in terms of a mathematical formula."[21] The Board of Appeal then

---

[19] *Id.*

[20] *Id.* at 74, 78.

went on to explain where it draws the line between unpatentable mathematical method and patentable technical process:

> A basic difference between a mathematical method and a technical process can be seen, however, in the fact that a mathematical method or a mathematical algorithm is carried out on numbers (whatever these numbers may represent) and provides a result also in numerical form, the mathematical method or algorithm being only an abstract concept prescribing how to operate on the numbers. No direct technical result is produced by the method as such. In contrast thereto, if a mathematical method is used in a technical process, that process is carried out on a physical entity (which may be a material object but equally an image stored as an electrical signal) by some technical means implementing the method and provides as its result a certain change in that entity. The technical means might include a computer comprising suitable hardware or an appropriately programmed general purpose computer.[22]

The *Vicom* decision is important, for it demonstrates that a computer-related invention is treated as any other invention. It is the "as such" language of Article 52(3) that makes this treatment possible:

> The provisions of paragraph 2 shall exclude patentability of the subject matter or activities referred to in that provision only to the extent to which a European patent application or European patent relates to such subject matter or activities *as such.*[23]

§ 10.5 —EPO Cases after *Vicom*

There have been several EPO Board of Appeal decisions since *Vicom* that demonstrate the viability of that decision, and test its limits.

In 1990 the EPO Board of Appeal decided two IBM software patent applications in favor of patentability. In *IBM/Data Processor Network*[24] the invention related to coordination and control of the internal communications between programs and data files stored in different computers connected as nodes in a telecommunication network. The Board of Appeal held that invention was of sufficient technical character to support patentability because the invention was concerned with the internal workings of processors and the way in which the particular application programs operate on the data.

---

[21] *Id.* at 74, 79.

[22] *Id.*

[23] Art. 53 Eur. Pat. Convention (Oct. 5, 1973) (emphasis added).

[24] IBM/Data Processor Network (T6/83, Eur. Pat. Office J. 1–2 1990).

[25] IBM/Computer-related Invention (T115/85, Eur. Pat. Office J. 1–2 1990).

In *IBM/Computer-related Invention*[25] the claims related to a method of decoding stored phrases and of providing a display of events in a text processing system. The method used a message building program, which the Examining Division considered to be a computer program and hence excluded subject matter. The Board of Appeal reversed. The Board found that patentable subject matter was present, holding that the signaling of conditions prevailing in a machine (word processing machine) was a technical problem and was therefore patentable subject matter.

Do not get the impression that IBM wins every patentability contest before the EPO. In *IBM/Document Abstracting and Retrieving*[26] the Board of Appeal affirmed the Examining Division's rejection of a claim directed to abstracting a document, storing the abstract, and retrieving it in response to a query. This claim was held to fall within the patentably excluded category of "schemes, rules and methods for performing mental acts" under Article 52(2)(c) EPC.

It is interesting that the Board rejected the invention under what United States patent law would call the "mental steps doctrine." It did not reject the claim as being a computer program per se. In urging patentability, IBM alluded to the following language from *Vicom*, on which the Board in that case found patentability:

> . . . if a mathematical method is used in a technical process that process is carried out on a physical entity (which may be a material object but equally an image stored as an electrical signal) by some technical means . . .[27]

IBM argued that the invention here involved comparable electrical signals representing stored information. The Board rejected this argument, finding that here the electrical signals do not represent a physical thing (for example, an image), but rather part of "the information content of a document, which could be of any nature."[28] "The claimed activity," the Board reasoned, "does not bring about any change in the thing operated upon (i.e. the document to be abstracted) but derives therefrom new information to be stored."[29] The Board was thus not willing to construe *Vicom* to hold that any manner of bringing about a change in a physical entity will *ipso facto* qualify as a technical process.

In another application, *IBM/Semantically Related Expressions,*[30] IBM tested the limits of the *Vicom* decision. The claimed invention was a text processing

[26] IBM/Document Abstracting & Retrieving (T22/85, Eur. Pat. Office J. 1–2 1990).

[27] Vicom/Computer-related Invention, 2 Eur. Pat. Office Rep. 74, 79 (1987).

[28] IBM/Document Abstracting & Retrieving (T22/85, Eur. Pat. Office J. 1–2, para. 13 1990).

[29] *Id.*

[30] IBM/Semantically Related Expressions (T52/85 Eur. Pat. Office J. R–8, 454 1989).

system for automatically generating semantically-related expressions. The Examining Division rejected the claim as being a computer program under 52(2)(c) EPC. The Board of Appeal affirmed. The Board characterized the subject matter of the invention as belonging to the field of linguistics:

> . . . the functional features of the individual system elements relate to the linguistic evaluation, on the basis of a linguistic relationship of input linguistic data, for the purpose of displaying a linguistic result, the actual processing involving only conventional techniques of storing, accessing, etc. coded data. No contribution is therefore made in a field outside linguistics nor outside the field of conventional computer performance.[31]

The decision in *IBM/Semantically Related Expressions* can be contrasted with the decision in *Koch & Sterzel/X-ray Apparatus.*[32] The invention in that case concerned computer control of a known x-ray apparatus. The claim recited a method of controlling the x-ray tube to achieve optimum exposure while protecting the tube against overloading. Under EPC opposition practice, Siemens and Philips sought to have the claims declared unpatentable as a computer program. Specifically opposer Philips argued that the only "technical effect" occurs at the end of the computing operation, so that the conventional x-ray apparatus and the computer program had to be looked at quite separately. Philips' argument resembles the reasoning expressed by the U.S. Supreme Court in *Parker v. Flook*[33] that inconsequential "post solution activity" will not render nonstatutory subject matter patentable.

The Board of Appeal did not agree with the opposers and the claims were allowed to stand. Rejecting Philips' argument, the Board stated, "[w]hen (in time) the technical effect occurs is irrelevant to the question of whether the subject-matter claimed constitutes an invention under Article 52(1) EPC. The only fact of importance is that it occurs at all."[34]

Philips even sought to challenge the decision in *Vicom,* arguing that *Vicom* renders Article 52(2)(c) EPC "totally ineffectual, because even an ordinary computer program used in a general-purpose computer could then be regarded as an invention under Article 52(1) EPC since each computing operation is carried out with the aid of natural, i.e. electromagnetic, forces."[35] This argument was rejected as well. The Board took the following view:

> . . . while an ordinary computer program used in a general-purpose computer certainly transforms mathematical values into electric signals with the aid of natural forces, the electric signals concerned amount to no more than a repro-

---

[31] *Id.* at 454, 458.

[32] Koch & Sterzel/X-ray Apparatus (T26/86, Eur. Pat. Office J. 1–2 1988).

[33] 437 U.S. 584 (1978).

[34] Koch & Sterzel/X-ray Apparatus (T26/86, Eur. Pat. Office J. 1–2, para. 3.2 1988).

[35] *Id.* at para. 3.3.

duction of information and cannot in themselves be regarded as a technical effect. The computer program used in a general-purpose computer is thus considered to be a program as such and hence excluded from patentability by Article 52(2)(c) EPC. But if the program controls the operation of a conventional general-purpose computer so as technically to alter its functioning, the unit consisting of program and computer combined may be a patentable invention.[36]

The metes and bounds of the *Vicom* decision were also tested by the *Merrill Lynch Application*.[37] The invention in that application was a business system for implementing an automated securities trading market. The examiner held the claims did not define a patentable invention because the claimed features would be present in a conventional business computer system and because they define essential functions required for the performance of a business method. Merrill Lynch argued that the claimed invention is not a computer program.

The Board of Appeal applied the *Vicom* case, construing its metes and bounds as follows:

> . . . it cannot be permissible to patent an item excluded by section 1(2) under the guise of an article which contains that item—that is to say, in the case of a computer program, the patenting of a conventional computer containing that program. Something further is necessary. The nature of that addition is, I think, to be found in the *Vicom* case where it is stated: 'Decisive is what technical contribution the invention makes to the known art.' There must, I think, be some technical advance on the prior art in the form of a new result (e.g., a substantial increase in processing speed as in *Vicom*).[38]

§ 10.6   EPO Guidelines

In the United States the Patent Office examiners follow the *Manual of Patent Examining Procedure* (MPEP) when examining patents. In Europe, the EPO examiners follow the *EPO Guidelines* for much the same reason. The current *EPO Guidelines* (the version of March 1985) contain several provisions regarding software inventions. One objective of the *Guidelines* is to harmonize examination practice throughout Europe. Like the MPEP of the United States Patent Office, the *EPO Guidelines* are not binding on the Board of Appeal, which is an independent body of a judicial nature. Quite the opposite, decisions of the Board of Appeal may lead to changes in the *Guidelines*.

Therefore, it is not surprising to find that the *EPO Guidelines* adopt many of the principles that the Board of Appeal decisions represent. See **§ 10.5.**

---

[36] *Id.*

[37] Merrill Lynch/Automated Trading Sys. [1989] RPC 194.

[38] *Id.*

The following are excerpts from the *Guidelines* that relate to computer programs.

C-II, 4.9a   In order that the requirements of Article 83 and of Rule 27, paragraph 1, subparagraphs (d) and (f) may be fully satisfied it is necessary that the invention is described not only in terms of its structure but also in terms of its function, unless the functions of the various parts are immediately apparent. Indeed in some technical fields (e.g. computers), a clear description of function may be much more appropriate than an over-detailed description of structure.

C-II, 4.14a   In the particular case of inventions in the computer field, program listings in programming languages cannot be relied on as the sole disclosure of the invention. The description, as in other technical fields, should be written substantially in normal language, possibly accompanied by flow diagrams or other aids to understanding, so that the invention may be understood by those skilled in the art who are deemed not to be programming specialists. Short excerpts from programs written in commonly used programming languages can be accepted if they serve to illustrate an embodiment of the invention.

Where patentability depends on a technical effect the claims must be so drafted as to include all the technical features of the invention which are essential for the technical effect.

Where patentability is admitted, then, generally speaking, product, process and use claims would be allowable. See however in this context III, 3.2 and 4.1.

C-IV 2.   Inventions

Article 52(2) 2.1   The Convention does not define what is meant by "invention," but Article 52, paragraph 2, contains a nonexhaustive list of things which shall not be regarded as inventions.

It will be noted that the exclusions on this list are all either abstract (for example discoveries, scientific theories, and so forth) or non-technical (for example aesthetic creations or presentations of information). In contrast to this, an "invention" within the meaning of Article 52, paragraph 1, must be of both a concrete and a technical character (see IV, 1.2(ii)).

2.2   In considering whether the subject-matter of an application is an invention within the meaning of Article 52, paragraph 1, there are two general points the examiner must bear in mind. Firstly, any exclusion from patentability under Article 52, paragraph 2, applies only to the extent to which the application relates to the excluded subject-matter as such. Secondly, the examiner should disregard the form or kind of claim and concentrate on its content in order to identify the real contribution which the subject-matter claimed, considered as a whole, adds to the known art. If this contribution is not of a technical character there is no invention within the meaning of Article 52, paragraph 1. Thus, for example, if the claim is for a known manufactured article having a painted design or certain written information on its surface, the contribution to the art is, as a general rule, merely an aesthetic creation or presentation of information. Similarly, if a computer program is claimed in the form of a physical record, for example of a conventional tape or disc, the contribution to the art is still no more than a computer program. In these instances the claim relates to excluded subject-matter as such and is therefore unallowable. If on the other hand, a computer program in combination with a computer causes the computer to operate in a different way from a technical point of view, the combination might be patentable.

It must also be borne in mind that the basic test of whether there is an invention within the meaning of Article 52, paragraph 1, is separate and distinct from the question of whether the subject-matter is susceptible of industrial application, is new and involves an inventive step.

2.3   The items on the list in Article 52, paragraph 2, will now be dealt with in turn, and further examples will be given in order better to clarify the distinction between what is patentable and what is not.

Discoveries . . . Scientific theories . . . Mathematical methods . . . Aesthetic creations . . . Programs for computers

The basic patentabiity considerations here are exactly the same as for the other exclusions listed in Article 52, paragraph 2. However a data-processing operation can be implemented either by means of a computer program or by means of special circuits, and the choice may have nothing to do with the inventive concept but be determined purely by factors of economy or practicability. With this point in mind, examination in this area should be guided by the following approach:

A computer program claimed by itself or as a record on a carrier, is unpatentable irrespective of its content. The situation is not normally changed when the computer program is loaded into a known computer. If however the subject-matter as claimed makes a technical contribution to the known art, patentability should not be denied merely on the ground that a computer program is involved in its implementation. This means, for example, that program-controlled machines and program-controlled manufacturing and control processes should normally be regarded as patentable subject-matter. It follows also that, where the claimed subject-matter is concerned only with the program-controlled internal working of a known computer, the subject-matter could be patentable if it provides a technical effect. As an example consider the case of a known data-processing system with a small fast working memory and a larger but slower further memory. Suppose that the two memories are organized, under program control, in such a way that a process which needs more address space than the capacity of the fast working memory can be executed at substantially the same speed as if the process data were loaded entirely in that fast memory. The effect of the program in virtually extending the working memory is of a technical character that might therefore support patentability.

Where patentability depends on a technical effect the claims must be so drafted as to include all the technical features of the invention which are essential for the technical effect. Where patentability is admitted then, generally speaking, product, process and use claims would be allowable. See however in this context III, 3.2 and 4.1.

§ 10.7   Japanese Intellectual Property System

In 1990 the United States Chamber of Commerce published a compilation work on intellectual property, entitled *Westview Special Studies in Science, Technology and Public Policy.*[39] In it, Michael Borrus, a contributing author, describes the Japanese intellectual property system as being significantly different from other industrialized countries. "The differences," Borrus writes, "can be traced at least in part to Japan's interpretation of the contribution of social value accorded imitation versus innovation." Borrus reports that "until recently, intellectual property in Japan has been considered more as a common good to be shared and used than as a right of exclusive possession accorded to the creator."[40]

This philosophical difference has the potential to create a great deal of misunderstanding. Borrus relates an interesting example, which highlights how misunderstanding arises on both sides. In 1982 IBM partcipated in a now famous FBI sting operation in which Hitachi was caught taking IBM technology. In the United States, Hitachi's actions were viewed as theft. However, in Japan, Hitachi was considered the aggrieved party, since appropriation of IBM technology was essential to Hitachi's socially valuable activity of creating superior IBM-compatible products. The fact that the FBI was involved was seen by the Japanese as proof that the United States government was trying to thwart Japanese industry.[41]

§ 10.8   —Salient Features of Japanese Patent System

Japan has a first-to-file patent system; that is, the first party to file an application is awarded the patent. The patent term is 15 years from the date of publication, but not to exceed 20 years from the filing date of the application. All applications are laid open to public inspection. Under the Japanese practice, applicants are essentially not required to cite prior art.[42] There are significant pre-grant opposition procedures available, which permit opposers to tie up applications for years—occasionally as long as ten years or more for new technologies.[43]

---

[39] U.S. Chamber of Commerce, Westview Special Studies in Science, Technology, and Public Policy (1990).

[40] *Id.* at 262; (citing Peter D. Miller, *Cavalier View of Patents Erodes Incentive,* Japan Econ. J. 23 (Oct. 22, 1988)).

[41] U.S. Chamber of Commerce, Westview Special Studies in Science, Technology, and Public Policy 262 (1990); (citing Clyde Prestowitz Jr., *Trading Places: How We Allowed Japan to Take the Lead* (1988)).

[42] U.S. Chamber of Commerce, Westview Special Studies in Science, Technology, and Public Policy 266 (1990).

[43] *Id.* at 266.

The Japanese patent system provides two levels of protection, the patent and the utility model. Patents are granted for the full 15-year term. Utility models are granted for a shorter 10-year term. The utility model is typically easier and less costly to obtain. In terms of infringement, there is no difference between a utility model and a patent. The technical scope of a patented invention is interpreted as being equal to that of a utility model, if their claim statements are the same. However, usually the utility model will have narrower scope; and the threshold of invention is lower with the utility model. Patents are awarded for inventions that rise to a "highly advanced creation," whereas utility models are awarded for inventions that are merely "the advanced creation of a technical idea."[44] Utility models cannot be obtained for process or method inventions, thus it is unlikely that many software utility models will be granted.

The Japanese patent system is closely tied to the Japanese Ministry of Trade and Industry, or MITI. The Japanese Patent Office (JPO) head comes from MITI, and the JPO reports to the MITI Minister.[45] MITI serves as the "official doorman [between the domestic and international economies] determining what and under what conditions, capital, technology, and manufactured products enter and leave Japan."[46]

§ 10.9 Software Patents under Japanese Patent System

The Japanese Patent Law provides that the purpose of the patent law is to encourage inventions by promoting their protection and utilization, to contribute to the development of industry. "Inventions" protected by the Japanese patent law are defined as "the highly advanced creations of technical ideas by which a law of nature is utilized."[47]

There is no express statutory provision or judicial precedent concerning the patentability of computer software or computer programs. However, effective July 1, 1993, the Japanese Patent Office has put new Guidelines in place, describing how computer software is to be viewed vis-à-vis the "law of nature" utilization requirement. Under these Guidelines computer software inventions are examined using the following test:

---

[44] *Questions and Answers on Japanese Patent Practice,* paper distributed by the Japanese Pat. Att'ys Ass'n (Nov. 1983) (following the Seminar on Japanese Pat. Prac. (Prosecution) sponsored by AIPLA in cooperation with the Japanese Pat. Att'ys Ass'n (JPAA) (Arlington, Va. and Los Angeles, Cal. June 15, 18, 1992)).

[45] U.S. Chamber of Commerce, Westview Special Studies in Science, Technology, and Public Policy 267 (1990).

[46] *Id.* at 264–65; (citing T.J. Pempel, *Japanese Foreign Economic Policy, in* Between Power and Plenty (Peter J. Katzenstein ed., 1978)).

[47] Cary H. Sherman, Computer Software Protection Law, 1991 Supp. JP-31, translating Japanese pat. law Art. 2 para. 1.

The following inventions are classified as statutory invention:

(I) Inventions in which natural laws are utilized in the information processing by software, i.e.:

(1) Execution of control with respect to hardware resources or processing accompanying the control, or

(2) Execution of information processing based on the physical or technical nature or properties of an object.

(II) Inventions in which hardware resources are utilized.[48]

The term object in Guideline (I)(2) above is not defined. The Japanese Patent Attorneys Association (JPAA) interprets this to mean that "any existing object such as a signal, character, image, picture, data, layout, pattern, shape, hardware or the like can be encompassed."[49] The JPAA notes that the statutory subject matter has been broadened by this Guideline, making it possible to patent concepts of a technical nature such as character recognition, communication format or protocol, structure of a pulse train, signal format, and so on.

These Guidelines do not, in the JPAA's view, open the floodgates to all types of software-implemented inventions. Inventions that are not considered to have utilized natural laws in the information processing by computer, and are also not considered to have utilized hardware resources are as follows:

When information processing is based on mathematical methods, schemes, rules or methods for doing business or performing mental acts, and the like, and also when the limitations imposed by hardware resources in a claim correspond to an inevitable restriction (mere use of hardware resources) resulting from the use of a computer, then, . . . the claimed invention is not considered to utilize natural laws.[50]

The enactment in 1993 of specific Guidelines permitting the patentability of software (if natural laws are utilized) is an interesting development in Japanese intellectual property law; but it merely represents the evolution in Japan's consistent line of thinking.

In the 1970s MITI did a study of computer technology, forming a Committee to Study Legal Protection of Software, in June 1971. This Committee published an Interim Report on the Legal Protection of Software in May 1972, which concluded that neither the copyright nor the patent systems

---

[48] *Questions and Answers on Japanese Patent Practice* 26, question 62, paper distributed by the Japanese Pat. Att'ys Ass'n (Nov. 1983) (following the Seminar on Japanese Pat. Prac. (Prosecution) sponsored by AIPLA in cooperation with the Japanese Pat. Att'ys Ass'n (JPAA) (Arlington, Va. and Los Angeles, Cal., June 15, 18, 1992)).

[49] *Id.*

[50] *Id.*

were suitable for software protection.[51] Notwithstanding the conclusion of the Committee, MITI, in December 26, 1975, promulgated Guidelines on the Criteria for Computer Programs as Inventions, which authorized patents on computer programs if a "law of nature" was used. Then, in 1982, MITI again promulgated a Guideline that a microcomputer that has been designed to achieve a particular purpose may be patented, and to the extent software has been developed as an integral part of the microcomputer, the software may be covered by the same patent which covers the microcomputer.[52] Thus the current Guidelines, while more detailed, still apply the "law of nature utilization" test.

This is not to imply that everyone within MITI believes that the Japanese patent system is well equipped to handle software inventions. Since the 1970s MITI has vacillated on this issue. For example, in 1983 MITI recommended a *sui generis* Program Rights Law should be developed to protect software, instead of either the patent system or the copyright system. MITI is a very powerful force within Japan. However, in this case the Ministry of Education (MOE) proposed that copyright law should be used. Powerful MITI capitulated to less powerful MOE. Some speculate that MITI capitulated under pressure from the United States, who feared that Japan's proposed Program Rights Law would provide weak protection to allow Japanese companies to pirate United States software technology.[53]

---

[51] Cary H. Sherman, Computer Software Protection Law, 1991 Supp. JP-32.

[52] *Id.*

[53] *Id.*

CHAPTER 11

WHAT SOFTWARE IS PATENTED?

§ 11.1   Software Patents of Microsoft Corporation

Microsoft began patenting its software in 1985. This was about two years after Lotus 1-2-3™ replaced VisiCalc™ as the spreadsheet of choice, and one year after IBM introduced the PC AT. That Microsoft intends to continue seeking patent protection for its developments is no secret. Microsoft's testimony during the Public Hearing on Patent Protection for Software-Related Inventions, January 26–27, 1994, makes this clear:

> While copyright has been and is an important and effective tool for the software industry, that does not mean that there is no role for patent protection. Indeed, there is a large and growingly important role for patent protection.
>
> Microsoft believes that the software patent law will continue to mature and we would trust rapidly enough to effectively support growing industry awareness and use of software patents.[1]

---

[1] U.S. Patent & Trademark Office, Public Hearing on Pat. Protection for Software-Related Inventions 68 (San Jose, Cal. Jan. 26–27, 1994). See **App. A.**

Because Microsoft is currently a dominant player in the software industry, it is instructive to see the kinds of software inventions Microsoft has already patented. Each of Microsoft's software patents issued to date is summarized below. Recognize that the following summary is intended only to give an overview of each patent. Carefully review the claims and specification, in light of the prior art and prosecution history, to determine precisely what each patent covers.

§ 11.2   —Letwin; 4,779,187; October 18, 1988

Letwin

Method and Operating System for Executing Programs in a Multi-Mode Microprocessor, U.S. Patent Number 4,779,187, issued October 18, 1988, assigned to Microsoft Corporation.

Objective.   To allow application programs originally written to run on a single-tasking system (for example, original IBM PC—Intel 8086) to run on a multitasking system (for example, IBM AT—Intel 80286).

Problem addressed.   When an application program written for single-tasking system terminates, it resets any changes it has made in the interrupt vector table to the state the table was in before the application program made the change. In a multitasking system, resetting the interrupt vector table in this way causes severe errors, because it ignores the possibility that other application programs may have been subsequently loaded (by multi-tasking) and are still running. These applications still running will likely crash if the interrupt vector table is reset to what the terminating application thinks is the correct state.

Invention or discovery.   A new interrupt handling method solves this problem by employing a dispatcher that maintains a client list corresponding to each interrupt vector. The dispatcher monitors the contents of the interrupt vectors to determine when an application program has changed the contents of the interrupt vector and takes appropriate action to keep the vectors from being corrupted when applications terminate.

Sample Claim.   1. A method of processing interrupts in a digital computer system including a processing unit, a memory, and a multi-tasking operating system, the processing unit including an interrupt vector table for storing the memory addresses of operating system routines or application program routines for servicing interrupts, the method including the steps of:

a. for each interrupt serviced by an operating system routine, storing the address of the corresponding operating system interrupt service routine in a corresponding client list in a dispatcher routine in the operating system;

b. for each operating system interrupt service routine, storing the address of the dispatcher in the corresponding interrupt vector;

c. periodically examining the interrupt vector table to determine if any application programs have edited interrupt vectors to replace the address of the dispatcher with the address of an application program service routine;

d. for any edits located in step (c), placing the address of the application program interrupt service routine on top of the client list for the corresponding interrupt and restoring the interrupt vector value to point to the dispatcher;

e. upon receipt of an interrupt, successively transferring control to the interrupt service routines until one of the routines services the interrupt; and

f. upon termination of an application program that has edited the interrupt vector table, deleting the addresses of the interrupt service routines of the terminated program from the client lists of the dispatcher and restoring the values of the interrupts as necessary to point to the dispatcher.

§ 11.3   —Letwin; 4,825,358; April 25, 1989

Letwin

Method and Operating System for Executing Programs in a Multi-Mode Microprocessor, U.S. Patent Number 4,825,358, issued April 25, 1989, assigned to Microsoft Corporation.

Objective.   To allow DOS application programs (real mode) and Windows application programs (protected mode) to better coexist, by providing a faster way to switch the microprocessor between real and protected modes.

Problem addressed.   The Intel 80286 (on which the IBM AT computer is based) has two modes of operation, a real mode used by DOS applications and a protected mode used by Windows applications. The 80286 microprocessor has no provided method to switch from protected mode to real mode, other than to reset the microprocessor—a relatively slow process similar to rebooting using [Ctrl]-[Alt]-[Del].

Invention or discovery. The mode switching technique determines as each program is loaded whether a mode switch is required. If required, the operating system generates a false triple fault error message, which causes the microprocessor to reset to the real mode much faster than via a conventional reset.

Sample Claim. 1. A method for operating a digital computer with an operating system program, said operating system program comprising a plurality of subroutines, said computer including memory, input-output devices, a system clock, initialization means to boot-up said computer, and a microprocessor, said microprocessor including a plurality of modes, a mode switch means capable of switching said microprocessor from a first mode to alternate modes but incapable of switching back to said first mode, and means for resetting said microprocessor, said resetting means causing said microprocessor to boot-up in said first mode, said method providing means for efficiently running on said computer applications programs adapted to said first mode concurrently with computer applications programs adapted to said alternate modes by switching between modes when necessary, said method comprising the steps of:

a. booting up said computer;

b. loading into said memory and said microprocessor operating system programs;

c. running a plurality of said applications programs on said microprocessor as required;

d. determining as each program is run whether a mode switch is required;

e. if a switch from said first mode to one of said alternate modes is required, activating said mode switch means;

f. if a switch from an alternate mode to said first mode is required, causing said microprocessor to reset by activating said resetting means by control means;

g. determining whether said resetting was triggered by said control means rather than by power-up, hardware faults, or a malfunction in the operation of the computer; and

h. if said resetting is determined to have been caused by said control means, causing said computer to bypass normal initialization routines during boot-up.

§ 11.4   —Notenboom; 4,955,066; September 4, 1990

Notenboom

Compressing and Decompressing Text Files, U.S. Patent Number 4,955,066, issued September 4, 1990, assigned to Microsoft Corporation.

Objective.   To compress Help files (user documentation) so they may be distributed on fewer disks.

Problem addressed.   User documentation, such as application program Help files are text files that take up a lot of disk space. If these files are compressed, fewer disks are required. However, once files are compressed, they must be decompressed before they can be read. Decompression takes time, which a user might find annoying.

Invention or discovery.   The three level compression technique compresses the following: (1) runs of identical characters, (2) frequently occurring phrases, and (3) frequently occurring bytes. Compressed information is located and decompressed using an intermediate lookup table of reference strings. When a reference string match is found, the lookup table tells where the compressed text is stored. Separate claims are presented on the three level compression and string matching decompression techniques. Claims 1 and 6 are illustrative.

Sample Claims.   1. A method of compressing a text file stored in a computer memory in digital form, comprising:

> generating a full text file having characters formed into phrases, said characters being digitally represented by bytes;

> generating a first level compressed text file from said text full file by replacing runs of identical characters with a run flag, the character and a repetition count;

> generating a second level compressed text file from said first level compressed text file by replacing frequently occurring phrases in said first level compressed text file with a key phrase flag byte and an index byte; and

> generating a third level compressed text file from said second level compressed text file by replacing frequently occurring bytes in said second level compressed text file with a unique string of bits.

6. The method of locating and decompressing text stored in the memory of a computer comprising:

comparing a sample string to a plurality of reference strings until a match is found;

stepping to a topic address in memory based on which reference string matches said sample string;

stepping to a topic address in memory based on which reference string matches said sample string;

stepping to an address containing compressed text stored in memory based on an address provided by said topic address;

retrieving compressed text from memory;

decompressing said text from compressed form to a standard full format form ready for display on a computer monitor; and

outputting said full format text.

§ 11.5 —Rupel; 4,967,378; October 30, 1990

Rupel

Method and System for Displaying a Monochrome Bitmap on a Color Display, U.S. Patent Number 4,967,378, issued October 30, 1990, assigned to Microsoft Corporation.

Objective. To display monochrome bitmaps on a color display quickly by minimizing the number of CPU to graphics adapter write operations.

Problem addressed. When the IBM PC was first introduced, two different display options were offered, a high resolution monochrome display option and a lower resolution color display option. A different graphics adapter was provided for each display option. More memory is required per pixel for color than for monochrome, hence a monochrome bitmap cannot be directly loaded into a color display adapter. The CPU must determine how to fill the monochrome bitmap into the larger memory space of the color adapter. This takes time and may be perceived as unacceptably slow on some computers.

Invention or discovery. The bitmap memory updating process converts the single plane bitmap (monochrome) into a multiplane bitmap (color) by setting all bits of the latch registers for each plane to the bit value of one of two colors, and by then performing an exclusive OR operation between each byte of the single plane bitmap and the value of the latch register.

Sample Claim. 1. A method of updating a multiplane bitmap memory using a single plane bitmap as input, the single plane bitmap having values 1 and 0 to represent two preselected colors, color1 and color0, respectively, the multiplane bitmap memory using the corresponding bits in each plane to form a multibit value designating the color in accordance with a preselected set of multibit color designations, the bitmaps having a corresponding logical unit and corresponding latch register for each plane of the multiplane bitmap, the method comprising the steps of:

  a.   identifying the planes of the multiplane bitmap for which the preselected colors have common bit values;

  b.   setting all bits of the latch registers for each plane to the bit value of color0 for that plane;

  c.   for each byte of the single plane bitmap, logically exclusively ORing the value of the latch register with a value of 0 for each plane identified as having common bit values and with the byte of the single plane bitmap for the planes not identified as having common bit values to effect the update of the multiplane bitmap memory.

§ 11.6   —Hargrove; 4,974,159; November 27, 1990

Hargrove

Method of Transferring Control in a Multitasking Computer System, U.S. Patent Number 4,974,159, issued November 27, 1990, assigned to Microsoft Corporation.

Objective.   To allow single-tasking DOS application programs to run more efficiently in a multitasking Windows environment.

Problem addressed.   Single-tasking DOS applications are not designed to share the computing resources with other concurrently operating programs, as must occur in a multitasking environment such as Windows. Forcing a DOS application to share resources is tricky, because a DOS application cannot be randomly interrupted. Doing this can cause the DOS data structures to become corrupted and cause the DOS application to crash.

Invention or discovery.   An inoperative instruction is inserted into a selected routine of the DOS program or DOS service handling routine. The multitasking operating system monitors the execution of the DOS program or service handling routine and interrupts execution—transferring control to itself—when the inoperative instruction is run. In this way the multitasking operating system gains control, suspending operation of the DOS application when that will not corrupt the application data structures.

Sample Claim.   1. A method of transferring control in a multitasking computer system having a system monitor and a plurality of programs executing under the system monitor, comprising the steps performed by a computer of:

writing an inoperative instruction into a selected routine of a program; and

monitoring the execution of the programs to detect an occurrent of the inoperative instruction and transferring control to the system monitor after detection of the occurrence.

§ 11.7   —Pisculli; 5,021,974; June 4, 1991

Pisculli

Method for Updating a Display Bitmap with a Character String or the Like, U.S. Patent Number 5,021,974, issued June 4, 1991, assigned to Microsoft Corporation.

Objective.   To update graphically displayed text in a window more quickly.

Problem addressed.   Updating graphically displayed text is more difficult than updating character-based text because not all graphically displayed letters take up the same amount of space. The computer cannot simply overwrite one letter upon another because portions of the original letter not overwritten will still be visible. To handle this, a conventional approach first paints a blanking (opaquing) bitmap over the letter to be replaced and then paints the new letter over the opaqued region. The conventional approach is slow.

Invention or discovery.   A stack data structure stores a virtual character for each character to be displayed. Each virtual character entry contains the phase, the width, and a pointer to the virtual character bitmap. The virtual characters are then combined in memory such that all of the display details are worked out before the display is physically updated on a column by column basis.

Sample Claim.   1. A method of updating a display bitmap in a columnwise manner to display a string of characters in a selected font with a font height, a bitmap being a matrix of bits defining a display pattern and having an associated width, each character comprising a plurality of virtual characters and having a character width, each virtual character having a virtual character bitmap and a virtual character width, each virtual character bitmap having a heights equal to the font height and a width equal to the virtual character width, each character having a character bitmap comprising the virtual character bitmaps for the virtual characters for the character, each virtual character having an associated phase based on the position within a byte in the display bitmap at which the first bit of the virtual character is to be displayed, the display bitmap being logically divided into one-byte wide columns and into scan lines, the method comprising the steps of:

generating a list having an entry for each virtual character that comprises the characters in the string, the entry containing the phase, the width, and a pointer to the virtual character bitmap; and

for each column in the display bitmap to be updated with the character string, repeating the steps of:

selecting the column;

combining the virtual character bitmaps for the virtual characters to be displayed in the selected column based on the phase, the width, and the pointer stored in the list for each character; and

updating each byte in the selected column to effect the display of a portion of the character string.

§ 11.8   —Letwin; 5,027,273; June 25, 1991

Letwin

Method and Operating System for Executing Programs in a Multi-Mode Microprocessor, U.S. Patent Number 5,027,273, issued June 25, 1991, assigned to Microsoft Corporation.

Objective.   To allow Windows applications to access the additional memory available on multi-mode systems while retaining software compatibility with single mode DOS systems.

Problem addressed.   The original IBM PC uses a single mode Intel 8088 microprocessor that can address one megabyte of separate memory locations. When the highest memory location is reached, at the one megabyte address, the next address higher wraps back around to the lowest memory location, like a cat chasing its tail. Later computer models, using more powerful multi-mode microprocessors (for example, Intel 80286, 386, 486, and so forth), are able to address many more than one million memory locations and hence they do not wrap from high memory to low memory at the one megabyte address. Thus these multi-mode microprocessors do not perfectly emulate the single mode processor.

Invention or discovery.   The operating system provides two ways of addressing the base address of the memory segment, depending on whether the application is running in real mode or protected mode. In one mode, the segment selector is set to address the base address of the segment directly. In the other mode, the segment selector is set to point to a value stored in memory, whereby the base address of the segment is addressed indirectly.

Sample Claim.   1. A method for accessing a segment in a multi-mode computer having segmented addressing, the computer having a memory, the computer having a segment selector to select the segment, the segment having a base address, the computer having a first mode wherein the base address of the segment is addressed by the segment selector and a second mode wherein the base address of the segment is addressed indirectly by the segment selector that points to a memory location within a mapping system where the base address of the segment is stored, the method allowing the segment to be accessed by the same segment selector value in both the first and second modes, the method comprising the steps of:

  a.   selecting an address that is a multiple of 16 to be the base address of the segment;

  b.   when the computer is in either the first mode or the second mode;

     1. setting the segment selector to a value so that the segment selector addresses the base address of the segment when the computer is in the first mode;

     2. storing at a selected memory location within the mapping system the base address of the segment, the memory location being selected so that it is pointed to by the segment selector as set in step (1) when the computer is in the second mode; and

     3. loading the segment into the memory at the base address; and

  c.   accessing the segment in both the first and second modes using the segment selector.

§ 11.9   —Notenboom; 5,109,433; April 28, 1992

Notenboom

Compressing and Decompressing Text Files, U.S. Patent Number 5,109,433, issued April 28, 1992, assigned to Microsoft Corporation.

Objective.   To compress Help files (user documentation) so they may be distributed on fewer disks.

Problem addressed.   User documentation, such as application program Help files are text files that take up a lot of disk space. If these files are compressed, fewer disks are required. However, once files are compressed, they must be decompressed before they can be read. Decompression takes time, which a user might find annoying.

Invention or discovery.   The three level compression technique compresses the following: (1) runs of identical characters, (2) frequently occurring phrases, and (3) frequently occurring bytes. Compressed information is located and decompressed using an intermediate lookup table of reference strings. When a reference string match is found, the lookup table tells where the compressed text is stored. This patent is a continuation of 4,955,066, discussed at § **11.4.** That portion of the term after the expiration of 4,955,066 has been disclaimed.

Sample Claim.   1. A method of creating a compressed text file stored in a computer memory in digital form, comprising:

> generating a full text file having characters formed into phrases, said characters being digital data;

> generating a first level compressed text file from said full text file by replacing frequently occurring phrases in said first level compressed text file with a key phrase flag byte and an index byte; and

> generating a second level compressed text file from said first level compressed text file by replacing each unique string of bytes in said first level compressed text file with a unique string of bits.

§ 11.10   —Padawer; 5,124,989; June 23, 1992

Padawer

Method of Debugging a Computer Program, U.S. Patent Number 5,124,989, issued June 23, 1992, assigned to Microsoft Corporation.

Objective.   To simplify finding certain classes of software bugs that are not evident until the program has run through many iterations.

Problem addressed.   Certain classes of software bugs (errors) are difficult to find, because they do not become evident until the program has run through many iterations. The first few times a program runs through an iteration or loop, the program seems to work flawlessly. However, one variable may become unacceptably large after many iterations, creating an error and causing the program to crash.

Invention or discovery.   The debugging program creates a debug history tape that can be run again and again, allowing the program to run through many iterations. At any point during execution the program can be made to suspend execution, allowing the values of variables and contents of registers to be examined.

Sample Claim.   1.   A method of locating and correcting errors in a software program, comprising:

a.   inputting a software program into a computer;

b.   executing a debug command on a line in said program;

c.   storing said debug command as a record on a debug history tape;

d.   repeating steps (b) and (c) a plurality of times to create a debug history tape of said debug commands and said line numbers;

e.   executing said stored debug commands by running said debug history tape on said program; and

f.   outputting a visual display to a user indicating the line in said program being executed by said debug commands as they are executed a second time.

§ 11.11   —Hall; 5,125,077; June 23, 1992

Hall

Method of Formatting Data from a Mouse, U.S. Patent Number 5,125,077, issued June 23, 1992, assigned to Microsoft Corporation.

Objective.   To implement a mouse that will connect to a serial port.

Problem addressed.   Conventionally the mouse is connected to the computer by a dedicated controller board. This type of mouse is sometimes called a "bus mouse." Operating power for the mouse is supplied directly by the computer bus. In connecting a mouse to a computer using the conventional RS–232 serial port, there is a need to supply operating power to the mouse. Battery power is impractical.

Invention or discovery. The serial mouse uses software drivers to maintain certain serial port lines at certain voltages, so that operating power for the mouse can be derived from the serial port lines.

Sample Claim. 1. A method of controlling a cursor on a computer display, the method including:

> providing a cursor control device having at least first and second buttons, a position sensor, and a serial encoder;

> coupling the cursor control device to a computer using an RS–232 interface that includes first, second, and third lines;

> under control of a software driver in the computer, maintaining the first RS–232 line at a first voltage and maintaining the second RS–232 line at a second voltage different than the first;

> deriving from the first and second RS–232 lines an operating voltage to power the serial encoder;

> formatting data from the position sensor and from the first and second buttons into a three byte packet to form a serial data stream using the serial encoder;

> said formatting step including formatting a first byte of said three byte packet to include a bit indicating a status of the first button and a bit indicating a status of the second button; and

> transmitting said serial data stream to the computer using the third RS–232 line while the first and second RS–232 lines are maintained under control of the software driver at said first and second voltages.

§ 11.12 —Randell; 5,125,087; June 23, 1992

Randell

Method of Resetting Sequence of Access to Extended Memory Disrupted by Interrupt Processing in 80286 Compatible System Using Code Segment Register, U.S. Patent Number 5,125,087, issued June 23, 1992, assigned to Microsoft Corporation.

Objective. To move data between real memory and extended (protected mode) memory to permit extended memory to be used in disk caching, for example.

Problem addressed.   The LoadAll instruction is an Intel-provided instruction that can be used to move data between real memory and extended memory. However, conventional use of this instruction requires that the interrupts must be disabled prior to executing the LoadAll instruction. It is undesirable to have the interrupts disabled for long periods of time and therefore, conventional use of the LoadAll instruction is limited to moving only small blocks of data at a time.

Invention or discovery.   The LoadAll instruction is used to load the code segment (CS) register and the code segment base address register with inconsistent data. More specifically, the code segment base address is loaded with the segment base address of a repeat instruction and the code segment selector is loaded with the segment address of code to be executed after the repeat instruction is executed. The interrupts are not disabled. Thus, when an interrupt occurs during execution of the repeat instruction, execution continues, not at the repeat instruction, but at the instruction pointed to by the code segment selector and the instruction pointer.

Sample Claim.   1.   A method of detecting the occurrence of an interrupt during the execution of a set of instructions on a processor with a code segment selector register and a code segment base address register, the method comprising the steps of:

loading the code segment selector register with the segment address of interrupt processing code to be executed upon completion of an interrupt routine;

loading the code segment base address register with the segment base address of the set of instructions;

executing the set of instructions;

upon the occurrence of an interrupt during the execution of the set of instruction, saving the value of the code segment selector register and executing an interrupt routine; and

upon return from the executed interrupt routine, loading the code segment base address register based on the saved value of the code segment selector register so that the interrupt processing code is executed.

§ 11.13 —Rupel; 5,138,303; August 11, 1992

Rupel

Method and Apparatus for Displaying Color on a Computer Output Device Using Dithering Techniques, U.S. Patent Number 5,138,303, issued August 11, 1992, assigned to Microsoft Corporation.

Objective.   To provide a more diverse range of colors in a color graphics display.

Problem addressed.   Windows provides device-independent graphics with a much larger number of active colors than is typically supported by the graphics adapter hardware. This large number of colors is mapped onto the fewer number of supported colors, resulting in similar, but different, colors being identically displayed. While it would be desirable to have a graphics adapter that supports more colors, this solution is not affordable by the typical personal computer user.

Invention or discovery.   Four picture elements (called pels) of a display are logically grouped together to create a super-pel. By varying the intensity level in each pel of a super-pel, the effective number of intensity levels for a given color is increased.

Sample Claim.   1.   A method of filling an area on a computer output device being pel-addressable and logically divided into super-pels, each super-pel comprising a 2-by-2 array of four pels, the pels being designated as an upper-left pel, an upper-right pel, a lower-left pel and a lower-right pel, each pel having three color components designated color one, color two, and color three, each color component capable of being set to one of a fixed set of intensities, the method comprising the steps of:

inputting an intensity;

selecting a base intensity that is within the fixed set of intensities for the color component and that is lower than the input intensity;

determining the number of pels in a super-pel to be filled with the selected base intensity;

selecting the determined number of pels of each super-pel to be filled with the base intensity wherein the priority of pel selection for color one is the lower-left pel, the upper-right pel, the lower-right pel, and the upper-left pel, for color two is the upper-left pel, the lower-right pel, the upper-right pel, and the lower-left pel, and for the color three is the upper-right pel, the lower-left pel, the upper-left pel, and the lower-right pel;

setting each selected pel of each super-pel to the selected base intensity; and

setting each nonselected pel of each super-pel to an intensity higher than the base intensity that is within the fixed set of intensities so that the effective intensity displayed is between the selected base intensity and the higher intensity.

§ 11.14   —Naidu; 5,146,580; September 8, 1992

Naidu

Method and System for Using Expanded Memory for Operating System Buffers and Application Buffers, U.S. Patent Number 5,146,580, issued September 8, 1992, assigned to Microsoft Corporation.

Objective.   To overcome the 640K memory limitation of MS-DOS.

Problem addressed.   The Expanded Memory Specification or EMS is a memory architecture that was jointly developed by Lotus, Intel, and Microsoft (sometimes called LIM-EMS memory or EMS memory). EMS memory provides additional data storage above the 640K boundary in regions called pages, which are available to be used by either a user application or DOS. Using EMS by both user application and DOS simultaneously can cause problems because one may overwrite the memory of the other. This could be solved by locking a page currently in use, but the EMS does not provide a locking function.

Invention or discovery.   The system allows DOS system and user buffers to simultaneously reside in EMS memory without conflict. A page frame is created comprising at least three pages. DOS system buffers are mapped into the highest page of the frame and user buffers are mapped into lower pages. The system detects whether any of the data read into the user buffers will overflow into the DOS system buffers. If so, the lowest page of the user buffer and the DOS system buffers temporarily exchange places.

Sample Claim.   1. A computer implemented method of transferring data between a user buffer and system buffer in a computer system having a plurality of user buffers and system buffers, the computer system having expanded memory comprising logical pages and conventional memory comprising physical pages, the computer system having an address space, the conventional memory being within the address space of the computer system, the user buffers and system buffers being stored in expanded memory, the method of comprising the steps of:

a. allocating a page frame in conventional memory for mapping of logical pages into the address space;

b. logically dividing the page frame into at least three pages, including a highest page and a lowest page;

c. mapping user buffers into the page frame;

d. for each page in the mapped user buffers, determining whether any of the pages need to have data transferred between a target system buffer;

e. if a transfer is needed with a determined page that is not the highest page of the page frame, mapping the target system buffer into the highest page of the page frame, transferring data between the determined page and the mapped target system buffer, and re-mapping the user buffer that was previously in the highest page back into the highest page of the page frame upon completion of the transfer; and

f. if a transfer is needed with a determined page that is the highest page of the page frame, mapping the target system buffer into the lowest page of the page frame, transferring data between the determined page and the mapped target system buffer, and re-mapping the user buffer that was previously in the lowest page back into the lowest page of the page frame upon completion of the transfer.

§ 11.15 —Rubin; 5,155,842; October 13, 1992

Rubin

Logical Event Notification Method and Apparatus, U.S. Patent Number 5,155,842, issued October 13, 1992, assigned to Microsoft Corporation.

Objective. To make Local Area Networks easier to use by automatically informing users and programs about conditions and events occurring on the network, for example, the status of printers.

Problem addressed. Prior local area networks require a user or program running on the network to request information about the status of the network. The programs providing this information are required to interrupt their processing to give the information. This slows down the network, particularly if many users communicate with a program while it is running.

Invention or discovery. An alert database is maintained by the network operating system. When events occur or when statuses change, the database is automatically updated. The database contains a look-up table of the addresses of all programs desiring to receive status updates. The alert software steps through the look-up table and writes a copy of the requested alert report data to all requesting programs.

Sample Claim.   1.   A method of monitoring events occurring on a computer network having a plurality of users and a plurality of devices coupled to said network, comprising:

performing a process under the control of an operating program;

entering an alert database function call from the operating program when the program causes or notices a logical event occurring on said network, said event being a power failure;

generating an alert report describing said event;

storing said alert report in a buffer; and

writing a copy of said alert report to a plurality of addresses, one of said addresses being a receiving program that notifies all users that the power has failed and that the system is on battery power, and another of said addresses being a receiving program that begins controlling network activities to provide an orderly showdown procedure.

§ 11.16   —Smith; 5,204,960; April 20, 1993

Smith

Incremental Compiler, U.S. Patent Number 5,204,960, issued April 20, 1993, assigned to Microsoft Corporation.

Objective.   To allow software to be written more quickly by speeding up compilation.

Problem addressed.   In writing software a compiler is used to translate the source code into object code. Software development often involves repeatedly using the compiler: testing the code, making minor changes to it, and then recompiling and testing again. Using a conventional compiler, a large program will take a long time to compile, even if only minor changes have been made to it.

Invention or discovery.   The compiler incrementally compiles only those portions of the source code that have been changed. The compiled object code for portions that have not been changed is retained and the newly compiled object code is patched into the object code file to replace the portions changed.

Sample Claim.   1. The method of incrementally compiling a source file into an object file comprising:

compiling a first version of a source file into a first version of an object file;

storing data corresponding to check points within said source file;

storing data corresponding to check points within said object file;

editing said source file;

recompiling a portion of said source file which includes said edited region of said source file and patching it into said first version of said object file to create a second version of said object file, said portion that is recompiled being selected using said stored check points within said source file and said stored check points within said object file.

§ 11.17   —Mason; 5,214,755; May 25, 1993

Mason

Document Processing Method and System, U.S. Patent Number 5,214,755, issued May 25, 1993, assigned to Microsoft Corporation.

Objective.   To improve the way text and graphics may be arranged on the page, with text automatically flowing around the graphics.

Problem addressed.   To give word processing software the power of full-fledged desktop publishing software, it is desirable to allow both text and graphics to be positioned on the same page. The text should flow naturally around the graphics, making the page appear as if it has been typeset. Text and graphics are inherently different, and prior word processors were limited by allowing text to be placed only on one side of a graphic image. The prior wordprocessors could not permit text to flow from one side of a graphic image to the other.

Invention or discovery.   Starting with a full page "default" layout rectangle, the method first identifies any regions with graphics and makes those regions off limits to flowable text. The default layout rectangle is then redefined as a set of smaller rectangles, within the confines of the original default rectangle, but not including any of the off limit regions. These smaller rectangles are then linked together and used to receive flowable text.

Sample Claim.   1. A method for generating a plurality of layout rectangles for a page in a computer system for processing documents, the page comprising absolutely positioned object and unpositioned data, the absolutely positioned objects having a predefined size and location on the page, the unpositioned data may include text characters and graphic objects, the layout rectangles to define areas into which the unpositioned data may be placed, the method comprising the steps of:

a.   defining a default layout rectangle to encompass the page;

b.   determining if any absolutely positioned objects intersect the default layout rectangle;

c.   if no absolutely positioned object intersects the default layout rectangle, generating a layout rectangle equal to the default layout rectangle;

d.   if an absolutely positioned object intersects the default layout rectangle,

  1.   generating a layout rectangle from the default layout rectangle such that the layout rectangle does not include an absolutely positioned object; and

  2.   redefining the default layout rectangle to exclude the generated layout rectangles; and

e.   repeating steps (b) through (d) until no absolutely positioned object intersects the default layout rectangle and wherein the generated layout rectangles define areas into which the unpositioned data may be placed.

§ 11.18   —Chung; 5,218,697; June 8, 1993

Chung

Method and System for Networking Computers Having Varying File Architectures, U.S. Patent Number 5,218,697, issued June 8, 1993, assigned to Microsoft Corporation.

Objective.   To integrate local area networks of different types, so that each individual network retains its own native environment.

Problem addressed.   There are several network architectures in popular use. Each has its own operating system and each has its own native environment, which users prefer or become accustomed to. For the most part, these architectures are incompatible. Ideally, a single integrated file server is needed that will make these architectures compatible while retaining the native environment of each, so that users will not have to learn a new system.

Invention or discovery.   A client-server solution is proposed that defines a central server and a foreign server. The central server is the main file server of the network. The foreign server provides file services to clients (for example, incompatible operating environments) that are not recognized by the central file server. The file service requests of foreign server clients are directly translated into file service requests in a format recognized by the central server.

Sample Claim.   1. An improved, distributed network comprising:

   a.   a central server having a central server file system, said central server including means for communicating with central server clients in accordance with a central server network protocol, means for converting central server network file service requests in said central server network protocol, communicated form said central server clients, into central server file system commands, and means for sending said central server file system commands to said central server file system; and

   b.   a foreign server, said foreign server including means for communicating with foreign serve clients in accordance with a foreign server network protocol, means for converting foreign server network file service requests in said foreign server network protocol, communicated from said foreign server clients, into central server file system commands, and means for sending said central server file system commands directly to said central server file system without routing the commands through the central server.

§ 11.19   —Padawer; 5,220,675; June 15, 1993

Padawer

Method and System for Customizing a User Interface in an Integrated Environment, U.S. Patent Number 5,220,675, issued June 15, 1993, assigned to Microsoft Corporation.

Objective.   To allow a user to customize a menu in a running application program by adding a menu item that will call an external application program.

Problem addressed.   Typically, an application program's menu is configured by its creators. There needs to be a way to allow users to add features to an existing program, whereby information may be passed from the existing program to the program supporting the new feature.

Invention or discovery.   While a first application program is running, a menu item referencing a second application program is added. Text strings generated by the first application program are stored in memory and assigned "handles" to which the newly added menu item attaches. The first application program saves the information it is working on in a source file and the second application program then operates on this source file, using a text string stored in memory that is referenced by the handle in the menu item entry.

Sample Claim.   1.   A computer system for allowing a user to customize a user interface of a first computer program for invoking a second computer program, the system comprising:

> means for displaying a menu with menu items that are available for selection by the user of the first computer program;

> means for storing an identification of the second computer program;

> means for adding a new menu item to the menu;

> handle means for linking the new menu item to the identification of the second computer program; and

> means for selecting a new menu item, including means for saving a source file before executing the second computer program, and means for executing the second computer program on the source file.

§ 11.20   —Koss; 5,231,577; July 27, 1993

Koss

Method and System for Processing Formatting Information in a Spreadsheet, U.S. Patent Number 5,231,577 issued July 27, 1993, assigned to Microsoft Corporation.

Objective.   To empower an application program to display different font attributes (for example, underlined, bold, italic) using less memory.

Problem addressed.   Conventionally every different font attribute (for example, underlined, bold, italic) requires a separate attribute code. In a spreadsheet, the user may want each cell to apply several different attributes. Assigning individual attribute codes on a cell by cell basis takes a great deal of memory because the necessary attributes must be stored with each individual cell, even though all cells may use the same attributes.

Invention or discovery. An "extended format" table of each possible combination of attributes (for example, bold only, bold plus underlined, bold plus underlined plus italic, and so forth) is stored as a linked list. Each cell in the spreadsheet contains a single index pointer that references the appropriate entry in the extended format table.

Sample Claim. 1. An improved method of formatting cells and characters in a spreadsheet, said method comprising the steps of:

allocating a worksheet having a plurality of cells containing data elements, some of said cells being associated with other cells in accordance with a predefined mathematical relationship;

allocating a table for storing format combinations which represent the appearance of said cells and said data elements within said cells;

combining bits of cell formatting information to create a default format combination;

generating an index to the default format combination using a predetermined hashing function;

storing the default format combination in the table according to the index; and

initializing each of said cells with the index to point to said default format combination.

§ 11.21 —Barrett; 5,247,658; September 21, 1993

Barrett

Method and System for Traversing Linked List Record Based upon Write-Once Predetermined Bit Value of Secondary Pointers, U.S. Patent Number 5,247,658, issued September 21, 1993, assigned to Microsoft Corporation.

Objective. To extend the disk operating system to support write-once memory such as flash-erasable, programmable, read-only memory.

Problem addressed. Flash-erasable, programmable, read-only memory is different from conventional disk memory. It can only be written to once. The conventional DOS file system assumes that disk memory has multiple-write capability. Conventionally, data is written to disk memory in blocks at a time, leaving portions of blocks unused. The conventional DOS file system will not work well for flash-erasable, programmable, read-only memory.

Invention or discovery. The system uses a secondary pointer to indicate that data stored in a file system data structure has been superseded. The secondary pointer points to a record that contains the superseding data.

Sample Claim. 1. A method of updating data stored on a computer memory file storage device with new data, the memory containing records of data, each record having a primary pointer and a secondary pointer, the records stored as a linked list that is linked by the primary pointers, the method comprising the steps of:

locating a record that contains data to be updated, the record being contained in the memory comprising a plurality of bits such that once a bit is changed from a predefined bit value to another bit value the changed bit cannot be individually changed back to the predefined bit value, the data including bits that have been changed from the predefined bit value to the other bit value, the secondary pointer of the located record having each bit set to the predefined bit value;

allocating a record to contain the new data, the record being allocated in the memory, each bit of the allocated record being set to the predefined bit value;

writing the new data to the allocated record; and

setting the secondary pointer in the located record to point to the allocated record to indicate that the new data in the allocated record is an update of the data in the located record by changing at least one bit of the secondary pointer from the predefined bit value to the other bit value

wherein the step of locating a record includes the steps of:

a. selecting a record at which to start a traversal of the linked list;

b. reading the secondary pointer for the selected record;

c. if each bit of the read secondary pointer is set to the predefined bit value, then selecting the record pointed to by the primary pointer of the selected record;

d. if each bit of the read secondary pointer is not set to the predefined bit value, then selecting the record pointed to by the secondary pointer of the selected record; and

e. repeating steps (b) to (d), until the selected record contains the data to be updated.

§ 11.22   —Michelman; 5,255,356; October 19, 1993

Michelman

Method for Hiding and Showing Spreadsheet Cells, U.S. Patent Number 5,255,356, issued October 19, 1993, assigned to Microsoft Corporation.

Objective.   To add hierarchical (outlining) display capability to a spreadsheet.

Problem addressed.   The homogeneous grid of rows and columns is sometimes unwieldy with large spreadsheets. It would be desirable if information could be organized in hierarchical, collapsible-outline fashion, so that details within the spreadsheet can be hidden or shown at the user's option.

Invention or discovery.   The spreadsheet software automatically identifies a dominant row that has a relationship to at least one subordinate row. The subordinate row may be selectively hidden (that is, not shown on the computer display). Note that unlike other Microsoft patents, this patent includes an extensive source code listing. The listing is written in the C language for the Borland Turbo C compiler.

Sample Claim.   1. In a computer having a display device, an entry device, and a processor for executing a spreadsheet program, the spreadsheet program causing a plurality of intersecting rows and columns to be displayed on the display device, some of the plurality of rows having a predefined relationship with other rows, the predefined relationship being either dominant or subordinate, a method of hiding selected ones of the plurality of rows comprising the steps of:

   a.   automatically identifying a dominant row having a dominant relationship to at least one subordinate row;

   b.   automatically selecting the at least one subordinate row having a subordinate relationship to the dominant row; and

   c.   hiding the selected at least one subordinate row such that the at least one subordinate row is not displayed on the display device.

§ 11.23   —Letwin; 5,257,370; October 26, 1993

Letwin

Method and System for Optimizing Data Caching in a Disk-Based Computer System, U.S. Patent Number 5,257,370, issued October 26, 1993, assigned to Microsoft Corporation.

Objective.   To speed up disk access by improving the way the read ahead disk cache determines how much data to read.

Problem addressed.   The read ahead disk cache is conventionally used to speed up disk access. When a disk access is performed, the operating system reads the data requested and also reads ahead by a fixed amount. If the read ahead amount is too large, time is wasted seeking data that is not needed. If the read ahead amount is too small, additional disk access operations are required. Some conventional systems attempt to monitor past disk access history so that the read ahead amount can be fine-tuned. This technique does not work when the computer is first turned on, because at that stage there is no past history.

Invention or discovery.   File access behavior is monitored for the file and recorded in a file access log that tells whether the file access was "sequential" or "sequential and fast." This information is stored in the file access log when the file is closed.

Sample Claim.   1. A method, performed by a computer having a cache, for caching data from a file stored on disk, the method comprising the steps of:

monitoring, upon closing the file, access information corresponding to the file indicating the file access behavior monitored;

maintaining, upon closing the file, access information corresponding to the file indicating the file access behavior monitored;

obtaining, upon reopening the file, the access information maintained; and

reading an amount of the data from the file into the cache, the amount based on the access information obtained.

§ 11.24 —Masden; 5,261,051; November 9, 1993

Masden

Method and System for Open File Caching in a Networked Computer System, U.S. Patent Number 5,261,051 issued November 9, 1993, assigned to Microsoft Corporation.

Objective. To speed up computer networks by improving the way batch files stored on the file server are processed by the workstation.

Problem addressed. Conventional batch files are executed one line at a time and a batch file must be closed prior to execution. When executing a batch file remotely, the client application (for example, on a workstation) and the file server exchange a series of eight request and acknowledge messages, for each line of the batch file. This creates a significant amount of network traffic and tends to slow down network operation for all users.

Invention or discovery. The batch file is opened and a copy of the entire batch file is sent to the remote workstation, where the remote copy is run without further delay—producing request and acknowledge messages. While this is occurring, the file server places the batch file in an opportunistic locked mode. Once the batch file has entirely executed, it is unlocked and closed on the file server.

Sample Claim. 1. A method of executing multiple batch file commands from a remote terminal, comprising the steps of:

    a. caching a batch file having the multiple batch file commands from a file server to the remote terminal;

    b. opening the batch file within the remote terminal when no other remote terminal has opened or requested to open the batch file; and

    c. locally processing any number of the multiple batch file commands within the remote terminal without closing or deleting the batch file within the remote terminal so long as no other terminal has opened or requested to open the file.

§ 11.25   —Fenwick; 5,261,101; November 9, 1993

Fenwick

Method for Calling and Returning from a Subroutine that is Invoked by Either a Near Call or a Far Call, U.S. Patent Number 5,261,101, issued November 9, 1993, assigned to Microsoft Corporation.

Objective.   To eliminate a source of programming error caused by mixing "near" and "far" subroutine calls.

Problem addressed.   The IBM PC family is based on the Intel architecture, which uses a segmented addressing scheme. To address a memory location, a segment address and an offset address are combined to generate the physical memory address. The combining of segment and offset is done so that the segment represents the most significant digits of the address. In small programs that need only to access 64K of memory or less, the segment portion of the address is fixed and needs to be specified only at the outset. In large programs that must access more than 64K, the segment portion of the address must be explicitly specified each time a memory location outside the current segment is addressed.

When calling subroutines that reside in the current memory segment a "near" call is made, in which only the offset is specified. The called subroutine returns when it is finished to the program which called it, by executing a "near" return. When calling subroutines that reside outside the current memory segment a "far" call is made, in which both segment and offset must be specified. The called subroutine returns when it is finished to the program which called it, by executing a "far" return. If the programmer accidentally mixes a near call with a far return, or a far call with a near return, the program crashes.

Invention or discovery.   The subroutine is designed with a near entry point and a far entry point. When invoked through the near entry point, the subroutine executes a near return upon completion. When invoked through the far entry point, the subroutine first stores an offset of a far return instruction. The subroutine then starts executing at the near entry point. When the near return instruction is executed, the subroutine automatically retrieves the stored far return offset, causing the processor to continue execution at the far entry point.

Sample Claim.   1. A method for invoking and returning from a subroutine on a computer having code segments, an instruction set, and an instruction pointer, the instruction set having a near call instruction for intra-code segment invoking of the subroutine, a near return instruction for intra-code segment returning from the subroutine, a far call instruction for inter-code segment invoking of the subroutine, and a far return instruction for inter-code segment returning from the subroutine, the subroutine comprising a plurality of instructions from the instruction set being stored in a code segment, the subroutine having a far entry point, each code segment having a plurality of locations for storing instructions, each location within a code segment having an associate offset within the code segment, the method comprising the steps of:

> executing the far call instruction specifying the far entry point of the subroutine to be executed;

> when executing the subroutine in response to executing the far call instruction specifying the far entry point;

> storing the offset of a location containing the far return instruction that is located in the code segment in which the subroutine is stored, the offset being less than 128 or greater than 65,407;

> executing the near return instruction to retrieve the location of the stored offset and to set the instruction pointer to point to the location of the stored offset; and

> executing the far return instruction pointed to by the instruction pointer to effect a return to an instruction following the executed far call instruction.

§ 11.26   —Rubin; 5,265,261; November 23, 1993

Rubin

Method and System for Network Communications Using Raw Mode Protocol, U.S. Patent Number 5,265,261, issued November 23, 1993, assigned to Microsoft Corporation.

Objective.   To eliminate some of the overhead associated with transferring files between incompatible systems connected to a local area network.

Problem addressed.   Different types of computers, running different, incompatible operating systems, can be connected together on a common local area network. This requires a protocol for sharing files among the incompatible systems, by converting to a common format. There are three problems with conventional file sharing protocols. First, there is high overhead associated with formatting and sending system message blocks (SMB) and network control blocks (NCB). Second, the use of small blocks is inefficient to transfer large blocks of data. Third, there is duplicate copying occurring as the transport system copies the data to the SMB buffer and then the redirector copies the data to the application buffer.

Invention or discovery. The transport is provided with a read request to send data from the first computer to the second, and with a receive network control block that directs the transport to store the next data it receives directly in the data buffer. The transport sends the read request to the first computer. The first computer stores the data identified by the read request in a data block without a header. The first computer transmits the data block over the communications line to the transport. Using information contained in the network control block, the transport stores the requested data without the header directly in the data buffer.

Sample Claim. 1. A computer implemented method in a computer system for transmitting data from a server computer to a consumer computer connected by a virtual circuit, the consumer computer having an application program requesting a read from the server computer, having a redirector, and having a transport, the application program having access to a data buffer allocated by the application program, comprising the steps of:

allocating and initializing a receive network control block for directing the transport to store the next data it receives directly in the data buffer;

transmitting from the redirector to the transport a read request to read data from the server and said receive network control block for directing the transport to store the read data directly in the data buffer, the read request indicating that the read data should be transmitted without a header;

in response to the step of transmitting, sending the read request from the transport to the server computer;

examining and recognizing that the read request indicates that the read data should be transmitted without a header;

storing the read data in a data block without the header;

transferring the data block from the server computer to the transport in response to the step of sending the read request; and

in response to the read request and the receive network control block and in response to the step of transferring, storing the data block directly from the transport into the data buffer.

§ 11.27 —Koss; 5,272,628; December 21, 1993

Koss

Method and System for Aggregating Tables Having Dissimilar Formats, U.S. Patent Number 5,272,628, issued December 21, 1993, assigned to Microsoft Corporation.

Objective.   To enhance the spreadsheet program by adding the ability to combine several tables of different configurations into a single master table.

Problem addressed.   In prior spreadsheet programs several spreadsheet tables may be combined into an aggregate master table, only if the individual tables each have the identical number of rows and columns and each have identical categories and divisions aligned along each vertical and horizontal axis, respectively.

Invention or discovery.   The spreadsheet allows aggregation of tables of different sizes and of different configurations. Rows and columns are automatically created in the destination table (master table) based on categories and divisions of one or more source tables. The user can specify categories for aggregation, or categories may be generated automatically, based on categories contained within the source tables. Once the desired categories are specified, the program creates mapping tables for rows and columns. The mapping tables comprise an array of pairs of values for linking source table and destination table locations. The program then conducts a binary search based on each pair of values in the mapping table, to find the correct location in the destination table and to apply the desired table mapping by performing the desired mathematical function on the values in the source and destination tables.

Sample Claim.   1. A method for aggregating tables in a compute system running a program, wherein the program uses tables to store and manipulate data, each table consisting of a grid intersecting rows and columns, and where each column has a heading called a division and each row has a heading called a category, said method comprising the steps of:

   a.   specifying a plurality of source tables for aggregation, each source table having at least one category and division;
   b.   generating a destination table template, said destination table template specifying desired categories and divisions of said source tables to be aggregated into a destination table;

c. creating a category mapping list that maps categories of said source tables to corresponding categories of said destination table template;

d. creating a division mapping list that maps divisions of said source tables to corresponding divisions of said destination table template; and

e. applying the category mapping list and the division mapping list to said destination table.

§ 11.28 —Rosenberg; 5,274,751; December 28, 1993

Rosenberg

System and Method for Printing Graphic Objects, U.S. Patent Number 5,274,751, issued December 28, 1993, assigned to Microsoft Corporation.

Objective. To improve graphics printing accuracy, so that a graphic image when shown on the computer screen will better match the size, shape, and position of the graphic image when printed.

Problem addressed. Computer display screens have a resolution that is substantially lower than that of a typical laser printer. The computer must perform calculations to translate the image on the low resolution screen to an image on the high resolution printer. Often this will involve rounding errors. For example, a one millimeter ruler on a 96 dots per inch (dpi) screen has a length of 3.78 dots—neither 3 dots nor 4 dots, exactly. The computer splits the difference, translating one millimeter as 3 dots at some screen locations and translating one millimeter as 4 dots at other screen locations. When images are printed on a laser printer having 300 dpi, or 600 dpi, these distortions show up. The printed image does not appear the same as the screen displayed image.

Invention or discovery. The system measures all distances from a predefined reference point (for example, the origin of a ruler displayed on the screen). The system assigns an absolute location value to all objects on the screen. The system translates the absolute location value into a printer value so that an object, which is drawn to dimensions indicated by the marks on the displayed ruler, will be printed out with the intended dimensions in spite of the inherent inaccuracies of the display screen.

Sample Claim. 1. A computer system for accurately printing on a graphics printer a graphic object displayed on a computer screen, the display screen being unable to accurately represent visually a selected unit of length measurement, said system comprising:

means for generating a ruler on the display screen, said ruler having an origin and a series of marks, said marks being displayed at nonuniform spacings along the length of said ruler and at least some of said marks having a labeled value indicative of an intended uniform spacing of said marks along the length of said ruler relative to said origin and expressed in the selected unit of measurement;

means for calculating intended location values of said marks, said intended location values corresponding to said intended uniform spacing of said marks along the length of said ruler relative to said origin;

measurement means for determining an intended location of the object displayed on the display screen by determining a particular one of said marks with which the object is aligned, and assigning to the object aligned with said particular mark an intended location value corresponding to said particular mark;

translating means for determining a printer location value for the object, said printer location value being related to said assigned intended location value for the object; and

means for transmitting said printer location value to the printer.

§ 11.29   Software Patents of Borland International

Borland International began patenting its software in 1989. Borland currently holds one patent. Like many of the Microsoft patents of this era, Borland's patent relates to solving the 640K memory limitation of MS-DOS.

§ 11.30   —Bennett; 5,189,733; February 23, 1993

Bennett

Application Program Memory Management System, U.S. Patent Number 5,189,733, issued February 23, 1993, assigned to Borland International, Inc.

Objective.   To allow large application programs to be run in the limited 640K memory space available under MS-DOS.

Problem addressed.   MS-DOS limits the size of an active application program to 640K of the computer's random access memory (RAM). To allow application programs larger than 640K to run, programmers use an overlay technique known as "code swapping." Portions of the application code that are currently executing are retained (resident) in RAM and portions that are not likely to execute are swapped to disk and not retained or resident in RAM. These nonresident portions are termed "suspended" portions.

The problem is to determine which portions of the code are the best candidates to be suspended. If chosen poorly, the application program runs slowly, due to the time required to retrieve portions of the code stored on disk.

Invention or discovery.   Space is allocated in memory for an entry stub used to access a code object that is required to be resident in main memory. If the code object is resident in main memory, then the address of that code object is stored as the entry stub. If the code object is not resident in main memory, then an executable instruction is stored as the entry stub. A memory manager processes each call to a code object by referring to its entry stub and executing the stored instruction if the code object is not resident.

In addition, a record of all resident code objects is maintained in a sorted, linked list. Code objects that are likely candidates to be suspended are placed at one end (the "suspend" end) of the list and code objects that are unlikely to be suspended are placed at the other end (the "keep" end) of the list. Each record in the list includes a flag that is set when the associated object is near the "suspended" end of the list. This object is said to be on "probation" from suspension. When an object is on probation, the stub vectors are set to trap all calls or returns to the object. If a call or return is made to an object on probation, the traps are removed and the object is removed from probation and its record is placed at the "keep" end of the list.

Sample Claim.   1. In a computer system having a main memory and a secondary memory for storing objects not present in the main memory, a method for execution of an application program in a limited memory space, said program including at least one code object capable of removal from the main memory during program execution, the method comprising:

a.   allocating space in main memory for an entry stub for accessing a code object which is required to be resident in the main memory;

b.   if a code object is resident at a location in the main memory, storing as the entry stub a vector to the code object at the location;

c.   if a code object is not resident at a location in the main memory, storing as the entry stub an instruction executable by the computer upon any calls to the code object; and

d.   processing each call to a code object by at least referencing the entry stub, whereby a call to the code object results in execution of the instruction by the computer when the code object is not resident.

§ 11.31   Software Patents of Lotus Development Corporation

Lotus began patenting its software in 1986. Lotus currently holds two software patents. The earlier of the two relates to improvements in the spreadsheet program. The later of the two relates to object-oriented database technology of the company's Agenda product. Lotus's founder, Mitchell Kapor, is one of the six named inventors of the later patent.

§ 11.32   —Klein; 4,788,538; November 29, 1988

Klein

Method and Apparatus for Determining Boundaries of Graphic Regions, U.S. Patent Number 4,788,538, issued November 29, 1988, assigned to Lotus Development Corp.

Objective.   To enable the user of a spreadsheet program to identify an irregularly configured region on the screen by placing the cursor within the region and letting the computer determine the boundary of the region.

Problem addressed.   When using a spreadsheet a user may wish to perform a command on an irregularly configured region of rows and columns on the screen. For example, the user may wish to ERASE THIS, and would like the computer to determine automatically what THIS is.

Invention or discovery.   The user selects an initial X-Y position on the screen using the mouse. The computer then uses a searching pattern, searching radially outwardly from the initial position until a blank cell is found in each radial direction. All non-blank cells located within the search region are then treated as the irregular region corresponding to THIS.

Sample Claim.   1. A computer display system having a central processing unit (CPU) coupled to display means including a display, said display having a plurality of selectively enabled and disabled display elements arranged in a matrix, such that each display element is identified by a unique X, Y address, comprising:

> memory means coupled to said CPU for storing a plurality of binary quantities, each of said binary quantities disposed in a memory cell corresponding to a display element, said binary quantities defining regions on said display;

cursor control means coupled to said CPU for selecting an initial X, Y address on said display, and corresponding memory cell in said memory means, to identify an area on said display where the boundaries of a region are to be determined, said initial cell being defined as a seed cell;

logic means coupled to said CPU for determining if said initial X, Y address corresponds to a disabled memory cell, and in such event said logic means incrementing said initial X, Y address to search outwardly to adjacent memory cells until an enabled cell is located, said enabled cell then being defined as the new seed cell;

said CPU searching radially outward in M directions from the X, Y address of said seed cell for N consecutive disabled memory cells, and said logic means setting in each of said directions, the last enabled memory cell prior to said N consecutive disabled cells, as boundary cells;

said logic means defining an initial rectangular region through at least two of said boundary cells; said logic means determining if P consecutive rows and columns of disabled memory cells bound said initial rectangular region, said CPU selectively extending the boundaries of said initial region in X and Y directions until said region is bounded by P consecutive rows and columns of disabled cells;

whereby the boundaries of a region on said display are determined.

§ 11.33   —Belove; 5,115,504; May 19, 1992

Belove

Information Management System, U.S. Patent Number 5,115,504, issued May 19, 1992, assigned to Lotus Development Corp.

Objective.   To make database systems easier to use by allowing data to be entered or modified while in the data viewing mode.

Problem addressed.   Conventional database management systems assign data elements to records that are part of a predefined data structure comprising different categories or fields. Data may only be entered in a data entry mode. Data may only be viewed in a separate report writer or view mode. It would be easier if the user could enter, modify, or delete data while in the view mode.

Invention or discovery.   A link data structure is provided to link elements of data (data objects) with categories of data (category objects). The data objects and category objects thus exist independently. The user can modify data through a view mode, and the system resolves any ambiguities using available information to determine the most likely intent of the user.

Sample Claim.   1. An item/category database system, comprising

means for storing independent data objects including category objects, item objects and view objects, along with networks of independent link structures, said category and item objects each containing character string representations of categories and items, respectively, and pointers to certain ones of said link structures, said link structures containing essentially only pointers to data objects and/or other link structures serving thereby to interconnect item and category objects in one cross-linked network representing a relationship between categories and their assigned items, and view and category objects in another cross-linked network,

means for defining views in relation to view objects, each view comprising at least one section of items assigned to a category represented by a particular category object to which a respective view object is linked within said another cross-linked network,

means for visually representing a defined view by displaying separately in each section each item of alphanumeric information represented respectively in each of the item objects already linked to the particular category object corresponding to the section,

means for entering new information into the database within the context of any given view by accepting new alphanumeric information as a free form character string entered under a section in the given view, storing a digital representation of said character string in a new item object and linking the new item object with the particular category object corresponding to said section by means of a new independent link structure within said one cross-linked network, and

means for further associating said new item object with pre-existing category objects by examining the character string of the new item object to match portions thereof with other category objects and linking the new item object to said other category objects via new respective link structures within said one cross-linked network.

§ 11.34   Software Patents of
WordPerfect Corporation

WordPerfect Corporation began patenting its software in 1990. It currently holds two software patents. Both patents relate to features of its word processing product. The first patent addresses how to print multiple fonts in a single document. The second patent relates to WordPerfect's equation editor.

§ 11.35   —Landes; 5,233,685; August 3, 1993

Landes

Method and Apparatus for Integrating Graphical and Textual Character Printing, U.S. Patent Number 5,233,685, issued August 3, 1993, assigned to WordPerfect Corporation.

Objective.   To allow a mixture of different character fonts within a single document to be printed.

Problem addressed.   Conventional word processing programs will print a predefined set of textual characters, or graphical characters separately, but not in an integrated manner.

Invention or discovery.   The printing engine of the word processing program makes a series of decisions to determine what character definition and printing technique is used to print each character. If the character can be printed in text mode, the printer's stored character definition is used. If the character to be printed can be split into two characters, by being overstruck to add a diacritical, then the base character is printed, an overstrike command is sent and the diacritical is added. If the character to be printed cannot be printed using the printer's character definition, a substitute font is selected and that is used to print the character. If no substitute font is available, the printing engine determines whether a secondary substitute character or a blank space is printed.

Sample Claim.   1.   A computer system for performing wordprocessing operations, the computer system comprising:

   a.   input means responsive to operator commands enabling an operator to specify any of a plurality of characters for inclusion in a document being created or edited;

   b.   printing means having the capability of printing characters in either text or graphics mode;

   c.   memory means associated with the printing means for storing a text mode definition for each of a subset of the plurality of characters that may be specified by the operator using the input means;

   d.   a first data storage means identifying each character having a text mode definition in the memory means;

   e.   processing means coupled to the input means, the first data storage means and the printing means for comparing each character selected by the operator with information stored in the first data storage means to determine whether, for each specified character, a text mode definition exits in the memory means and,

  i. if said definition exists, sending data to the printing means identifying the character; or

  ii. if said definition does not exist, taking alternative action comprising sending data identifying an alternative character to the printing means for printing in graphics mode or sending data identifying said alternative character in a substitute font to the printing means for printing in text mode.

§ 11.36   —Martel; 5,251,292; October 5, 1993

Martel

Method and Apparatus for an Equation Editor, U.S. Patent Number 5,251,292, issued October 5, 1993, assigned toWordPerfect Corporation.

Objective.   To add scientific formula and mathematical equation editing to a wordprocessing program.

Problem addressed.   Editing scientific formulas and mathematical equations is difficult using a conventional word processor. Formulas and equations use many Greek alphabet characters and other special symbols not commonly used in conventional text. Placement of these characters and symbols in proper relation to one another on the page is critical to convey the formula or equation author's intent. Producing properly formatted formulas and equations is very difficult using conventional text-oriented wordprocessors.

Invention or discovery.   The equation editor uses a textual description to represent the characters and symbols used in scientific formulas and mathematical equations. The textual description language also includes terms used to designate relative character and symbol placement.

Sample Claim.   1. An equation editing system implemented on a digital computer for enabling a user to edit a mathematical equation to be placed in a document and to display the equation as it would appear in final printed form, the system comprising:

  a. display means comprising an editing window, a palette window and a display window;

  b. memory means;

  c. microprocessor means;

d.   storage means;

e.   input means including a standard computer keyboard whereby a user can enter a textual description of the equation;

f.   a first portion of the memory means being adapted to store the textual description of each element of the equation entered by the user;

g.   the editing window being associated with the memory means and being adapted to display the textual description of each element of the equation as it is entered by a user;

h.   a second portion of the memory means being adapted to store predefined keywords in an equation editor grammar that may be used to construct the textual description, the grammar being composed of tokens which include the keywords;

i.   parser means containing stored grammar rules describing sequences in which the tokens of the textual description may be combined;

j.   lexical scanning means for causing the microprocessor to successively compare tokens of the stored textual description with the keywords and, when a token corresponds to one of the keywords, for passing a unique value representing the token to the parser means;

k.   the parser means being adapted to receive keywords from the lexical scanning means, process those keywords according to the stored grammar rules and generate data structures describing the appearance of the equation in a printed document and the display window;

l.   means for causing the equation to be displayed in the display window;

m.   the palette window containing multiple selectable menus which enable a user to use the input means to select keywords for editing said textual descriptions; and

n.   means for causing the display means to display the mathematical equation in the display window simultaneously with the textual description of said mathematical equation in the editing window.

§ 11.37   Other Software Patent Examples

In 1993, Patent Office Group 2300 (the computer and software patent group) issued 3,613 patents in classes 364 and 395.[2] Many of these patents involve software-related inventions. No attempt is made here to give a comprehensive analysis of all software patents issued to date. There are simply too many. Rather, the following sections provide a snapshot of a few of the more interesting ones. The first is of a very famous software patent that predates the computer by nearly one hundred years.

---

[2] Statistics courtesy of United States Pat. & Trademark Office.

§ 11.38 —Precomputer Software Patent

Whether software requires a computer before it is eligible to be patented is still the subject of much debate. One view is that software, apart from the computer, is not patentable subject matter, but that once loaded into a computer, the software changes the computer into a machine that is patentable subject matter. Another view is that *software is a machine* and that the computer is merely the power source (like a battery or pump) that energizes the machine.

> So a program is a kind of machine, in particular a 'software' machine. There is nothing a program can do that a mechanical machine built out of gears and sprockets can't, but the software version can be built using a programming language on a computer terminal.
>
> *   *   *
>
> The physical computer is nothing more than a (metaphorical) power source for the software machine.[3]

The modern digital computer was successfully reduced to practice in the 1940s. Long prior to this, Samuel Morse obtained several patents on his telegraph invention. The Supreme Court of the United States, in the celebrated case of *O'Reilly v. Morse,* found this claim to be valid:

> Fifth. I claim, as my invention, the system of signs, consisting of dots and spaces, and of dots, spaces, and horizontal lines, for numerals, letters, words or sentences, substantially as herein set forth and illustrated, for telegraphic purposes.[4]

The specification described Morse's system of signs as follows:

> These are the characters, recorded, and how they are read: - — is A, — - - - is B, - - is C, — - - is D, - is E, - — - F, — — - is G, - - - - is H, - - is I, — - — - is J, — - — is K, — — is L, — — is M, — - is N, - — is O, - - - - is P, - - — - is Q, - - - is R, - - - is S, — is T, - - — is U, - - - — is V, - — — - is W, - — - - is X, - - — is Y, - - - - is Z, - - - - is &, and such is the alphabet.[5]

Morse's fifth claim covers a machine coding system for conveying intelligence. At a very fundamental level, telegraph machine code and computer machine code are the same thing. Present day computer machine code uses a binary system, that is a system having two digits. If you count Morse's dots, dashes, and spaces, Morse's machine code uses a ternary system, that is a

---

[3] David Gelernter and Suresh Jagannathan, Programming Linguistics 2 (1990).

[4] O'Reilly v. Morse, 56 U.S. 62, 85, 112 (1854).

[5] *Id.* at 94.

system having three digits (the dot, the dash, and the space). Genetic machine code, with which DNA sequences are written, uses a quaternary system, having four digits (A, T, C, G). Possibly the machine code of future creations of humankind will be quaternary.

This may be disputed, but Morse's telegraph patent may well be the first software patent—issued nearly one hundred years before the modern digital computer was invented.

§ 11.39   —Data Structure Patent

Data structure is an organizational scheme, such as a record or an array, applied to data so that it can be interpreted and so that specific operations can be performed upon that data.[6]

The Data structure is a fundamental building block of computer software. It is difficult to imagine computer software that does not have at least one data structure. In some instances the data structure is the novel aspect of a software invention. **Section 11.40** contains an example.

§ 11.40   —Ebling; 4,864,507; September 5, 1989

Ebling

Method and Apparatus for Process Manufacture Control, U.S. Patent Number 4,864,507, issued September 5, 1989, assigned to Marcam Corporation.

Objective.   To use a computer to monitor and control a manufacturing process, taking into account the materials consumed during manufacturing.

Problem addressed.   Conventional computer-aided manufacturing is said to lack the ability to model the full range of manufacturing processes.

Invention or discovery.   The computer models the manufacturing process as a data structure capable of representing one-to-one, many-to-one and many-to-many relationships between consumed resources and elements produced by the manufacturing process. The disclosure of this patent contains an enormous number of pages of computer program documentation, making it one of the largest jumbo patents issued to date.

---

[6] *Computer Dictionary* 110 (Doyle, Smith, DeJong, Carey, Magee, Fuchs, McEvoy eds., 1944).

Sample Claim.   1. A processing apparatus for manufacturing process control, comprising:

A.   first input means for inputting digital signals representative of one or more resource elements consumed in said manufacturing process,

B.   second input means for inputting digital signals representative of one or more resource elements produced by said manufacturing process,

C.   third input means for inputting digital signals representative of manufacturing relations associated with said manufacturing process between at least one consumed resource and a set of one or more produced resources, said manufacturing relations including at least one of an operational relation, a planning relation, and a financial relation,

D.   product modeling means, coupled with said first, second and third input means, for generating and storing a production model comprising digital signals representative of said manufacturing relations, said production modeling means including means for generating digital signals representing one-to-one, one-to-many, many-to-one, and many-to-many manufacturing relations between consumed and produced resource elements, and

E.   output means, coupled with said production modeling means and with said first and second input means, for generating output signals representative of at least selected portions of said manufacturing process, including manufacturing relations associated therewith.

§ 11.41   —Algorithm Patent

Whether a software algorithm is patentable subject matter has generated considerable controversy. *Gottschalk v. Benson*[7] may be responsible for generating the controversy, although that case did not hold software patents, per se, are unpatentable. For a full discussion, see **Chapter 9.**

    Clearly, some software algorithms are patentable, as the following examples demonstrate. The first example, Pardo, 4,398,249, is a very early software patent, applied for in 1970. The Pardo patent may well be the first spreadsheet invention to be considered by the Patent Office. The second example, Karmarkar, 4,744,028, involves a very clever mathematical algorithm.

---

[7] 409 U.S. 63 (1972).

§ 11.42   —Pardo; 4,398,249; August 9, 1983

Pardo

Process and Apparatus for Converting a Source Program into an Object Program, U.S. Patent Number 4,398,249, issued August 9, 1983.

Objective.   To allow business people without computer programming experience to solve problems using a computer.

Problem addressed.   In 1970 when this application was filed, computer programming was very difficult. There were no easy to use spreadsheet programs designed for business users.

Invention or discovery.   This invention may be the first spreadsheet program. The user places formulas and data in boxes (for example, spreadsheet cells). The algorithm of the invention examines the formulas located in each box in turn, and alters their order of presentation to the computer, so that the computer can execute the formulas as a standard computer program. Note that the Court of Customs and Patent Appeals (CCPA) reviewed this patent and held it to constitute patentable subject matter. See *In re Pardo.*[8]

Sample Claim.   1. A process of operating a general purpose data processor of known type to enable the data processor to execute formulas in an object program comprising a plurality of formulas, such that the same results will be produced when using the same given data, regardless of the sequence in which said formulas are presented in said object program, comprising the steps of:

a.   examining each of said formulas in a storage area of the data processor to determine which formulas can be designated as defined;

b.   storing, in the sequence in which each formula is designated as defined, said formulas which are designated as defined;

c.   repeating steps (a) and (b) for at least undefined formulas as many times as required until all said formulas have been designated as defined and have been stored;

   whereby to produce the same results upon sequential execution of the formulas stored by said process when using the same given data, regardless of the order in which said formulas were presented in the object program prior to said process.

---

[8] 684 F.2d 912 (C.C.P.A., 1982).

§ 11.43   —Karmarkar; 4,744,028; May 10, 1988

Karmarkar

Methods and Apparatus for Efficient Resource Allocation, U.S. Patent Number 4,744,028, issued May 10, 1988, assigned to AT&T Bell Labs.

Objective.   To solve very large resource allocation problems with minimum computation time.

Problem addressed.   Routing telecommunications traffic over a complex worldwide network can involve many, many resource allocation decisions. At every node of the network there may be several different choices of where to route the signal next. To a mathematician, it is a resource allocation problem. Conventional simplex methods and elliptical methods for solving the resource allocation problem run into difficulties when very large systems are involved. Computation time grows exponentially as the number of network nodes increases.

Invention or discovery.   The "geometric" algorithm of the invention defines the problem as a polytope having a plurality of facets, corresponding to the planes of the problem constraints. The algorithm starts a point in the interior of the polytope and takes successive steps in the interior of the polytope along a trajectory towards the optimum allocation point. Since the size of successive steps is not limited by the adjacent vertex spacing (as in the simplex method), much larger steps can be taken, fewer steps are needed, and the time required to identify the optimum allocation is shortened.

When reading this patent, it is obvious that the inventor was concerned that the invention might be characterized as an unpatentable mathematical algorithm. To avert this, the inventor cites "prior art examples of the use of such mathematical models to characterize physical systems" to include "the use of equations to construct radio antennas or to control rubber-molding operations."[9] You will probably recognize these famous prior art examples as the MacKay Radio antenna invention[10] and the Diehr rubber molding invention.[11]

Sample Claim.   1. A method for allocating the available telecommunication transmission facilities among the subscribers demanding service at a particular time so as to reduce the total cost of operating said transmission

---

[9] Karmarkar, U.S. Pat. No. 4,744,028, col. 1, lines 58–61 (1988), *assigned to* AT&T Bell Labs.

[10] MacKay Radio & Tel. Co. v. Radio Corp. of Am., 306 U.S. 86 (1939).

[11] Diamond v. Diehr, 450 U.S. 175 (1981).

facilities, where the available transmission facilities, the subscribers, and the total cost are related in a linear manner, said method comprising the steps of:

tentatively and iteratively reassigning said available telecommunications transmission facilities to said subscribers so as to reduce said total costs at each said reassignment,

each said reassignment being determined by normalizing the previous assignment with respect to constraints on said allocations,

terminating said iterative reassigning steps when said costs are below a pre-selected threshold, and

allocating said transmission facilities in accordance with the reduced cost assignment.

§ 11.44   —User Interface Patent

The user interface defines the connection between the human user and the computer. Microsoft Windows has a graphical user interface that provides this function. Most software inventions rely on an existing user interface, such as the one provided by Microsoft Windows. Thus most often the user interface is standard and does not form part of the invention. There are exceptions. The following patent is an example where the user interface is the invention.

§ 11.45   —Atkinson; Re 32,632; March 29, 1988

Atkinson

Display System, U.S. Patent Reissue Number 32,632, reissued March 29, 1988, assigned to Apple Computer, Inc.

Objective.   To provide a mouse (pointing device) operated menu selection system.

Background.   This patent concentrates primarily on mechanical aspects of an improved mouse. The original application was filed July 19, 1982 (issued August 7, 1984 as Patent 4,464,652). The patent was reissued March 29, 1988, to delete all claims pertaining to the improved mouse. The surviving claims pertain to a computer-controlled display (menu) system.

Invention or discovery.   The user selects a menu title by pointing to and pressing the mouse button. The computer display system then either executes the menu title, if it is an immediate command, or displays a set of sub-commands for user selection. If sub-commands are presented, the user selects one, by continuing to depress the mouse button while dragging the cursor to a selected a sub-command. The user then removes pressure from the mouse button, thereby signaling the computer display system to executed the selected sub-command.

Sample Claim. 11. In a computer controlled display system having a display wherein a plurality of command options are displayed along a menu bar and sub-command items corresponding to each option are displayed once said option has been selected, a method for selecting an option and an item, comprising the steps of:

a. generating and displaying said menu bar comprising said plurality of command options;

b. positioning a cursor on said display using a cursor control device for movement over a surface, the movement of said cursor control device over said surface by a user resulting in a corresponding movement of said cursor on said display;

c. signalling said computer of an option choice once said cursor is positioned over a first predetermined area on said display corresponding to an option to be selected, said user signalling said computer by placing a switch coupled to said display system in a second position while moving said cursor control device over said surface such that said cursor is over said first predetermined area;

d. generating and displaying said sub-command items corresponding to said selected option;

e. positioning said cursor over a second predetermined area corresponding to a sub-command item to be selected, said switch being maintained in said second position until said cursor is positioned over said second predetermined area;

f. placing said switch in a first position once said user has positioned said cursor over said second predetermined area;

whereby an option and an item associated with said option is selected.

§ 11.46   —Multimedia Patent

The multimedia industry was outraged by the Compton's New Media patent (Reed, 5,241,671), which many perceived as encompassing the entire multimedia industry. Whether this is so, you can judge for yourself. Responding to industry protests, in December 1993, Patent Commissioner, Bruce Lehman, ordered a nearly unprecedented reexamination of the Compton's New Media patent.

§ 11.47   —Reed; 5,241,671; August 31, 1993

Reed

Multimedia Search System Using a Plurality of Entry Path Means that Indicate Interrelatedness of Information, U.S. Patent Number 5,241,671, issued August 31, 1993, assigned to Encyclopaedia Britannica, Inc.

Objective.   To provide an interactive CD-ROM search system in which graphical and textual information can be accessed with equal ease.

Problem addressed.   Conventional CD-ROM search systems, the patent states, lack the tools to interactively search both graphical and textual information stored in a single database. Text search modes cannot access graphical information and graphical search modes cannot access full textual information.

Invention or discovery.   The search system provides multiple textual entry paths for searching textual information and multiple graphical entry paths for searching graphical information. Specifically, the main menu offers eight separate and interrelated entry paths, allowing textual information to be accessed through graphical entry paths, and allowing graphical information to be accessed through textual entry paths. The eight entry paths include the following: Idea Search, Title Finder, Picture Explorer, Topic Tree, Feature Articles, World Atlas, History Timeline, Researcher's Assistant.

Sample Claim.   1.   A computer search system for retrieving information, comprising:

means for storing interrelated textual information and graphical information;

a plurality of entry path means for searching said stored interrelated textual and graphical information, said entry path means comprising:

textual search entry path means for searching said textual information and for retrieving interrelated graphical information to said searched text;

graphics entry path means for searching said graphical information and for retrieving interrelated textual information to said searched graphical information;

selecting means for providing a menu of said plurality of entry path means for selection;

processing means for executing inquiries provided by a user in order to search said textual and graphical information through said selected entry path means;

indicating means for indicating a pathway that accesses information related in one of said entry path means to information accessible in another one of said entry path means;

accessing means for providing access to said related information in said another entry path means; and

output means for receiving search results from said processing means and said related information from said accessing means and for providing said search results and received information to such user.

§ 11.48   —Business Methods Patent

The Patent Office does not consider methods of doing business to be patentable subject matter.[12] Nevertheless, a computer-implemented system useful in business may be patentable. The classic example of such an invention is the Merrill Lynch, Musmanno patent.

§ 11.49   —Musmanno; 4,346,442; August 24, 1982

Musmanno

Securities Brokerage-Cash Management System, U.S. Patent Number 4,346,442, issued August 24, 1982, assigned to Merrill Lynch.

Objective.   To provide a brokerage/cash management system that automatically invests free credit cash balances in a money market fund and that permits consumer transactions using charge cards and checks.

Invention or discovery.   Subscriber's credit card charges and checks drawn against the bank are accumulated by the bank and periodically transmitted to the brokerage house. The brokerage house establishes a credit limit against which each subscriber may use the credit card and checks. The credit limit is updated based on the subscriber's expenditures.

Sample Claim.   1.   In combination in a system for processing and supervising a plurality of composite subscriber accounts each comprising a margin brokerage account, a charge card and checks administered by a first institution, and participation in at least one short term investment, administered by a second institution, said system including brokerage account data file means for storing current information characterizing each subscriber margin brokerage

---

[12] § 706.03(a) (5th ed. Mar. 1994).

account of the second institution, manual entry means for entering short term investment orders in the second institution, data receiving and verifying means for receiving and verifying charge card and check transactions from said first institution and short term investment orders from said manual entry means, means responsive to said brokerage account data file means and said data receiving and verifying means for generating an updated credit limit for each account, short term investment updating means responsive to said brokerage account data file means and said data receiving and verifying means for selectively generating short term investment transactions as required to generate and invest proceeds for subscribers' accounts, wherein said system includes plural such short term investments, said system further comprising means responsive to said short term updating means for allocating said short term investment transactions among aid plural short term investments, communicating means to communicate said updated credit limit for each account to said first institution.

APPENDIXES

A.   United States Patent and Trademark Office Transcripts of the Public Hearings on Use of the Patent System to Protect Software-Related Invention

B.   Software Classification System of the United States Patent and Trademark Office

C.   Letter of Thomas Jefferson to Isaac McPherson Dated August 13, 1813

UNITED STATES PATENT AND TRADEMARK OFFICE TRANSCRIPTS OF THE PUBLIC HEARINGS ON USE OF THE PATENT SYSTEM TO PROTECT SOFTWARE-RELATED INVENTION

United States Patent and Trademark Office

Public Hearing on Use of the Patent System to Protect
Software-Related Inventions

Transcript of Proceedings

Wednesday, January 26, 1994
Thursday, January 27, 1994
9:00 a.m. to 5:00 p.m.

Before
Bruce A. Lehman
Assistant Secretary of Commerce and
Commissioner of Patents and Trademarks

Location:
San Jose Convention Center
408 Almaden Avenue
San Jose, California

United States Patent and Trademark Office

Public Hearing on Use of the Patent System to Protect Software-Related Inventions

Transcript of Proceedings

Wednesday, January 26, 1994
Thursday, January 27, 1994
9:00 a.m. to 5:00 p.m.

Before

Bruce A. Lehman
Assistant Secretary of Commerce and
Commissioner of Patents and Trademarks

Location:
San Jose Convention Center
408 Almaden Avenue
San Jose, California

UNITED STATES PATENT AND TRADEMARK OFFICE
Public Hearing on Patent Protection for Software-Related Inventions
San Jose, California — January 26-27, 1994

Table of Participants

Before: Bruce A. Lehman
                Assistant Secretary of Commerce and
                Commissioner of Patents and Trademarks
                United States Patent and Trademark Office

The Panel: Ginger Lew
                General Counsel-Designate
                United States Department of Commerce

                Lawrence Goffney
                Assistant Commissioner for Patents-Designate
                United States Patent and Trademark Office

                Micheal K. Kirk
                Assistant Commissioner for External Affairs
                United States Patent and Trademark Office

                Jeffrey P. Kushan
                Attorney-Advisor
                United States Patent and Trademark Office

Recording
Technicians: Karl Henderscheid
                Support Office Services
                52 Second Street, Third Floor
                San Francisco, CA 94104
                (415) 391-4578

Trascriber   Milton Hare
                Rogershare Transcribers
                541 Maud Avenue
                San Leandro, CA 94577
                (510) 357-8220

UNITED STATES PATENT AND TRADEMARK OFFICE
Public Hearing on Patent Protection for Software-Related Inventions
San Jose, California — January 26-27, 1994

Witnesses

January 26, 1994

Mr. Clark
VideoDiscovery

Mr. Poppa
StorageTek

Mr. Ryan
Intellectual Property Owners, Inc.

Mr. LeFaivre
Apple Computer
Computer and Business Equipment Manufacturing
Association

Mr. Lopez
Interactive Multimedia Association

Mr. Heckel
Abraham Lincoln Patent Holders Association

Mr. Kohn
Borland International, Inc.

Mr. Brotz
Adobe Systems Incorporated

Mr. Troesch
Fish and Richardson

Mr. Sabath
World Intellectual Property and Trade Forum

Mr. Benman
Benman & Collins

Mr. Baker
Oracle Corporation

Mr. Silverman
Intel Corporation

Ms. Caldwell
Software Entepreneurs Forum

Mr. Chiddix
Time Warner Cable

Mr. Fernandez
Fenwick and West

Mr. Antoniak
Solar Systems Software

Prof. Hollaar
University of Utah

Mr. Henry
Wolf, Greenfield & Sacks, P.C
Boston Patent Law Association

Mr. Cassamassima
Exxon Production Research Company

Mr. May
Iconik Corporation

Mr. Brown

Mr. Irlam
League for Programming Freedom

Mr. Yoches
Finnegan, Henderson, Farabow, Garrett & Dunner

Mr. Shay
Morrison & Foerster

January 27, 1994

Mr. Fiddler
Wind River Systems

Mr. Warren
Autodesk, Inc.

Ms. O'Hare
Mr. Glenn
Intellectual Property Section of the State Bar of California

Mr. Lippe
Synopsys

Mr. Boyle
Multimedia Development Group

Mr. Laurie
Weil, Gotshal & Manges

Mr. Patch
Sun Microsystems, Inc.

Mr. Byrne
American Committee for Interoperable Systems

Mr. Gimlan
Fliesler, Dubb, Meyer & Lovejoy

Mr. Cronan
Taligent, Inc.

Mr. Neukom
Microsoft Corporation

Mr. Morgan
The Prudential Insurance Company of America

Mr. Stallman

Mr. Casey
Silicon Graphics, Inc.

Mr. Sterne
Sterne, Kessler, Goldstein and Fox

Mr. Siber
IBM Corporation

Mr. Lachuck
Poms, Smith, Lande & Rose

Mr. Aharonian
Source Translation and Optimization

Mr. Cole

Mr. Graham
International Federation of Industrial Property Attorneys

Mr. Lemon
Network Computing Devices

Mr. Schlafly
Real Software

Mr. Brand
Reasonings Systems, Inc.

Mr. Judd
Mentrix Corporation

Mr. Higgins
Cooley, Godward, Castro, Huddleson & Tatum

Mr. Grace
Tetrasoft International

UNITED STATES PATENT AND TRADEMARK OFFICE
Public Hearing on Patent Protection for Software-Related Inventions
San Jose, California -- January 26-27, 1994

--oOo--

JEFF KUSHAN: We're ready to begin the hearings today. We're very pleased to be out here on the West Coast. What I'd like to do is to introduce the Vice-Mayor of San Jose, Blanc Alvarado, so we could begin the program.

--oOo--

VICE-MAYOR BLANC OALVARADO

VICE-MAYOR, CITY OF SAN JOSE, CALIFORNIA

VICE-MAYOR ALVARADO: Well, good morning to all of you. It's wonderful to see as many of you here today. Hopefully more people will come in during the course of the hearings, because indeed what is happening here in our city today is very very important not only to the software industry, but certainly to the nation and to the country as a whole.

Commissioner LEHMAN, distinguished officials from the Patent and Trademark Office, ladies and gentlemen, I am Blanc Alvarado, Vice-Mayor, City of San Jose and it is my pleasure to welcome you to our city known as the capitol of Silicon Valley for hearings on patents for software-related inventions.

As you all know, for the past decade the computer software industry has evolved into one of the nation's fastest-growing industries, and today U.S. software firms lead the world in innovation and market share. Silicon Valley firms develop one-fourth of the world's software, and to maintain leadership in this vital industry, a commitment to innovation on the part of each and every one of us is essential.

It is quite a privilege for San Jose to host the first landmark public hearing on patent protection held outside of Washington, D.C. This is the first in a series of public hearings which will result with your input and good advice in a revamping and updating of a system that at best I would say is somewhat out of date. We commend the Patent and Trademark Office for recognizing Silicon Valley's critical role in the world software industry, and I would also like to recognize the efforts of our own Office of Economic Development in bringing these hearings to San Jose.

The dialogue that will take place today and tomorrow and throughout the public hearings in other parts of the country is as you know extremely important to the software industry, to our regional economy, and certainly to the nation's economy. We wish each and every one of you a very very successful public hearing, and we encourage you to speak candidly, to give us your best advice so that those that are here from the Patent Office will be able to take your recommendations, your input in the most serious step further up ahead, to look at how the system for patenting inventions can be improved. We wish you success, encourage you to stay for the two days, and also encourage you to invite other people who are not here presently to attend as well. Thank you very much for being here.

COMMISSIONER LEHMAN: Thank you very much.

--oOo--

COMMISSIONER BRUCE LEHMAN

COMMISSIONER OF PATENTS AND TRADEMARKS

COMMISSIONER LEHMAN: On behalf of President Clinton and Secretary of Commerce Ron Brown and all of us at the Department of Commerce and the Patent and Trademark Office, I'd like to thank the Vice-Mayor and the City of San Jose for providing this great spot to have these hearings and providing the technical and physical assistance that we really needed to come here from the political and legal capitol of the United States to the technological capitol of the United States which really is right here in Silicon Valley. And I think it emphasizes what we would like to think is a growing cooperation between the political capitol and this technological capitol, and particularly the President's commitment to work with California to make certain that California can be everything that it possibly can be.

President Clinton has made the development and competitiveness of America's high-tech industries the cornerstone of his economic program, and he talked about that last night in his State of the Union Address. Promoting these industries will lead to the highway to high-tech jobs for Americans, more high-wage, high-tech jobs, and will insure continued competitiveness for our industries into the future.

In fact, you know, we're not far from the mountains of the Gold Rush. In the Nineteenth Century it was the wealth in the ground that created the wealth of California and the nation. As we move into the 21st Century, it's the wealth of the human mind which is going to be our most precious natural resource. That wealth doesn't mean a whole lot if it doesn't have a conception of a modern up-to-date legal system which defines the rights that individuals have in their creations. That system needs constant revising and constant modification, and that's why we're here, right here in the heart of Silicon Valley, where we see a tremendous potential for pursuit of the Clinton Administration's goals.

Much recent concern has been expressed over the patent system to protect software-related inventions. These concerns range from claims that the patent system is incompatible with software development to skepticism over the ability of the Patent and Trademark Office to accurately gauge innovations in this field of technology. However, to date, there has not been a forum in which those having concerns could air them with the hope that they would be heard, evaluated, and used to develop future policy. These hearings are intended to provide that forum. We're really quite serious about having this opportunity to really hear from people in the business about what they think about the current state of the intellectual property system, what they think needs to be done to improve it.

Before we begin I'd like to provide you with a little information about the Patent and Trademark Office, our operations and our plans for the future. The Patent and Trademark Office is an agency of the Department of Commerce. It's a very old agency; it was founded in 1790. It's one of the first agencies of the Federal Government. It's a part of the team that the President has assembled to promote technological innovation and exploitation to increase our exports and to enhance the overall competitiveness of U.S. industry. The Commerce Department is also leading the Administration's initiative to accelerate the development of our nationwide electronic superhighway. The President also talked about that last night in his State of the Union Address. This Information Superhighway, and of course Silicon Valley and the intellectual property system is very much a part of that, will

UNITED STATES PATENT AND TRADEMARK OFFICE
Public Hearing on Patent Protection for Software-Related Inventions
San Jose, California — January 26-27, 1994

be the basis for our information-based high-tech economy of the 21st Century.

Our office plays an integral role in this team, and Secretary of Commerce Ron Brown has given us the following mission:

First, we're to administer the laws relating to trademarks in order to promote industrial and technological progress in the United States and strengthen our national economy. Secondly, we are to develop and advise the Secretary and the President on intellectual property policy, including copyright matters, and of course that's part of what we're here about today. And finally, in cooperation with other trade agencies of the government, the International Trade Administration in the Department of Commerce, we are to advise the Secretary and other agencies of the Government such as the United States Trade Representative on the trade-related aspects of intellectual property, and we just finished, as you probably know, a very successful effort that culminated in Geneva last month to provide a new trading regime for the world which will very much benefit high-tech industries, particularly the computer software industry.

The new focus of the President and the Secretary of Commerce on technology-based economic growth makes this a very exciting time for me to be leading the Patent and Trademark Office as its commissioner. It also places a serious obligation on us, however, to ensure the proper functioning of the patent system, especially in the rapidly-developing areas of technology. We have devoted a substantial amount of effort and resources to improving quality of examination for our software-related inventions, though I must say there are some inherent problems there which are very difficult to address, and just to point out what one of them is, particularly in this area of computer software-related inventions is that a lot of what is known in this area is in the area of trade secrecy. It's not written down anyplace. It's not even in prior patent applications, and so we have a very difficult time sometimes making determinations -- what is the existing state of technology? And as most of you who are here know, that's a critical requirement in order to be able to issue a patent, to know what is in fact new, what is a new innovation that should warrant protection.

Our Computer Systems and Applications Examining Group headed by Gerry Goldberg, who is here with us today, has been at the center of this effort. This group currently employs over a hundred and sixty examiners who bring with them a wide range of expertise and experience. We use stringent hiring standards to ensure that our examiners come into our office with the proper background, and then provide training from experts in the field to ensure that they keep abreast, not only of the state-of-the-art technology, but also of current legal standards. These examiners are responsible for the examination of a steadily-increasing number of patent applications being filed by inventors in this field. In 1991 we had 6,600 applications. In 1992 we had 7,500, and last year we had over 8,300. That's out of a total of about 190,000 patent applications in all fields of technology in our office.

We have also worked hard to remain receptive to public and industry concerns, and I think this can be seen through our extensive efforts to improve our prior art collections, conduct training for our examiners and recently to respond to intense industry concern over the issue of patents.

We will soon forward to Congress a legislative package. We'll make our reexamination process more open to third-party participation. These changes will make reexamination a more attractive option for, those having reasons to question the validity of any particular patent. We will also be changing the patent term to run from twenty years from the date of filing rather than seventeen years from the date of grant. This is a change that is good for the United States. We believe that it will prevent the disruptive effect of patents that are issued long after they have been filed, due to administrative delays in the processing of the patent applications, delays that are often deliberately arranged, sometimes by patent applicants who want to extend ultimately the reach of their patent further than it ought to go.

We recognized this benefit when we agreed to a change recently in the GATT-TRIPS context where we agreed to an international standard of twenty years from filing as the standard that all countries would attempt to achieve. But as an extra bonus, by making this change, we have been able to convince -- and I just back from Tokyo last week -- we've been able to convince the government of Japan to loosen their rules regarding filing patent applications. This will greatly assist U.S. inventors in their efforts to gain patent protection in Japan. And I should add that intellectual property protection in foreign markets like Japan is a very vital part of our effort to encourage and promote U.S. exports, because what we have to promote is often the technology itself, which is not going to be very valuable unless it's protected by an internationally-recognized regime of intellectual property laws.

Finally, our hearings today, I would like to think, emphasize our desire to remain receptive to the needs of our users and our public. Of course we, I think, will find out in the next few hours that sometimes those recommendations that we get from users in the public aren't always in harmony; I'm sure that we're going to hear differences of opinion, and we are going to have the task of sorting through those differences and coming up with a policy that works.

I'd like to just make an observation about the nature of the intellectual property system before we proceed, and that is that I don't think there's any question about it, that intellectual property protection, patents and copyrights, have been a major part of the economic growth of America from the very beginning. When I walk into my office every morning, I see the patent model of Thomas Edison's light bulb sitting there, greeting me as I walk in the door, and out of that, great industries have been built. I see mid-Nineteenth Century inventions, inventors like Eli Whitney. That innovation is increasing in the United States, and it's always been protected by the patent system and encouraged by the patent system. The purpose of the patent system is to incent innovation, not to disincent it. And patent law is a very delicate instrument. If it doesn't work right, if the threshold of patentability is too low, there's too much confusion in the system, it may actually end up disincenting innovation rather than incenting it. The best kinds of patent systems is a patent system that is clear, that everyone understands, that requires very little litigation to use it, and it is our concern that we're not quite seeing that

UNITED STATES PATENT AND TRADEMARK OFFICE
Public Hearing on Patent Protection for Software-Related Inventions
San Jose, California — January 26-27, 1994

kind of a patent system, particularly in the software-related inventions area, that has caused us to be here in Silicon Valley today, and we're going to do everything that we can possibly do to try to make this the best system that we can.

Finally, before we call our first witnesses, I'd like to introduce the people who are here with me at this table this morning, and I'd like to start at my far right with Michael Kirk. Mike is currently our Assistant Commissioner of Patents for External Affairs. He has been responsible for some time for all of the policy and legislation in international matters in the office. President Clinton has nominated him to be the Deputy Commissioner of Patents, and as such he's going to lead an effort to deal with these policy problems and make our intellectual property system all that it can be.

Next I'd like to introduce Ginger Lew, to my immediate right. Ginger Lew is our new General Counsel for the entire Department of Commerce. She works directly for Secretary of Commerce Ron Brown. Ginger is from the Bay Area. She was a practicing lawyer out here, has worked in this area of law herself, and I think is an illustration of the kind of technology-oriented, California-oriented people that we have in our administration who I think are going to be very receptive to the concerns of people out here.

Next I'd like to introduce Larry Goffney. Larry is our new Assistant Commissioner for Patents. His responsibility will be to supervise the patent examining corps. He'll have about three thousand people working for him, including all the examiners and support staff who examine the software-related inventions. Larry has taught law around the United States, he has a an engineering and a law degree, he was a patent lawyer and a partner in a very prominent law firm before coming to our office, and we're very excited about the prospects that he brings to our office and his understanding of these issues. And finally you have already been introduced to Jeff Kushan who is on the staff of our Office of Legislation and International Affairs who has been the sparkplug who's really pulled all of this together, and I know that this room I think seats about a thousand people, so -- I think the Vice-Mayor was a little concerned that we didn't have a good turnout, but I think that when you think of how many people the room seats that we're having a pretty good turnout, so it indicates that Jeff has done his job of getting the message out so that all of you know that we're here to listen to your concerns.

The people who will be testifying over the next two days should have received a schedule indicating the approximate time that they have been assigned to give their remarks. A final list is available at the entrance to the room. I imagine most of you got it, and I would encourage all of the people who are scheduled to testify here to be here at least twenty minutes before your assigned time slot. We're going to try to keep to this schedule as much as we can, but hopefully you'll give us a little bit of leeway either way. Each person will have eleven minutes to speak, and the computer monitor in front of this podium here, this computer monitor that you see sitting in front of Jeff, will display a green screen for nine minutes, and then it will turn yellow during your last two minutes, so that you'll know that you'll have to start wrapping up, and then when the screen turns red the time will be up. I would encourage everybody to try to cooperate with us and stick to these time limits so that we

can be fair to everybody. Unfortunately if one person goes over too much then that really is at the expense of others, and we're not going to have a very balanced hearing. I think eleven minutes ought to be pretty good time for people to get most of their comments in, but of course we're not limited to these oral comments, and I would encourage anyone who has further additional written comments to give them to us and anybody who's not here, anybody that anybody here knows is not here who has views about this should certainly feel free to send in their written comments and they can consult the Federal Register notice which was published on December 20th, 1993 for more information about this. We may have copies of that out here for those of you who don't have it, and Jeff can certainly get that for you if we don't.

The notice has been widely circulated through the Internet, and it can be retrieved at our ftp site, which is comments.uspto.gov. The transcripts for these hearings will be available after February 7th, 1994, and paper copies will be available from our office for a charge of $30.00. I'm sorry we have to charge that, but it's unfair to ask our patent applicants to pay that fee, so there will be a $30.00 fee which is basically our charge of reproducing them, and the transcripts will also be available through our ftp site that I just gave to you.

Once again I'd like to welcome everybody here today. It's a real pleasure for us to be out here, and I think this is going to be a very productive exercise, that we are going to in fact learn much information that will help us turn those dials of law and policy in Washington so that they're totally finally tuned, and we can provide all of you out here we're looking to to create the wealth of America for the next century, with the kind of intellectual property system that you need to do your job properly.

In calling our first witness, I'd like to say even though everybody has eleven minutes to speak you don't need to use all the eleven minutes, don't feel that you have to do that. To the extent that you leave us a little more time, we might be able to ask a question or two if we feel motivated to do that. So with that explanation, I'd like to call on our first witness, who is Joe Clark, the Chairman and CEO of VideoDiscovery, and welcome, Mr. Clark.

--oOo--

JOE CLARK

CHAIRMAN AND CEO, VIDEODISCOVERY

MR. CLARK: Thank you very much, Commissioner LEHMAN. My clock says 9:28, and that's what it says on the sheet, so I congratulate you the good timing of your remarks, and I'll try to do the same.

I really appreciate the opportunity to come and talk to this group. I have a publishing company in Seattle, Washington that publishes multimedia products for science education, and we're pretty well-known at this time throughout the country, and we're totally frustrated by our experiences with the patent system. And so what I would like to do during my time is kind of share with you personal experiences that we had in order to illustrate some of the problems that I think are inherent in the current patenting process, and then I'd like to recommend two or three different solutions.

Now, you've sort of preempted my remarks, and I'm really

UNITED STATES PATENT AND TRADEMARK OFFICE
Public Hearing on Patent Protection for Software-Related Inventions
San Jose, California — January 26-27, 1994

appreciative of it. It's the first time that I've heard that the Patent Office was drafting legislation that would take care of most of these, but there's one part of it that I want to try to deal with and maybe ask you a question about.

On the plane on the way down I thought it was in some way almost poetic that I was headed down to California. I was a little bit anxious about earthquake country, you know, in fact I didn't sleep very well last night. But I thought about the earthquake thing as not being too dissimilar from the situation we find ourselves in with the patent system, that is to say, in the last year and a half we've heard some rumblings coming from the Patent Office with patents like the Grass Valley patent and the Optical Data patent and then the Compton patent which sort of got a 7.3 on the Richter scale as far as I could figure out, and my big worry is that there's no end in sight, that is to say, given the secrecy in the Patent Office, we don't know what to expect tomorrow, next week, next month, and so on.

In my case, I experienced a situation where a patent was called to my attention that literally could drive me out of business. I started VideoDiscovery in 1983. I worked very hard for ten years to get it to the point it is at, with sixty people, and for somebody to have a patent that was a club that could just close down my operation didn't set well with me. I didn't know much about the patent system until about a year ago when I got a letter from my competitor that called attention to the award of two patents, and they indicated that they thought we might be infringing on their patents and suggested that I contact their technical person to see about licensing the technology.

Well, they had two patents. One of them was for a method of instruction that we lovingly call the Socratic Method, and the other patent was for a method to customize a curriculum, using a computer to do it, and we thought that that had been a process that had been going on for a long, long time.

So my immediate reaction was confusion. In the first place I couldn't believe that anybody would patent these things. If I could have the Number 3 slide, please. I just want to describe this one patent for you. The patent on the Socratic Method, as I say -- this is not the way it's described, it's described as a method of instruction -- was composed of a trilog, and the trilog had three components. One was a random-accessible reservoir of information like a video disk player -- could have been a CD-ROM or a hard disk, I guess, or maybe a textbook, a teacher was the second component, and the students were the third component. The way this system worked was that the teacher was given instructions where to go on the random-accessible reservoir of information, withdrew the information, passed it on to the students, the students responded, and then they would go back to this system.

Now, they got a patent for this. I couldn't believe it. And my first reaction was anger, disgust, you know, disbelief, and so on. More recently I've modified my position where I believe that the, the Patent Office is indeed not the culprit, but the victim in a system. Any system that operates in secrecy like that where they can't confide or consult with the members of an emerging industry, for which there's no prior art, no experience, no informed judgment on the part of the examiners, is ultimately a victim to this thing where they

have to -- they, they can't distinguish obvious from unique and are almost obliged to issue the patent.

So the point there is that I think that if we would remove the veil of secrecy, which I hope is part of the legislation package, and I'm not sure that is attached to, you know, ultimately or necessarily to first-to-file process, so I'd like a clarification about that, but that is really critical, to support change in our industry. At one point it was the computer industry, it was the biotechnology industry, it was the software industry, the multimedia industry, what's going to happen next week, next month and so on, but whatever the new, emerging industry is, unless that law is changed so that there's some better process, we're going to face the same kind of dilemma.

Let me come back to the history on my case. As soon as we got that indication, as a small company I did not have many attractive alternatives. One was litigation, which was very very expensive, and I could literally not afford that, and the other one was the reexamination process. In talking to no less than ten patent attorneys over the course of last year, I never got one that recommended reexamination process, and so I'm very happy that the Patent Office recognizes the problem with that and is going to include more third-party involvement in that reexamination process. But that was one of my recommendations.

As it happens, when we filed in Court in August to ask the Court to find these patents invalid based on the obviousness of the patent and the existence of prior art, the other party had sixty days to respond; and on the sixtieth day they decided to donate the Socratic Method back to the public where it belongs. The second patent, however, they asked for reexamination in the Patent Office. That puts us in a terrible position. We know that the inventor has a tremendous advantage through the reexamination process as it exists. We also have some trumps, some prior art that we know that will knock that out, and we don't know whether to provide it to the Patent Office or to save it for litigation if it emerges from the Patent Office. So you can kind of see our dilemma on that thing.

So a recommendation that I would have is to change the process so it's published prior to award. That would solve the problem and serve existing, you know, changes and so on (sic). Second recommendation would be improve the examination process. I think that that's being considered, and so on. But a compromise position, and something that I would like to see for immediate relief -- I'm talking we need Federal aid now, an immediate relief to get us out from under this anxiety, is either a hiatus on any more patents coming out for multimedia -- that would be preferable -- if you can't do that, then I'd like to see the Commissioner empowered to constitute a commission and do peer review of any patents that have come up. The Commissioner would identify new emerging industries, all right? And when they saw that, because there's no prior art, because there's no experience with the examiners and so on, that they work with the industry leaders in that particular industry, to develop the prior art collection, to set the guidelines for what's patentable, to review patents as they come out.

So I hope that you can sympathize with the position of a small business person who has gone through the fear and the anxiety of having something like that ripped out from under

UNITED STATES PATENT AND TRADEMARK OFFICE
Public Hearing on Patent Protection for Software-Related Inventions
San Jose, California — January 26-27, 1994

them. I feel I've been extremely lucky to get my resources together and to be able to operate in this system.

Thanks very much for your attention; I'd be happy to answer questions.

COMMISSIONER LEHMAN: Thank you very much, Mr. Clark. In terms of this reexamination process that you're concerned with right now, I think one of the problems that we have in reexamination right now is that generally speaking we limit the prior-art references in a reexamination to those that are submitted by the person who is seeking reexamination, and that creates a problem for third parties.

MR. CLARK: Aha!

COMMISSIONER LEHMAN: So in this situation it sounds to me like the patentee kind of got the leg up on you by being the first to request reexamination. Is that problem.

MR. CLARK: Yeah, I don't disagree. Yeah. I don't disagree that I was outmaneuvered, you know, but -- yeah, you're right. You're right.

COMMISSIONER LEHMAN: I really appreciate that. Does anybody have any other comments? If not, thank you very much for coming down here and sharing these thoughts with us.

MR. CLARK: Thank you.

COMMISSIONER LEHMAN: Next I'd like to call Mr. Ryal Poppa, the Chairman and CEO of Storage Tek.

—oOo—

RYAL POPPA

STORAGE TEK

MR. POPPA: Good morning, and thank you very much. I'm going to be answering principally the Question 4 on whether the circumstance or the framework of the current patent law preserves competition.

Quick background on Storage Tek, we are a twenty-five-year-old company, start-up, much like you see here in the Valley. We do about one and a half billion, have ten thousand employees. We belong to many organizations, the CCIA, Computer and Communications Industry Association; ESIS and ASIS, the European and the American Committees on Interoperable Systems; AEA, American Electronics Association; and the IEEE, the Institute of Electronic and Electrical Engineers. All of these are very pro-competitive in their attitudes, and that's the principal reason we belong to them.

For the record, we have over three hundred programmers cranking out programs all the time, we have lots of patents and we have the same risk everybody else does. In the industry though we do build principally data storage devices that are attached to all the major mainframe manufacturers of the world, eighteen at this time, and many networks. We do support patents in every sense, as applied to the area of software, with one exception. We believe we have to have continued decompilation rights to maintain interoperability when needed. Modern APIs or mandatory APIs would do the job -- application program interface -- but frankly most companies do not want to do this, but that would be a solution in addition to decompilation.

In supporting the thesis of "pro competition" I want to give three illustrations.

One is old Ma Bell; we all know what it was like in the old days, very bureaucratic, very successful, it was the stock of widows and orphans, but it was a stifling, stultifying, noncompetitive environment. The new Bell of course is growing, marvelously. It is competitive. The competitive juices are flowing. And think of all the new services in the last twenty years that we have become accustomed to. Auto-answer, FAX, networks, fiber-optics, cellular, ISDN, et cetera, et cetera. New companies; MCI, the WilTel's, the Sprints, et cetera, and new related industries defined by companies such as Novell with software, and NSC for high-speed data transmission, McCaw for cellular, Hayes for modems and the list goes on and on and on as you well know. But this flowed out of a pro-competitive stance, a break-up of a company, and it led ultimately to [DarvdaNet], InterNet, and the information highway. That was the genesis of that kind of program. Today we've globalized that communications capability all over the world and we continue to do so by freeing our telecommmunications capability.

A second illustration is, in my principal industry, computers, leader of the industry, IBM, fell upon hard times. We all are aware of that. They are correcting that problem and will clearly return to health. But they fell into a pattern of being in the sixties and seventies highly competitive, and then they went into a protect mode, where they were trying to hold onto their base, hold onto their customers, and as a consequence, they fell behind, they became anticompetitive, and as a consequence, they began to lose the competitive juice, and even today some of the comments made by their own officers saying that we have lost the will to compete. They're getting it back, they will return, but it was because they lost their desire to win. Part of that was the intense, massive fight over copyrights and patents, protecting in the court, fighting in the courts rather than fighting in the customer arena to save the customers and keeping them happy. No new ideas were allowed in the seventies and eighties. Where did the PC come from? or the mini? or the workstation? Not out of the big companies. They came out of the start-ups, where they could get the proper patent and copyright protection. But oftentimes decompilation is part of that because you have to maintain interoperability -- very fundamental issue.

I sincerely hope that Lou Gershner understands that there's a smothering effect of too extensive use of patents and copyrights. It destroys the design capability of the company because they don't look to get their products to market quickly, they design poor patents and protection, and therefore it doesn't really work to their great benefit. In the last six years, we along with many of our colleagues, have opposed the forces in Europe that have been seeking to use copyright and patent protection to limit competition, and as you well know, the EC finally came down on the point that decompilation is legal, desirable, when necessary for interoperability, and that's the only thing we look for -- no piracy, no cloning, no copying, no replacement of the program, but interoperability. That must be preserved.

The last example is the information highway. This is not an economic debate in the way it was between Bell and IBM, but rather it is a competition of ideas, of interchange, of the exchange of relationships over the Internet, as you -- if you follow it and see what goes on, it is used in many, many ways.

I would add a challenge to you, because of that Internet. Looking for data the way you are, and in your opening statement you said you're actively looking for ideas from our society, put out on the Internet a question. Should decompilation be allowed for the purpose of interoperability, but clearly not for piracy, cloning or replacement of the basic software? I think you'll get a very strong eighty-to-ninety-percent positive response that it should be. The reasons are you have organizations like the IEEE with two hundred and forty thousand members who have voted and publicly stated they support decompilation when required. The same with ASIS, the same with CCIA. In the case of CCIA we have sixty-seven companies -- I happen to be Chairman of that -- most of the RBOCS, all but one, AT&T, Univac, Amdahl, Storage Tek, and we have approximately a million employees represented, and they would vote for decompilation and maintaining it as a, a necessary option. Remember the alternative is a mandatory API. That could be something that could be legislated, but if not --

COMMISSIONER LEHMAN: Could you explain that?

MR. POPPA: Applications Program Interface?

COMMISSIONER LEHMAN: Right. Well, API, but what would be a mandatory API?

MR. POPPA: Well, literally in law saying that a second vendor or a third vendor would have rights of access to the base code so that they could understand it, so that they could build their code to interact with it and interoperate with it. Today most companies are locking that up on an object-code-only basis, and not allowing us to see it.

COMMISSIONER LEHMAN: To some degree this is an antitrust issue, and my colleague, Ann Binghamen, who is the Assistant Attorney General for Antitrust over in the Justice Department has indicated that she's going to put together a task force to start working on these problems, and it may well be that this sort of mandatory API idea should be explored in that context. In a sense that's more of a, I think, an antitrust kind of a solution to this problem as opposed to an intellectual property solution.

MR. POPPA: We think that's a good alternative. We would also hope that within the structure of the PTO we could get a clear distinction, as they have done in the EC, but I don't think they did it as clearly as they should. They left it a little unclear, such that some people are going to be able to say, Well, Gee, for interoperability I can really replace the program. We are not in any way supporting that position; only that we should be able to access the program so that we can look at it and make sure that we can make our programs talk to each other. Nothing beyond that.

My last point, and it's really a picture worth a thousand words: a terminal device we're all well-familiar with. It is a very standard device, but it also comes with an information network, with a very standard interface. It's a telephone. But when you take patents and copyrights and you tighten them down such that you could not in any way see the inside of the machine, what we do is we cover up the access port, we take the network, we cut off this end so you can't see the interface, and we say, Now, Mr. Engineer, make them

interact. And that doesn't make any sense, because it isn't just a telephone, it's a computer with three million instructions in it, and this network has on the line hundreds of terminals with other millions of instructions, and therefore decompilation and interactivity must be maintained. Please.

Thank you very much.

COMMISSIONER LEHMAN: Thank you very much. Do any of my colleagues have anything they want to add? Thank you very much. Thanks for coming over.

MR. POPPA: You bet.

COMMISSIONER LEHMAN: Next I'd like to call William Ryan who is representing the Intellectual Property Owners Incorporated, but is directly with AT&T.

--oOo--

WILLIAM RYAN

INTELLECTUAL PROPERTY OWNERS, INC.

MR. RYAN: Good morning, Commissioner LEHMAN, and members of the Panel. My name is William Ryan, I'm a general attorney at AT&T. I'm here, however, as you say, representing the Intellectual Property Owners. They are a nonprofit association located in Washington whose members are companies, including AT&T, other companies as well as universities and individuals who own and are interested in patents, trademarks, copyrights and trade secrets. IPO presents these remarks in support of the continued strong patent protection for computer program-related subject matter.

There can be little doubt that the computer software industry is an important and growing economic force in this economy, in fact for year 1992 it was estimated that just the packaged software industry accounted for some seventeen billion dollars in revenue, and importantly about half of that was from sales oversees. However, the amount of revenue in the software industry is not limited just to the packaged software. There is indeed a great deal of other software that goes on that is less visible but nonetheless very very important. I make reference to control software for manufacturing systems, for controlling the telephone network, for the ubiquitous microwave ovens and the VCRs and intelligent-talk telephones and many many other applications.

The sales and revenues for devices or the software component of these devices and systems by many estimates well-exceeds a hundred billion dollars a year. Even one level higher in the scheme of things, the services provided by both the equipment and many of the underlying processes, again referring to such things as the financial systems, the telephone network and the entertainment business, are increasingly based on software infrastructure underpinning it. Therefore, the effect on the economy of decisions made relating to software have implications much beyond the kinds of software sales that might be accomplished in local over-the-counter sales.

We don't come by this cheaply, though. Software research and development is very expensive. Among the hundred top packaged software companies it's been estimated that an average of seventeen percent of revenues flows through to support continued R&D. And many companies not

UNITED STATES PATENT AND TRADEMARK OFFICE
Public Hearing on Patent Protection for Software-Related Inventions
San Jose, California -- January 26-27, 1994

traditionally thought of as software companies -- and again only by example I'll refer to AT&T, we have an R&D budget of approximately three billion dollars per year, and some sixty percent of that is devoted to software efforts, and we are not exactly thought of as a software company.

With this kind of economic importance at stake, it's clear that the managers of our business have to seek ways in which these large investments can be protected. One way that it's been adopted of course is the well-known copyright as it has been applied for example to the mass-market software, and it's been done very successfully by and large. Less publicized though is the need to protect and the vulnerability in fact of the other software investments, some of which I referred to before, the large systems software and the embedded software in many, many applications.

So then the question is asked, Why isn't copyright protection sufficient to protect the software investment? Well, it should be clear from the very words of the Act itself that the copyright is intended to protect the expression. It does in no event protect the systems, the methods, and other aspects of functionality within the software. Importantly too, copyright suffers from a limitation that it is not as precisely defined as patents, although the arcane language we practitioners use to define our inventions in patents is sometimes criticized, nevertheless it is precise, and with copyright protection there is no such precision. It's a very much looser judgment that business people have to make as to where the boundary is for their protection.

Moreover, the Supreme Court has made it very clear that patents are the preferred mode for protecting the functionality, the implementations of ideas as against the expression of the ideas, which the Copyright Law can protect. We think that computer program-related subject matter is, and has been, protected well in the past, by patents.

Many people think that software protection for software commenced only perhaps in 1980 or '81 with the Diehr decision, but that is not true. We have been filing applications in the computer-related industries for decades, going back at least until the 1950s. And it's proved very effective. One of the questions in the Notice of Hearing was, what experiences have we had, and by and large the experience has been good. We've been treating software inventions for some time in precisely the same way as we protect and treat inventions in other areas. In fact, in many ways it's hard to tell whether an invention is a software invention or not. I'll deal with that just a little bit later.

Why are the patents for software-related inventions particularly important? Well, they're not particularly important for software any more than any other inventions, for example, investors seeking to sponsor a start-up organization or a new enterprise within a larger company would like to have some certitude about what it is that they can hope to have some protection for and where their investment, how their investments can be protected.

Also, importantly, is the disclosure aspects of patents. One of the functions served by patents is to disclose to the public. Before an allusion was mentioned to the secrecy that often attends patents. Well, in many ways the contrary is true. Patents themselves of course contain disclosure, but also in an organization like mine again, we encourage

publication of technical ideas, in fact last year we published some forty-four hundred technical articles. Many of these would not have been published if we could not also have concurrently filed patent applications so that the publication of the technical papers would not compromise the value of our inventions included in the disclosures.

Patents are important in many other ways, one of which is the -- they provide a vehicle for developing of the ubiquitous alliances that are present in the software and hardware industries. They provide a medium, in fact, for people to come together and exchange value so that they can work together to get a cooperative result. Often this helps people and companies get into new markets and establish businesses that would not otherwise exist.

Again, some people have said that software inventions should be treated differently. We think not. In some respects, in fact to treat the software industry as an industry raises more questions than it answers. As I mentioned before it's much of an enabling technology in many domains, in telecommunications, in entertainment, in finance, in manufacturing and process control, software is often a common denominator. And the earlier-mentioned national information infrastructure, the highway likewise is largely a software development, and it's been going on for some time.

Some people suggest that a solution is that we should have a new statute, one especially tailored to software problems. We think not. These sui generis proposals have arisen in the past and have been bandied about for some time and in one case applied to a different subject, the Chip Protection Act is an example. We think these raise more problems than they solve as well. We think the existing scheme is workable and is fair and appropriate. If we were to adopt the sui generis scheme we'd have to live through many of the uncertainties that we've had in both the copyright and patent realm for these last twenty years. We may have to live through the same issues tried from a different perspective. Moreover, the many other of our industrialized countries, the European countries for example and Japan, have statutory schemes that are roughly equivalent to our present protection for software-related inventions. Patents are available there to about the same extent they are here.

The recently-enacted NAFTA and GATT treaties also have dictates in them that would suggest that we cannot get too far out of whack. We must have a level of protection consistent with what is currently provided by the patent statute.

The questions posed in the Notice of Hearing, in some cases have been dealt with; in other cases they deal with details of claim formats, which I'm not prepared to deal with now, but which we will respond to in our extended remarks.

In concluding then, we'd like to say that consistent with the findings of the final report of the Advisory Commission on Patent Law Reform, to the Secretary in 1992, the current statutory regime for the protection of rights, both copyrights and patents and other matters as well, is adequate; it is working and it is working well, but not perfectly. If the experience of the last ten years teaches us anything, it is that we can't predict with any certainty what directions the information processing industry will follow in response to new technology and new global political and business trends. This vast changing environment requires

UNITED STATES PATENT AND TRADEMARK OFFICE
Public Hearing on Patent Protection for Software-Related Inventions
San Jose, California -- January 26-27, 1994

the U.S. patent laws and implementing procedures to be technologically neutral and flexible enough to avoid major discontinuities.

Thank you.

--oOo--

COMMISSIONER LEHMAN: Thank you. I have a question, and that is that, you mentioned that the exclusivity provided by the patent system encourages you to publish because obviously you can make the information available and then you can be certain you'll be protected, and of course that's been a traditional trade-off in the patent system; you disclose, and you get protection.

One of the suggestions which was made by Mr. Clark at the very beginning of the hearing and that's floating out there is that in this particular area where it's very hard to keep up with the technology, where a lot of the prior art is not easily findable, is that we have some kind of prepublication prior to the issuance of the patent. That, if we were to do that, that obviously to some degree abrogates that traditional deal, because certainly you know that you might get the patent but you're not certain that you're going to get it prior to the disclosure, and I'm wondering if you have a reaction to that.

MR. RYAN: Well, that's a risk that the parties would have to take, of course, knowing when they file their application that there's a possibility they will have in effect given away the genesis of the invention and for one reason or another are not able to get a patent. That's a risk the filing party would have to take.

COMMISSIONER LEHMAN: Do you think that the advantages though of prepublication would outweigh the negatives of that risk?

MR. RYAN: It would have to be evaluated on an individual basis, but I think in many cases that's the case. We publish much more broadly in the technical literature than we do in the patent literature.

COMMISSIONER LEHMAN: Thank you very much.

Next I'd like to call Richard LeFaivre, the Vice-President of the Advanced Technology Group of Apple Computer who will be representing the Computer and Business Equipment Manufacturing Association CBMA.

--oOo--

RICHARD LeFAIVRE

APPLE COMPUTER, AND,

COMPUTER AND BUSINESS EQUIPMENT
MANUFACTURING ASSOCIATION

MR. LeFAIVRE: Thank you, good morning. My name is Rick LeFaivre from Apple Computer and today I'm actually wearing four hats, first as a computer scientist with twenty-five years' of experience in software technology as a researcher, a professor and an R&D director, second as Vice-President of Advanced Technology at Apple Computer. My organization is responsible for a large percentage of the patents that are granted to Apple, and the protection of the innovation that we do is very important to me. In particular over the years we've seen a marked shift in our innovation focus from hardware to software, and so I'm very interested in the topic of these hearings in particular.

Third, I'm the founding member of the Executive Committee

of the Software Patent Institute. As you may be aware the SPI was founded to provide training in software technology and access to prior art, to help insure that those software patents that are granted are of high quality, and we're working very closely with Gerry Goldberg in that task. I should point out that the Software Patent Institute has chosen to take a neutral stance on the broad issue of the patentability of software so the views I'm about to express do not necessarily reflect those of the SPI.

Finally and most importantly I will be testifying today on behalf of the Computer Business and Manufacturer's Association CBMA, and let me give you a little background of this group. CBMA is a trade association whose members represent the leading edge of high technology companies in the computer business equipment and telecommunications industries in the U.S. In 1992 CBMA's twenty-six members had a combined estimated sales of more than two hundred seventy billion dollars, which represents about four and a half percent of the U.S. gross national product. CBMA member companies employed approximately a million workers in the U.S. in this past year.

The computer industry performs about twenty percent of the total private-sector R&D investment in the U.S. That figure is about five times the investment of the aerospace industry, three times the investment of the health care industry, and four times that of the chemical industry. This investment allows our members to rapidly advance the capabilities of their products and to get access to, and compete successfully in, a very tough international marketplace. It also results in significant numbers of jobs just within R&D alone. I'm here today because patent protection for new computer functions is absolutely crucial to all our members. Software-related inventions fit within our present patent system and patents issued under a sound application examination process support the Constitutional mandate of promoting the useful arts and sciences. CBMA members file for and obtain patents for software-related inventions. They also enter into agreements to utilize such patents held by others. Because our companies typically have broad product lines, they address patent issues in many areas of technology. They see no reason to treat software-related patents differently from patents related to other technologies.

In the first question set forth in the hearing notice, there are a number of subparts relating to claim subject matter and claim formats. CBMA's response to this question is simply that if the claim is drawn to the solution of a real-world commercial problem, and the claim functional steps or elements as a whole meet the strict legal requirement to be new, nonobvious and useful, then a patent should issue. The function claimed, not the format, is what is important. It shouldn't matter whether new, nonobvious and useful process steps are claimed in the context of a program or a disk or claimed in a hardware or method format, or in the context of a semiconductor chip. Software-related inventions are valuable to the purchaser not for what they communicate, but for the functions they perform. The functions are what are important and what should be assessed for novelty and nonobviousness.

Relative to Question 2, our members have integrated their software-related patents into their overall patent portfolios and practices so that separating out their impact is quite difficult. However, this integration itself demonstrate that these patents are just like all others. They are sought when the inventor or his or her employer believe that the investment in obtaining the patent will be returned. Conversely, CBMA members often must respect the software-related patents of others, which they do in the same manner as further technologies.

Regarding Question 3, the standard for patent eligibility for software-related inventions should be maintained at the same level as for all other technologies. An alteration in that standard would negatively impact investment in our industry. If the standard were to be restricted severely it would disarm CBMA member companies in their dealings with foreign competitors because licenses under U.S. patents are used to negotiate access to foreign markets and foreign technology. Obtaining patents for software-related inventions in our principal competitor countries is generally equivalent to that of the U.S.

Software-related technology will be one of the leading technologies of the 21st Century. Discrimination against this technology would set a terrible example sure to be rapidly adopted by the developing world. To now have the leading country in software creation and patents declare that such inventions are excluded from the statute, despite falling within the terms of statutory subject matter, or are to be treated differently from patents involving other technologies, would reverse much of the hard-fought progress that has been made over the last decade in improving intellectual property protection throughout the world.

Relative to Question 4, patents provide the relatively broad protection necessary to bring in risk capital for new and useful inventive functions that are generally defined in terms of processes or methods of operation. This protection should be afforded only after a detailed examination to insure that the claimed functions are truly novel and nonobvious. This, by the way, is one of the places where the SPI is trying to work with the Patent Office to make that process more efficient. In contrast, copyright protects only the expression contained in the computer program, as it does for other literary works. High-level functional processes are expressly excluded from protection by statute. Thirdly, trade secrets provide the necessary protection to facilitate the disclosure of confidential software-related designs to employees, joint venture partners and others within the structure supporting that confidentiality.

Thus, each protects different aspects of the intellectual property. The inventor, who may not wish to or be able to author a complete software product, deserves protection. The author of a program deserves protection from piracy and plagiarism. Those with confidential information, willing and able to keep it confidential, should be able to protect that value against those from which it has a fiduciary relationship.

Finally, with regard to Question 5, CBMA supports continued reliance on the tested, well-developed protection of patents, copyrights and trade secrets. We strongly support continued improvement in the patenting process for software-related inventions. But nothing suggests the need to treat software differently. A new and untested regime would fail to provide inventors and authors with any certainty of protection for an extended period of time while judicial precedent was developed to determine the scope of the law.

Additionally, international protection for our software research and development is critical. There is no certainty that a new protection system could be implemented worldwide, whether through multi- or bilateral negotiations. The hard-fought protections in the GATT, TRIPS and NAFTA treaties regarding literary work protection for programs and the issuance of patents without discrimination based on technology were just obtained last year. It is inconceivable that such protections would now be abrogated with the ink hardly dry on these provisions by the adoption of a sui generis protection.

In closing, our message to you is this: Don't cut back on patent protection for software-related inventions because some invalid patents may have been issued. The current reexamination process and the Federal Court system do provide mechanisms for the removal of these mistakes. We believe that further training for examiners, and access to a larger library of prior art can and will reduce the possibility of future mistakes. Overall, the system is working and should be improved, not abandoned. If the standard for patentability is changed for software-related inventions, or if patent protection is dropped in favor of some new form of protection, it will severely and negatively impact CBMA members, our industry and the country.

Thank you for letting me submit these remarks and we look forward to continuing to work with the Patent Office on these issues.

COMMISSIONER LEHMAN: Thank you very much. I have one question if you have a moment, and that is that, there's obviously a difference of opinion about the application of the patent system to the software industry that is represented in the room, we've already heard it this morning and I think we're going to hear more testimony about it. Apple certainly is a company, and I gather that CBMA is a company now that very much favors patent protection for software, and Apple's certainly a very important, successful part of American enterprise today.

One question that I have is that obviously the purpose of patents is to incent people to invent and to make investments. And can you point in your own experience to an example where that has happened? Has the patent system actually been a factor in a decision to go into a new technology, the fact that it might be patentable? Has it been a factor in getting financing from capital markets?

MR. LeFAIVRE: Yeah, that's a good question. Apple thinks a lot about patentability of any technology, software or any other, in looking at some of our innovations. We do feel that there has been a lot of investment made in technologies that, to be quite honest have been appropriated, copied, whatever, by other companies, that have not helped our situation in the marketplace, I think it's fair to say, and so we certainly are interested in trying to evaluate the patent potential of different technologies as we develop them, so I wouldn't point to any particular issues or topics, but yes, we certainly take that into effect when we're looking at technology investments.

UNITED STATES PATENT AND TRADEMARK OFFICE
Public Hearing on Patent Protection for Software-Related Inventions
San Jose, California — January 26-27, 1994

COMMISSIONER LEHMAN: So that is an important part of Apple's decision-making process.

MR. LeFAIVRE: Yes. I think that's probably true for all companies now.

COMMISSIONER LEHMAN: Thank you very much.

MR. LeFAIVRE: Okay? Thank you.

COMMISSIONER LEHMAN: Next I'd like to call Mr. Tom Lopez who is President of the Interactive Multimedia Association.

--oOo--

TOM LOPEZ

INTERACTIVE MULTIMEDIA ASSOCIATION

MR. LOPEZ: Thank you. Mr. Commissioner, my name is Tom Lopez. I'm Chairman of Mammoth Microproductions of Seattle, Washington, a multimedia development company. I'm also President of the Interactive Multimedia Association. The Association's general counsel, Brian Cann, who also directs our Intellectual Property Project, is with me today to help answer any questions that you may have.

The Interactive Multimedia Association is a 290-member trade association headquartered in Annapolis. We are here today because the patent system has cast a cloud over our emerging industry, an ambitious and motivated industry which seeks to transform the way we play, learn, work, think and communicate. We're specifically concerned about the impact of patents on the flow of information and fundamental principles of free expression, on the impact of patents on enabling environments, in particular the development of the national information infrastructure, the need for a patent system that is publicly accountable and open to industry input specifically through pre-grant publication and peer review, knowledgeable and informed about its operation and its economic and social impact, and sensitive to competing values and policies.

We bring a unique perspective, because our membership spans the whole of the multimedia industry, from large computer companies to small publishers and developers. This makes it impossible for the IMA to take positions on issues such as the merits and proper scope of software patents where we encompass many different views. However, we have historically been especially concerned with needs and perspectives of developers of multimedia also known as content-driven software. Multimedia developers provide the creative spark that is driving multimedia into homes, schools and businesses. Therefore, we do not address competition within the software industry, we address the impact of patents on content, on the organization, expression and communication of information.

Multimedia developers depend upon computers, networks and operating systems, authoring tools and other software environments. They build on technological platforms developed by others. Like traditional publishers, they add value through research, selection, organization and coordination, by aggregating rights, by creating original material and by expressing whatever ideas they believe will move the market, the body-politic or the soul. They use interactivity as their grammar. It is how computers speak to people, it is how people speak to computers. It is how people speak to other people through computers.

Historically, copyright law has provided a level of protection to the software developer. Unlike copyright, patents control the private use of patented processes. Unlike copyright, independent creation is not a defense to patent infringement. Patents therefore control not only original implementations, but also the users of such original implementations. Patents even control the use of products of the process. The extraordinary power of patents resonates across an increasingly-integrated and interdependent digital environment, putting everyone downstream of the underlying technology at risk. Content-integrators, publishers, distributors, even users. Indeed, typically end-users are the direct infringers. The upstream providers are technically only contributory infringers. For example, in the recent case of the Optical Data patent, interactive method for the effective conveyance of information in the form of visual images, the direct infringers were the hundreds of thousands of teachers in classroooms, and by extension the local school districts and all of us as taxpayers.

The Computer and Business Equipment Manufacturers Association described this problem sixteen years ago in arguing against patents for algorithms. Quote. The computer has become the engine which assists in running our society and in the future will assist man in numerous areas totally unrelated to the usual application of today's computers. These applications and computer uses should not be clouded by problems resulting from unwitting infringement by computer users. End quote.

Looking at the list of speakers today, it is clear that users are not represented at this hearing except for multimedia developers. Multimedia developers are on the front lines of the user community, because they're developing content-driven product and services. To the extent that they are successful, they become targets for patentees. Content-oriented developers get protection from copyright, not from patents. They need protection against patents. How do they get it?

For the first time, errors and omissions insurance to cover patent infringement is available from the American International Group for multimedia products. The cost is fifty thousand dollars per product, with a fifty thousand dollar deductible. That's a formidable barrier for an independent developer, a regressive tax on interactive expression. Such insurance, costly as it is, does not cover patents of which you are aware you may be infringing. This unfortunately is another good reason, along with the threat of triple damages for wilful infringement, to avoid reading patents entirely, a sad comment on a system originally intended to spread technical knowledge.

And while we are concerned with the impact of patents on publishing and First Amendment values, we share with others a concern for the related problem of patents on broad abstract processes. Such patents are extremely difficult to interpret. They often purport to preempt basic functionality so as to preclude others from designing around the patent. Usually their claims are over-broad, but can be narrowed only at great expense to those who would challenge them.

These abstract system-level patents threaten the development of common standards, specifications and architectures, including our Association's own work on cross-platform compatibility. They create information bottlenecks, or tollbooths, in the vision of a national information infrastructure. Mindful of the history of blocking patents in the development of the radio and the aircraft industries, we note that the highly complex and interrelated nature of the information infrastructure makes it very vulnerable. Broad patents are especially suspect in the case of software where functions can be implemented in a wide variety of ways and where independent creation is commonplace.

This problem, along with the threat that patents still pending may be inadvertently incorporated in standards or infrastructional systems, would be greatly alleviated by pre-grant publication. The secrecy of the present application process is an anachronism, and a primary cause of the present uncertainty and insecurity. We plan to address this issue further in the February hearings on examination processes.

We're grateful to the Commissioner for holding this public hearing and dealing openly with the issues as a matter of public policy. We're also pleased to see a serious effort to develop patent policy within the larger context of economic development and the Administration's vision of a national information infrastructure.

We would like to close by expressing our support for a strong patent system. By that of course we do not mean a system that in the name of incenting novelty oozes uncontrollably into every corner of human life. We mean a system that knows its limits, that functions spectacularly within those limits and that does not debase the concept of intellectual property by incenting gaming and speculation. We mean a system that works in the real world, that acknowledges its regulatory nature and is tailored to the economic characteristics of the operating environment. We mean a system that operates proudly in public view, that is understood and acclaimed not only by patentees, their agents and their attorneys, but by the tens of millions who also contribute to our economy and society and face tough competition unarmed by patent monopolies.

Thank you very much.

COMMISSIONER LEHMAN: Thanks. You said that you felt that with the exception of the Interactive Multimedia Association that we didn't have on our witness list real representatives of users of the system. Who are we missing? Who would you count in that category of users?

MR. LOPEZ: For instance, teachers who use the products of multimedia developers, people who are users in the home who I think would be very upset to find out that they perhaps are infringing on patents without knowing about it.

COMMISSIONER LEHMAN: How might they be infringing on, on —

MR. LOPEZ: If they are actually the people who are taking the actions which would be against the patent, as teachers would be in using the products that would violate the Optical Data patent as an example.

COMMISSIONER LEHMAN: Thank you. I also wanted to ask, just to clarify your position a little bit more, is your position that you would not be in favor of such a drastic step as doing away with patentability of software-related inventions.

MR. LOPEZ: No.

COMMISSIONER LEHMAN: So you really feel what we need to do is to reform the system to make certain that, that we have a clearer scope of patentability and that we have better procedures, primarily pre-grant publication for making sure we capture the prior art.

MR. LOPEZ: Exactly. I think as Mr. Clark has indicated in his testimony, one of the greatest problems for multimedia developers today is the uncertainty that exists, and when this uncertainty exists it inhibits the investment and the -- not only of intellectual energy, but also of capital.

COMMISSIONER LEHMAN: My colleague, Ginger Lew, who's our General Counsel for the Department of Commerce and on Assistant Secretary of Commerce has a question.

GENERAL COUNSEL LEW: In Mr. Poppa's testimony he mentioned the possibility for the need of mandatory API -- ADI, and I wanted to know if the Association had any position on that.

MR. LOPEZ: The question is does the Association have any position on mandatory APIs regulated by law? Brian.

UNMIKED VOICE: No.

MR. LOPEZ: No, we do not at this point.

COMMISSIONER LEHMAN: One comment I'd just like to -- maybe it's more of a comment, we have a little more time here, and you may have a response to it. We haven't focused very much on that, and I don't think our questions did, but a previous witness I believe it was indicated that they thought it was very important to have the Courts to flesh out the patent system. There are elements in patent law at the moment, for example, the fact that, even assuming we spruce up our examination process, right now you can go to the Court of Appeals through the Federal Circuit, and basically get de novo review of our Patent Office decisions. The Court can second-guess the patent examiner, judges who are not even remotely experts in a given technology.

Secondly, we have a number of legal doctrines, like the Doctrine of Equivalence, which some have argued cloud the certainty in the patent system, and I'm wondering if you have any comment about the impact of those on your industry. Do those kinds of problems that occur in enforcing -- understanding how the Courts will interpret a patent, do they create uncertainty that creates problems for you?

MR. KAHIN: We really haven't addressed the problems, the technical problems you've described, at that level. I think the concern in the judicial evaluation is more focused on a very high presumption of validity of the patent examiner's determination, and -- that carries over into the judicial system. So that once that determination of nonobviousness based on the referenced prior art is made, it can't be overcome except by clear and convincing evidence. So that that high presumption is a disincentive to challenging the patent in Court.

COMMISSIONER LEHMAN: Actually I think the situation is a little different than that. I think we have maybe a little bit the opposite problem with the Court of Appeals. The Court of Appeals for the 12th Circuit has de novo right to review the patent and I'm not sure that they always do use that clear and convincing evidence standard that you

UNITED STATES PATENT AND TRADEMARK OFFICE
Public Hearing on Patent Protection for Software-Related Inventions
San Jose, California — January 26-27, 1994

discussed.

MR. KAHIN: But it's very expensive to get that far, to get to the Court of Appeals for the Federal Circuit. Most of our members have enough trouble getting to a patent attorney, let alone filing suit in a District Court.

COMMISSIONER LEHMAN: Thank you very much.

MR. KAHIN: Thank you.

COMMISSIONER LEHMAN: Next I'd like to call Mr. Paul Heckel, Acting President of Abraham Lincoln Patent Holders Association who is from Hyperracks, Incorporated.

--oOo--

PAUL HECKEL

ABRAHAM LINCOLN PATENT HOLDERS ASSOCIATION

MR. HECKEL: Thank you. If somebody can display these slides?

COMMISSIONER LEHMAN: Charlie Van Horn from our office will.

MR. HECKEL: Thank you.

COMMISSIONER LEHMAN: I think you testified at our hearings on harmonization.

MR. HECKEL: Yes, I did. And --

COMMISSIONER LEHMAN: By the way, for those of you who don't know, Secretary Brown issued a statement yesterday, or on Monday, I guess this is Wednesday already, in which he indicated that we would not at this time proceed with international negotiations which would require the United States to change to a first-to-file system. I think it's important to bring this out at this point because these, this process of obtaining public input does make a difference. There are some people who don't think it makes a difference, but we had hearings on the question of patent harmonization, and we heard public testimony, Mr. Heckel testified, he had a very strong position on that, which I recall was somewhat consistent with the position that the Secretary has taken here on our recommendation, and so we have changed our policy, and so these hearings can make a big difference.

I should add, just as a footnote on that, that that doesn't necessarily mean that we won't at some point reconsider the question of a change in our system, but we concluded on the basis of those hearings that we had that we weren't really getting a good deal, that we weren't getting harmonization, and that the disadvantages to the U.S. creative community were not outweighed by the comparable advantages that we would receive as the proposed harmonization treaty was presently constituted. So this is a serious exercise, and thanks for joining us again, Mr. Heckel.

MR. HECKEL: Thank you, Commissioner LEHMAN, and I was there, and I felt at the time that it was very useful to get input from a lot of different people, and I feel that it's very good that you hold these hearings too. I think an awful lot of what has been spoken is really not supported by the facts, and I think it's useful for people to come there and to provide a reasonable basis for their opinions, because I think a lot of the time it doesn't stand.

Well, I'm Paul Heckel, and I'm here basically as Acting President of an organization called ALPHA, which is an organization of software patent holders. We only have about twenty members, but fourteen of our members are patent holders. I think ten or twelve of those actually had founded companies based on their patents. Two of our members were on the board of directors of the Software Publishers Association. Three of our members had their patents attacked by the League for Programming Freedom in several of their publications, me being one of those people. In fact, it was those attacks that really started to bring me in, to get interested in the issue, and as I suspect the Commissioner may know, I wrote two articles, one on the Communications of the ACM and one in Computer Lawyer on the software patent issue to try to bring out some of those facts and I'll bring out some of those facts later.

Clearly ALPHA strongly supports software patentability in pretty much all the forms that are there. We've also had an opportunity to look at the statements of the American Bar Association, the Software Entrepreneurs Forum and the Intellectual Property Section of the California State Bar and we concur in their positions as well.

Basically we feel we should have software patents. Inventiveness should be judged by the content of the invention and not by the color of the technology, as a variant on Martin Luther King's famous quote. We believe, by the way, that the quality of the examiner's position should be a more high-status position. We believe that trying to increase the pay and increase the professionalism of examiners is desirable. We all want a system which will make it clearer and less uncertain for everybody. Nobody, patent-holder or potential infringer alike, gets any advantage out of infringement.

Now I want to talk a little bit about some of our members because I know you're interested in personal experience.

For example, Mike and Susan Morgan found a company called MacInTax, developed a couple of products. Because they had patents on them they told me that, as Susan told me, she said, with her venture capitalists, when the venture capitalists asked us how we could protect ourselves against say Microsoft coming out with a competitive product and stealing our market, the fact that we had applied for patents put the problem to bed. It made the VCs feel much more comfortable, and that's a big difference. They have since sold out, they started another company.

Reed Hastings is another person. He founded a company here in Silicon Valley called Purer Software. He started, he made it profitable, he raised a couple million dollars from venture capitalists, the fact that he had patents made that possible; certainly it helped him a great deal. Currently he's facing a potential litigation problem with one of -- somebody in his market said, "Why don't we add his patented feature to our product?" and so he's having to deal with those problems.

Another is Dr. Marcusson who is a patent-holder and a physician. His -- when Oracle recently announced its product for the Information Superhighway they used something that he had designed for teaching medicine. It was called "Salvaging a Patient with a Stab Wound to the Heart. It was running on a Hypercard-like environment. He's had a lot of experience with inventors. He's a specialist in repetitive-strain injury, so he's familiar with that controversy which is going on. But what he has said is that, "I have seen first-hand emotional and financial damage done to independent inventors whose inventions are ripped off by big companies," and he said he "fears that many small inventors will be the roadkill for the Information Superhighway," which is the talk that I take, and having heard the previous talk I'm concerned that if their position is taken that it could very well happen that way.

Hal Nesley is actually an investor, but he's invested in four start-ups which have software involved, one has a patent, the other three are in the process of getting patents.

So those are some examples. In my own case, I started a company relying on patents. It gave me more confidence to start the company since I had the patent or was going to get the patent, I thought, and it gave my investors confidence. They told me it was one of the reasons they decided to put money into it. We brought products to market, as did the other people that I have been talking about, and we then found out we were infringed by Apple, we got in some litigation and I've described it in my book that some people here I'm sure are aware of, and we settled and they took out a license. Then we got involved with IBM; that situation still is not clarified.

But I guess I'd like to go into what I really found out when I examined the patents that Mr. Stahlman attacked in some of his articles. And I particularly refer to the ACM article. If we can have that slide now. I went and I called. They gave an example of nine patents, and I went and I called the patent-holders on each of those nine patents. I found out some interesting things. I want to refer specifically to it. That chart is in Computer Lawyer, and this afternoon I'll have copies of Computer Lawyer out there for people to look at so they can see the chart. But based on that chart we have some conclusions.

One. All nine patents protected commercial products. Every one that they brought up that they said is an example of a bad patent and absurd patent. Two. Software stimulated new business formation. Four of those nine patents were held by companies that were started precisely to develop the technology that was in the patents, and a fifth company had only been in business for two years when it filed the patent. So five of the nine companies really were independent small start-up phase companies that were using patents. Okay? I think that that's strong evidence, based on a sample selected by the people who are condemning patents that software does stimulate new businesses.

Second, I would argue that they stimulate the introduction of fundamental technology. I think three of those patents introduce technology that was fundamental, at least in the sense that it was widely seen throughout the industry, and I'll talk about one of those later. By the way, I've talked to several inventors in different technologies, and I referred to a lot of that in my Harmonization testimony, and I found out in many ways that the problems faced by software developers or software inventors are very similar to the problems faced by inventors in other technologies. They're made more severe by the prior art problem and the newness of the technology, but fundamentally they're very very similar problems, and the way the trade system treats them is very similar.

My last point is an interesting one. Can I see the next slide, please? Small entities are exceptionally cost-effective in encouraging innovation, especially compared to Federal

funding, and I will give you the example. It might be a little hard to see there, but if you look down the first column we have the number of commercial products. The first item is four for large entities. Next is five for small entities, and below that we have zero for Federally-funded. None of the nine patents cited a product that had a Federal patent behind it, and as you know, if you develop something under Federal law funding, you can get patents on it, you do have rights to use those patents in the commercial marketplace.

Now I looked at what I call the efficacy of the invention, and I used the fact that somebody has asserted a patent as a measure of efficacy, because a lot of patents aren't asserted, and I found two of the large company patents were submitted, and all five of the small-entity patents were asserted. So I use that as a measure of effectiveness, because we're going to look at taxpayer cost effectiveness.

Now if you look at Federally-funded we gave one there just so you don't have a number of zeroes, so the numbers work out in some sense.

Now we looked at the cost, and in 1989 the Federal funding of the Patent office was two million dollars, and so we allocated those costs and we got thirty, fifty thousand -- I can't quite read those numbers there, for those numbers, and then we divided to get the efficacy. By the way, the Federal funding of computer science in that year was four hundred and eighty-seven million dollars. So if we look at the cost-effectiveness of it, and the large entities had a cost-effectiveness thirty-three thousand, the small entities had a cost-effectiveness of two hundred and fifty thousand and Federally-funded had a cost-effectiveness of one point o three. Which says that a dollar spent in the tax -- to help the Patent Office really brings back more innovation. Now clearly if the Patent Office was clearly funded, the numbers would probably knock down to something like thirty-three and two hundred and fifty, which is still a very large number compared to one.

Now I fully recognize that this is only nine numbers. It's a very small sample, but remember, these numbers were picked by Mr. Stahlman and the League for Programming Freedom to say that it's bad for innovation, and there's a very very strong prima facie argument that it does encourage innovation. So those were the results of those numbers.

I want to talk now about a specific patent, which is the spreadsheet patent that I'm sure a lot of people have heard about. It's been described as the automatic recalculation patent, and when first suit was filed on it in 1989 it was attacked widely in the press as obvious and it was well-known in the prior art and stuff like that. By the way, I called the inventor, I got a copy of the patent, and I said, Who's talked to you? Nobody in the American press had even called this person although widely his patent was attacked in the press, and it was clearly easy to find him as all you had to was get a copy of the patent. So it doesn't give me a great deal of confidence when I hear these press stories about these horrible patents.

So since then I've learned a certain amount about the patent. In my opinion, that patent is to the modern computer spreadsheet what the Wright Brothers' invention was to the airplane. It might not have had a visual display; they used a teletype terminal. They started out with a concept of Basic, and instead of executing the statements in the numbered

UNITED STATES PATENT AND TRADEMARK OFFICE
Public Hearing on Patent Protection for Software-Related Inventions
San Jose, California -- January 26-27, 1994

order, they said, Why not take the statement numbers, break them in two, use both halves as indexes into an array, and then calculate the formulas in the order which is natural, and use it to solve business problems. That seems quite clear from reading the patent. They developed a product, they brought a product into the marketplace, and they had real users; okay? But they had a problem with the patent system. By the way, they filed the patent in 1970, twenty-four years ago, they have yet to see dime one for an invention which is in many ways responsible for the success of Apple, because VisiCalc helps out Apple Computers, the success of Lotus. They have yet to receive dime one.

This is what happened to them. They got a Notice of Allowance from the Patent Office. Then the Benson decision came down, and then the Patent Office took their patent away from them, because of the Benson decision. They then appealed it, pro se, through the Courts, and got a decision at the CCPA called in re parto, which says that just because the inventiveness is in an algorithm or in the software does not mean it's not patentable -- that's an important decision as I'm sure everybody involved with software patent knows, it was done pro se without an attorney by those inventors. Now they are in trial, and in July I went to hear a one-day --

COMMISSIONER LEHMAN: Yeah, I think, Mr. Heckel, I think we're going to have to --

MR. HECKEL: Turn me off?

COMMISSIONER LEHMAN: Yes.

MR. HECKEL: Okay, I'm sorry, can I just briefly --

COMMISSIONER LEHMAN: Is our machine on? I'm not sure if it's working right.

VOICE: It was on but we gave you a few more minutes because we tied up in the beginning.

MR. HECKEL: I'm sorry. I just want to say that I saw in Court their patent attorney in my opinion perjure himself on the stand to testify against his clients, to save himself from a malpractice suit. I saw that in July. The decision hasn't come down. I hope when the decision comes down you read it, Commissioner, Examiner, and look at that patent lawyer and consider whether or not this is what you want to have representing clients out there in the field.

Thank you very much, Commissioner.

COMMISSIONER LEHMAN: Thank you very much, Mr. Heckel. You know, we do have a procedure in the Patent Office for hearing complaints against people for not carrying out their professional responsibilities, so it's certainly available to people if they wish to use it.

Next I'd like to call Mr. Robert Kohn, the Vice-President and General Counsel of Borland International.

--oOo--

ROBERT H. KOHN

BORLAND INTERNATIONAL, INC.

MR. KOHN: Thank you, Commissioner LEHMAN, for the opportunity to testify today. I'm Bob Kohn, Vice-President of Corporate Affairs of Borland International, a leading developer and marketer of desktop and client-server computer software including D-Base, QuattroPro, Paradox, InterBase and Borland C++. I worked in the entertainment

and computer software industries my entire career. My experience in the software industry includes many types of application, utility software for both mainframe and desktop computers. After a brief period of private practice and as Associate Editor of the Entertainment Law Reporter, I joined the legal department of Ashton-Tate Corporation in 1983. Until its acquisition by Borland in 1991, Ashton-Tate was one of the world's largest computer software companies. In 1985 I left Ashton-Tate to become Associate General Counsel to Kandell Corporation, a leading supplier of IBM mainframe software, and in 1987 I joined Borland as General Counsel.

I want to emphasize that I am sensitive to the need for the intellectual property protection on both a professional and personal level. My professional career is focused on protecting the valuable intellectual property assets of software companies. I'm also an author myself, having recently written a reference book on music licensing that was published by Prentice-Hall. To call order 1-800-223-0231. So I can certainly appreciate the need to protect intellectual property. And I hope I've made my point. If you need the number again I'll have it available.

COMMISSIONER LEHMAN: Be careful, you know, works of the United States Government are not copyrightable, so if you get your stuff involved with ours you might have a problem.

MR. KOHN: I'll try not to read my -- I'll try not to read my book into the record.

I'm testifying today in my capacity as Vice-President and General Counsel of Borland, a publicly-traded Silicon Valley company. On behalf of Borland I want to comment specifically on Question 4 in the Hearing Notice, and if time permits more generally on questions regarding the scope of protection for visual aspects of software programs.

Question 4 asks whether the present framework of patent, copyright, trademark and trade secret law effectively promotes innovation in the field of software. Like all other software companies, Borland invests heavily in both the creation and acquisition of new software products, and like other companies Borland needs strong government enforcement of existing intellectual property rights, especially in foreign markets, in order to protect its investments.

But it is particularly unproductive at these hearings and at other forms for public debate on these issues to hear two extreme views espouse. One group, generally small companies, argue for no protection or perhaps at best very weak protection. A second group, generally very large companies, addresses the issue of scope rather than enforcement, arguing that broader protection for software is necessary, and indeed the broader the protection the better. We believe that much of the polarization you have heard and will hear is the result of a confusion of what is being debated.

Protectionist interests in particular confuse enforcement of what is an undisputed intellectual property right with the underlying scope of intellectual property protection. We in the industry all understand that software as a product is particularly susceptible to unauthorized duplication. We therefore need strong enforcement of existing intellectual

UNITED STATES PATENT AND TRADEMARK OFFICE
Public Hearing on Patent Protection for Software-Related Inventions
San Jose, California — January 26-27, 1994

property rights to make sure that we are protected against the pirating of our software. But issues concerning the enforcement of intellectual property rights must not be confused with issues concerning the scope of intellectual property protection. It is too easy to wrap oneself in the proverbial American flag of antipiracy and anticonterfeiting enforcement. There is no dispute that strong antipiracy enforcement is required to promote the resources necessary for research and innovation. But it does not follow that because strong enforcement of intellectual property promotes innovation, a broader scope of intellectual property protection will also.

We should understand that many of those who very responsibly argue for limitations on the scope of intellectual property protection are not trying to defend pirates. They are, rather, trying to make a medium under which the proper scope of intellectual property protection as established by Congress and the Courts is respected and strongly enforced by the Administrative Branch of government.

This distinction between the enforcement of existing rights and a broadening of the underlying scope of protection was recently addressed at the 1993 Berkeley Roundtable on the International Economy in which the Vice-President, the Commerce Secretary and the Commissioner all participated.

The Report of the Roundtable on Maintaining Leadership in Software states the distinction between enforcement and scope very clearly. I'll include a block quote in my written testimony which begins with the following sentence: "Industry representatives argue that the importance of protecting intellectual property from theft by commercial counterfeiters and unscrupulous users must be distinguished from issues concerning the proper scope of intellectual property protection."

Unfortunately Question 4 in the Hearing Notice, in our view, heightens rather than diminishes the confusion and polarization. Question 4 seems to be based on a premise that strong protection for existing intellectual property rights necessarily implies a greater scope of intellectual property protection, and further that a greater scope of intellectual property implies a greater amount of innovation.

Implicitly, Question 4 neglects the important role that competition plays in encouraging innovation. We believe that the implication inherent in Question 4 should be the subject of much greater scrutiny and analysis. Within the industry we all, or at least most of us, agree that greater enforcement of intellectual property is necessary. What has fractionalized the industry is the attempt by some to use the need for greater enforcement to attempt to expand the scope of underlying intellectual property rights, particularly within the copyright area. As the Commissioner is aware, just two weeks ago the head of the Antitrust Division of the Department of Justice, Assistant Attorney General Ann Bingamen gave a major speech on the occasion of the sixtieth anniversary of the founding of the Antitrust Division. The Assistant Attorney General recognized the polarization within the industry that has been caused by attempts to increase the scope of intellectual property protection.

She said, "The substantive reach of the exclusive rights granted under the intellectual property laws also has been a matter of particular concern and ferment in the software industry. The Courts and the agencies have been faced with difficult decisions about the scope of both patents and copyrights in this field, as is clear to anyone who has paid attention to the long series of important court decisions on computer software copyrights, including Whelan, Altai, and the recent decisions in Lotus v. Borland, now under review in the 1st Circuit. The scope of copyright protection for computer software has we believe important competitive implications as well as important implications for the incentives to innovate."

We are particularly heartened to hear Assistant Attorney General most eloquently state her concern about attempts to increase the underlying scope of intellectual property protection. Again, please permit me to quote what she had to say. "Given my strong belief in competition, I think the courts should be hesitant to read the statutory grant provisions expansively, but should recognize the anticompetitive potential of restrictive practices at or beyond the borders of clearly-conveyed statutory rights."

While the Assistant Attorney General was directly addressing only the courts, we believe the same cautions should apply to the Administrative Branch of government as well.

Many questions to be addressed at these hearings deal with the visual aspects of computer screen displays. In evaluating the proper scope for protection for the individual aspects of computer programs, we believe that the Patent and Trademark Office would do well to consider the analytical framework employed by the engineers and computer scientists as opposed to the lawyers and judges in the software industry.

As the Commissioner is aware, much of the original and seminal work in graphical user interface analysis and design was done at Xerox Corporation in the 1970s. The research at Xerox formed a wealth of user interfaces far beyond just those of Xerox's products. Apple's MacIntosh and Lisa, Hewlett-Packard's New Wave, Microsoft's Windows, X-Windows, IBM's Office Vision and OS/2 to name just a few. Much of the research at Xerox was published in scholarly papers for distribution both inside and outside of Xerox. The most famous of those papers, entitled "A Methodology for User Interface Design," was published by Xerox Palo Alto Research Center in January of 1977. Because of the enormous importance of this paper, I'm going to attach it to Borland's written comments and ask that you consider it as part of these proceedings.

The Xerox research produced a methodology of interface design that is based upon what Xerox researchers called a taxonomy or classification for user interface analysis. This taxonomy is designed to permit analysis and evaluation of what each aspect or component of a user interface does. The taxonomy was created for software analysis and not for any legal purpose, but remarkably it dovetailed seamlessly with the overall intellectual property scheme of patents, copyrights and trade secrets established by Congress.

As the Xerox research concluded, every user interface has three separable components; one, the user's conceptual model; two, the control mechanism or command invocation of the product; and three, the visuals, or the information display. The user's conceptual model is the abstraction selected by the software developer which users can relate to

UNITED STATES PATENT AND TRADEMARK OFFICE
Public Hearing on Patent Protection for Software-Related Inventions
San Jose, California -- January 26-27, 1994

the task they are trying to perform.

For example, the spreadsheet metaphor is the conceptual model that underlies Borland's QuattroPro line of products. Under our intellectual property scheme, the conceptual model of a particular piece of software would not be protectable at all except of course insofar as it may be protected by trade secret or under the terms of a contract or confidential relationship. The command invocation or control mechanism of the user interface is the mechanism that extracts the functionality built into the software. It is a set of actions and results defined in particular relationships to one another. Menu items and keystrokes are part of the control mechanism and were clearly identified as such by the Xerox research published in the mid-seventies. Indeed, the control component was originally called the command language.

Under the intellectual property scheme established by Congress, the control mechanism of the software product falls within the ambit of patent law, specifically utility patents. In order to secure utility patent protection over a control mechanism, an inventor should be required to satisfy the statutory requirements of novelty, advancement over the prior art and so forth. For example, if the user entered a database by first clicking on the picture of the door to simulate knocking, and then clicking on the picture of the door-knob to simulate turning it, the sequence of steps would be part of the control mechanism and must satisfy the rigors of patent examination if it is to be protected. If the command mechanism does not meet the rigors of patent protection, it should not be protected by any other form of intellectual property protection such as copyright.

Finally, in Xerox's terminology, there are programs of visuals. The screen displays of many sophisticated user interfaces have a truly separable visual or expressive component. Images that can be manipulated through animation techniques.

The Congressional scheme provides for protection of these visuals, and under both statute and the case law, the visual display of the computer program may be protected by copyright law if and only to the extent its artistic features can be identified separately from and are capable of existing independently from the utilitarian aspects of the software program. Note that the definition of computer program under copyright law is a set of statements or instructions to be used directly in a computer in order to bring about a certain result. The screen display is a certain result of the set of statements or instructions that comprise the underlying computer program and must therefore independently qualify as a work of authorship.

Those are my two paragraphs. Thank you for the opportunity to appear here today and I would be happy to answer your questions.

COMMISSIONER LEHMAN: Thank you very much, Mr. Kohn. I just note you refer to Question 4 in our Federal Register Notice which states that -- which asks the question, Does the present framework of patent, copyright and trade secret law, A, effectively promote innovation in the field of software, and, B, provide the appropriate level of protection for software-related inventions. I don't read those as implying that we should raise the level of protection; in fact I read those as an open-ended question as, What is the appropriate level? and that may well be a lower level. It may be no level at all, and I think the questions we've asked would suggest that we do have an open mind about that.

MR. KOHN: I'm glad to hear that the Commission has an open mind about these issues. I think that, looking at the background section of the hearings, I don't have it in front of me, specifically emphasizes the innovation that's promoted by protecting intellectual property, and the point that I made is that there is absolutely no reference whatsoever to the importance of competition in promoting innovation, and you mentioned earlier, to an earlier witness, that -- you suggest that the competition issues might be more appropriately addressed under Antitrust provisions, but it is an intellectual property issue, and that's precisely what Ann Binghamen had said in her speech. It is an intellectual property program, we are after all talking about government-granted monopolies.

COMMISSIONER LEHMAN: Thank you very much. I'd like to take a five-minute recess before we reconvene for the rest of the morning's hearings, and our next witness, when we come back will be, I believe, Douglas Brotz from Adobe Systems.

(Recess)

COMMISSIONER LEHMAN: Next I'd like to call Douglas K. Brotz who is the Principal Scientist of Adobe Systems, Incorporated right here in the Valley.

--oOo--

DOUGLAS BROTZ

ADOBE SYSTEMS, INC.

MR. BROTZ: Good morning, Mr. Secretary and members of the Panel. My name is Douglas Brotz. I'm Principal Scientist at Adobe Systems, Incorporated, and I am representing the views of Adobe Systems as well as my own. Adobe is a software company based in Mountain View, California. We are most well-known for our PostScript language and interpreter which provides foundation for desktop and electronic publishing.

Although I am a computer scientist, I became involved in patents when Adobe was contacted by another company regarding Adobe's possible infringement of a patent. I'm currently Adobe's technical advisor to our patent attorneys.

Let me make my position on the patentability of software clear. I believe that software per se should not be allowed patent protection. I take this position as the creator of software and as the beneficiary of the rewards that innovative software can bring in the marketplace. I do not take this position because I or my company are eager to steal the ideas of others in our industry. Adobe has built its business by creating new markets with new software. We take this position because it is the best policy for maintaining a healthy software industry, where innovation can prosper.

The problems inherent in certain aspects of the patent process for software-related inventions are well-known, the difficulties of finding and citing prior art, the problems of obviousness, the difficulties of adequate specifications for software are a few of those problems. However, I argue that software should not be patented, not because it is difficult to do so, but because it is wrong to do so.

The software marketplace requires constant innovation regardless of whether the computer programs can be

UNITED STATES PATENT AND TRADEMARK OFFICE
Public Hearing on Patent Protection for Software-Related Inventions
San Jose, California -- January 26-27, 1994

patented or not. Indeed, the fundamental computer programs and concepts on which the entire industry is based were conceived in an era when software was considered to be unpatentable.

For example, when we at Adobe founded a company on the concept of software to revolutionize the world of printing, we believed that there was no possibility of patenting our work. That belief did not stop us from creating that software, nor did it deter the savvy venture capitalists who helped us with the early investment. We have done very well despite our having no patents on our original work.

On the other hand, the emergence in recent years of patents on software has hurt Adobe and the industry. A "patent litigation tax" is one impediment to our financial health that our industry can ill-afford. Resources that could have been used to further innovation have been diverted to the patent problem. Engineers and scientists such as myself who could have been creating new software instead are working on analyzing patents, applying for patents and preparing defenses. Revenues are being sunk into legal costs instead of into research and development. It is clear to me that the Constitutional mandate to promote progress in the useful arts is not served by the issuance of patents on software.

Let me illustrate this burden with some figures. The case Information International Incorporated v. Adobe, et al., was filed five years ago. Last year the trial court ruled for Adobe, finding no infringement. In December the Appeals Court for the Federal Circuit unanimously affirmed that judgment. Yet, in that time, it has cost Adobe over four and a half million dollars in legal fees and expenses. I myself have spent over three thousand five hundred hours of my time -- that's equivalent to almost two years of working time -- and at least another thousand hours was spent by others at Adobe. The Chairman of the Board spent a month at the trial. This type of company behavior would not be high on anyone's list of ways to promote progress.

This state of affairs might be acceptable if there were a corresponding benefit for patents in the software industry. However, I see none. Companies that have trumpeted their fundamental software patents are not leaders in software innovation. Conferring monopoly positions in an industry that was already the most innovative of all will promote stagnation rather than increased innovation. When companies turn from competing by offering the best products to earning money by the threat of patent litigation, we will see our best hope for job creation in this country disappear. An industry that still generates tremendous job growth through the start-ups of two guys in a garage will not continue to grow when a room for a third person, a patent attorney, needs to be made in that garage.

There does exist a perfectly adequate vehicle to protect creator's rights in this industry, the Copyright Law. The nature of software is that it is a writing, an expression of mathematical ideas. The copyright law protects this expression, and it does so without requiring costly and time-consuming proceedings. For people working in the fast-paced software industry, the way a copyright is created is idea. While feverishly working to meet deadlines, there is no need to explain what you've done to a government agency. The very act of writing the software confers the copyright on it.

Furthermore, the copyright law confers the correct level of protection on computer software. Regardless of what current regulations may say, the fact is that all computer programs express mathematical algorithms. Every part of every computer program manipulates numbers with logic. Any software that performs any task does so through mathematics. It is inconsistent to hold that mathematic algorithms are unpatentable while granting patents on systems composed of software.

If the Patent Office were truly following the law it would recognize the inherent mathematical nature of software and it would not grant patents to software-based inventions. In the last decade the Patent Office has been granting patents on software and algorithms regardless of superficial attempts to cast claims as systems methods or processes. The Supreme Court did not say in Diamond v. Diehr that pure software inventions are patentable. By adopting this position in its recent practice, the Patent Office has made a dangerous step that could decimate the very industry it wishes to protect.

Whenever the Patent Office grants a software patent, it grants a right to the patent-holder to devastate innocent businesses. Due to the arcane nature of this technology, our courts find it very difficult to distinguish frivolous software patent lawsuits from legitimate ones. As a result, a frivolous plaintiff is in a very strong blackmailing position, where a defendant can look forward either to an extortionate settlement or enormous legal costs. An excellent remedy would be to change our law to allow a successful defendant to recoup legal costs in patent cases. Until that day arrives, at least our Patent Office can refrain from granting these dubious patents.

We have heard today from proponents of software patents who will claim that these patents can protect the independent inventor. This belief is a delusion. The expensive patent process protects large, methodical corporations that can afford to apply for scores of patents much more than it protects the poorly-capitalized lone inventor, and when that inventor tries to produce his invention he may well find that those large corporations can ruin his own business with their large software patent portfolios.

In summary, these are my main points:

The software industry thrived without patents, creating its fundamental base in an era of no software patents; software patents harm the industry, with no corresponding benefit; software embodies mathematical algorithms; the law, starting with the Constitution, argues against patents for software-related inventions; and last, the proper form of protection for software is copyright.

As a postscript to the figures on the patent lawsuit that I discussed before, the final figure is actually not in. Although Adobe has been successful twice already, the plaintiffs are asking for reconsideration of the unanimous appeal judgment against them. These kinds of festering sores are what our country can ill-afford when we are trying to lead the world in creative industry.

Thank you.

COMMISSIONER LEHMAN: Thank you very much, Dr. Brotz.

UNITED STATES PATENT AND TRADEMARK OFFICE
Public Hearing on Patent Protection for Software-Related Inventions
San Jose, California — January 26-27, 1994

You've indicated that you think that the copyright system works very well to protect software. An earlier witness, Mr. Kohn from Borland, indicated that he felt that there were serious problems with the existing copyright system, and in particular he felt that it shouldn't protect screen displays, for example.

Other witnesses have indicated that they're very concerned about, I believe, the witness from Storage Technology indicated that he was very concerned about the decompilation issue. He very much believed that one should be able in effect to copy software in the decompilation process in order to produce interoperable works. I'm wondering, since you really believe that we should focus on copyright, if you have views on either of those two issues.

MR. BROTZ: Yes. I certainly do. I agree with Mr. Kohn that we should not confuse strong enforcement of copyright rights with broadened scope of copyright rights. I agree that some plaintiffs have tried to stretch the scope of copyright beyond where it ought to go. I firmly support his position, in fact, that copyright law should protect us against piracy and the kinds of threats that copyright law was intended to protect us against.

In answer to your other question about decompilation and interoperability considerations, I believe that the evidence always cited for the importance of interoperability is that companies that do not provide for interoperability fall of their own weight. I do not see that as an argument for insisting that companies therefore make themselves interoperable. If strong rights are granted to all aspects of the written computer software, then a company could choose what level of protection it wanted and how far to assert its rights and whether they wanted to open their interface or not. If they make a wise decision and offer enough interoperability, they'll do well; if they make an unwise decision, they won't, and it's up to them to decide whether they want to succeed or not.

COMMISSIONER LEHMAN: In other words, your view is that the licensing system deals with this problem, that if people don't adopt intelligent licensing processes, then they will suffer the economic consequences which will be negative and will encourage basically licensing that creates more open systems.

MR. BROTZ: That's right. And I would oppose having a law that straitjackets the way in which these kinds of licenses or accesses must be made.

COMMISSIONER LEHMAN: Thank you very much. Does anybody else have any questions? Thank you.

Next I'd like to call Hans Troesch, partner in the law firm of Fish and Richardson.

—oOo—

HANS TROESCH

FISH AND RICHARDSON

MR. TROESCH: Good morning, Mr. Commissioner, distinguished Panel. My name is Hans Troesch. I'm here speaking on my own behalf. My partners have reminded me of that.

Many years ago I earned a Masters Degree in Computer Science at the University of Michigan, and for close to ten years, regardless of my various and more fancy job titles, I considered myself principally to be a computer programmer. Today I'm an attorney and a member of the patent bar. I practice patent, copyright and trade secrets law, as we already mentioned, with the law firm of Fish and Richardson.

I'm here today because I would like to offer my own views on a few of the questions that the Patent Office has invited the public to address at these hearings. As a preliminary matter, I must confess my own deep concerns about the present fate of software inventions in the Patent Office. I believe that the logical, almost musical nature of software technology provides unique opportunities for advocacy and for confusion in a system that is based on a more structural, may I say more sculptural view of the world, but that is a topic for another day.

Today I will merely state my hope and belief that the Patent Office will rise to the challenge of finding and keeping qualified examiners, securing access to the vast body of software-related prior art that is not of record in the Patent Office, and of developing delimiting doctrines of novelty, obviousness and enablement in ways appropriate to the peculiarly flexible genius of software technology.

I would like to address Question I at this point in the Office Notice, and to state my view that a computer program, that is to say, a set of instructions that is executable on a computer, to achieve a result, should be considered a machine within the meaning of Section 101 of the Patent Statute, and should therefore be eligible for patent protection, without resort to the additional and often redundant limitations to computer processors, read-only memories or data input-output devices.

On the issue of eligibility for patent protection, I dare say such a change in the form of the law would not greatly expand the scope of protection available to inventors, at least not to those inventors who can afford the kind of legal talent testifying at these hearings.

Those of us who know what we are doing can get computer program machines covered. The process we have to go through may be painful to watch, may be expensive, but we can do it. For that reason I would promote my suggestion principally as one that will improve the quality of the analysis of software-related ventures, and the doctrine under which those inventions are examined.

On the issue of infringement we would have to be a bit more subtle. If we allow claims to be made to computer programs per se we must be careful not to create a risk of infringement by traditional print media and their successors in electronic publishing. The publication for human readers, whether or not on paper, for the patent-protected computer program, should not by itself be any kind of infringement of the patent.

I would like to turn now to one of the specific questions raised for today's hearing. What aspect of a mathematical algorithm implemented on the general-purpose computer should or should not be protectable through the patent system? I believe that a machine made up of computer program instructions that usefully transforms data or information should be protectable under the patent laws in all its novel and nonobvious aspects. Given the importance of information processing to our economy, it would be perverse for us to continue to deny direct protection to a

UNITED STATES PATENT AND TRADEMARK OFFICE
Public Hearing on Patent Protection for Software-Related Inventions
San Jose, California — January 26-27, 1994

technology that is so important to our information processing prosperity.

This leads me unavoidably to the question of what is novel and unobvious in a computer program. I believe that our greatest challenge lies in these two questions, regardless of how we answer the question previously posed.

For myself, I would not consider novel and nonobvious merely to transpose to a computer something previously known to be done by hand, or in one person's head, or collectively by a group of people. But if the method for transforming information is truly new, then the doctrines that limit or preclude protection solely because the method is a computer program seems unwarranted.

It has been suggested that allowing mathematical algorithms to be protected would remove laws of nature from the public domain and give an unwarranted universal scope of protection to a patented technique. Personally I find those rationales peculiar. Taking the computer programmer's informal definition that an algorithm is a predetermined set of steps to perform a function, and that a mathematical algorithm is one that operates on mathematical objects, such as numbers, triangles, continuously differentiable functions, then granting protection for a new, previously-unknown and nonobvious set of steps withdraws nothing from the public. And if the patent reaches over a broad range of applications, that would merely correspond to the broad usefulness of the new algorithm.

In any other technology this would be grounds for praising the inventor, not for denying protection. I would submit to you that if someone were to object to a patent on the transistor on the ground that it would have too many uses, you would find that objection incomprehensible.

One final point that might be kept in mind before whence it comes to an alarm about the potential breadth of claims to mathematical algorithms: a naked mathematical algorithm claim would seem to be the ultimate engineering claims, and therefore particularly susceptible to being rejected or invalidated, because any prior art that shows the algorithm steps being applied in any context would invalidate the claim. Personally I would be surprised if any patent practitioner would ever rely solely on a naked algorithm to protect his client's interests.

The Patent Office also poses the variant of this question, limiting it to the implementation of the algorithm to a special purpose rather than a general purpose computer. If the problem is bad patents, this does not seem to be a solution. If one begins with a computer program that should be unpatentable because it is not new, or because it is obvious, one should not in my view be able to achieve patentability merely by attaching to the program the input-output devices that are conventional for the process that the computer performs.

In other words, one should not be able to save an old or obvious bread-baking program merely by attaching a digital thermometer to it. Conversely, if the program is new and not obvious, then the conventional addition of necessary computer hardware and other devices is redundant to the claim, at least insofar as patentability is concerned. Such additional limitations would not in fact limit the scope of protection available to the inventor, unless parenthetically

the claims are poorly drafted. But such a redundant edition of apparatus to the program claim does create a potentially substantial distraction for the patent examiner who, in the terms of my example, in searching the art of digital thermometers, may completely miss the point about bread-baking.

Finally, I would like to say a word about whether we should replace patents with a new form of protection for computer software. My one-word answer is no. Patent law can deliver predictability, definiteness and uniformity. Under copyright law we cannot protect your ideas, at least not without doing some violence to traditional copyright principles, and we are subject to forum shopping in thirteen circuit courts of appeal. Under trade secrets law, we can protect our ideas, but are subject to the law as developed in any of fifty different state courts and their Federal counterparts. We're never quite sure what the protected ideas are and are at risk of having someone rediscover or reverse-engineer our inventions out from under us. But under the patent laws we can get warning about what is protected expressed with reasonable clarity and applied with national uniformity. It would be unfortunate if such a sound concept were to be crippled because we were too slow in learning to apply its fundamental principles to the challenges of software-related inventions.

Thank you.

COMMISSIONER LEHMAN: Thank you very much, Mr. Troesch. That was very helpful.

The next person on our list is Brett Glass, but we're not sure that Brett Glass is here. If you are, will you please stand up and identify yourself and come forward? If not, we will move on to Robert Sabath, President of the World Intellectual Property and Trade Forum.

--oOo--

ROBERT SABATH

WORLD INTELLECTUAL PROPERTY AND TRADE FORUM

MR. SABATH: Mr. Commissioner, distinguished Panel. My name is Robert Sabath. I speak today in both my capacity as President of the World Intellectual Property and Trade Forum and as a solo practitioner in the patent field. I'm also on the Executive Committee of the California State Bar's Intellectual Property Section, but as you know, Mary O'Hara and Michael Glenn will testify at these hearings on behalf of the State Bar. Additionally I speak as Legal Issues Editor of QuickTime Forum, a multimedia developer's publication.

The primary topic today is the use of the patent system for the protection of software-related inventions. The central objective of my remarks is to encourage greater flexibility within the framework of the law in promoting the patenting of software-related inventions as well as pure software inventions.

Patents themselves are the best prior art against subsequent applications for a patent grant. Anything that artificially limits the development of the body of prior art relied upon by the patent and trademark office has the effect of slowing the progress of technology in critical fields. Software is clearly a key and strategic industry for the United States. It's no secret that software itself in the development of the industry were not caused by the patent incentives, but still, the patent

UNITED STATES PATENT AND TRADEMARK OFFICE
Public Hearing on Patent Protection for Software-Related Inventions
San Jose, California — January 26-27, 1994

system is part of the incentive structure which is necessary to the continued development of many software firms.

Moreover, the efforts of the United States Government to promote U.S. trade interests abroad and even to advocate changes in the intellectual property laws of other countries are severely undermined if the U.S. intellectual property laws and regulations fail to encourage successes of key U.S. industries at home. One such key industry is clearly software.

I do ask for your indulgence, Honorable Commissioner, in addressing a slightly broader question than the primary topic indicated above. As a sole practitioner I've come close to the plight of the solo inventor affected by the substantially increased PTO fees promulgated by prior administrations. Particularly the maintenance fees are believed to be a disincentive which may dissuade individuals from even initiating the process of obtaining patent protection.

But the cost of patenting which is born today by inventors and companies is softened by the Silicon Valley spirit of self-help which has characterized the American spirit since the days of George Washington and Thomas Jefferson.

An example of this self-help is the Sunnyvale Patent Information Clearinghouse. Self-help, and necessity, have additionally spawned in Silicon Valley a substantial venture capital community which is selectively supportive of the efforts of individual inventors. This spirit of self-help is additionally shown by many local firms and companies which have opened offices in Washington, D.C., and its surrounding communities of Virginia and Maryland.

We do salute you, Mr. Commissioner, and distinguished Panel for coming here to California. We clearly need your help, not just with regard to improving the laws and the regulatory environment as it relates to patents, but also with regard to the infrastructure in which patent and invention processes play themselves out in the United States.

The U.S. Government has facilities, buildings and courthouses throughout the nation. These facilities and buildings have many purposes. Federal courthouses now hear patent lawsuits in San Jose as well as in San Francisco, and in cities throughout the country.

It is clear that our country has developed elaborate mechanisms for facilitating and resolving disputes between litigants and patent lawsuits. However, we have done pitifully little at the Federal level to enable the solo inventor to search for prior art and effectively to limit the scope of claims to his fields or her fields of rightful entitlement. Mr. Commissioner, accordingly we're very happy to have you here today in this convention center.

We believe as a minimum the West Coast deserves a branch of the USPTO having at least search facilities to support the software, the semiconductor and the electronics industries that have developed the infrastructure of the American West so extensively. Perhaps the availability of public search rooms for inventors is not a matter for the Department of Commerce, but rather for the Department of Education. But whether the Commissioner of Patents and Trademarks takes the initiative or whether another Federal agency takes the lead, it is clear that many communities in our country need access to the technical collections and patents of the Federal Government.

The facilities for obtaining prior art in Sunnyvale are clearly needed. But in most communities of America, such facilities are nonexistent. Moreover, solo inventors are seldom in a position to invest in a state-of-the-art CD-ROM system or computer search services in view of their high cost. The Information Superhighway offers a bright vision of a technological future. Will there be facilities to provide public access to information carried in this superhighway?

The Patent Office can provide such facilities to bring the fruits of this superhighway of information to our inventors, to the young in America who thirst for knowledge and progress, and to the public at large.

The physical facilities of the Department of Commerce and the United States Patent and Trademark Office are needed in our local communities to implement the purposes of the intellectual property laws of our country. America wants to build its future by educating the inventors of the future. We need public search facilities for the electronic arts wherever major electronics developments are being made, in California, in Austin, Texas, in Dallas, in Colorado, along with many other communities across America.

We need biotechnology search facilities in Emeryville, California, and in Cambridge, Massachusetts, and in other communities of the nation, and we need software search facilities in the nation's software development centers including but not limited to such areas as Seattle and Silicon Valley. The German example for one shows that search facilities and examination facilities need not necessarily be located in the same cities.

The resources and the facilities of the PTO should be distributed at various locations across America to provide public access to the prior art regarding technological developments which have already become known. We salute you, Mr. Commissioner, for coming to California to address the vital subject of patenting software-related inventions in this public forum. The California economy is improving, but it remains disastrously understimulated. Because of the size of California's economy it can either drive or hamstring recovery on the national scale.

The questions raised at this public hearing have a direct and vital bearing on the economic well-being of California. We thus appreciate your coming to guide these hearings.

To focus more definitely on the subject of patenting software-related inventions, it is my belief and that of many participants in the World Intellectual Property and Trade Forum that there is no substitute for the development of an increased body of software art available to patent examiners. With a properly classified and complete body of prior art the searching and the examination of new patent applications will be enhanced.

The World Intellectual Property and Trade Forum salutes the corrective action of the Commissioner in connection with the reexamination of Compton's multimedia patent. This reexamination process clearly shows that even though applicable prior art was not initially available to the examiner, there are mechanisms for addressing questions of patentability even after grant of a patent, but certainly it would be optimal if the applicable art had been found and addressed during actual examination.

One way to ensure an effective and complete body of prior

UNITED STATES PATENT AND TRADEMARK OFFICE
Public Hearing on Patent Protection for Software-Related Inventions
San Jose, California -- January 26-27, 1994

art in the field of software patents is to relax the policies of the PTO with respect to the patentability of mathematical algorithms. Considerable room for relaxation is available even within the bounds of current case law on the subject. Many new inventions beneficial to the developing field of software may currently not even be the subject of patent applications because of the chilling effects of the PTO's restrictive approach to the patentability of software.

Insufficient software prior art limits the ability of the PTO to examine effectively future software-related patent applications, including pure software patent applications. The distinction between hardware and software approaches to the same problems has blurred technologically. This distinction should be blurred and eliminated in the bureaucratic spaces of the Patent and Trademark Office as well.

Patent examiners should rely less heavily on the Section 101 as a basis for rejecting software-related inventions. With an increasing body of prior art established by greater flexibility in allowing software-related patents, examiners will be encouraged to make substantive office actions based upon technical art rather than merely implementing policy articulated by agency representatives.

One object of the patent system is to encourage progress in the arts by publication of inventions. The effect of patent grant is to add to the body of detailed technical information comprised in issued patent documents. When a Section 101 rejection is successfully asserted by the PTO, the practical effect is to deny future software developers of the benefit of full patent disclosure. This hampers the development of new ideas in many technical fields, including multimedia software generally and even biotechnology which is to an extent dependent on progress in the field of data systems for its instrumentation to be effective.

We thank you again, Honorable Commissioner, for coming here and conducting these hearings.

COMMISSIONER LEHMAN: Thank you very much, Mr. Sabath. I just point out that we do have patent depository libraries all over the United States and I think there are several on this area, probably one at Stanford and Berkeley, and they actually have everything we have in the Patent Office there, and that is available to the public. In addition, we're automating the Patent and Trademark Office, and in fact right now if you're in Arlington you can go into the -- in fact, Group 2300 is fully automated already, and if you go into our patent search room in Washington, we've got a facility there where you can actually get computer retrieval of the patent documentation and we have plans to extend that to the patent depository library so that you'll be able to come out here and do the same thing. And eventually, hopefully in a few more years, we'll actually have this service available through the Internet. We're not quite there technologically yet, but every engineer and computer scientist in Silicon Valley will just be able to, in a few keystrokes, get access to our patent database. We think that's not only going to help people understand what the patent prior art is but hopefully it will give them access to some of the technology more easily than they otherwise would have, so we are indeed, I think, making some progress on that problem.

Thank you very much.

MR. SABATH: Thank you.

COMMISSIONER LEHMAN: Next I'd like to call Mr. William Benman of Benman & Collins. And Mr. Benman is the last speaker for this morning. We're pretty much right on target on our time. Thank you for joining us.

--oOo--

WILLIAM BENMAN

BENMAN & COLLINS

MR. BENMAN: And as someone that hasn't had breakfast, I assure you that my testimony will be brief!

Commissioner LEHMAN, thank you for hearing me on the question of the patenting of software-related inventions. I commend you for taking testimony on this important topic.

I'm a partner with the intellectual property law firm of Benman, Collins and Sawyer, with offices in Palo Alto, Los Angeles and Tucson. We have prepared and prosecuted numerous applications on software-related inventions, and we offer this testimony in the hope that our experience in this regard maybe of some value in connection with your effort to sample public opinion on this topic.

Since the early 1980s, we in the community of patent lawyers who are preparing and prosecuting patent applications on software-related inventions observed two thrusts, one in the direction of copyright protection as the primary if not sole form of legal protection for software, and the other in the direction of patents where patent protection was available. We notice that those companies that were patent-conscious were most likely to exploit the patent option. Many of the companies which did not utilize the patent option were often new or young software companies which were not patent-conscious per se. The plight of these companies was compounded by their reliance on counsel from lawyers that were typically not patent lawyers with experience in the field. These lawyers held themselves out as experts in computer law and high-tech law, but typically held a mistaken notion that software was not patentable, although patents had already been issued for software-related inventions. To this day, many uninformed attorneys either advise their clients that patent protection is not available for software, or they criticize the patent system as too costly and cumbersome for the protection of software. As a result these attorneys have either generally steered their clients away from patents as an appropriate form of protection or neglected to advise their clients to seek counsel from an attorney having experience in the patenting of software. Hence, for many years now, many software publishers have been lured by the ease and low cost of copyright protection without being properly advised of the shortcomings of same nor the availability and advantages of patent protection.

As early as ten years ago we began to suspect that the copyright holders would someday become aware of the limitations of copyright protection when it became necessary to enforce the copyrights. We expected that they would seek a more substantive form of protection such as that currently afforded by the patent system. This has now come to pass as the software industry has become aware of the shortcomings of copyright protection often as a result of painful and costly court battles. The lawyers guiding these firms away from patents have now essentially painted

- 21 -

UNITED STATES PATENT AND TRADEMARK OFFICE
Public Hearing on Patent Protection for Software-Related Inventions
San Jose, California — January 26-27, 1994

themselves into a corner, having failed to stretch the scope of copyright protection to cover substantially more than the form of the software and not the underlying inventive aspects thereof. These attorneys have now marshalled some software publishers behind their effort to escape from the situation by criticizing the current patent system as unwieldy for software, advocating instead some new form of protection for software that would protect the underlying concepts without a rigorous examination process. They are supported in their efforts by recent admissions by the Patent Office of a shortage of prior art in PTO files to facilitate the examination of software-based applications. It would appear that many now desire the ease and low cost of the copyright system with the substantive protection afforded by the patent system.

It would clearly be adverse to the public interest, in our view, to grant such monopolies without a substantive examination of the application. Yet, in our view, any system which involved a substantive examination of such applications would be essentially equivalent to the present system. Hence we seek to speak for those attorneys who are registered to practice before the Patent and Trademark Office and experienced in the protection of software in expressing our view that the present system of examination for software-related inventions and innovations is, though not perfect, adequate and appropriate for the protection of software.

First we feel compelled to mention that many of the concerns in the industry would be adequately addressed by educating the industry about the patent process by those qualified to do so. We believe that it is unethical for any attorney to advise a client not to seek patent protection for inventions whether software-related or not, if the attorney giving the advice is not skilled in the field.

The process by which attorneys are admitted to practice before the Office is intended to protect the public interest by ensuring that those that hold themselves out as qualified to practice before the office are indeed so-qualified. Unfortunately the software industry has grown up on an unhealthy of poor counsel with respect to intellectual property issues pertaining to software. It is no wonder then that it now has a bit of indigestion and needs some relief. We feel that the present system of examination if properly administered can provide that relief, and allow me to briefly address some of the perceived problems with the present system.

One of the perceived problems is that the Patent Office will issue patents on inventions already in the public domain. That's been touched on by some of the speakers earlier this morning. Another problem is that the patent process is costly and therefore available only to big companies, and a third often-heard complaint is that the patent process is too slow.

First, with respect to the concern that the Patent Office will issue patents on innovations that are known and used by others in the industry, let me say that to the extent that this is a real problem, it is no different for the software industry than for other areas of technology. There are at least three levels of safeguards by which this perceived problem may be addressed by the current system. First, the Patent Office is currently in the process, as I understand, of providing the

examining corps with the capability to search beyond PTO files to the on-line computer-searchable databases, such as those accessed through the Dialog system. This will facilitate a more thorough examination of the prior art including technical literature, new-product announcements and et cetera, minimizing ab initio the probability of a patent issuing on an innovation which lacks novelty or is obvious in view of such art.

To the extent that the innovation is known by others but is not published and therefore inaccessible to this approach, the next level of safeguard should be considered. However, it should be noted again that software-related applications do not differ from other applications in this regard. The second safeguard is afforded by the current reexamination process. Those who are aware of prior art which might render a patent issued on a software-based application invalid may initiate a reexamination of the patent, and I commend you for your intent to improve that process. A third safeguard results from the practical realities of patent enforcement. The cost of patent litigation are sufficiently high that one holding a patent of questionable validity on software would think twice before instituting a court battle when advised of prior art which would invalidate the patent. Hence there are clearly several current safeguards to address this first concern.

The second concern, that the patent process is costly and therefore only available to big companies must be considered in light of the fact that in other areas of technology, patent filings by small companies and individuals are quite high. In recognition of the value of innovations provided by small entities and individuals, those that qualify are entitled to pay reduced filing fees. In addition, it will soon be appreciated that in the software industry, as in other industries, the total cost of procuring a patent, typically somewhere between five thousand fifteen thousand dollars depending upon what part of the country you're in, is small compared to the value of patents and certainly small compared to the cost of copyright litigation. While patents are more expensive to acquire than copyrights, the old axiom, "You get what you pay for," comes to mind.

Finally with respect to the concern that the patent process is too slow, we have a suggestion. You might consider an expedited examination on the basis of a higher filing fee for those that would like to see their patents issued quickly or be prosecuted quickly.

Our concerns as practitioners with the patent system relate to the manner by which the examiners are currently applying the PTO test, and the extent to which the current PTO test is out of conformity with the position of the Court of Appeals for the Federal Circuit, and in that regard I'd simply like to complete my remarks by saying that we're very much encouraged by the position taken by the Board with respect to the Veldhuis opinion, to the extent that that is in conformity with the Arrhythmia decision of the Court of Appeals for the Federal Circuit.

So to conclude, it's our opinion that what is needed in the system is an adoption by the patent office of a test that's consistent with the case law, a cadre of examiners that understand how to apply this test, and in this regard I should note that I think Mr. Goldberg has done an excellent job of training the examiners, but -- they're coming along, but with

UNITED STATES PATENT AND TRADEMARK OFFICE
Public Hearing on Patent Protection for Software-Related Inventions
San Jose, California — January 26-27, 1994

a little more help from us practitioners on the outside I think they'll get it right at some point. But I would advise any company or individual with a software-related invention to consult with a qualified attorney, experienced in the preparation and prosecution of software-related patent applications with respect to the advantages and disadvantages of the various forms of protection.

With these elements in place, all concerned will recognize the viability of the current system of examination with respect to software-related inventions and innovations.

Thank you.

COMMISSIONER LEHMAN: Basically it's your position that we don't have much of a problem, right now, as I understand it.

MR. BENMAN: That's basically my position. I favor the current system. I think that when we get the bugs worked out, when you access the other sources of prior art, everybody will find that the system works pretty well.

COMMISSIONER LEHMAN: Do any of my colleagues have any questions or concluding remarks for this morning? If not, we will reconvene at 2:00 o'clock, at which time we will hear from Mr. Jerry Baker, Vice-President of the Oracle Corporation.

(Noon recess)

--oOo--

JANUARY 26, 1994
AFTERNOON SESSION

--oOo--

COMMISSIONER LEHMAN: Looks like we have a somewhat-dwindled group, but still an impressive audience for this afternoon. Thanks for sticking with us.

Our next witness, to start us off this afternoon, is going to be Jerry Baker, Senior Vice-President of the Oracle Corporation, and please accept our apologies, Mr. Baker, for our starting a couple minutes late. Do you want to come forward?

--oOo--

JERRY BAKER

ORACLE CORPORATION

MR. BAKER: Good afternoon, distinguished representatives of the United States Patent and Trademark Office, and members of the public. I am Jerry Baker, Senior Vice-President of Oracle Corporation and head of the company's product line development organization.

Oracle is now a one and one half billion dollar company employing over eleven thousand people worldwide. At Oracle we believe that patents are inappropriate means for protecting software and are concerned that the patent system is on the brink of having a devastating impact on the software industry. In our opinion, copyright and trade secret law is satisfactory to protect the developer's rights in software and to promote innovation in our industry.

I commend you, Commissioner LEHMAN, for the foresightedness to recognize this imminent threat, and to hold these hearings. This Administration has shown tremendous strength of character by raising such fundamental questions about its mission and objectives, and I applaud you for doing so. As we proceed through these hearings let us always keep sight of the U.S. Constitutional mandate for the patent system, to promote the progress of science and useful arts. I cannot find any evidence that patents for software will tend to achieve this purpose, indeed, every indication is to the contrary.

I will attempt to explain Oracle's thesis within the framework of the questions the PTO has propounded for this hearing. First, you ask, "What aspects of software-related invention should or should not be protectable through the patent system?" The examples specified in the question illustrate part of the problem. Software is fundamentally different from what the PTO is used to seeing. In many other industries the policy rationale for patent protection is understandable. In exchange for making their inventions available to the public, patent holders are rewarded with a seventeen-year monopoly, giving them exclusive right to this new technology. In cases where an inventor has committed substantial capital resources to the invention, this opportunity to monopolize the commercial application of the invention is justified not simply as a reward but as an incentive to motivate the developer to dedicate time and money necessary for innovation, design, production, marketing and distribution.

This policy, however, does not fit well with the software industry. Unlike many manufacturing-intensive industries, innovation and development of software products is very

UNITED STATES PATENT AND TRADEMARK OFFICE
Public Hearing on Patent Protection for Software-Related Inventions
San Jose, California -- January 26-27, 1994

rapid. Although there may be substantial development expenditure, there is an absence of tooling and production is accomplished almost instantaneously. As a result, software improvements are quickly incorporated into new versions, making product cycles very short. Because a patent takes two or more years from application to issuance, well into a product's projected life cycle, patents do not motivate companies to invest in the development, design, production and distribution of their products. In this environment a seventeen-year monopoly is completely out of context with industry reality.

Software varies from manufacturing in another key aspect. The engineering and mechanical inventions for which patent protection was devised are often characterized by large building-block inventions that can revolutionize a given mechanical process. Software seldom includes substantial leaps in technology, but rather consists of adept combinations of several ideas. A complex program may contain numerous established concepts and algorithms as well as a multitude of innovative ideas. Whether a software program is a good one does not generally depend as much on the newness of each specific technique, but instead depends on how well these are incorporated into the unique combination of known algorithms and methods. Patents simply should not protect such a technology.

The scope of what is protectable is a core issue with tremendous impact to anyone in the software industry. Oracle's answer to your question is that none of the cited examples should be protectable with the possible exception of Example F, which is not truly a software innovation, but rather an otherwise-patentable invention that just happens to be implemented on a computer.

Next, although Oracle has not yet been a defendant in a patent infringement suit, it is probably just a matter of time before we are. Our engineers and patent counsel have advised me that it may be virtually impossible to develop a complicated software product today without infringing numerous broad existing patents. Since the validity of many issued software patents is highly questionable and because Oracle is a company with sizeable resources with which to defend a lawsuit, many patent holders must be reticent to litigate an infringement action against us. Further, as a defensive strategy, Oracle has expended substantial money and effort to protect itself by selectively applying for patents which will present the best opportunities for cross-licensing between Oracle and other companies who may allege patent infringement. If such a claimant is also a software developer and marketer, we would hope to be able to use our pending patent applications to cross-license and continue our business unchanged.

But not all infringement plaintiffs are in the software business, and we would be forced to either pay royalties or risk an expensive lawsuit. Thus, to answer your next question, only if patent eligibility standards were dramatically limited could we expect to see a positive implication in the industry. And most positive would be for no software to be patentable at all.

Your next question takes us back to the Constitutional issue. Do software patents promote innovation in the field of software?

The U.S. software industry has evolved to a multibillion dollar industry that leads the world in productivity and accounts for a substantial portion of the U.S. GDP. The software industry has advanced the efficiency of other industries through the proliferation of computing and computer-controlled processes. All of these gains have come prior to the application of the patent process to software, and consequently without patent protection for software. Software companies succeed only because they continue to be innovative in bringing new and better products to the market, and these very market forces will continue to drive the software industry without patenting of software.

Finally, you asked whether a new form of protection for computer programs is needed. We do not believe one is necessary. Existing copyright law and available trade secret protections have proved very well suited to protecting computer software and they have done so in a manner that is not disruptive to software development. Copyright protects software as soon as it is written, without the expenditure of time and money on prior art searches and registration. Since computer software is considered a work of authorship under copyright law, the entire software program including each portion of code as well as the derivatives thereof are protected from copying. Developers may write software code without fear of infringing the rights of others, so long as they do not copy other developer's works. Copyright law encourages innovation since it allows everyone to take advantage of improvements in technology while protecting developers from having their specific works copied or appropriated.

At the same time, trade secret law protects developments that have not been disclosed beyond the development team. Many companies are successful in using trade secrets to establish market prominence, while the competition hurries to catch up.

Oracle has recommended that patent protection be eliminated for computer software and computer software algorithms because software patents are failing to achieve the Constitutional mandate of promoting innovation and indeed are having a chilling effect on innovative activity in our industry and because software is fundamentally different from manufactured products and these differences justify different treatment under the law.

Nevertheless, if patent law continues to apply to software, we believe that fundamental changes must be made in patent policy and procedure. Our recommendations in no way endorse the use of patents for protecting software, but the recommended changes could serve to assuage the existing problems if patents must ultimately affect software development.

However, we believe that making the necessary changes to the patent system will prove to be highly difficult to achieve. Patent law must be consistent throughout the world, and if it is to be applicable to software, it should encompass much shorter periods of protection than exist now, unified prior art searching capabilities, equal standards of novelty, the elimination of patent rules that allow patent flooding, and identical standards for prior-use restriction.

Because the evolution of software moves very quickly, the term of software protection should be cut back accordingly from the current seventeen years from grant date to three

UNITED STATES PATENT AND TRADEMARK OFFICE
Public Hearing on Patent Protection for Software-Related Inventions
San Jose, California -- January 26-27, 1994

years from the application date, that is, the application period must be dramatically reduced. A balance of fifty years protection for direct copying of code would continue to be provided by copyright law.

Also key to the success of the patent system for the software industry are the following changes. First, the prior art capabilities of PTO workers must be vastly improved to conform effectively the novelty and nonobviousness of the software patent that is the subject of applications. New classifications as well as an effort to record the current state of prior art would be necessary. This is conceptually a daunting task. Most software innovation is not recorded for public availability. Instead it is held as trade secrets.

The Software Patent Institute has been formed to build a database to assist the PTO with finding prior art, and while the SPI's intentions are admirable, it is inconceivable that developers, small and large, will be willing to give up their trade secrets or even to devote the substantial time needed to evaluate, draft and submit evidence of existing art to the SPI database.

Second, because the unusual speed with which software innovations are incorporated in products, the PTO's patent review process must be made more efficient. It should take no more than six months from application to registration. In the software industry where a patent application typically takes two or more years to process, the patented invention is frequently either widely used or obsolete by the time the registration is issued and the public discovers it is protected by a patent.

Third, examiners skilled in computer science and software programming must be trained on the nature of software inventions and the state of existing art. Many more qualified examiners must be employed at the PTO. Compensation rates equal to those provided by the industry are essential to recruit qualified personnel and to retain them at the PTO.

Fourth, the PTO in conjunction with industry must establish additional committees to clearly delineate the standards of novelty and nonobviousness that will be required for software inventions to receive patents.

Thank you for affording me the opportunity to speak today. I again commend the PTO for its willingness to face this very difficult but extremely important issue.

COMMISSIONER LEHMAN: Thank you very much, Mr. Baker. I really appreciate your coming to us. I would love to ask a bunch of questions, but I think since we got a little bit of a late start we move on, so, thank you.

Next I'd like to call Carl Silverman, Chief Counsel at Intel Corporation.

--o0o--

CARL SILVERMAN

INTEL CORPORATION

MR. SILVERMAN: I thank you. Good afternoon. My name is Carl Silverman, Chief Counsel, Intellectual Property for Intel Corporation. We understand that the Patent and Trademark Office is interested in obtaining public input on issues associated with the patenting of software-related inventions, and we're pleased that the Patent and Trademark Office invited us here today to briefly testify.

Software technology has become an integral part of virtually

all of U.S. industry, as innovators strive to develop new and improved products in today's competitive, worldwide marketplace. Now, this technology includes pure software, and software which is combined with hardware, so for example, Intel Corporation, like other successful high-technology companies, invests the efforts of its engineers and large sums of money, the shareholders' money, to develop software-related technology. In 1993 alone, Intel Corporation invested nearly one billion dollars in research and development, including a substantial amount in software-related technology. We also, we, Intel Corporation, also invested nearly two billion dollars in capital to build factories so that we can build these advanced products.

These advanced products include products such as our Pentium processor. This is a microprocessor with more than three million transistors on a single chip. This microprocessor product includes software technology in the form of microcode and other computer programs.

Now, to protect and encourage this kind of vast U.S. investment, and I'm referring to both the technical as well as the financial aspects, and, to promote the development of new and improved products, we at Intel believe that software-related technology should continue to be afforded the opportunity to obtain patent protection.

The patent system has consistently provided an incentive to expend the kind of technical and financial efforts previously testified to to develop new technology, including software-related technology. In the United States the Patent and Trademark Office carefully examines every patent application against prior art to insure that only the novel and nonobvious inventions obtain patent protection. Software-related technology is no different.

We support the current statutory law concerning patents as well as its interpretation by the courts as relating to software-related inventions. We are currently aware of no alternative to the patenting of software-related inventions that will better-serve our industry than the current patent laws.

Further, we believe it would be a mistake to treat the patenting of software-related inventions differently than the patenting of other utility inventions. In this regard, Patent and Trademark Office and the courts should be left free to develop the extent of patent protection for software-related inventions and its enforceability on a case-by-case basis until such time as it is apparent that the courts are not up to the task. This time is not at hand, rather, the courts for the most part are both interested and concerned about protecting innovative technologies such as software-related inventions.

Now, this is not to say that the current system for patenting software-related inventions is not without opportunity for improvement. For example: We understand that the Patent and Trademark Office is working to improve its library of software prior art so as to improve its ability to examine patent applications in this area. We support this effort. We urge the Patent and Trademark Office to increase its capability to examine software-related patent applications by taking whatever steps necessary to establish the best prior art software library and to increase and-or redeploy the number of patent examiners who are knowledgeable in this

UNITED STATES PATENT AND TRADEMARK OFFICE
Public Hearing on Patent Protection for Software-Related Inventions
San Jose, California -- January 26-27, 1994

crucial area.

On behalf of Intel Corporation we thank you for providing us with the opportunity to present our views on this subject, and we are delighted that the Patent and Trademark Office has encouraged this free flow of ideas so that we as a country can do the right thing here.

Thank you.

COMMISSIONER LEHMAN: Thank you very much, Mr. Silverman.

What's your view on the idea of prepublication that has been mentioned several times this morning here, that that would be one way of making certain that we wouldn't overlook some priority that we might already have missed.

MR. SILVERMAN: I apologize, Mr. Commissioner, for not being here this morning; I know generally the subject of publication, and oftentimes patent applications end up being published anyway as they're filed in non-U.S. jurisdictions, and I think that is perhaps a vehicle which would simplify some of the issues that are involved here. So I think we're open on that one.

COMMISSIONER LEHMAN: So you don't find that inherently offensive at Intel.

MR. SILVERMAN: No, I don't.

COMMISSIONER LEHMAN: One other question, too, and that is, you know, I remember the last time that I was in San Jose actually was sixteen years ago, and we were at the other end of downtown here at the old Santa Clara County Courthouse, and we had the first set of hearings. At that time I was Counsel of the House Judiciary Committee, and we had our first set of hearings that led ultimately to the legislation that became the Semiconductor Chip Protection Act of 1984, and Intel was a primary component of that. You were having problems with unauthorized reproduction of your semiconductor chips way back then, and ultimately Congress responded by creating a new form of intellectual property protection, and I'm wondering if you have any thoughts as to how that system is working and is the existing patent, copyright and mass works protection regime adequate, or in your particular area do you feel a need for either a strengthening of the mass works legislation or some alternative to that?

MR. SILVERMAN: The Mask Works Act, I think, was very necessary at the time in which it was created, and I think it's been successful with regard to those who would copy other person's or company's products. I think it's been effective there. I think these days, however, it forms a piece of the overall intellectual property protection available in this country. I think it made a lot of sense to do that then. I don't think it makes any sense to do a similar type of protection mechanism for software-related inventions.

COMMISSIONER LEHMAN: Basically you feel that you have an existing intellectual property regime with these three forms of protections that meets your needs, and it's really a question of tightening up on it, and I know you have strong international concerns, but it's really a question of enforcement and tightening up; there's no really fundamental problem with it.

MR. SILVERMAN: That's correct.

COMMISSIONER LEHMAN: Okay. Thank you very much.

Next I'd like to call Kaye Caldwell, President of the Software Entrepreneurs Forum. Maybe you can tell us a little bit about what your forum is, too. It seems to me you were at the Bree conferences before, weren't you?

--oOo--

KAYE CALDWELL

SOFTWARE ENTREPRENEURS FORUM)

MS. CALDWELL: Yes. I work with a lot of different software organizations and I'm speaking for the Software Entrepreneurs Forum today. I'm the President of that organization. I'm also the Legislative Awareness Director. SEF, as we this Software Entrepreneurs Forum, is a ten-year-old nonprofit organization of over one thousand present and future software developers. Nearly all of them are located in the Silicon Valley. We have monthly dinner meetings which attract over two hundred people and we've had as many as six hundred people. We also have eleven special-interest groups that each hold monthly meetings on a variety of technical and business topics. Our members are mostly small companies, and I think our idea of small is probably not the same as your idea of small. By small I mean one to five people in the company, very small.

The U.S. software industry is unique in that it includes a large number of very small companies. We have a thousand members just in the San Francisco Bay Area. Many of these small companies are responsible for the most creative new software developments. In the early days of microcomputer software development, nearly all software was created by individuals working on their own with one or two associates; yet these types of development environments were responsible for early word processors, spreadsheets and accounting software. In earlier generations of hardware, I'm told that it was also the case that one- or two-person companies were a major factor in leading innovations. Even today much software marketed by large software companies is initially developed by small, independent software developers.

SEF's mission is to help these small companies succeed. While SEF is local to Silicon Valley, we feel that SEF members are representative of the thousands of software entrepreneurs throughout the United States. Our members have different opinions on software patentability, indeed you're hearing from at least two of our members at other points during this hearing. Some of our members are patent holders and are strongly in favor of broad patent software protection. Other members are against software patents entirely. However, there are issues on which SEF members are in general agreement. Our members feel that the patent system favors large companies over small companies, and we feel that it's important that the patent system both in theory and in practice should not give big companies an advantage over small ones.

Most of our concerns have to do with Patent Office practices, and we understand that this subject is scheduled for hearing in February. We do appreciate the opportunity to speak on these issues today.

To the degree that software is patentable, SEF members want the patent system to produce good, clear patents, especially where the patents are important. We want patents to be issued and infringement issues resolved

UNITED STATES PATENT AND TRADEMARK OFFICE
Public Hearing on Patent Protection for Software-Related Inventions
San Jose, California — January 26-27, 1994

expeditiously.

Uncertainty as to the validity or scope of a patent hurts patentee and possible infringer alike. It makes it difficult to make decisions, to raise capital, to develop business plans and to make business decisions. Patents of uncertain scope or validity are much more damaging to small companies than large ones. Small companies can rarely afford a good legal analysis on a patent's scope and validity, and an uncertain situation can often put a major part of the small company's net worth at risk. The current patent system seems to encourage litigation. We feel that it's important to improve the patent system so that it becomes more self-enforcing.

While we realize that much progress has been made recently in the ability of the Patent Office to deal with software patents, initial progress needs to be made. In proposing the following recommendations for consideration we're less concerned with the specific suggestions than we are in highlighting what we see as problems and in stimulating the Patent Office to solve them.

Our first recommendation would be that the Patent Office should continue to improve its prior art database by adding to it textbooks, scholarly articles, user manuals of commercial products and nonpatent prior art cited in existing and pending software-related patents. This would be particularly effective if such art could be added to the PTO's computerized database, but also be useful to review the trade publications for the last ten years to identify significant software products or product enhancements so that their manuals could be included in the database.

Our second recommendation is that we realize that patent examiners must have both technical ability and a knowledge of how to apply legal principles to determine patentability. We encourage the Patent Office's recruiting of examiners with computer science knowledge. We encourage the Patent Office to continue to improve the quality and expertise of its patent examiners and software. We particularly suggest increasing the pay and professional stature of examiners so that more examiners see it as a professional career rather than just a stepping stone to private practice; I think you've heard those suggestions earlier also.

We also suggest putting a high priority on identifying and expeditiously examining patents which are likely to be asserted. We feel that it's important to identify crucial patents and to focus patent office resources on them as the place that will have the most real-world effect. The accelerated patent examination appears to be a mechanism for achieving this, but in practice the accelerated examination does not seem to be having the desired effect. We believe the criteria for making the accelerated examination also serve to select those patents which are likely to be asserted, those patents being reexamined, reissued, or where the patent holder says there's a suspected infringer.

The performance criteria for the Patent Office should give more weight to the examining of high-priority cases rather than simply counting numbers of patents examined. We suggest that expediters be responsible for getting accelerated patents through the system so they don't get stuck on individual desks. This and other problems could be reduced by tracking patents based on the length of time they've been in the Patent Office rather than their length of time on a particular desk. In brief we believe it's good public policy to identify those patents that are likely to be asserted and examine them promptly and thoroughly so as to reduce the uncertainty of the scope of those patents. This way the patent can take a place in the free-enterprise system as a negotiable commodity of reasonably-certain scope.

We understand that the Patent Office is trying out a preexamination interview. As we understand the way it works, prior to the examination the examiner, the patentee's lawyer and possibly the patentee have an interview where they attempt to convey what the invention is and to identify where relevant nonpatent prior art might be found. We commend this idea, which we think has potential to both speed the examination process and create a better-quality patent. We also commend the Patent Office for trying out new ideas on an experimental basis to try to improve the patent process.

We understand that the level of skill and the art needed to determine obviousness should be supported by printed publications. We also understand that the determination of obviousness is a legal question. However, we encourage the patent office to try to use software professionals and academics to help locate relevant printed publications which would document the level of skill in the art.

We also encourage the Patent Office to provide further education for patent applicants, which includes actual case examples illustrating how applicants can pursue the question of nonobviousness. Particularly important would be actual examples outlining the examiner's reasoning in determining nonobviousness.

We feel that there's a need for better education of the public on patents in general and software patents in particular. The reexamination process should be highlighted as a normal part of the process. The role of prior art in the reexamination process should be made known to the public and to the press in order to reduce the concerns of possible infringers.

The Commissioner has ordered a reexamination of the Compton's Multimedia patent. We applaud this action as it shows a respect for the legitimate concerns of possible infringers, especially small ones. We propose that the Commissioner, as a standard policy, order reexaminations of patents at no cost on request by small entities which both present evidence that they've been given notice on the patent and produce prior art or other evidence of invalidity.

In the interests of reducing the time and expense it takes to determine the validity and scope of patents, we propose that the law be changed in the following ways. A, have Federal judges remand all validity issues to the Patent Office for reconsideration. The courts should still be able to review such actions. B, require that anyone representing a possible infringer who has prior art on a patent send that prior art to the patent office for submission into the patent's file wrapper. The penalty for not doing so would be that the possible infringer could not use such prior art to challenge the validity of the patent. C, limit the number of reexaminations on any one patent to two except under extremely unusual cases, in order to bring forth prior art at an early point; require rather than allow that the Patent Office consider all previously-unconsidered art in a file

UNITED STATES PATENT AND TRADEMARK OFFICE
Public Hearing on Patent Protection for Software-Related Inventions
San Jose, California -- January 26-27, 1994

wrapper at any reexamination, provided such prior art is filed at some time prior to three months after the reexamination notice is published.

Finally, we would encourage the Patent Office to take full advantage of public participation in the patent process by making their internal prior art database available on electronic form via the Internet as well as placing notices of reexamination on the Internet. You spoke about this earlier today, and mentioned that this was a goal to be achieved several years down the road. Here in California there was a law passed last year that went into effect January 1st to put all pending legislation on the Internet. Last Friday that system went on-line. It took them three weeks. You might want to speak a little bit to Jim Warren who's testifying tomorrow morning. He was very much involved in getting this legislation passed and in getting this system implemented. So I think he could probably tell you something about that process.

We expect that the effects of these suggestions would be to force out prior art early on so as to more quickly determine the scope and validity of the patents.

Commissioner LEHMAN, I'd like to thank you for holding these hearings here in Silicon Valley and for giving us the opportunity to speak. Thank you.

COMMISSIONER LEHMAN: Thank you very much. I want to commend you for a very interesting catalogue of suggestions, and I think it's very gratifying how a group of individual inventors like yours, not a big corporation, can really give so much thought to something like this and come up with so many very intriguing recommendations that we're going to be looking at, and on that question of the -- putting our system on the Internet, I would just make an observation that the quantity of data in our files is a little bit larger than the legislation currently pending before the California Legislature, and there are a few more technical problems, but one of the things maybe if I can put in an advertisement, we have openings for two positions now in the Patent and Trademark Office, basically the two top people who ran our information systems program for the last seven years have retired. So we're recruiting for new people to take this over.

Obviously I think one of the problems we have now, there was a suggestion earlier that maybe we ought to move the Patent Office out here, and maybe we should move at least Group 2300 out here. I don't know. I see Gerry Goldberg is saying that wouldn't be such a bad idea, after all we went through in Washington last week. But this certainly is where the talent is, so I think we'll be publishing these openings pretty soon, and I think we'll do some aggressive recruiting out in this part of the world; and maybe you can help us to get ourselves up to snuff technologically. Maybe it won't be three weeks, but maybe it won't have to be the years that it's taken us thus far to make these improvements.

Anyway, I wanted to thank you very much for your excellent suggestions that are really appreciated. Thanks.

Next I'd like to ask Mr. James Chiddix to come forward, who is Senior Vice-President for Engineering and Technology of Time-Warner Cable.

--oOo--

JAMES CHIDDIX
TIME WARNER CABLE

MR. CHIDDIX: Good afternoon. My name is Jim Chiddix. I'm Senior Vice-President for Engineering and Technology at Time Warner Cable. Time Warner Cable is the second-largest cable operator in the United States.

COMMISSIONER LEHMAN: Can I ask, are you headquartered in New York or here?

MR. CHIDDIX: Actually in Stamford, Connecticut.

COMMISSIONER LEHMAN: Oh, really.

MR. CHIDDIX: We serve more than seven million subscribers in thirty-six states. Our parent company, Time-Warner, is the largest owner and distributor of copyrighted material in the world, and intellectual property rights are something for which we have great respect.

Two years ago we built the first one hundred and fifty-channel cable system in Queens, New York, and that remains the most advanced cable system in the world today. Currently we're building the country's first electronic superhighway, which we call the full-service network, in Orlando, Florida, and there we'll offer a host of high-speed two-way interactive services including video on demand, interactive shopping, and distance learning. Time Warner Cable plans to spend more than five billion dollars over the next five years to deploy full-service networks in the majority of our service areas across the country.

The Administration and members of Congress have indicated that building such networks is a national priority. In our experience, however, the current patent system is working against the development of an advanced communications infrastructure. Ever since we announced our full-service network plans, we and our suppliers have received a number of inquiries from individuals and companies who purport to have patent rights that cover basic but to us obvious elements of the information superhighway as well as traditional cable systems.

I'd like to describe for you two of these patents. The point is not whether these patents are valid or invalid, or whether any particular use is infringing or not infringing, although we firmly believe that nothing we are doing infringes on any valid patent. They do serve to illustrate the current patent system is out of balance and that rather than promoting the progress of science and useful arts, that system is stifling such progress.

My first example involves the Cutler patent. The Cutler patent purports to cover many uses of optical fiber to transmit television signals to receivers in the home. This patent was granted in 1979 and will expire in 1996. The use of fiber, of course, is basic to the electronic superhighway and has also been used for many years in traditional cable systems. Indeed, Time Warner Cable has been a pioneer in the deployment of broad-band optical fiber in cable systems. The inventor of the Cutler patent did not invent optical fiber.

Rather he merely filed a patent for using fiber to transport video signals to the home. The patent statute says that patents are not to be granted if the subject matter as a whole would have been obvious at the time the invention

UNITED STATES PATENT AND TRADEMARK OFFICE
Public Hearing on Patent Protection for Software-Related Inventions
San Jose, California — January 26-27, 1994

was made to a person having ordinary skill in the art to which subject matter pertains. I'm not a lawyer, but it seems to me that the idea of using optical fiber to transport video signals to television sets is not only obvious, but also inherent in the fiber optic medium itself, which was conceived as an information conduit. If such a patent were valid, I would think it would also have been possible to obtain patents after the invention of television for using the medium to transmit drama, sports or news programming. These, however, are merely self-evident uses that are inherent in the medium of television, just like video transport is inherent in the medium of optical fiber.

My second example involves the Starside patents which purport to cover a wide variety of features used in connection with electronic program guides. Electronic program guides are on-screen guides that provide program listings for channels that are broadcast or provided by a cable system. Starside is a number of patents, but the features I discuss here are purportedly covered by a patent granted in 1987 and another that is currently pending before the Patent Office.

Pursuant to this patented application, Starside apparently claims and seeks protection for the following electronic program guide features. First, the ability to move a cursor of automatically-varying size about on an onscreen program guide, to highlight a particular program on the schedule and then press a button on a remote control to tune the channel on which that program is being transmitted. Second, the ability to combine two or more criteria, such as sports and football, to obtain a listing of the times and channels on which programmings filling those criteria will be telecast.

Again, to me these features seem obvious and inherent in the technology that provides them. Daily newspapers have long provided channel listings, often using a grid format that shows what programs are on what channel at what time. In addition, individual broadcast channels and cable systems have long-telecast on-screen programming schedules. When a television viewer uses such a schedule he finds a program of interest, identifies the channel, and punches the number into the remote. The Starside system merely does this tuning process automatically through a straightforward transfer of the process to a computer. Similarly, when I want to watch football games on television, I simply scan the program schedule for such programs. It would be a simple but somewhat time-consuming task to write out a list of such programs, but again, preparing lists from data based on multiple criteria is a simple, straightforward and obvious computer application.

Under existing law, patents for what I've just described may be valid or invalid. As I said at the beginning of my remarks, however, in either case, such patents present impediments to progress. If such patents are found to be valid, surely the patent system has gone too far in providing protection for what would seem obvious to a layperson, let alone to a person have ordinary skill in the art. The result of awarding such patents at best results in added costs for no added value, if a license is obtained, and at worst prevents consumers from fully realizing the benefits of technology if a license cannot be obtained at a reasonable price.

If such patents would ultimately be found to be invalid, however, the patent system would still not be working

properly. Some of the Starside patents are currently being challenged in court. Business, however, cannot come to a halt in the meantime. Also, litigation is costly, slow, and never free from risk.

Rather than expend time and money on litigation, many prudent business people will choose to avoid the problem. Indeed, one of our suppliers of set-top boxes has informed us that rather than challenge the Starside patents, they will instead defeature the boxes they are making for one of our cable systems, removing ability of those boxes to provide some of the features that Starside claims are covered by its patents. This is not an uncommon or irrational decision. This supplier will be spending many millions of dollars to manufacture these new boxes. Even though they believe that Starside patents are not valid, it is simply not worth the risk and the cost of fighting them in court. Of course our supplier can always attempt to obtain a license for these features, but again this would result in added cost for what in our view provides no real added value.

So in our view, the present system of patent protections is not optimally promoting innovation in the field of software-related inventions. Rather, the current system is in some important instances stifling innovation, increasing costs and leading to defeaturing rather than fostering the development of new and better products and services. However, it is not the framework of the system that is the problem. The statutory tests of obviousness, and the person of ordinary skills standard, in themselves strike the proper balance.

What is needed then is not a new framework for patent protection for software-related inventions, but a more rigorous application of the present standards. For one thing, obviousness should include routine applications of a given technology regardless of whether there is prior art showing that particular application. For another, any invention that merely transfers a series of routine tasks to a computer should also be viewed as obvious.

As your Notice for these hearings states, the computer software industry has evolved into a critical component of the U.S. economy. Indeed, the importance of this component is growing greatly every day as the computer, cable and telephone industries continue to converge. If the United States is going to continue to be a the forefront of these crucial industries, it is imperative that the patent system be restored to its proper balance so that it can properly foster rather than frustrate innovation.

Thank you.

COMMISSIONER LEHMAN: Thank you very much, Mr. Chiddix. Time-Warner's certainly a company, unlike some of the other people who have testified, who is well-able to use every legal technique at its disposal to protect its rights, and does so if it has difficulties. I'm, I -- it's interesting to me that you haven't -- you have never apparently used the reexamination system to attack some of these patents that you disagree with. Is that because you did not feel the problem was in the prior art that was examined, that it was more the legal standard that was applied by the patent examiner, or is there some other reason why you failed to use the existing examination system?

MR. CHIDDIX: These are both very current cases, and I'm

UNITED STATES PATENT AND TRADEMARK OFFICE
Public Hearing on Patent Protection for Software-Related Inventions
San Jose, California — January 26-27, 1994

not sure that all avenues have been explored. The obviousness argument is one though that even reexamination may not be fully armed to deal with.

COMMISSIONER LEHMAN: I take it you don't share the view of some of the witnesses that we should completely eliminate software patents, rather, we should tighten up on the legal standard of patentability for software patents.

MR. CHIDDIX: Yes. That's correct.

COMMISSIONER LEHMAN: Thank you very much. Are there any other questions? If not, thank you very much.

Next I'd like to ask Wallace Judd, the President of Mentrix Corporation to come forward if he would please.

Is he not here? In that case I think we'll move on to Robert May, Ikonic Corporation. Is he here?

Okay, well, then we're -- this is why we ask people to be here at least twenty minutes ahead of time, the scheduled time, because we can see what happens.

The next person on my list is Pete Antoniak of Solar Systems Software. He's not here? Mr. Antoniak is not here? Is Professor Hollaar here? Good. Since you had to come all the way from Utah, you're —

MR. HOLLAAR: Early.

COMMISSIONER LEHMAN: You're early. So you'd help us out and maybe some of these other people will arrive. Thank you very much, Professor, for joining us.

—oOo--

LEE HOLLAAR

UNIVERSITY OF UTAH

MR. HOLLAAR: My name is Lee Hollaar. I'm a Professor of Computer Science at the University of Utah where I teach the Senior Software Development Laboratory and also teach computer intellectual property law within the Department of Computer Science. I also conduct research into information retrieval systems. I've been involved with computers for almost three decades and received my Ph.D. in Computer Science in 1975 from the University at Illinois. I'm also a registered patent agent working with the Salt Lake law firm of Van Cott Bagley Cornwall and McCarthy primarily with computer-related inventions. I hold one United States patent and I have another patent pending. The views I'll be expressing are my own and not necessarily those of the University of Utah or any other organization.

First I'd like to thank the Commissioner's staff for the opportunity to testify regarding these important matters and to commend them on holding these hearings. I'd also like to congratulate the office for making their decision to accept comments electronically and to make the comments and transcripts of these hearings available on the Internet.

Today what I'd like to do is cover a few points from my dual perspective as a computer scientist and also a patent practitioner. I'll be following up this testimony with written comments.

One of the things I would like to mention is that there are a number of assumptions that seem to be taken for granted about the differences of software and its patentability that may not actually be true, and should be examined. One is that there's the assumption that computer software is a fast-moving technology and that therefore a lesser patent

term -- I've heard three years suggested -- may be appropriate. Interestingly enough, about two weeks ago Butler Lamson gave an address at the University of Utah, he's one of the inventors of the Alto Computer and a number of other innovations from Xerox Park, and he indicated that from at least his point of view much of the innovation going on in computers is not the result of computer software, but the computer hardware now available at much faster speeds with more memories, enabling techniques that were known in the laboratories many years ago to be possible now and to be available to the masses. In fact he made the statement which many people disagreed with, but it certainly caught people's attention, that from his point of view with the exception of spreadsheets there's been no surprises in computer science since 1975. It's interesting to note that anything which you filed an application on in 1975 and a patent would have issued, the patent would have been expiring about this time. It's also interesting to note that the fundamental books on computer algorithms, written by Donald Knuth came out when I was a graduate student approximately two decades ago. Again, if everything in those books was patented, the patents would be expired by this time.

Much of computer science I see, my students and so forth, consists of reinventing wheels. A large amount of that is because people don't check prior art and a large amount of that is because there's no good prior art collections to check, and I think -- and I will comment on this -- that this is one of the problems that has been caused by the two decades of the Patent Office having at best ambivalent attitudes toward the patentability of computer software and not using the patent system to draw the trade secrets and the other art into the printed publications of U.S. patents. I was involved with developing a computer system in 1969 which is still running. If I had patented every technique in that computer system, and it still represents the basis for a state-of-the-art system, those patents would have expired five or six years ago on it.

Comment has been made that patents can restrict developers, and that's certainly the case, but that's true on every patent in every area of art. It's not particularly true for computer science in any respect. The comments have been made about bad patents, patents which have prior art problems, poor examination, again these exist in every art unit. Perhaps it may be worse in the computer art area because there was this period of time when the Patent Office was denying computer patents and therefore not building their prior art collection, not encouraging the submission of patent applications which would mature to patents and go into the prior art collection on it.

In my recent practice I've found the inexperience that people have talked about with the examiners to be diminishing and I've found that the examiner's doing quite a good job given the constraints of trying to examine very complex art in a wide variety of areas. I think also that the patent office has received bad press due to both people who should know better and also the people providing the information not knowing enough about the patent system. Too often comments are based on the title or at best the abstract of the patent, and not the claims, which indicate what the true invention is. Often this is compounded by press releases

UNITED STATES PATENT AND TRADEMARK OFFICE
Public Hearing on Patent Protection for Software-Related Inventions
San Jose, California -- January 26-27, 1994

from patentees trying to make their patents seem more important than it really may be.

There have been a number of problems caused by the past PTO position on patents. One, as I mentioned, is the poor prior art collection, which has been difficult, because in many cases computer inventions aren't as self-revealing as mechanical invention. When you sit down and sue a spreadsheet or another computer, you're aware that you're using a spreadsheet, but you may not be aware of the order that cells are being recalculated or the particular algorithm that is being used for justifying the text. The patent system would have eliminated this problem by forcing inventors, in trade for the patent monopoly, to reveal their trade secrets, to reveal how this would work, thereby giving a prior art collection for people who want to develop follow-on systems, and because of the distinctive claiming of patents as opposed to copyright, providing an indication of what an inventor can do to avoid the patent and yet produce an improved product on it.

Computer scientists suffer from a poor tradition of publishing their algorithms, especially those involved in industry, and also in looking at prior art. I often think that many of my students wouldn't know where the library is on campus if you ask them, and when they start out on a project the idea of going to the library is not the first thing that crosses their mind, and certainly the idea of doing a patent search to see what's in the prior art and see how to accomplish things is far from their mind.

I think that while the Software Patent Institute should be congratulated for what they're doing, their idea of collecting prior art is doomed to failure because especially for old inventions, it is very hard to determine what is prior art or what are the novel things. In the typeset system I wrote many years ago there were probably hundreds of things which may be novel or may at least be prior art for future inventions, and it would be hard to enumerate them.

Other problems caused by the past PTO position is both in the disclosure and in particular in the claims' obtuse language, unclear claims, as attempts to avoid a perceived perception of the PTO position on Section 101, claiming things which are clearly software programs as computer building blocks. I think of one patent issued to Thompson where not only is the source code listed, but they tell you how to build it out of computer modules from Digital Equipment, out of flipflops for this searching technique. No one believes that that's how they intended to implement the invention. More importantly, the Section 101 babble often takes the steam out of the examiners. After fighting the 101 fight there may be very little fight left in them for the proper 102 and 103 questions. I recently reviewed the file wrappers of two patents for a client who wanted to know their scope, and was shocked by how little prosecution history there was after the 101 arguments had been resolved, even though one patent had a continuation application filed and had been pending for a number of years on it, virtually no 102, 103 arguments after the initial 101.

I think the patent system has produced distortions in copyright laws, courts have held it necessary to provide protection beyond literal copying so that we have decisions like Whelan or the current Lotus against Borland decision, trying to extend copyright perhaps too far from its intended purpose, and as I said we have the loss of past disclosures because the Patent Office wasn't accepting patent applications, which has caused much reinventing of past techniques.

The solutions? I think one is to eliminate much of the current 101 confusion, and in fact go back to the basic principles of inventorship, that patents are, if there is something useful being produced, should probably meet the 101 test, and the real battle of whether the patents should be issued should be tried on 102 and 103 issues.

The comments have been made about laying open files during prosecution, and I strongly support that. I think it's the one hope we have for getting the prior art. Both laying it open at some fixed period of time such as eighteen months has been suggested to eliminate the so-called submarine patents, and also laying it open sometime after initial examination by the Patent Office. I would make sure that the file isn't laid open before the first office action such that the applicant has a chance to withdraw the application based on the position of the Patent Office and the prior art that's been found, and make an intelligent decision of whether to keep it as trade secret.

I would recommend that there be a period after the office determines that a patent is allowable that people can submit prior art for consideration by the examiner. This could be done by using technology to widely distribute the notice that this patent is about to issue and a representative claim and has some method for retrieving of the application, perhaps tied in with the project ongoing for the electronic filing of applications. This shouldn't be an advisory procedure, but a way of having the prior art brought to the attention of the examiner. I think in my case of the old system that I have, I certainly could see if there was an application and claims whether I had prior art on that and submit that to the attention of the Office much easier than I could go through a very complex system and identify every piece of prior art such that it could be searchable by the Patent Office.

That concludes my remark, thank you.

COMMISSIONER LEHMAN: Thank you very much, Professor, that was some really very helpful testimony. Appreciate you coming over here to California to talk with us. Thank you.

Next I'd like to ask Dennis Fernandez. Is he here? For Fenwick and West? Okay.

Welcome.

--oOo--

DENNIS FERNANDEZ

FENWICK AND WEST

MR. FERNANDEZ: Good afternoon, ladies and gentlemen, my name is Dennis Fernandez. I am a registered patent attorney at the Silicon Valley-based technology law firm of Fenwick and West. I am speaking today on my behalf.

Before practicing law I was an electrical engineer and a technical manager for several years at various companies in the computer and electronics industry including NCR, AT&T, Digital Equipment Corporation, Raytheon, RayCal Limited, where I did semiconductor chip design and processing as well as managed marketing and distribution of semiconductor chip products. Currently I specialize in patent prosecution and litigation in the semiconductor chip industry.

As you know, in this highly competitive electronics industry, intellectual property protection has become a very important part of doing business. This afternoon, I wish respectfully to share with you a few brief comments based on my practical experience in the semiconductor industry. As an electronics engineer and also as a legal counsel I believe I can provide many comments on how software patents have already or might in the future impact the business interests of semiconductor and software companies in the Valley, and because of the limited time which has been allotted for speaking I direct my comments only to a few points which are relevant to chip design software.

I believe these comments may reflect the interest of companies who do business in the area known as electronic design automation, or, EDA. EDA products refer generally to sophisticated software written for automating the highly complex process for designing and testing semiconductor chips and related system boards.

In this EDA context, I offer comments on the following three areas, number one, special technical need for software patent protection; number two, practical timing problems in U.S. patents, and number three, apparent effect of software patents on innovation.

First point, which is special technical need for software patent protection. Because of the highly functional nature of technical innovations that are developed for EDA software products, patenting seems to be an appropriate way for legal protection. For example, EDA software typically includes software programs for synthesizing logic circuits, generating test program vectors or simulating digital and analog system components. These software functions involve fairly abstract ideas, which would not be protectable ordinarily under copyright law, but would be protectable under patent method or apparatus claims if sufficiently inventive. Thus, due to the largely functional nature of innovations in EDA software, I believe that patent protection is appropriate.

Second point. There are practical timing problems in U.S. patents. There appear to be two practical problems which may apply to EDA companies with respect to timing related to U.S. patent applications. First, the seventeen-year patent duration may be too long. In the context of the EDA industry, where software products typically have product lives that are less than half this duration, it might be more appropriate to provide a shorter period of exclusivity. Second, the current two- to three-year backlog in the United States Patent and Trademark Office, especially in the electronic and software arts, may pose some problems to companies in the EDA industry, both for those companies who wish to enforce their patents during the market window available for their software products, and also for those companies who wish to learn about the existence of relevant patents and thereby avoid them.

Third and last point, the apparent effect of software patents on innovation. In the highly competitive EDA business, particularly in the Silicon Valley, it has been my experience in a number of recent cases that the presence of relevant software patents do not necessarily serve to impede or deter competitive product development. Typically, clients in this business tend to be fairly sophisticated in our understanding of patent enforcement matters. Furthermore, these individuals are aggressive entrepreneurs who are doing pioneering technical work in product development and are typically backed financially by venture capitalist institutions. These individuals often find ways to design around even what appear initially to be fairly broad patent claims. Also, it has been my experience that such EDA clients are often able to obtain reasonable licensing terms or raise reasonable arguments for invalidity based on relevant prior art, thereby providing themselves with opportunities to make, sell or use their EDA products, possibly without legal liability. It does not seem to me, therefore, that software patents have necessarily stifled competition, at least in the electronic design automation industry at this time.

This concludes my prepared comments. I thank you very much for your consideration.

COMMISSIONER LEHMAN: Thank you very much, Mr. Fernandez. So basically the bottom line is that you really don't think we need fundamental changes in the system, but you think we might want to deal with certain issues regarding the EDA industry like the appropriateness of length of terms.

MR. FERNANDEZ: Term limits. Yes.

COMMISSIONER LEHMAN: Yes. Thank you very much.

Next I believe that Pete Antoniak has arrived now from Solar Systems Software, so we can put him back on the agenda. Come forward, please.

--oOo--

PETE ANTONIAK
SOLAR SYSTEMS SOFTWARE

MR. ANTONIAK: My name is Pete Antoniak and I'm a professional engineer. I'm looking at the agenda today and see a lot of CEOs, chairmans of boards, and lawyers, patent agents, et cetera. I see very few engineers and software developers.

COMMISSIONER LEHMAN: You can probably help us a little bit if you just make sure that that mike you're talking into –

MR. ANTONIAK: Can you hear me now? Everybody? Good. You see very few engineers, software developers. I develop educational game software. I also teach, consult and program for others in order to supply this software habit of mine. For the past ten years I've been making about a third as much of money as I was making as an executive for GTE Sprint, and I do this because I'm looking for the big payoff, developing the great American software.

Approximately six years ago I started development of an educational game concept that I thought was quite unique and I was totally aware that nobody else had done anything like I was doing. I attended a seminar up in San Francisco, I believe by Prentice-Hall, in which I believe somebody from this panel or somebody from the Patent Office gave a talk and encouraged people like me to go ahead and get patents on our software. I was sent some brochures and literature and it seemed like a fairly friendly environment. I said, By golly, I'll do it. I'm the type of guy that repairs my own car and so I went to it.

When I developed my program, and I can understand from people out there that, you know, I'm a little naive in this, I

UNITED STATES PATENT AND TRADEMARK OFFICE
Public Hearing on Patent Protection for Software-Related Inventions
San Jose, California — January 26-27, 1994

wanted a program that could make an educational game out of any type of material, any subject, any grade level and any language. Particularly I wanted a game that did not require the need of a keyboard, no typing required. And I came up with a very interesting concept. My game used objects on the computer screen that represent abstract ideas and concepts. The player moves the objects around on the screen to represent their relationships. The concept I developed is simple, compelling and fun, and not only was there no prior art, but even to this day, and this is six years after development there still is nobody even doing anything like I'm doing. I have essentially no infringers.

I purchased and read the book called Patent It Yourself by David Pressman, which is kind of a bible in this industry of people who are inventors like me. I also learned that David was a fellow-member of Mensa, lived in San Francisco and for a fee of seventy-five dollars a review, now one hundred, would review my application. I spent six months developing an application, writing and rewriting it. He had about three or four times to review it and I sent it in as a patent application.

My first office action came about six months later when all my claims were rejected on the basis of prior art. Now anybody in this business understands that this is very common. I was upset at the time, extremely upset, but have since come to understand that this is normal. I can't complain about this as I was told by somebody in the Patent Office, this is the way the game was played.

However, what I can complain about is the fact that none of the prior art had anything to do with computers. I was confronted with such things as jigsaw puzzles, board games, card games, and classroom wall charts. One of the prior art patents was a few months short of one hundred years old. I spent a great deal of time writing responses, and it was very frustrating. It was unbelievable to me that anyone could even connect my program with the prior art that was being used. I felt that there was some kind of a logic gap between me and the examiner. In the end the examiner maintained that my arguments were not persuasive enough and I got a final rejection.

I phoned the examiner, and during the interview it came out that she was a mechanical engineer, did not have a computer and didn't know much about computers in general. She told me that her expertise was in games. I presented a logical set of arguments to get her to admit over the phone that the prior art she was using was absolutely not applicable to my claims.

She then stated that she was sure that there was something out there, perhaps in child development books or something that duplicated my computer game on a table, with three-by-five cards, a pencil and perhaps a teacher to look over as a referee or a judge. If she had the time she would find it. I said that a table was different from a computer in that a table could not know where those three-by-five cards were, whereas the computer screen did and could do instant evaluation well beyond the capabilities of a teacher. She said that I should explain that if I was to reapply. Well, essentially what I was doing defending an invention that didn't exist but only in her mind and which she didn't really tell me about.

She finally requested a different examiner. David Pressman also advised me to request a different examiner. He even made a few derogatory comments about my examiner being young and experienced. This was the luck of the draw and I just had to live with it.

I resubmitted, respectfully requesting a different examiner, waited six months, and the first Office action came back, and you guessed it, I had the same examiner. I went through another frustrating round going back and forth. I felt sometimes like I was arguing with a brick wall and there was some sort of a hidden agenda that no matter what I said that I wasn't going to get a patent.

After the final rejection the second time, I traveled to Crystal City, had an interview with the examiner and her supervisor. I arranged to use a computer store across the street from the Patent Office and demonstrated my software. I quickly became aware, to my dismay, from the examiner's reaction to the program, that she really didn't even understand what it was that I had submitted, and more importantly how it worked. This was moot, however, because just prior to the demonstration her supervisor had promised that if I were to resubmit again that I would get a different examiner.

I resubmitted a third time, and again was rejected in the initial office action. However, the tone of the rejection is different. It was obvious that the new examiner had read the application and understood it. He pointed out discrepancies in grammar between the original application and the claims. He pointed out some tactical errors in the claims and he recommended ways to correct things. The prior art he introduced seemed more pertinent to the claim and the invention. I almost cried, not that I had been rejected a third time, but because at least I had someone whose attitude was not, "How do we get this guy out of here," but, "How do we get this application in proper order to be patentable."

In the next two weeks I will submit a file wrapper continuation and start Round 4. The last thing my new examiner told me, however, when I called him up, was that he is now under pressure because of the Compton's fiasco, whatever you want to call it, and that he'd probably be throwing a lot more prior art at me. I'd rather take a stoic attitude about my experience with my Patent Office. I'd like to say that an easy patent that has not been exposed to a lot of prior art is not a patent that would stand up to a challenge; this has often been said, that if you get a patent too easy you may have a problem with it later on. However, I believe that the type of prior art used in my case was so nonapplicable as we go to the background, the experience of the examiner, that for all intents and purposes I am starting over, having wasted four years, many thousands of dollars in fees, approximately eight man months of my time that I could have been using in development, in marketing a product.

My claims are not earth-shaking. They're not controversial. They only protect my program. I will note that even though, and I'd mentioned before, I haven't shown it to a lot of people, I'm always aware of what's going out there, I've yet to find anybody that would be considered an infringer of my product. I'm a little guy; I'm the inventor. I'm the software-equivalent of the inventor, and my bottom line in all this is that if the Patent Office is doing a good job -- I'm not recommending a lot of changes to the Patent Office --

UNITED STATES PATENT AND TRADEMARK OFFICE
Public Hearing on Patent Protection for Software-Related Inventions
San Jose, California -- January 26-27, 1994

it's just if they're doing a good job, you know, I would -- I would probably have a patent right now, or at least I would know I couldn't get a patent right now. Right now I've spent a lot of time on absolutely, you know, nonsensible things. And I kind of consider, like when I took Latin in high school, you know, it's one of those things to give you some discipline. I can certainly write a claim. Jeez, you know, I can do very well. Matter of fact, as a member of the Software Entrepreneurs Forum I even had a conference about a year and a half ago in which we had the whole afternoon devoted to doing patents. I brought in a patent agent and we discussed these things. I'm pretty much up on it. However, I'd rather have a patent, rather have the, you know, the rights thereto, that I may attain to.

Anyway, that's it, and that's my bottom line, and if I have any time left, I can entertain any questions.

COMMISSIONER LEHMAN: Thank you very much, Mr. Antoniak. I would just say that the patent system is not set up to be a pro se system, and we have a lot of problems in that and we're here to help solve those. But part of being a good patent lawyer is to understand the art of lawyering, and oftentimes that involves making certain that your claims are drawn in such a way that you get to the right patent-examining group -- doesn't sound like your patent originally went to Group 2300 -- and that it get to the right examiner, and I'm very sympathetic with your difficulties that you had, but I think that when one attempts to bootstrap their case and you try to do brain surgery self-taught that you're inevitably going to run into some difficulties, that are hard for us to try to address in the system.

MR. ANTONIAK: Let me add that all along the way I was using a patent agent to review everything I set in. First it was Pressman and then it was a registered patent agent here in the Valley who has done software for the last twenty years. I looked to the Patent Office like a pro se inventor. In reality, though, everything was checked and rechecked and gone over by a patent agent who gave sound advice. All along the line they were saying, "Yes. This is definitely patentable. Matter of fact, what's somewhat ironic is that when I submitted my thing to Dave Pressman the first time around, he said somebody else had also submitted something that he said was absolutely not patentable, and what he was surprised was he sent it in and got a patent right off the bat with very little problems. I've run into that individual because it turned out I know him anyway, and Dave was surprised that mine had such a hard time getting a patent. Again, the wording was right, everything was pretty much right, my logic was right.

I think that the term pro se inventor, you know, have said, "Okay, here's a category, we don't have this guy the, you know, the professionalism that you'd give perhaps a patent attorney who can call us on it." Now that's my, that's my personal judgment on this, and I could well be wrong, but this is an experience; a lot of emotions and a lot of energy's gone into this, and -- you know, what can I say? I've been -- I've been to Vietnam and I've learned a lot from that, too. So.

COMMISSIONER LEHMAN: Well, I'm sorry you had that difficulty and I'm hopeful as a result of these hearings we'll get the problem fixed. Thank you very much.

MR. ANTONIAK: Thank you.

COMMISSIONER LEHMAN: Next I'd like to call Mr. Robert May from Ikonix Interactive, I believe.

--oOo--

ROBERT MAY

IKONIC INTERACTIVE

MR. MAY: I want to thank you very much for coming out to Silicon Valley and also for slipping me in unannounced. I'd expected to be out of town today and at the last moment my travel plans changed.

I want to give a quick perspective on the lay of the land from Ikonic Interactive. We're a software developer located in San Francisco. We're a multimedia developer with about nine years of experience in this business. Current clients include Time Warner for whom we're designing the user interface and software for the full-service network in Orlando, Florida; Dow Jones for whom we just recently completed the redesign of the Wall Street Journal for PDAs; a variety of other projects. So we're intimately acquainted with some of these issues and I'd like to just give you a snapshot of some of our perspective.

I spent my morning on the phone with one of our clients negotiating contracts, and I should say, number one, I am not an attorney, and it's only through the tutelage of Kate Spellman up at Steinhart and Falconer, our IP attorney, and David Hayes down here at Fenwick and West that I know just enough to be dangerous, but notwithstanding that, I often rush in where angels fear to tread, and I wanted to discuss two key issues that we face every day, and just to give you some data with which to make some decisions.

I should also say in the spirit of full disclosure, we do have a software patent application under way, another one that we're considering, and I come here as a supporter of the notion of software patents, and more specifically, interface patents. Notwithstanding that, a single biggest problem I'd say from a business exposure standpoint is that we are often asked by our clients to indemnify them, that we have not incorporated prior art or other patents in our work. Given the way that the prior art search has to be conducted at this point it's very very difficult for us to indemnify our clients to that, and I would respectfully suggest two possible solutions to that.

And the first would be that in my midnight reading of patents and patent law, which I've been doing the last year or so, I've learned that things like the Compton's patent have many many many claims attached to them, and it's very very difficult to understand, let alone plan for the implications of those claims. Originally as I understand it, patent law was designed to address inventions that were reduced to practice, and it seems to me that it might be a useful distinction to separate claims very specifically to those that are actually reduced to practice and are shown to be reduced to practice and those that are speculative and looking for future technologies. And as a nonattorney I've got a very difficult time when I'm faced with trying to judge that and then promise in a contract that I will in fact not -- not infringe on those claims.

Number two, recently the FCC decided to free up 10(k)s and other public filing information and make that available on the Internet; previously it was available on Meade and I believe maybe Lexis and Nexis. Currently I'm not aware of a way to research patent information by public, without signing onto Lexis, undergoing quite an expensive search process, and insofar as it is public information I'd like to urge you to make that information available on the Internet and make it available publicly.

Second issue that we're confronted with very frequently, and this wraps around both patent issues and copyrights and others --

COMMISSIONER LEHMAN: Can I ask you a question. What kind of information for somebody like you would be useful? You know, there's everything from the full text of prior-issue patents and all of the company technical drawings to, you know, abstracts of the patent. What kind of -- when you're talking about making things available on the Internet, what kind of information of that type would be useful to you?

MR. MAY: Yes, sir. Given the example that I just gave, from a business person's perspective, I'd like to see the whole thing, because I'm being asked to indemnify my client against all claims. A helpful start would be the abstract, but lamentably, I've got to be familiar with the art to the extent that I can be. It would help me very much if there were to be drawings, et al. Does that answer your question?

COMMISSIONER LEHMAN: Yes. Yes, it does.

MR. MAY: Okay. The second area that we experience in day-to-day is again as I said, broadly a problem across both patent law, copyright law, and I'd like to just raise it in the context of patent law here today, and that is the difficulty between what current practice is and what we'd like to see practice moved to, and that is the concept of work made for hire wherein typically a small company like ours is doing work for a larger client, who attempts to get us to engage in that work under work made for hire, which means that, as you know, they own all patent rights and copyrights and trade drafts, et cetera. Very difficult to conduct business in this way and to grow a business in this way.

So we've been successful ourselves and I urge other folks out there in our business to move to a license strategy where in fact we retain the rights to underlying key concepts and intellectual property that we develop and license that in perpetuity on a royalty-free basis to our client.

One of the key problems with that approach is the ambiguity in copyright law between what's called look and what's called feel, and I would urge you and the folks you work with to turn your attention to that ambiguity and try to address that, and the specific case in point is that when we're faced with producing a project for say Time News On Demand for Time Warner, it's one thing to grant them the rights to look at that program and morally and ethically and by all other business means. I'm absolutely committed not to producing work for another client that copies and looks the same as the work that I do for my initial client. At the same time, in the pursuit of my business, we often enjoy the discovery of elements that help us do the job better for the next person, and the current ambiguity in copyright law makes it very difficult to parse out, to separate out what is look from what is feel, and feel, as you know, in the Apple Microsoft Case has been pulled out to mean basically menu command structures, things like that.

So that's the underlying structure that we need to have in what we call our multimedia toolbox in order to ply our trade, and to the extent that we are forced by circumstance or by the size of our business in the marketplace to give up those rights in a work-made-for-hire scenario, it's very difficult for us to ply our trade in the future. Like the carpenter being told that they can't use a particular jig that makes them drill holes faster, it cuts down on our efficiency and our ability to carry on our business.

So I wanted to bring these two points to mind just to give you a snapshot of what it's like out here on the frontier of the Information Superhighway, but these are key issues for us and I'd welcome your attention to those.

COMMISSIONER LEHMAN: Part of that problem that you have, and I don't mean in any sense to suggest there isn't merit to your substantive ideas about scope of copyright protection, but is part of the problem there that in your situation when you mentioned Time Warner, they're a client, you're a small company, a small entrepreneur, that you just don't have the marketing power basically to avoid being, you know, strong-armed into signing work-made-for-hire agreements that would mean that you have to give away more than you'd like to give away. I mean is that one of the reasons this becomes really acute? You just -- Ideally, you know, you don't have to -- you work under conditions that you want to work under and you can say, Well, I'm sorry, I'm not going to give away some of my techniques that I would otherwise give away, but you just can't do that because you don't have the market clout. Is that a problem?

MR. MAY: Well, I think it's tempting to paint the big company as the bad guy and the little company as the Don Quixote. I would suggest from personal experience that large companies in point of fact, once this distinction, this difficulty is raised, they're willing to look at solutions that work for both sides. There is a reflexive tendency to turn to work made for hire as something that quote has been done in the past, and it's always been good enough. Happily we've been able to negotiate positions with our clients that enables us to move forward, but yes, I think in some instances you're correct, if you're a smaller company, if you haven't been able to build your multimedia tool kit and you come in with just a hammer and saw sometimes it's easy to be bulldozed, to mix my metaphors.

COMMISSIONER LEHMAN: Thank you very much.

MR. MAY: Thank you. Appreciate it.

COMMISSIONER LEHMAN: Next I'd like to, back on our regular schedule here, and I'd like to ask Mr. Steven Henry from Wolf, Greenfield & Sacks, came all the way from Boston.

--oOo--

STEVEN HENRY

WOLF, GREENFIELD & SACKS, P.C.

MR. HENRY: Thank you, Mr. Commissioner and distinguished panel members. I'd like to begin my comments just by stating who I am. I'm a patent attorney in a large intellectual property firm, approximately forty-five professionals, about half of whom deal with the computer industry, hardware and software. We have considerable experience in our client's experiences on all sides of these matters.

UNITED STATES PATENT AND TRADEMARK OFFICE
Public Hearing on Patent Protection for Software-Related Inventions
San Jose, California -- January 26-27, 1994

To back into my remarks, I am a strong advocate of the patent system and I have seen it work time and again in the software industry as well as other industries. I have seen no fundamental differences in the software industry other than tentativeness in applying the existing rules, and the problems that other speakers have addressed with respect to the ability of examiners to get at the prior art, which is indeed a serious problem. I don't believe the software industry operates under substantially different economic principals than any other industry, or that the people in that industry are driven by a different human nature.

Professor Hollaar addressed many of the points, made many of the recommendations that I would like to make to this body, and I certainly endorse what he said. I'd like to, before proceeding, go one step further and address a topic or two that he did not address, and specifically the issue of reexamination as a cure for defective examination in the first place. If one looks at the statistical studies that have been done of reexamination, and one takes into account the kind of anecdotal experiences that we have had, reexamination is tilted in favor of supporting the conclusions originally reached by the Patent and Trademark Office, not through any intentional bias, but that's what the statistics indicate; and number two, it is severely limited and was intentionally limited when it was fashioned, limited to consideration of patents and printed publications. The problems of examiners not understanding what they're looking at not addressed, the opportunities for testimony are not provided. If one has an initially-weak examination and it is then reinforced by a faulted reexamination system, we've compounded the problem; we haven't addressed the problem. Though it takes money principally to free up manpower to hold hearings and to broaden proceedings, I believe that there is no cure for the problem other than the money, the time and the increased training.

In written remarks we will address the overall legal and theoretical issues raised in your Notice. I'd like to take a few minutes to talk about some practical, anecdotal experience.

COMMISSIONER LEHMAN: Can I ask a question? You know, you're talking about the money that would be involved and the change of procedure that would permit us and maybe encourage us to take oral testimony and to get at nonwritten prior art, but to some degree -- life is not, you know, totally fair, but to some degree, and I assume that would partly be on the motion of the parties seeking reexamination if you wanted to have reexamination just on the basis if you couldn't afford, for example, to support coming to Washington, getting witnesses there and so on and so forth, you could still go forward with the written record. I mean it's not automatically implying a greater burden, financial burden for everybody.

MR. HENRY: Certainly the requester could go on a written record if the requester so desired. It may well be that the Commissioner should consider some way of developing a fund wherein if the examining group thought it would be appropriate to have a hearing of some sort, and the requester is not able to bear that expense, that there may be other resources brought to bear to be able to fly appropriate witnesses in. Because I think faith in the system is something that's extremely important and right now that's what's lacking. It's lacking in part because of media attention

on a few glaring mishaps in the system, they're not the rule, they are the exception, but it so happens that the exception gets the attention.

To turn to some of the times we've seen the system work, I'll try to give a synopsis of a few experiences, hopefully without identifying the companies. In our first case I have a client that's a small software company on the West Coasts, initially financed through the founder's own resources. This is a utility type of software, improving hardware performance and reliability. They filed a patent application; a hardware company that they were working with decided to flex its muscles a bit and threatened to design their own product, notwithstanding the patent application. However, once we had an indication of reasonable allowable claims we were able to negotiate them back into the fold.

A few months later, despite the success of the product, as we all know, it's extremely expensive to get software into the marketplace and marketing expenses were just eating up the company's cash.

The company went to look for investors. Every single investor refused to get actively involved until knowing that there would be strong patent protection, because the one thing that makes software unique is how easy it is to copy. And I'm not using copy necessarily in the copyright sense, but analyzing it and taking what's there.

This was a situation where fortunately the system and some public servants in the patent and trademark office, very sensitive to issues such as this, responded and dealt expeditiously with the response we had filed to an outstanding action, and indeed allowed very broad claims, and our client is at this point closing the financing which was the difference between life and death for the company.

We represent university clients also. Universities will generally not be able to license their technology unless they have chances of protecting it. They are not known to be litigious; it is out of respect for the patent system and access to future technology generally that a licensee signs up. We've seen a number of instances where software developed at universities was licensed by the very developers who knew the potential, went out, formed their own companies, and that was a revenue stream that was formed back to universities; and that revenue stream is very important.

We have investors come to us, any number of times, thinking of investing in software-related companies, and their question again is, "Is this protectable? If I'm going to put in my millions and millions of dollars and all of my effort, will someone else be able to come along and walk off with it?"

In those situations where our own investigations of prior art or the Patent Office investigations of prior art make it questionable that strong protection is available, generally an investment is not made. Where, however, it appears that protection is available, an investment often is made. We don't want investors to start getting gun-shy about investing because subsequently we find out that the examination -- search process in particular -- is defective. The best thing we can do at this point is everything reasonably possible to beef up that process.

That will have carryover effect, as Professor Hollaar mentioned, with respect to the copyright system. The copyright system is drawing a great deal of fire because of the look and feel and its progeny and uncertainty. Investors and business people look for certainty, and it's our job to move the system in the direction where they feel a lot more comfortable with it.

Thank you.

COMMISSIONER LEHMAN: Thank you very much.

Basically it's been your testimony, and it's very strong, that in your experience representing clients you've seen a number of very specific examples where investment in innovation would not have occurred had it not been for the patent incentive.

MR. HENRY: Absolutely.

COMMISSIONER LEHMAN: Thank you very much.

Next I'd like to call Sal Cassamassima, General Counsel of the Exxon Production Research Company.

--o0o--

SAL CASSAMASSIMA

EXXON PRODUCTION RESEARCH COMPANY

MR. CASSAMASSIMA: Thank you, Commissioner LEHMAN, and thank you particularly for pronouncing my name correctly. I know it's a struggle to get that one right the first time. My name is Sal Cassamassima, and I'm the General Counsel of Exxon Production Research located in Houston, Texas. I'm here to present testimony on behalf of Exxon Production Research, which for the sake of brevity I'll refer to as EPR.

I'm going to address the subject of patent protection for software-related inventions and more particularly on the patentability of inventions containing mathematical algorithms. This is a very important subject to EPR, and we appreciate this opportunity to present our comments on the subject. We will also submit more detailed comments, written comments for the record by the March 15th deadline.

Our comments will focus on the subject of inventions containing mathematical algorithms, and we will recommend that the Patent and Trademark Office clarify and liberalize its guidance on the subject to better align with the views of the Federal Circuit.

Let me tell you first a little bit about EPR and why the subjects addressed here today are important to us. We are a wholly-owned affiliate of Exxon Corporation and we're engaged in basic and applied research related to oil and gas exploration and production technology.

Our company and many other companies in the oil and gas industry are among the most intensive users of advanced computer technologies and applications. For example, in exploring for oil and gas, there is an increasing need for highly accurate representations of subsurface formations, particularly in geologically-complex areas. Meeting that need in recent years has been an enormous challenge for industry, particularly with oil hovering around fifteen dollars a barrel.

That challenge is being met by rapid advances in the application of leading edge computer technology and the processing of geophysical data which you probably know is obtained from seismic surveys. For example, so-called three-dimensional or 3-D seismic provides much more

accurate depictions of complex geologic formations than was ever possible with more conventional two-dimensional, 2-D seismic. Advanced computer applications are also being used on the production side of our business to predict oil and gas reservoir drainage and to model enhanced oil recovery techniques by computer simulations.

In pushing the frontiers of this new technology, EPR is constantly challenged in several areas that are computer-related.

First is the hardware itself. Seismic surveying and the ensuing data processing require enormously powerful computers such as supercomputers and massively parallel computers. To obtain these various depictions of 3-D seismic you really have to have an enormous amount of number-crunching capability. In fact, we think our industry is second only to the Defense Department in the use of MPPs and supercomputers.

Secondly, the industry must develop the software to both process the data and convert it into readily-analyzable forms; and this is where we come in. Closely related to hardware and software development is the ongoing challenge to develop sophisticated mathematical algorithms which are the key to enhancing analysis of seismic or reservoir data. The algorithms we develop do many critical things in analyzing seismic and reservoir data.

For example, the algorithms enable the computer to process data more efficiently. They compress data or rearrange data to make it more readily processible, and they enable the processing of poorly-conditioned data by removing noise or other irrelevant signals.

Development of these algorithms and their integration into the hardware and software usually involves very major investments in both time and money. The synergistic combination of more powerful computers and software enhanced by mathematical algorithms has resulted in a quantum leap in oil and gas exploration capabilities. Many companies are now reexploring mature producing areas such as the Gulf of Mexico because the new technology enables the discovery of reservoirs that were heretofore unknown because of their complex subsurface geology.

The type of inventions we seek to protect generally relate to methods for analyzing seismic or reservoir data using mathematical algorithms which yield a desired output, such as an accurate 3-D depiction of the subsurface. For example, these methods may accurately identify salt domes, highly faulted formations, and other complex subsurface anomalies which reveal oil and gas deposits. Patent applications claiming methods for analyzing seismic data using mathematical algorithms have always been among the most perplexing cases for the Patent and Trademark Office to review. In some cases, the Office in applying the so-called Freedom Walter Abel test, two-part test, has held such claims to be patentable subject matter under Section 101. In other cases, very similar cases, the Patent and Trademark Office has found the test not to be satisfied.

It was thought by many in the industry that some clear guidance would be forthcoming from the Patent Office when the Federal Circuit issued its opinion in the Arrythmia Research v. Corazonix case which some other speakers mentioned today. However, we have been disappointed that

UNITED STATES PATENT AND TRADEMARK OFFICE
Public Hearing on Patent Protection for Software-Related Inventions
San Jose, California -- January 26-27, 1994

the Patent and Trademark Office often does not appear to follow the reasoning of Arrythmia, thereby creating a great deal of uncertainty in this important area of the law, and I realize that consistency is the hobgoblin of little minds, but in the area of Section 101, the threshold of patentability, consistency is very important.

COMMISSIONER LEHMAN: I think that consistency in the Patent Office is an extremely important part of customer service, so I don't think that cliche is applicable to us at all, and I think this is a very good point that you're making.

MR. CASSAMASSIMA: The types of inventions that are the subject of this controversy all have one thing in common. They deal with algorithms which yield a useful result. For example, in many of our inventions seismic signals are analyzed to accurately depict subsurface geology. In the arrythmia case, electrocardiograph signals were analyzed to detect the susceptibility to excessively rapid heartbeat, which is known as tachycardia, a very life-threatening illness. In other cases, we might see techniques for mathematically analyzing molecular structure to screen for chemotherapy agents. But let me give you a hypothetical example that may be more meaningful, given recent events. I'll describe this hypothetical invention: A method of analyzing seismic data to predict earthquakes, said method comprising combining seismic signals using Formula X, mapping said combined said combined seismic signals using Formula Y, comparing said map seismic signals using Formula Z with a database of historically-mapped signals to determine the probability of an earthquake.

Now of course I have no idea what X, Y and Z formulas might constitute, but needless to say, that would be a rather dramatic invention.

Question: Is the method I just described patentable subject matter? And I would say that under current Patent and Trademark Office policy, the answer is hard to concern. Should it be? In my opinion, absolutely yes. The method that I just described, claimed, is not an abstract idea of a law of nature. It is a process for analyzing real physical data to yield a highly-useful life-saving result, the prediction of earthquakes. The earthquake claim does not seek to protect a generic technique for analyzing data. It does not claim a purely mathematical method of identifying a data anomaly by comparing sample data to generic databases. What it seeks to protect is a process for determining the probability of an earthquake by comparing in a quantifiable manner actual seismic data with reference databases. By grounding the claim in seismic signal analysis the claim comes to life as a patentable process, and it's protected by the Patent Act. It does not matter whether there is a discernable physical component to the claim itself.

Inventions, such as the ones I have described, our type of inventions, the Arrythmia case or the hypothetical, all have the requisites of patentable subject matter. They are new and useful, and granting patent protection to them would foster innovation and technology development, the very purpose of the patent law. Absent patent protection, the time and the resources to develop such new and needed technology might not be forthcoming.

We therefore recommend that the Patent and Trademark Office dispense with the two-part Freeman-Walter-Abel test and issue new guidance that embraces a statutory basis for determining patentable subject matter under Section 101. The guidance should be simple and as broad as the statute and judicial precedent permit. We recommend that the word "process" be given its literal meaning and let the guidance dispense with the notion that a method claim containing a mathematical algorithm cite some physical step. Only algorithms which solve abstract or generic math problems should be deemed nonstatutory. The guidance should also direct that the algorithm be viewed in the context of the specification as a whole, in the claims preamble. With that approach, method claims of the type contained in arrythmia and the ones I've described would be statutory subject matter.

Finally, the guidance should make clear that in the absence of legislative limits by Congress, the Patent and Trademark Office will not impose nonstatutory or policy constraints on what processes are worthy of patent protection. Such guidance would eliminate the present uncertainty and would provide a boost to the type of technology that will come to dominate the Information Age in the years ahead.

Thank you very much.

COMMISSIONER LEHMAN: Thanks very much, Mr. Cassamassima, I really appreciate all your very specific recommendations. We'll examine those.

Next I'd like to call Christopher Palermo, another Fish and Richardson attorney. Is he here? I guess not. In that case we'll move on to Neil Brown. Mr. Brown? We're ahead of schedule now.

MR. BROWN: Sorry about that. I was expecting twenty minutes, but --

COMMISSIONER LEHMAN: I know; we're a little further ahead in the schedule than we thought, mainly because the preceding witness wasn't here.

--oOo--

NEIL BROWN

INDEPENDENT SOFTWARE ENGINEER

MR. BROWN: Well, I have a lot to say. First of all, I'd like to thank you all for being here. I have a lot to say and I appreciate the opportunity to say it to you directly. It's been a long time since I've been on stage; sorry. My name is Neil Brown. I'm an independent software engineer. I work as a contractor for software development companies and I do development of my own. I did programming for fifteen years and I've been getting paid for it only in the last six.

Although I can't speak for all of us, I can speak for some of us, and I can certainly speak for all the friends I've talked to who feel very similar to the way I do. I represent the ultimate source of all revenue for every person who profits from the software industry, however indirectly, the developers; if somebody wasn't writing the software, there wouldn't be a single software patent lawyer that could possibly make a penny. This is why I -- what I, what the League for Programming Freedom and what the Free Software Foundation, neither of which I'm a member, have to say is important. We power this industry; we're the dynamo which causes it to exist, and in order to keep our jobs, in order to continue marketing software, we must make clear what we need before its too late.

I'd like to address the questions that you've asked, as I

UNITED STATES PATENT AND TRADEMARK OFFICE
Public Hearing on Patent Protection for Software-Related Inventions
San Jose, California — January 26-27, 1994

indicated from not listing affiliations, I'm not speaking on behalf of anyone other than myself and those in the software industry whom I have found to agree with me.

On the question, Topic A, Question 1, Example A, "What part of mathematical algorithm implemented on a general purpose computer can be patented?" My response: None whatsoever.

The technique of long division where one writes the number to be divided down, puts a little bar under it, and writes the number to divide into it, next to it, writes notations and partial answers, gradually arriving at a more complete answer, can clearly be described in a fashion executable by a computer. It's not at all hard for most developers to write a graphical front end for long division, so this is a useful, I mean the question of whether or not division is useful is, is not worth debating. It's a useful tool to accomplish a useful goal, and real money is made from using it, but what would happen to your education? How would you have learned division if the school that was trying to teach you that suddenly found itself being attacked by another school who claimed to own that very method?

A mathematical algorithm performed on a special-purpose computer; can you patent a calculator? I do seem to remember that the beginning of the digital revolution was really noticed when pocket calculators starting causing slide rules to disappear. If only one company had been able to produce calculators, would the price have dropped from four hundred dollars to fifteen in only a couple of years? If only one company could own the legal right to build a machine to perform mathematical calculations, where would the software industry have gotten its start?

Topic A, Question 1, Example B, sorry, Example C and C-2. "Can you patent the disk on which a computer program is stored?" Again, with the calculator, if it were possible to patent the concept of a calculator, if it were possible to patent the calculator that has the ability to execute more than one program, where would the software industry be today? How do you define what a program is? Do you define it as being able to push the sine key and get the sine of the number? Do you define a separate program as one in which you can press the cosine key and get the cosine of that number?

Question 2. "What impact, negative or positive, have you or your organization experienced from patent issues on software-related inventions? On several occasions I have found myself being unsure of whether or not I was able to use a particular algorithm, specifically the compression algorithm embedded in the program known as Compress, within software. There have been many questions raised and lots of time spent chasing after whether or not the company could somehow use this and escape any royalty obligations.

"What implications, positive or negative, can you foresee in maintaining or altering the standards for patent eligibility?" This is Question 3. Well, I see small guys getting squeezed out. I see innovation becoming more and more difficult, because every one of the hundreds of ideas that the developer goes through while writing an application, every one of the little techniques that he goes to use or goes to put together with another, he has to go and call up Legal to find out if that's been patented or if it might be covered by a patent. The software industry is not going to progress very

rapidly if people like me spend all their time on the phone to Legal asking if we can do this.

"Does the framework of patent, copyright or trade secret law," Question 4, "effectively promote innovation in the field of software?" Yes. "Does it provide the appropriate level of protection?" A qualified yes. The qualification is that it provides too much protection, potentially.

Question 5. "Do you believe a new form of protection for computer programs is needed?" My answer is no. The water is muddy enough.

On Topic B. I agree with all concerns that access to prior art is difficult, or is outmoded. The difficulty of determining whether or not two programs are equivalent or similar is extremely difficult. I deem it intractable. There are so many languages out there, there are so many sophisticated ways of expressing algorithms that it's hard enough just to understand one, but comparing two? Doing this for every program out there that seems to possibly be related to an application can take forever. The very concept of, is there anything out there at all that does what this does, is extremely difficult to solve, and I deem it to be intractable for software in general.

Topic B, Question 1. No, I don't think that the patents and printed publications provide examiners with sufficient collection of prior art, and as I said before, it can't. The work on software interface patents, if you allow patenting of the idea of having a hammer on a desk and deem it a different invention if the hammer is the drawer of the desk, how is somebody using that desk going to be able to get their job done? How is somebody going to be able to design -- How is anyone going to be able to get the job done if their job is to design a new desk and they have to go and find everyone that has similar functionality available at the top of their desk? The patent which has control information such as page numbering and position on the page and document being edited available on the screen, the very idea of having many pieces of information available for manipulation of the information is the whole idea of an interface. You want to be able to provide as much ability for the user to manipulate the raw material they're working with as apparently is possible. You want all of these tools to be easy to get to and easy to work with, and if someone comes with a formalism for making all of these things available, then if any means of providing that same functionality is deemed equivalent, then how can progress possibly happen?

I do have lots more to say, as I said, but --

COMMISSIONER LEHMAN: Well, maybe I can help you to wrap up in just asking you, I have a little confusion in your statement to us; in the answer to Question 4 you basically seem to say that the present framework is okay, but I have the impression that you basically don't think that -- that you think there are a lot of problems with the patentability of software just generally. Is it your position that software should not be patentable?

MR. BROWN: Software patents are a blight. They're a problem. They get worse.

COMMISSIONER LEHMAN: So basically you think that copyright protection is --

MR. BROWN: Copyrights and trade secrets.

COMMISSIONER LEHMAN: -- is okay, and trade secrets,

UNITED STATES PATENT AND TRADEMARK OFFICE
Public Hearing on Patent Protection for Software-Related Inventions
San Jose, California — January 26-27, 1994

but that basically the difficulties from trying to work with the patent system applied to this industry are so great that it virtually makes it impossible to use it as an effective technique for protection that developers like yourself can really work with.

MR. BROWN: Yes. How many houses would you build if every time a carpenter went to build a house, every time a carpenter went to take up a tool he had to pay a point one percent royalty on the gross profit on that house, or the gross revenue on that house?

COMMISSIONER LEHMAN: We appreciate your coming and sharing these comments. Thank you.

MR. BROWN: Thank you very much.

COMMISSIONER LEHMAN: Next I'd like to ask, if he's here, Gordon Irlam, representing the League for Programming Freedom, which our previous witness referred to in his statement.

--oOo--

GORDON IRLAM

LEAGUE FOR PROGRAMMING FREEDOM

MR. IRLAM: Good day. The League for Programming Freedom's an organization of roughly six hundred people within the software industry. It's a combination of software developers employed by various companies and small people who own their own business which typically are anywhere between like one or two people up to fifty or a hundred people, and they also have a number of members that are either academics, researchers or students. The League for Programming Freedom has two main policy areas it's concerned with. It has a belief in doing software development on the basis of competition and between different implementations of what could be the same technology, and we believe by doing that that such software is going to be in a sense like economically more efficient impact, if you can get multiple products that will represent the same technology; and prices -- and efficiencies are going to be driven up by the competitive ventures involved.

So to do that we believe in what you might term a traditional literal aspects doctrine of copyright. That's very useful for software developers. It basically means if you copy code, you know, you can't do that, but if you wrote the code yourself, that's all you need to know. You can then go out and sell it, and you're safe in the knowledge that you can, and you won't be sued later on. You know you owned it.

So based on this belief the League has two positions. We're opposed to the look and feel copyright, and extensions that seem to have been happening over the past few years, and we're also opposed to software patents. And we take various actions to try and raise these issues and submit these to courts and so on.

Fundamentally I think this whole question of software patents is being approached in what might be the wrong direction. In fact I think the whole issue has to be looked at as one of economics, and not either based on, you know, the direct, uh, interests of any party or, uh, you know, you've got to stand back a bit and take a big picture view of, you know, what effect do software patents have on competition and market structure. So therefore I'm rather disappointed, but as far as I know, there hasn't been anybody with any

economic background that's been speaking on these matters. And you know, I think it would be really important if the Commission or whatever could like seek out people with an economic background that can provide the input on these matters. And so I think, you know, if you start analyzing patents and in particular software patents from an economic standpoint, then you'll get a lot of benefit. But I think it should be obvious that every industry has different economic characteristics. This is both like market size, market structure, with availability of market information, extent of competition, and there's just a huge range of economic parameters that differentiate, for instance, the pharmaceutical industry from the software industry, and you know, because of this, the application of patents to one industry might be sound public policy, but the application of the same rules to another industry will have an adverse effect on the overall public welfare.

So for instance, one of the big things about computer software is it's protected by copyright in a way that pharmaceuticals, for instance, aren't. And that provides a good basis for allowing different people to develop different products and compete, so you know, the important thing is if you look at it from an economic standpoint, every industry's different, and so the impact of patents will be different on every industry; and I contend that in the software industry, patents are harmful.

And I believe it's because, based on my experience, the software industry appears to be a highly competitive industry, and I feel software patents have potential to stifle this competition in terms of they can take away profits from, you know, some of the firms, perhaps significant value to the industry, and they'll be transferred to firms that don't add a lot of economic value.

I think the important thing about software is it's not so much new ideas that are important; it's building real products that solve customer problems, and I'm a software engineer in my regular employment, and my job doesn't consist of trying to come up with new ideas all the time. There's just hundreds of ideas. It's trying to implement those ideas, build real products that solve real customer problems and, you know, if they solve them well, that both they integrate well with other products and are -- and easily usable. I think if you look at the last ten or twenty years with like the microcomputer revolution, that's what it's really all been about, you know, the firms that have been successful are the firms that have been able to take ideas and turn them into something that's useful for end-users, and add value that way. So you know, the successful firms are companies like Microsoft, Novell, Borland, Adobe, and you know, the list goes on, all these new companies that have, you know, typically been started some time in the last ten to fifteen years.

And so when you start looking at software patents you'll find that it's quite disturbing because if these are the companies you want to attract, if you actually start to count which companies have how many software patents, you'll find things that are quite alarming in terms of the companies that you'd imagine should be being rewarded by the patent system for developing real economic value hardly hold any patents. And indeed, many of them don't even hold any patents at all. And even the large company such as

UNITED STATES PATENT AND TRADEMARK OFFICE
Public Hearing on Patent Protection for Software-Related Inventions
San Jose, California -- January 26-27, 1994

Microsoft count very few patents. And on the other hand, if you look at companies like Hitachi and IBM and AT&T which people within the software industry will tell you have been more or less totally inept at bringing their software ideas to market, they can come up with ideas but they just can't implement them successfully in a way that fulfills real customer needs.

And so I think if the software patent system continues, then it's going to have a very adverse effect in terms of resources from the economy are going to be diverted away from the firms that are adding real value and put towards these very large conglomerates which are like multifactored concerns that have large patent hierarchies.

And so because of this I think, you know, the patent system's got to be analyzed from an economic point of view and, you know, in the case of software I believe that that's -- the patents are harmful to the software industry and I think the best solution will be to make software nonpatentable.

You know, I'd like to just mention briefly on the issue of economics, there seems to be very little real research into like the fundamental functioning of the patent system in terms of I know there was a study way back in I think 1958 by Fritz Matlock (phonetic) that, you know, did an economic evaluation for the Senate, and raised an awful lot of questions about the patent system, which I think was good, but then they tended to be just left off, and I feel, you know, if someone had taken those questions and started evaluating them and gathering real data, we'd be in a much better position today to actually know what the state of the patent system is, exactly how it works on deciding important public policy issues such as this.

All right. In the remaining time I'd like to just read, if I may, one or two things by some of our members who haven't been able to attend today, have sent. Okay.

So this is from James Hellman (phonetic) who's a member of the League for Programming Freedom, and he says, "A couple of years ago I was involved in a start-up that was shut down by a bogus software patent. We were well on our way to having several hundred thousand dollars of private-placement venture capital. Out of the blue another company was awarded an extremely broad software systems patent for an obvious concept through substantial existing prior art. We received a cease and desist letter and our funding evaporated. The sad thing is that the company that received the patent were so incompetent that they went out of business shortly afterwards. Business success should be determined by who has the best ideas, best implementations and best marketing

Okay. Have you got any questions?

COMMISSIONER LEHMAN: No, other than to say that I think you make a very good point about lack of really effective economic analysis about how the patent system works. It is something that is lacking. I know we've attempted to survey the literature on that subject, and there really isn't any. It's interesting that certainly this hearing was made available to everybody; we're within a few miles of one of the great research institutions in this area of the country. Nobody, no professor, no great economist saw this subject as worthy of advising us on and it's a problem we have, frankly, it's a problem, and unless we go out and commission

the work to be done I'm not sure that we're going to get that kind of information, but it does put us at some kind of disadvantage so we have to do the next best thing and that is get the kind of anecdotal information that we're getting here today from people like you and other witnesses. The difficulty with that is that we're hearing exactly the opposite thing from several different witnesses. We heard people earlier who testified that it's an absolute fact that there would not have been investments made in innovation, companies would not have been formed if they had not had the patent incentive. You've given us in your letter that you just read to us an assertion of an exact opposite situation. So we'll have to sort through all of this.

MR. IRLAM: I believe there will be value if, you know, longer term, the Patent Office was to maybe develop some of its own skills at doing like economic analysis for its like policy section or whatever that may exist.

COMMISSIONER LEHMAN: Well, we may well have to do that. Thank you very much.

Next I'd like to ask Mr. Robert Yoches to step forward, who has, I assume, come all the way out there from Washington, Finnegan, Henderson, Farabow, Garrett & Dunner.

--oOo--

ROBERT YOCHES

FINNEGAN, HENDERSON, FARABOW, GARRETT & DUNNER

MR. YOCHES: Thank you, Commissioner LEHMAN, it is indeed a pleasure not to be in Washington, D.C. today because of the weather, and also a pleasure to be before this distinguished Panel. For the record my name is Bob Yoches and I am a partner of Finnegan, Henderson, Farabow, Garrett & Dunner, although I speak today not as a representative of that firm, not as a representative of my partners, and not as a representative of any of the clients of the firm. Instead I offer my own views based upon having practiced in the area of intellectual property for patents for fourteen years, and in that capacity I've been before the Patent Office in prosecution, I've litigated patents in the software and computer area, I've licensed patents in those areas, licensed in and out technology, I've been involved in copyright registrations, copyright licensing and litigation, and I've been involved in trade secret litigation. I've represented both large companies that have been well-established, small companies and start-up companies. I've also represented domestic companies and foreign companies, and I've represented those that had intellectual copyrights and those that were concerned with other parties' intellectual property rights. And based upon that experience I'd like to offer some observations about the applicability of the patents and the patent law to the software-related inventions. I'm going to restrict my remarks to perhaps unique aspects of software that make patents appropriate or inappropriate, as opposed to addressing any of the general attacks on the patent system itself. I'm not under the impression that there's any large-scale movement to rid ourselves of the patent system, so let me address myself to the specific aspects of software and the specific aspects of how the patent system impacts software.

I note that in the discussions today and the testimony given there are three characteristics of software that I think are

UNITED STATES PATENT AND TRADEMARK OFFICE
Public Hearing on Patent Protection for Software-Related Inventions
San Jose, California – January 26-27, 1994

important, especially from the aspect of how best to implement the Constitutional directive. One is that software is pervasive in our technology. It pervades our lives, it pervades our jobs, it pervades all other types of technology that hithertofore we've considered different. We've heard somebody from the petroleum industry talk. We've heard about a case involving software and the medical industry. There is software in the banks, software in stock exchanges, there's software in your automobiles. Not only does software now pervade our lives, it will do so more in the future.

A second observation is, you cannot extricate the software and treat it separately, in other words, I question whether we can talk intelligently about software-related inventions, software's such an integral part of our lives. And lastly, the last observation generally on software is that although software has some unique aspects, so does every other type of technology; certainly biotechnology has unique aspects. Certainly chemistry and pharmaceuticals have unique aspects, but I think there are some things about software that it has in common with other innovations and with other technologies that are particularly important to how patents will affect that.

One of those characteristics is software is extremely useful; it is, as I indicated before, pervasive, but it has the potential, and has already actualized much of that potential for dramatic impacts on our life.

Second, the more we know about software, and I think there is some testimony on this point also, the more that is known about software, the greater will be the development in order to avoid ploughing ground that's been ploughed, and the faster will be the rate of that improvement.

Given those observations then, what role do patents play and can they play? And I think patents have already played, and will continue to play, a role in three major aspects. The one generally starting from what I just talked about is in publication. We heard a speaker this morning testify that indeed one large company allowed publication of ideas because they were protected by way of patents. In addition to that, however, and I think a much stronger point, is the fact that the patents themselves are publications of the ideas, and publications in a very important way that really hasn't existed. They are publications of information in a structured format by way of the Patent Office's own classification system. As the Commissioner spoke this morning, the fact of the matter is that because we have relied so long on trade secrets there is perhaps a lack of this structured database. The way to solve that is not to avoid the patent system, but rather to embrace it, and to look at and perhaps adopt many of the recommendations that have been made here on how to improve the accessibility to prior art.

The second issue, and this has been a key issue here, is that of investment, and rather than repeat what's been said, it has been my experience that not only do investors, and by investors I not only include venture capitalists, but also large concerns that are interested in some sort of partnering agreement, but these type of investors care more about patents than they do about trade secrets, if in all honesty copyrights are kind of a wash. They're there anyhow, it doesn't make much difference.

But given that, there's often a choice between whether to

keep processes secret or obtain a patent on it, I find investors like patents much better, for two reasons. One is, they don't like dealing with trade secrets because they have to sign a confidentiality agreement and a lot of investors won't do that. The second reason is, and I think even more compelling, is that the investors are afraid that the trade secrets will have a short lifetime. They can easily be lost. They can be lost in an instant by an inadvertent publication. They much prefer patents.

The third area that I think that patents play in software is that of innovation. There's been I guess some dispute here on whether software is fast-developing or slow-developing, but I think there is one observation we can make, and that is, it's generally easy to change software. It's more flexible to change software than hardware, indeed that's why so many of our developments have software in it. Well, of course one of the options that the patent system offers, and one of the opportunities it offers, is that if there's a patent out there, and you don't feel like paying the license fee for it, you are encouraged to design around the patent, and indeed the Federal Circuit has indicated that a key aspect of the patent laws is the designing-around.

Software, by its nature, by the ease and quickness by which you can modify your procedures and modify your algorithms, is particularly adapted to designing around other patents, and particularly adapted to then promoting new developments. It has been my experience, in summary, that the patents have served the software type of developments very well, and I believe in general that the Patent Office, especially in Group 2300 with which I've had the most experience, has also done a good job of serving the system well, but I notice, I think, two problems currently, with the Patent and Trademark Office in the area of patent protection of software-related inventions. The one is, I believe in the Section 101 area as I think other witnesses have indicated, that there is a reluctance, and almost stubborness by the Patent Office to taking the most contrary position that they can on whether subject matter is patentable, and indeed in the form paragraphs which the patent and trademark office uses as a bases for its rejections, it had been able to pick and choose among different cases, especially cases from the 1970s, to support their positions.

I think that's contrary to the trend of the law. I think it's contrary to two major Supreme Court cases, the most recent cases in this area. Because in the Jacobardi case, as the Notice indicates, the patent laws are supposed to extend to anything under the sun made by man, and in the Diehr case, there was a direction that we're supposed to look at the claim as a whole and not dissect it into its old elements, meaning its mathematical algorithms, and its new elements. And I do not believe currently that the Patent and Trademark Office is following that, and I think that the result has been, at least in my experience, two things. One is frustration by some applicants because they have abandoned their application rather than pursue this to the Board, and for those people that have pursued to the Board, at least in our firm, they've been very successful, and all it's resulted in is an additional expense to those applicants.

The other issue, and I think the Patent Office I understand the last week made I think a major change, is the Patent Office I understand now allows or will allow Group 2300 to hire computer scientists as examiners. I think that's a very good step. However, it's my understanding though that if you're a computer scientist out practicing in the world you may not currently sit for the Patent Bar. The belief is that you don't have sufficient technical training. I think that should change, and certainly if you're qualified enough to examine patents, you ought to be qualified enough to prosecute those patents in front of the Office.

Thank you very much.

COMMISSIONER LEHMAN: Thank you very much. Mr. Yoches, for coming all this way to share those thoughts with us.

Next I'd like to call our final witness of the afternoon, Jim Shay of the firm of Morrison and Foerster.

--oOo--

JIM SHAY

MORRISON & FOERSTER

MR. SHAY: I find myself in the very difficult position of playing clean-up and of trying to say something new, because many good things have already been said and many of my remarks I think only serve to reinforce those things, but perhaps that's useful as well. My name is Jim Shay, I am with the law firm of Morrison & Foerster in San Francisco. We represent the Multimedia Development Group, a trade association based on San Francisco, as well as other clients in the software and multimedia industry. My comments today are my own, however. They do not necessarily represent the views of the firm or its clients.

I am a patent attorney. I spent three years as a patent examiner before entering private practice. I've also served as inhouse counsel for a medical technology company, and I've worked in a variety of technologies in a variety of ways, prosecution, litigation, licensing, representing individual inventors, large companies and investors.

I believe in the value of patent protection as a tool for spurring innovation and for helping inventors, whether corporate or individual, obtain the benefit of their contributions. In my opinion this principle applies as much to software-related inventions as to any tangible mechanical, chemical or electrical invention.

Specifically, the software industry as a whole and software companies and developers individually benefit from the patent system. The software industry I'm referring to is not just the companies whose primary products reside on floppy disks or CD-ROMs. In my view the term software industry includes any suppliers of products incorporating programmable microprocessors, products such as medical monitors, animated toys, automobile electronic ignitions, audio products, just to name a few. Advances in microprocessor technology have made software ubiquitous and protection of patentable inventions embodying that software is therefore of concern not only to companies writing and selling software per se, but also to all manner of high, medium and low-tech companies serving a variety of markets.

As the PTO has acknowledge in conducting these hearings, there appear to be a particularly high amount of concern over the validity of software patents. A good example is the public reaction to the Compton's new media patent, a patent

I came to know very well in my position as counsel to the Multimedia Development Group. I participated in question and answer sessions about the Compton's patents with members of the MDG's Executive Committee and with individual members of the MDG. Many expressed many strong, negative opinions about the conduct of the Compton's patent applicants before the PTO and about the ability of the PTO to examine and issue valid patents in the subject area.

My review of the file history of that patent, however, showed no evidence of any particular lapse or failure on either part. Nonetheless, the consensus of nearly all to whom I spoke was that the broadest claims of the Compton's patent could not possibly be valid, and that anyone associated with the multimedia industry would agree. The eventual disposition of the Compton's patent remains to be seen. The discussion surrounding that patent, however, has pointed to some possible deficiencies in the current patent system, especially as applied to software-related inventions.

First, as other people have noted, patent examiners do not have easy access to the best prior art for software-related inventions. The best prior art consists of actual software, operators manuals, research papers and the like. These references are not generally accessible to patent examiners.

Second, the PTO's relative lack of experience in software-related inventions because of the relative newness of the patentability of software makes it difficult for an examiner to determine how one of ordinary skill in the art would have approached the problem that patent claims address. Often it is the feeling that an invention would have been obvious that leads an examiner to find the most pertinent prior art references, to make the most compelling argument regarding the unpatentability of the claims. This disconnect between the gut feelings of the patent examiners and the gut feelings of skilled artisans in the software industry undermines the industry's faith in the PTO.

I would now like to make some recommendations based on these observations. These are not new, these will merely reinforce other recommendations made earlier today.

First, operating within the current statutory framework, I believe that the PTO and the software industry could benefit greatly from a more formal interaction. Specifically, the software industry operating through industry groups such as the Multimedia Development Group, could provide the PTO with kinds of prior art references that the PTO currently lacks. I have spoken to many members of these groups who at least now are expressing a willingness to work with the Patent and Trademark Office if the PTO will work with them in compiling these prior art references. Such a program would require the industry groups to dig up and send, and the Patent Office to accept and classify, prior art references related to the past and present software inventions.

In addition, the PTO and industry groups should cooperate to train examiners working with software inventions. I'm aware, for example, of training programs offered by the Software Patent Institute. I also believe that the PTO should undertake the task of teaching the software industry about the patent process so that the industry can use the existing process more effectively. One of the most surprising things I learned in the Compton's process was how little people

UNITED STATES PATENT AND TRADEMARK OFFICE
Public Hearing on Patent Protection for Software-Related Inventions
San Jose, California — January 26-27, 1994

actually knew about the patent system.

To the extent that the PTO is willing to support statutory changes and as I learned this morning, you are, I believe that a system of pre-grant publication and opposition proceedings would help improve the quality of software patents. This one aspect of change is the one thing mentioned more often by more people in discussing the current patent situation. A less radical statutory change would seem to be opening the reexamination process to provide for full participation by interested parties in addition to the patent owner. I advocate the use of oral testimony. Experts in the field can be the best source of prior art, and this would be useful in the reexamination process. This change could encourage the submission of all relevant prior art instead of the current practice of withholding the best prior art for use in license negotiations and in District Court infringement proceedings.

In conclusion, while the emphasis of our remarks has been on the deficiencies I perceive in the patent system, I should state that I believe that there is much right with the current system. Our proposals will only be minor changes to a system that has served us well in promoting the useful arts.

Thank you.

COMMISSIONER LEHMAN: Thank you very much, Mr. Shay, I appreciate those very specific recommendations.

I'd like to thank everybody in the audience for having the interest in what others had to say, to stay all day and be with us, and we'll reconvene tomorrow morning at 9:00 o'clock, and our first witness at that time will be Jerry Fiddler, CEO and Chairman of Wind River Systems. Thank you very much

—oOo--

United States Patent and Trademark Office
Public Hearing on Patent Protection for Software-Related Inventions
San Jose, California -- January 26-27, 1994

UNITED STATES PATENT AND TRADEMARK OFFICE

PUBLIC HEARING

ON USE OF THE PATENT SYSTEM

TO PROTECT SOFTWARE-RELATED INVENTIONS

January 27, 1994

COMMISSIONER LEHMAN: Good morning. Welcome to our second day of hearings on the use of the patent system to protect software-related inventions.

Yesterday we had an excellent series of speakers. I think we all learned a lot here, those of us who came from the Commerce Department in Washington. You all gave us a wide variety of opinions and I know that today is going to be just as good and we're going to be armed with all the information we need to improve our patent system when we get back to Washington.

I'd like to just, for those of you who might not have been here today, briefly introduce who we are here on this panel.

I am Bruce Lehman. My official title is Assistant Secretary of Commerce and Commissioner of Patents and Trademarks.

And to my immediate right is Ginger Lew, Assistant Secretary of Commerce and General Counsel of the Department of Commerce Designate, and Ginger Lew was a practicing lawyer until a few months ago up here in the Bay Area and knows this area very well and knows a lot of the industries and businesses that are involved very well.

And then to my far right is Michael Kirk. Mike Kirk is the current Assistant Commissioner of Patents and Trademarks for External Affairs and the President has nominated him to be the Deputy Commissioner of Patents and Trademarks.

And to my left, immediate left, is Lawrence Goffney, and Larry Goffney the President has nominated him to be our new Assistant Commissioner for Patents. He will be running the entire patent operation, with over 3,000 employees at our Patent Office in Washington, and will play a very critical role in the development of these policies.

And then finally Jeff Kushan is a Staff Member of our Office of Legislation and International Affairs and he is the person who did a lot of the leg work in setting this up and his name is listed, as you know, on the Federal Register Notice.

I'd also like to -- I don't know if Gerry Goldberg is here yet this morning -- but I want to observe the presence of Gerry Goldberg, who is the Director of Group 230, or 2300, which is the Software Examining Group.

Is Gerry --? I don't see him around here yet. Okay, well, he'll be here later. I think many of you know him and I'm certain he will be available to you if you have private comments to make to him.

Finally, I'd like to introduce the young lady in the blue suit who just came in is Ruth Ford, who's our Director of Media Relations, and I know we have a number of media and press people who've been here and if you have any needs that need to be dealt with, Ruth will be happy to assist you with that.

So I'd just like to basically review again the ground rules that we're going to be operating with this morning.

The people who will be testifying today should have received a schedule indicating their approximate time that they've been assigned to give their remarks and I think we even have that on a table up front. The list is available there.

And I'd encourage all of the people who are going to be talking with us today to be here at least 20 minutes before your time, your assigned time slot. And sometimes we get going a little bit -- we get speeded up, maybe somebody didn't show up and so then we end up having our schedule advanced beyond what we thought it would be.

Each person will have 11 minutes for their presentation and the computer monitor in front of us here will display a green screen for 9 minutes and then it will turn yellow and when the screen turns red that means that the 11 minutes is up. And I encourage everybody to be cooperative with us if at all possible and try to stick to those limits. Otherwise we'll sort of have to politely ask you to wrap up.

To the extent that you can finish before 11 minutes, it's not such a bad idea because it gives us a little more freedom to have a dialogue and ask questions and get really a better sense of where you're coming from and understand your testimony better.

In addition to, of course, these oral comments, we're open to additional written comments from everybody, and additional written comments from all those who are going to be testifying today, maybe something is said by one of the other people that you feel you have to follow up on, and those can be submitted to us in our office and I think the address for all of that has been indicated in the Federal Register Notice that has been circulated through the Internet and was in the Federal Register Notice itself.

That Notice can be retrieved from our FTP site, which is: Comments, period, USPT O, period, GOB.

The transcripts of the hearings will be available after February 7th and paper copies will be available for a charge of $30. The transcripts will also be available through our FTP site.

Once again, I want to welcome everybody here, and it's wonderful to see that we have this kind of interest for a second day in how we can improve the legal basis for high technology in the United States.

I'd like to call on our first speaker, who will be Jerry Fiddler, CEO and Chairman of Wind River Systems. Welcome, Mr. Fiddler.

--oOo--

JERRY FIDDLER

CEO/CHAIRMAN

WIND RIVER SYSTEMS

MR. FIDDLER: Thank you.

I just dashed in the door. Traffic was terrible.

I stand before you not as an expert in intellectual property law. I'm not a lawyer. Most people in this room know far more about intellectual property law than I ever will. Rather, I wish to speak to you as an expert software engineer and the founder and CEO of a successful software company, Wind River Systems.

Wind River Systems is a 30 million dollar public company, with 40 percent of our revenue from overseas. We create software for embedded systems, the microprocessors found inside our cars, fax machines, telephones, robots, factories,

United States Patent and Trademark Office
Public Hearing on Patent Protection for Software-Related Inventions
San Jose, California — January 26-27, 1994

consumer electronics. According to Software Magazine, last year we were the 92nd largest software company in the US.

My perspective on software patents is simple: stop issuing software patents. Software patents should not exist. I say this for a number of reasons.

First and foremost, I look at the reasons patents exist, which is for the benefit of society. Certainly there are fields where patents are essential because of the large investment involved for creation of technology and the ease of copying that technology. In such situations, patents incent the major investments necessary for those inventions which benefit society.

This doesn't apply to software. Availability of patent protection is not necessary to incent creation of software. Copyright and trade secret protection are entirely adequate and more appropriate. Yes, major investments are necessary to create software, but that investment is primarily involved in quality implementation and support of the software, not development of the algorithms and ideas that might be patentable. Therefore, unlike a drug, for instance, it's not substantially cheaper or quicker to copy a program's functionality than it is to develop the original.

The deal society makes with the inventor, "Tell us about your invention and you can have a monopoly for 17 years," is not a fair deal today when it comes to software. In a field changing as fast as software is today, 17 years might as well be a millennium. The deal might as well be phrased, "Tell us about your invention and you can monopolize it forever," so the fact that we, society, know about it is meaningless.

In fact, patenting of software is actively harmful to society. People don't need software monopolies. They need software that's open, compatible, and that adheres to their expectations and standards. They need the software equivalent of expectations like "accelerator on the right, brake on the left". Patenting of software could only impede these goals.

Furthermore, patenting of software will not accelerate its creation or advancement. Rather, it will impede that advancement, which is far better driven by the free market than by monopoly.

Imagine where we would be today if patents had been granted on technology or concepts critical to word processors or spreadsheets. Rather than the sophisticated and elegant tools we now have available thanks to competition, we would still be using something very much like the primitive first versions of those tools. Worse still, we must remember that word processors and spreadsheets have been largely responsible for spawning an industry and making the personal computer a part of most of our lives. The quality and advancement in those tools have created opportunities for computer manufacturers and for other software vendors who can sell to users who have computers primarily to run those primary tools.

It's not too strong to say that if there had been strong patent protection for the first word processors and spreadsheets, the personal computer industry today might be five to ten years behind where it is. As another example, if aspects of TCP/IP, the network protocol, had received patent protection, today the Internet might very well not exist.

Creation of software will also be impeded by the difficulty of writing software that doesn't inadvertently trip across a patent somewhere. This is true in other fields where patenting is less controversial, but it's far worse in software. It's not unusual for a program to be a million lines long and consist of many thousands of subroutines and functions. Algorithms and ideas are embodied in each of those components and in combinations of them. Some of these algorithms may be studied in school or found in books, but many are developed "on the fly" as the program is created. Many of these subroutines and functions might be far afield from the purpose of the program as a whole.

An operating system, for instance, might contain routines for sorting and searching, handling queues, parsing text, controlling hardware, testing memory, et cetera. It will be impossible to know which of these routines, algorithms and ideas violate a patent, because every programmer would need to understand every software patent -- every software patent that's active. Software is simply too complex, composed of too many pieces which are too easy to create, to lend itself to being broken down into patent-sized chunks.

I can easily envision a world in which progress in software is totally blocked by a web of patents owned by a very few very large companies; not the best or the most creative companies but rather those with the most lawyers. In a world like that it would be completely impossible to start and build a company like mine -- and this nightmare could come to pass very quickly.

To date there has been little litigation regarding software-related patents. God help us all when that litigation does begin. Judges and juries will be asked to rule on whether a large complicated program, potentially millions of lines long, written in an obscure computer language, violates an arcane patent. The claimed violation will be built into the very fiber of the program, hidden within the program's structure and data in complex and subtle ways. One expert will say one thing, another expert will say the opposite, neither judge nor jury will be competent to understand the nature or veracity of the patent, much less which expert is closer to the truth. The patent will have been issued by an examiner who is not expert in the specific software field and might not understand the concepts essential to operating systems, fuzzy logic, or whatever the specific field is, much less the prior art. The chances of a fair and informed decision will be vanishingly small.

Software is, perhaps, more analogous to literature and music than it is to mechanical invention. It would be silly to think about patenting the first-person novel or the sonata form, yet there are software patents already that to a software engineer are just as absurd.

As a software company CEO, I am perfectly content to compete based on the quality of the software we create and the support we provide for it. I am fully satisfied with copyright, contract and trade-secret protection for the software we write. We have begun to work on some patent applications because I think we may need them for defensive purposes, but I would far rather we didn't need to do so.

If software patents become prevalent, it will seriously interfere with our ability to continue improving our products and our ability to continue developing new ones. It will also interfere with our ability to provide openness and compatibility to our customers -- a key part of the value we

UNITED STATES PATENT AND TRADEMARK OFFICE
Public Hearing on Patent Protection for Software-Related Inventions
San Jose, California -- January 26-27, 1994

provide to them.

The best possible result of these hearings for us, for our customers and for society would be for software patents to simply go away.

COMMISSIONER LEHMAN   Thank you very much, Mr. Fiddler. I would just make an observation and ask a question.

You indicate where would we be if we had had patents on the spreadsheets, and so on and so forth, and I think that suggests that I think it's one of the reasons why we may not have patents on spreadsheets and the idea of a word processing program, and so on, is because those particular items were not patentable, they didn't meet the test of patentability.

And I think herein lies a lot of the problem when you say software shouldn't be patentable. Well, it well may be that there's a lot of confusion as to where that threshold is drawn, and that indeed some software-related inventions could and, you know, are very appropriately patentable, but there seems to be a lot of confusion about where the test, where the threshold, what kind of innovation meets the test of novelty and unobviousness, where that's drawn.

And how would you feel about a more vigorous examination of where that line of nonobviousness is drawn?

MR. FIDDLER: You know, obviously, to the extent patents exist, I'd like them to be as narrow and as well-defined as possible. Clearly, that's in everybody's benefit.

But I think that, yes, it's true that probably the concept of a word processor is not a patentable concept, but there certainly are key components of those that very well may have passed patent law, particularly as patents seem to be being issued, you know, very recently.

There are, I think, that even if the Patent Office is perfect, even if it issues only patents that are entirely appropriate, are entirely correct, are novel and nonobviousness, and so forth, which is I think a very unlikely place to get to, but even if we can assume that the PTO is perfect in those respects, I still think that it will have -- it makes it far more difficult to create software.

If I sit here, I mean you can set for me a problem and say please write a program that does something, and, depending on the problem, in somewhere between five minutes and a couple hours I may be able to do that. Is what I have done patentable? Maybe. Maybe there's an idea in there that is, maybe there isn't.

To find out if there is, it will take me far longer to find that out, and there's no way in the world I can be familiar with it and it will be very difficult for me to find it. It may be in a field far away from the one in which I'm working. It will multiply my work not by 10 or 20 or 50 percent, but potentially by thousands of percent.

COMMISSIONER LEHMAN   How is that any different, really, from an engineer that's working in electronic components of aircraft in --

MR. FIDDLER: I think it's different --

COMMISSIONER LEHMAN -- in Seattle where there's obviously a lot of innovation and they're constantly asked to design all kinds of gizmos and do things and yet that's an area clearly where there's been patentability for a long period of time and they aren't, you know, suggesting that somehow or

other engineers can't make a move and put pen to paper or turn on their workstation without consulting the legal department?

MR. FIDDLER: I think it's different in a couple ways. For one thing, copyright doesn't work for them and it works fine for us. For another thing, it's far easier to create software ideas and to make them work.

When I start and write a program, I may write however many lines of code it is, I may start with a design and do that, and I may actually have it debugged within a very few minutes. I can make changes to it by saying, "Change this line of code." I can make it work in a very few minutes. That's very different than a hardware concept or building something in hardware, where the turnaround time is much longer, the number of concepts probably embodied -- certainly the number of novel concepts embodied in any specific project are probably much smaller.

As I said, a very small number of programmers, two or three or five programmers, can certainly write a million-line program with many thousands of ideas that may potentially be patentable. Have they been patented? Have they not been? Is there prior art? Isn't there? It's almost a question of luck and almost impossible to find out and it will make it extremely difficult to work to create these kinds of programs.

COMMISSIONER LEHMAN Thank you very much.

MR. FIDDLER: Thank you.

COMMISSIONER LEHMAN Gerry? I wanted to have Gerry Goldberg stand up, the Director of Group 230. He's an important person for all of you to know. He'll probably be back here, I would guess, following up on some of the aspects that will come out of these hearings to try to improve our procedures.

So Gerry is our point man on software. I hope you all get to know him, if you don't already.

Next I'd like to ask Jim Warren of Autodesk to step forward.

Oh, I think we think you're the person who got the Internet legislation for the California legislation passed --

MR. WARREN: That's correct.

COMMISSIONER LEHMAN -- passed in three weeks?

MR. WARREN: It's been online.

COMMISSIONER LEHMAN We've got a couple of job openings at the Patent and Trademark Office, so I mentioned that yesterday, maybe we ought to --

(Laughter)

MR. WARREN: We're going after the campaign disclosure information now.

--oOo--

JIM WARREN
AUTODESK, INC.

MR. WARREN: Mr. Chairman and other distinguished representatives of the Department of Commerce:

My name is Jim Warren.

First, I am a Member of the Board of Directors of Autodesk, a multi-national software company specializing in computer-aided design. As a 400 million dollar company,

UNITED STATES PATENT AND TRADEMARK OFFICE
Public Hearing on Patent Protection for Software-Related Inventions
San Jose, California -- January 26-27, 1994

we have been recently identified as the sixth largest PC software publisher in the world. I am presenting its recommendations.

Secondly, I have been a computer professional since 1968, have founded multi-million dollar companies in Silicon Valley, and have held numerous leadership roles in personal computing essentially since its inception in the 1970s, in the mid 1970s.

I was founding President of the Microcomputer Industry Trade Association, received the Electronic Frontier Foundation's first Pioneer Award, hold graduate Degrees in Computer Engineering, Medical Information Science, Mathematics and Statistics.

I was founding Editor of microcomputing's first software periodical, was founder of the first, first free newspaper and the first subscription newspaper, InfoWorld, and founding host of television's oldest Computer Weekly, as well as founding the world's largest public microcomputer conventions and chairing them in the first decade of the industry.

My remarks are excerpted from three parts of my prepared statement; namely, principles, pragmatics and some specific recommendations. I am not speaking as an intellectual-property attorney. I am speaking as a technological innovator with proven experience and as a long-time observer of this industry. I've written approximately 60 to 70 articles about the future of this industry that have received wide circulation, in excess of 220,000 copies per issue.

We all know that software is somehow different from all traditional inventions. The difference -- but how does it differ from the devices that are surely what the framers of the Constitution envisioned when they mandated patent protection? The difference is that all traditional inventions enhance our physical capabilities, whereas software mimics the mind and enhances our intellectual capabilities. This is what makes software different from all patentable devices and this is what justifies sui generis.

Let me define what software is for the purpose of our discussion, based on its functionality, its utility, the useful character of its art: software is what occurs between stimulus and response, with no physical incarnation other than as representations of binary logic.

The fundamental question is: Do we want to permit the monopoly possession of everything that works like logical intellectual processes? I hope not.

The mind has always been sacrosanct. The claim that intellectual processes of logical procedures that do not primarily manipulate devices, as in Diamond vs. Diehr, can be possessed and monopolized, simply extends greed and avarice much too far.

What frightens and infuriates so many of us about software patents is that they seek to monopolize our intellectual processes when their representation and performance is aided by machine.

I respectfully object to the title of these hearings, "Software-Related Inventions". The title illustrates an inappropriate and seriously-misleading bias. In fact, in more than a quarter century as a computer professional and observer and writer in this industry, I don't recall ever

hearing or reading such a phrase -- except in the context of legalistic claims for monopoly where the claimants were trying to twist the tradition of patented devices in order to monopolize the execution of intellectual processes.

To pragmatics.

There is absolutely no evidence whatsoever, not a single iota, that software patents have promoted or will promote progress. And I provide examples in my paper.

Of the thousands of programmers I have known in the last quarter century, I have never heard a single one say they didn't develop a program because they could not monopolize its functionality.

Of the thousands of programs I have known about as a multi-decade industry observer, I don't know of a single one that was innovative enough to promote progress, much less perhaps qualify for a patent as a useful art, that couldn't find funding.

The system was not broken when there were no software patents.

Now, however, there is growing evidence that software patents have begun to harm and deter progress. And I provide a number of examples, including the company for which I am speaking, Autodesk, holds some number of software patents and has applied for others, which, of course, remain secret under current US law. However, all are defensive and an infuriating waste of our technical talent and financial resources made necessary only by the lawyers' invention of software patents.

Autodesk has faced at least 17 baseless patent claims made against it in recent years and has spent over a million dollars defending itself, with millions more certain to pour down the bottomless patent pit. Fortunately, we have the financial and technical resources to rebuff such claims. We rebutted all but one of the claims even before the patent holders could file frivolous lawsuits and will litigate the remaining claim to conclusion.

Your Office has issued at least 16 patents that we have successfully rebutted and we never paid a penny in these attempted extortions that your Office assisted, but it is an enormous waste of resources that could better be invested in useful innovation.

COMMISSIONER LEHMAN   Could I ask a question about that?

MR. WARREN: Out of your time or my time?

COMMISSIONER LEHMAN   It can be out of your time -- out of my time.

MR. WARREN: That's what I was -- oh, okay, thank you.

COMMISSIONER LEHMAN   We have a procedure for re-examination of patents. It sounds to me like what happened here --

MR. WARREN: I was about to recommend that.

COMMISSIONER LEHMAN   Well, we have that now, you know. In other words, were those 16 --

It sounds to me like what happened here is that people basically threatened you with lawsuits and, you know, you got your lawyers all geared up and basically scared them away before you went to court, but left it there. Whereas, one of the things that you could have done, under our existing procedures, is that you could have come into the Patent and Trademark Office and petitioned for re-examination of those patents and have them held invalid.

Did you consider doing that, and, if you didn't, why?

MR. WARREN: I am certain that we did the least expensive thing that we could do.

And I have no specifics. You'll have to talk to our legal eagles on that, or have to ask our legal folks on that. But this is an enormous —

Incidentally we not only invested our financial resources, we invested our technical talent. Instead of them creating something, they had to go research prior art to fight off these frivolous claims. That ain't right.

Back to my prepared remarks.

That does not reward innovation nor promote progress. Furthermore, software patents can probably deter progress, and I provide a number of examples.

Finally, there is an intense danger that software patents pose to our industry's global competitiveness, and I detail how.

To specific recommendations. Okay, this is the goodies.

Let us agree that those who hold software patents probably prefer patent protection -- IBM, I think, is the largest holder and MicroSoft is the second largest -- and those who spend their time and resources creating technical innovation and national progress rather than creating patent applications and litigation probably prefer unfettered freedom to innovate.

Let us also agree that the Constitutional intent -- very important -- is to "promote progress". So let us disregard who wants what for self-benefit and act on principle. We propose as a principle that those processes that are exclusively intellectual and exclusively algorithmic, even when mimicked by machine, must not be monopolized.

We offer two recommendations, the second having 12 parts, so to speak, the 12 Apostles of redress of the current problems.

The first recommendation: Issue a finding that software, as I have defined it, implements intellectual processes that have no substantive physical incarnation, processes that are exclusively analytical, intellectual, logical and algorithmic in nature; plus the clearly stated Constitutional intent to declare that -- and use those findings to declare that the Patent Office acted in error when it granted software patents; declare that software patents monopolize intellectual and algorithmic processes and also fail to fulfill the Constitutional mandate to promote progress; declare that software as a mimic of the mind cannot be patented.

Second, until and only until software patents are definitively prohibited, reject or freeze all such applications pending conclusive action on the following 12 points:

(1) Redress serious errors of previous administrations.

Issue a finding that there have been extensive and serious errors of judgment in a large percentage of software patents granted in the past and immediately recall all software patents for re-review and possible revocation.

Encourage industry assistance. And I offer some comments about how and some legislation that's needed.

Make the information available via the Internet and solicit maximum public input.

(2) Mandate disclosure upon filing.

Issue a finding that it unconstitutionally suppresses progress to hide software threats in secret filings for one to five years. Note that most of the other high-tech nations with which we compete require disclosure upon filing or very soon thereafter.

Require disclosure upon filing or at least within, say, 90 days of filing. This will give software developers essential early warning of possible danger. It will also allow them to provide badly needed prior art, perhaps years before the patent might be granted and become a threat.

Let it be the responsibility of those seeking lengthy monopolies to defend the truly novel and truly non-obvious character of their innovations in a public patent-application review process. Do not continue to force that responsibility onto all other practitioners after the fact.

(3) Recommendation 3. Require disclosure of complete source code and documentation upon filing.

That will slow this stuff down.

Reiterate that the -- (Laughter).

That was not in my prepared remarks.

Reiterate that the major function of the patent system is to assure complete public disclosure of innovation in order that all may benefit and progress be promoted.

Issue a finding that software patents require full disclosure of complete original source code and complete internal documentation. Then require its disclosure, preferably upon filing or perhaps 90 days later, but at least upon the granting of the software patent. Note that this implements the "best mode" requirement.

Software patent disclosures in the past have often failed to fulfill this minimum requirement; therefore, require such disclosures from all present software patent holders. Those who decline to so disclose in a timely manner must have their patents invalidated as being improperly granted.

(4) Prohibit filings after any public exposure.

Issue a finding that most of the nation's high-tech competitors prohibit patent filings after any public exposure of their proposed innovation.

Further, find that patentable innovation in software is unclear, vaporware is rampant, early disclosure is common, sharing of disclosed innovation is almost universal, and possibly infringing development using such disclosures is almost inescapable. Use that finding to prohibit any filing after the date of any public exposure.

Recommendation (5) Reduce requirements for challenging software patents.

Find that the evaluation of what constitutes new, novel and un-obvious innovation in software is highly subjective and essentially impossible for the Patent Office to judge, since the Office does not have the 50 years of prior art that exists.

Change the standard for invalidating software patents from a requirement for "clear and convincing evidence" to no presumption of validity at all -- which is usually the case if the experience of well-funded defendants who can do the adequate research, such as Autodesk, is any measure.

UNITED STATES PATENT AND TRADEMARK OFFICE
Public Hearing on Patent Protection for Software-Related Inventions
San Jose, California -- January 26-27, 1994

(6) Reduce the protection period.

Issue a finding that 17-year software protection patents are clearly unreasonable where, in an industry where significant innovation can often be created in months, most innovation has minimal costs relative to traditional inventions, manufacturing and distribution is trivial, products can be shipped within weeks of being finalized, great profits can be attained in less than a year, the life of a product typically is only a few years, and all of the growth of the industry, from inception to Diamond vs. Diehr in 1981, was barely three times the 17-year monopoly period.

Shorten the one-time protection period to no more than, say, two years. Sui generis is justified.

(7) Replace -- wow, I'm still in the green -- or no I'm not -- or have I run out of time?

COMMISSIONER LEHMAN I was giving you your maximum.

MR. WARREN: Oh, sorry about that. May I finish the other remarks very quickly?

(7) Replace first-to-invent with first-to- file.

Issue a finding that this nation is almost alone in granting monopolies on the basis of first-to-invent. If the patent system is justified and public disclosure has merit, then encourage it by awarding monopolies only on the basis of first-to-file-and-disclose, but, of course, retain the principle that prior art always invalidates a patent.

(8) Declare that useful intellectual communications cannot be monopolized.

This is the look and feel issue. We don't want to protect it under patent any more than we want to protect it under copyright, when they are not primarily aesthetic and not primarily artistic and not primarily for controlling equipment. And I address that more properly.

(9) To promote continuing progress, mandate cross licensing.

If you are going to grant monopolies over our algorithmic processes, then at least mandate that we can use them under license from the monopolists. And I suggest how.

In particular, we suggest mandatory licensing rates not exceeding, say, 5 percent of a licensee's profits prorated across all cross licensers for a given product.

(10) Provide a nationally accessible prior-art collection.

I'm sure you heard that from 50 other people. If you don't have the resources to do it -- and make it available across the Internet -- if you don't have the resources to do it, then inform Congress that you are unable to perform your assigned functions without endangering national progress.

(11) Exercise much greater due diligence with regard to software patents.

You must stop leaving it up to endless threats, defenses, court battles among those who can afford them to ascertain which few patents might be valid, which is too often determined only by the relative wealth of the combatants.

(12) And finally, create a large public advisory body, a commission of volunteers who are technologists, those who produce the nation's progress in this area, not just intellectual-property attorneys.

Seek them from a broad spectrum of software publishers, great and small producers, including individuals.

These recommendations require Congressional action, and this industry has been politically asleep, but continuing software patent debacles are beginning to awaken it, most especially its innovators, and we certainly have the financial resources, the communication tools and the tenacity to seek effective redress as we finally organize and choose to act.

However, the needed Congressional action can be greatly facilitated by supportive recommendations from your Office. Please draft them soon. But not cloistered inside the Washington Beltway, rather with extensive Internet circulation of all drafts and discussion.

Let us stand on each others' shoulders rather than on each others' toes.

Thank you.

COMMISSIONER LEHMAN Thanks very much, Mr. Warren. We gave you a few extra minutes there --

MR. WARREN: I appreciate that.

COMMISSIONER LEHMAN -- because of my intervention.

I want to thank you for coming out here. I think we'll look at your recommendations very carefully and I think with regard to this idea of, first of all, I hope you will appreciate the fact that we're not inside the Beltway right now --

MR. WARREN: Every two days outside we appreciate.

COMMISSIONER LEHMAN -- we have a little capacity to innovate, even Washington lawyers can come up with a few good ideas every once in awhile.

And secondly, I think that we do need to have closer, a better means for communicating directly with the innovative community and not just for patent lawyers, and so we need to do a little innovative work to figure out the mechanisms for doing that ourselves and I really appreciate your comments. Thanks.

MR. WARREN: Ask us for help -- I mean all of the industry -- and we will help.

Thank you.

COMMISSIONER LEHMAN Next I'd like to ask Mr. Michael Glenn, from the Intellectual Property Section of the State Bar of California, to step forward. Maybe he can defend the lawyers.

--oOo--

MARY O'HARE

CHAIR, EXECUTIVE COMMITTEE

INTELLECTUAL PROPERTY SECTION, STATE BAR OF CALIFORNIA

MS. O'HARE: I am not Michael Glenn. He felt as though he needed some company up here.

Assistant Secretary and Commissioner Lehman, my name is Mary O'Hare. I am the Chair and am speaking on behalf of the Executive Committee of the Intellectual Property Section of the State Bar of California.

The Section is voluntary, comprised of more than 3700 attorneys practicing in the various intellectual property fields of copyrights, trademarks, trade secrets and patents. Our members represent, for the context of this hearing, individuals, non-profit organizations, small and large businesses.

We are proud that our organization was one of the first to have Commissioner Lehman as its keynote speaker and we thank you for holding these hearings in California.

All too often in the past, as Commissioner Lehman has noted, California, and sometimes the needs of its attorneys and clients, more than 2600 miles away from the Patent Office, have been felt to be out of sight and out of mind. Nonetheless, California has been the center of the United States cultural and technical renaissance of the late 20th century. California's two largest industries, entertainment and technology, are also the United States' two largest export engines.

We in the Section hope that these hearings will signal the Office's willingness to have easy, open access to the Patent Office for Californians, a privilege until recently primarily enjoyed by the Washington, DC, patent bar.

While I am Chair of this Section, my intellectual property expertise has been gained in the context of a motion picture entertainment practice. Commissioner Lehman, we know you have a sense of humor, we know you know that we've been through an earthquake recently, but the tragic earthquake in Southern California may have rattled our homes, our offices and our psyche, but let me assure you that Californians are tough, we are not so rattled as to ignore the importance of your presence here and that's why we are here or to presume to have a motion picture attorney address you on matters at the Patent Office.

Therefore, I am privileged to present Michael Glenn, an officer of our Section, who is a patent attorney in the Silicon Valley who has represented both individual inventors and large corporations before the Patent Office for the past 14 years.

His qualifications are set forth in our written statement and he will present the statement of the Section.

Thank you.

COMMISSIONER LEHMAN Thank you.

—o0o--

MICHAEL GLENN, ESQ.

MR. GLENN: Commissioner Lehman, today's hearings have been convened to receive comments from the public on patent protection for software inventions. Rather than respond to the specific questions raised in the Notice of these hearings, we will address the important, broader issues that form the context in which the issue of patent protection for software inventions arises.

These issues include: (1) the expertise and ability of the Examining Corps, especially with regard to the difficult task of applying complex legal principles to emerging and sophisticated technologies; (2) the availability of task appropriate tools and resources to the Examining Corps; (3) the need to make Patent Office services and resources readily available to the public; and (4) the understanding that the US Constitution, in providing the Congress with "the power to promote the progress of science and useful arts by securing for a limited time to authors and inventors the exclusive right to their respective writings and discoveries", did not limit the types of discoveries for which a grant of

exclusive rights would be secured.

Preliminarily, it must be observed that patent myths abound and the Patent Office should use its best efforts to dispel these myths. These hearings are one excellent way to raise the general level of public understanding of the US patent system. However, the primary job of the Patent Office is to examine patent applications. A quality examination and precise application of the patent laws by the Patent Office are necessary to assure that the interests of both the public and the inventor are properly served.

First, while recent efforts to improve the quality of the Patent Office services, especially the quality of the Examining Corps and as a result the quality of patent examination and patents issued by the Patent Office have not gone unnoticed, more needs to be done.

Because the process of examining a patent application necessarily demands both a high level of technical expertise and a thorough understanding of the legal standards that are applied during the examination, the Patent Office must continue to attract and retain Examiners who not only have the technical knowledge necessary to understand the invention, but who also understand the legal framework within which the Patent Office functions. To this end, ability and merit should be the most important standards by which Examiners are hired, promoted and retained.

Secondly, we encourage the Patent Office to do more with regard to improving the quality of the patent examination process.

For example, in many technical areas a search of issued US patents alone cannot reveal the most relevant prior art. In rapidly developing technology, such as computer software and biotechnology, where the enforceability and availability of intellectual property rights in the past have been uncertain, the most relevant art may be found in industry journals and in proceedings of professional societies and institutes.

The Examining Corps should be encouraged to search all relevant information sources. Intensive training in using these information sources should be provided the Examining Corps such that the most relevant priority is applied by the Examiners to every patent application filed with the Patent Office.

Thirdly, since the Patent Office is also a tremendous depository of knowledge, we encourage the Patent Office to explore the possibility of giving the public throughout the United States free or inexpensive access to the Patent Office database through an online source such as the Internet.

At present the few public patent depositories scattered across the US are underfunded, understaffed and resource-constrained. For example, online searching is not available at the Sunnyvale patent depository here in Silicon Valley and those wishing to perform a computerized search of the now available CD-ROM database there are limited to only 20 minutes of use.

The Patent Office search room in Washington, DC, is not accessible for the public at large, attorneys and inventors who live, work and invent in California. Ready public access to such publicly-owned information would allow inventors to make informed decisions about whether or not they should pursue patent protection, would allow those seeking to enter a new market to review the patent literature before entering upon a course of action that could lead to a wasteful, potentially disastrous patent infringement lawsuit, and would allow those seeking to license technology to have access to the marketplace of ideas contained in the Patent Office database and be better able to establish a fair value for such technology. As important, the public would become more familiar with and better educated concerning the patent system.

Fourth, from time to time an issue may arise when a recently-issued patent is publicized as part of a marketing campaign by a successful patent applicant or as part of an ideological debate concerning the applicability of patent laws to the technology protected or the breadth of coverage afforded the invention by the patent's claims. As a result a discussion ensues concerning the wisdom of extending patent protection to new and emerging technologies. We caution the Patent Office not to allow the mere existence of a public debate alone to provide a rationale for establishing separate rules for such technologies.

This discussion is not new. In the days of the Wright brothers there was the fear that the future development of aviation would be seriously impeded if Wilbur and Orville should be allowed a basic patent on their invention. As we all know, this was not the case. As Wilbur Wright put it: "When a couple of flying machine inventors fish, metaphorically speaking, in waters where hundreds had previously fished, and spending years of time and thousands of dollars finally succeed in making a catch, there are people who think it a pity that the courts should give orders that the rights of the inventors shall be respected and that those who wish to enjoy the feast shall contribute something to pay the fishers."

With regard to enforceability of patent rights for new and emerging technologies, the Patent Office must show leadership. The Statutory mandate of the Patent Office is clear: novel and unobvious inventions that comprise patentable subject matter must be granted a patent. As a general principle, patentable subject matter cannot be limited to known technologies, but, as stated by the Supreme Court in the Chakrabarty case, must also encompass "anything under the sun that is made by man." Otherwise, only old technologies will be found to comprise patentable subject matter, at which point the patent system will lose all meaning.

It is the ownership of invention that spurs innovation, not just the promise of exclusivity afforded by patent grant, but more significantly, in the incentive to avoid a patent by inventing around the patented invention.

Finally, while the patentability of software inventions has long been an interesting topic of discussion, first in the courts and the Patent Office and now in the press, much of the discussion may be caused by misunderstanding and confusion. We suggest that some of the misunderstanding stems from the confidential nature of the examination process. In many areas it is not possible to perform an infringement search to clear a new product because the most relevant patents are still pending in the Patent Office and not available to the public.

The Patent Office could explore opportunities for involving the public in the examination process to avoid any surprise attendant with the grant of broad-reaching patents. For example, the Patent Office may want to consider the pre-grant publication of patent applications and/or pre-grant public opposition hearings.

We applaud the Patent Office decision to re-examine a recently issued patent on its own initiative in light of new art discovered after issuance of the patent. As an organization we have no opinion regarding the outcome of the re-examination, we only applaud this bold and welcome policy on the part of the Patent Office to pursue excellence. The ultimate outcome of such actions will be to improve the stature and regard with which a United States patent is held. This in turn will provide more certainty concerning the validity of an issued patent. Reducing the likelihood of a successful attack on the validity of a patent should encourage early settlements of patent disputes and strengthen American industry by strengthening the incentive to innovate rather than to litigate.

In closing, the Patent Office must continue to serve the needs of a broad range of applicants, from independent inventors to multi-national corporations, while taking into account the effects of a fast-changing global economy.

Patents not only protect inventions, they also protect employment and national wealth. The United States is a technology leader because of the incentives it provides to those persons who take the effort and risk involved in bringing new inventions to the marketplace. Of all the nations in the world, the United States has the only significant software industry, the only significant biotech industry, and the only significant microprocessor industry, to name a few. These industries form a mighty technology river that has human creative energy as its source. The American experience shows us that such creative energy requires incentive. The role of the Patent Office is paramount because the Patent Office is charged by law with providing incentives for this creative energy by protecting patentable inventions.

We pledge that if you involve California's inventors and practitioners in the ongoing discussion of Patent Office procedure and policy, your job will be easier and we can together ensure that the patent system and the Patent Office fulfills the Constitutional proviso of promoting the progress of science and the useful arts, all to the economic benefit of the citizens of California and the rest of the United States.

Thank you.

COMMISSIONER LEHMAN Thank you very much.

Next I'd like to call Mr. Lippe of Synopsys.

--oOo--

PAUL LIPPE

GENERAL COUNSEL

SYNOPSIS

MR. LIPPE: Thank you, Mr. Chairman.

By way of introducing myself to the Panel, let me say that I've sat where you're sitting. I used to be Chairman of a thing called the Colorado Air Quality Control Commission and having sat through two days of stupifyingly dull testimony about aromatic emissions of oxygenated fuels, I respect your stamina and your willingness to sit through this stuff.

UNITED STATES PATENT AND TRADEMARK OFFICE
Public Hearing on Patent Protection for Software-Related Inventions
San Jose, California — January 26-27, 1994

COMMISSIONER LEHMAN Well, there's a big difference. That may have been stupifyingly dull, but this isn't. It's intensely interesting. It really is.

MR. LIPPE: So I'm going to try not to echo the comments that you've heard before, but I do want to stand in strong ratification of some of the critiques that Mr. Fiddler from Wind River made about the software patent system.

The problem is, from my perspective, the legal system --

COMMISSIONER LEHMAN Can you tell us just a little bit about Synopsys?

MR. LIPPE: Yeah, I will.

The broad problem is that the legal culture and the legal domain is so different from the technical innovation world that when you try to bring them together, at least from the technical people's side, it doesn't work very well.

I'm General Counsel of Synopsys. Synopsys is an electronic design automation software company. I'm also the head of a little thing called "The Public Affairs Committee of EDAC". EDAC is our industry trade association. It stands for EDA Companies. There are about 40 companies in EDAC, ranging from very raw startups to some half a billion dollar companies. EDA is probably one of the two or three principal domains within what your Notice refers to as "computer integrated design".

It is a strategically critical-technology area for the United States, and Synopsys is, in the new parlance, clearly a national technology champion. We make software which is used in the design of complex electronics parts and our customers are in the semiconductor computer systems and telecommunications industries. People such as Sun, Hitachi, IBM, Intel, Siemens.

Synopsys itself was founded about seven years ago, and, in the term of art, industry analysts expect that we'll do around 200 million dollars of revenue this year. We are probably the second fastest growing company in the computer-aided integrated design sector, the fastest growing company in EDA, and we are considered to be one of the hot companies in our field.

The reason I'm speaking today is I want to challenge what I think has been the animating idea behind the move towards enhanced intellectual property protection and patent protection and that is that enhanced intellectual property protection is per se beneficial for US companies.

And my challenge comes not as an intellectual property lawyer, although I am a lawyer, and not as a technologist, because I'm not a technologist, but as somebody with some deep experience in the political sector who's given some thought to what mix of policies makes the most sense to advance America's industrial interests.

And as somebody taking a political approach, I think it's important when you examine these policies, to think of — to focus on the outcomes and who wins and who loses and not so much on the product, as well as what the ideas are that are advanced by the various speakers.

The concern that I've got, and I think the gentleman from Wind River and other people have, is that the startup process and the innovation process is inherently fragile, and, as the domain becomes increasingly littered with patents, to have the ability to kill companies at each stage of the

process. There are various what you might call choke points, at the financing stage, at the various financing stages, and at the stage of trying to begin to sell to customers, and it's all too easy for innovative companies to be blocked from bringing their products to market. And I want to talk about that a little more.

The fundamental assumption that enhanced protection for patents is favorable to US industry is an idea that I think gained currency in the late '70s and early '80s and it was based on the notion, the basic idea -- and I hope I don't offend anyone by saying this -- that Americans invent and Japanese copy, and the way to make America stronger is to help to enhance intellectual property protection. My fear is that we've gone too far, that we've moved towards more aggressive patent enforcement, at the same time we've moved towards less aggressive anti-trust enforcement, and that the remedy, the inherent remedy for patent of monopoly protection and the nature of patents being issued is not -- we've gone too far.

And the other thing to focus on in terms of the software industry is that software, as the gentleman from Microsoft used to say but won't say today, is a natural monopoly. Being first to market confers an enormous advantage in terms of the ability to set the standard, there are high barriers to entry, high fixed costs and low variable costs, so you've already got a huge head start if you're first to market.

It's not clear to me that there's, as some of the earlier speakers have said and I agree with, that you're really furthering the goal to encourage people to innovate by conferring additional monopoly.

And there tends not to be a lot of success in the software industry for copiers, clones, and followers. I think you'd be -- there are very few examples of people who followed, who have executed a following strategy copying other people's technology, that have been successful in software.

Some of the ideas that underlie increased protection for patents, I think, are misconceptions, at least in the domain where we live.

First, the key idea that I think is wrong is the notion that invention per se is what's important. If you go to a venture capitalist in Silicon Valley and you say "I've invented something", they've got zero interest in that because they recognize that the whole Silicon Valley paradigm is based on the notion that what matters is customer-delivered innovation, which is very different from the level of invention that you need to get a patent, and that's why today the perception of the people in this room who are on the anti-patent side is that most patents are going to big companies who don't sell the products, they get the patents out of their industrial labs and then this group of people that you might call the lone inventors.

But what really creates value for the United States and for the customers is when you deliver the technology to customers in a way they can be used and that, that has not been the focus of the patent law, for good and sufficient reasons, in the past.

The second thing that I think, at least in our domain, that is a misconception is that people actually read patents and use them to advance the wrong technology. No engineer I've ever known has been willing to read other people's patents,

UNITED STATES PATENT AND TRADEMARK OFFICE
Public Hearing on Patent Protection for Software-Related Inventions
San Jose, California -- January 26-27, 1994

and most people feel, at least in our field, that patents don't describe things with enough particularity to know how to copy them anyway.

The third problem is the patents, as you've heard over and over again, I won't belabor the point, have been very incremental, they haven't been significant, and so there's so much overlap space between the existing patents.

And the fourth misconception and I think the most important one is that the patent system protects small companies. As I said earlier, the patent process is fundamental in the legal process, a lot of lawyer bashing goes on, some of it justified, much of it not, but in any case recognize that the process of delivering innovation to the customer is a totally different culture, it's a totally different process, than that required to obtain and enforce a patent.

That doesn't mean that obtaining and enforcing patents is a bad thing, but it's always going to be a diversion of energy and resources, as Mr. Warren said, from that process of delivering innovation to customers, and the litigation process is almost always going to favor the bigger guy because he's got the resources and he's acculturated to going through that kind of drill. Small companies hate it. Engineers, most engineers I've ever known hate it, and they're very uncomfortable and they're very vulnerable to this kind of process.

The other point is that the legal system doesn't really comprehend the technology. We happen to be the leaders in our field, we're glad of that, but the consequence of that is that, of the ten people in the world who understand what we do, eight of them work for us, none of them work for the Patent Office, and it's very unlikely that anybody who's got that kind of leading edge expertise would want to work for the Patent Office, no disrespect to the folks in the Patent Office, but they would like to be building the products and, you know, doing the things that people around here do.

So there's an enormous amount of randomness in the system because the legal system cannot adequately -- and cannot be expected to -- adequately comprehend the technology at the level that our folks do. That randomness, then, introduces enormous transfer costs and friction costs because it doesn't really afford, the current system, doesn't really afford us a lot of inexpensive ways to resolve the issue.

There's an article in "Electronic Engineering Times" which talks about patents in the EDA industry. The EDA industry is probably the most, maybe along with desktop software publishing, American-dominated industry. 99 percent of worldwide revenues from American companies, and it is absolutely a strategic technology industry, central to everything happening in electronics today, but the people who hold the patents by and large are Japanese companies, with the exception of IBM which is the largest patentholder. Well, these Japanese companies happen to be our customers, they're not our competitors because they don't sell any products, but it is a little worrisome that Hitachi's got 49 patents in this area and they don't sell anything and we've got zero patents in this area. So if we were an earlier-stage company, it would be even more worrisome because the ability of the large company to block the small company creates a lot of uncertainty.

And I was always taught and always believed that in the law predictability has got to be one of the principal goals of any well-conceived legal system and right now people feel like there's very little predictability in the system, instead there's a lot of randomness.

The other thing that's happening in terms of where the world is going in our domain, and I don't know how to deal with this one, to tell you the truth, there's what I call "hardware/software convergence". We're able to represent in software things that were formerly only represented in hardware and so we now have sort of a confluence of the most patent-oriented domain, which is electronic parts, and the least patent-oriented domain, which is software, and it's very confusing.

We've also got the reality that the traditional US patent holders, in particular IBM and AT&T, are no longer as constrained as they have been historically about their anti-trust worries and have been aggressively going after people.

So, you know, one of the anomalies is that there's a very significant technology called RISC, Reduce Instructions Set Computing, it was invented by IBM in 1975 in Fishkill, and that's great but they didn't do anything with it, they left it in the closet for eight years, until Sun brought RISC to market and made a very significant technology shift and delivered a lot of value to customers through RISC. Well, IBM went after Sun and they were able to get Sun to pay them royalties on the technology, but the really important event that occurred was, not the conceptualization and creation of RISC in the lab, it was Sun creating the market and delivering the value to customers around RISC.

In terms of suggestions, you know we've all got sort of overlapping suggestions so I won't belabor the point, I think some of the suggestions that were made were really good, but I think we ought to be thinking, and I would ask you to consider, I don't know how you get there, that some kind of sales is a requirement, that there be some kind of -- I think first-to-file is not going to solve any of the problems, but some notion of first-to-deliver-value as opposed to just having an invention in the lab. Especially where we've got this three-year black hole, where somebody can file a patent and everybody else is shipping products and then three years later people find out that they've got a problem with the products, and obviously Compton's Multi-Media Patent is an example of that.

So my focus point is that intellectual property protection per se is not necessarily a good thing for America. It's good for some companies, it's not good for others.

I think on the whole the thing that we are best at, which is the smaller-company innovation, it is a very worrisome trend and a lot of companies are very concerned about it. I think it poses a significant threat to hurt the job creation and innovation and company creation machines that we've got going, and I'd like you to look for ways to rein back where we are.

COMMISSIONER LEHMAN Thank you very much.

Next I'd like to call Tim Boyle, Executive Director of Multimedia Development Group.

--oOo--

TIM BOYLE

UNITED STATES PATENT AND TRADEMARK OFFICE
Public Hearing on Patent Protection for Software-Related Inventions
San Jose, California -- January 26-27, 1994

EXECUTIVE DIRECTOR
MULTIMEDIA DEVELOPMENT GROUP

MR. BOYLE: Good morning.

My name is Tim Boyle and I represent the Multimedia Development Group. I'm the acting Executive Director of that Group.

The Multimedia Development Group is a market-development oriented trade association. It's located in San Francisco. Our members are primarily interested in the software side of this industry.

We represent about 400 companies that build the software for multimedia titles. These include about 200 multimedia developers and publishers, 50 technology companies, about 150 service providers, including accountants, public relations firms, marketing research firms, and over 25 law firms. We also represent 20 to 25 educational, nonprofit and governmental organizations.

Our mission is to help the emerging multimedia software companies become commercially viable by facilitating the communication between the parties who develop, fund, service, sell and, in your case, regulate these titles.

I would like to thank you for the forum and we appreciate the fact that you are soliciting our opinions.

I'd like to address three points today.

The first is the need to stimulate the creative processes in this industry and the commercial structures that support them through an equitable code of intellectual property.

Secondly, the need for this code to meet the digital challenge by distinguishing between what is a patentable invention and a copyrightable creation.

And finally, some suggestions for your consideration, such as the possibility of incorporating some of the precepts of academic science into the work of the Patent Office, in particular the concept of peer review.

I'd like to start by saying that we support patent protection for inventions that integrate software with other elements. I would also like to let you know that the furor on the Compton's New Media patent claim comes in part from our community. While we note with pride that Compton's New Media is a member of our organization and we wish to see their creations appropriately protected, the majority of our members believe that the ideas at issue in that claim are better protected by copyright rather than patent.

Compton's Multimedia Encyclopedia is a very clever and extremely innovative use of the new vocabulary of digital communications. As such, it represents a unique and creative arrangement of fundamental elements that constitute this new vocabulary of the artist and the author in the digital age.

Graphical screen elements, windows, buttons and such, search and navigation methodologies, multiple views of databases, are part and parcel of this new vocabulary. It is their use in the expression and representation of ideas that creates value, and this value, our membership believes, must be protected. We look to the Patent Office to identify, understand and protect the fundamental concepts of this new media. These concepts properly belong in the public domain because they are the alphabet, the building blocks of our new media.

The multimedia developer community has a vested interest in protecting their intellectual property from unfair copying or infringement and to ensure that the concepts on which they are based can be freely exchanged. We believe that one can only properly assess the patentability of a work after reviewing that work in the context of all the work which has gone before it.

There was a much simpler task in the industrial age and this is now much more difficult in the information age that we're moving into.

How would theatre have developed if the concept of plot were owned by someone? I mean William Shakespeare never could have afforded a license. It is the innovator and society who will suffer if we fail to protect the novel ideas or fail to recognize the obvious in this new media.

I'd like to close with a few suggestions that we have for the Office. The first is opening up the patent application process. The current process has been characterized as "secretive". We would like to see that characterization changed.

We would also suggest peer review. In academic science a discovery is accorded recognition only when it has passed the test of peer review. If you'll remember "cold fission". That was taken care of by the scientists.

We recognize that there is a problem that open review presents for inventions with great commercial potential, but there are other members of our industry who have put forward a number of proposals in that regard. Our organization endorses the general concept of peer review as an important element in the evaluation of software patent applications.

And the third and final suggestion is building a definitive library of prior art. The Multimedia Development Group has published a call for prior art and we would like to offer your Office access to any an all materials that we received. We would like to establish an ongoing relationship to ensure that your Office has access to any prior art it requires.

The Multimedia Development Group's purpose is to represent the interests of the multimedia community and to grow this industry. We would like to extend our hand to assist you in gaining access to and understanding the needs of that community. We would like to have as strong a relationship with our Patent Office as the one enjoyed by the metal fabricating inventors of the industrial age. That Patent Office created the basis for the most explosive economic growth that the world had ever seen, and this Patent Office has the opportunity to dwarf that achievement by creating the basis for a global information economy.

Thank you for your time.

COMMISSIONER LEHMAN: Thank you very much.

By "peer review" do you mean that we would have like a panel of multimedia -- say we had a multimedia patent application -- we would have a panel of multimedia developers who were actual developers out there who we would convene somehow or other or we would send around the patent application to them the way in an academic setting they might send around a paper?

If you were a biochemist, you know, and you were about to

UNITED STATES PATENT AND TRADEMARK OFFICE
Public Hearing on Patent Protection for Software-Related Inventions
San Jose, California — January 26-27, 1994

publish a paper in science, the editor sends it around to three other scientists to look at it and to make comments and corrections. Usually the author of the original paper doesn't even know it, who the people are. Is that the kind of thing that you're talking about?

MR. BOYLE: That is one way to go about it and I would want that reality factor in there.

The other method is a scholastic review, but not in the traditional, old school sense. We have a school, San Francisco State University, that is providing 50 courses and training over 900 students a semester in multimedia. They have a group of people, many of them our members, who understand this. That school or an institute of that type, and there are many around the country, would be very happy to act as the agent to tell you what had happened in the past.

COMMISSIONER LEHMAN Well, I think part of what you're talking about there is better communication, better education of our Examining Corps, and more fluid and constant communication between the Examining Corps and the people in it with people who understand these industries.

MR. BOYLE: Right.

COMMISSIONER LEHMAN Now, for example, we could send some people from the Examining Corps out to attend this course that you just described.

I think one of the things -- and I don't want to open up, you know, an unmanageable floodgate here -- but I think these hearings are a very formalized kind of procedure, but I like to think of them as sort of the beginning of the process since it's so clear that we need to have better communication with our customers. That will solve some of our problems right there, if we just kind of have better communication with them, and that's why I think that we're going to have to.

I mentioned Mr. Goldberg was here and I think on an informal basis, we're not like a court, you know, you can only hear us in a hearing room, we can have informal contacts with industries and people and I encourage those of you who are in the room to get to know some of the Patent Office people who are here and sort of start to develop where you bring us into your peer group a little and we'll try to cooperate with that.

Obviously, we have to be doing our job, we can't be running around the country on junkets all the time, but we -- but it's important for us to develop better means of communication. Of course, electronic communication, Internet style of communication, too, is an important part of that. Anyway, I appreciate your comments and I have a little better understanding what you mean by "peer review".

MR. BOYLE: And I also would suggest that opening up the Patent Office electronically as widely as possible is going to give you access to that community. And you have many trade associations and professional development societies that would be happy, that are looking forward to working with you.

And I think everybody understands that we're on -- that this is the beginning of something new. My favorite is that the theme song of multimedia is "Something's happening here, what it is ain't exactly clear", and that is the state we're in.

Thank you.

COMMISSIONER LEHMAN Thank you.

Next I'd like to ask Mr. Ronald Laurie, Attorney at Weil, Gotshal & Manges, a prominent member of the intellectual property bar, to step forward.

--oOo--

RONALD S. LAURIE, ESQ.

WEIL, GOTSHAL & MANGES

MR. LAURIE: Thank you, Mr. Secretary.

I'd like to address the issue of patent protection for software-related inventions generally rather than the specific questions raised in the Notice.

The views expressed are personal, they're my own, and they don't necessarily represent the position of either my law firm or any particular client.

By way of introduction, I worked in Silicon Valley for 33 years, initially as a programmer and software designer and later as a patent lawyer focusing on computer technology. I currently teach a course at Stanford Law School entitled "Intellectual Property Protection for Information Technologies".

I have previously served on advisory panels to the National Research Council and the National Academy of Science in connection with software protection, and I was the only patent lawyer on the Advisory Panel to the Office of Technology Assessment in its recent study "Intellectual Property Protection for Software".

When one listens carefully to the impassioned arguments against quote "patenting software" unquote, it becomes apparent that the arguments and the basic intellectual property policy positions which underlie them can be classified into three categories:

First position: patents are bad. Second position: software patents are bad. Third position: bad software patents are bad.

The first position is most often heard in the halls of academia and raises fundamental social and economic issues which go far beyond the scope of the present inquiry.

The second position is often advanced by some, though not by any measure all, of the software companies that emerged and flourished during the early and mid '80s as a direct result of the commercial introduction of the microprocessor at a time when the industry generally and incorrectly believed that software-based inventions were unpatentable as a class.

The third position is the one most widely held today and for obvious reasons the easiest to defend.

In the heat of the debate over software patents, the boundaries between the second and third positions tend to blur, but I submit it is critically important to address them separately.

I respectfully submit that the second position is legally unsound and that the third while correct does not represent an insoluble problem. In support of my thesis, I offer the following:

Premise one: U.S. patent law does not protect software. Rather, it protects processes and machines that are quote "within the technological arts" unquote. In one of the first cases to consider the question of whether inventions involving computer programs constituted patentable subject matter. Judge Giles Rich, who was one of the principal architects of the current patent statute, introduced the phrase, "technological arts" as the modern equivalent of the constitutional term "useful arts," and is therefore defining the outer boundaries of patentable subject matter, both under the Constitution and under Section 101 of the Patent Act. That case was, In re Musgrave, decided in 1970.

Over the more that two decades since Musgrave, Judge Rich's formulation has remained unchallenged by any subsequent decision, although unfortunately it has been ignored by many. Thus any process that is not sufficiently applied the physical environment in which it operates to qualify as being quote "within the technological arts" unquote, constitutes unpatentable subject matter.

The critical distinction then is between applied technology and abstract ideas. Examples of the latter include; laws of nature, scientific principles, methods of doing business, printed matter and unapplied mathematical relationships.

Premise two: Computer implemented solutions to technological problems in the form of processes and/or machines typically exist along a design spectrum, ranging from pure hardware, that is random logic, to pure software, that is an externally-loaded computer program running on a general purpose digital computer.

Intermediate points along the spectrum involve designs which may be described as special purpose computers and which combine elements of hardware and software in varying proportions, using random logic, array logic, such as PLAs and PALs, microcode and firmware, firmware being fixed programs stored in internal read-only memory.

The particular point along the design spectrum that represents the optimum solution to a given problem is determined by a variety of factors, such as cost, speed, size, flexibility and so on. Moreover, the optimum design point moves over time as competing implementation technologies evolve at different rates. For example, in the mid '70s, complex video game functionality was implemented entirely in random logic. After the arrival of the microprocessor, the very same functionality was realized using firmware.

Finally, technologies such as logic synthesis are becoming available, by which a software solution can be quote "translated," unquote into an equivalent hardware solution, and vice versa. It should be self evident that as a matter of legal policy, the law should not promote artificial distinctions that the technology does not recognize.

And I should point out that Mr. Lippe's company is in the business of making a product which in effect translates software into hardware. Another example which I think illustrates the point is the technology of neural nets, which was originally created as a pure hardware solution and has evolved now into a software technology.

Premise three: The fact that a particular solution can be expressed mathematically or is a series of logical operations should be irrelevant to the patentability of the solution.

In 1972, based on what many commentators believe to be an erroneous interpretation of its prior decisions involving laws of nature and scientific principles, the U.S. Supreme Court announced, in Benson v. Gottschalk that a patent claim

describing a process which, quote, wholly preempts a mathematical algorithm is nonstatutory; that is, does not define patentable subject matter under Section 101 of the Patent Act.

The result of this formulation has been over two decades of confusion and inconsistency in the case law involving the patentability of software-implemented processes. The fact is that mathematics is a language, albeit a very precise one, and like other languages can be used to describe concepts and relationships that are technologically applied as well as those of a more abstract nature that are not so applied.

As noted by Professor Chisholm in an article called The Patentability of Algorithms, the real issue is probably not one of subject matter under Section 101, but rather one of indefinite claiming of the invention under Section 112. Under the constitutional standard within the technological arts, it is the subject matter of the invention and not the language chosen to describe it that should determine the presence or absence of patentable subject matter.

Premise Four: Even if a particular software equipment and solution represents patentable subject matter, in order to justify the exclusionary benefits conferred by a patent, it must also pass the test of novelty and nonobviousness over the prior arts.

And Commissioner, you have pointed this out to several of the speakers, that there is significant difference between the patentability of software as a class and the patentability of any particular software invention.

This is the key factor that interrelates the second and third positions, i.e., software patents are bad versus bad software patents are bad; that is, even if a software implemented solution is sufficiently technologically applied to pass muster under the statutory subject matter test, in order to quality for patent protection, the solution must also be novel and nonobvious to a person of ordinary skill in the art.

It is submitted that given the objective to be accomplished and accepted principles of software design, the great majority of the software written today would not pass the nonobviousness test. Thus, the effectiveness of a patent system in a particular area of technology is directly related to the degree to which the examining authority -- in this case the Patent & Trademark Office -- has access to the most relevant prior art. To the extent that there are or can be created mechanisms through which the Patent & Trademark Office can access the widest body of software-related prior art, the system will work.

A number of such mechanisms have been discussed during these hearings, and they include PTO access to the growing number of commercial and public databases of software technology, private sector assistance in supplementing the PTO internal database, early publication of patent applications coupled with third party submission of prior art.

The important point is that the problem of bad software patents is mechanical and not inherent. That is, over time it can be engineered away or at least reduced to a commercially tolerable error rate.

Finally, Premise Five: A very heavy burden of persuasion should be placed on anyone who advocates that a particular kind of technology should be exempted from the normal operation of the patent system.

UNITED STATES PATENT AND TRADEMARK OFFICE
Public Hearing on Patent Protection for Software-Related Inventions
San Jose, California — January 26-27, 1994

In 1980, in the Chakrabarty case, the U.S. Supreme Court interpreted the patent copyright clause of the U.S. Constitution to require that the scope of patentable subject matter should be as broad as possible — anything under the sun that is made by man.

Those who maintain that software based invention should be excluded as a class from patent protection argue that software is different. It's different, they argue, in terms of its essential character -- it's logical. It's different in terms of the creative process by which it comes into being — it's authored rather than engineered. Or it's different in terms of the underlying economic model governing its production, distribution and life cycle.

These differences have been discussed and debated at gatherings of distinguished software developers, computer scientists, economists and legal scholars and practitioners under the sponsorship of a number of governmental agencies, including the National Research Council, the National Academy of Science, the Office of Technology Assessment, the U.S. Congress and the U.S. Patent & Trademark Office.

Despite the fact that the positions on both sides have been eloquently expressed, the results are inconclusive. The primary reason is that there is no hard data available to support the anti-software patent position, and the evidence is anecdotal at best. Clearly, software is different, but is it different enough from all other technologies to justify a special exemption from the normal operation of the patent laws.

Given the unavailability for reliable data on the societal costs and benefits of patenting software-implemented technology, we are presented with a situation where important policy decisions must be based on fundamental legal principles. In such a setting, we must conclude that those who would withhold patent protection from technologically-applied processes and machines, that happen to be implemented partially or wholly in software, have failed to satisfy the burden that the Constitution, the Supreme Court, and sound legal policy have placed upon it.

Thank you.

COMMISSIONER LEHMAN: Thank you very much for an excellent statement, Mr. Laurie.

There was something I was going to ask, and I may have to follow up now on it because it slipped my mind. But I think that was a good description of -- you parsed out the problem very well.

MR. LAURIE: If I could address a point that came up yesterday, relating to the role of competition in intellectual property law, and where the competition is more appropriately addressed under the anti-trust laws or under the intellectual property laws, I'd like to say that I think that there is, there are many places in intellectual property law where competition plays a role, and the patent law of misuse is an example, and as shown by the Seiko v. (Accolade) case in the Ninth Circuit, in the copyright law under fair use, competition plays a very important role.

Thank you.

COMMISSIONER LEHMAN: Thank you.

Next I'd like to ask Lee Patch, the Deputy General Counsel of Sun Microsystems to come forward.

—oOo--

LEE PATCH
SUN MICROSYSTEMS

MR. PATCH: Mr. Commissioner and colleagues, my name is Lee Patch. I speak today on behalf of Sun Microsystems, a 12-year-old $4 billion Silicon Valley-based manufacturer of computer workstations and related software products.

Sun invests approximately one-half of its substantial R&D budget in software development, particularly UNIX-based operating systems, development tools and application programs.

I serve as Deputy General Counsel and Chief Intellectual Property Counsel at Sun. I have the responsibility there for the patent activities.

You've heard and will no doubt continue to hear today widely diverging opinions concerning the virtues, or on the other hand, great evils of software patents, and you will note no lack of emotion and commitment to the speakers on either side of the issue. It's quite remarkable, I believe, that the normally quiet, calm environment of the patent practice and of the software development community has been so disrupted in recent years by loud and impassioned philosophical debate on subject matter that historically and traditionally had been only of interest to esoteric patent practitioners.

We've seen luminaries such as Mr. Warren take time out of his busy schedule to speak to you very passionately about evils of software. What I'd like to take with you from these hearings, if nothing else, is that from the perspective of a company like Sun Microsystems, the system is indeed broken and needs addressing. The current operation of the system is creating an unacceptable amount of uncertainty within the software and computer industries, and as I'm sure you will appreciate, business executives who routinely or daily make million dollar, multimillion dollar gambles on issues of technology or on issues of the marketplace, hate the need to take gambles and to make bets upon the outcome of a legal system.

In the face of this problem with the system, you have heard radically different proposals for solution, ranging from abolition of software patents outright to rather modest suggestions of improvement in the searching capabilities that exist within the Patent & Trademark Office.

I would like to summarize if I could what I believe to be the three fundamental problems that have been the subject of much testimony before you this week. The first problem that I believe has been identified and addressed significantly relates to the quality problem within the Patent & Trademark Office. The second problem that I would like to address, which has been discussed previously, relates to the surprise problem, that is of considerable concern to the software industry. And finally, I'd like to address briefly the subject of the tied-hands problem, which is another aspect of the frustration you may be hearing this week.

To the subject of the quality problem, I would say in my experience that it is indeed the case that low quality software patents are routinely being issued -- I should also mention that none of those are being issued to my

UNITED STATES PATENT AND TRADEMARK OFFICE
Public Hearing on Patent Protection for Software-Related Inventions
San Jose, California — January 26-27, 1994

company -- but they are indeed being issued. Largely it appears, due to the fact that prior art is not available or being overlooked or being misunderstood, and secondly, because it's a widely-held view that the nonobviousness standard that is being applied is simply too low a threshold.

COMMISSIONER LEHMAN I hate to interrupt your train of thought, but what is the -- I should probably ask some other people this, but -- what is the relationship of the Court of Appeals or the Federal Circuit to that? Do you think they're not giving us the right kind of guidance that they should give us on the obviousness standard here? Or is this our problem more?

MR. PATCH: I believe it's a merged problem. I believe that the Court of Appeals for the Federal Circuit has lowered that standard, and unduly so, and I also believe that the standard is by no means uniformly being applied within the Patent & Trademark Office.

In my role as corporate patent counsel, in-house counsel, I spend considerable time defending against infringement charges, and I have had personal opportunity to confront most of the famous bad software patents that you will and have here heard about, including such as the exclusive or patent, and the Soderblom patents and AT&T Pike patents, and other like the Mark Williams byte order patent. There's a list of them which have been widely disseminated as problem patents. I have personal experience in having rebutted and defended against charges of infringement with relation to many of those. From that experience, I would like to offer a few observations for your benefit.

First, there is indeed a quality problem that exists, and it is costing the industry a great deal in terms of lost cycle time, a lot of expensive effort being undertaken that would ideally not be necessary.

That having been said, I'd also like comment that no, it is not the case that in the software industry the sky is falling. We have not reached a stage where these types of problems are bringing to a screeching halt progress in the industry. Our confrontations with this group of questionable patents were fortunately all resolved prior to litigation, and where there was some payment, they were relatively inconsequential amounts.

A third observation I'd like to mention is that to address these kinds of infringement charges, which are perceived to have little merit, it's often quite necessary in my position to do some mining in the memories of a series of old and experienced practitioners of this art, who I happen to have at my disposal inside the corporate environment.

There is not a great deal of public documentation, patent or otherwise, that serves as a ready vehicle or mechanism for solving these problems when they arise. A lot of dusty basements have to be explored and old computers that haven't been powered up for many years have to be discovered and reactivated in order to deal with these problems as they exist today.

The last observation I wanted to make is that the quality problem that I believe to exist is not unique to the software industry. In my business questionable patents are being enforced not just with respect to software inventions but in the hardware arena and the semiconductor arena, there is a considerable amount of that going on, driven not so much by

the nature of the technology but by the nature of the economic interests and an opportunity being presented to people to realize some very significant money to the bottom line.

The second issue I wanted to mention briefly was, as I said, the surprise problem. And that's a very real source of frustration as you've heard at length this week. The industry feels as though it's being kept in the dark for long periods of time, and then surprised by some unanticipated patent jeopardies. This is clearly the result of delayed publication on the one hand, coupled with the ability in the Patent Office for an applicant to prolong the prosecution for an inordinate period of time, with no penalty, without loss of legal rights. This creates an environment where surprises become the rule rather than the exception to the industry.

Finally, the third issue of the tied-hands problem has also been mentioned, and I'd like to simply summarize my experience as an in-house counsel as it relates to that. When a low-quality patent is perceived to have issued in the software industry, most feel powerless to do anything about it. There exists today no quick, cost-effective mechanism to remedy this situation. The court system is typically unavailable unless you've already been accused and would be able to initiate a declaratory judgment action. And even if it was available, it's viewed as slow, expensive and lacking expertise.

The current Patent Office re-examination procedure, which has been discussed, is frankly considered in the industry as a trap to the unwary, and it is consciously avoided in most cases of the type that I mentioned. It's viewed as biased in favor of the patent applicant, and it's also viewed as dangerous, as a spoiler of otherwise powerful prior art. Frankly, the best prior art that you know about you would never offer up into the current patent re-examination procedure. You hold that back quite consciously.

COMMISSIONER LEHMAN Why is that? Because you don't want to disclose it because it's trade —

MR. PATCH: No. If you have a good reference, your very best reference, you don't wish to throw it over the fence to the Patent & Trademark Office and —

COMMISSIONER LEHMAN You want to save that for litigation.

MR. PATCH: You wish to have an opportunity to advocate aggressively the significance of that reference, and the Patent & Trademark Office re-examination proceeding simply does not provide that, and as a result of that lacking, good references are spoiled and no longer of significant use to you later in litigation.

COMMISSIONER LEHMAN And is that why a lot of people just choose to forego the re-examination process and go into litigation then directly?

MR. PATCH: Absolutely, absolutely.

A couple suggestions as to how you might address some of these problems: The quality problem unfortunately is the most difficult of the three. It's not one that can be solved overnight, it's not one that can be solved with the wave of the legislative wand. It requires, like in operating a business, daily, consistent execution. And that is your challenge, Mr. Commissioner, in implementing a solution to the quality problem that exists today.

UNITED STATES PATENT AND TRADEMARK OFFICE
Public Hearing on Patent Protection for Software-Related Inventions
San Jose, California -- January 26-27, 1994

The notice problem is one which I think creates a great deal of the emotion that you're seeing displayed today, and one which can be directly addressed and resolved. Since it's fundamentally due to the delay in the publication, plus the process in the Patent & Trademark Office which allows one to prolong extensively the prosecution history, the solution should be quite clear. Publish patent applications early and secondly, discourage prolonged prosecution by measuring the life of the patent from its filing date. If somebody wishes to prolong their prosecution for eight or ten years after that, it's at their own jeopardy.

This may sound in some regards like a call for harmonization, but I don't wish it to be misunderstood as such, because I'm a strong advocate of harmonization only when there's a specific identifiable problem being resolved by such harmonization.

I'd also suggest that the software industry would probably be a supporter of the idea of implementing a very short time period prior for publications after filing, perhaps shorter than even the current European and Japanese model of 18 months.

Concerning the tied-hands problem, the proposal or suggestion that I have is really in two parts -- a minimal approach and then a more comprehensive approach. The minimal approach would involved converting the existing re-examination procedure into an inter partes procedure, where opportunity for equal advocacy and appeal would be available. I would also strongly recommend that you permit a much broader range of prior art to be introduced into the proceeding. Even when a challenged company would like to take advantage of the re-examination procedure in our industry, it's very commonly the case that the form of the prior art that we have available to us is not acceptable in the re-examination procedure, and I would recommend you open it up much more widely, allow oral testimony, allow physical demonstration and make it a true inter partes procedure. Address all issues relating to validity and reference to prior art.

Finally, I would remove any appearance of a bias in favor of the patent applicant. I would do so by changing the trier of fact in the re-examination procedure, and I would strongly recommend you upgrade it and so the credibility of the Patent & Trademark Office is enhanced and prolonged.

The more aggressive approach that I would recommend would be a full-fledged opposition approach. Time for challenge to a patent should be set for a reasonable period after its issuance. I would recommend a speak-now-or-forever-hold-your-peace approach to that opposition procedure. Companies can come forward during the time allotted, challenge with their best shot, and thereafter the issue has been resolved before the Patent & Trademark Office, no longer subject to repetitive review by every court that might have the patent presented before it. This will have the benefit of unburdening the courts from dealing with frankly issues they are not well-positioned to deal with, and it would streamline subsequent court proceedings to deal with issues relating principally to infringement.

COMMISSIONER LEHMAN I think we're running a little over, so maybe we can wrap up.

MR. PATCH: I only have one more comment, and I will excuse myself. Sorry.

The term of the patent in an opposition such as I've recommended should be extended for the period in which the opposition goes forward to avoid abuses of well-funded challengers keeping an opposition going for a long period of time.

Thank you.

COMMISSIONER LEHMAN Thank you very much. Those were interesting ideas. If you were here yesterday, you know, we announced actually that we have already taken one of your suggestions, and that is that we are going to be submitting legislation to Congress to deal with the so-called submarine patent problem in part by moving to a system 20 years from filing will be our new patent term, and that will at least in part address that difficulty. And then it turned out to be kind of a win-win situation because we were able to get the Japanese to make some concessions to us in return for our agreeing to do that.

And I'd like to also just use this as a forum to make a point about harmonization process. We announced earlier this week that we were going to suspend the patent harmonization exercise that we had been engaged in with the World Intellectual Property Organization which would have required us to change to a first-to-file system in the United States. That's not because this administration or I am opposed to harmonization. In fact, quite the opposite. Clearly the best patent system for Americans would be one in which you could file a patent in our Patent Office and then with great certainty and trustworthiness get very, very rapid protection everywhere else in the world that would be sound and that you could trust and so on.

That was not the deal that we had cut in the last administration, that wasn't the harmonization exercise that we were engaged in. And so we're basically going back and we're not going to abandon the principles of the system that many Americans feel favor them until we really have a system in which we receive very, very tangible results in other patent systems. And indeed this illustration of where we move to -- or we agree to do something that is also in our benefit in this case, I think the 20-year term from filing, we have received the tangible benefit from the Japanese.

I am very optimistic that we will, in fact, achieve true harmonization at some point in the not too distant future, but it won't happen if we just simply make all the changes unilaterally. So since you raised that point, I just wanted to explain where the Patent Office was on that. Thanks.

Yeah, I guess Christopher Byrne, Senior Intellectual Property Counsel for StorageTek, who is representing the American Committee for Interoperable Systems, ACIS.

--oOo--

CHRISTOPHER BYRNE

STORAGETEK -- ACIS

MR. BYRNE: Good morning. I'm Chris Byrne, Senior Intellectual Property Counsel for Storage Technology Corporation, or StorageTek. I am testifying today on behalf of the American Committee for Interoperable Systems, or ACIS, to which StorageTek belongs. ACIS sincerely appreciates this opportunity to provide testimony.

UNITED STATES PATENT AND TRADEMARK OFFICE
Public Hearing on Patent Protection for Software-Related Inventions
San Jose, California -- January 26-27, 1994

By way of introduction, I am an electrical engineer and a lawyer, and a registered patent attorney before joining StorageTek as patent counsel in 1991. I spent six years on the Intellectual Property Staff of the Hewlett-Packard Company.

I will address Topic A, Questions 4(a) and 5: Does the present framework of patent, copyright and trade secret law effectively promote innovation in the field of software? Do you believe a new form of protection for computer programs is needed?

Because these questions are two sides of the same coin, I will respond to them together. ACIS members include numerous innovative high technology companies such as Sun Microsystems, NCR and Broderbund Software. My own company, StorageTek, is headquartered in Louisville, Colorado, which is about five miles east of Boulder. We employ thousands of people worldwide, and we had 1993 revenues of approximately $1.4 billion. StorageTek designs and manufactures high performance data storage and retrieval systems for mainframe, mid-range and networked desktop computer systems.

Our customers include many Fortune 200 communication, transportation and financial companies. In fact, if you recently made a phone call, bought an airline ticket or bought or sold securities, chances are that records of your activity is stored on one of our products, awaiting ready access and retrieval when necessary. Our competitors include IBM, Hitachi and Fujitsu.

Like other ACIS members, we rely heavily on our nation's intellectual property system to protect our most valuable assets: the innovations of our engineers, particularly our software engineers. Without adequate intellectual property protection, we could not protect and recover our substantial investment in research and development. For instance, at StorageTek last year, we invested approximately 10% of our revenues in R&D -- that's over 140 million dollars. Without that R&D investment, we simply cannot stay competitive and in business. Indeed, last November Vice President Gore himself toured our substantial R&D facilities and personally previewed key technology which we believe will facilitate his grand vision of the information superhighway.

While all ACIS companies believe in strong intellectual property protection, we also believe in balance. We believe that overprotection is as threatening to innovation as underprotection. The need for this sophisticated balance is particularly important with respect to software, which is so pervasive in our economy and critical to its growth in our national leadership and high technology.

ACIS believes that it would be a dangerous act of underprotection to deny patent protection to software subject matter per se. But it is an equally dangerous example of overprotection to fail to expeditiously implement needed corrections in the way we currently do software patents, if not all our patents. Those needed corrections are well known, and ACIS has gone on record in support of them. They include:

Improving the software prior art database so that it is accurate, timely and includes both patent and nonpatent prior art. The quality of the software patent database will be directly related to the quality of the software patentability examination by the PTO.

Working to raise the skill level of PTO examiners who are charged with the vital and difficult task of examining software patent applications. One way to accomplish this is with site visits by examiners. For instance, last year two groups of examiners, one from Art Unit 2308 led by Michael Fleming and another group from Art Unit 2507 led by Bruce Arnold, visited StorageTek. They spent valuable time with our engineers and our patent committee learning how we do R&D and how we make our decisions about which inventions to seek to patent. We were very favorably impressed with the legal and technical expertise of the examiners, who too often are merely names at the end of an office action.

To our mutual benefit, the examiners learned about the challenges we face in innovative R&D and we received a much better understanding of the difficult nature of the examiners' work. Educational visits by examiners is one way to raise those skills.

Implementing key procedural reforms to prevent applicants from secretly and indefinitely submerging their applications in the PTO until they are ready to ambush the public -- and I think your 20-year limit is going to go a long way toward solving that problem. Otherwise we need to speed the examination process and include accompanying public notice of possible patents. Many such procedural reforms are considered as a function of possible harmonization of patent law, but such reform in this country should proceed with or without harmonization.

And just a footnote here: I think one of the very positive fallouts of this meeting has been the offline interaction among participants. And just as an example, yesterday I spent some time brainstorming with my counterpart at Silicon Graphics, Tim Casey, and Rob Stern, an attorney in private practice from DC, and just over lunch we were talking about the problems that we have with the Patent Office and we were brainstorming possible solutions, and a number of those were things like regionalizing the Patent Office, industry-sponsored technical colleges for examiners, expedited application procedures, possibly limiting patents to one independent claim, and the automation requirements of the modern patent system. And one of the conclusions that we came to was that we definitely believe that the water glass at the PTO is half full as opposed to half empty, and we think that hearings like this are going to be an important first step towards filling the glass.

But all the good work that we undertake to improve software patents will be simply undermined if we do not address another balancing issue, and that is the proper balance between patent versus copyright protection of software. This is because copyright, if misapplied, can achieve patent-like protection for software functionality. This misapplication is particularly dangerous when we consider that there is no examination for copyright as there is for patents; a copyright registration does not specify the boundary line of protected expression in a work, whereas a patent is explicitly bounded by the terms of its claims; and copyright protection outlasts patent protection by at least a factor of four.

This de facto patent protection under copyright is

UNITED STATES PATENT AND TRADEMARK OFFICE
Public Hearing on Patent Protection for Software-Related Inventions
San Jose, California — January 26-27, 1994

particularly pernicious with respect to interface specifications. Unlike novels and plays, which stand alone and do not need to interact with other works, computer programs never stand by themselves; they function only by interacting with a computer environment. If the developer of an environment can use copyright to prevent other developers from conforming to the system of rules governing interaction within the environment -- to its interface specifications -- the first developer can gain a patentlike monopoly without ever subjecting his system of rules to a patent examination. In the absence of competition, the first developer would have little incentive to develop more innovative and less costly products. Moreover, this result is particularly dangerous to a company such as mine.

StorageTek designs and manufactures data storage peripherals which interface with the computers made by the dominant American, European and Japanese computer vendors. With de facto patentlike copyright control of their operating systems, these vendors have the potential to therefore control functional access to that interface and therefore exert market control over subject matter, i.e., the peripheral device, which is completely beyond the scope of the copyright itself. This is dangerous overprotection of software via copyright.

StorageTek joined ACIS because of our concern that the courts and the U.S. government were losing sight of the importance of maintaining a balance between incentives and competition in the area of intellectual property protection of software, particularly copyright protection.

From the outset, it was our believe that the proper application of traditional copyright principles such as the idea/expression dichotomy, merger, scenes a faire, and the fair use doctrine would yield the appropriate scope of protection for software. Recent court decisions have validated this.

The Second, Ninth and Federal Circuits have all found that copyright does not protect functional interface specifications. Further, the Ninth and Federal Circuits have found the reverse engineering technique known as disassembly to be a fair use and proper means to achieve functional interoperability. In our view, the Altai, Sega, and Atari decisions are not radical departures from traditional principles; rather, they return copyright to its proper course. We expect that the First Circuit will soon be consistent and overturn Judge Keeton's decision in Lotus.

Despite this positive trend in the case law, however, we fear that the U.S. government has allowed its laudable goal to improve the balance of trade to inadvertently divert its attention from the ultimate goal of our patent and copyright system: promoting the progress of science and the useful arts, as explicitly provided for in Article I, Section 8, Clause 8, of the U.S. Constitution.

We applaud the manner and spirit of these hearings, therefore, as solid indication that the U.S. government clearly appreciates that more protection is not necessarily better. We are also encouraged that Assistant Attorney General Bingaman has established a task force to review and reformulate the Antitrust Division's policies on intellectual property and antitrust. We applaud her observation that the scope of copyright protection for computer software has important competitive implications.

In summary, we see no need for a sui generis software protection law. Until recently, courts applied copyright in a manner that overprotected software, but the Altai, Atari, and Sega decisions corrected that aberration. Bad software patents also dangerously risk overprotecting software, but let's not throw out the baby with the bath water; let's move quickly to implement needed improvements in the way we do our software patents.

Thank you for this opportunity to present this testimony for your kind attention. I would be glad to answer any questions.

COMMISSIONER LEHMAN   Thank you very much. Appreciate your sharing that with us today.

Next I'd like to ask Gideon Gimlan from Fliesler, Dubb, Meyer & Lovejoy.

--oOo--

GIDEON GIMLAN

FLIESLER, DUBB, MEYER & LOVEJOY

MR. GIMLAN: Honorable Commissioner, distinguished members of the panel, may name is Gideon Gimlan, and I do not come here to represent any particular organization. It's true that one of the labels I wear, if you want to define where I am coming from, is that I am a patent attorney with the law firm of Fliesler, Dubb, Meyer & Lovejoy of San Francisco and Sunnyvale. This particular firm represents numerous high technology companies located in Silicon Valley and elsewhere. The work of the firm and my own work includes the preparation and prosecution of software-related patent applications in a variety of areas, including networked computer systems, graphic imaging systems and mainframe computers.

I have to add the immediate legal proviso that these comments are my own personal views based on general experience, and not those of any member of the law firm or of any clients represented by the firm.

I come before you wearing an additional label -- this is part of my general experiences -- that prior to becoming an attorney, prior to so-called defecting into law school, I was also an engineer who worked in the field for over seven years. I would characterize the nature of the work that I did as being a hardware/software engineer. And the reason I use that characterization is that a lot of the work assignments that I followed through with included the step of choosing whether to implement particular functionalities in software or hardware.

Insofar as the experience I've had from that background, I'll have to repeat what Ron Laurie so eloquently phrased, is that there is a spectrum, continuous spectrum, in terms of what we define as hardware and software, and it's almost impossible to cut that spectrum in half and define some line that separates something from being hardware or software.

Also, while I'm on that topic, it brings back to mind while I was working as a hardware/software engineer, Mr. Fiddler, who was here before, mentioned something about word processing being a old and obvious technique that shouldn't be patentable. I unfortunately go back to the days when people were doing affordable word processing with hard-wired machines back in the early '70s. The original

UNITED STATES PATENT AND TRADEMARK OFFICE
Public Hearing on Patent Protection for Software-Related Inventions
San Jose, California -- January 26-27, 1994

versions of affordable word processing came in the form of the IBM magnetic card, and there were a lot of companies who came out during that time and started to produce hard-wired word processing that eventually led to software types of devices. Generalized computer has taken it over, but the origins of it really lie in hardware in terms of having affordable word processing capabilities.

The question that I really wanted to focus on here today was Question No. 3 in your requests for comments: What are the implications of maintaining or altering the current standards for patent eligibility for software-related inventions?

And I'd like to retitle that as "What is the current PTO practice? And where is it leading us to in the software arts?"

My own personal experience is that, insofar as anticipation and obviousness are concerned, the examining corps treats software-related inventions no differently than other kinds of inventions. The legal tests for 102/103 determination are fairly well-established and most examiners treat software-based cases with the same uniform fairness as hardware-based cases.

The issues of finding good prior art in software area is no different than that in any other art. As an aside, in terms of quality, I find that the European patent office tends to find closer prior art for particular inventions than does the United States Patent Office, but again, that applies to general subject matter and is not specific to software-related cases.

Insofar as Patent Office inquiries into 35 USC 101, what constitutes statutory subject matter, I fail to see any across-the-office uniform consensus on what is or is not statutory, the OG guidelines notwithstanding.

The treatment of statutory subject matter question appears to vary greatly from examiner to examiner. Some examiners are lenient in what they consider to be statutory, while others seem to be on a witch-hunt for a 101 basis of rejection. This injects a considerable degree of uncertainty into the application process. You cannot predict the outcome of a 101 issue with any degree of confidence. It very much depends on which examiner you draw for your case.

Perhaps "software-related" isn't the proper term for what I am trying to address here. The problem more properly fits under the broader rubric of algorithm-related inventions and should the PTO be expending so much time and energy trying to weed out claims that arguably extend or encroach into nonstatutory areas.

I suggest that the answer is no. The Patent Bar and Examining Corps are wasting client money and taxpayer money arguing over metaphysical abstractions. That to technologists in the field sounds like we are debating over how many angels dance on the head of a pin. The case of In re: Iwahashi serves as a good example. It was not strictly speaking a software-related case because the claim preamble started off with, "An autocorrelation unit, dot dot dot, comprising."

But if one wished to take some license and rewrite the preamble to start with, "A computer comprising," and I note that that was done in Example B of the PTO request for comments, then in my mind this should not materially alter the gist of the invention.

Any digital signal processor, including the one in Iwahashi, can be viewed as a computing machine, or quote "computer" if you choose, one could then go out on a limb to call each invention that uses a digital signal processor as being software-related because its operations can be described in algorithmic terms.

Notice that I didn't say controlled by a computer program or controlled by quote "software". There are those skilled in the art who will argue even today that a computer program can be used as a description of the operations to be carried out by the machine, and the description does not necessarily have to form part of the machine that actually performs the described operations. The machine's control lines could just as easily be driven by combinatorial logic as from a memory source.

In the end, it should make little difference that an invention is implemented in hardware, software, or in-between-ware. In the eyes of the electronic circuits that carry out a given invention, there really isn't any functional difference. A set of electrical signals are first supplied to the DSP machine. Perhaps the input signals originate from a memory device like a ROM or a floppy disk, perhaps they come from an x-ray machine. Irrespective of origin, the signals are somehow transformed by the machine. Then they are output, perhaps for return to memory, perhaps for routing to some other immediate use, such as creating a real-time high-definition video image.

One inventor recently looked at me with bewildered eyes when I tried to explain some of the 101 concerns related to his particular case, and he said, "I don't understand, data is data, what does it matter whether it comes from an x-ray machine or from memory? What is government up to?"

And in that quote I've taken some literary license to replace what the actual source of the question was, but okay.

I think the problem and the answer lie in how we as human beings come to appreciate the subtle implications of a given invention. We need to step back and ask, Has the inventor come up with a faster or cheaper way of doing things even if the improvement is found in software? Has the inventor compressed the physical size of an apparatus so that something smaller can now do the job of something that previously had to be much larger? Has the inventor obtained a higher level of resolution than was previously feasible?

We see in hindsight that these kinds of improvements -- faster, smaller, cheaper, better resolution -- have brought us the miracle of affordable palm-top computers, ones that have pen-based graphical user interfaces, and ones that, arguably, give even the technical neophyte access to the powers of the digital revolution because of their intuitive nature.

I think we can all agree in hindsight that these are the kinds of innovations that our patent system is supposed to protect and foster. But when we turn away from past glories and look to the next invention, we are somehow daunted by the enigma of this thing we call software. We are all, in a sense, blind men beating at a pachydermial beast, each finding something different based on the angle from which we approach it. Some say this software stuff is more like the punched paper in a player piano, or like the music recorded

UNITED STATES PATENT AND TRADEMARK OFFICE
Public Hearing on Patent Protection for Software-Related Inventions
San Jose, California — January 26-27, 1994

on a vinyl record. Others say it's more like the mathematical proofs of their college calculus classes. Yet others say it's something that is still in its infancy, that will grow and evolve into something we still do not fully understand.

Of course, in the meantime, software applications keep pouring into the Patent Office. So what should we do? Should we tell those who craft new software to go away? You are not welcome at the Patent Office? Should we direct every algorithm-smith over to the line at the Board of Appeals? Every examiner has his or her own personal angle on how to deal with this problem.

This leads to a haphazard system which gives inventors -- particularly those that have had the misfortune of being assigned to an "anti-algorithm" or "anti-software" examiner -- the impression that they are not receiving uniform, fair treatment. It is absurd in the mind of many technology gurus that an invention is okay if implemented in hardware but suddenly becomes unaccepted because it is implemented in software.

The pat answer, of course, for inventors who face such examiners, is that they can always go to the Board of Appeals, and if not satisfied with the results there, they can go higher to the Federal Circuit. But that doesn't happen with regularity. What really happens is that many patent-worthy cases fall by the wayside, not because the applicants agree with the examiner's 101 position — and as a side comment, I sometimes wonder if even the examiners themselves agree with their official position — but because of monetary considerations, it's just too expensive to go forward any further and appeal.

One could argue that this problem could be taken care of by well-to-do corporations, that they should lead the charge into the courthouse and help us create better law, but that doesn't always work. Some corporations are afraid to get on the bad side of a key examiner. Even those that are brazen think twice about pouring more time and money into an application that is already twice rejected by an examiner. Most inventors, and corporate executives for that matter, do not have the experience or patience to grapple with the kind of metaphysical questions that are posed when a Section 101 rejection is raised. For example --

COMMISSIONER LEHMAN: Mr. Gimlan, we're running out of time.

MR. GIMLAN: Oh, I am, okay. Then let me skip to my proposal then. I think that the ongoing witch-hunt at the patent office for nonstatutory subject matter is in essence driving technology gurus away from the system. They simply don't understand it and will bypass the system.

My proposal is that unless particular claim in an application is clearly limited to the practice of a mathematical algorithm, the Patent Office should allow the applicant to disclaim within the body of the claim that portion of the claimed system or process that falls outside the scope of

35 USC 101, and then allow the case to go to issue as is, assuming there are no other bases for rejection.

After the patent issues, we should let experience and the advice of technical gurus help us to decide whether an accused device falls within the scope of a claim as interpreted under 101, or whether that accused device is

protected because in order to enforce the claim, you would have to transmute its meaning such that it becomes a claim to a mathematical algorithm.

COMMISSIONER LEHMAN: We can certainly take everything and read it over very carefully with the specific suggestions.

MR. GIMLAN: Okay, thank you, Commissioner.

COMMISSIONER LEHMAN: We really thank you for sharing this with us today.

This idea that we have created a sort of artificial determination for patent -- an artificial subject matter, in a sense, for patent lawyers to avoid the, in order to deal with these 101 determination problems is clearly something that we've heard from other witnesses here. This is worthy of looking into.

Next I'd like to call Tom Cronan, Secretary and General Counsel of Taligent, Incorporated.

--oOo--

TOM CRONAN

TALIGENT, INC.

MR. CRONAN: Good morning, Mr. Commissioner. My name is Tom Cronan, and I'm the General Counsel and Secretary of Taligent, and I'm testifying today on behalf of Taligent.

I must say after listening to yesterday's session during the morning, it is with some trepidation that I approach the stand this morning. As a lowly high-tech copyright lawyer, I guess it's malpractice per se to be even testifying here today.

What we're going to talk about is the patent system and how the patent system is critical to stimulating investment in the software products and technologies areas.

We will recommend some refinement to that system. We want to have a system that is designed to support high technology, this industry which gives us high-tech, high-wage jobs. We want to continue to be the world technology leader in software. I will talk about both start-ups and large companies and how the patent system benefits both.

We want to stimulate investment, that's what we're all about. There's lots of various interpretations of whether the patent system will help or hurt venture capitalists and others make decisions on whether to invest in software. We certainly have an opinion on that that we'd like to share with you today.

So I'm going to discuss three things: Why software is important to new ventures, why software patent protection and related inventions is important to new ventures, why the patent system attracts investment, and the refinements that we discuss to the current system.

Taligent, as an example, is a new, founded in 1992, small, starting with 170 employees -- we now have 350 employees and by the end of this year will have 450 employees -- innovative, high-tech, high-risk venture. We're going into an extremely competitive marketplace, we're going to have an object-oriented operating environment that will compete with Microsoft's offerings, clearly the dominant player in a lot of competition in the area.

We are going to compete on the basis of innovation. We are going to try and establish a foundation technology for

APPENDIXES

UNITED STATES PATENT AND TRADEMARK OFFICE
Public Hearing on Patent Protection for Software-Related Inventions
San Jose, California -- January 26-27, 1994

the industry, a new type of technology that will be an operating environment that's open and extensible at all levels, based on a brand-new technology.

As I was sitting here this morning listening to our first speaker talk about the fact that two of his programmers could program a million lines of code, I was thinking about our own efforts. We have been developing this technology before the company began -- it's been now six years in development. And by the time we're done, we will have a very elegant program with 750,000 lines of code. I would think that some of our developments may be a little obvious than those this morning, which were the million lines of code.

This architecture is being developed from the ground up -- a clean sheet of paper. That's why it's going to be innovative, that's why it's foundation technology. We're not unique. There's going to be lots of other foundation technologies that will have to be established for the information superhighway, and they will not be done by garage shops. They will be done by larger ventures, by people in the industry who understand the technology, who understand the risks. We could have never attracted venture capitalists to our venture, we are too risky. We're funded by the industry, like now three separate large companies in the industry who will be funding us.

So as we look at our architecture, as we look at our developments, we see ourselves very much like the beginning processor developers. We're looking at an architecture that's extensible, we're looking at functions and features that are new, and we think that software should be protected in the same way as hardware.

We don't think there's any material difference and we think that the policies of the patent system are in favor of protecting software the same way as hardware.

Next I'd like to talk about why that patent system attracts investment.

The software industry is different than some other industries. It has a very front-end loaded investment. You have to invest all of your risk capital before you know whether or not your product is going to be competitive, before you know whether or not anyone will buy your product. So you have a lot of risk and you have a lot of uncertainty.

If you add on that additional risk and uncertainty associated with not knowing whether or not you'll be able to protect your new and innovative product from a major competitor, you may not have any investment at all. The market risks are very high, and if competitors can take a utilitarian function which you spent a lot of time and effort designing, as we mentioned, and use those against you without having the same R&D expenses, you would not be able to support these investments.

The other reason, policy reason, is as we look at this technology, copyright law will not be adequate to protect the types of object-oriented programming that we're developing. We have designed our system so that in object code developers using our development environment can go in and modify almost every portion of our system. The entire architecture is open. We cannot protect it by trade secret. There will be those, I'm sure, who will argue that the entire system is an interface. That raises some copyright issues -- as us lowly copyright lawyers know.

We think that the patent law encourages disclosure. In the absence of patent protection for this technology, I would certainly advise my client to make sure that we keep as many of the interfaces closed and not open as possible, make sure that most of the important functions aren't disclosed in documentation.

With the patent system, we're able to disclose those not only in the patent applications but we also will want to make sure that for those important utilitarian aspects that we can't afford to patent, that we'll publish and establish the prior art in those areas.

We want to make sure that the United States continues to be the world leader. As you probably have read, there is now more R&D dollars going into software ventures and software technology in Silicon Valley than hardware. That wasn't true two years ago; it's true now and it increases every year, and this investment is dependent on having a system that protects that technology.

One other point I would make on this is, an earlier speaker said that there was presumption that the first to market would win. I would challenge that presumption. If you look at Excel, if you look at Word, I do not believe that they were the first spreadsheet or the first word processor on the market, but they have substantial market share.

Next I'd like to go back and talk about some refinements that can be made to the current system. There's been lots of suggestions that have been offered today, and I would like to just offer a few additional suggestions, and also some endorsements of some of the suggestions that have been made.

We applaud the Patent Office's initiatives on education. We have been very active with Gerry Goldberg in trying to educate the Patent Office. We spent time, money and effort sending Mike Patel, our VP of Advanced Technology, back to the Patent Office. He educated a large number of people for half a day. His talk was not about Taligent; it was about object-oriented programming from its inception. And he was a professor for eight years before he came to Taligent, so he had a very good background.

It was so well-received that the Patent Office invested in sending 17 senior supervisors out to Taligent and to other companies in the Valley. They spent a day and a half at Taligent understanding our technology in great detail. And most of the responses we got from them were extremely positive.

And I was there for the wrap-up of that session, and I heard one of the senior supervisors saying, "You know, this is great, we learned a lot, we now have new innovative ways to deny your claims."

One of the other things that I think would really help the Office -- and I know that you have begun this and we think you should continue it and with even greater speed -- hire more computer science graduates who don't have engineering degrees. These are the type of people who understand this technology, the type of people that should be evaluating these types of inventions.

I think that some of the other problems of obviousness, there are lots of issues with obviousness, but one of the

UNITED STATES PATENT AND TRADEMARK OFFICE
Public Hearing on Patent Protection for Software-Related Inventions
San Jose, California -- January 26-27, 1994

things, consistency and having people that understand the technology better would certainly help the nonobvious issue.

In addition, I have one other proposal that's a little different than some of the proposals. To deal with this problem of having all of the prior art not found anywhere or searchable by advanced technology -- and I know that you're trying to put together databases in advanced technology -- we would propose a human database.

There are people, there are consultants, there are people who can be hired who have lots of expertise and lots of industry experience in the relevant areas that a lot of the software patents will be filed on. These people, because of Internet and because of advanced technology, don't even have to be located with the Patent Office; they can be reached through advanced electronic communication, so that people in California who have a general reluctance to move back to Washington, D.C., especially after the snow storms of this winter -- except of course the people in Los Angeles -- can be reached by Internet.

Finally, on publication, we would be in favor of publication prior to issuance. I think that one of the issues that hasn't really been addressed is that there needs to be some certainty in this publication scheme, a publication scheme that would be tied to when the patent issued and publication prior to that would have a great deal of uncertainty because of the great deal of uncertainty in when the patent is processed through the Patent Office and when it gets issued.

It would be important to understand whether or not your product is out in the marketplace before the patent issues, and before the publication. So I think having a set time period, like 18 months, or some other time period that's appropriate for the industry, is the best way to proceed.

So let me just conclude. We think that protecting software-related inventions is critical to investment and for ensuring certainty on return in those investments. We propose some refinements to the current system; we think with those refinements we should be able to enhance competitiveness of the software industry in the United States, particularly the high risk, high level of investment foundation technologies, such as our company, which will be needed for the information highway.

Thank you.

COMMISSIONER LEHMAN Thank you very much, Mr. Cronan, for sharing those ideas with us.

Next I'd like to ask William Neukom, Vice President of Law and Corporate Affairs for Microsoft Corporation to come forward.

--oOo--

WILLIAM NEUKOM

MICROSOFT CORPORATION

MR. NEUKOM: Good morning. My name is Bill Neukom. I'm Vice President of Law and Corporate Affairs at Microsoft Corporation.

I appreciate having the opportunity to be here to present the current best thinking of our company on the subject of this hearing. If I'm making points that are not clear or deserve some comment or questions, please don't hesitate to interrupt. I think I'm scheduled to go most of my allotted time with my prepared remarks, but I want to communicate while I'm here this morning as best I can.

Microsoft is a developer and marketer and supporter of a very wide range of systems and applications software products for personal computers. By having helped to make it easier for users to work with their personal computers for an increasing number of purposes, the company's products have been able to contribute to what's sometimes referred to as the "PC revolution," which has occurred in the past 12 to 15 years. The growth of the company has paralleled an even more important statistic, which is the increase in the number of people who use personal computers in this country. About a million people were using personal computers in 1980; by today we estimate that probably 90 million or more people are using personal computers.

The software industry is a major contributor to the economy of this country. In the last five years, virtually every study of the key technologies of America's present and future have identified the vital role of computer software industry. Software is characterized by both its very rapid technological innovation and by the widespread use of that technology in downstream markets. Computer software improves the competitiveness of other industries in this country and around the world because it helps to make -- our products help to make those enterprises more efficient and more innovative, and it's the continuous evolution and enhancement and improvement of software products that permeates much of the economy of this country.

The US software industry has experienced quite remarkable growth. Measured over the past ten years, it is the fastest growing industry in this country by any rational measurement; it is now larger than all but four or five industries in this country's economy. The growth has been fueled by strong export performance by US companies; 75% of the world's sales of pre-packaged software come from US software companies; and the 100 largest American software companies earn more than 50% of their revenues from offshore sales.

The key to much of this is strong intellectual property protection, which we and our colleagues and competitors in the industry view as essential for US software industry to continue to compete globally and continue to play a leadership role in this nation's economy.

On this morning's subject of patent protection for computer software, we believe that the existing laws in the form of the statute and the regulations and the case law provide both an adequate and an appropriate framework in which to assess the patentability of software-related inventions. This is not to say however that the existing system cannot be improved, and we commend the patent office for its willingness to take a constructive view of that challenge.

We appreciate the Patent Office's commitment to the improvement of the examination process by increasing the number of examiners and the expertise of the examiners in software technology and providing better technical training for the examining corps.

We also agree that or support the Patent Office's decision to pursue some reform of the re-examination process. I read in the Commissioner's opening remarks from yesterday that there is some legislation forthcoming and we look

UNITED STATES PATENT AND TRADEMARK OFFICE
Public Hearing on Patent Protection for Software-Related Inventions
San Jose, California -- January 26-27, 1994

forward to reviewing that and supporting it in a constructive manner, assuming it does things which we think are beneficial to the process. The advantage of reforms to the re-examination process are measured both in terms of a more efficient determination of patentability, but have the very handsome byproduct of reducing the threat of expensive and protracted litigation.

We believe the software industry would benefit from greater availability of prior art; this is not a novel subject to you experts or to the audience, but patent applicants need to know more about prior art, the office needs to know more about it, and parties to infringement actions or threatened infringement actions could benefit from better, earlier information about prior art. We are a participant in the Software Patent Institute's efforts to gather that prior art, and we are trying to exhort our colleagues and competitors to step up and make more technical information available, so that it can become part of a richer and more relevant database of prior art.

And finally, we think that the industry would benefit from a reduction in the average pendency of applications before the Patent Office. We don't presume to think that that's an easy matter to accomplish, but we think it's important; the more prompt issuance of patents will provide industry participants with a better return on their substantial investments in technology and in the patent process itself. That is particularly material for an industry like ours, which is so fast-moving and where today's invention is next year's afterthought.

With a commitment from both the industry and from the Patent Office to implement these kinds of changes and perhaps others that have been suggested or will be thought of, we believe that the existing system can mature in a fashion that effectively achieves the constitutional goals of stimulating and protecting innovation in a competitive context.

Let me try to respond to each of the questions that have been published for these hearings. Question one asks, What aspects or specific examples of software-related inventions should be protectable via the patent system?

Without addressing each example individually, Microsoft notes that this inquiry appears to subsume two basic issues. First of all, should patent protection be available in some form for inventions embodied in software; and secondly, if so, how should protection be characterized? As to the first issue, we do not believe that patent protection should be withheld from an invention that otherwise meets the statutory requirements for patentability, simply on the basis that the invention is or may be embodied in software. I think that point is reasonably well resolved by the courts and by the Patent Office at this stage.

With regard to the second question: The characterization of the protection, we favor claims structures that clearly recite those aspects of computer software-related inventions that are novel and unobvious, and allow an accused infringer to readily identify the activity or activities that may be proscribed under the claim. The success of a particular claim in meeting these objectives may depend, however, less on the form and more on the substance of the claim and the supporting specification.

As to question number two, the impact of software-related patents on the industry, Microsoft has never initiated an action for patent infringement. We have, however, unfortunately been the defendant in several lawsuits involving software-related patents. The defense of those suits has consumed considerable of our resources, resources we'd prefer to use in positive and constructive research and development efforts. Even so, we are committed to the existing patent system as a reasonable and responsible vehicle for protecting software innovation, particularly when that process is viewed in light of the ongoing effort being made by the Patent Office and the courts and more and more, I'm pleased to say, by the industry to improve the systems application to our technology.

The dichotomy illustrated by our position reflects the equity that we think can be achieved by the existing system in balancing the competing interests of protecting innovation on the one hand and preserving competitive freedom on the other hand.

One potential way of lessening the negative impact of software-related patents on the industry would be to consider again this subject of reform of the re-examination process. The threat of litigation involving a patent of questionable validity can be particularly damaging to a smaller company, which may not have the financial or the human resources to effectively challenge the patent's validity in the federal court process. Although the existing re-examination process affords a potential defendant an alternative venue in which to contest a patent's validity, the utility of the current re-examination process is limited by its ex parte nature and the limited scope of prior art that can be considered.

The Patent Office, the Patent Bar and industry participants should carefully consider whether these and other limitations on the existing re-examination process should be overcome.

Question number three addresses the implications of maintaining or altering the standards for patentability of software-related inventions. Microsoft believes there are several advantages to the maintenance of the existing standards. We're not suggesting they should be frozen, but we believe that they are fundamentally sound and there are reasons to continue to rely on them in the main.

Workability. Although the expression and application of the existing standards may not yet have fully matured, the standards have evolved slowly over a number of years and do provide a stable framework in which to assess patentability of computer software-related inventions. Improvements have already been made. The Patent Office has already taken steps to improve the quality of examinations, as we've noted, and the software industry is working to enhance the effectiveness of the Patent Office's application of existing standards through, among other means, the work of the Software Patent Institute.

Thirdly, this is a way to avoid greater near-term uncertainty. Both the industry and government have made considerable strides in understanding and applying the existing system, particularly in the last few years. The introduction of some new statutory or regulatory standards would almost certainly present a new set of uncertainties or ambiguities,

UNITED STATES PATENT AND TRADEMARK OFFICE
Public Hearing on Patent Protection for Software-Related Inventions
San Jose, California -- January 26-27, 1994

making a major revision perhaps more unsettling to the industry, at least in the short and perhaps the midterm.

And finally, there are investments that have been made under the current standards by industry members, and significant changes to the patent standards might compromise the value of those substantial investments.

Question four asks whether the existing framework of patent copyright, trade secret protection effectively protects and promotes innovation in the software field. Microsoft response to that would be, yes, it does. The importance in the growth of the software industry described earlier in my remarks has not occurred in a legal vacuum, as I'm sure you are all aware. As noted in the Patent Office's discussion of Topic A, the Supreme Court held in 1981 that the mere presence of a software-implemented mathematical algorithm in an invention does not automatically preclude the invention from being eligible to receive patent protection. Similarly, the copyright statute has expressly addressed the subject of computer programs since 1980. The maturation of the industry under the existing legal framework suggests that the framework is appropriate and that it is reasonably effective.

While copyright has been and is an important and effective tool for the software industry, that does not mean that there is no role for patent protection. Indeed, there is a large and growingly important role for patent protection.

Microsoft believes that the software patent law will continue to mature and we would trust rapidly enough to effectively support growing industry awareness and use of software patents.

The final question asks whether a new form of protection is required for computer programs. Microsoft does not believe that a new form of protection is required; the existing patent system has a long history which reflects an appropriate balance in protecting inventive technology. The system has served American industry well. We are aware of no compelling reasons at this time why it should not be continued to be applied and approved as it is applied to the field of computer software.

Thank you for this opportunity to share Microsoft's current thinking on this very important subject.

COMMISSIONER LEHMAN: I've a question to ask if you'd just hang on for a moment.

Yesterday we had a witness from the League for Programming Freedom, who displayed a chart indicating, showing who had applied for patents and who hadn't, and not surprisingly, the chart showed, for example, that IBM had the most number of patents, AT&T had the next number, and then it went down to some of the companies that we associate more with the mass market software industry, like Microsoft and Lotus and Novell, Borland, Next, Oracle, etc. And he noted that Microsoft only had thirteen patents. Lotus only has seven, Novell has one, WordPerfect has none, for example.

And the implication of that was that basically the patent system has played virtually no role in the stimulation of this fabulous industry that you've talked about, and of course that's part of the Article 1, Section A, mandate is to stimulate progress in the arts, and that, in fact, this particular witness, a computer programmer, felt that it was having a counter stimulative influence because programmers didn't

want to even touch their keyboard before they consulted the legal department.

Microsoft obviously did develop to where it is now without significant patent protection. Do you see something, is there something that's changing in the industry that is causing you now to take a look at patents? What is different about now, today, than the early 1980s when you first came out with your first products?

MR. NEUKOM: I think what's different, in terms of patents is that our industry and certainly my company has become much more aware of the value of patenting software-related inventions. I think as a whole the industry relied extensively on trade secret and copyright protections. It's important to remember, particularly in terms of the mass market kind of software that you describe, that this is a very, very young industry. We tend to think of this as an industry which has always been about the size and had about the reach that it currently has in the mid 1990s, but when you realize that graphical computing, for example, personal computing, has really only come of age in the past four or five years, and portable computing has really only come of age in about the same timespan, you realize that this is an industry which has grown so fast and diversified so quickly that to think about the early '80s is to think about generations-old forms of the current industry.

And there were questions, as I know the Commissioner knows full well about the copyrightability of software, there were some questions among lawyers about the patentability if software. As those questions have been resolved by the courts, the companies have had to pay attention to that. I think that the companies at the top of that list, the IBMs and the AT&Ts tend to be companies which are hardware companies as well, who have a culture of patents and the companies toward the bottom of the list are more purely software companies who didn't come into the industry with that sort of culture and awareness of the values of the trade-offs of patents, and so we're essentially as an industry, I think, catching up with the patent process, and I think that there has been a very material increase in attention paid by the legal staffs to the prospect of patenting software.

We will soon have six patent lawyers in my department, and that's grown from a group which had none in it two and half years ago. We've always relied on outside counsel and will continue for purposes of applications and prosecutions because of the nature of the work involved in writing those claims, but it's certainly much more center-of-screen for law departments and I think that companies are making informed decisions about where they want to spend their scarce legal resources in terms of protecting their intellectual property rights.

I think that there will be -- the hardware companies went through this, I think, in a somewhat transferable piece of history where they were filing an increasing number of patent applications and as they were issued, there came a time when some of those companies had to reach cross-licensing kinds of accommodations with each other. But we, at Microsoft, take the view that to the extent that there is important technology, that seems to us to be patentable, we do want to raise the level of awareness among our technical people to be in touch with the law department, for us to decide whether to pursue an application. I think that's generally happening around the industry. The number of patents issued, of course, is only a sense of how many are in the process, and I think the industry itself is putting more resources in the effort.

COMMISSIONER LEHMAN Microsoft obviously as a big company takes it a little bit on the chin because, the big guy, everybody is concerned about Microsoft's market power and size. That's come up in the discussion of issues, such as decompilation, for example, in the copyright side, where one of the things that we've heard very strongly is that we've had a lot of the testimony that oftentimes -- by the way, testimony from people who feel that there should be no patent coverage for software, but sometimes from people who think there should be patent coverage, too. We've had a lot of suggestions that the copyright law should be construed very narrowly also, so that only literal code is covered.

And then we've also heard some testimony about the decompilation issue too, that there ought to be access to products through that process, and I wonder if you have a comment on that.

MR. NEUKOM: Generally speaking, our view is that software ought to be treated by the copyright law and process the way any other original creative expression is treated, and not distinguished by the nature of its technology. And I think that the courts have been sensible about developing and reinforcing that notion, in terms of broadening an exception for reverse engineering or decompiling.

We are very concerned about that, not just in the law of this country but in the law of other countries, and as the panel knows, that matter is currently the subject of some serious consideration in Japan, and we are very much concerned, for example, in that context that an already none-too-strong copyright law may be further weakened by a too-broad exception for decompiling, which would essentially expose US -- this is not a Microsoft issue, this is a US software publishers' industrywide issue -- would lay open our technology to a shortcut by Japanese and other software companies who could bring to market products which would compete with a very unfair advantage, an advantage of not having had to spend the research and development resources to create and invent the expression and the ideas that go into that product.

COMMISSIONER LEHMAN Thank you very much.

MR. NEUKOM: I hope that's responsive.

COMMISSIONER LEHMAN Finally, next I'd like to ask Charley Morgan to step forward, Vice President of OPEB Funding for The Prudential Insurance Company of America.

I think, Mr. Morgan, you're one of a kind. You're our only insurance person.

--oOo--

CHARLES MORGAN

THE PRUDENTIAL INSURANCE COMPANY OF AMERICA

MR. MORGAN: Good morning, I'm Charles Morgan, I am Vice President, OPEB Funding. OPEB Funding is a business unit of the Prudential Asset Management Company. We fondly know of it as PAMCO. PAMCO is a wholly-owned subsidiary of The Prudential Insurance Company of America, the largest insurance company in the United States. PAMCO offers investment management and related administrative services to US employee benefit plans, foundations, endowments and other domestic and foreign institutional clients.

I have to say I've done a lot of flip-flops this morning and yesterday, listening to the other people talk as to whether I'm really relevant here. I think I'm going to be asking you to make a fairly significant shift in context as I give you my remarks. I'm really here to give you an anecdote -- sort of a horror story.

We are an old industry. The insurance industry in this country has been around for hundreds plus years, Prudential has been around since 1875. We have old products that have been expressed on paper, copyrightable, that are now finding, in manual systems to implement those old products, they are now finding new expression in electronic form, implemented through new systems that also use software and computers. And here I am, a former tax lawyer, who now finds himself running a small business with The Prudential. Prudential has 100,000 employees; my little business has eleven employees. So I listened to the conversations about big organizations against the little guy, the innovator, and wonder where I fit because I am both. I am not a patent lawyer, and I am not a software expert. All I know about software is that I use it every day.

As I mentioned, I work in OPEB Funding, O-P-E-B stands for Other Post Employment Benefits. OPEB Funding offers institutional investors financing solutions for their retiree healthcare liabilities. If you read the paper today, Clinton and his agenda includes healthcare reform, it's a big part of my life.

My work is different from traditional pension benefits, this is post retirement healthcare benefits that I work with. Our primary product is a flexible premium group life insurance contract. The contract offers the employer participating life insurance, but also a broad array of investment accounts similar to pension accounts. Typically it is purchased by a trust, and the employer uses that trust to finance the cost of those benefits.

Now, our product development work for this product that we're selling began in 1987. We're highly regulated. We had to file with state insurance departments for approval of our forms, their content are dictated in large part by the states. Our first state approval occurred in 1989, in April. Our first product installation occurred in August of 1989. Our system development work paralleled that timeframe, and built on existing Prudential systems already used for very similar products.

Now, I should note that our product took a very old idea; that is, a life insurance contract and a trust to fund employee benefits, and updated it by employing a group insurance wrapper rather than an individual policy wrapper. And that was a significant innovation only because legal impediments in our industry were perceived to say it was not possible to do it. We did it.

I then turned to our lawyers and I said, "How do I protect this innovation?" They said, "You cannot, you cannot patent a life insurance contract. You can copyright it, but you can't patent it".

Much to our surprise, you issued a patent, we call it the (Premit Patent) in 1992, covering a system employing a VEBA trust, V-E-B-A, which in turn purchases variable life insurance contracts to fund retiree healthcare benefits. An employer contributes money to the VEBA and obtains a tax deduction. The money is invested in the insurance contracts, eventually it's distributed in the form of healthcare benefits through a health claim system.

The patent owner has approached our clients and prospective clients, advising them that we would owe him royalties as a percentage of the investments in our group variable life insurance product, and that we would try to pass the cost back to them, which we would.

The inventor -- or the invention, that is, covered by the patent is comprised of numerous elements, including a VEBA trust, a variable life insurance contract, a couple of healthcare liability calculation systems for financial accounting and tax accounting purposes, a death claim collection system and a health claim payment system among other elements. Significantly, the patent owner has focused on collecting royalties solely from Prudential and exclusively with respect to our group variable life insurance contract; that is, the life insurance contract segment of this invention.

Now, why would we, Prudential, owe the patent owner royalties on this? All we're doing is selling a variable life insurance contract. We do not perform most of the functions comprised of the segments in the invention. While it is true that we do have death claim systems, those systems are inherently connected with the business of selling and administering life insurance contracts. We also have healthcare systems connected with our group health insurance businesses. But it would be merely coincidental if we happened to administer a health claim system for a client who purchases our variable life insurance product.

The focus of his royalty claims on the insurance contract segment of this, quote "invention" unquote, suggests that he merely wanted to patent a variable life insurance contract, something that we thought was not possible. To accomplish his objective, he merely surrounded the contract with sufficient quote "system trappings" unquote, to justify issuance of the patent on his invention and persuaded you to issue it. Now, he has not implemented any of those systems, he has merely patented the concept.

The patent fails on three conditions of patentability. The invention is not new. It is perfectly obvious to a person in the field, and it is merely a method of doing business. The Prudential has been in the business of selling life insurance since 1875. We've been in the employee benefit business since the 1920s. We have worked with pension liabilities for more than half a century. We have worked with healthcare liabilities for decades. Individual life insurance products have been used to fund pension liabilities since at least the 1940s. The Internal Revenue Service even issued a ruling, what we call PS No. 58, in the 1940s, to cope with pension funding with pension trusts investing in life insurance contracts.

Now VEBAs, an important part of this supposed invention, came into unique prominence for funding retiree healthcare liabilities in the late 1980s, only because Congress enacted ERISA in 1974 and DEFRA in 1984, thereby curtailing the

other tax-motivated devices employed previously. Originally called "Retired Lives Reserves", several IRS rulings in the 1960s and early '70s established the foundations of the tax deductions that ultimately were codified by DEFRA in 1984. Life insurance policies and VEBAs were favored funding instruments for Retired Lives Reserves even before Congress codified the rules. The essential role to be played by VEBAs prospectively was obvious to anyone in the insurance industry, the benefits consulting community, anyone who had worked with pension plans, trusts, life insurance and Retired Lives Reserves. VEBAs are not new, they're not unusual. A VEBA is just name that Congress put on a 501C9 trust in the Internal Revenue Code. You go read it, and that's the label in the section.

The primary purpose of the trust is to secure the asset from the employer's creditors so employees like you and me will get the promised benefits. Section 501 of the Internal Revenue Code has been there ever since 1954 and has antecedents going back to the '39 code.

The Prudential has been a leader in the development and use of record keeping and other systems required to support life, health and annuity and pension products. We employed the earliest computers doing the 1940s for statistical purposes, during the '50s we installed the earliest machines from IBM. Our computer systems became a substantial part of our business in the '60s with the automation of our policy and group pension administration.

Prudential developed the first medical and dental claims systems in the United States in the '70s. One of our major life insurance systems contains tens of millions of lines of code, that require 750 people simply to maintain in.

In our group insurance and PAMCO operations alone, we have more than a hundred major applications in development or under maintenance. Our annual budget for systems applications runs into the many hundreds of millions of dollars. If I'd had time to research it, I'd daresay we're upwards of a billion annual.

Notwithstanding that big investment, we have not pursued patents within Prudential, we haven't stockpiled them. And I asked our patent lawyer how many he was aware of, he knew of none.

I was interested in the picture painted yesterday, the big guy against the little guy, as I said, we have not been using these as a tactic, and we may well have to turn to that.

In my little business, when confronted with this patent I have only a few very unpleasant options. I can shut myself down, I can spend a lot .of money on lawyers, pursue royalty litigation or litigation to get rid of the patent or I can pay a royalty which is what I see as nothing more than a ransom, extortion.

THE PTO re-examination process was not available to me for the reasons that Lee Patch mentioned this morning.

Now, I only have two more brief paragraphs with my suggestions, but they're echoes of what you have heard already today: You need to introduce rigor into your research of prior art. People like us are available to you, you ought to seek us out and learn a little bit from the community that is affected by the patent application. I agree with those comments wholeheartedly. I am not a patent lawyer. It was obvious to me that that's something you need

UNITED STATES PATENT AND TRADEMARK OFFICE
Public Hearing on Patent Protection for Software-Related Inventions
San Jose, California — January 26-27, 1994

to do, and I applaud these hearings as a first step in hearing about that sort of thing.

I don't see the software patenting issue as the real issue, I see the real issue is research into obviousness and newness.

That really about sums up my comments except to say that in the financial services community, we have a very broad spectrum of products which at one extreme or the other have significant differences. At any point in between those two extremes, the line drawing exercise for you and me is incredibly difficult. And applying new expressions to age-old products like this needs to proceed with care.

COMMISSIONER LEHMAN Thank you very much.

MR. MORGAN: Okay. Thank you.

COMMISSIONER LEHMAN Next up and finally, our final witness for the morning is Les Earnest.

--oOo--

LES EARNEST

MR. EARNEST: Les Earnest, speaking for myself.

Based on my 40 years of experience in the computer system development, much of it before software patents were introduced, I believe that the alleged connection between such patents and the stimulation of innovation is tenuous at best and probably negative. Let me confess that even though I oppose the continuation of software patents, as a defensive measure I've applied for some that have been granted.

When I entered the field as a programmer in 1954 there were only about a hundred of us in the whole world, and each of us was turning out thousands of inventions each year, or maybe it was hundreds depending on your standards, but a lot. Software was given the same kinds of protection as other documentation, namely copyright and trade secret.

It was certainly a good thing that there were no software patents because my colleagues and I could have papered over the field and retired for 17 years or so to collect royalties. Since patents didn't exist, we kept working and had quite a good time doing it, sharing ideas and standing on each other's shoulders to see how high we could reach.

In 1956 I went to MIT to help design the Sage Air Defense System, it was a technological marvel full of inventions, both hardware and software. It was the first real-time computer system and depended on the large software system that was cooperatively written by many people. That was the first such system.

This project helped transfer a lot of technology from MIT to IBM, but almost nothing was patented. Dozens of Sage systems were eventually deployed around the country, each with a vacuum tube computer that covered a floor area about the size of a football field and an air conditioning system to match.

It is fortunate that this power, that the Soviet Union, never attacked the U.S. in that era, because the marvelous technology in Sage had several Achilles' heels that would have caused it to fail catastrophically under attack. However, those short comings were kept well hidden from Congress and the public, and as a result the so-called command control communications technology became a major growth industry for the military industrial complex.

The most recent example of that line of development being the grossly defective Star Wars system, but that's another story.

Beginning in 1959 I developed the first pen-based computer system that reliably recognized cursive writing. I believe that it was more reliable than the 1993 version of Apple's Newton. But the idea of getting a patent on such a thing never occurred to me or my colleagues. It wouldn't have done much good anyway because the computer on which it ran filled a rather large room, and the 17-year life of the patent would have expired before small portable computers became available.

In order to cope with a personal shortcoming, I developed the first spelling checker in 1966.

(laughter)

I didn't think that was much of an invention and was rather surprised when many other organizations took copies. And, of course, nobody patented things like that.

When John McCarthy and I organized the Stanford Artificial Intelligence laboratory, and I served as its executive officer for 15 years, there was a great deal of innovation that came out of there, including the first interactive computer-aided design system for computers and other electronic devices, early robotics and speech recognition systems, the software invention that became the heart of the Yamaha music synthesizer, document compilation and printing technologies that later came to be called desktop publishing. The Sun workstation was invented there. And the guy who invented public key cryptography was in our lab.

Few of these inventions were patented in the early period, but we later began to file for such coverage. The pace of innovation I note has necessarily slowed over time as the technology matures, but concurrently, of course, the amount of patent protection has increased. I suspect that these changes are connected.

Yesterday in this forum, my friend Paul Heckle said that software patents stimulate new businesses. I'm afraid that Paul has that backwards. In fact, new businesses stimulate software patents. Venture capitalists want the comfort of patents on products that are being brought into the market even though know-how is far more important in most cases.

In 1980 I co-founded Imagen Corporation, which developed and manufactured the first commercial desktop publishing systems based on laser printers. We filed for software patents to try to appease the venture capitalists, even though it was not actually important to our business, I believe. Of course, they didn't understand and the lawyers were happy to take our money.

Based on my experiences, I also joined the League for Programming Freedom to help resist the patent conspiracy and I later served for a time on its board of directors.

In summary, for many years there has been a great deal of innovation, there was a great deal of innovation in the computer software field with no patents, under the quote, stimulation of software patents the pace now seems to have slowed. I believe that there may be a connection, not only because of the time that must be devoted to covering and deciding what to cover and filing a patent application, but also because patents are owned by other organizations, many of them in fact based on prior art, and constitute a

UNITED STATES PATENT AND TRADEMARK OFFICE
Public Hearing on Patent Protection for Software-Related Inventions
San Jose, California — January 26-27, 1994

mine field that must be carefully navigated. I recommend a return to the good old days when success depended on moving faster than the other guys rather than trying to catch them in a trap.

Thank you.

COMMISSIONER LEHMAN Thank you very much, Mr. Earnest.

That will conclude our morning session, and we'll reconvene at 2 o'clock, at which time our first witness will be Richard Stallman.

(Luncheon recess taken)

COMMISSIONER LEHMAN We can get underway. It seems to be a usual human tendency of somehow or other always running a couple of minutes late. So perhaps we can start right out again by calling Richard Stallman forward, please.

I assume you're -- you're just listed as Richard Stallman, but I assume you still have the affiliation with the Free Software Foundation?

--oOo--

RICHARD STALLMAN

FREE SOFTWARE FOUNDATION

MR. STALLMAN: I guess I'm just speaking for myself because, yes, I am involved in software development with the foundation, and I guess this is probably the opinion of the foundation too since I'm its president.

(laughter)

COMMISSIONER LEHMAN Great. Well, welcome, and why don't you proceed.

MR. STALLMAN: Okay. Each year the government creates new bureaucratic programs. Each is created for a purpose. That doesn't mean it serves that purpose or that it is worth the cost.

It's hard the close down unnecessary bureaucracies because people presume they must do some good. It's easy to admit a government program has drawbacks, but many won't seriously consider whether it does its job at all.

Thus we see, in the announcement of these hearings, the supposition that software patents are helpful. We are asked whether they protect software developers enough. Patent lawyers chose the word "protection" to imply that patents are beneficial.

I'm not a lawyer. I'm a programmer, considered a good one. I am here to explain why software patents impede software development and retard software progress. Software is like other fields of engineering in many ways, but there is a fundamental difference: Computer programs are built out of ideal mathematical objects. A program always does exactly what it says. You can build a castle in the air supported by a line of zero mathematical thickness, and it will stay up.

Physical machinery isn't so predictable, because physical objects are quirky. If a program says to count the numbers from one to a thousand, you can be sure it will do that. If you build a counter out of machinery, a belt might slip and count the number 58 twice, or a truck might go by outside and you'll skip 572. These problems make designing reliable physical machinery very hard.

The result is that software is far easier to design per component than hardware. This is why designers today use software rather than hardware whenever they can. This is also why teams of a few people often develop computer programs of tremendous complexity.

People naively say to me, "If your program is innovative, then won't you get the patent?" This question assumes that one product goes with one patent.

In some fields, such as pharmaceuticals, patents often work that way. Software is at the opposite extreme: A typical patent covers many dissimilar programs and even an innovative program is likely to infringe many patents. That's because a substantial program must combine a large number of different techniques and implement many features. Even if a few are new inventions, that still leaves plenty that are not. Each technique or feature less than two decades old is likely to be patented already by somebody else. Whether it is actually patented is a matter of luck.

The only way a programmer can avoid this mess is by sticking to things that are obsolete. You may not recall the state of the computer field 17 years ago since most people didn't pay attention back then, there were no personal computers. If you were a hobbyist you might get a computer with a few thousand bytes of memory. If you were lucky it might run basic.

This shows another way that software is different, it progresses very quickly. A program three years old is becoming obsolete, and one that's six years old looks Stone Age. A 20-year monopoly for anything in computers is absurd.

In other fields a new technique may require development, building one device after another until you understand how to make the technique work. If a steel part functions badly and you think copper might be better, you can't type "replace steel with copper" and try the new device a minute later. The need to recoup the cost of this development is part of the usual argument for patents.

In software, an individual technique usually doesn't need much development. What we do develop are products that combine a new technique with dozens of other techniques. When a second programmer decides to use the same technique, he will have to do just as much development as the first programmer. Firstly, because he's probably using a different combination of techniques with that new one, and secondly, because the first programmer probably kept the results of development a trade secret.

The patent system is supposed to help by discouraging trade secrecy. In software, patents don't do this. Today, just as in 1980, most developers publish general ideas and keep the source code secret. Here is a copy of a compiler that I wrote with a few friends. It's printed four pages per sheet to make it manageable. This program is mainly the work of four people, another dozen helped substantially, and others occasionally. The two principal developers were not working on this full-time.

This compiler and its output are probably being used on more than a million computers today. Major companies such as Intel and Motorola have adopted it and now add to it. The U.S. Air Force is funding extensions to it. Many widely used systems are compiled with it. Just a few lines of code can be enough to infringe a patent. This compiler has 10,000 pages -- how many patents does it infringe? I don't know, nobody does.

Perhaps you can read the code and tell me?

(laughter)

I know of one patent it infringes, I found it along with some near misses in a list I saw by luck. I believe I have prior art for that patent, but I can't be sure what a court would say. I don't dare tell you the patent number, because if I were sued, I couldn't pay for the defense. I would lose by default.

An invalid patent is a dangerous weapon. Defending a patent suit typically costs a million dollars and the outcome depends mostly on legal technicalities.

I've had at least one patentable idea in my career, I know this because someone else patented it years later. It's a feature for using abbreviations in a word processor. A couple of years ago, the users of the word processor XyWrite received a downgrade in the mail. XyWrite had an abbreviation feature, the developer removed it when threatened by the patent holder.

They knew about my earlier published work; why didn't they fight the patent? Sometimes a business can't afford to have a lawsuit that will drag on for years. At those times, even if the patent is invalid, you lose.

These patents are invalid because of luck. It was pure luck that these ideas were published by one person before they were patented by another. And it was luck that the ones who published didn't patent instead.

This is an important point: What is patented and what is not is mainly a matter of luck. When you develop a large system and you need to combine a large number of techniques and features, whether or not you can use each given one is a matter of luck.

The carelessness of the Patent Office in dealing with software is well known. So some people assume that if the PTO only did a better job, everything would be okay. They say we that we should wait while the invalid patents spew out, and eventually the PTO will understand software and do the job right.

There are two flaws in that suggestion: The PTO will not do a better job, and that would not solve the problem if they did.

Some years ago a professor I know patented Kirchoff's current law, which says that the electric currents flowing into a junction equal the currents flowing out. He did this to confirm, privately, his suspicion that the PTO could not handle the field of electronics. He never tried to enforce the patent which has since expired. I will disclose his name if you give assurances that he and his lawyer will not get in trouble for this.

Kirchoff's laws were formulated in 1845. If the PTO couldn't understand electricity after a century, how can we expect it to understand software in another decade or two.

(applause)

Computer scientists look at many software patents and say, "This is absurdly obvious". Defenders of a patent system reject our opinion. "You're using hindsight," they say. "You're more skilled than a typical practitioner." What we consider obvious patents are not errors, they reflect a different definition of "obvious". It's not going to change.

What if the PTO stopped making mistakes and issued no more invalid patents? That would not solve the problem because all new techniques and features, those not known today, would be patented just the same.

Suppose the PTO were perfect, suppose that it is the year 2010 and you're a software developer. You want to write a program combining 200 patentable techniques. Suppose 15 of them are new, you might patent those. Suppose 120 of them were known before 1990, those would not be patented any longer. That leaves 65 techniques probably patented by others, more than enough to make the project infeasible. This is the gridlock we are headed for.

Today's PTO mistakes are bringing us to gridlock sooner, but the ultimate result is gridlock even with a perfect PTO.

I have explained how patents impede progress; do they also encourage it? Patents may encourage a few people to look for new ideas to patent. This isn't a big help, because we had plenty of innovation without patents. Look at the journals and the advertisements of 1980 and you'll see. New ideas are not the limiting factor for progress in our field. The hard job in software is developing large systems.

People developing systems have new ideas from time to time, naturally they use these ideas. Before patents they published the ideas too for kudos. As long as we have a lot of software development, we will have a steady flow of new published ideas.

The patent system impedes development. It makes us ask for each design decision, "Will we get sued?" And the answer is a matter of luck. This leads to more expensive development and less of it. With less development, programmers will have fewer ideas along the way. Thus, patents can actually reduce the number of patentable ideas that are published.

A decade ago the field of software functioned without patents, it produced innovations such as windows, virtual reality, spreadsheets and networks. And because of the absence of patents, programmers could develop software using these innovations.

We did not ask for the change that was imposed on us. There is no doubt that software patents tie us in knots. If there's no clear and vital public need to tie us up in bureaucracy, untie us and let us get back to work.

I'm finished. I hope I didn't exceed my time.

COMMISSIONER LEHMAN No, you didn't. Thank you very much.

Does anybody else have any questions of Mr. Stallman?

Thank you very much.

(applause)

COMMISSIONER LEHMAN Did you write this entire 10,000 pages worth of code?

MR. STALLMAN: No. As I said, about four people did most of the work. In what's here, I and one other person did most of the bulk of the work. And then there were like two or three others who did substantial pieces, and a dozen who did significant pieces.

By the way, with this goes another stack -- this tall -- of

UNITED STATES PATENT AND TRADEMARK OFFICE
Public Hearing on Patent Protection for Software-Related Inventions
San Jose, California — January 26-27, 1994

machine descriptions for particular target machines, but I didn't include them because they have a lot more different contributors.

COMMISSIONER LEHMAN And what do you do with this? How do you make this available to the public?

MR. STALLMAN: It's on the Internet. You can FTP it and run it. Many organizations distribute it. We also supply it on compact disks.

COMMISSIONER LEHMAN So that's how you make most of your work which is dedicated to public domain as I understand it, pretty much.

MR. STALLMAN: It's not public domain, but that's getting into a digression, it's free software.

UNMIKED VOICE: Can you go back to the microphone?

COMMISSIONER LEHMAN I apologize, I should have asked that.

MR. STALLMAN: I don't want to get into free software because it's a digression I think for the most part, and it leads into an area where I have views that are definitely a small minority's views. What I've said I think most programmers would agree with. I've stayed away from my controversial beliefs.

But, yes, I distribute free software, and because of that I generally can't licence even one patent. Other software developers can muddle through if they have to license a few patents, gets to be enough and they get crushed.

But I can't — I get stopped dead by even one.

COMMISSIONER LEHMAN Have you been sued yet?

MR. STALLMAN: No, but I've had to stop distributing software because I've seen other people being threatened for the same patents. I didn't wait till I got sued. People often wouldn't actually sue a charity. After all, I am the president of a charity, and they might feel it would look bad to be suing us, so instead they would just sue our users. Right? And how would I feel if I were trying to help the public, giving them something that's a trap, a trap for getting sued.

COMMISSIONER LEHMAN Have any of your users been sued, of your work?

MR. STALLMAN: They haven't been sued for the programs that we write, but for other free software we use they have been threatened. They received letters from AT&T, everyone using XWindows got threatened by AT&T and by Cadtrack. So even though we didn't write that software, it's an essential part of the system we're trying to build.

COMMISSIONER LEHMAN Thank you very much.

Our next witness is Timothy Casey, Senior Patent Counsel with Silicon Graphics.

MR. STALLMAN: Would you like to keep this? It's an exhibit, we'll offer it to you, but we'll throw it away if you don't want it.

COMMISSIONER LEHMAN It seems like a shame to throw it away, but I think that it's going to be hard for us to take it back to Washington.

MR. CASEY: I'd be happy to recycle it for you.

(laughter)

COMMISSIONER LEHMAN But we can put it in a museum here in San Jose. Well, since it's available actually on the Internet, we can just call it up there, if we need it. Please go ahead.

—oOo—

TIMOTHY CASEY
Senior Patent Counsel
SILICON GRAPHICS

MR. CASEY: Hello, I am Timothy Casey, Senior Patent Counsel with Silicon Graphics, and representing their views.

Silicon Graphics is the world's leading supplier of visual computing systems targeted for technical, scientific and corporate marketplace. The company pioneered the development of color three-dimensional computing, transforming it into practical and affordable mainstream solutions that improve the productivity and increase operational efficiencies across a broad array of industries, even though as of late, we seem to have gained our greatest notoriety from our involvements in films like Jurassic Park and Terminator 2.

I would also like to point out that the company was originally founded on an exclusive grant of a patent from Stanford University that's since run out, but we did have our basis around the patent.

Although Silicon Graphics designs and manufactures personal computers, workstations, servers and supercomputers based on our own designs for RISC processing technology, a large part of our overall development effort is now focussed on software, including, display, communication, development tools, operating systems, applications and user interface technologies.

Naturally, Silicon Graphics files a large number of patent applications related to both our hardware- and software-based inventions, and has a vested interest in maintaining such protections. But rather than use my time to further expand on the horrors or virtues of software patents, I would rather state that we are spending too much of our time in these hearings I believe, discussing the ill patient and not enough time discussing the disease. And shooting the patient I don't think is an adequate solution.

Software as incorporated into the patent system is not the great villain that many people would like us to see, but rather a misunderstood giant. As I mentioned earlier, most computer system manufacturers today invest a majority of their research and development efforts on software technologies in order to further distinguish their hardware products from their competition. I truly hate to think what would happen to this industry and this nation's economy, if less than half of this development effort was subject to patent protection.

It is also important to consider that in practical terms, software is not really different from hardware. It's just that the Patent Office understands hardware and is better prepared to adequately examine hardware-related cases in most situations. Patents have been granted on transistors, resistors, capacitors, clock circuits, filters, and the like, all necessary building blocks of many electronic designs. But has that seriously impeded the electronics industry? Why is software so different?

Are not most software products composed of basic

UNITED STATES PATENT AND TRADEMARK OFFICE
Public Hearing on Patent Protection for Software-Related Inventions
San Jose, California -- January 26-27, 1994

elemental blocks of code arranged in new ways to perform new tasks, much like the hardware elements of any modern electronic product? The reason software patents have developed into such a controversial topic is primarily because a number of overly-broad software patents have been allowed to issue. And why is that?

Well, we can argue that the prior art is inadequate, and that is true. And we can argue that the statutory subject matter tests are inadequate, and that is also true. But I would argue that one of the biggest causes is the fact that the Patent Office has not had the most important tool it needs to adequately examine software patents; and that is examiners who have the same fundamental understanding of basic software elements as they have of basic hardware elements.

I find it absolutely amazing that the Patent Office has issued so few overly-broad software patents given the level of training of many of the examiners and the complexity of the application subject matter. While I understand that the Patent Office has already undertaken steps to hire computer science majors in the future to help solve this problem -- which I loudly applaud -- there are many additional measures that can be taken to improve the services of the Patent Office, both with respect to already issued software patents, and any applications that might be examined in the future.

Some of these measures include revamping the re-examination process, so that re-examinations can be used to achieve the goals for which they originally intended. One step would be to make re-examinations an inter partes proceeding. Another would be to make them less expensive, both in terms of fees and the formal requirements of a re-examination request that presently force potential applicants to seek exceedingly expensive professional assistance in order to comply with the regulations.

It may also be in the country's best interest if an amnesty period is implemented over the next year or so during which applicants could institute a re-examination of any software patent, based on new art, meeting the requirements -- which may indeed need some revamping -- by simply filling out a one-page application form and filing a minimal fee, say of $500 instead of the present fees which is well over 2,000, I believe.

Second, instituting some form of prepublication of applications for the purpose of eliciting industry comment, such as publish issue patents on a tentative basis pending the discovery of new art during the comment period.

Third, establish routine industry-supported education programs to provide continuing education for examiners, even up to and including advance degree study for examiners who commit to an extended tenure with the Patent Office.

Silicon Graphics has participated in both bringing people to the Patent Office to do presentations on graphics technologies for the examiners. And we have also hosted a number of examiner groups at our office in Mountain View to attempt to give them additional education on our industry and our technologies. And I applaud the Patent Office's efforts in that area.

Four, employing technical specialists with broad industry knowledge and allowing them to roam between examining groups so they can provide expert assistance when needed to less highly trained examiners.

Five, allowing examiners more exposure to a variety of technologies instead of pigeon-holing some of them in narrowly constructed examination areas.

Six, providing the examiners with better technical tools, such as network computer systems that allow examiners to do key element searching of both text and graphics on a single screen at the same desktop system that they use for word processing, video teleconferencing, and Internet communications.

Seven, introducing legislation to turn the Patent Office into a government corporation, so that the Patent Office can attract and maintain examiners at competitive pay scales to the industry without being constrained by the Civil Service pay guidelines, and allowing the Patent Office to actually keep and utilize all the money it raises from user fees.

Eight, instituting new limitations on the maximum number of claims permitted in an issued patent, such as three independent claims and no more that 30 total claims, in order to simplify the examination process and reduce the burden of accused infringers who are often forced to prepare opinions on patents with hundreds of primarily duplicative claims.

Nine, instituting per-page surcharges for patent applications with more than 35 pages of text and 10 drawing figures to force applicants to be more succinctly-descriptive of their inventions.

As long as I am on the subject of steps that the Patent Office can undertake to improve its services to its clients, I will introduce two additional measures that should be considered: namely, instituting a new type of expedited patent application, and regionalizing the Patent Office.

Silicon Graphics recently obtained a patent on some technology that was critical to the protection of one part of our systems, and that we knew has already been duplicated by after-market suppliers of such parts. Despite filing a Petition To Make Special with our application and being extremely diligent in our efforts to shepherd the application through the Patent Office as soon as possible, it still took eight months from the filing of the application for it to finally issue as an enforceable patent.

Now, you may think, "Eight months, that's pretty fast". But it would have been done in two or three months had it not been for the fact that it took three months to get from the mail room to the examiner and another four months to get from the examiner to the final print. The examiner completed the entire examination of the patent in less than one month.

In a similar case, we have a patent application on a fairly simplistic mechanical assembly sitting in the Patent Office since July of '91, despite the filing of a Petition To Make Special. During the pendency of this application, that mechanical assembly was copied by a number of other companies. Although this only resulted in a small amount of competition for us in a relatively narrow market for this part, it was a greater concern for us because the knock-off products are not always of adequate quality, it could cause damage to our customers' systems when used, for which we would ultimately be responsible for correcting in order to maintain our customer loyalty. This would not have been

UNITED STATES PATENT AND TRADEMARK OFFICE
Public Hearing on Patent Protection for Software-Related Inventions
San Jose, California — January 26-27, 1994

the case had this application been allowed to issue.

The reason the one application took eight months and this other application has taken over two and a half years is because the Petition To Make Special Process only applies to the examination and not the remainder of the Patent Office process. What is needed therefore, is a new type of application that not only gets expedited when in front of the examiner, but throughout the entire process. I would be more than happy to pay a higher fee, such as a 1,000 to $1,500 in filing fees for such an application in these types of situations, because I would surely make that up in outside counsel fees when the attorneys have to relearn the technology two or three years later after we get a final office action.

My last suggestion is that the Patent Office seriously consider working to regionalize the Patent Office. No one in Washington can truly appreciate the difficulties in communicating with the Patent Office from the West Coast. Because of the time differences between the two parts of the country, and the new flexible hour programs instituted by the Patent Office, which I do think is a good idea, there's only a one-hour period each day, typically between 1:30 to 2:30 Pacific Standard Time, during which a practitioner on the West Coast or an applicant can expect to get ahold of an examiner on the telephone. Because of this, it has sometimes taken over a month to arrange a telephone interview with an examiner.

My colleagues on the East Coast however, can call at much more convenient hours, or even walk over to the Patent Office for an in-person visit, something which would cost me well over a thousand dollars to attempt. Given these restrictions, I hate to imagine what the independent inventor or startup organization on the West Coast thinks of our patent system.

Some other benefits of a regionalized Patent Office would include: An ability to draw from a larger pool of potential examiners; new economic growth in the parts of the country selected for the new Patent Office sites; and greater public accessibility to the Patent Office records and examiners, as well as greater exposure for the examiners to the relevant industries. It would certainly cut down on your costs of sending examiners across the country.

I hope these suggestions prove to be useful guides to the Patent Office and as an invitation to the Patent Office to consult with West Coast companies and practitioners and applicants for addition solutions that could be implemented by the Patent Office to resolve our present difficulties, but also to raise the Patent Office to new heights of service.

Thank you for this opportunity.

COMMISSIONER LEHMAN Thank you.

Do you think it would be a good idea, for example, to have Group 2300 located here in this area?

MR. CASEY: I would imagine that a majority of their clients are in this area so it would probably be a good idea, or at least some portion of them.

COMMISSIONER LEHMAN There were some reactions I had to certain things that you said, but I don't want to take away from some of the other -- we are already I think making changes along the lines of some of the things you've recommended, and certainly part of it has to do with our

automation system and other reforms that we are making. But thanks very much for your help.

MR. CASEY: Thank you.

COMMISSIONER LEHMAN Next I'd like to call Robert Sterne of Sterne, Kessler, Goldstein and Fox.

--oOo--

ROBERT GREEN STERNE, ESQ.

STERNE, KESSLER, GOLDSTEIN & FOX

MR. STERN: Good afternoon. I am Robert Greene Sterne. And my testimony represents my own views as an attorney in private practice with over 15 years of experience representing almost exclusively U.S. companies in high technology electronic and computer technology. Based on my experience in the trenches, I believe that U.S. companies of all sizes, particularly startups and those creating leading edge technologies are served best by an intellectual property system that provides a broad scope of protection and strong enforcement remedies.

Having heard much of the testimony in these hearings, I would like to state that I agree with those speakers who have stated that technological innovation is fostered by a broad scope of intellectual property protection and by strong enforcement of such exclusive rights. I don't want to replow this ground today. Rather I would like to focus on a few points which I believe need further discussion so as to round out the record of these hearings.

First, from a purely selfish professional viewpoint, and I say this purely -- patent attorneys benefit financially from the uncertainty that exists concerning patent eligibility for emerging electronic technology, and from the complexity that the present patent rules create. So I ask you all to please make the system more precise and simpler for everyone.

Second, the panel seems to find war stories helpful. Let me give you one that I am involved in concerning a startup that is in the process of raising 100 million dollars. Patent applications are being written and product clearance studies are being done which are absolutely critical to this financing. The venture capital people would not feel comfortable in investing their money if they did not believe that they were free of infringement and had an excellent chance of obtaining broad patent protection for their innovation.

Now, this is not an isolated event. More and more, the financial community is requiring that the intellectual property portfolio of a startup electronic company be sufficient to provide a proprietary position and be free of infringement problems in order for necessary capital to be raised. As you know, startups and companies in emerging areas of electronic technology, Mr. Commissioner, create a disproportionate number of new jobs in this economy. We need to protect this process through a strong intellectual property system which will encourage investment and the creation of real wealth.

My experience is that without strong intellectual property, the business community will invest in less risky ventures outside of high technology electronics.

Third, the case law and the Patent Office position concerning so called "mathematical algorithms" which, if found, create nonstatutory subject matter status for otherwise inventive electronic technology, frankly, is illogical and pernicious. No one, and I repeat no one, in my opinion, either inside or outside the Patent Office can draw the bright lines that the rest of the public believes should be capable of being drawn concerning patent eligibility as it relates to mathematical algorithms. This uncertainty is unnecessary and totally unsatisfactory.

For example, when I debated your solicitor on this subject before the Maryland Patent Law Association last October, he stated that the law of mathematical algorithms was so complex that even he had to review the cases each time he had to deal with the issue.

This uncertainty hurts innovation in this country.

On a substantive level, the alleged distinction between patentable algorithm inventions and unpatentable mathematical algorithm inventions makes no sense in reality. Every physical system, I repeat, every physical system and process can be represented mathematically. In fact, that is how physical systems and processes are modeled today in all industries using computer-aided design and manufacturing tools. To say that a product or process made by man is not statutory merely because the label "mathematical algorithm" is stuck to it, begs the question completely. Furthermore, all one has to do is pick up any two technical dictionaries and one will find that there is no agreement as to what the term "algorithm" and what the term "mathematical algorithm" each means.

So in addition to not reflecting what happens in the technical world, there is the added problem that there is no definitional certainty concerning algorithm and mathematical algorithm.

The Patent Office has a duty to discharge its constitutional mandate of promoting progress in the useful arts by making sure that the definition for statutory subject matter for electronic technology encompass anything and everything under the sun made by man in this technical area. Otherwise, critical emerging areas of technology, such as digital signal processing, voice recognition, computer graphics, compilers, multimedia, virtual reality, handwriting analysis, encrypted communications, and information retrieval, just to name a few, will be denied patent protection despite their innovation, because a patent examiner or an infringer will be able to stick the label "mathematical algorithm" on the otherwise patentable invention.

You, Mr. Commissioner, must be make sure that the people reporting to you seek broad interpretation of patentable subject matter in this electronics area like that being given in the biotechnology and other emerging areas of technology.

Fourth, I often say that electronics is applied functionality in the electronic domain. Implementation of this functionality is merely a design choice in most cases in terms of hardware or software. The choice of how to implement this inventive functionality depends on many factors, but it is the functionality that is the invention, and one should never forget that.

We should stop the endless debate of saying that hardware inventions should be treated differently by the Patent Office than software inventions. The alleged inventive distinction between hardware and software is ludicrous to those in the electronics industry.

Furthermore, we have the same definitional problem that we had with algorithm and mathematical algorithm. No one can agree upon the definition of what is hardware and what is software. The reason for this is simple. As the technology evolves, the blurred boundary between hardware and software implementation changes and shifts.

Fifth, opponents of so called "software patents" argue that the patent of software operates to remove well-known software inventions from the public domain because the Patent Office does not have an adequate database to properly examine them.

The PTO needs to continue to enhance its database in this area of technology as well as in all emerging areas of technology such as biotechnology, but denying patent protection for software inventions due solely to the database inadequacies is akin to throwing the baby out with the bath water. The examination process needs to be improved rather than restricting statutory subject matter for computer-related inventions.

Now, I would like to offer you a ready-made solution which is Rule 56. Under Rule 56, applicants must provide the Patent Office with the best art of which they are aware. Often, this art submitted under Rule 56 includes nonpatent literature. This nonpatent literature in most cases is better than the patents contained in the Patent database, because patents by definition are several years behind the technical literature. Thus, the Patent Office can significantly enhance its search database by feeding in the technical literature obtained under Rule 56.

Six, you inquired in Part A about claim formats, and I will address this in detail in my written submissions.

Let me make just two high level comments: First, claiming should be flexible. The goal should be to define the invention so as to fully protect the inventor while providing the precision that the public so critically needs in determining whether or not they are infringing. The present rigidity often exhibited by the Patent Office in terms of specialized claim formats in emerging electronic areas prevents one or both of these goals from being met. Let's stop putting form over substance, and let's start putting effective claim drafting back into the picture.

Let me give you just one example: The so-called computer program product claim is critically needed so as to allow the patentee to charge the infringer with direct infringement where only software is being sold on media or being transmitted electronically over networks such as the electronic superhighway.

The Patent Office should be seeking ways to have these types of claims made permissible, rather than engaging in a bureaucratic exercise that is tantamount to a war of delay and attrition in denying these types of claims.

Seventh, your twenty-year term proposal is excellent. But it must be accompanied with a rock-solid commitment from the Patent Office to significantly lower the pendency period of patent applications. Leading edge electronic companies in this valley and elsewhere now operate on product development cycles at 6 to 9 months. That is the time it takes from coming up with an idea to releasing a product into the marketplace.

Our firm routinely prepares over 200 U.S. patent applications on complex electronics each year. And we know from experience that it takes two to three years to typically get these applications through the Patent Office.

Mr. Commissioner, that's too long. I predict that if we cannot get pendency period down, the electronics industry will pull away from the patent system because it will take too long for them to get protection.

Finally, the patent system is of enormous benefit to the electronics industry in encouraging and protecting innovation. I think that the system needs to be worked on and improved, but I think overall everything is working out well. It's just that we need to make the system in terms of eligibility more precise.

Thank you very much.

COMMISSIONER LEHMAN Thank you very much.

Next I'd like to call forward Victor Siber, Counsel to the IBM Corporation.

--oOo--

VICTOR SIBER

SENIOR CORPORATE COUNSEL

IBM CORPORATION

MR. SIBER: Good afternoon, and thank you for the opportunity of allowing me to deliver my comments this afternoon.

I am Victor Siber, Senior Corporate Counsel for the International Business Machines Corporation. My comments do represent the views of IBM.

The IBM Corporation spent 6.5 billion dollars on research and development in 1962. In that same year, over 22,000 software programmers were employed by the company, and we sold approximately 18.5 billion dollars of software products and services. So obviously, we are intensely interested in the subject matter of these hearings.

We protect the detailed expression in every one of our software products by copyright. And approximately 3 to 5 percent of these programs contain new and unobvious functions that are protected by patent. Patent coverage on these inventive functions protects our investment, gives us important business leverage, as well as access into foreign markets.

I understand that this hearing was scheduled, in part, to address questions raised by some broad software patents that have recently issued. These patents are alleged to cover old processes. The response by some is to call for changes in the law to prevent the issuance of patents in this technology.

In the short term that would hurt the U.S. computer industry. And in the long term all industries that use computers to gain competitive advantage will suffer.

The argument over these controversial patents is not that they cover unpatentable abstractions. These patents cover quite useful functions, which others in the industry want to use. The issue, and the key to the controversy is something quite different: whether these patents cover truly new and nonobvious functions and thereby add something to the useful arts. In the final analysis that is the job expected from the U.S. Patent and Trademark Office. And it is a job that is doable.

The United States was the first and continues to be the global leader in computer hardware and software technology. This technology is important not only in itself, but as a driver of innovation in other fields. And today, it is facing stronger and broader global competition. As the industry matures and competition from overseas increases, patents will be the key to protecting the most valuable US-originated innovations.

You have posed a number of questions at the today. Beginning with Question 3 relating to altering the standards for patent eligibility for software-related inventions, I want to make it clear that we completely oppose such a proposal.

Going into the next century, the key inventions will be in information processing. Altering the standards for patent eligibility for software-related inventions will shift investment away from this area.

The purpose of research and development in any technology is to gain an advantage over your competitor. But if your competitor can legitimately copy the fruits from your R&D and can create a product that can compete head-on with your product while you are still trying to build a market for the product, then you've lost.

The long term value of R&D in the marketplace is in the new functions implemented by software. If such new functions are protected, investment flows to the industry. If not, investment will dry up.

There are several other points I want to make on this issue. We can't divorce computer program-related inventions from computer hardware and other microprocessor inventions. The overlap between the two is so great that cutting back on one automatically cuts back on the other.

An alteration in the standards for patent eligibility will also put the courts and your office in a quandary. That is because computer program-related inventions can be implemented in either hardware or software. Applicants will simply cast their patent claims in terms of electrical circuitry. And if you limit claim coverage over computer program implementations of circuit inventions, you will turn electrical patents into nullities, because the circuit functions can be implemented by a programed computer.

Furthermore, if process patents cannot reach computer implementations of the process steps, there will be a negative impact on every industry that uses computer-controlled industrial processing or uses microprocessors in their products.

From an international standpoint, a cut-back on patent eligibility for computer program-related inventions sets a truly unfortunate precedent for the developing world. It would violate GATT and NAFTA provisions that prohibit discrimination of patent eligibility based on technology. The biotechnology area provides a graphic example of what happens when countries limit protection for a technology. Leading European companies working in this area of technology simply moved their biotech R&D operations to the United States.

Concerning the issue of sui generis protection, replacing patent protection for new and unobvious program and process functions, and replacing copyright protection for the original expression contained in computer programs with

UNITED STATES PATENT AND TRADEMARK OFFICE
Public Hearing on Patent Protection for Software-Related Inventions
San Jose, California — January 26-27, 1994

some form of sui generis right would be devastating to the industry.

In a single act, U.S. industry would unilaterally be disarmed relative to our competitors in Japan and Europe. We would lose patent priority rights in the 114 countries of the Paris Convention, and we would lose the copyright protection automatically afforded American program works in 102 countries as required by the Berne Copyright Convention.

As you know, the Trilateral Work Studies conducted jointly by the U.S. PTO and the Japanese Patent Office and the European Patent Office, concluded that the standards for patentability in the area of software-related inventions are generally the same except at the far margins.

The Japanese Patent Office has published for opposition in the last six years approximately (45) patent applications on software-related inventions, while the European patent office has issued approximately 2700 patents since 1980 which have resulted in multiple European member country patents.

The majority of these software-related patents in the European Patent Office and the great majority in Japan are issuing to non-U.S. companies. Without U.S. patents of a reasonable scope to bargain with, U.S. companies will potentially lose access to those markets.

With the introduction of a sui generis system, there would be —

COMMISSIONER LEHMAN   Can I ask a question? Why do you think that is, that the majority of those patents -- we issued 8,600 patent this last year in the United States, so clearly we've got 8,600 people, and I think I cited those statistics before, two years ago it 6,500 or something like that. Clearly, we have the inventions, but people aren't seeking. American's aren't seeking patent protection in those foreign markets, why that is?

MR. SIBER: I think there's a questions of maturity of the industry, many smaller companies are not familiar with the process of filing overseas, possibly may not be able to afford it or feel they can't afford it.

Secondly, it is natural, particularly in Japan to have a large number of Japanese patent holders where the filings of large Japanese companies is very high.

COMMISSIONER LEHMAN   So, but IBM, I assume does file in those.

MR. SIBER: Yes, we do.

COMMISSIONER LEHMAN   And pretty extensive. I would assume when you file a patent application here, you file there too, since you're a worldwide company.

MR. SIBER: Correct.

COMMISSIONER LEHMAN   Is that generally true? Are there situations where you don't file there and you would file here?

MR. SIBER: We do not file a counterpart patent in Europe and Japan for every patent that we file in the United States. It is selective, it is a selective process. We too have budget limitations, even though we just turned a substantial profit last quarter.

(laughter)

COMMISSIONER LEHMAN   Sorry, to interrupt.

MR. SIBER: With the introduction of a sui generis system

there would be an extended period of uncertainty, the bane of businessmen and investors, as the body of case law were developed interpreting the new sui generis law and determining its scope.

Additionally, there would be a complete absence of effective international protection for the new right. The internationalization of a sui generis law would require a sui generis treaty. Such a treaty would be negotiated without any of the international consensus on what sort of protection regime would be appropriate. As you know, the primary multilateral treaty to date for a sui generis right, The Treaty on International Property in Respect of Integrated Circuits, known as the Washington Treaty, was strongly influenced by developing countries that were hostile to IP protection generally. The result was a treaty so flawed that not one single major chip-producing nation supported it.

The only remaining way to internationalize that sui generis chip-protection right was through reciprocity. But reciprocity has it rewards and its vices. The European community now points to the reciprocity provisions in the U.S. Semiconductor Chip Law to justify its discrimination against America's authors through the reciprocity provisions in the E.C. Directive on Copyright Term Extension, and for denying U.S. authors the benefit of unfair extraction right in the draft E.C. Directive on Database Protection, and in refusing to grant movie and music producers and authors their fair share of the blank tape and movie levies.

Finally, regarding the series of claim format examples in Question 1, we believe that the format of the claim should be viewed from the perspective of patentable subject matter. If the claim as a whole is directed to a machine, article of manufacture, or a machine-operated process, then subject matter eligibility should not be an issue. The focus of the examiner should be on the normal statutory tests of novelty, nonobviousness, and utility of the claim as a whole. And to insure compliance with the formality requirements of 35 USC 112.

Specifically, a claim directed to an article of manufacture comprising computer-usable medium and a plurality of computer-readable program code means for causing a computer to effect a plurality of specific and interrelated functions should be eligible for patenting under the statute. Such an article of manufacture constitutes a machine part that is commercialized separately. And it should be protected separate, like other machines parts, if it meets the statutory test of novelty and nonobviousness.

In summary, the patent system is designed to instigate the invention of new nonobvious and useful functions that add to the arts. The key to seeing whether the system is working is to see if there is strong competition in the marketplace; to see if new products are introduced in the market on a regular basis; to see if employers and investors vote for the system with their pocketbooks by funding new development work.

As for my company, we rely heavily on the patent system to protect our investment in new products. And we are negatively impacted probably more than most by poorly-examined patent applications. Thus, we want the issuance of poorly-examined patents curtailed. And that is clearly doable if the PTO would invest in hiring and training the best possible examiners, as well as in the creation of an

UNITED STATES PATENT AND TRADEMARK OFFICE
Public Hearing on Patent Protection for Software-Related Inventions
San Jose, California -- January 26-27, 1994

adequate database for software prior art.

Thank you for the opportunity. I would be delighted to answer any questions.

COMMISSIONER LEHMAN Thank you very much, Mr. Siber. Is there anybody else that wants to ask something?

Thank you very much for joining us today.

Next, I would like to call on Mr. Ewald Detjens, CEO of Exemplar Logic, Incorporated.

--oOo--

EWALD DETJENS

CHIEF EXECUTIVE OFFICER

EXEMPLAR LOGIC, INCORPORATED

MR. DETJENS: Thank you.

My name is Ewald Detjens. I am with Exemplar Logic. Opinions being expressed are both mine and those of the company.

Thank you very much for holding these meetings in the first place. It's a good opportunity to express the views of a large group of people that I don't think have been really addressed at this point.

I'd like to go through a little bit of the background of myself and the company, talk a little bit about the history of software and how the patents have crept into it, then talk about the effect on my industry and talk about the sort of conflict I see, and finally conclude.

And to not leave you in any suspense, I'll give you the conclusion right up front. I'd like to make life easier for you, I'd like there to be no software patents at all, and to back off from the ones that have been issued. I think that the copyright/trade secret law as is is totally effective for my industry and has been working quite well for us.

Exemplar Logic is a startup, it's totally privately-held, self-funded, we've been boot-strapped up. We're profitable, it's one of the things you can still do in software with very minimal money, is to get a software business going and create a new product in an area that didn't exist before.

We do logic synthesis for field programmable gate arrays, a very dynamic and emerging segment of semiconductor marketplace right now. I have been active in a number of trade organizations, IEEE, ACM, American Association for the Advancement of Science. I have written a number op-ed pieces on the area of software patents, and those have been in electronic magazines like EE Times, ASIC and EDA. I've gotten a lot of feedback from people in the industry about this already.

In terms of the history, I think it's pretty clear that the legislative intent had been to have software be copyrighted and not patented. And certainly, the Constitution does not provide any mandate for patents for software any more than it provides a mandate for patents for literature.

The courts have sort of slowly changed this over the years as the whole issue of software being integrated into physical machinery created problems for some people. I think those problems can be addressed without getting to the whole general issue of software patents. I think you can still protect that machinery with the special-purpose software that's in it without affecting the rest of the software industry that's been extremely successful given our current structures.

Now, as I've mentioned, it seems like some of the players here, the programmers in the world have not been very informed of this process as it's been happening. It's been decisions that are out of the realm of your typical software engineer, and it's been in the realm of the lawyers. And I was almost a bit concerned to see the list of people speaking here today being very dominant on the side of lawyers versus the software people.

I think that certainly the fury you're seeing over the Compton patent is just the tip of the iceberg, it's a much greater percentage beneath the surface. The issues revolving around software patents will be affecting more and more people as we go on.

In particular, it has some definite effects on my industry. It's sort of like changing horses in midstream, so it's very difficult for us to have things covered both by patent and software, and know exactly what we should be doing, and to be left with the situation of prior art not in place and known by the wider public.

I think that if you do have the necessity for doing software patents in the future, it will certainly slow down the pace of innovation. It's going to make programming far harder than it is today. It's going to drive the cost of software up. It's going to lock us into old systems for far longer than we are. A sort of analogy is, we would be locked into DOS for many years, into the next century before Windows or something could come out so we could get rid of some patents so the next generation software could appear.

So some of the people looking at the short term interests in patent -- I mean certainly, a patent is a good thing because it provides you an unfair advantage, but you look at the overall industry, I think it's going to provide very detrimental effects compared to the short term effects some individuals might see for their company looking in the narrow focus.

Some of this is kind of hard to explain. I mean, I think there have been other people that have gotten up in front of you and explained how difficult software development is, and certainly the state of the art hasn't advanced a lot in the last few years as far as just pure development is concerned. There aren't any magic bullets here going forward. The systems are getting more complex and we don't have any tools to deal with the larger complexity that faces us. So it's sort of a bleak view for the programmer out there.

COMMISSIONER LEHMAN What do you think was the single most important magic bullet in this industry in the last 20 years? Was there ever such a thing? Was there ever an innovation that was just so fundamental that --

MR. DETJENS: Well, it's kind of hard to say. There's been a number of things promoted as being a magic bullet. Certainly, object-oriented programming, that paradigm has been one recently. I believe it's a very effective method of doing programming. I don't think it's something that gives you an order of magnitude improvement. Maybe it makes it twice as effective or something. And yet, we're seeing demands on us for providing systems that are 10 times more complex, detailed than they have been in the past.

And the average size of a program is going way up in the number of bytes and the deliverables. If you look at it, it's incredible. What used to be delivered would fit on one little floppy. And now, for your average word processor, they include billions of files with it that have all kinds of added functionality for a huge realm of people.

CD ROMs are sort of an expression of this. You see many people switching to CD ROMs. You can't deliver software effectively on floppies any more, nobody is going to take 40 floppies and be inserting them just to get going with their program.

So there doesn't seem to be any magic bullets really on the horizon, and we're still programming almost as ineffectively as we did in the early '60s in some sense.

The best thing that has happened has not been a software thing, but it's been the fundamental hardware has gotten better, and that's helped us out. We can do programs, if the hardware speeds up by 10 times, we can deal with writing a program that's 10 times slower in getting it to market faster.

COMMISSIONER LEHMAN Actually, that's what I thought your answer would be that the hardware, that the magic bullets have tended to be more in hardware. And hasn't hardware classically been protected by the patent system, and most people aren't proposing that that be changed?

MR. DETJENS: No, no. I don't think any software engineer would venture into the realm to say that patents should be backed off for any other type of thing, certainly not computer hardware at all.

COMMISSIONER LEHMAN I didn't want to get you off the track too much.

MR. DETJENS: No, that's okay.

So one of the interesting things in terms of the op-ed pieces I've been writing, too, has been the feedback. And so far it's come down a hundred percent, a hundred percent. The people that were pro software patenting were the programmers out in the profession and the people that were -- excuse me, did I say that correctly? The people that were against patents were the software people, and the people that were for patents were the lawyers.

And this to me is amazing. I thought it was sort of benign at first, but the question is who benefits from this? And the lawyers are driving it certainly. You can see that the programmers are getting more and more annoyed by this kind of thing.

I don't think that Exemplar would really exist the way it does today, if we didn't -- if we did have software patents in general use, I don't think that you can boot-strap a company in our industry any more that way. You would need far more funding to just prevent against somebody suing you.

Certainly, one of the biggest problems for us is, even if it's an invalid patent, the onus is on the infringer, which means that somebody has an invalid patent and they tell me that I can't proceed with my program. It's up to me to dig out the prior art, go through a very expensive court procedure to do something about that. So that's going to provide just an incredible negative impact for the sort of garage-shop industry where a lot of new types of companies have been spawned.

So just in summary, I would like to say that the preference of the majority of the programmers out there in the world that I have been talking to is that we should not have software patents. The copyright/trade secret are working and are

excellent methods for software protection.

Thank you very much.

COMMISSIONER LEHMAN Thank you very much.

I would like to next call on Michael B. Lachuck, of Poms, Smith, Lande and Rose.

COMMISSIONER LEHMAN We know when you have four last names you must be a lawyer. Michael Lachuck of Poms, Smith, Lande and Rose.

--oOo--

MICHAEL LACHUCK

POMS, SMITH, LANDE & ROSE

MR. LACHUCK: Pick four, right.

Good afternoon, Mr. Commissioner and distinguished panel.

I am a partner in the intellectual property law firm of Poms, Smith, Lande and Rose. And I will be speaking today solely on my own behalf based on my own experience and those of some of my partners.

I would like to depart at least a little bit from some of the comments that you've heard from so many other patent lawyers that have had an opportunity to speak at these hearings. Virtually, every one of those attorneys has said to you that they've been able to obtain patents for software-related inventions, and frankly, my experience has been no different.

I would like to point out that what this means is that irrespective of what the Patent Office decides to do, clever patent drafters will always a way to disguise a mathematical algorithm or some other form of software-related invention either as a piece of hardware, or as some form of methodology having significant post solution activity necessary to get a patent.

The problem is one that simply isn't going to go away, it can to a certain extent be curtailed. What I would like to do is make some suggestions on how the Patent Office might be able to change its practices to alleviate this problem.

There are two issues I would like to address: One, is specifically how the Patent Office might change its practice, and the second is how the Patent Office might propose legislation to effect remedies available in patent litigation.

Speaking to the first issue of patent practices: at the office, several people have come up here and suggested that applications might be laid open during the pendency of the application and before a patent issues.

I would like to argue against this practice for three specific reasons: the first reason is that this practice would shift the fundamental contract between the patentee and the U.S. government concerning the grant of a patent in the first place. Currently, the application is obliged, or rather the patentee is obliged to provide a specification having an enabling disclosure, one that teaches the public or those reasonably skilled in the relevant arts how to make and use the invention. In exchange for this, he's awarded certain rights and remedies under the patent laws. Now, if the application is simply laid open, the same standard or obligation of teaching merely avails the application of a possibility of obtaining a patent at some later date based on the presence of prior art that they, themselves, may or may not be aware of.

UNITED STATES PATENT AND TRADEMARK OFFICE
Public Hearing on Patent Protection for Software-Related Inventions
San Jose, California -- January 26-27, 1994

Secondly, I would like to most strenuously point out that if the practice of laying open an application for public comment were to follow current practices of re-examination procedure, it simply wouldn't work. The problem is that right now the public has only one bite at the apple. They can submit prior art of a certain form, prior patents and printed publications, and they are allowed to comment exactly once on the relevancy of this art to the application.

Thereafter, the process again becomes an ex parte process where the applicant's advocate, some skilled patent attorney is able to argue with the examiner over whether or not that art is in fact relevant or does make the invention obvious. The ant-like persistence of patent attorneys is legendary, as even the well known jurist Learned Hand once noted. This process of allowing the ex parte communication between the patent applicant's advocate and the examiner, is a decidedly risky proposition.

What I would like to propose instead is that the re-examination process be modified to allow representatives of the public or interested members of the public to participate in that further communication that takes place between the applicant's advocate and the Patent Office examiner, more or less in the manner that litigation motions currently proceed; that is, the public would be afforded an opportunity to submit prior art and comment on its appropriateness or applicability to the application. Thereafter, the applicant's advocate would be afforded an opportunity to comment and then the public or their representatives would be afforded an opportunity to respond to the applicant's comments.

I am concerned that if this isn't done in some fashion or other, then the suggestions that have been made concerning the submission of prior art to the Patent Office, particularly in this area where there appears to be a dearth of prior art, isn't going to change very much.

Under current circumstances, the district court judges typically afford great weight to the decisions of the Patent Office examiner. Unfortunately, the public representatives are never provided an opportunity to debate or address the subsequent arguments that are made by an applicant's representative. The result is that very few litigators suggest filing a re-examination application. The best prior art is lost, and the patent is simply strengthened.

Turning to the subject of patent remedies. I would like to suggest a drastic reduction or elimination of injunctive relief in patent enforcement litigation. The threat or promise of injunctive relief drastically distorts the economic value of a patent and the attendant costs of litigation. It's been my personal experience, and the experience of every patent attorney I have ever talked to that the cost of litigation is directly related to the potential liability exposure of the defendant.

Patent infringement litigation, because of the threat of injunctive relief typically becomes a venture company-type lawsuit. The client does insist on a most vigorous defense proportional to the risk that they face. If potential liability exposure for patent infringement litigation were reduced to a few thousand dollars, the cost of litigation would drop to some small fraction of that value.

The basis for award of injunctive relief is based solely on tradition, dating back to old English law, which now, in the hands of a patent owner who frequently does not market any product, is ludicrous. The effect of patent infringement litigation with the threat of injunctive relief is to waste a tremendous amount of American wealth and resources. It is time to bring this practice to heel.

(applause)

Thank you for the opportunity to speak to you today, and I thank you also for your taking the time to personally come out here and hear from so many representatives of the industry.

COMMISSIONER LEHMAN Thank you very much. I should add that I've been waiting for somebody to make the point that you did. And I am somewhat surprised that it has not been made before, and that is that there is a deal in the patent system, and that is that one does not really give up their trade secrecy rights until they are certain that they've got the patent. And certainly to go to a prepublication system would create a hiatus in which that bargain in effect would be jeopardized.

But I do find it interesting that thus far, you're the only person who's raised that. That by and large the wave of testimony has been, I gather, that it's worth taking that risk in order to improve the availability of the prior art to the patent examiner.

Anyway, thank you very much.

MR. LACHUCK: I would like to address that one comment. I suggest that if the statutes were amended to provide that any patent infringement litigation were automatically stayed pending re-examination, then the need to have post issuance examination or comment by the public, the need to have the application laid open would be alleviated.

The current reasoning I think that exists for people wanting to have an application laid open during the pendency of the application is to avoid the situation where the trial court judge decides to continue with the litigation while the re-examination takes place. And as things currently stand, there's also the threat of preliminary injunctive relief, so if you get rid of that threat, it would probably be a more practical alternative to allow the same public comment through re-examination.

Thank you for your time.

COMMISSIONER LEHMAN Thank you.

Next, I'd like to call on Gregory Aharonian, from Source Translation and Optimization.

--oOo--

GREGORY AHARONIAN

SOURCE TRANSLATION AND OPTIMIZATION

MR. AHARONIAN: I run a consulting service up in the Boston area, dealing with software re-use technology transfer, and more recently software prior art and software patenting.

And to summarize how I feel with what's been said today, I am for software patents, for better prior art, open re-examination, and I'm against prepublication.

No, I am not a patent lawyer, or have any software patents on file.

The chief asset of my consulting business is what I consider

UNITED STATES PATENT AND TRADEMARK OFFICE
Public Hearing on Patent Protection for Software-Related Inventions
San Jose, California -- January 26-27, 1994

to be the largest software prior art database in the country. I have information on over 15,000 government, corporate, and university research programs, 5,000 patents, and over 100,000 journal, article, technical reports and books and other such things in which software technology might be described. I monthly monitor the output of about 150 corporate academic and government research labs and about 250 journals.

The problem of software prior art is very, very nontrivial, and I think that's why so many other government agencies have had problems over the years dealing with the similar issue of how do you track all this country's software technology.

I have many more comments on the art of software prior art, and I'd like to speak about them in February hearings in which it's more appropriate. What I would like to speak about now is kind of observations on having examined so much software over the years on a few of the issues that have been brought up today.

One, is I think it's going to be very difficult to change the rules to deal with software patents. There's already a current set of statutory guidelines that are pretty well-reasoned, pretty consistent, certainly comprehensive, if you read all the court cases. But I don't feel that they're working well, for the following reasons: I've examined over 5,000 software patents as part of my technology transfer business, and I've seen a lot of very trivial software concepts actually getting a patent. I've seen many software patents with very broad claims, I've seen things that are as close to a pure math algorithm as possible with maybe one claim in there for a piece of hardware, and I see more and more business practices being awarded software patents. And in some cases, I see pure source code being patented. In 1992, the Air Force got the patent for the difference in source code between two versions of a public domain program at Ames. And I consider that to be fairly trivial.

If you try to come up with more rules to guide the process of awarding software patents, I think you're just going to come up with more ways for patent lawyers to get around the rules. It's tough to treat software any differently than any other technology, and I think you have a lot of problems.

So in general, based on just examining a ton of software in the past 10 years, I'm not sure there's much anyone can do in terms of trying to come up with more rules, it's very difficult.

And on the practical side of the patents I've examined to date, I could probably successfully challenge 25 percent of them on software prior art and a few related issues. There's a lot getting through that should not be awarded.

Of course, my phone is not off the hook, asking for my services to challenge software patents, so I still don't think to date it's a big problem. I think it's being exaggerated because of stunts like the Compton incident, which is great for PR, but not much more.

The second issue I would like to address is that of what one of the earlier speakers, Robert Sterne, testified that there's really no difference any more between hardware and software, and that if you try to change the software patent rules in isolation without treating the hardware patent rules, you're not going to do anything. You're going to leave a big loophole for people to get around the hardware rules by just doing things over on the -- or getting around the software rules by doing things over in the hardware world. It's even happening today.

Existing technology now in the market where I can take a circuit schematic, which anyone would consider a piece of hardware for the most part, automatically convert it into a computer representation language and then convert it once more into an algorithm which I think most people consider to be software.

Similarly, there's other technology out there that let's me take an algorithm written to a traditional language like Pascal or C, covert it into another intermediate language and feed that into a hardware design tool, and get out an integrated circuit. So here I'm starting out in the software world and ending up in a hardware world. To me, it becomes impossible to find what software or hardware is.

And quite recently, in fact, last week a company in Germany announced a tool that integrates -- and that's the overhead I have up there -- computer-aided software engineering tools which is the domain of the software world with hardware design tools, so that within one tool set I can type algorithms, draw circuits and go back and forth and not really care at all, the computer will take it all and account for me.

And with such a tool I can design a new device, and with a cleverly-drafted set of claims, where I have a broad independent claim that talks about systems and methods and things of that nature, dependent claims somewhere that actually mention hardware and software, I can protect infringements in both worlds with one patent. So to make these distinctions between hardware and software, I think is a mistake.

And in fact, there are a few of these design tools in which it should be possible within a year or two to not only allow the user of the tool to generate either an integrated circuit or a computer program, but at the same time a patent application. And if you want to have a million software engineers and electronics designers having an automated patent generation tool on their hands, it's going to become a possibility quite soon. And I'd hate to think of the headaches you're going to have then.

One other thing, the equivalence of hardware and software also complicates the issue of software prior art, because if these mappings are true and you can go back and forth between the two domains of hardware and software, and conceivably someone's circuit schematic somewhere could serve as software prior art in another case.

And I track both software and hardware, so it's no big difference to me, but if the Patent Office intends to seriously treat the problem of prior art, it will not be able to do software prior art separate from hardware prior art. It is all one field of computing devices.

Now, one thing I would like to suggest is currently I publish over the Internet a news service dealing with patent information. Each week I mail out to about a thousand sites on the Internet the titles and numbers of the latest patents coming out of the Patent Office. In Boston there is an APS terminal that I can use for free, which is very nice. And just once a week I go down there, and dump off a couple files

UNITED STATES PATENT AND TRADEMARK OFFICE
Public Hearing on Patent Protection for Software-Related Inventions
San Jose, California -- January 26-27, 1994

worth of data, broadcast it out over the Internet. It's a very well-received service, I offer it for free since it doesn't take too much of my time. And the main demand is for people who are trying to find out more information on software patents.

At best, if someone actually cared to make an effort to find out what was being patented in the software world, you would go to a local patent repository and use one of the CD ROMs, (Casus Bib) or something, and those tend to be five or six months out of date at the typical repository. And people tend to want more recent information.

So the various calls to get the APS system on the Internet will be very well-received in the Internet world, and there are many out there glad to help out with the process.

So In general, I don't think there's much you can do to change the rules of dealing with software in isolation. The current rules are a good set of rules. I'm not a patent lawyer, but rules are rules. I don't think you're going to be able to do too much better. You can change some of the procedures, and many people are calling for that. But dealing solely with statutory type things, I don't think it's going to have much of an effect.

And certainly, if you had seen a lot of the software patents I've examined over the past four or five years, it's hard not to conclude that they just don't work. I think the open re-examination process will help, but I think you're grossly underestimating the amount of paperwork and headaches that that's going to entail.

If everyone in Internet, at the request of someone, decides to forward their pet document to the Patent Office, I mean, you'll get a million people sending in something that pertains to one particular patent. You could fill up this hall many times over for each case.

That's all that I have to say.

COMMISSIONER LEHMAN Thank you.

One thing actually I had meant to ask one of the other witnesses, but since you indicate that you see a lot of patents issued that you're quite convinced would not meet the nonobviousness test -- our decision to reexamine the Compton case was a very unusual one, but the Commissioner does have the power to order re-examination himself. What would you think of as one method of attempting to clean the files of allegedly nonpatentable incorrectly issued patents if we had some kind of a program where maybe we work with people like you and attempted to identify some of these patents that we issued, we ordered our own re-examination?

(applause)

MR. AHARONIAN: Well, I think it's a great idea, and certainly would love to bid on a contract to do that. There are two practical problems I see with that.

The first is, I'm actually an inventor in the world of electric power equipment. That's how I got into a lot of this patenting stuff. I don't think the problems of prior art in the software world are any worse off than in some of the other fields.

For example, many of the high temperature superconducting patents for devices being issued today would be invalidated by low temperature superconducting device patent

applications dating back to the '30s and '40s. Most of those patents no one knows about anymore. You really can't get at them through APS or any of the CD ROMS or anything else. They're literally lost unless you go look for them. But they couldn't validate many of the new high temperature superconductor device applications. So I could argue that if you're going to consider doing that in the world of software, you could do it in all the fields because they all have that same problem. And most information dating back before the early '60s or so in any field is literally off the abstracting services of anyone, and it's a big problem.

The second problem is, while I've been out here I've been kind of working the venture capital circuit so I could actually raise some funding to actually start a business for providing software prior art and services. I'm going around looking for $10 million, it's a very expensive process to keep track of everything. And I happen to be good at it, I mean if anyone else was going to go do it, I would say it would cost 20 million or more. I've been doing it for 10 years, I have 10 years of leg-work out of the way. It's a very expensive thing.

I know the Defense Department spends $10 million a year just trying to track all of its software, and they haven't had much luck. The DOE, NASA, all the agencies have not had much luck. It's a very difficult process of tracking it all.

And I'll give you a case that will explain why it will be difficult when the re-examination process opens up: In the signal processing world there's a technique called a "Fast (40 A) Transform, it is used all over the place. In my life I've seen 200 different implementations of this one algorithm, and as an algorithm it's not very complex to begin with, three or four indented loops where some math goes on. When I do my service, I have to look at these 200 algorithms and figure out which four or five I'm going to include in my database. To make those type of decisions in all the different aspects of software is very complicated. You need the type of person who's not trained anywhere. I mean, I didn't go to school to learn this, I had to look at the stuff over the years. So the types of decisions that have to be made in these re-examination processes are very complex, require tons of data, and I'm not sure it even can be done, but I think you're going to try your best anyway.

COMMISSIONER LEHMAN Thank you very much. Next, I'd like to call George Cole.

--oOo--

GEORGE COLE, ESQ.

MR. COLE: Good afternoon. The first problem area I would like to address is the paucity of adequately-educated patent examiners. I realize, and I presume that we are familiar enough with the problem, I don't have to detail it. A hundred and sixty examiners are simply not enough to examine thousands of patents every year, to keep up with the literature and expanding number of technical fields to remain abreast of continually changing and adapting common law, and in addition, to eat, sleep, get lunch and a few things like that.

The problem is particularly acute in the area of software-related invention, which is why we're here today. It's so bad there's a serious possibility that the current approach will be abandoned perhaps in favor of alternatives such as privatizing the process. We could try giving it to all

UNITED STATES PATENT AND TRADEMARK OFFICE
Public Hearing on Patent Protection for Software-Related Inventions
San Jose, California -- January 26-27, 1994

the people in Ann Arbor where their database is to give them a trade secrets database of computer inventions, which would then serve as the basis for seeing whether or not a right to sue existed.

Frankly, I'm in favor of improving the review process not weakening or abandoning it. It costs society far less to have a determination made during an impartial review process than through adversarial patent litigation. What the PTO needs, what we need the PTO to have is more people with the knowledge needed in the patent review process. We need the process to continue to keep the current legal and technical standards, to improve on them, particularly the technical standard, particularly in fast-advancing fields such as computer software.

Yet, we face an inherent problem in the current system that will keep us from solving it by just adding more examiners. That's because to become a patent examiner you need a scientific degree, a Bachelor's degree, and the legal education. Virtually all who have such dual qualifications pick them up in that order -- science first, then the law. Very few do it in the opposite order which is what I did, law first and then a science. In my case a Master's in computer science at Stanford in '87, six years after I had a law degree from Michigan. The order most prospective examiners gain their dual backgrounds matter, and I'll get back to it in a moment.

The old approach would have been simply adding more examiners, this is necessary, and I would suggest that with some creativity on the part of government and business, we can find the money to do it. I mean, suppose every patent issues gave the government a four percent royalty. But this is not going to be an effective solution overall. It doesn't use the advances in communications that we have, it doesn't react to societal trends.

For one thing, there are often far more rewarding opportunities available to people who have dual training. For example, if you want to practice in Washington, D.C., you're giving up the weather that you've got outside today in favor of an East Coast Winter.

COMMISSIONER LEHMAN I should note; you know, we don't require them to be a lawyer to be a patent examiner. Maybe we should, but we don't. All you have to have is the technical background, so you don't really have to have the dual training.

MR. COLE Don't need the dual training. And then when the review process comes in and the examination goes through.

The other problem is -- I'm sorry, let me continue with this line for a moment. Another approach would have been to abandon, as people suggest, giving patents in computer software. If the U.S. was the only country where that was going to have an effect, it would be something that makes sense. But since it is not the only country where software patents can issue, and only larger companies can realistically and consistently press for patents abroad, and then by international treaty enforce them in the United States, this is going to put us at a severe disadvantage.

Our most valuable resource in software is in intellectual creativity, and it's going to end up possibly completely stifled by this. As the companies go outside, enforce the patents there, get them there and then come in and squelch it here.

One prior speaker announced how that happened in a slightly different field, where they came away from the area where they do not afford protection to the U.S. I would rather not see that happen the other way around.

Another approach would be, we get rid of the legal and technical evaluation that goes on. Now, patent examiners may not have to have a legal background, but you're going to have to pay some attention to what the courts are doing along the way, or in a challenge there is going to some review of what the current state of the law regarding software algorithms is. The courts aren't going to come up with a solution in the near future, I suspect.

A real problem in a way is that the background that the patent examiners have is a Bachelor's and this just isn't enough nowadays. It used to be enough, it used to be just like a basic college degree was enough to be on the leading edge of our society, but by the time the science makes its way from the lab to the educators into the curriculum and into the students, it's dated. It's going to be maybe five years behind the times, and the undergraduates aren't going to be able to keep up with the leading edge because they're still too busy picking up the fundamental basis so they can understand the leading edge.

So we have that delay built in, and it's just going to get worse if you sit there and ask the patent examiners to pick up a graduate degree. They're going to add more years to the time, but that's also going to add the pressure for them to go elsewhere. So how do we provide the benefits of this process that gives both the evaluation, but copes also with an inherent limitation on the number of people that you've got?

What I'd like to suggest; the Patent Office consider finding means to leverage its personnel, just as the federal judiciary can call on special masters, or judges pro tem to extend the effectiveness of the cadre of full-time judges. The Patent Office should look for ways to use the thousands of individuals who have technical advanced education in our society, not as full-time patent examiners working solely for the government, but additional personnel called in and paid for as needed. When you need more computer science people, you get more computer science people. When you need more biomechanical people, you get more biomechanical people. But you don't have to commit to a full-time government career service job. And perhaps you could get the specialist fees paid for by the people who are applying, or as one person suggested, if they're going for a special process, if they want the technical specialty, if they want speed, let them pay for it, but call it in from outside.

The patent examiners job then changes from doing all the work on every application, him or herself that he gets, to managing the process, to getting the patent applications, coordinating and consulting with the technicians, consulting with legal scholars if a complex legal issue seems to appear and then coordinating the results. Is there a concern over maintaining traditional secrecy of the patent process?

I point out that researchers have lab assistants or graduate students, law partners have associates. I suggest, since they've already faced and solved this type of problem in dealing with confidentiality and tracing of information, the Patent Office could find a solution to this.

There a lot of individuals throughout this country who could be called on to assist. Fees could be paid to them, maybe you arrange a tax waiver instead if they'd like that. You've got professors at universities, you've got legal scholars at law schools, researchers in governmental labs, graduate students in science or law who might work on an in internship basis.

With the modern technology available facsimile transmission could allow the PTO to coordinate such efforts throughout the country. The Patent Office then becomes the coordinator rather than the sole worker of the information process and allows them to master the information and the rapid changes that are coming through, not to be overwhelmed.

The second area that I would like to address is some of the problems in the current regulations which attempt to provide protection against inadequately trained individuals serving as patent attorneys. And frankly, this is an area that's probably worse seen in the software area than in many other area.

Section 10.7(a)2(ii) requires an individual who seeks to be registered to practice before the Patent and Trademark Office to establish to the director satisfaction that he or she possesses the legal, scientific and technical qualifications necessary to enable him or her to render applicants for patents valuable service. There is no requirement in the statute or regulations that this competency be maintained. The examination of a would-be patent attorney is only an initial hurdle; once passed, it acts as a lifetime assurance the attorney possesses the necessary qualifications. This may have been enough when science did not advance rapidly, it is not adequate anymore.

Furthermore, the PTO presumes that a patent attorney is competent in the field of science underlying a patent the attorney is prosecuting before the Patent and Trademark Office. It can be left to the client to discover his patent attorney lacked the scientific competency to adequately evaluate or prosecute that patent.

The PTO, though it initially requires the attorney to show the scientific field, does not maintain that information, does not retain it, and does not check it against the application. That protection for the public is abandoned after the first hurdle.

Nationally, the Patent Bar is a uniform bar, you've got to have it that way. But you run into a problem for attorneys who want to keep up a scientific background, who want to study in the field and have to keep up an education for current legal standings. Continuing legal education in most states just does not allow, the course work simply is not there that focuses on a technical side. It's a rare exception to come across it. I was lucky, there have been some in California.

This places an additional burden on attorneys who are trying to keep up the legal and technical background. I am submitting, and it's in the written comment, a proposed amendment to the regulation currently existing that addresses these problems. I urge your attention to it. It tries to balance -- I'm not saying it's a perfect solution -- but it tries to balance the needs that I've addressed.

Do you have any questions at this time?

COMMISSIONER LEHMAN No. Thank you very much. I'll just point out that we do have a substantial number of people with advanced degrees in our Examining Corps. We have at least 38 people with Master's degrees and at least 5 Ph.D.s, maybe more. And obviously they're there to help guide those who don't have that. And we're recruiting for people all the time with more education.

My sense is that our problem -- there's been a lot of discussion, a lot of suggestion that we need to have more attractive compensation structure et cetera, therefore we don't want to be a part of the government. I am not sure that's true. I think our capacity to hire people at up to about $90,000 a year as a patent examiner.

Now, in order to do that they have to have a variety of qualifications, they have to have an advanced degree, they have to be in an area that's been designated hard to get, which generally I think this area is, a variety of things. And then even that includes I think a bonus payment that we give them as well. But my impression is that -- and we're never going to compete, nor should we take from Silicon Valley the folks who can go out there and make -- start companies that will make millions of dollars and create thousands of jobs, we don't want them examining patents.

My sense is that to get a competent technologist who can understand the art here, that probably we ought to be able to get people in that range that I just described. But that's not our most critical problem. Though, it has occurred to me from time to time that maybe one of the, sort of a drastic solution about reinventing government would be that we should be moving the Patent Office to Silicon Valley, would be that we could contract out patent examiners. You know, we could hire law firms to do it, or consulting firms and in various areas.

I have a feeling that we wouldn't automatically improve our quality in doing that, but we certainly have an open mind to all kinds of solutions whatever they may be. But we are steadily working on this problem, and I appreciate the suggestions of people like you. So thanks very much for coming here today.

And let me say, when it comes to drastic solutions like that, you know part of my job is I also am a policy maker, but I'm also in effect the CEO and head of an institution with 5,000 people, and their lives and their families are involved in this, and we're not going to take steps that are going to disrupt these people's lives. You know, I think we have an obligation to -- we have problems with our workforce to do that in a way that's fair to the people who work there.

Next I'd like to call Barry Graham, who is an attorney with the International Federation of Industrial Property Attorneys, or an attorney who I assume is representing the International Federation of Industrial Property Attorneys.

MR. GRAHAM: That's correct.

--oOo--

BARRY GRAHAM, ESQ.

INTERNATIONAL FEDERATION OF

INDUSTRIAL PROPERTY ATTORNEYS

MR. GRAHAM: Good afternoon. As the 22nd witness today and the 47th witness overall, I thank you, Commissioner Lehman, and the members of the panel for your patience and continued interest in all the speakers that

UNITED STATES PATENT AND TRADEMARK OFFICE
Public Hearing on Patent Protection for Software-Related Inventions
San Jose, California — January 26-27, 1994

went yesterday and have gone forward today.

Should the United States continue to provide patent protection for software-related inventions?

The answer should be clear; yes, the United States should continue to provide such patent protection. Patent's own software-related inventions are beneficial. The ongoing evolution of patent jurisprudence with regard to software-related inventions is sound and should be allowed to continue.

The United States section of the Federation International De Consul and Propriete Industrial, that is FICPI. And in English it is International Federation of Industrial Property Attorneys, appreciated the opportunity to express its views on the subject of patenting software-related inventions.

FICPI was created on September 1, 1906, as an association of industrial property attorneys in private practice. It's principal aims are: One, to enhance international cooperation within the profession of industrial property attorneys in private practice, promote the exchange of information, and harmonize and facilitate relations between members.

Two, to maintain the dignity of its members and the standards of the profession of industrial property attorneys in private practice on an international scale.

And three, to express opinion with regard to newly proposed international and national legislation insofar as it is of general concern to the profession. The members of the Federation deal generally with all matters in the field of industrial property in the countries in which they practice and in other countries through associates. And especially to the extent permitted by their national laws with A) filing and prosecution of applications for patents and utility models where applicable, trademarks and designs, and the maintenance of such industrial property rights. And B) advising in matters relating to industrial property rights, and those concerning unfair competition, licensing, no-how, and transfers of technology.

FICPI has as its members, the leading representatives of the private practice bar in all major countries of the world. The United States section of the Federation, known as FICPI/US, consists of over 100 U.S. attorneys in private practice who specialize in intellectual property law. The member of FICPI/US, such as myself, come from both small and large law firms.

With respect to software-related invention matters, the members of FICPI/US in their private practices represent small startup companies as well as small, medium and large established companies. Representation includes: obtaining patent protection on software-related inventions, asserting patents on software-related inventions, and defending against the assertion of such patents, as well as general counseling on software-related inventions with respect to U.S. intellectual property law.

For the record, I am Barry Graham, and am a partner in the law firm of Finnegan, Henderson, Farabow and Dunner, in the firm's Washington, D.C. office. My partner Bob Yoches spoke here yesterday.

The following represent the view of FICPI/US, and not necessarily the views of the World Federation, my law firm or myself. The World Federation however, has spoken actively in support of protection for software-related inventions by use of the patent laws.

The views address briefly question No. 4 of the public notice focussing on the patent system; FICPI/US believes, based upon actual experiences various members have encountered in representation of clients in the U.S., that the present framework of the patent system as it has and continues to evolve has and will continue to effectively provide innovation in the field of software by providing adequate protection to software-related inventions.

The patent system promotes innovation by assisting startup companies and establishing themselves by obtaining needed capital to operate and grow, based in part at least on company assets in the form of patents on software-related inventions developed by the companies. These startup companies can then continue their research and development on new software-related inventions, using the startup monies obtained.

For example, and inventor developed a neural network system for forecasting stock price movement, the system uses a math program. After learning that patent protection was possible on software-related inventions and was beneficial, the inventor filed for patent protection. Based on the filing, the patent applicant's business went forward successfully generating income.

The patent system also promotes innovation by helping startup companies and established companies protect their commercial products and thereby promote the development in bringing to the market new commercial products. For example, a small company developed a TV rating system, the company sought patent protection on its new system which included software. The company has now been able to go into the market and compete against established systems such as the well known A.C. Nielsen Company system.

Another example involves a well established company. The company developed a software-based BUS protocol for its line of computer systems, and obtained patent protection on the protocol. The company licenced the protected technology, and has used monies generated from its licensing to fund further activities.

The patent system, vis-a-vis software-related inventions, is not perfect. It has the same weaknesses and problems as does the system in other technologies. Quote/unquote, bad patents issue along with good patents. The PTO's efforts towards improving the Examining Corps and the prior art searching ability of the PTO with respect to software-related inventions are appreciated and encouraged. The PTO's efforts to clarify and refine what it understands as standards of patentability of software-related inventions to be, are also appreciated and encouraged.

Those undertakings coupled with the efforts of the federal courts in providing guidance in the evolution of patent jurisprudence have and will continue to provide a sound patent system for software-related inventions. These efforts will in turn help foster innovation in the ever burgeoning field of software, all to the benefit of the United States. The evolution should be allowed to continue without artificial or quick-fixes to an already adequate patent system.

Furthermore, it should be noted that the United States has with success encouraged countries within the international

UNITED STATES PATENT AND TRADEMARK OFFICE
Public Hearing on Patent Protection for Software-Related Inventions
San Jose, California -- January 26-27, 1994

community to adopt laws which allow patent protection for software-related inventions. If the United States were now to dismantle its own laws on patent protection for such inventions, our country would lose much credibility within the international community.

On behalf of FICPI/US, I thank you, Commissioner Lehman, the panel members and all of those at the PTO responsible for these hearings, for setting up the hearings and for the time allowed for my comments presented today for the Unites States section OF FICPI.

COMMISSIONER LEHMAN Thank you very much for your compliment, and thank you for coming.

Next I'd like to call Edward Y.W. Lemon, III. He's a software engineer with Network Computing Devices.

--oOo--

EDWARD Y.W. LEMON, III,

SOFTWARE ENGINEER

NETWORK COMPUTING DEVICES

MR. LEMON: Howdy. I would like to thank you for providing me an opportunity to give my comments. My name -- normally, people call me Ted Lemon.

COMMISSIONER LEHMAN I assume that's the way you wanted me to announce you, Edward Y.W. Lemon, III, no?

MR. LEMON: No. It just says that on my passport and voting record.

COMMISSIONER LEHMAN Just Ted, okay.

MR. LEMON: So anyway, I am software engineer at Network Computing Devices, speaking just on my own behalf, not on the behalf of Network Computing Devices.

And I'm basically here to give you a message that I think is very important. I know quite a few software engineers, I know very few that argue in favor of software patents. I believe that we do not need patents on software. Most of us don't want patents on software, and I believe that patents will actually hurt us very badly.

For example, the IBM guy just mentioned that in 1965 -- that was the year I was born, by the way -- they sold 18 billion dollars a year in software. 1965 was 15 years before Diamond vs. Diehr, the first software patent that's widely acknowledged.

COMMISSIONER LEHMAN I think he might have gotten that date wrong. I think he meant -- he said 1962. I think he meant 1992 because I don't think in 1962 -- they said they had a 6 billion dollar research budget, I don't think in 1962 IBM sold 15 billion dollars worth of stuff, or if they did it was just about that. So I think he was -- I think it was probably 1992. I should have probably clarified that point.

MR. LEMON: In any case, I actually have to say that I found that number quite astounding too, because I didn't think that the entire market was that big in 1962, but I was willing to take it.

However, the software market has grown dramatically over the course of the last two decades, and I don't think that that growth can be attributed to software patents in any way.

Let me see if I can come up with a couple of other examples here. As another person mentioned a few minutes ago, the difficulty in developing software is not in coming up with interesting new innovations. The difficulty in developing software is taking innovations, putting them together and producing a complex system that does what you want. That's a very difficult thing to do, but I don't know of any way that you can really patent it.

And certainly, I would like to see great rewards being given to people for doing that thing, but again, the patent system is not the way to provide those rewards.

Now, on the subject of how patents will hurt us, I can give you a couple of examples from my personal experience. I've worked at four companies in my life, starting with a company back East called New Media Graphics Corporation, and of those four companies three of them have been sued by a company known Cadtrak.

Actually, I am not sure that this actually proceeded to a lawsuit, they may have settled before a lawsuit was made, but I know for a fact that all three of those companies have been approached by Cadtrak, have been told that they were violating or infringing on the Cadtrak patent and have paid substantial sums of money to Cadtrak for the privilege of not being sued essentially.

The Cadtrak patent is widely acknowledged by most people, I've never heard of anybody saying that the Cadtrak patent is an example of a patent that should have been issued. It's a very old patent.

COMMISSIONER LEHMAN Does that mean you think that that Cadtrak patent was an invalid patent?

MR. LEMON: Yeah, I think that it fails the test --

UNMIKED VOICE: We have prior art on it.

MR. LEMON: And in addition to the prior art which this person has mentioned, it clearly fails the test of obviousness. It's based on a simple mathematical principle and there is no other way to do the thing which the Cadtrak patent claims to do. And not only is there no other way to do that, but the thing that you want to do is very obvious, drawing a cursor on the screen.

COMMISSIONER LEHMAN So but the essence of the problem here then is that there's been a statement here that there was a patent issued that didn't meet the test of patentability.

MR. LEMON: Right.

COMMISSIONER LEHMAN And now, in effect it's being used to extort money out of people, and they just, you know, buy into the extortion scheme and then they pay up rather than solve it.

It reminds me a little bit of the old thrillers that you used to see on television when I was a kid about the Mafia holding up the candy store, and people would let that happen, you know, getting protection money out of them. And every once in a while the vigorous prosecutor would come along and the uncorruptible police officer and stop the business. Maybe that's my role to do that --

(laughter -- applause)

MR. LEMON: Well, that would certainly be appreciated.

COMMISSIONER LEHMAN -- but it doesn't necessarily mean that the answer in those days would have been to do away with the law.

UNITED STATES PATENT AND TRADEMARK OFFICE
Public Hearing on Patent Protection for Software-Related Inventions
San Jose, California — January 26-27, 1994

MR. LEMON: That's absolutely true.

COMMISSIONER LEHMAN: And so as I mentioned, we do have a capacity to take some look at these things ourselves, and maybe we should start doing that more. Anyway, please go ahead.

MR. LEMON: Well, a further example on that subject is another patent which I'm sure you've heard bandied about here before which is the Natural Order Recalc Patent. I don't know that the Natural Order Recalc Patent is obvious, and I think there may exist prior art, but nonetheless, the Patent Office wasn't aware of the prior art. And if there hadn't existed prior art, one might argue that the Natural Order Recalc Patent would be valid.

However, the Natural Order Recalc Patent, is a technique which I personally independently invented, and I'm not saying this to blow up my own ego, I'm just saying that I personally invented it and thought nothing of it, when I had been working in the industry for a year.

It's a very simple concept, and I can't think of any other way that you could solve the problem which is intended to be solved. However, it's complicated enough that I could easily see where it could be granted a patent. And if this is not an example of something like that, then certainly there are other patents which would be valid under the current scheme of things.

Now, the problem with that is that, as I was saying before, software is built of large complicated systems, and these systems require small building blocks like the Natural Order Recalc Patent. The Natural Order Recalc Patent is a trivial part of most of these software systems.

The difficult part of creating software systems is having a user interface that people can use, making sure that it doesn't break when you give it the wrong input, designing a whole system of processes. Many of which one could easily imagine patenting, designing this whole system of processes to produce a final end product.

Now, there are of course parallels in other industries, but the difference is that in the software industry, these processes are not only -- these simple processes that we use to build the systems are processes that one would come up very easily simply in the process of designing the whole system. They're not something where you would have to go out and learn about someone's new technology and incorporate that technology.

To be honest with you, I very rarely do any research at all personally. I never look up prior art in the field. I mean, I read journals to some extent, but in general the journals speak about these systems that I'm telling you about, they do not speak about the small simple techniques.

And so when I create a program, that program is made up of things which have been — I mean, I have examples here — which have been patented, and which one could easily argue are patentable. And unfortunately that means that in the process of building this valuable thing, I am subject to being sued by people who have created small tiny things which are of no value.

And that means that in theory at least when I write a program, I have to go research all the little nuts and bolts that I use to build the program. I have to go learn about all

these things. I don't have time to do that. And frankly, I don't think that most people that are working in the software industry in startup companies have either the time or the money to do that.

The result being that there is a — if software patents become as widely used as patents on things like systems within automobiles or something like that, then essentially the entrepreneurial spirit of the industry will die.

I have this dream that someday I will be able to start my own company and sell software. I happen to be a believer in free software, so the mechanism for that may be a little bit difficult.

(laughter)

But I believe that the way the industry has been in the past, I should be able to form that company and I should be able to make a good living at it. However, if software patents become as prevalent as patents in cars and hardware for that matter, I won't be able to form that company, and I won't be able to make a living. And that is why I do not want to see software patents continue as they appear to be.

And one other thing, I wanted to address a point that somebody else brought up earlier. Just because something is done in software does not mean that the hardware patent is equivalent, or rather just because something can be done in software does not mean that the patent on the equivalent hardware is equivalent. Because the hardware implementation is generally much more useful, and if it isn't, the software will outsell it.

So if you have a patent on something which can be done better in hardware, then by all means do it in hardware. And if you don't have a patent on something that can be done better in hardware, then the fact that it can be done in software will mean that your hardware won't sell. So I don't see any reason why we should be concerned about the fact that hardware and software can do the same things. It's really not relevant.

I think that really concludes what I need to say here. So if you have any questions, I would be happy to answer them.

COMMISSIONER LEHMAN: Thank you very much. I appreciate your taking the time to share your concerns with us.

You know, I would like to make a point, -- a number of witnesses ago, made a point that we have, you know, it seems like half the people are lawyers who are here testifying, I'd like to point out that in no sense was our witness list rigged. We put out an announcement, we put it out on this Internet, we tried to make it available to everybody.

So basically what you see in terms of the people who are here are people who have an interest and took it upon themselves to come and share their time with us, and their thoughts with us. And by the way, I really appreciate that. I'm getting paid for sitting here, some of you aren't -- some of you are, some of you aren't. And we appreciate the fact that some of you did take out of your own time and your own busy lives to come here and talk with us.

The world is imperfect, I wish we could sort of drag out all the people that probably had other things to do who might be able to enlighten us, but that's just the way it goes. But I do think we're getting a pretty good picture, a pretty good cross section of views on this. Even though there are awful lot of lawyers here, we're hearing from a lot of non-lawyers too.

So our next witness is Roger Schlafly of Real Software. You have the real software that really should be patented then I guess.

MR. SCHLAFLY: Yeah, right.

COMMISSIONER LEHMAN: The original software.

--oOo--

ROGER SCHLAFLY
REAL SOFTWARE

MR. SCHLAFLY: My name is Roger Schlafly, I am self-employed and a software developer and nobody is paying me to be here.

I have a Ph.D. in mathematics and I have worked for both small and large companies. I have one issued patent, and I have been sued for patent infringement. I have a couple of patents pending, and I have some pending patent litigation.

Most of the discussion so far has come from software companies who've argued about whether software patents are good for the industry, and from patent lawyers who favor patenting everything. There have also been a number of good suggestions for improving the system, but most of these apply equally to nonsoftware patents. Instead, I want to focus on some legal and technical issues related to the scope of software patents.

First of all, I want to say that software patents are not as new as everyone seems to act that they are. The first Patent Act explicitly made processes eligible for patents, and the government's been getting process patents for 200 years. Processes are indistinguishable from algorithms, many process patents are enforced.

For example, the Polymerase Chain Reaction, PCR invention which won the Nobel prize in chemistry last year was a process patent. It was upheld in court and was sold for $300 million. It is a recipe for cooking DNA, but legally it is indistinguishable from an algorithm path.

For an older example, Samuel Morse's patent on the telegraph was upheld by the U.S. Supreme Court in 1853. Morse specifically claimed the system of dots and dashes we now know as Morse code. This was a software patent.

My next point is that many software patents are not algorithm patents, and much of the discussion of the legality of software patents focuses on the patentability of algorithms, but actually many if not most, claim a system or an apparatus or a machine. Even if we could reinstate the anti-algorithm bias of the Benson Decision, it would not eliminate software patents.

Many of these software patents, especially the nonalgorithm patents are legally indistinguishable from traditional nonsoftware patents. Many special purpose electronic circuits and chips are designed using software techniques, and they often have microcoded programs etched onto chips. Nobody is seriously suggesting that patent protection should not be available for electronic gadgets.

I don't see how you could justify protection for a special-purpose circuit and deny protection for software on general-purpose computer that performs the same function.

My next point is that the law does not have to change with new technology. Many people here have argued that software is different from other technology and therefore requires a sui generis protection scheme. I think this is a big mistake.

For 200 years copyrights and patents have served to protect intellectual property without any fundamental change in the law. I only know of two cases where sui generis protection scheme was created as a result of industry pleading that some new technology required it.

One, is plant patents. As you know, it was eventually decided that ordinary patents suffice for animal inventions, so the notion that special patents were needed for plants turned out to be unnecessary.

The other case is The Semiconductor Chip Protection Act, eventually though, it turned out that ordinary copyright law was sufficient to protect complicated chip designs, and this special law turned out to be unnecessary also.

Thus, I think you should reject the notion that the law must change to keep up with changing technology unless there is clear and compelling evidence to the contrary.

One advocate here of the sui generis system was Oracle, and to tell you where they're coming from, I want to quote from their policy on software patents. They say, "New developments influential to the software industry frequently emanate from individuals and small companies that lack substantial resources".

So from this I suggest that here they are one billion dollar company, what they want to do is get their innovation for free and not pay for it.

Okay. My next point is that mathematical algorithms are not distinguishable from other algorithms. The Benson decision tried to make this distinction, most everyone including the Court of Appeals for the Federal Circuit and the recent Arrhythmia decision, agreed that this was nonsense. All computer algorithms are essentially mathematical in character.

I see we have up in the podium the Knuth bible on computer algorithms, and it's impossible to say that some of these are mathematical and some of them aren't. There's just no distinction there. Fortunately, all these are in the public domain.

My next point is that many software patents should have failed the novelty or nonobviousness test. For example, the Benson patent, which was rejected by the Supreme Court in 1972 for being unstatutory subject matter, was for an algorithm for multiplying by 10. It consists of noticing that the decimal number 10 is equal to one-zero one-zero in binary notations. So that on a binary computer multiplication by 10 can be accomplished by two shifts and an add. This trick is obvious to any skilled programer. If anyone had tried to publish the trick as a research result, he would be laughed at.

A lot of patents seem to merely consist of taking some well known method and putting it on a computer. These are not novel. Any method can be put on a computer, that is inherent in the nature of computers, and people shouldn't get patents just for the idea of computerizing something.

Now, I want to talk about some of the specific claims that were in the Notice of Announcement for this hearing. The last one, Invention G seems to be in this category of just computerizing something. It claims an accounting system implemented on a computer. It is obvious that any accounting system can be implemented on a computer. Accounting systems are normally not patentable and it shouldn't make any difference that it is implemented on a computer. So I don't think that claim should be patentable.

Inventions A and B are for mathematical algorithms. Patents for these were thrown out by the Benson decision and reinstated by later decisions. Current practice is to look unfavorably towards these, but to allow them as long as the claim mentioned some hardware. The hardware mentioned might be merely some memory chips. Many older patents have drawn elaborate diagrams of flip-flops and other electronics hardware, but the Patent Office seems to be getting more lenient about this all the time.

It seems to me that the hardware requirement is not serving any useful purpose anymore, it is not required by the law, and does not serve to limit the claims in any meaningful way. It might as well be abolished.

Invention claim C-1 and D-1, directly claim a computer listing. I think this is a mistake and should not be allowed because it confuses patent and copyright protection. Copyright law protects program listings. If someone else sells a similar program, such a claim will not provide any useful guidance as to what constitutes an infringement.

On the other hand, copyright law provides a framework for deciding what plagiarism is. Software patent claims should distinctly claim the invention as with other patent claims.

The alternate version of the claims for that invention, Claims C-2 and D-2 more reasonably describe the software invention. I don't see that it makes any difference whether such a claim directly refers to a computer program, or something more tangible such as a disk. The legal scope of the claim will be the same. The traditional Patent Office tangibility requirement is not accomplishing anything useful here, it should be dropped.

Invention E is a computer data structure. I think the arguments for and against this are the same as for mathematical algorithms. Much as people may not like it, I don't see any basis under current law for rejecting these claims.

Invention F is a computational diagnostic method performed on a computer. If it is a genuinely novel invention, it shouldn't be rejected just because it uses a computer. An MRI device might be in this category. Computer calculations perform a necessary part of MRI scans, but most of the novelty lies elsewhere.

A great many electronic devices use microprocessors with software. But the claim in Invention F is very similar to the claims in the Meyer and Weissman patent which was rejected by the Court of Customs and Patent Appeals in 1982 for unstatutory subject matter. That invention was not really a diagnostic device, but a computer program for inputting medical test results comparing them to a list of known (ontcomps) and applying a simple criterion for determining whether the patient has a problem.

It might be acceptable to grant a patent for some very clever novel way of implementing such a criterion, but the Patent Office should not give a broad patent for something like this. It is completely obvious that there are many criteria to chose from, and that any criterion can be computerized.

In sum, whether anyone likes it or not, it's my opinion that software-related patents will continue to be issued because that's the law. The best we can do, is improve the system by trying to give patents only for truly novel and nonobvious inventions.

COMMISSIONER LEHMAN Thank you very much.

Next I would like to ask Wallace Judd of Mentrix Corporation to come forward.

--oOo--

WALLACE JUDD

MENTRIX CORPORATION

MR. JUDD: Thank you. My name is Wallace Judd, I am president of Mentrix Corporation. I am the holder of a patent that's not for software. I am also a programmer. And even though our software company in Nevada City, California, is very small, the testing and training that we provide impacts over 800,000 people annually in the United States. So even small software companies have a fairly large impact.

I would like to ascertain, are all of you up there lawyers?

Yeah. It's been interesting to me the dichotomy --

COMMISSIONER LEHMAN Sorry, we run the world, it's just -- I think about 90 percent of the presidents are, you know.

MR. JUDD: Well, you know, but this is interesting. It's curious to me because all the programmers --

COMMISSIONER LEHMAN Julius Caesar was a lawyer, you know. The pharaoh was a lawyer, you can't get away from that.

MR. JUDD: Well, all the programmers seem to be opposed to patent for software, and all the lawyers have testified in favor of it. And I think that bodes somewhat inauspicious for my plea to request that you not protect --

COMMISSIONER LEHMAN I think we just heard from one that was in favor of patent protection.

MR. JUDD: Beg your pardon?

COMMISSIONER LEHMAN I think --

MR. JUDD: Mr. Schlafly was in favor it, he was the only one.

COMMISSIONER LEHMAN There were a few others.

MR. JUDD: He's in firmware.

Today, I am going to outline --

COMMISSIONER LEHMAN You make a point, though. There is no question about it that the lawyers seem to very much in favor of patent protection. Companies tend to be somewhat split, and programmers who've testified, though not all, a majority of them have testified against it.

We have noticed that fact.

MR. JUDD: Today I am going to continue to outline some procedural questions with regard to software patents that I believe are essentially unanswerable. Then I am going to show some instances over the past several years in which software patents simply did not work. And finally, I will try

UNITED STATES PATENT AND TRADEMARK OFFICE
Public Hearing on Patent Protection for Software-Related Inventions
San Jose, California -- January 26-27, 1994

to discuss the disastrous impact of allowing software patents on software development.

The first, the issuance of a patent revolves around several salient points: establishing the time of invention, documenting the invention, and establishing the nonobviousness of the invention to a practitioner in the field.

In the world of software we shall see that all of these I believe are essentially unanswerable. With the physical objects the time of invention is the achievement of the working model, or the creation of a drawing of a working model. In software the time of invention is unknowable. If it is the writing of code exhibiting the claims, what if the code has bugs? Has the invention been discovered? How many bugs are allowable? How major can the bugs be to disallow establishment of the claim? Does the code have to be free of bugs? If so, then DOS 6 wouldn't qualify, and certainly most of my Windows software wouldn't qualify.

In essence, you've got an unanswerable question here; when has the claim been established in software?

Suppose you develop a stark prototype, just the skeleton of a program that demonstrates the claims, how robust must this prototype be? Must it demonstrate all features, the salient features? I can see people rushing down to your offices with two-page executing code sketches making exorbitant claims for their little hack.

Documenting the invention is another issue. What language would programs have to be submitted in? Does the Patent and Trademark Office have to compile the code to execute it? How can an examiner test the claims of the patented code? What if the code doesn't do what it claims to do?

To mount an acceptable challenge do I have to execute the patented code and show it doesn't work?

What if I don't happen to have the compiler for that code? What if the language is unique? What if the code exists only on a virtual machine? How can I then demonstrate that the code does or doesn't work?

Should the Patent and Trademark Office define acceptable languages in which submissions should be made? If so, that will guarantee that most discoveries are years behind the times since many leading edge applications are programmed in languages designed for a special purpose that don't have a wide following.

What's obvious to a practitioner in the field, if I obtain a patent for a software training program which monitors the user's every action, is it obvious that simply by adding a scoring algorithm I have a test? It's obvious if you think about it and yet, patents have awarded independently for testing and training programs.

What level of expertise is exhibited by a practitioner in the field? The degrees of modification to make the one I just suggested are obvious to a computer 101 programmer, and yet the questions is would they be obvious to an examiner?

The Commissioner this morning pointed out to Jerry Fiddler that there are no patents on spreadsheets or word processing programs, and I think that was an appropriate thing to point out. However, in my field there are patents being awarded for training programs, for testing programs, and for help systems all of which are obvious and have been in practice for a number of years.

In fact, apparently this field is getting patent protection where word processors and spreadsheets did not get it. So there's a real problem, there's a real issue here in my particular area.

COMMISSIONER LEHMAN I'd like to make a point about this, and I don't mean this is critical of you, but we're obviously supplying this forum and we're obviously getting the message from various people about frustrations they have and unhappiness they have with the system. But one thing I hope that people will leave here with, those who are still in the room, is the notion that we're not on Mars or someplace. If people are unhappy with the system, you know, we're never more than a letter away, and now even with Internet we're an Internet message, an electronic mail message away.

So I think that if people in the business start to see things that they don't like, like the issuance of patents in this area, even without having to use the re-examination procedure, I'd like to think that people can write a letter to the Commissioner of Patents. And you can be certain that if start getting lots of letters and we get complaints we'll start to look into these things. That as it is, you know, it seems like we sort of have to read about things in the newspaper, or they have to really get disastrous before we know about the problem.

So I just hope that one of the sort of teaching points that can come out of this is that dialogue is a two-way street. We're going to try to have a more open ear, but we encourage people to communicate with us too, when they perceive that things are not going the way they'd like them to go.

I'm sorry to interrupt you, you can have the rest of your time back.

MR. JUDD: That's all right.

Robert Greene Sterne earlier testified that it is the functionality that is the invention when testifying with regard to the distinction between software and hardware, and the fact that there was no essential distinction between the two. And yet, I would like to make an argument for the opposite case.

In fact, if you invented a unique way of trapping mice, you get revenues for 17 years, but you can't protect the notion of trapping mice. If somebody comes along with a better mousetrap, you can't prevent them from trapping mice and licensing their trap if it doesn't violate your method. Copyright protection for software and for circuit designs is adequate. You just don't want somebody to steal your code or your circuit design. Stealing the goal, the objective, the function of the patent is as old as patent itself.

You trap a mouse with a string, I'm going to drown those little suckers, voila, I've got a patent. Okay? You cannot patent the notion of trapping a mouse. And I think the same thing is true here. We don't have a problem with the distinction between hardware and software. That in fact, if you copyright a circuit design, that is effective protection for that particular idea.

Since I have only read reviews of the Compton's patent, please understand that my next remarks are based on hearsay not close analysis of the patent itself. Nonetheless, I believe the issues I raise are germane, whether or not the details of the patent as I present them.

- 92 -

UNITED STATES PATENT AND TRADEMARK OFFICE
Public Hearing on Patent Protection for Software-Related Inventions
San Jose, California -- January 26-27, 1994

The problem with the Compton's patent is that there claims are so broad as to virtually disallow any other method of index access to a CD ROM. Essentially, they want to patent the idea of trapping mice, not their particular mousetrap.

But as any basic database programer knows, there are dozens of ways to create indexed access to data, whether the data is on a CD ROM, a hard disk, in random access memory or stored in magnetic donuts, the principles are identical.

The fact that the Patent Office would grant a patent on access to a CD Rom simply shows that the examiner doesn't understand the generality of random access storage devices.

Another famous or infamous patent software case is the Apple Microsoft litigation with regard to Windows and the Macintosh Look and Feel. The case I felt was truly ridiculous since the Look and Feel of the Macintosh were established at Xerox Park years before the Macintosh was invented. Yet the litigation sucked up millions of dollars, tens of millions of dollars worth of legal fees per year for a number of years. All you had to do was drive up Pagemill Road, run the old Park examples and you would see a Macintosh system. And yet, apparently nobody did that.

Now, how do I know this? The answer is, I worked at Xerox Park in 1979 and '80, then was hired by Apple to work on the Lisa system, which was the precursor to the Macintosh. At Park, I worked on teaching the Star interface to users, so I am particularly qualified to comment on that particular issue.

At Apple our implicit charter was to emulate the Xerox system. Any programmer with two eyes and an index finger, would have looked at the Star System in the Macintosh and thrown the case out of court, yet it consumed millions of dollars in litigation.

Any person looking at the issue of software patent who is familiar with both Xerox's Star System and Apple's Macintosh would have to conclude that the millions spent on litigation between Apple and Microsoft would have done more good spent almost anywhere else in our society.

UNMIKED VOICE: Here, here.

MR. JUDD: Although, over a hundred million dollars were spent or will be spent on these cases, our society is no better off as a result of this litigation.

Increased cost, if patent law is the standard form of protection awarded software there will be clearly a dramatic increase in defending a software product from infringement claims. Today at lunch, as a matter of fact, I was privy to find out that we are infringing a patent issued in 1992 for a help system. Now, this is a computer-assisted learning support system filed in Tokyo, Japan -- of course, the system that we're infringing it with was invented in 1985, and incidentally had the examiners been familiar with the prior art back to 1981, the help system for Lotus 1-2-3, version 1.0, was a perfect example of this very patent and the series of claims contained therein. So in essence, what's going to happen is a small software company such as I is going to have to hopefully be able to notify the Commissioner, or at the worst case, spend $2,000 having this claim re-examined.

The sheer number of potentially patentable aspects of a computer program would make it prohibitively expensive to research them all. While a computer chip or a tire or a drug may have several different arenas of patent law to research, the number of arenas impacting software are exponentially more. Assuring that your software is free of infringements would require research into database maintenance, disk access, user interface, memory managers, interrupt handling, queueing theory, and literally dozens of other programming issues. Writing a few lines of code would require days of research to see whose code you might have infringed.

Another impact will be in marketing delays caused by a year of uncertainty until everyone comes out of the woodwork who might have invented something remotely related to your program. Suppose software is patentable. What's the optimal low finance strategy for a person such as myself? Obviously it's to sandbag it. File patents 360 days after I've documented a program; then if my claims are allowed, I can sue all the folks who have big marketing bucks in similar programs. It's not an enhancement for society. If you manage to establish priority, you've got their marketing investment already engaged behind your license program.

To summarize, I've shown elements critical for establishing a patent are indeterminate. I've illustrated the problem with patent enforcement, using the Compton's and Apple vs. Microsoft cases, and I've shown several disastrous impacts that can be predicted from widespread use of software patents. As a software developer, I beg you, keep patent law out of software. Don't let legal entanglements destroy the software industry as they did the private airplane industry. Clarify that the protection available to software developers is copyright, not patent.

COMMISSIONER LEHMAN   Our next witness -- we're getting near the end of the day here -- is Russell Brand, Senior Computer Scientist & Product with Reasonings Systems, Incorporated.

Mr. Brand, if you'll bear with me a little bit, I'm going to leave the room for about three minutes and I'll be right back, and if there is any chairing work that needs to be done, hopefully my colleague, Commissioner Goffney, will take that over. So I'll be right back and I hope you'll forgive me for missing your opening part of your remarks. Thanks.

Why don't you proceed.

--oOo--

RUSSELL BRAND

REASONINGS SYSTEMS, INC.

MR. BRAND: Mr. Commissioner, members of the panel, my name is Russell Brand, I'm a Senior Computer Scientist and Product Manager at Reasonings Systems in Palo Alto. I've been a programmer for more than 15 years. I speak only for myself and not for my company.

I'm here today to speak against software patents, as most programmers seem to, and am here primarily to talk a little bit about part of the history that seem to have been lost. Before I start with my prepared remarks, there are enough issues that have been raised in the few hours that I've been in the room that I think are worthy of attention, that I had not considered carefully before coming here, did not realize they were issues.

The system that my company sells is a hundred times larger than the stack of paper you see there on the side. The

UNITED STATES PATENT AND TRADEMARK OFFICE
Public Hearing on Patent Protection for Software-Related Inventions
San Jose, California -- January 26-27, 1994

system that I write reads source code so the people who own the source code can figure out what it does. Often the source code that we read is a factor of twenty larger than that, written by a team of a hundred people over ten years. If we could in any manner figure out what it did easily, if someone could do that, we'd be out of business. It's hard, even with all the help of the people there, to know everything it does. It would be impractical to find out what patents it infringes. If you could give me a good machine description of every software patent, I don't think, even with my tools, and my tools are the best in the world by perhaps twenty years, I could go through the software in an automated fashion, and find out what patents are being violated.

There have been questions as to whether there are distinctions between numerical and non-numerical algorithms. I think the late Admiral Grace Hopper would turn over in her grave to think that there is no difference and that we couldn't understand the difference. She brought the industry forward perhaps thirty years by the realization that computers could work with characters and could do things that were not fundamentally thought of as mathematical. I learned while sitting in the office that a tool that I wrote in an afternoon about two years ago to help me deal with dyslexia, to fix some of the spelling as I type it, probably violates two patents. There is nothing nonobvious in it. There was a problem; I spent an hour to solve it. Should I stop using it now? Should I rely on the patent having been invalid?

There's been talk about changing the rules to narrow the edges a little bit. You're dealing with programmers as one of the groups best suited to find ways around rules. Working around social rules, working around machine restrictions, that's part of what makes us programmers. You're also dealing with lawyers, who are probably the second best group at working their way around rules, and I imagine that microtuning and managing the procedures is not going to help much. It will buy you six months or nine months, and someone will find the new bugs, and there are more of them who will be looking for ways around it than there can possibly be of you trying to fix up the rules.

In addition to being a full-time programmer, six to ten hours a day, five to seven days a week, I'm also a law student three nights a week. I bring a laptop with me to class; when class gets dull, I work on programming. I have an open lawbook next to my terminal while waiting for compiles. I have determined that it's going to take me only probably five years part-time to learn enough about law to speak intelligently on this, and I imagine to understand what's going on with algorithms would take someone without scientific training ten or fifteen years. All of my free time now goes into understanding legal issues, primarily issues of information privacy, constitutional issues, but also in the patent issues.

There's been questions about how do we find the prior art. If in my field I could get via Internet all the new patents nominally in my field, and could send back by Internet mail, here are the things that we have done ten years ago, here are the articles, check it against my databases online that I use so I know who to cite when I write articles. It would take me a little effort; I could do that, I wouldn't need to

charge anyone to do it because it's a small increment over what I'm normally doing, and it's keeping me aware of the current research, and I imagine specialists in a hundred other fields could do the same thing.

Part of what the users of my system do when they are studying software to find out what's good and what's bad, is they introduce defects and see how many of them are found. We send our system for testing, we put in ten defects; if the testers only find eight of those ten defects and they find a hundred other defects, we can bet there are twenty other defects that weren't found.

At this point there is at least a wide belief that many of the software patents should not have been granted. My statistical study, grabbing patents at random and reading them, is more pessimistic that anyone else's prediction in the room. Nineteen out of every twenty I've read are voidable on at least three grounds.

Perhaps it's time that we start introducing ridiculous patents, like the (Letvin Kirchoff) current law patent into the system and see how many get through. And if more than one percent of them get through, then we should address it as a quality control problem, as we would address a quality control problem in any other industry.

To move on to the history, which is the basis of prepared remarks that I'd like to make, I'm on a number of committees that run conferences, annual conferences large and small for professional organizations. I had a very hard time getting speakers for one of my conferences this year, a state of the art technical conference. More than half of the speakers that I approached said they couldn't speak this year because of patent-related restrictions placed upon them by their company's corporate counsel. In previous years, ten years ago when this series started, no one had any problems. People talked about what they did. This year I lost half of my best speakers. It's going to be another two or three years to find out what they are doing, and so everyone working in that same field isn't going to be able to build on that research as quickly.

One of the speakers, in order to give a talk, managed to hack his internal legal system and get a publication out, such that they started their one-year clock from that date running, and he was able to talk publicly. He had to hack his internal legal system in order to make the information publicly available and allow us to build on his knowledge in the field.

Five groups of my colleagues doing work in cryptographic technique have moved or are in the process of moving their work outside the United States. They say the patent restrictions and the export restrictions in combination here prevent them from doing development, prevent them from doing marketing, prevent them from starting a company. They'll move it to Europe. By the time they finish building it, most of the patents they care about will have expired; they'll bring it back and start selling it.

Two months from now I'll be giving a half-day tutorial at the Computer Freedom and Privacy Conference sponsored by the ACM. The tutorial will be on election fraud. In it we'll talk about some of the techniques that could be used to prevent election fraud. Many of them are cryptographic, and I believe at this point all of them have restrictions based on patents that would prevent them from being used, and all of them could be constructed from information that was in the literature before any thought of patenting those things came out.

Last year I gave a tutorial at the Computer Freedom and Privacy Conference on privacy of data about individuals, and we talked about what could be done cryptographically to better protect the data. And again, the best techniques are protected by patents and you can't license these patents to use in good and strong ways. The licensing restrictions are not just, we want so much money, but we want to control the way you use the patents. So that level of privacy, a level of a fair voting system, a level that will allow people to speak in an anonymous, safe way, and to prove who they are is held hostage to a patent system that will keep us from entering the next level of participatory democracy, hold it up at least another three years, perhaps another ten.

Lastly, I'd like to talk about what I see as the coming age of defensive patent portfolios. At this point companies get defensive patent portfolios so that they can force other people to cross-license to them. Individual programmers like myself, I don't have such a portfolio. I'll need to join someone who has it so that I can cross-license everything I need so that I can publish. If I have an individual patent, it won't do me any good because I can't build anything without that cross-licensing. So the patent will afford me as an individual developer no protection, but afford the large companies, the companies IBM, AT&T, HP, with giant defensive portfolios the ability to control the new technologies that come out, whether they've invented it or not.

In perhaps a related issue, people in my area tend to think of patents and the software look/feel copyrights at the same time. We look at the history of the look/feel copyright. It was validated by the court to protect video games, a video game named "Scramble," that I enjoyed playing when it first came out. And it's been extended and extended. If we look in the same manner, the first software patent that was granted, Diamond vs. Diehr, it was a computer system, part of process control. The idea was that a statutory bar on numerical algorithms would not prevent it from being part of a combination patent. We have gone from computers stopping you from getting patents, to the computer part being okay, to now anything once you put a computer in it, it's a form. Well, you couldn't copyright a form, it's on a screen, now I can get a look/feel copyright. It's an equation; you can't patent an equation, it's part of a computer program with no physical relation to the world. The rules say you can't patent it, but 1400 such patents were granted. The rules, as they were written, would provide a valuable service; the rules, as they are executed, especially with the giant defensive patent portfolios, do a disservice to developers and to the American public as a whole.

Thank you.

COMMISSIONER LEHMAN Thank you very much for sharing that with us, Mr. Brand.

Next, Willis Higgins, with the law firm of Cooley, Godward, Castro, Huddleson & Tatum.

--oOo--

WILLIS HIGGINS, ESQ.

COOLEY GODWARD LAW FIRM, PALO ALTO, CALIFORNIA

MR. HIGGINS: Thank you very much, Commissioner Lehman, ladies and gentlemen. I should state first that I'm a partner at the Cooley Godward firm and I've headed the firm's electronics and software patent prosecution practice, but will add the views that I express in my written statement and here at this oral testimony are personal and do not represent the views of the firm or any of its clients.

In general I'm going to follow the order of my prepared statement, but I'm not going to read it into the record. At this point I think you've heard enough discussion on this issue that if I were to read this into the record, that would probably put you all to sleep.

I think that a fundamental issue that merits some discussion is the distinction between the way the copyright system works administratively and the way the patent system works administratively, because I think that difference has very significant policy implications. Of course, the copyright system, being a registration system, there is essentially no administrative record that a court can rely on to decide the cases of nonliteral copyright infringement, the so-called look and feel cases. What that means is that a Federal District Court judge or, even worse, a Federal District Court jury is put in the position, to a certain extent, of the patent examiner and has to take a look at the copyrighted work, other similar earlier copyrighted or noncopyrighted works, the prior art, if you will, and then attempt to distill what's the contribution of the copyrighted work in question, and all of this with nothing in the record as an aid to determining what is the proper scope of this copyrighted work and has that been infringed in the nonliteral similarities between the copyrighted work and the alleged infringing work.

On the other hand, in the patent system at least the courts start with a headstart. There is an administrative record, there is a testing of the alleged inventive subject matter against some prior art and an attempt to define in the patent claims what the scope of that work is. And for that reason, I think any attempt to eliminate patents for software is going to cause a lot of problems by throwing these difficult questions back into the copyright arena, and the courts have struggled for years to devise tests that will make the determination of the scope of these copyrights easy, and they simply haven't been able to do it, and the nature of the intense in fact inquiries required to make those judgments I think means that they're just not going to be able to come up with easy tests in that area, so that the inherent nature of the patent system and the copyright system say that it's absolutely essential for the patent system to play a significant role in the protection of American intellectual property.

I think, and I've developed that theme further in two publications that are attached to my prepared statement. But the second area I'd like to talk about, I haven't developed in those publications, it's developed to some degree in the statement, and that concerns the implications to be derived form the institutional practices in the Patent Office and what conclusions should be drawn from those institutional practices with respect to how the examination of software-related patents are handled. Of course, we all know that the time that examiners can devote to each patent application is limited. The examiners, of course, are

UNITED STATES PATENT AND TRADEMARK OFFICE
Public Hearing on Patent Protection for Software-Related Inventions
San Jose, California -- January 26-27, 1994

on a form of a quota system in which their performance is measured by disposals. Now what the means is that, if examiners are handicapped with respect to other examiners by extra procedures that don't apply in other art areas, it gets very difficult to provide a good objective measurement standard for their performance.

Fundamentally what I'm talking about here is the whole issue of statutory subject matter and the very complex set of rules that have been developed with respect to that, and, of course, anyone who reads the guidelines, reads the case law, sees that extremely fine distinctions are drawn in the case law and it's very difficult to conclude is this claim on the right side of those guidelines or on the wrong side of the guidelines.

Based on my practical experience, I find that too often in the examination process, most of the effort is directed to testing on the 101 issues and on claim language, and very little attention is devoted in many cases to measuring the contribution against the prior art to determine whether that contribution is new and unobvious. And, of course, given the limited time that examiners have available for each application, if they're in effect forced to deal with these extra issues of statutory subject matter, that means that they're going to have less time available to deal with the truly significant issues of is it new and is it useful and has the new and useful contribution properly been defined in the claims that are before the office.

So the suggestion that I would make is in terms of statutory subject matter is follow the lead suggested by the Supreme Court that essentially the patent system should cover anything under the sun developed by man, and move on to the really significant questions of judging against the prior art. And I think most of the comments, most of the comments that I've heard, and no doubt most of the comments that you've heard earlier are not that the Patent Office is calling it wrong in the statutory subject matter area, but calling it wrong in some cases with respect to prior art that either wasn't available or that wasn't properly evaluated. So that I think is the sum and substance of the second area I wanted to discuss.

The third area I want to talk a little bit about is the form and content of patent applications, although as set forth in the notice of these hearings, that's really going to be more primarily the subject of your next hearing, but I think there are some policy issues here as well.

Again, in determine what kind of form, what kind of format should be used in patent applications and deposits of source code if they're going to be used, what's important, I think, is to make a judgment call on whether a particular form, format or procedure adds value to the process. Does it do something to give us stronger patents. So, for example, requiring applicants to deposit source code in a very rigidly defined microfiche format probably doesn't add a whole lot of value to the process. Why not allow the applicant to deposit the source code, if it's going to be deposited, on disk in machinery to perform so that it can be more easily accommodated in online databases and other machine searchable tools. So again, as an example here, look to the question of what value is being added by the procedures, and I would say that requiring one form over another as opposed to what's the content of what you're submitting doesn't add

value any more than the debate over the fine lines in statutory subject matter adding value.

So in summary, what I would say is that in order to strengthen our patent system, we should cut to the chase, get to the questions of novelty and unobviousness over the prior art, and I think as an interim measure, what we as patent attorneys have to do is assume a proactive stance. We've got our Rule 56 obligations that say that we should call the attention to the Patent Office of prior art that we know about. If we want to obtain good, strong, valid patents for our clients, we've got to do more than that. We've got to go out and look for the prior art and get it in the record so that it's considered and overcome. And if we do that, coupled with increased efforts on your part to develop your own prior art databases, then I think the end result will be a much stronger patent system.

Thank you very much.

COMMISSIONER LEHMAN   Thank you very much, Mr. Higgins, for taking the time to think through all of this and give us your comments.

Finally, our last witness of the day and of the entire two days of hearings is Mr. Joseph Grace of Tetrasoft.

--oOo--

JOSEPH GRACE
TETRASOFT

MR. GRACE: Thank you, Commissioner Lehman, for this opportunity to get some thoughts out on software patenting. I feel like after hearing these comments that -- well, first I should say, I don't have a vested interest in software patents; I have a future vested interest in the sense that I'm starting a company.

I find the system daunting and counterproductive from my perspective, and it keeps me up late at night because it's hard enough starting a company with natural disasters, but when somebody can hold a man-made disaster over your head, i.e., you write some software and somebody says 16 years down the road on their patent that you owe them money -- they're not just flushing your dream down the drain, they're flushing your employees down the drain, they're flushing your customers down the drain and they're flushing your suppliers down the drain. To me, that just doesn't make sense. And even if you do succumb to that, and you don't go the way of spending a fortune on lawyers -- I'll try to mention this only once -- I don't believe that the software industry should subsidize the legal services industry. So, if you don't go down that path, which you won't because it will cost you more money to go down that path even if you're in the right, than it would just to knuckle under to some patent challenge, you still end up spending money you shouldn't have to spend. And that money may be going to a competitor who hasn't even earned it, okay? And this is for a system that basically doesn't work.

If I wrote the software to represent this system, it would be riddled with race conditions, okay? That's a bozo no-no in software design, and it would have deadlocks; that means you're going to court. If you want to know an example of a race condition, you could have two companies --

By the way, I don't think these comments are limited strictly to software. I think you're going to see this problem crop up in other industries as they start using computers as intellectual development tools, because the computers are going to accelerate their development. The reason we're seeing it in software is because software is already accelerated by using computers.

For example, one of the worst race conditions that you have two companies developing something and spend $10 million on it, seven years of people's lives, whatever. Somebody gets the patent first. The patent system says they deserve the reward for that innovation. I disagree. I think the market deserves the reward of both innovations, and both companies deserve the chance to try to build on their opportunity.

Anyhow that's my background, that's why I'm here today because this stuff keeps me up late at night. I don't think it's such an incredibly complicated issue. From here on out I'm going to try not to give you my perspective, though this will definitely be a slanted presentation. I'm going to try and give you some information that I have, that I think could help you understand why there are so many conflicting attitudes and opinions, and how all these people can be basically telling the honest truth. And this is a little slanted, but with the sole exception possibly of the lawyers, since of all people they have the most incredible vested interest in maintaining a system which subsidizes their industry, even at the expense of the software industry.

The title is "Software Patents and Why They Should Be Abolished." The reason is they are unconstitutional. The Constitution says in Article 1, Section 8, Clause 8, The Congress shall have power to promote -- to promote -- the progress of science and useful arts by securing for limited times to authors and inventors the exclusive right -- and I would put that in quotes because that's a sort of nebulous idea -- to their respective writings and discoveries.

The key word in that is "promote." If the system stops promoting growth, the system is unconstitutional. Now, the lawyers may say, "Well, it's grandfathered in because the Congress already established the patent law." Well, that may be true, but that's a legal perspective and not a practical perspective.

Let me define patents further. The basic idea of patent, as I see it, which I think is pretty accurate, is promoting innovation, which is a factor in business and an important one, over free competition, which is a principle of business, and you don't sacrifice that principle lightly, okay? Whoever came up with the patent idea decided that it was worthwhile to promote innovation, even at the expense of free competition, my basic claim is that was a wise idea and it has served its purpose. But it's now outgrown and outlived its purpose and it's time to move on to productivity without patents, because now they're becoming counterproductive and slowing people down. And the reason basically is because it used to be that patents were few and far between -- I call that sparce, okay? Now our industries have matured enough that the patents, the ideas and the technologies and the innovations are coming very rapidly -- that's dense. You're having people trip all over themselves.

As soon as you get into that situation, there are interdependencies between these patents, so when you add a patent, you're not adding N goes to N+1 complexity,

you're going from N to N times N+1 complexity. That's a fact in computer science; that's called factorial growth. And that's heinous, okay? We're not talking linear growth add one, we're talking factorial growth. If you've got thousands of patents and you multiply those by another thousand in complexity, which is what all the inter-relationships between the patents are, you've got a problem. And that's why you can't keep up with the patents, and that's also why you're not going to be able to, ever.

Well, I'm going to drift through this, because I bet I burn more time than I expect.

I call this the Medusa effect. You've heard plenty of views on those conflicting accounts. Each of these views is like an eye of the Medusa. And Medusa is the Medusa of unfair competition, okay. We're sacrificing free competition for the Medusa of unfair competition. The nature of the system is that its outgrown and outlived its usefulness. It's degenerated into a win-lose industrial paralyzing influence. Basically that's the nature of our patent system. I call this degenerate influence the Medusa effect. It's all the same system but the view is different and conflicting from each eye. Each of our presenters is a different eye. The head is overcrowded with eye stalks, and worst of all, every seeing person in the vicinity of Medusa has genuinely high blood pressure -- that's the entrepreneurs who don't have portfolios of patents, okay?

Living near Medusa makes for a scary, unhealthy and unproductive situation, i.e., unconstitutional. The software industry already suffers from the Medusa effect today, due to the interference of the software patent system. That's like interference between patents except the system is doing it to an entire industry.

I would like to see this situation rectified and simplified, i.e., the elimination of patents from software.

Two challenges: To rectify this situation entails two challenges. The first challenge, of course, is to see the forest for the trees. Or in the case of Medusa and software patent, to see the whole Medusa instead of just some eye stalks. I shall try to solve the problem for you in the first part of my presentation shortly.

The second challenge is to fix the system. To fix the system is left to you; if I had the authority, I'd take care of it myself. This talk, unfortunately, is the limit of my contribution so far, but I have a feeling this will be around for ten years and I'll be back.

Fortunately, by applying -- the principle I'd like you to apply is the "kiss" principle, which is "Keep it simple, silly," and that means get rid of the system. The first challenge is eyeing the Medusa of unfair competition; that's being able to see it. I'd like to read a fragment of a New York Times article by John Markoff. He says:

Critics now say that the system is creating a public policy contradiction. On one hand the Clinton administration is eager to foster competition in telecommunications. On the other, the agency continued to grant 17-year monopolies just as it did when technologies involved at century-long intervals.

That's the crux of the problem. Mr. Markoff identifies the basic dilemma for the patent system: Times change. The tradeoff in sacrifice of free and fair competition to promote

UNITED STATES PATENT AND TRADEMARK OFFICE
Public Hearing on Patent Protection for Software-Related Inventions
San Jose, California -- January 26-27, 1994

innovation may no longer be a prudent tradeoff. Times change and the patent system has done its job to build an innovative, industrious, technological base. Now the patent system needs to step aside and let commerce generate the rest of its momentum instead of gumming up the works with unnecessary and counterproductive litigation.

I'd like to mention four books -- I think this stuff was covered very well in the Markoff article for an overview. In habit four of the Seven Habits of Highly Effective People, which is "think win-win." Right now we've degenerated into lose-lose-lose. The patent holder loses because the society doesn't grow; its competitors lose because they can't even get into the market; and the customers lose because nobody is delivering service as rapidly as they could have.

The next book is the <u>One-Minute Manager Builds High-Performing Teams</u>. This is by Ken Blanchard. I would like to see some situational management understanding applied to this. He goes by stages as well. In the early stages you need directive, coercive management, and in the most latter stages, you need hands-off management.

And the third book that I think applies is <u>Crossing the Chasm</u>, by Jeffrey A. Moore. He uses a multistage system as well. I think we've left the early adoptive cycle of his technology life adoption cycle, which is where patents are beneficial, and we have entered the early majority part of the cycle, where they start to gum up the works because the industry can maintain its own momentum. That's the basic gist.

I think you should take a look at this: Where we started, where we are today, and where we need to go. And I think you need to look at it in terms of stages, and I think if you do, you'll begin to understand why there are so many conflicting remarks. People are coming at this from different stages, and the software engineers are coming at it from the most current stage. And I think that holds value.

How do you kill the Medusa? You use this understanding as a mirror to look at her, and you slay her. And the weapon I would use to slay her is Akim's razor. That goes by the name of the kiss principle as well, and it's also known in legal circles as necessary and sufficient, and only necessary. And what we have now in the patent system is no longer necessary. Besides which, it's also insufficient.

Thank you very much for this opportunity to talk.

COMMISSIONER LEHMAN: Thank you very much, Mr. Grace.

I'd like to thank everybody who has testified over the last two days, even those who aren't here, all those who have come to watch the process. I'd like to think it's a process of open government; I'd like to think it's a process of customer service. I hope you'll help us at the Patent & Trademark Office to improve our customer service by taking the advantage of keeping in touch with us over the weeks and months to come.

I can tell you this: I'm not sure that I'm going to propose next week to abolish the Patent Office, but I can assure you there are going to be some real and substantive changes that are going to come out of this process, and you will see those in the coming months. Some of them will be administrative changes that we can make; some them we can make right

away, just simple policy changes. Others require work.

For example, the full potential of the Internet and electronic communications, even if we change our policies with regard to what we can hear from, who we can hear from and what we can get from them require technological improvements at the Patent & Trademark Office that will require an expenditure of capital, it will require money. So some things will be phased in, some things will happen very quickly.

The next category of changes that you're going to see is that we are certainly going to be coming up with some legislative proposals to change the statutory system. For example, were we to decide not to have software patents or to eliminate the Patent Office, I think those would have to be legislative changes and we'll have to go to get Congress' approval. I'm not suggesting we're going to necessarily propose either of those two alternatives, but we are going to be proposing to Congress some changes which will make the system work better.

So those are two examples of the things we're going to do. The final one is we're going to definitely be more aggressive in the Patent & Trademark Office in not only developing our own legal policies, but in working with the various courts, and the Court of Appeals for the Federal Circuit in particular, in trying to help them develop clearer legal standards and do their part in resolving some of these problems.

So in the next months and certainly during the remainder of this Clinton presidency, you can look forward to a series of changes in the areas that I've just outlined, and you'll be able to have many opportunities as these changes unfold, as the decision-making process unfolds, to give us feedback, to let us know what you think. I am a little scared to say that in this group, because I have a feeling the probably the Internet system and the computer system is going to break down at the Patent & Trademark Office with all of the feedback that we get, but let's try and see how it works.

Thank you very much for coming, and I look forward to continuing to work with you all for the next three years. Thanks.

(Public hearing concluded)

UNITED STATES PATENT AND TRADEMARK OFFICE
Public Hearing on Patent Protection for Software-Related Inventions
San Jose, California — January 26-27, 1994

Index to Participant Testimony

United States Patent and Trademark Office

Public Hearing on Use of the Patent System to Protect Software-Related Inventions

Transcript of Proceedings

Thursday, February 10, 1994
9:00 a.m. to 5:00 p.m.

Friday, February 11, 1994
9:00 a.m. to 12:30 p.m.

Before
Bruce A. Lehman
Assistant Secretary of Commerce and
Commissioner of Patents and Trademarks

Location:
The Marriott Crystal Forum
1999 Jefferson Davis Highway
Arlington, Virginia

APPENDIXES

UNITED STATES PATENT AND TRADEMARK OFFICE
Public Hearing on Patent Protection for Software-Related Inventions
Arlington, Virginia — February 10 & 11, 1994

Table of Participants

Before: Bruce A. Lehman
             Assistant Secretary of Commerce and
             Commissioner of Patents and Trademarks
             United States Patent and Trademark Office

The Panel: Lawrence Goffney
             Assistant Commissioner for Patents-Designate
             United States Patent and Trademark Office

             Micheal K. Kirk
             Assistant Commissioner for External Affairs
             United States Patent and Trademark Office

             Jeffrey P. Kushan
             Attorney-Advisor
             United States Patent and Trademark Office

             Michael Fleming
             Supervisory Patent Examiner
             United States Patent and Trademark Office

Transcription Services by:

AMERICAN REPORTERS
NATIONWIDE (800) 929-0130
WASHINGTON METRO (703) 644-7636
FAX (703) 866-7049

UNITED STATES PATENT AND TRADEMARK OFFICE
Public Hearing on Patent Protection for Software-Related Inventions
Arlington, Virginia -- February 10 & 11, 1994

Witnesses

February 10, 1994

PAUL ROBINSON
Tansin A. Darcos & Company

KEITH STEPHENS
Taligent, Inc.

MARK TRAPHAGEN
Software Publishers Association

ROB LIPPINCOTT
Interactive Multimedia Association

E. ROBERT YOCHES
JEFFREY A. BERKOWITZ
Finnegan, Henderson, Farabow, Garrett & Dunner

STEPHEN L. NOE
Caterpillar, Inc.
Intellectual Property Owners, Inc.

JOHN J. HORN
Allen-Bradley

RICHARD NYDEGGER
Workman, Nydegger & Jensen

ALLAN RATNER
Philadelphia Patent Law Association
Ratner & Prestia

DIANNE CALLAN
Lotus Development Corporation
Business Software Alliance

R. DUFF THOMPSON
WordPerfect Corporation

RON REILING
Digital Equipment Corporation

RICHARD JORDAN
Thinking Machines Corporation

A. JASON MIRABITO
Boston Patent Law Association

JONATHAN BAND
Morrison & Foerster

LEONARD CHARLES SUCHYTA
Bellcore, Bell Communications Research

VERN BLANCHARD
American Multisystems

EDDIE CURRY
IMAGESOFT, INC.

February 11, 1994

D.C. TOEDT
Arnold, White and Durkee

JOSEPH HOFSTADER
League for Programming Freedom

TIMOTHY SCANLON
JOHN J. HORN
Allen-Bradley

R. LEWIS GABLE
Welsh & Katz

JOHN E. DeWALD
The Prudential Insurance Company of America

DAVID L. CLARK
Aquilino & Welsh, P.C.

ALLEN M. LO
Finnegan, Henderson, Farabow, Garrett & Dunner

SAMUAL ODDI
Northern Illinois University
College of Law

BERNARD GALLER
University of Michigan
Software Patent Institute

GREGORY AHARONIAN
Source Translation and Optimization

UNITED STATES PATENT AND TRADEMARK OFFICE
Public Hearing on Patent Protection for Software-Related Inventions
Arlington, Virginia -- February 10 & 11, 1994

PROCEEDINGS

MORNING SESSION

(9:11 a.m.)

COMMISSIONER LEHMAN: Good morning. My name is Bruce Lehman and I am the Assistant Secretary of Commerce, and Commissioner of Patents and Trademarks.

Welcome to our second round of hearings on the use of the patent system to protect software-related inventions. Two weeks ago we held two days of hearings in San Jose, California, the capital of the Silicon Valley. Those hearings focused on the patent system and how it was being used in the field of software.

This round of hearings will focus on the standards of patentability and the examination process, as well as the treatment of the visual aspects of software under our design and utility patent systems.

The common goal for all of our hearings is to find out how the patent system is working for this field of technology and to get your suggestions for making it work better.

President Clinton has made the development of and competitiveness of high tech industries in the United States a cornerstone of his economic program. Promoting these industries will lead to high tech, high wage jobs for Americans and will ensure continued American competitiveness in the industries of the future.

Our Secretary of Commerce, Ron Brown, has assembled an excellent team to work on initiatives toward that end and I am pleased to be a part of that Commerce Department technology team. The software industry is already meeting the President's goals for creating competitive high tech domestic industry. So we've got a good thing going already.

Statistics show that since 1987 employment in the software industry has risen at an annual rate of over 6.5 percent and now employs well over 400,000 people. In 1992 revenue from the sales of programming services, pre-packaged software and computer integrated design was over $50 billion. U.S. software firms dominate the world's software markets, holding over 75 percent of the market for pre-packaged software.

It is interesting that up until the middle of this century the wealth and economic strength of the United States came primarily from the exploitation of our natural resources and we had a lot of them in those days. In the 21st Century, our economic strength will come from tapping our most treasured resource, the wealth of the human mind, and we will be concentrating on conserving our natural resources.

To do this, however, we must encourage innovation and provide our innovators with the legal protections they need to successfully exploit their innovations. This is especially true in the intensively competitive and fast-paced computer and software industry.

Indeed, innovation is the life blood of this industry. It is what separates successful firms from unsuccessful ones.

Innovation, however, is a fragile commodity. Without effective legal protection our software industry would not enjoy the dominance it now does in the global market, nor would consumers enjoy the high quality and extremely usable software products that are available on the market today.

Our intellectual property systems were established over 200 years ago to promote and protect innovation in all fields of technology. If these systems are functioning properly, they will provide an appropriate level of protection and encourage innovation.

From what we have heard recently, this may not be the case for our patent system in the field of software-related inventions. This is why we are seeking public input -- to identify the problems that exist and to hear suggestions on how to address them.

Two weeks ago we held the first round of hearings, as I mentioned earlier, in San Jose, California. No clear consensus emerged from those hearings, but many suggestions were made regarding how the patent system could be improved for the software industry.

Some people testified that the patent system was not working at all, that it neither encouraged nor assisted software development. Others suggested that companies only sought patents for defensive purposes. If true, this runs counter to one of the primary reasons for the patent system, which is to encourage innovation.

On the other hand, several people testified that the patent system was essential for successful software development efforts. We heard large and small companies tell us that without patents they would not be able to attract or effectively protect investments in developing new software-related technology. I think we also were hearing that the industry might be on the verge of a shift to more patent dependency and more usefulness in the patent system.

However, even people who generally supported the patent system commented on the need to improve the quality of issued patents. Some people expressed skepticism over the ability of the PTO to accurately gauge software innovation. Others commented that the Patent and Trademark Office does not have access to enough prior art or that adequate collections of prior art simply do not exist.

We are committed to addressing these concerns and to taking whatever measures are necessary to ensure the proper function of the patent system. I would like to say, just yesterday, I know, the Chairman of our House Subcommittee, Chairman William Hughes, discussed these hearings and he indicated his willingness to work in partnership with us, to the extent that legislation is required to assure the proper functioning of that system.

My goal is to ensure that patents will be instruments that you can take to the bank literally. From what we heard in San Jose this may not be the case for patents in the field of software-related inventions.

We intend to address these concerns through three levels of action. First, we will improve our examining operation

- 1 -

to ensure high quality examination. Second, we will pursue appropriate legislative reform to ensure the efficient functioning of the patent system. And finally, we intend to work with the Judiciary to improve the interpretation of patent rights in the context of enforcement.

Many useful suggestions were made in San Jose two weeks ago and I expect to hear many more in the next two days -- today and tomorrow. For example, many people stressed the need for reform of the reexamination process. We recognize the need for making reexamination a more attractive option for those having reasons to question the validity of any particular patent and are presently studying a number of suggestions and proposals in that area.

Many people pointed out in San Jose that the obviousness standard, as interpreted by our examiners and by the court, seems to be inconsistent with the realities of the industry.

We recognize that an effectively functioning patent system requires a standard of nonobviousness that is rigorous and reflective of industry norms. However, we also recognize that the courts are the primary source of guidance on the basic question of obviousness.

As such, we intend to work with the courts to ensure that the obviousness standard is applied rigorously, not only in the context of examination, but also when patents are enforced. I mentioned that was part of our three-part program.

Several suggestions were made regarding the improvement of our operations. I would like to note that we are already responding to some of these suggestions. For example, many people have called for the PTO to improve its ability to find and retrieve prior art.

One step we've taken towards this goal is the creation of our electronic information center in Group 2300. This facility will provide an easily accessible structure through which we can improve our collections of and access to the prior art.

However, extensive work with industry and other groups is beginning to pay off in the form of specific commitments to providing information, like in-house textbooks, old software user manuals and access to information on early programming techniques.

We also heard that we need to attract and retain more qualified examiners by providing more competitive salaries and improving the stature of the examiner position. Toward this end, we have just changed our standards so that we will hire for the first time computer scientists as examiners.

We are also in the process of expanding our examiner enrichment program to provide our examiners with greater exposure to other aspects of the Patent and Trademark Office and technical programs in other government agencies. That is just the beginning. We have a real quality of life improvement program underway here for our patent examiners that hopefully will translate into better quality of examination.

Another specific area targeted by people testifying in San Jose was the need to improve the administrative processing of patent applications. People stressed the importance not only of insuring the timely consideration of patent applications but the timely processing at every stage of the patent application process. This falls squarely within our new focus on customer service.

One example of a program that we are studying now is the pre-examination interview. We are conducting a trial program to evaluate whether this step can help reduce the delays and assist pro se inventors.

Before we hear from our first witness, I would like to introduce you to some of the members of our own panel, people who are here from the Patent and Trademark Office.

First, I would like to introduce on my left Michael Kirk. Mike is our Assistant Commissioner for External Affairs. Presently he's in charge of our Office of Legislation in International Affairs. But President Clinton has nominated him to become Deputy Commissioner.

Under our new reorganization that we are implementing in the Patent and Trademark Office, he will be in charge of -- basically the policy czar for the Patent and Trademark Office and will have reporting to him not only the Office of Legislature and International Affairs, which he now runs in the Office of Public Affairs, but also the Solicitor's Office, the Board of Appeals and our quality review operations so that we can bring all of these together into a single unified policy entity that will help work on policy aspects of these problems and provide better service to all the people who look to us in the Patent and Trademark Office for leadership.

On my immediate right is Lawrence Goffney, our Assistant Commissioner for Patents-Designate, who the President has nominated to run our patent operation, by far the largest, over half of the whole Patent and Trademark Office, with over 5,000 employees. And, of course, Group 2300 and this particular subject matter falls directly under Larry Goffney's jurisdiction.

The other fellow sitting here at the table with us is Jeff Kushan, an attorney in our Office of Legislation, International Affairs, who many of you may have talked with. He's the point man for day-to-day contact on this particular issue. And anybody who has any questions or follow-up on this can get ahold of him, and his number is 703-305-9300.

I also would like to introduce somebody who is not sitting at the table, but who is absolutely a lynch pin to this whole effort, and that is Jerry Goldberg --- Jerry wants to stand up -- who is our Group Director for Group 2300.

Finally, even though he is not sitting there right now, I would like to note that Mike Fleming was in Group 2300. There he is right there. Mike is going to be, anybody that has any scheduling issues or questions or whatever, whether a hearing is going on -- if you might, stand up again, Mike, so they can make certain they know where you are. Are you going to sit there or over there? He's going to sit

UNITED STATES PATENT AND TRADEMARK OFFICE
Public Hearing on Patent Protection for Software-Related Inventions
Arlington, Virginia — February 10 & 11, 1994

right over here in the corner. You should just approach Mike and he'll see that you get taken care of.

People who will be testifying over the next two days should have received a schedule indicating the approximate time they have been assigned to give their remarks. A final list is available at the entrance to the room. I expect most of you have already picked it up.

I would encourage all the people scheduled to testify to be here at least 20 minutes before your assigned time slot. The reason for that is because we've already had a couple of people because of this weather who can't come. So obviously if we have a person who can't come, that's going to move us up a little bit. That's been our experience so far with these hearings, these and other similar hearings. So please be here at least 20 minutes before your assigned time slot.

Each person will have eleven minutes to speak. The computer monitor right there in front of the podium will display a green screen for nine minutes. Then it will turn yellow. And when the screen turns red we would very much like you to have concluded your comments by that time. I encourage everybody to do that because it's really only fair to all the other witnesses. And generally speaking, these hearings have been pretty good at that. I hate to have to gavel people to a halt. So if you'd really cooperate with that, I'd really appreciate it. I think eleven minutes is a pretty good amount of time.

I want to emphasize that, you know, these eleven minutes aren't your only chance to -- they may be your only chance in the spotlight with an audience, but they are not your only chance to communicate with us. You know, this isn't the court where this is your oral argument and that's it. We certainly welcome further written comments. Certainly at the Patent and Trademark Office we like to be accessible even on a day-to-day oral basis. I've just introduced a bunch of people to you -- Jerry Goldberg and Jeff Kushan.

I would also like to introduce Charlie Vanhorn who is sitting over there. Charlie is our Chief Patent Policy guru in the Patent Corps. I know many of you already know these people. I'm sure that over the next weeks and months they look forward to having a dialogue, continued dialogue, on these issues.

If you check the Federal Register Notice of December 20, 1993, you will find all the information about how to send us more comments if you want. That notice is not only available printed in the Federal Register, but it's also been widely circulated through the Internet and it can be retrieved from our FTP site, which is COMMENTS.USPTO.GOV.

Transcripts for these hearings will be available after February 21 and paper copies will be available from our office for $30.00 and transcripts will also be available for free through our FTP site on the Internet.

Once again, we welcome everybody to our hearings today. I'm really gratified at the turnout that we've been having. We had a very large audience in San Jose. We get a

normal 60 people who testified and I'd say that we had at any given time at least 100 people in the room, and probably at the maximum we had 300 or 400 and a lot of them stuck with us. So there's obviously interest in the industry in this. We're gratified about that.

We also understand that that imposes on us an obligation to really make these hearings meaningful and to follow up in the ways that we've already started, that I've outlined to you in my own opening remarks.

So with that I'd like to call our first witness to come up and share his thoughts with us, and that's Paul Robinson, who is the Manager of Data Processing and Chief Programmer of Tansin A. Darcos.

PRESENTATION BY PAUL ROBINSON

TANSIN A. DARCOS & COMPANY

MR. ROBINSON: Good morning, Assistant Secretary Lehman, Mr. Kushan, the staff here, members of the audience, people reading this report in the future and anyone else I've forgotten. My name is Paul Robinson. I am Chief Programmer for Tansin A. Darcos & Company, a software development firm which specializes in text processing applications.

I also do work on commercial philosophy and metaphysics of computer systems. My special interest and my personal hobby is collecting compiler and other program sources. My reasons for this are that these all solve problems.

By reading the manner and method other people solved other problems it gives me insight into how to solve mine. This is a common practice in the computer world in order to, as the expression goes, not reinvent the wheel. I assume this is common in other industries. In fact, this is most likely the reason that we have the patent system.

Someone is granted the exclusive right over commercial use of their invention for a limited term in exchange for telling the world about it. For most computers, every application, such as word processing or spreadsheets, has at least two and possibly three or more different applications fighting for market share.

The fights in this industry are usually referred to by the expression dinosaur mating dances, as huge companies fight for market share by releasing new programs to introduce new features that the companies believe the customers want.

Version 3 of Turbo Pascal was an excellent language compiler and less than 40K. Version 4 would fit on one 360K diskette. Today, Turbo Pascal Windows Version 1.5 takes 14,000K of disk space.

The program that is most probably the premier application for graphics design is Corel Draw, which has so much material it is being released on not one, but two 500 megabyte CD ROM diskettes. But there are probably still niches for smaller companies to move into.

With the rapid changes in the marketplace it is necessary to be ready to have new programs and new releases of old programs out to encourage people to move to the next

UNITED STATES PATENT AND TRADEMARK OFFICE
Public Hearing on Patent Protection for Software-Related Inventions
Arlington, Virginia -- February 10 & 11, 1994

release. In some cases, companies make more money from upgrades and need to do so to stay alive. These kind of cycles mean new releases have to out very quickly, in a matter of weeks to months.

With this kind of rapid development cycle, delays in a release of a program could be fatal and the time available to create the work is sometimes barely enough. Until recently, the only legal issue that anyone had to worry about was copyright infringement. This could be avoided by creating new work from scratch.

Now we have another issue altogether. A programmer can independently create something without ever knowing about any other developments, and yet be sabotaged by the discovery that the method they have used is patented. This is a standard problem that all industries have had to face and it is part and parcel of living in an industrial society.

But there is another problem. A computer program is the written instructions by a human being to tell a computer how to perform a particular task. As such, there are only two parameters -- the input supply to the program and the expected output. Everything else is literally a figment of someone's imagination.

This bears clarification. A computer program is the means of manipulating the internal data passed through a computer system. There is no requirement that the manipulations have any correspondence to the real world. In this, the real world, doing anything requires the expensive movement of people and goods from one point to another, the possible refinement of materials into other materials and the expenditure of energy and resources.

Doing anything in a computer is merely the essentially cost-free movement of electron paths from one direction to another. It brings forth the approbation of the concepts of the math, man and manual camped into reality, a world in which anything is possible.

We can see this in the current discussions going on about violent computer games where someone goes about maiming, shredding and killing their opponents in graphic detail. Then when the game is over, nothing in the real world has changed except the clock.

One of my favorites happens to be the game Doom, where the weapon of choice is a 12-gauge shotgun, but a chain saw does a nice job on people near you. We have seen it in motion pictures, such as Total Recall, where if one is acting within a part of a computer program you cannot be certain what is real and what is fantasy.

The movie Brainstorm had simulations of sexual contact, apparently indistinguishable from reality.

There are things that can be done within a computer program that cannot be done in the real world or would have undesirable consequences. As such, we should ask whether the patent rules which are designed to apply to real world conditions where doing something requires the expenditure of energy and resources should apply where the known rules of the universe do not apply. Because the entire design starts from scratch, the designer doesn't just get to play God, he is God.

Despite the ease under which someone can do something, we still live under real world constraints. Once a design choice is made, it is very expensive in time and effort to change it. Worst, because most programs have interactions that cover every part, a change to one part can cause unexpected and even undesirable side effects in unknown and unexpected places.

Computer programs may be the stuff that dreams are made of, as Shakespeare has used. But once placed in a concrete form, as written in software instructions, it's just as expensive to repair or change as if it were carved out of real materials. It may be necessary to change the rules on patents to comply with conditions that exist for computer programs. I can think of a couple of suggestions.

There has been talk of instituting first-to-file in order to "harmonize" with the systems in other countries. I think that this is not a good choice. Most countries have fewer patents and provide protection which is much narrower than our system does. This would also mean that if someone does invent a new and useful technique for use in a computer application would be unable to collect any royalties from someone else who is using the same invention who thought of it after they did, but started using it before they filed.

The two really large problems that exist in our system are probably two-part -- the secrecy under which patent applications are filed and the problems if a program uses parts of several patents which might not be discovered until later.

As I mentioned earlier, computer programs are created out of the figment of someone's imagination, then mass copied the way an original painting can be reproduced by lithograph. A single large application might have a dozen people working on it or thousands of people working on it, and upwards of 50 different features, and might have upwards of 200 or more different parts. Any one of those might be infringing on zero, one or more patents, depending on what the claims are.

I doubt seriously that all but the largest corporations have the resources to do 200 patent searches on a single software application, which would be prohibitive for a small company because it is likely that a large program could infringe dozens of patents due to the continued development of ever larger applications that do multiple simultaneous functions.

But more than that, you can't do patent searches on works which are under application form until after the patent has been issued. And more importantly, with more than 1200 patents issued every week, checking them all for possible interconnection would make it impossible to do any serious work, although that might provide somebody with an idea for a magazine.

Seventy years ago fears that the major piano manufacturer would tie up the entire song market and create other companies from creating player piano roles caused Congress to institute compulsory licensing. This may be an idea whose time has come again.

-- 4 --

Therefore, it might be considered to make two possible changes to the patent law with respect to computer programs. Perhaps to implement a standard compulsory license, perhaps 10 percent of the manufacturer's suggested list price, and to eliminate secrecy provisions in the filing of patent applications.

Either of these could certainly help the situation. Eliminating secrecy and publishing applications once filed would let people know about pending applications. They could endeavor to avoid infringements in advance. It might also allow them to file inferences early if it turns out that they invented the concept earlier while it is still cheap to do so; and would allow people to be aware of what is being developed, which would comply with Article I, Section VIII of the Constitution where patent protection was designed to "encourage the improvement of the useful arts."

The other option of setting a standard royalty, via compulsory license, would eliminate the worries of someone infringing upon an existing patent or multiple patents or one that is filed after their work is created. It would also grant to inventors an income stream from those who use their inventions which started before they filed their application, but after they reduced the invention to practice.

It would also limit liability and exposure to sustainable limits. As it stands, if someone develops a program that infringes upon 40 patents and they each want a 3 percent royalty, it isn't hard to see that 120 percent of the program's income is not going to be possible.

Thank you. Any questions?

COMMISSIONER LEHMAN: Thank you very much, Mr. Robinson. You obviously put a lot of thought into that statement and had some very interesting ideas. Thank you very much.

I'd like to next call on Keith Stephens, corporate counsel to Taligent, Inc.

PRESENTATION BY KEITH STEPHENS

TALIGENT, INC.

MR. STEPHENS: Mr. Commissioner, my name is Keith Stephens. I'm corporate counsel of Taligent and I will be testifying today on behalf of Taligent, Inc. I'm a computer scientist and engineer by training and have earned my living as a systems engineer, as an inventor and subsequently as a marketing rep before I saw the light, went back to law school, took the patent agent's exam and became an attorney. Currently I'm employed by Taligent to protect their intellectual property.

Taligent is a joint venture, similar to many other small innovative companies in the Silicon Valley. It's increasingly important for small ventures o be able to protect their intellectual property.

Today I would like to talk about transforming the legal chaos associated with software-related inventions into a system with much better legal certainty by continuing to refine the examination process, and issuing quality patents

allowing software investors to obtain a better return on their investment, and encouraging investment in American software technology.

Can I have my second slide? I have three major points. First, it's important for the Patent Office to hire the best people. Second, to provide them with the best tools. And third, to tune the examination process.

The Patent Office needs to hire computer science majors and I applaud your efforts in that area. However, they need to get computer science majors with industry experience. This will give them a historical perspective on the prior art.

In addition, they need to continue the efforts that Jerry Goldberg and Group 2300 have made in bringing industry experts into the Patent Office to teach classes on particular technologies that they come into contact with. We sent Mike Pitel, who was a university professor at Chicago. He came and taught a class on object oriented programming, not just a class to introduce them to the technology, but also to teach the history of object oriented programming and give them a perspective so that they would be in a better position to examine our patents.

We also worked closely with Groups 2300, 2500 and 2600 to bring a set of examiners out to the Silicon Valley to introduce them firsthand to technology experts. However, as Tom Kronium pointed out in the Silicon Valley, this is a two-edged sword. As Gary Shaw quipped, this provided him with new and innovative ways to reject our claims.

Now in addition I'd like to encourage examiner/attorney communication. It's so important for examiners to up front understand exactly what the invention is that I would like to encourage them to be more open in contacting attorneys so that they can find out from their first source exactly what the invention is.

Corporate America doesn't work in a vacuum. Corporate America -- it's always the case that we consult experts within and without before we make any kind of a decision. Similarly, as an attorney, when I receive an invention disclosure I don't just snap to a decision on that disclosure. I'll consult the experts within our company as well as ask general questions to maintain confidentiality of what the state of the art is outside.

And finally, I'll also, if I know someone in the Patent Office that's an expert in the area, contact them and ask them what they know about it. Similarly, I would encourage the Patent Office to create a human database of experts, both inside and outside of the Patent Office, and communicate with them through phone, Internet, querying a wider audience to determine exactly what the prior art is.

This could be done through a contractual basis or just generally by contacts and asking open-ended questions. But I would also encourage them to continue the confidential status of patents until they issue.

Secondly, I think it's important to give the best tools to the examiners. It's very encouraging to see examiners starting to get access to Internet. Electronic mail is a tool that everyone in the industry uses as a common practice.

UNITED STATES PATENT AND TRADEMARK OFFICE
Public Hearing on Patent Protection for Software-Related Inventions
Arlington, Virginia — February 10 & 11, 1994

I would even venture to say that had Internet been available that the multimedia technology, state of the art, would have made it in the Patent Office in a much more timely manner.

Secondly, commercial databases such as those in the Group 2300, Orbit, Dialogue and Lexus should be used as a regular basis amongst examiners. But in addition the Patent Office should pursue getting industry databases from such companies as AT&T and IBM, so that they can effectively search the technical disclosure bulletins of these companies. The result will be quality patents and a confidence in the appropriate claim scopes issuing in the patents.

Third, I'd like to talk about tuning the examination process. It's very important to standardize the examination process and encourage examiners to take advantage of contacting attorneys using the databases to find out what the state of the art is in the area and inquiring of experts, both within and without at the Patent Office to make their determination as to novelty and obviousness.

Then in addition it would be very good to have a common format of acceptable standards to file patent applications so that we could electronically file patents. This standard could be such as WordPerfect or a word standard document that we could transmit electronically to the PTO and eliminate a lot of the paper shuffle associated with patent applications and speed up the processing of these applications.

Then, too, I would encourage the improvement of practical application of the law in the Patent Office. Hiring people with industry experience is naturally going to elevate the current obviousness standard and the novelty standard once people have a knowledge of what the prior art really teaches.

And then I would encourage the Patent Office to modify their examination process, to remove the bias currently associated with the reexamination process, to encourage us to utilize the reexamination process as opposed to using a more costly approach of going to the CAFC or other Federal District Court type of an approach.

These changes, which are slight modifications to the current examination process, will result in much better patents being issued.

So in summary, I would encourage communication with attorneys in the Patent Office, better communication with the outside world. I would encourage the utilization of a human database through a setup so that the PTO could have access to better prior art. And then I would encourage the best possible tools being provided to the Patent Office so that they'd be in a better position to know what the prior art is and to also assess what is truly new technology versus just reinventing the wheel.

And finally, tuning the process associated with examination of processing patent applications. This will eliminate the current chaos associated with software-related inventions, improve the legal certainty associated with issued patents, and make the PTO much prouder of their work product.

Let's remember who created the patent system and let his words control. Thomas Jefferson said, "Where a new invention promises to be useful, it should be tried and afforded the best possible protection to allow progress in the technology and to allow the fruit of the labor to be realized by the inventor of the technology."

This will encourage investment in software, will result in more software-related high pay, high tech jobs and finally, will increase American competitiveness in a global economy.

Thank you.

COMMISSIONER LEHMAN: Thank you very much, Mr. Stephens. I didn't hear in your list of proposed reforms, which actually Mr. Robinson suggested, and that was the idea of some kind of disclosure prior to publication of the patent, of the information in the patent application. Pre-publication as a technique to make certain that we let the world know what's going on and make sure we get the prior art. What would be your view about that?

MR. STEPHENS: My view on that is I don't think that pre-publication is necessary to reach your common goal that I think everyone here will agree with, is to issue the best quality patents with claims of the scope that the inventor is entitled to.

That can better be achieved by providing the appropriate tools to examiners and providing them access to the experts in the area, even possibly putting together a contractual relationship between the Patent Office and various human experts that are available in industry, so that the confidentiality of the application will not be compromised.

But the information will be available to examiners to make sure that the issuance of the patent has the appropriate claims or the appropriate scope of claims.

COMMISSIONER LEHMAN: Thank you very much. Does anyone else have any questions?

(No audible response.)

COMMISSIONER LEHMAN: Next I'd like to call Mark Traphagen, counsel to the Software Publishers Association.

PRESENTATION BY MARK TRAPHAGEN
SOFTWARE PUBLISHERS ASSOCIATION

MR. TRAPHAGEN: Good morning, Mr. Commissioner, members of the panel, and those of you in the audience. Thank you for the opportunity to appear today to speak about patent protection for software-related inventions. My name is Mark Traphagen and I am counsel for the Software Publishers Association.

Patents for software-related inventions have been highlighted by the media in recent months. For example, last year the U.S. Patent and Trademark Office granted a patent to Compton's New Media of Carlsbad, California for a system of retrieving information for multimedia works.

Now Compton's New Media is a member company and SPA has no position on the merits of this patent which is

UNITED STATES PATENT AND TRADEMARK OFFICE
Public Hearing on Patent Protection for Software-Related Inventions
Arlington, Virginia — February 10 & 11, 1994

now being reexamined. But it is worth noting that Compton's New Media is not alone in seeking patent protection for software, as several other companies have been reported in the trade press to own patents for software with important applications in multimedia. And since 1987 more than 10,000 patents have been issued on nearly 35,000 applications filed in classes 364 and 395.

In 1992 alone almost 2,000 patents were issued on 8,000 applications filed. And lest one think the patent applications for software patents are a phenomenon unique to the United States, the Japanese Patent Office issued as many as 12,000 such patents in 1990.

Since it was founded in 1984, SPA's been a leader in advancing the interests of its members, primarily through copyright law. And copyright law has been popular, more popular than patents, among software developers and publishers because its protection is relatively inexpensive and free of formalities.

Copyright law alone, however, cannot protect all of the aspects of intellectual property and software technology because it is limited to creative expression in code, screen displays and other graphic output. In particular, Section 102(b) of the Copyright Act provides that "in no case does copyright protection for an original work of authorship extend to any idea, procedure, process, system, method of operation, concept, principle or discovery regardless of the form in which is described, explained, illustrated or embodied in such work."

Now it's precisely these functional aspects of software technology that are sought to be protected by patent law. While like copyright law, patent law does not protect ideas in themselves, it does protect the machines, methods, processes, and apparatus that implement these novel ideas. This protection is extended, however, only to innovations that satisfy the statutory requirements of novelty and nonobviousness.

SPA has over 1100 members and represents not only large, well-known software publishers and developers, but hundreds of smaller companies and organizations as well. SPA members include not only those organizations that have sought patent protection already, but also those who will do so in the future and those whose products are potentially affected by patents held by others.

SPA called on the elected Board members of its consumer, education and multimedia sections to join a software patent working group and assist SPA's government affairs committee in formulating our position on patent protection for software-related inventions.

The success of the patent system in encouraging technological and commercial progress in other fields suggests that it would be prudent to try improving the patent examination process before changing the statutory underpinnings of the law. Whether patent owner or patent user, many agree that the patent examination process can be procedurally improved.

SPA applauds the efforts the U.S. PTO has made to make these improvements, including those announced by you today, Mr. Commissioner, and those that Jerry Goldberg, the Director of Group 2300 and I have discussed earlier by telephone.

SPA supports these efforts to improve the patent examination process and commits itself to the following three-step process to help the U.S. PTO continue to solve these problems.

First of all, SPA will continue to support the efforts of the Software Patent Institute, a nonprofit organization developing a software technology prior art database. You will be hearing later on in the day from a Mr. Galler, who I've worked with before on this issue and who is Chair of the Software Patent Institute.

Second, SPA will call on its broad membership to contribute nonproprietary information about software products to the Software Patent Institute.

And third, SPA will provide educational and training opportunities in the field of software technology to U.S. PTO examiners.

Many difficulties or many objections to the current system of patent protection for software-related inventions stem from difficulties in uncovering prior art. Typical complaints focus on the unavailability of pertinent prior art and an expanded prior art collection would help the U.S. PTO make more informed judgments about whether a particular invention meets the statutory tests of novelty and nonobviousness.

These difficulties are not unique to software technology, but developing a comprehensive prior art database has proven more difficult for software than other disciplines, such as biotechnology.

In the early days of the software industry, patent protection was not as widely used as it has been for other technologies. The primary focus instead was on copyright protection for creative expression and trade secret protection for other aspects of the technology.

As a result, much pertinent prior art may not reside in prior patents but in publications and limited circulation documents such as technical manuals. The difficulty has been compounded by related problems, in particular inconsistent terminology in the technology.

The first step in SPA's program will be to continue to support the effort to build a non-patent prior art database in the field of software technology. The SPA is an Executive Committee member of the Software Patent Institute, which has been recognized for its efforts to provide the best available prior art in the software technology field for use by the PTO and the public.

Up until now the PTO has lacked such a source to fill this need. The Institute is compiling a database of software technologies from descriptions of software techniques and processes contributed by the software industry, government, and academia.

The Institute's work is now producing results that promise to improve the ability of patent examiners to conduct research into non-patent prior art. On January 15th the

UNITED STATES PATENT AND TRADEMARK OFFICE
Public Hearing on Patent Protection for Software-Related Inventions
Arlington, Virginia — February 10 & 11, 1994

Institute made its prior art database available on-line and has demonstrated it to the U.S. PTO and the American Intellectual Property Law Association.

As the second step in its program SPA will call on its membership to contribute nonproprietary information about software prior art to the Institute. SPA is in an excellent position to assist this effort because it is the principal trade association of the personal computer software industry.

SPA has over 1100 members in North America and Europe, ranging from large well-known companies to hundreds of smaller companies, all of which develop and market consumer, business and education software. Their cumulative knowledge is unsurpassed and should reinforce the already significant resources incorporated into the Institute's database.

The third step in SPA's program will help address concerns about the level of skill of patent examiners handling applications for software-related inventions. SPA would like to assist the U.S. PTO in educational and training programs designed to keep software patent examiners conversant in this rapidly developing technology.

To begin this effort, SPA will extend scholarships for U.S. PTO patent examiners to attend the SPA Spring Symposium and other conferences. These conferences feature many seminars devoted to emerging technologies. The upcoming seminar in particular includes seminars on risk unix systems, wireless and interactive networks, and I think typically the role of patents in software development.

The SPA program would compliment the academic training now being offered by the Software Patent Institute and other groups. Mr. Goldberg, the Director of Group 2300, has been very receptive to this initiative and in return has invited SPA's software patent working group on a tour of the PTO. I am pleased to say that we will be glad to accept.

In closing, the most important concern about patents for software-related inventions for SPA members whether they be patent owners or patent users is the integrity of patent examination. SPA is hopeful, as others have been, that the current problems of patent protection for software-related inventions can be addressed by improving U.S. PTO's access to non-patent prior art and information about ongoing developments in software technology.

We look forward to a continuing relationship and a free flow of information between the U.S. PTO and our members. Once again, Mr. Commissioner and members of the panel, thank you for giving SPA the opportunity to testify on this important issue. I will be happy to answer any questions you may have.

COMMISSIONER LEHMAN: Thank you very much, Mr. Traphagen. Does anybody have any questions on the panel?

(No audible response.)

COMMISSIONER LEHMAN: If not, thank you very much for your sharing with us.

Next I would like to ask Rob Lippincott, Executive Vice President of the Interactive Multimedia Association to come forward.

PRESENTATION BY ROB LIPPINCOTT

INTERACTIVE MULTIMEDIA ASSOCIATION

MR. LIPPINCOTT: Good morning, Mr. Commissioner, members of the panel, ladies and gentlemen. My name is Rob Lippincott. I'm Vice President for Content at Ziff/Davis Interactive, which is an on-line information services provider and multimedia publisher. I also serve as Executive Vice President of the Interactive Multimedia Association.

The Association's General Counsel, Brian Kahen, who also directs our intellectual property project is here with me today to answer any questions you may have.

As a traditional magazine and newsletter publisher, Ziff/Davis has built a business on the value added by the work of editors and writers doing research, selecting, highlighting, linking information, by aggregating rights, by creating original material, and by expressing the opinions which they believe will influence the market, change the flow of business or touch human souls.

As multimedia information publishers we have come to view interactivity as perhaps the fundamental principle of the new media. It is how editors and developers use computers to speak to people. It's how people use computers to get the information they need, and it's how people speak to other people through computers.

It's how communities grow and how markets are formed, perhaps most importantly. Interactivity, per se, cannot be considered a patentable process. It's how we communicate. It's this perspective that I find shared by the majority of my fellow IMA members and from which I offer the following testimony on their behalf.

The IMA, the Interactive Multimedia Association, is a U.S. based trade association with more than 280 member companies and organizations, representing all of the areas of the multimedia industry. Its mission is to promote the development of interactive multimedia applications and to reduce existing barriers to the widespread use of multimedia technology.

Multimedia draws on traditional content industries -- movies, television and music, as well as traditional publishing -- which have been and which promise to be powerful export industries for the United States. These are creative industries which function very effectively and comfortably to date, largely dependent on the copyright law for intellectual property protection.

And as my colleague Tom Lopez testified in San Jose, a number of the creative people in our emerging industry feel rather threatened by abstract process patents which they believe give patentees leverage over content developers and publishers.

Our concern is not software patents in general, but patents which constrain and control human expression and the flow

UNITED STATES PATENT AND TRADEMARK OFFICE
Public Hearing on Patent Protection for Software-Related Inventions
Arlington, Virginia -- February 10 & 11, 1994

of information. Under the European patent convention, patents are not granted for "schemes, rules and methods for performing mental acts, playing games or doing business, programs for computers or presentations of information."

While we have similar judicially created exceptions in our law, in certain instances they have been eroded if not eliminated. The result is that we have a patent system that has in certain instances stretched the system beyond its resources and capabilities some might argue, to in fact regulate those abstract functions.

From the perspective of a number of our members, our multimedia developers and producers, the patent system is a one-size-fits-all system for creating property rights that is indifferent to its impact on the industries it seeks to regulate, directly or indirectly. Software is treated in much the same way as chemical compounds, but it has persistent problems in the examination process.

Broad patents, especially patents that preempt functions that cannot be designed around, should not be granted without an extraordinary level of quality control, preferably in the form of peer review, much as has been spoken of earlier today.

Whatever the practical limitations on the knowledge and expertise of examiners, they ought to be able to identify such broad claims and route the applications accordingly. Broad patents are inherently regulatory in nature. It is imperative that the claims be precise and that the examination be thorough. Such patents must be widely acknowledged and respected within the field and the industries that they affect.

Pre-grant publication for both broad and narrow patents is an absolute necessity in the software area because the patent database is so limited. In Europe and Japan and virtually everywhere else in the world patent applications are published before the patent is granted. Many of the patents that trouble the multimedia industry because of their breadth would never stand up to pre-grant publication.

In 1966 the President's Commission on the Patent System recommended against granting patents for computer programs for practical reasons. "The Patent Office now cannot examine applications for programs because of the lack of a classification scheme and the requisite search files. Even if these are available, reliable searches would not be feasible or economic because of the tremendous volume of prior art being generated."

Twenty-eight years later, and a significant twenty-eight years in our industry, the situation remains largely the same because the search files have never been completely developed and the volume of prior art has naturally grown exponentially.

However, the U.S. PTO began to grant patents on software processes liberally without addressing the practical problems. Pre-grant publication is an alternative, which could in due course elicit sufficient prior art to make such a database feasible.

Furthermore, we have the beginnings of an information infrastructure that can make pre-grant publication

inexpensive and effective. The patent system should be an integral part of this infrastructure.

The problems with subject matter and those of examination tend to go hand-in-hand. While we applaud the fact that last month the PTO finally began hiring examiners with degrees in computer science, this didn't happen until 12 years after the PTO liberalized its policy on software.

With the PTO granting patents on multimedia designs, business methods and educational methods by rights it should admit MBAs and Masters in instruction design as patent examiners. Given past experience, we would not expect this to happen any time soon. But the notion suggested in question two that an examiner trained in electrical engineering can deduce the level of ordinary skill in these arts from reading a few journals and patents is clearly insupportable.

The relevant art or arts should be identified by the applicant. The examiner should be identified with a cited art and their final signature should, in fact, affirm that they are skilled in those arts.

There are a number of other considerations we don't have time to note here, but will do so in writing. We will do so with the understanding that other industries may feel differently about the operation of the patent system. Other industries may feel the opportunity to maintain trade secret protection outweighs the need for a better examination process. We respect their views because we feel that the system should be tailored to promote innovation, not simply to validate preconceived rights through the threat of exorbitantly expensive lawsuits.

As the Commissioner has suggested in San Jose, there is a dearth of economic analysis of the patent system, but there are costs that are real, and for multimedia designers, frightening.

Stanford Professor John Barton estimates the average cost of patent litigation at $500,000 per claim per side. The cost of insurance against an inadvertent patent infringement is a minimum of $50,000 per multimedia product with a $50,000 deductible. That's a marketplace measure of the tax that the patent system places on our industry.

This figure is likely to be five or ten times the cost of conventional errors and omissions insurance which covers most other liabilities. This figure functions as one benchmark that multimedia developers will look to to gauge the Patent and Trademark Office and the administration and their efforts to protect the expression in the multimedia age.

We look forward to working with the Patent and Trademark Office to perfect the process that we must support as an industry. Thank you, Mr. Commissioner and members of the panel, for this opportunity to express the concerns of multimedia developers and publishers.

COMMISSIONER LEHMAN: Thank you very much, Mr. Lippincott. We appreciate your comments. They were so thorough that I don't have any questions. You answered all of them.

UNITED STATES PATENT AND TRADEMARK OFFICE
Public Hearing on Patent Protection for Software-Related Inventions
Arlington, Virginia -- February 10 & 11, 1994

MR. LIPPINCOTT: All right.

COMMISSIONER LEHMAN: Next, I'd like to ask Mr. Robert Yoches from Finnegan, Henderson, Farabow, Garrett & Dunner to come forward.

PRESENTATION BY E. ROBERT YOCHES

FINNEGAN, HENDERSON, FARABOW, GARRETT & DUNNER

MR. YOCHES: Thank you, Mr. Commissioner. My name is Bob Yoches and I am with Finnegan, Henderson, Farabow, Garrett & Dunner; and I am presenting my own views today, not the views of the firm, and not the views of the clients of the firm.

What I would like to address specifically are Questions three through six of topic B. However, the testimony I give may apply to other topics as well.

Questions three through six really address the issue of whether the examination standard for patents on software-related inventions should differ from patents on other technologies. I don't believe it should. The primary reason is, I don't think it's possible and I don't think it's warranted.

I don't think it's possible because as many other witnesses in San Jose testified, it is difficult, if not impossible, but certainly impractical to distinguish between software-related inventions and inventions based on other technologies. Certainly the history of software has arisen many times as an evolution from hardware to firmware and finally to software.

Moreover, we found, and many witnesses have testified, that software is ubiquitous. It is in many different technologies and it is in many different aspects of the life. It is no longer a separate and identifiable part of the technology that can be treated differently.

More to the point though, if some distinction were made, I fear that what would result is some sort of game playing. In the Patent Office we saw this in the 1970s where clever patent agents and patent attorneys tried to get around the reluctance of the Office to grant software-related patents by changing the specification and claims to make it look not like a computer, even though that's what the invention was.

Another problem that I see arising from having different standards for examining patent applications for certain inventions is in the area of litigation. Because I think if you have a higher standard for examining applications for software-related technology that what you'll do is cheapen the patents on the other technology, because there isn't a patent lawyer around who when attacking a patent on a non-software-related technology won't point out to the jury or judge that this patent didn't receive the special treatment that the Patent Office gives to computer patents.

Attorneys representing patentees that have a patent based on the software-related technology will argue just the opposite, that this patent received that special attention that the Patent Office has reserved for computer related inventions.

The other practical problem I see in having different standards for examination is one in the Patent Office, and that is a training problem. I don't need to tell you how difficult it is to train the examiners with regard to issues of 102 and 103 and obviousness and novelty.

If they have to learn not one, but two different standards, and if they also have to use their judgment of when to apply the one standard as opposed to the other standard, I think that the training costs and the quality of examination will drop.

There is, however, I think a larger problem in even asking the question of having different standards and that's a philosophical problem, because the questions are based on the underlying assumption that there's something wrong with software-related patents that issue from the Patent Office now. I don't know that that's been shown.

Certainly there's no question but software is a different technology than other technologies, but you could make the same argument about any technology. I don't think that there's been a demonstration, other than by some anecdotal indications that the software patents are any better or worse than patents related to any other technology.

In fact, to the contrary, I have found that especially in Group 2300 with Director Goldberg, that there's been an increased effort and an intense effort to improve the examination process. In fact, as you may know, the AIPLA and the Patent Office held a joint program last fall, a program we hope to continue, where there was an open dialogue between the Office and between the practitioners to try to improve communications and improve the examination process.

More to the point, however, changing the standard for examining patents will not really address the problems which have been raised. Those are the lack of prior art and the inability to retain examiners.

And now to the specific questions. Question three asks whether the Patent Office should impose a special duty, a higher duty, on applicants having a software-related invention to disclose information. I'm not quite sure what's being indicated there because the current duty is quite high. I assume that the additional duty would require some sort of a search.

However, most of the places that patent attorneys search are the same places that the patent examiners would search. So I don't know that you'd get a better examination process. What you would get, however, is a lot more charges of fraud on the Patent Office because information that should have been discovered wasn't discovered and given to the Patent Office. And as the Federal Circuit has already noted, charges of inequitable conduct and fraud are a plague on the patent system.

Question four asks whether the standards of novelty and obviousness accurately reflect the inventive activity in that area. I think they have to. The standards which the Patent Office is supposed to apply are independent of a particular

UNITED STATES PATENT AND TRADEMARK OFFICE
Public Hearing on Patent Protection for Software-Related Inventions
Arlington, Virginia -- February 10 & 11, 1994

technology and they involve what the state of the art is and they involve what the level of ordinary skill in that art is.

And the way those standards are supposed to reflect the particular technology, it's just supposed to be applied to that technology. So the state of the art and the computer technology will track whatever those changes are and the level of skill will also track those changes.

Question five asks whether we should implement, I suspect, a per se rule, that if the underlying process is known that merely implementing on a computer is not patentable. Again, I don't think so. I think that the present legal standard which asks the Patent Office and asks the courts to look at the claim as a whole is the proper one because I can imagine situations where either because of difficulties and practicalities or because of common knowledge in the art, it was not thought possible or a good idea to implement a certain process on a computer.

Although I can't give you a specific example from real life, one that came to mind on my way over here is the idea of a product I had just seen, which is supposed to improve the grammar and the style of writing. Now certainly English teachers have been doing this for years. It's a known process of how to improve grammar and style.

But implementing it on a computer, I suspect, is pretty difficult. Although there is a product out there and maybe it's prior art now, I don't think that we should have a per se rule saying that type of product does not merit patent protection.

Finally, Question six addresses the general question of whether the PTO should change its examination procedures for novelty and obviousness in this area, and there are three subparts. The first asks whether the Patent Office should require applicants to conduct a search and distinguish their inventions from the prior art in the search.

Now the Patent Office already has a procedure for doing this if you want to get expedited examination. What I think will happen is two things. One is, if this rule existed right now I would pay the extra fee, which is not too much, and get the expedited examination.

I don't know whether the Patent Office examination though of software-related patents would improve, because again the searches that are conducted generally are from the same database as the examiners use.

Question B asks whether the Office should impose a special requirement on applicants to show that their inventions are distinct over the prior art independent of their computer implementation. I have addressed that before. The invention is the invention as a whole and, indeed, part of the invention may rely on how it was implemented by a computer.

Question C asks whether the PTO should be allowed to establish that a software-related invention is not novel or obvious using a lower standard, in other words, not a prime facie case. I'm a little confused here because I don't know what could be a lower standard.

The prime facie case merely asks the examiner to do two things. One is to find art that shows each one of the claim elements; and, two, show that there's some motivation for combining those elements. I suspect the lower standard could either be removing the criteria for motivation or allowing the examiner to reject applications based on his or her gut feel.

In my experience, both occur right now. Whether they should or they shouldn't is another issue. But I don't think it's appropriate that, again, you should be applying different standards here. I don't believe that the result will be any better patents. It will just be a longer and more drawn out examination process.

My conclusion is this. I believe that if you adopt more stringent or even different examination standards for a certain class of inventions, whether it be software-related or others, that you'll be opening up a Pandora's Box that will create many more problems than it's intended to solve. Thank you.

COMMISSIONER LEHMAN: Thank you very much, Mr. Yoches.

Next I'd like to ask Stephen Noe, counsel to Caterpillar, Inc., representing Intellectual Property Owners, Inc. to come forward and share.

PRESENTATION BY STEPHEN L. NOE

CATERPILLAR, INC.

MR. NOE: Thank you. I am Stephen Noe, but I am sort of Stephen Noe as well, Intellectual Property Council for Caterpillar, that well-known earth moving and computer company in Peoria, Illinois.

Today I'm representing the Intellectual Property Owners, a nonprofit association whose members include companies, universities, individuals who own and are interested in intellectual properties.

My testimony has been approved by the Board of Directors for IPO for presentation as an IPO position as well. Caterpillar is a member organization of the IPO and is truly an interested party in its own right, as both a producer and major user of computer software.

Today's hearing -- I have to thank Mr. Yoches for shortening my necessary presentation. But I want to amplify some of the things he said. Today's hearing presupposes the continued availability of patent projection for the computer software implemented inventions, a position strongly endorsed by the IPO and focuses on the examination of those applications.

However, implicit in this series of hearings is the suggestion that software is somehow different from other technologies and must be treated in some special way. I disagree. Considering some of the remarks made at the recent hearings in San Jose and even some this morning, just agreeing on what is and what is not software-related technology may be an exercise for Humpty Dumpty from Alice in Wonderland where a word means just what I choose it to mean. Nothing more nor less.

UNITED STATES PATENT AND TRADEMARK OFFICE
Public Hearing on Patent Protection for Software-Related Inventions
Arlington, Virginia – February 10 & 11, 1994

For purposes of my testimony I'll use software or software-related technology in the broad sense, to include discreet software products like word processors or speaker timing computers, highly complex custom software that controls manufacturing systems and imbedded software that controls engines, anti-lock braking systems, perhaps your microwave oven.

One can readily come up with other examples, some of which may look and feel more or less what we think of as software traditionally, but all of which lie along a continuum of software-related technology. Whether an automobile engine is controlled by a camshaft or a microprocessor it makes little difference to the driver of that automobile who only cares that the engine run well and reliably.

Patent policy should not be the factor that forces a manufacturer to choose which tool to use to control that engine. The IPO supports treating software-related technology like any other technology within the scope of the patent system. Continued patent protection of software-related technology is important to the United States' industrial competitiveness.

The PTO should process applications for patents on software no differently than applications in any other technology, either in examination procedure or in the way the statutory tests are applied. In particular, the IPO rejects the proposal that software-related patent application should be subject to special tests or standards governing novelty, nonobviousness or disclosure.

The first noticed question related to the adequacy of prior art. Patents and more significantly printed publications do provide a sufficient and representative collection of prior art to assess novelty and obviousness. Examiners access to and understanding of the printed publications is the issue, not the existence of the publications.

Several avenues are available to and should be used by the PTO to improve its access to and its ability to apply software-related prior art.

These include supplementing its own collections with non-patent references, reclassifying and computerizing those collections as necessary, encouraging the development of readily accessible prior art collections outside the Office, collections such as that we have heard discussed this morning being put together by the Software Patent Institute in Ann Arbor, Michigan, training its existing examiners in the technical programming skills necessary to understand and properly apply the prior art references that they do find, and hiring as fully qualified examiners computer scientists or others who are trained in software technology.

A number of these activities are currently being implemented and the IPO applauds and encourages these efforts. Jerry Goldberg has been especially active in this area and I've spoken with Jerry many times about this.

The hearing notice also asks if a special duty of disclosure should apply to applicants for software-related inventions. Such a burden would be neither fair nor workable. Even knowing when the duty applies would be difficult and subject to interpretation. There simply is no bright line separating software-related inventions from other inventions.

Instead, there is a continuum of software-relatedness, which encompasses products of all descriptions. Developers who implement their inventions using software should not be penalized for doing so by the patent system.

The notice then moves to focus on the PTO examination procedures, the area that Bob Yoches specifically addressed. Once again, there simply should be no special standards or tests applied to or duties imposed upon applicants in software-related applications.

The difficulties in examining these applications result from examiners unfamiliar with the technology attempting to examine applications using incomplete prior art collections. These difficulties can and should be corrected by supplementing the art collections and improving the expertise.

A mandatory duty to search for, disclose and discuss prior art in software-related applications would be a powerful incentive to characterize inventions as other than software-related in an attempt to avoid the burdens and disadvantages of that duty. Examiners will try to impose the requirement; applicants will try to avoid it; and the quality of examination and classification will suffer.

One item of software-related technology the PTO should follow closely and make early use of is the national information infrastructure of the high speed data highway. I noticed in Commissioner Lehman's comments that this has begun. The Internet is being used by the PTO already.

A major problem underlying the difficulty in examining software-related patent applications is information related. The PTO does not have sufficient access to the best prior art information and the public has no convenient access to the PTO search files. The proposed data highway could close this information gap, providing a common resource to searchers, both within and outside of the PTO.

As Mr. Lippincott pointed out earlier this morning, this technology could even offer a cost effective way to implement early publication of pending applications, allowing interested parties to review the applications and provide relative art. This approach would take advantage of the knowledge of those most informed in the field of software technology and most concerned about the issuance of software-related patents.

What difficulties the applicants face in complying with existing disclosure requirements? The best mode requirement in U.S. law used to be a non-issue. The best mode issue seldom arose in patent contests. However, recent judicial opinions have caused quite a stir in this area and patent practitioners have responded as they believe necessary to protect their clients. Some in an abundance of caution feel the need to submit program source or object code listings.

The PTO cannot unilaterally resolve this matter. Resolution must await legislative or judicial clarification. However, the Office could begin accepting code listings on standard machine readable media containing printable files.

UNITED STATES PATENT AND TRADEMARK OFFICE
Public Hearing on Patent Protection for Software-Related Inventions
Arlington, Virginia -- February 10 & 11, 1994

The PTO should not, however, require patent applicants to confirm to any standardized disclosure format for such applications. No one format can be the best for all the wide range of software-related technology. What would simplify examination in the Office might well complicate others' understanding of the resulting patent or complicate litigation relating to that patent.

The issues commented on here today are important ones for all of American industry, because software permeates every facet of technology today. Industry needs the assurance of patent protection for innovative developments, software-related or otherwise, to maintain and improve technological leadership. Software-related technology is not inherently different from any other new technology that the patent system has faced and adapted to in the past and will be called upon to deal with in the future.

The problem that exists today lies not with the technology, but with the initial PTO reluctance to meet it head on. The PTO resisted until the courts insisted. Had the patent system and the technology grown side-by-side as is the usual case, there would be no hearings today.

Now the PTO is a bit behind the curve, but progress is being made. This is the time to accelerate, support and encourage the adaptation to this technology, not to make a special case of it.

Who can say what the next generation of innovation will bring. What will be the software issue of the future? With appropriate training, tools, and hiring practices the PTO can examine software-related applications just as capably as anything else and the patent law can remain technology neutral as it must. Thank you.

COMMISSIONER LEHMAN: Thank you very much, Mr. Noe. What is IPO's position with regard to the issue of pre-publication?

MR. NOE: I feel it supports the concept of pre-publication provided that it's done with sufficient safeguards to the applicant. For example, the applicant should have the opportunity to withdraw the application prior to publication if that is to come to be.

COMMISSIONER LEHMAN: Thank you very much.

I'd just like to observe that there already are differences in examination procedures among different examining groups and different technologies, certainly in Group 1800 which does biotechnology and we do a lot of searches of DNA sequences. We have an examination technique and procedure really that is quite different. So we can distinguish between the technologies without necessarily changing legal standards among the technologies.

Next, I'd like to call John Horn, Patent Counsel for Allen-Bradley Corporation. Are you representing Allen-Bradley or yourself, Mr. Horn?

PRESENTATION BY JOHN HORN

ALLEN-BRADLEY

MR. HORN: I'm representing Allen-Bradley this morning, sir. Good morning, my name is John Horn. I'm Patent Counsel for Allen-Bradley Company, which is a manufacturer of industrial automation equipment, such as programmable logic controllers and including an increasing number of software products.

Allen-Bradley has observed a strong trend in the industrial control business towards replacing functions accomplished by hardware with software. Industrial control hardware and industrial control software can and frequently do have very similar functionalities.

Consequently, patent claims can closely correspond between hardware and software based inventions. In view of the above, we believe new software based functions should be patentable in the same way as new hardware based inventions are patentable.

However, we also believe that it is important that patent examiners should look to hardware based prior art and that previously existing hardware based functionality should always be viewed as highly relevant to the allowability of software based claims. Novelty should it not be predicated on the coding of functions previously implemented in hardware.

Although new functions which may be enabled by software's special capabilities should be patentable when they rise to the level of being novel and non-obvious improvements on previous hardware based techniques.

It appears to us that inventions and patent claims focusing on the software art form itself, such as programming techniques, may at least temporarily require some new procedures for identifying prior art. Allen-Bradley supports the idea of establishing new mechanisms for identifying prior art pertinent to software inventions in order to assist in getting the best prior art into the hands of the examining corps.

However, Allen-Bradley also believes that software inventions should be treated in like fashion to inventions in other technological fields and higher standards for patentability of software inventions should not be adopted. Software would appear to us to be a new and distinct type of technological art form. As such, it may have some growing pains at the Patent Office and elsewhere.

Nevertheless, software inventions need protection to promote creativity and protect the investments of innovative developers. Consequently, we would like to encourage the Patent Office as well to recognize software as independently capable of having patentable elements, such as specialized data structures, when such elements are novel and non-obvious.

Separately, Allen-Bradley does not believe computer program code listings are an effective way to describe software inventions. In general, such listings we have found to be arcane and too difficult to decipher to enable most software inventions to be understood and used.

Thank you. Allen-Bradley looks forward to working with the Patent Office in trying to improve the patenting process.

UNITED STATES PATENT AND TRADEMARK OFFICE
Public Hearing on Patent Protection for Software-Related Inventions
Arlington, Virginia -- February 10 & 11, 1994

COMMISSIONER LEHMAN: Thank you very much, Mr. Horn.

Next, I'd like to call forward Mr. Richard Nydegger for the Digital Equipment Corporation. He's going to be replacing Ron Ryland who was scheduled to represent Digital this morning. You need to correct your representational status here, Mr. Nydegger.

MR. NYDEGGER: Yes, I will. Thank you.

PRESENTATION BY RICHARD NYDEGGER

WORKMAN, NYDEGGER & JENSEN

MR. NYDEGGER: Good morning, Mr. Commissioner, members of the panel, and fellow participants. My name is Rick Nydegger. I am a patent attorney and I practice with the law firm of Workman, Nydegger & Jensen in Salt Lake City, which specializes in intellectual property law. I'm also an Adjunct Professor of Law at the University of Utah, College of Law and I am a past-Chair of the Electronic and Computer Law Committee of the American Intellectual Property Law Association. I currently serve on the Board of that Association.

The views which I express today, however, are my own views and I appreciate this opportunity to participate in this proceeding and to add my comments to the record of these hearings.

First, I wish to make a few introductory comments, which I will then follow with specific comments in response to the subject of this hearing, namely standards and practices used in examination of patent applications for software-related inventions.

Much has been written and said by way of criticism about overly broad patents having been granted by the PTO for software-related inventions. However, it should be remembered that these types of problems are not unique to software-related inventions alone, but have existed and will exist in connection with any type of new and rapidly emerging technology.

Indeed, in the celebrated Telegraph case that was decided by the Supreme Court in 1854, the eighth claim in Samuel Morris' patent on the telegraph was ultimately invalidated as being overly broad, although granted initially by the Patent Office.

However, equally important though often overlooked is the fact that the first seven claims in Mr. Morris' patent were upheld, thus providing broad protection for a new technology which spawned a whole new industry.

In a similar fashion, in 1888 Alexander Graham Bell's patent for the telephone was also challenged as being overly broad. Claim five of Bell's patent was contained in a mere five lines which simply read, "The method of and apparatus for transmitting vocal or other sounds telegraphically as herein described by causing electrical emulations, similar and formal vibrations of the air accompanying the vocal or other sounds."

Yet in upholding that claim the Supreme Court said, "It may be that electricity cannot be used at all for the transmission of speech except in the way Bell has discovered it. And that, therefore, practically his patent gives him this exclusive use for that purpose. But that does not make his claim one for the use of electricity distinct from the particular process with which it is connected in his patent. It will, if true, show more clearly the great importance of his discovery, but it will not invalidate his patent."

Those skilled in the art of prosecuting patent applications for software-related inventions will readily appreciate the similarities between the claims and the issues raised in the telegraph and telephone cases and the issues raised by the claims in many software-related inventions.

I cite these historical examples merely to point out that criticism and charges of overly broad patents that are issued by the Patent Office are not something new, particularly when dealing with fundamentally new and rapidly changing technologies.

Yet the fact remains that in both these cases, as in many others, protection under the patent system was broadly afforded to these emerging technologies on which entire industries were ultimately founded.

That's not to say that the U.S. patent system as it presently exists is without problems that need to be carefully examined. Indeed, I strongly support the increased efforts being made by the Patent Office, including these hearings, to become more customer oriented and to create a stronger sense of partnership with American inventors at all levels.

However, when examining the problems that may exist under the patent system there is a need for temperance and we should be slow to illuminate or narrowly circumscribe protection for any new or emerging technology simply because the newness of that technology makes it difficult to search, difficult to disclose or difficult to apply statutory standards of eligibility or patentability.

With these remarks in mind, I turn to some particular comments on examination standards and practices that will, it is hoped, suggest possible ways to strengthen the patent system and the way in which the patent system can serve to both reward and foster innovation as well as to continue to strengthen our country's economy and the ability to compete in an increasingly competitive global marketplace.

Specifically, I wish to direct my remaining comments to four areas. One, improving access to relevant prior art; two, improving the experience, training and retention of qualified examiners; three, reducing the present emphasis on pendency time and adopting early publication procedures; and four, expanding third party participation in reexamination and opposition proceedings.

On point number one, improving access to relevant prior art, for pure software systems such as application programs, computer operating systems, network operating systems, database management systems to name just a few, access to prior art other than patents or printed publications is needed because many such pure software techniques have not been documented or published in traditional ways. Much is already being done to rectify those problems.

UNITED STATES PATENT AND TRADEMARK OFFICE
Public Hearing on Patent Protection for Software-Related Inventions
Arlington, Virginia -- February 10 & 11, 1994

Efforts such as the APS classified search and retrieval system, private efforts such as those that Dr. Bernard Galler with respect to the Software Patent Institute and others are commendable and are helping to develop an adequate prior art database.

The PTO has and should continue to request voluntary submission of product descriptions, user manuals, administrator guides and programming guides and soft copy from software developers for addition to the PTO's library.

The current reclassification efforts with respect to software-related inventions have been successful. And Director Jerry Goldberg and his team in Group 2300 of the PTO have been doing an excellent job of reclassifying software-related technology within the Patent Office.

In addition to the extent that such a source has not already been considered, a classification system which takes into account classifications proposed by the IEEE and the ACM might be considered. These classification systems represent industry efforts to classify software-related technology.

Continued effort in all of these areas is needed. Another way to provide patent examiners with access to the most complete up-to-date prior art is to solicit the assistance of those most interested in seeing to it that patents with overbroad claims do not issue, by providing for publication prior to grant and by providing an opportunity for interested parties to submit relevant prior art before issuance. This is discussed further in point three below.

On point number two, improving the experience, training and retention of qualified examiners, patent examiners who are not well qualified or trained or who lack adequate resources will not be able to adequately assess an invention's patentability.

Thus, patent examiners need to have proper background in the software-related arts and every effort needs to be made to retain well-qualified and experienced examiners. One way to ensure that patent examiners have proper training in the field of software-related technology is to recognize computer science as a science for the purpose of serving as a patent examiner. I was pleased to hear that things are moving in that direction currently.

Another important step toward improving the examining corps' performance level in the field of software-related technology is to improve the retention rate of examiners. On-the-job training builds examiner confidence and examiners should be encouraged to stay on the job.

I believe the PTO should consider conducting a comprehensive study to find ways of increasing the retention rate of well-qualified, trained and experienced examiners and to provide adequate resources in terms of physical support facilities and personnel to permit efficient and thorough examination to be carried out.

On point number three, reducing the present emphasis on pendency time and adopting early publication procedures, the PTO should decrease the present emphasis on pendency time concurrent with adopting early publication procedures. The current emphasis by the PTO on pendency time is, I believe, misplaced since a patent is an important means for disclosing details concerning new technology.

The important question is not pendency time, but rather time to publication. This concept is recognized in the patent laws of most major industrial countries which provide for publication of an application 18 months after the priority date.

Delays in publication can mean that the technology disclosed in a patent is not available to the public in a timely fashion, which may delay further development of the technology and may also lead to problems with so-called submarine patents.

The present emphasis on reducing pendency time by the PTO has a number of undesirable consequences on the examination process. For example, if a patent issues within the approximately 18 month pendency time as now suggested by the PTO, prior art from foreign patent tribunals is most likely not available for consideration by the U.S. examiner.

Having this prior art is particularly important in the software-related arts and would further help to protect against issuance of overly broad patents. It would make for a more complete examination and higher degree of confidence in the validity of an issued patent for such inventions.

It is thus suggested that consideration be given by the PTO to publishing applications 18 months from the priority date. This publication should be contingent upon providing a search report prior to publication to permit the applicant to amend or withdraw the application prior to publication.

Following publication the applicant should be entitled to recover damages for use of the invention after publication but prior to issuance in the event of infringement. Examination could then take place in a more contemplated environment.

It should be noted that early publication can also operate as an early notification to others working in the field of the potential issuance of the patent, allowing them to factor that into their business decisions and thus minimizing the problems with submarine patents as noted above.

On point number four, expanding third party participation in reexamination proceedings, the PTO should consider changing the current procedures governing reexamination. The problem of patents that are issued with overbroad claims could be reduced by changing the current procedures governing reexamination.

Third parties are reluctant to institute reexamination because of the essentially ex parte nature of such proceedings. The PTO should expand the ability of third party petitioners to participate in reexamination after the petition for reexamination is granted. If such a reform were made, the use of reexamination would increase and the reliance on the courts would decrease.

UNITED STATES PATENT AND TRADEMARK OFFICE
Public Hearing on Patent Protection for Software-Related Inventions
Arlington, Virginia -- February 10 & 11, 1994

In conclusion, Mr. Commissioner, I believe that the above-proposed changes would serve to greatly strengthen the U.S. patent system in ways that would appropriately further the progress in science and useful arts as contemplated under the Constitution and in ways that would continue to help U.S. industry to effectively compete by protecting the investment of U.S. companies in important new technologies of the type typified by the software and electronics industries. Thank you.

COMMISSIONER LEHMAN: Thank you very much, Mr. Nydegger, for those thoughts and for coming all the way from Utah to be with us.

I'd like to mention a couple of housekeeping items at this point. I'd like to remind the speakers that if they have prepared remarks it would really be helpful to us. If you haven't already given them to us, if you would give them either to Jeff Kushan right here or Mike Fleming who is circulating around here someplace, who I introduced before.

Also, for any members of the press or media who are here interested in this, I'd like to note that Ruth Ford is our Director of Media Relations. I don't think she's here in the room right now, but will be very happy to help you with anything you need. And you can reach her at the Commissioner's office at 703-305-8600.

Next, I'd like to ask Allan Ratner, the President of the Philadelphia Patent Law Association from Ratner & Prestia to come forward.

PRESENTATION BY ALLAN RATNER

PHILADELPHIA PATENT LAW ASSOCIATION

Mr. RATNER. I'm Allan Ratner of Valley Forge, Pennsylvania. I'm representing Ratner & Prestia. We're a firm of 13 attorneys, 7 of whom specialize and mainly work in software, computers and sophisticated electronics.

I'm also representing the Philadelphia Patent Law Association. That's a 400 member association with members in New Jersey, Pennsylvania and Delaware. I'm familiar with the views of our membership and I state for the record that at this time these remarks are being considered by the Association and will be soon acted upon by the Board.

I personally have been prosecuting and licensing software-related inventions for more than 25 years and have seen the continuous growth of the law and the practice and changes in the law and the PTO practice as time goes on. I've seen this positive evolution continuing to better protect the public interest and better protect the burgeoning technology, the software technology.

My remarks -- in considering protection for software it's important to view the industries impacted by any potential changes in the patent law. First, what products fall under the umbrella of software-related inventions. The request for comment refers to the software industry and programming services, prepackaged software and computer integrated design.

However, there is no single software industry. Certainly there is a large expanding prepackaged software industry and the U.S. patent system should reflect policies that encourage and protect innovation within this industry. But equally important are those many industries that produce machinery and electronic systems in which imbedded microprocessors and microcontrollers use control functions.

In 1992 a single U.S. manufacturer sold nearly 250 microcontroller chips, each of which is used to provide control functions in a hardware system.

The list of products controlled using these imbedded chips is virtually endless. The following is a brief list, intended only to show diversity. Every one of these systems is controlled to some extent by software executed in the imbedded microprocessor or microcontroller. Every one of them is a software-related invention.

We have telephone CT scanners; MRI systems for imaging the human body; televisions and TV converter boxes; electronic test signal generators; automobile subsystems, including ignition systems, anti-lock brakes, traction control, airbags; chemical process control equipment; agricultural equipment; microwave ovens; facsimile machines; sewing machines; dishwashers; signal processing equipment; camcorders; automatic bank teller machines.

We have clients in many of these fields -- small clients, emerging companies, mid-sized companies and large companies -- all of which use patents to protect their technology.

The trend toward increased use of software in imbedded chips is expected to continue as the cost of chips decreases. The decision to use chips is a design choice and is determined by such factors as cost, design delays, comparing software against the same functions in hardware, such as ASICS. They also consider whether the functions of the product will change frequently, in which case software reduces life cycle development costs.

Thus, it is impossible to define a single software industry. Admittedly, at one end of the spectrum there are application software developers who have low capital costs and who are able to bring their products to market rapidly.

Nonetheless, at the other end, U.S. auto manufacturers, for example, rely on software to improve the comfort and safety of their cars. Few industries have higher capital costs than the auto industry and delays in bringing new products to market are common.

For example, testing of airbags in an actual car is neither fast nor expensive and, of course, software controls the operation of the airbag. There are countless other industries that rely on software-related inventions which do not have low capital costs or short development cycles and any attempt to define a software industry is bound to fail.

Furthermore, the industries that use imbedded microprocessors and controllers are in need of the protections offered by the patent system that are not available through other forms of IP protection.

UNITED STATES PATENT AND TRADEMARK OFFICE
Public Hearing on Patent Protection for Software-Related Inventions
Arlington, Virginia -- February 10 & 11, 1994

Defining separate standards for patenting hardware and software is likely to result in inadequate protection for software-related inventions that do not fit neatly into the precise pigeon holes of hardware systems and software systems.

Although it is more common to see hardware circuitry replaced by software implementations, this is not a one-way street. As computer aided design techniques improve, a growing number of hardware designs are created by implementing functions in software from which designs for dedicated hardware are automatically generated.

Given the ability to implement many algorithms in either hardware or software elements that are functionally equivalent, there is no compelling reason for penalizing an inventor that selects one implementation over another. On the contrary, the inventor who identifies that a software implementation is better, i.e. less expensive or faster to bring to the marketplace, has given something more valuable to society than the inventor that discloses a functional equivalent -- but more expensive -- hardware embodiment.

The fact that the inventor has disclosed a software embodiment of the invention that is easier to implement increases the value to the public and the inventor should be rewarded.

35 U.S.C. 112 requires that the inventor disclose the best mode. Ever increasingly, the best mode for many machines and systems include software elements. A software solution to a control function may be the preferred mode. 112 requires disclosure of that software embodiment. Without protection for the inventive concepts that are in software, there would be little incentive for inventors to disclosure software-related inventions in the United States industries.

Thus, the fundamental constitutional mandate for promoting progress in the useful arts would not be met. In this way the contributions of software engineers, control engineers and systems analysts have been rewarded and encouraged.

Coming out to Part B, they seem to reflect a response to a number of criticisms, many of which reflect the public's misunderstanding with respect to standards applied in the examination of software-related inventions.

Both the PTO and the Patent Bar should emphasize that hardware and software-related inventions have been and continue to be subject to the same standards with respect to novelty and unobviousness during examination. It has never passed muster to take a known system or a known process and without more implement that system or process in software. A conventional hardware system by itself ported over into software is still a conventional system.

There is no public policy reason to define a higher standard of patentability for a software-related invention than for any other invention. Now some patents covering software-related inventions have been questioned because the Code is written following well-known programming skills. This is not and should not be the standard for patentability used by examiners.

The relevant field of the invention is usually never computer programming itself, even for inventions in software application programs. The field may be systems engineering; operating systems; networks; database architecture; electronic design; automatic control system design; electromechanical system design; chemical process engineering or others.

The inventor very often is the system architect, the person who conceives of the system and its concepts. The programmer acts as a technician under the inventor's direction -- a technician.

A valid concern has been raised that examiners do not have access to a comprehensive base of prior art. One approach to solving this problem is to improve the access to materials within the PTO's library, which presently is quite extensive, as well as improving access to on-line prior art databases that increase the examiner's productivity.

These techniques are being implemented and more funds should be put into them. Perhaps the single most effective method of providing a more comprehensive base of prior art to the examiner is to enlist the assistance of other parties who have a stake in the outcome if a patent is issued. These parties include both third parties and the applicants themselves.

With respect to third parties, the current patent law presents obstacles for third parties who would otherwise be inclined to submit prior art. With adequate safeguards -- that's important, with adequate safeguards -- early publication of all patent applications may be one way to enable third parties to submit prior art during the pendency of applications. This particular way has problems but that is being considered.

Increased third party participation in post issuance reexamination proceedings may also encourage the submission of prior art by third parties. Thank you.

COMMISSIONER LEHMAN: Thank you very much, Mr. Ratner, for those really thoughtful comments.

Next, I'd like to ask Dianne Callan, Deputy General Counsel of the Lotus Development Corporation to come forward. She will talking with us on behalf of the Business Software Alliance.

PRESENTATION BY DIANNE CALLAN

LOTUS DEVELOPMENT CORPORATION

MS. CALLAN: Good morning, Mr. Secretary. My name is Diane Callan and I am Deputy General Counsel of Lotus Development Corporation. I am speaking to you this morning on behalf of the Business Software Alliance.

On behalf of the BSA I would like to thank you for convening this hearing to consider these important issues and we appreciate the opportunity to speak to you.

The BSA was organized in 1988 to promote the continued growth of the software industry through its public policy, education and enforcement programs in the United States

UNITED STATES PATENT AND TRADEMARK OFFICE
Public Hearing on Patent Protection for Software-Related Inventions
Arlington, Virginia -- February 10 & 11, 1994

and in more than 50 countries throughout North America, Europe, Asia and Latin America.

BSA members are actively involved in nearly all aspects of microcomputer software development, including production of operating systems, application software and networking software.

The current BSA members who are participating in this statement include ALDUS Corporation, Apple Computer, Inc., Autodesk, Inc., Intergraph Corporation, Lotus Development Corporation, Microsoft Corporation, Novell, Inc. and WordPerfect Corporation.

In the last five years every government, academic and industry study of technologies that are key to America's futures have identified the vital role to be played by the software industry. Software is characterized by both rapid technological innovation and widespread use in downstream markets.

Software innovation improves the competitiveness of other industries which utilize software products to make them more innovative and more competitive. The benefits of continuous software innovation permeate much of the American economy.

In March of last year the BSA released a study prepared by Economists, Inc. entitled "The U.S. Software Industry/Economic Contribution in the U.S. and World Markets." Based on government and industry information, the study reviewed the economic contribution made to the American economy by U.S. core software industry. By core software we mean prepackaged software, custom computer programming services and computer integrated design.

The Economists' study found that the core industry is the fastest growing industry in the United States, is now larger than all but five manufacturing industries, is contributing to the economy of virtually every state in the nation, and is achieving tremendous success in the international marketplace.

Notwithstanding this impressive record, the software industry's role in the growth of the nation's economy will be even more critical in the future as new and more advanced technologies continue to evolve.

The BSA has several views which we would like to share at this hearing. First of all, we believe that strong intellectual property protection is essential to the continued health and growth of the software industry. Software is difficult and expensive to create, yet easy to steal or duplicate.

Moreover, the real value of the software and the principal assets of a software company are not its tangible factories or raw material inventories. Apart from its employees, buildings and computer equipment, the assets of a software company are intellectual property, the technology embodied in the computer programs that are their products.

Second, the BSA does not believe that a new form of protection for software-related inventions is necessary or desirable. There is, however, an urgent need to improve

the operation of the United States patent system as it pertains to software-related inventions.

Patents continue to be issued, which do not appear to meet the statutory mandates of novelty and nonobviousness. And these patents impose a substantial cost on the software industry and on society as a whole. Those aspects of the patent system that permit long gestation periods for patents also cause economic cost to society without providing commensurate benefits.

Let me emphasize that members of the BSA have widely divergent views as to the values of patents being granted for software-related inventions. However, all the members recognize that the current patent system does not adequately deal with such patents.

Therefore, these comments which are the minimum common points agreed upon by the participating BSA members primarily suggest procedural changes to the operation of the patent system to improve its effectiveness regarding the protection of software-related inventions.

The BSA respectfully suggests several changes to improve the effectiveness of the system. First, the patent system should run for a fixed time from the filing date. An important problem with the patent system is the issuance of patents after inordinately long application periods, brought about by continuation and continuation in part applications and occasionally interference proceedings.

Whatever the cause, the result is that the sudden appearance of a patent years after the technology to which it relates has been developed and commercialized is an important problem for the industry.

At that point design around possibilities may no longer be feasible and the patent consequently can assume an enormously enhanced power to disrupt long established expectations for a full 17 years from the issue date.

The BSA supports the Commissioner's intention to establish a fixed term from the original filing date, as that would give the patent owner a strong incentive to have her patent issued promptly and would in any case reduce the likelihood of the stealth patent that suddenly appears having lain hidden in the PTO for 15 or more years.

Furthermore, the spur to an applicant to timely present all claims and applications stemming from a single disclosure would promote additional efficiencies in the examination process. The BSA is gratified to learn that the PTO will support legislation embodying this concept.

Our second suggestion is that the examination process should be improved as to the content of the prior art database, the accessibility of this database to the examiners and the training and treatment of the examiners. Most of the prior art regularly available to the PTO examiners comprises collections of patents and publications.

However, especially in the field of software-related patents, much of the relevant art exists not as patents or publications but rather as companies internal technical manuals, reference works, bulletins and other similar documents.

Thus, often the most relevant prior art is not readily available to the examiners of software-related patents. Groups such as the Software Patent Institute have undertaken to compile databases with these types of software-related patent prior art.

It is important, especially in this area, that the PTO expand the universe of the prior art on which it relies and to improve access to that universe. The BSA hereby offers to provide ongoing assistance in establishing and providing content for suitable databases as well as examiner training and software tools for searches in these databases.

Our third suggestion is that applicants should be encouraged to conduct a patentability search before filing and to present the results of that search to the PTO before the application is examined.

Because of the quantity of prior art relating to software-related inventions, as well as the diversity of the nature and location of such prior art, we think that the applicant should be encouraged to conduct a reasonable prior art search and to present those results.

Our fourth suggestion is that an opposition procedure should be established with provisions that ensure expedited results. A third party may often be aware of prior art not readily accessible to the PTO and may also be the entity with the greatest interest in preventing the issuance of a patent covering what is in the prior art.

The BSA believes that providing an opportunity for submissions during prosecution, as is done in the EPO after publication of the application and the EPO search report, would facilitate a more complete view by the examiner of the relevant prior art.

In addition, once claims are allowed an opposition period of sufficient duration to permit reasoned investigations pertaining to those claims would provide the public with a timely and efficient opportunity to submit relevant information pertaining to the claims as they are expected to issue.

Our position, however, is premised on some assumptions. First of all, the fact that a period for filing an opposition has expired without any oppositions having been made would not in any way affect the presumption of the validity of the patent.

Second, that any opposition activity or proceeding would take place in an expedited manner, so that the opposition process cannot be used, as in some countries, including Japan, to unduly delay the issuance of the patent.

And finally, any opposition proceedings would include appropriate procedural safeguards to limit the potential abuses of the process.

The last suggestion that we would like to present today is that the examination procedures should be strengthened and expanded substantively to include non-prior art validity issues.

The current examination process, as was discussed earlier, is generally not viewed as a viable option by opponents to a patent due to the largely ex parte nature of the process. The BSA urges that reexamination be modified to provide more of an inter-parte proceeding, allowing opponents to a patent to feel more comfortable in relying on the procedure to efficiently resolve their concerns in what may be the most efficient forum.

Further, the scope of the reexamination proceedings should be expanded to additionally cover all prior art categories as well as non-prior art, validity and enforceability issues. For example, inequitable conduct regarding an applicant's nondisclosure of material prior art during the prosecution of an application.

The BSA acknowledges and supports the Patent Office's intent to forward to Congress legislation making reexamination a more attractive vehicle for challenging a patent's validity. We appreciate the opportunity of speaking to you.

COMMISSIONER LEHMAN: Thank you very much, Ms. Callan, for sharing that with us. It was a sufficiently complete statement that I really think I understand it and don't really have any questions where you stand.

Before I call our next witness, I just want to say that since we're running a little bit ahead, we may be able to get through to shorten our afternoon session if we can call some of the people who are scheduled to appear this afternoon. I have a list of some people -- Richard Jordan, Jonathan Band, Vern Blanchard, and Jeffrey Berkowitz.

If any of you are here, what I'm going to do is, after the next witness I'm going to at least call one or two of you. And if you're able to, then we can, you know, get your testimony included in the morning session.

With that I'd like to call next R. Duff Thompson, who's the Executive Vice President and General Counsel of the WordPerfect Corporation.

PRESENTATION BY R. DUFF THOMPSON

WORDPERFECT CORPORATION

MR. THOMPSON: Thank you, Mr. Secretary. My name is Duff Thompson. I am speaking to you today on behalf of WordPerfect Corporation, for which I serve as the Executive Vice President and General Counsel. WordPerfect appreciates the opportunity to participate in this hearing regarding the patent process. We certainly applaud the efforts of the Commissioner and others to bring these issues to light.

WordPerfect Corporation is a Utah company employing approximately 5,000 people worldwide. It is the leading supplier of word processing software in the world and other key business applications. WordPerfect is a member of the Business Software Alliance, as has been mentioned, and we support the positions that Ms. Callan has just expressed.

On behalf of WordPerfect, however, I want to emphasize certain points she has made and to add a couple of others. First, WordPerfect Corporation believes with the Business Software Alliance that strong intellectual property protection is essential to the U.S. software industry to

UNITED STATES PATENT AND TRADEMARK OFFICE
Public Hearing on Patent Protection for Software-Related Inventions
Arlington, Virginia -- February 10 & 11, 1994

continue to grow and provide jobs and export revenues for this country.

Because of the ease of copying, software piracy is endemic, not only in this country but around the world. Software companies need vigorous intellectual property protection to secure the fruits of their labors.

Second, like the Business Software Alliance, WordPerfect Corporation does not believe that a suigeneris form of protection for software-related inventions is a viable solution to the problems that exist with the current legal regimes, including patents.

Recent experiences of two types highlight the reasons for these concerns. First, the 1976 amendments to the Copyright Act, an existing statute I might add, took well over a decade to become enacted. Given the number and diversity of views on technical, financial and legal matters relating to software protection and software patents, it seems likely that a new statute could easily be a decade in the making.

During that time we would still have to get along with the system we now have. And as we know, a decade in the software industry is virtually an eternity. Moreover, even if a suigeneris act were enacted, it would necessarily introduce enormous uncertainties into the subject until years of case law development had clarified the many inevitable issues.

We have lots of uncertain areas now within the existing legal framework, but those uncertainties would seem very small indeed compared to the issues that a clean slate approach to this subject would introduce.

WordPerfect in sum believes that the existing statute, regulations and case law are capable of providing an adequate framework for assessing the patentability of software-related inventions.

WordPerfect also believes, however, that two major deficiencies in the application process which have led to enormous expenditures of nonproductive effort and money by software companies need to be addressed.

Time and again software companies have had to respond to patents that should not have been issued because they are, in fact, obvious over very close but non-cited prior art, and to patents that issued a decade or more after the initial application was filed during which time entire related industries have developed, unaware of what I have called buried land mines.

These consequences must be avoided if the health, growth and worldwide competitiveness of the United States software industry is to continue.

First on the issue of the obviousness of some of the patents. Too many software-related patents have issued despite the existence of very close prior art, art which was not found during the examination process. Mr. Secretary, you, yourself, have highlighted what has become the most glaring example of this type of patent in the Compton New Media patent issued in August of '93.

You ordered a reexamination of this patent because it cased a "great deal of angst in the industry." The PTO to its credit departed from normal procedure when it decided to consider additional prior art from the public during the reexamination of the Compton patent.

This action clearly demonstrates the PTO's recognition of the underlying problem, that much of the prior art in the area of software-related inventions is not embodied in patents while existing searching techniques focus on patents. Clearly, the archive of prior art in relevant areas needs to be significantly improved. And the PTO's ability to access that prior art must be greatly enhanced.

In speaking for the BSA, Diane Callan mentioned the possibility of industry assistance to the PTO in setting up databases for prior art with respect to software-related inventions, in providing necessary software tools to ensure meaningful access to those databases and in assisting with training of examiners in these areas.

I'm here today to tell you the WordPerfect Corporation is also ready to participate in that enterprise. We are ready to do our part in helping the PTO improve the examination process. I encourage all similarly situated software vendors to participate in a like manner.

In addition, WordPerfect believes that giving third parties the right to file oppositions to allowed applications would further benefit the PTO and the public. Oppositions would in essence deputize the concerned public. They would enable people with the best knowledge of the subject matter to submit prior art which was not located by the examiner.

In this way the PTO would be assisted, often by experts in the field, in identifying the most relevant prior art. At the same time the interested public has the opportunity to prevent the issuance of an undeserved patent that would otherwise become a scarecrow in the art.

Again, consistent with the BSA statement, WordPerfect's support for the availability of an opposition proceeding is based on the expectation that first the failure of a party to file an opposition would not in any way affect the presumption of validity of an issued patent, either as to that party or generally; and second, any opposition that is filed would be completed in a relatively short period, so as not to unduly delay the issuance of the patent.

Second, on the land mines issue a very small proportion of patents carry a substantially and unfairly disproportionate weight upon being granted. These are often patents that are issued 10, 20 or even more years after the initial application was filed. Often such patents rest buried in prosecution or the public, not knowing about them, develops whole industries related to their subject matter.

Such patents often don't really issue so much as blow up in the unsuspecting public's collective faces. Enormous royalties are often demanded by their owners who have been watching the industry develop, and in many cases drafted claims to read on the products and processes of those industries, taking advantage of accidental disclosures in their applications that can be stretched and tortured to support claims they never considered making until others made the inventions.

The patents then go into expensive and protracted litigation. Two examples make this point. The first is, in 1990 Gilbert Hyatt's patent for a computer on a chip issued. The original application had been filed in 1970 when most of today's computer companies were not yet even contemplated. Yet industry analysts have estimated that Hyatt's patent portfolio may be well worth over $100 million during its 17-year life.

A second example, Jerome Lemelson owns a number of these long hidden patents. For example, his Patent Number 753 covering a bar code scanner issued on July 7, 1992 from a continuation application filed in 1989. However, the original application was filed in December of 1954 and was followed by 11 continuation, division and continuation in part applications

In 1992 alone Lemelson's attorney, who according to the American Lawyer Magazine earned more that year than all the combined partners of Krabath, Swain & Moore and Winston & Strong combined -- I assume to the chagrin of the partners at Krabath, Swain & Moore and Winston & Strong -- negotiated over $400 million in settlements regarding Lemelson's patents.

A racketeering and anti-trust suit filed against Lemelson cites Lemelson's attorney as having written that "Some of Lemelson's pending patent applications were being refined to encompass explicitly the processes that manufacturers were already using in their factories."

Even Judge J. Plager, Circuit Judge of the U.S. Court of Appeals for the Federal Circuit acknowledged this problem in a recent interview by the Journal of Proprietary Rights. As you may know, Judge Plager did not have a patent law background prior to taking the bench on the Federal Circuit. Even so, during the interview on May 12, 1993 Judge Plager supported the idea of switching to a fixed patent term from the date of filing, noting that even in the short time that he had been on the court, which is approximately two plus years, he had picked up "some of the things that go on, the delays that are built into or allowed by the system, all of the things that you can do to game the system."

Thus, WordPerfect wholeheartedly welcomes the PTO's inquiry into legislation which would change the life of a patent to one that expires after a fixed period of time from the original filing date of an application or its earliest parent.

Similarly, WordPerfect urges the PTO to support the publication of all pending applications a fixed time after their filing dates. In these ways, most of the buried land mines would be disarmed or at least have their explosive power lessened, enabling the public to travel a safer landscape of software development.

Finally, WordPerfect requests that the PTO consider one additional item not mentioned in the BSA presentation. That is the vast extension of patent claims by unreasonable application of the doctrine of equivalence to cover software-related inventions which are vastly different in spirit and content from the invention disclosed in the patent.

WordPerfect recognizes that the doctrine of equivalence has a place in patent law and that there are times when the choice between implementing an invention in hardware or software is determined by a variety of factors which do not alter the basic nature of the apparatus or process in question.

However, in other cases the basic nature of the invention as described in a "hardware" patent is qualitatively different from a software implementation. In those cases I suggest the doctrine of equivalence has been applied beyond any reasonable scope.

Thank you for the opportunity to present these remarks.

COMMISSIONER LEHMAN: Thank you very much, Mr. Thompson. I'd like to ask you a question or two if you don't mind.

First, a fairly short one, and I think you've obviously given us the answer, but just to put it on the record, when we were in San Jose, one of the witnesses presented a chart and it showed all of the patent applications that had been filed by various computer software companies. As might be expected, it showed that we had, you know, the largest number in companies like IBM, General Electric, Digital Equipment and so on.

The point was made that some of the most rapidly growing and innovative companies in the business in the last ten years have filed very few applications. You got down to Microsoft and -- I don't know -- there were maybe 13, I think, or 15 applications and the Lotus Development Corporation had about 7; WordPerfect had none. And this was used to indicate that -- basically as a result, I think the message was that certainly the microcomputer industry could do just fine without any patent protection at all.

And yet I don't hear you saying that. Is it your view that the industry has matured to the point that, you know, patents should be a part of the options available to you now, even though you have not -- obviously, any applications that you may have pending are confidential -- but you haven't had any issued?

MR. THOMPSON: We actually have had three issued. I am not sure where that information came from.

COMMISSIONER LEHMAN: I guess the information we got then was incorrect.

MR. THOMPSON: Yes. We actually have had a number issued and we have a number in process.

This is a difficult question, Mr. Secretary, because we're asking really at the base root whether or not we believe patents are a helpful aspect of this industry. I think that it's been the position of the owners and most of the employees of WordPerfect Corporation for a number of years that patents are not good news for the software industry.

UNITED STATES PATENT AND TRADEMARK OFFICE
Public Hearing on Patent Protection for Software-Related Inventions
Arlington, Virginia -- February 10 & 11, 1994

However, I believe the time for making that argument passed many years ago and we are now at a point where we simply have to say, if they are part of the landscape how can we best ensure that they become a workable part of our business plan.

I have to say that WordPerfect Corporation has been surprised. There is a certain lag effect in the patent process, isn't there? There's not a real hurry up and let's start getting our patent portfolio in shape. There's a certain lag effect here and it takes a period of years for companies to develop process and methodology to see that patents are made a part of the everyday development process.

And certainly that's the case of WordPerfect Corporation. Three years ago WordPerfect Corporation essentially had one patent application in process. Today we have many. We are considering hiring in-house patent counsel. We consider it an unfortunate circumstance, but a necessary circumstance.

COMMISSIONER LEHMAN: I gather then that the reason that you're filing patent applications is by in large from a defensive point of view?

MR. THOMPSON: Absolutely right.

COMMISSIONER LEHMAN: Some of the other witnesses in San Jose indicated the same thing.

The next question I wanted to ask concerns, you referred to the Commissioner's order of reexamination in the Compton's Multimedia case. Again in San Jose we heard a number of situations listed, a number of patents which had been issued, which some of the witnesses there, at least one or two, thought were similarly questionable.

Obviously, one of the things that we could conceivably do is to make better use of that, of our own powers to order reexamination and perhaps make a review of some of the patents that are -- where there is some question about whether or not we have gotten all the prior art. What would you view about that be? Would you encourage or discourage us from using that Commissioner ordered reexamination?

MR. THOMPSON: I think that's a healthy thing for the industry and certainly the most efficient thing that can be done at this point in time. As you may know, WordPerfect and other companies are being threatened, a number of claims of infringement on patents that we believe simply should not have been issued and the prior art searches that we have done, I think, would be very useful for the PTO.

COMMISSIONER LEHMAN: But I gather that in those cases you haven't chosen to use the reexamination procedure yourself.

MR. THOMPSON: Not yet, no.

COMMISSIONER LEHMAN: And I asked also about that in San Jose and I'm -- just in the interest of time; I don't want to spend an hour on cross examination here, so I'll lead the witness a little bit -- the answer that we got as to why companies who feel that they have prior art that clearly might invalidate some of these patents, they don't want to bring that to our attention by requesting reexamination themselves is because they think that the present procedure basically is not their best shot for utilizing that prior art and they don't want to disclose it in that kind of a forum. They'd rather save it for the infringement law suit itself.

Do you find that figures into your strategy about whether or not to use reexamine?

MR. THOMPSON: I think that's right. I believe if we had a better sense of the reexamination process and certainly had the sense that it was an expedited process, one which could bootstrap us ahead of where we would be through the private negotiations in the litigation that would be something we'd be very attracted to.

COMMISSIONER LEHMAN: Well, unless any of my colleagues have any questions, thank you very much.

MR. THOMPSON: Thank you.

COMMISSIONER LEHMAN: As I indicated, we are running a little bit ahead of time and it would be very helpful to us in getting through our afternoon more quickly if we could fit in at least one or two of the afternoon people. So I've indicated that Richard Jordan -- is Richard Jordan here?

MR. JORDAN: Yes, I am, sir.

COMMISSIONER LEHMAN: Great. Would you mind coming forward? Presumably you'll be as prepared now as this afternoon.

Richard Jordan, Patent Counsel to Thinking Machines Corporation. I hope you'll notice this new level of customer service that we have here.

MR. JORDAN: Thank you very much. It's very much appreciated.

COMMISSIONER LEHMAN: We're on the Internet. We've got all our hearings printed up. We've got refreshments in the lobby. We haven't yet gotten them for free, but we're working on that.

PRESENTATION BY RICHARD JORDAN

THINKING MACHINES CORPORATION

MR. JORDAN: Mr. Commissioner, ladies and gentlemen, my name is Richard Jordan. I'm Patent Counsel with Thinking Machines Corporation. By way of background, Thinking Machines Corporation was founded in 1983 to develop, manufacture and sell massively parallel super computer systems. Thinking Machines products are an outgrowth of research undertaken principally by its chief scientist, Danny Hillis while he was a graduate student at MIT.

Since Thinking Machines announced its first product, the Connection Machine, Model CM-1 super computer in 1986 the company has had excellent revenue growth and revenue from massively parallel super computers is believed to be the largest of any company.

However, it should be noted that its revenue is much less than that of a number of other companies in the computer industry, both domestic and foreign, including companies in

UNITED STATES PATENT AND TRADEMARK OFFICE
Public Hearing on Patent Protection for Software-Related Inventions
Arlington, Virginia -- February 10 & 11, 1994

the traditional super computer field as well as those principally known for selling computers and more conventional architectures, many of which I should say are developing products that are competitive with Thinking Machines.

Over the past several years the computing power of massively parallel computing technology has been emphasized by a number of awards relating to Thinking Machines' technology. Since 1990 the IEEE, the Institute of Electrical and Electronics Engineers, has given its Gordon Novell Award for computing speed to several teams, including Thinking Machines employees for programs processed on a connection machine super computer and for compiler technology.

The importance of massively parallel computing technology has also been recognized by articles in journals such as the Scientific American and newspapers such as the New York Times and the Wall Street Journal.

A connection machine computer achieves its computing power through a combination of hardware and software, unlike a conventional computer which uses one or only a few powerful data processors on masses of data, the hardware of a connection machine computer includes tens, hundreds, or even thousands of microprocessors which operate in parallel on relatively small amounts of data that are distributed to them.

The individual microprocessors are interconnected by a data routing network which allow them to share data as necessary and the software effectively coordinates the operations of the individual microprocessors and the routing network to achieve tremendous computing power.

While the hardware is important to the computing power achieved by a massively parallel computing system, at least as important as the advancement in software techniques. Many advancements have come in the development of parallel algorithms and computing techniques; the pattern of assignment of data to processors to minimize processing time; techniques for rapidly routing data through the routing network; compiler techniques; the development of high level languages and compilers to make massively parallel computers easy to use.

Thinking Machines currently has a staff in excess of 500, of whom approximately one-third are involved in hardware and software engineering development. Of these engineers only about 30 percent are involved in what might traditionally be referred to as hardware development, while fully 70 percent are involved in software development.

In addition, a number of other employees actively develop software in Thinking Machine's large customer service group developing software techniques specifically for or with customers. It is manifestly evident that Thinking Machines software development effort represents a very significant portion of its investment in massively parallel computing technology and Thinking Machines believes that patent protection provides an important tool to help protect this investment.

Thinking Machines further has an ongoing program to encourage its developers to publish papers and articles describing new parallel processing techniques. This provides information on new uses for massively parallel computing technology and techniques and may also help to enhance the professional standing of its employee authors within their professions.

Published papers represent divulgation of technology for which Thinking Machines has provided often considerable investment. And Thinking Machines believes that patent protection can be an important tool to protect this investment as well, particularly in view of the substantial degree of competition that's developing in the marketplace.

Thinking Machines, unlike some larger companies, does not require its employee's papers to be cleared, that is scrutinized to determine whether they describe technology which the company may wish to protect, before the papers can be sent out for publication, but it does actively file for patent protection on technology to be described in the papers.

Thinking Machines recognizes that computer software is also protected by copyright, but it believes that copyright will not provide the degree of protection required to protect its investment. First, the scope of copyright protection is far from clear and has been made less clear in recent years in view of the Second Circuit's opinion in the Computer Associates case. It's generally said that copyright protects the expression of a work and not its idea.

While these words are easy to say, it's very difficult to apply them in practice. Furthermore, the application of 17 U.S.C. Section 102(b), which exempts from copyright protection ideas, processes, methods and so forth regardless of the form in which they're described, further renders uncertain the degree of protection provided by copyright.

Much of the value in the program related techniques developed by Thinking Machines is not in the detailed computer program code, which is clearly protected by copyright, but in the algorithms, programming techniques for which copyright protection is far less clear. Similar ambiguities are not present in patent protection.

Furthermore, patent protection is important in view of the publishing by Thinking Machine's employees, which disclosed the algorithms and techniques to the world and particularly to the competition and in view of the fact that copyright protection may not protect against reverse engineering.

Accordingly, Thinking Machines believes that patent protection for computer program related inventions is an important tool to protect its investment. That being said, Thinking Machines believes it important that the patent system maximize the likelihood that the patents issued are valid, that the claims are directed to new, useful, and nonobvious technology in accordance with the statutory mandate.

It does no one any service if patents are issued that do not meet the statutory standard. While no one can reasonably

UNITED STATES PATENT AND TRADEMARK OFFICE
Public Hearing on Patent Protection for Software-Related Inventions
Arlington, Virginia -- February 10 & 11, 1994

expect that any institution run by human beings can be 100 percent perfect, we believe that enhancements can be made to improve the system.

And I might mention that while we're here discussing patent issues relating to computer software-related inventions, these same problems can arise in connection with computer hardware and indeed in any technology. The problems may be exacerbated somewhat in the software area since the PTO for a number of years was reluctant to consider computer program related inventions to be statutory subject matter -- a reluctance that to some extent still continues -- which delayed its development of a prior art database in this area.

However, there is no industry in which all of the technology is patented or otherwise published. Several changes to U.S. procedure may be appropriate to provide for early publication of the applications. This would have two advantages. First, it would ensure more timely publication of the technology, making it available to those working in the industry. A publication delay of one to one-and-a-half years after submission to a paper is not atypical for engineering and scientific journals, but for patents, particularly in this subject matter, a much longer delay is more typical.

With developments in computer technology moving as rapidly as they are, the patent disclosure after such a lengthy delay may be somewhat less valuable as a source of technical information.

Second, early publication can also operate as early notification to others working in the field of the potential issuance of a patent, allowing them to favor that into their business decisions.

The potentially lengthy delays to patent issuance under current practice in the United States means that others working in the field would not be notified that a patent application is pending that may cover something they are developing until the patent actually issues, which can be a number of years after its original filing date and perhaps after much time and money has been invested in the potentially infringing enterprise.

Third, early publication followed by an examination in a more contemplative environment than would be possible in the current push for a reduction in the pendency period would provide a better patent upon issuance. For example, if a patent issued on the original application with the approximately 18 month pendency period as currently suggested by the PTO, the prior art from foreign patent offices would most likely not be available for consideration by the U.S. examiner.

Having this prior art is particularly important in the computer area. It makes for a more complete examination and a higher degree of confidence in the validity of the patent. Typically such prior art is not available until around 18 to 24 months after the priority date and an 18 month pendency time would mean that the art would not be available until just around the time the U.S. patent would be issuing.

If the art were deemed material and the application still pending, the applicant would likely have to file a continuation application to get it considered, which could delay issuance to the patent and publication of the technology for an even greater amount of time and require additional expenditure by the applicant of another filing fee.

On the other hand, if the U.S. patent had already issued the only ways to have the art considered would be by reexamine or reissue, both of which can be costly. In addition, it puts too much stress on the Patent Examining Corps which can have problems with retention of examiners.

These problems can be alleviated by a few relatively simple changes to the prosecution procedures and the PTO. First, they can publish the application 18 months from the priority date, preferably with a search report so that the applicant can have it and ideas to the likelihood of being able to get a patent.

In addition, the public should be brought into the process at some point, perhaps by way of an opposition proceeding just before or after issuance. It would alleviate the secrecy problem, things going into the Patent Office. But you have to make sure that oppositions are conducted and restricted here as to procedures and time frames, otherwise they can run on interminably.

Another way that the system can be improved is by holding ongoing dialogue such as these hearings to get input from the Bar and others who have interest in the patent system.

Wearing another hat, I am also Chairman of the Electronic and Computer Law Committee of the AIPLA and our committee leadership has for a number of years been meeting with the group directors and others in the electrical examining groups to discuss issues of mutual concern. We expect to hold another meeting in April, of which we hope to discuss among other things, some of the issues raised by the notice for these hearings.

An outgrowth of earlier meetings was a program held last October in conjunction with the AIPLA's annual meeting that was extremely well attended by examiners from the Examining Corps and by members of the AIPLA.

At the program a number of problems and practice issues of concern to the Examining Corps and to the Bar were discussed in detail. Each side, so to speak, learned quite a bit of the problems and perspectives of the others and the program received quite good reviews and we hope to have more of them. Thank you very much.

COMMISSIONER LEHMAN: Thank you very much. Those were very helpful comments and I appreciate your be willing to give them in advance of your prepared time.

MR. JORDAN: Thank you very much.

COMMISSIONER LEHMAN: I'm going to try to call one more person in the morning session. Is Jonathan Band here?

(No audible response.)

COMMISSIONER LEHMAN: How about Vern Blanchard?

(No audible response.)

COMMISSIONER LEHMAN: Jeffrey Berkowitz? Mr. Berkowitz, great. Mr. Berkowitz is an attorney with Finnegan, Henderson, Farabow, Garrett & Dunner.

Yesterday we had a meeting with the unions at the PTO and we big -- we were sitting on the Partnership Council and we had a big discussion about who should get represented and how many representatives they should have on this.

It's interesting that we have a disproportionate representation from Finnegan, Henderson, Farabow, Garrett & Dunner. I think this is about the fifth witness that we've had in the course of these four days of hearings. It will be interesting to see this other face of the firm.

PRESENTATION BY JEFFREY A. BERKOWITZ

FINNEGAN, HENDERSON, FARABOW, GARRETT & DUNNER

MR. BERKOWITZ: Good morning, Mr. Commissioner, and other distinguished members to this panel. I'm Jeffrey Berkowitz, Associate with the intellectual property firm of Finnegan, Henderson. And like my colleague, Mr. Yoches, my comments today are my own and not those of the firm.

I'd like to talk a little bit today about Question Number 10 in Topic B for today's hearing. In Question Number 10 the PTO asked for comments on how they should handle the submission of computer program code listings, specifically the PTO seeks comments on the following four items:

One, should the PTO require a submission of program code listings;

Two, should the PTO require a submission of code listings in machine readable format only;

Three, should program code listings be included in patent documents or should they be made available only through a publicly accessible database; and

Four, what hardships would patent applicants face if these requirements were imposed?

In my opinion, the PTO should not require a submission of program code listings. The following discussion concerning my opinions on the first item of Question 10 necessarily provides my opinion on the remaining items.

Currently, applicants may file program code listings with the PTO, and I emphasize the word "may," because these listings, particularly when in machine readable format can take hundreds of pages, maybe even thousands of pages. It is clear that the PTO must deal with substantial financial, printing and logistical problems when an applicant chooses to submit a program listing.

In an effort to deal with these problems, the PTO promulgated 37 C.F.R. Section 1.96 under which program listings must be included in the application itself, either in the specification or as part of the drawings if the listing is under 11 pages in length.

If, however, the listing is 11 or more pages in length then the listing may be submitted in the form of a microfiche appendix, which will not be part of the printed patent, but will become available to the public once the patent is issued. Some applicants choose to submit program code listings regardless of the number of pages to ensure that their applications comply with the statutory requirements of Section 112, first paragraph.

However, if a programmer of ordinary skill in the art could write a program without undue experimentation from the disclosure of the program list application, that is an application for a software-related invention absent a program listing, and if such a listing is not required to satisfy other statutory requirements, for example, the best mode requirement of Section 112, second paragraph, then the applicant would not need to file a program code listing for the invention.

Based on this reasoning, many applicants typically choose not to file program code listings. A requirement for program listings would prevent applicants from filing applications until product development is complete, which would further delay the process of filing applications, examining applications, and issuing patents for software-related inventions.

In many of the software-related patent applications that I've written and prosecuted, inventors have not yet completely developed their software-related inventions to be patented prior to the filing of the application.

Thus, there is no final program listing to be submitted with the application. This should not prevent the applicant from filing an application on his or her invention. In this regard, it is important to note that in other technologies applicants can and do file patent applications without having completed product development.

Applicants also choose not to file program code listings because filing the listings would make the entire program available to the public, which in some cases may divulge important trade secrets or other information that the applicant may not need to specifically divulge in order to secure patent protection.

Even if applicants choose to submit machine readable listings, such listings may be reverse engineered. As long as a programmer of ordinary skill in the art can write a program without undue experimentation from the disclosure of a programless application and if such a listing is not required to satisfy other statutory requirements, then the applicant should not have to file a program code listing for the invention and divulge important trade secrets.

Furthermore, a requirement for the submission of program code listings, regardless of the form of the listings will only further increase the PTO's burden in connection with both the examination of software-related inventions as well as the practical aspects related to storing program code listings and making those listings available to the public.

Examiners do not have the time to study program listings, regardless of the form in which they are submitted to the PTO, nor does the PTO have resources to waste in storing the program code listings and making them available to the public.

Some of the hardships associated with mandatory requirement for submission of program listings are apparent from the above discussion. There are also a number of problems associated with the current microfiche requirements that are worth mentioning. First is the availability and cost associated with the microfiche appendix requirements outlined above.

When an applicant chooses to submit a program listing of 11 or more pages, he or she must locate a company that provides the microfiche services, a task that is not so easy, and spend additional money to have the listing put on microfiche, a cost that may be high depending upon the length of the program listing.

Instead, if the PTO believes that it is necessary to require appendices for program listings, I suggest that the PTO consider more practical approaches, such as submission of program listings on a CD-ROM or other mass storage device and in a format that may be used by examiners to inspect efficiently and effectively the program listings.

I believe these and other approaches are less expensive and more accessible to inventors of software-related inventions than the archaic microfiche appendices instituted in the current rules.

Finally, I'm also concerned that requiring submission of program code listings would lead to litigants unnecessarily raising issues concerning a program listing should the PTO adopt a submission requirement. This, however, is beyond the scope of these hearings. Thank you for your time this morning to present my views.

COMMISSIONER LEHMAN: Thank you very much, Mr. Berkowitz.

I understand that Ron Reiling is now here. Perhaps you could finish up the morning for us, Mr. Reiling. Ron Reiling is corporate counsel to the Digital Equipment Corporation.

PRESENTATION BY RON REILING

DIGITAL EQUIPMENT CORPORATION

MR. REILING: Good morning, Mr. Commissioner and members of the panel. Greetings from a snow-filled and bitterly cold Boston. I'm representing Digital Equipment Corporation. We are, as you may know, one of the larger suppliers of network computers and software in the world and we invest heavily in research and development to come up with new products and we rely heavily on the patent system to protect that investment.

We are vitally interested in software-related inventions because we spend hundreds of millions of dollars a year in this area. Creativity and innovation drive technology and industrial progress. Thus, the importance of adequately rewarding the world's best minds by safeguarding their software-related inventions through patents I believe will increase dramatically in the years ahead as technological advances in this field accelerate.

In today's global highly competitive marketplace, some believe that we are witnessing a fundamental shift in business history. They are, we say, progressing from managerial capitalism to intellectual capitalism. They believe that the importance of intellectual capital will ultimately cause a dramatic shift in the wealth of the world from material resources to those who control ideas and information, that is intellectual property.

A fundamental feature of the patent system is that it establishes a basis for this intellectual effort to be regarded as an asset and to be traded in the marketplace. Thus, an effective patent system which promotes creativity by providing a beneficial and stimulating environment for inventors is essential for the information age.

This environment will produce a constant stream of new products and competitive processes forging the growth of a vigorous American economy.

Turning now to the specific issues, Digital believes, one, that software-related inventions should be treated the same as any other invention; that no legislative changes are necessary in order to properly protect software-related inventions; that increased training, as well as expanded content and better classification of the prior art available to the examiners would improve the examination process.

We feel it's important that patents can be obtained on all software-related inventions, those at the operating system level, at the application system level, those pertaining to storage or the transmission of information, such as memory data structures, packet switch networks, magnetic and optical media.

We also believe that the standards for patentability applied by the PTO for software-related inventions should be the same as those applied to any other technology. It would be a mistake to single out any technology and treat it in a discriminatory manner.

The issues related to software-related inventions have been evolving for almost 20 years. It appears that we are finally approaching a point in this evolutionary process where predictability may be possible. It would be misguided in our view to attempt to redirect software-related patenting at this time by altering the established standards of review.

However, the PTO appears to have recently changed its standard of review in certain of the software-related inventions by ignoring novel software-related steps or means in the claims, thereby finding the claims anticipated by prior art that does not disclose the ignored claimed features.

This is basically a reversal of the PTO's longstanding claim as a whole analysis in novelty determinations. What's happening in our view in these cases is that the PTO has imported 101 type considerations back into the 102 and 103 considerations.

The PTO has also asked whether the implementing of a known process, technique or method on a computer should be patentable if but for the use of the software the overall process, technique or method is known. I believe the correct answer is yes and that's provided, of course, the software recitations in the claim present a new and nonobvious invention. It should not be the PTO policy or procedure to exclude software limitations from novelty determinations.

On another point the PTO should not impose any special duty on the patent applicants for software-related inventions under Rule 56. Such applicants should not be required to conduct a patentability search. After all, Rule 56 already encourages all applicants in all technologies to examine carefully the closest prior art information.

With respect to the way a software-related invention is described no special requirements should be proscribed or required. Typically block diagrams are a useful to communicate the software steps and functionality of relationships of components included in software inventions.

Blocks within the diagrams should be deemed adequate illustrations to support elements of both method and apparatus claims. Program code listings should not be encouraged. They should be accepted provided the specification standing alone provides a clear and understandable description of the invention.

With respect to administrative matters, we believe it is vital that the PTO invest in quality. The PTO has recently shown improvements in timeliness and quality of examinations, but further improvements are essential. Congress should approve the hiring and training of more examiners and ongoing qualification assurance programs, including continuing education requirements should be adopted.

The examiner should improve on the quality of Office actions by including better explanations of rejections. Providing only conclusory statements of prior art rejections does very little in advancing the determination of patentability.

Needless to say comprehensive patentability searches are essential and we see some improvement in the PTO in the last few years. However, too often patent offices in other nations encounter references, including U.S. references, which should have been located but were not during the search by the PTO. This has to change.

Another possibility is the creation of an electronic database where one could include software-related documentation and make this database accessible to the public, so that people could add to the database over the Internet, for example.

The patenting process we all agree should include public involvement and we think the mechanisms to accomplish this are already in place, but perhaps are not adequately utilized. For example, we could encourage the public to cite prior art in accordance with Section 301 or the reexamination process might be redefined to provide an incentive for early challenges to issued patents.

One concept might be to substantially reduce the fees in the first three months over a patent's life to encourage people to use reexamination.

In conclusion, software-related patents are of great significance to American industry. We have a vast and vital interest in software-related patents, in valid software-related patents, and the industry is more than willing to work with the PTO in accomplishing this objective. Thank you.

COMMISSIONER LEHMAN: Thank you very much, Mr. Reiling. I appreciate your suggestions, the idea of sort of a development of an open-ended electronic database that you could get public input in is a very interesting idea.

That concludes our morning set of hearings. We're going to reconvene promptly at 2:00 this afternoon. I hope since we have heard several of this afternoon's witnesses, I hope that anybody that is in the room this morning that is going to be here this afternoon will realize that, you know, they may be called maybe even more than 20 minutes -- I hope more than 20 minutes -- before their assigned time schedule so that we can conclude our business this afternoon early.

Thank you very much.

(Whereupon, at 12:06 p.m., the above-entitled hearing was adjourned, to reconvene at 2:00 p.m., this same date.)

UNITED STATES PATENT AND TRADEMARK OFFICE
Public Hearing on Patent Protection for Software-Related Inventions
Arlington, Virginia -- February 10 & 11, 1994
AFTERNOON SESSION

(2:14 p.m.)

COMMISSIONER LEHMAN: We're about to begin our afternoon session of our third day of hearings on patent and software-related inventions. Before we call our first witness, I'd like to note the fact for those who are here that we have a distinguished visitor with us and that is Roland Deer, who is a Director in the European Patent Office.

Mr. Deer, welcome to the United States. We're glad you have an interest in our proceeding.

(Applause.)

COMMISSIONER LEHMAN: We made quite a bit of progress this morning and apparently our first witness that we had scheduled for this afternoon, Michael DeAngeli has not arrived and, therefore, we are going to go on to Jason Mirabito, Board Member of the Boston Patent Law Association. So if you would join us, please, Mr. Mirabito, maybe we could hear from you.

PRESENTATION BY A. JASON MIRABITO

BOSTON PATENT LAW ASSOCIATION

MR. MIRABITO: Is that where you want me?

COMMISSIONER LEHMAN: That's right.

MR. MIRABITO: I'm sorry I wasn't here this morning. My trip here took 24 hours to get from Boston here.

COMMISSIONER LEHMAN: Did it really? I guess we had some other people from Boston this morning who had a lot of problems.

MR. MIRABITO: I missed a hearing before the Board of Appeals this morning at 9:00, so I made it for this.

COMMISSIONER LEHMAN: We're sorry about that. Just relax now. Tell us what you think.

MR. MIRABITO: Thank you. Good afternoon, Commissioner, gentlemen. My name is Jason Mirabito and I am a partner at the Boston patent law firm of Wolf, Green, Field & Sax. I'm here to testify on behalf of the Boston Patent Law Association, which is an Association of some 400 members, of which I am the past-President.

In the short time available to me today I wanted to concentrate solely on the issues of Topic B. While I was trying to prepare my remarks earlier yesterday, figure out what I wanted to say, I questioned, why is this area different from other areas and why does this area seem to be so fraught with problems that other areas of technology have not been.

An example of that is the biotechnology area. I guess I came to the conclusion that in the biotechnology area, where there has been a lot of patent activity in the last ten years, the general thrust is to publish. If you don't publish, you perish. And perhaps in this area this is an area in which if you do publish you do perish. That is due, I think to some extent to the trade secret licensing status and much computer software.

I think what's -- I don't mean this literally, of course, because certainly computer software programs aren't published, but the underlying processes of them are not generally published.

Our organization recognizes that sometimes shortcomings in both the examination process and the process of uncovering prior art is partly due to this trade secret status of many software developments. We do not believe, however, that the difficulty in searching for prior art should militate and argue in eliminating protection for computer software and that software only be deprived of the protection which is guaranteed to them and to other technology holders.

We should remember that some, I guess it's 20 years ago now, in the '70s through until 19-, really early '80s, the issue of computer software patentability was again before the Patent Office and the Patent Office at that time took an attitude which I would suggest is negative towards the patenting of computer software. It finally took a Supreme Court decision to change that around.

As I see Topic B there are two main themes there. The first theme being what can be done to better examination and what can be done to better the discovery of prior art. And the second is the disclosure of software inventions.

As to the first series of questions, we suggest that the Patent Office needs to be appropriated more funds and the Patent Office, like every other agency always likes to hear that. But I think those monies are needed to better index software technology and to train examiners.

COMMISSIONER LEHMAN: Can I interrupt you?

MR. MIRABITO: Sure.

COMMISSIONER LEHMAN: You know, we don't receive appropriated funds. We're by law fully fee funded. Does that mean you think we should increase the fees to support this?

MR. MIRABITO: Definitely not. I've always found it interesting that this is one of the few agencies that's required to be somewhat self-sufficient while every other agency -- although I understand now the FDA, they're talking about the FDA charging for the analysis they do. But I've always found that very curious that we're expected to, we the public are expected to, fund an agency. The defense agency certainly does not have that problem.

I think if the Patent Office gets the required funds and gets the better training for the examiners, particularly hiring more computer software trained examiners, people with majors in computer science, I think the Patent Office can do what the biotech group did earlier and will rise to the occasion.

With respect to the issue of so-called hidden prior art, this is a very real problem. There are allegations that the so-called prior art has been sitting in software programs and on people's computers for years and years. I think to the extent it's true -- and I think there is some truth in it -- that it is very difficult to search some computer technology, that the Patent Office should, as the Commissioner did

recently in the Compton's patent case, order reexamination.

We, as an organization, are in favor of an expanded reexamination procedure within the Patent Office that would include all the traditional reasons for unpatentability. This would require a slight change to the reexaminations statute and procedure, but not very much at all.

Secondly, I think another thing which may ameliorate the problem that may exist with so-called bad patents being issued is when the United States, if it does go to a publication system, I think a publication system would eliminate some of those problems because then people would be advised of potential patent rights and then have a right to make opposition to those rights.

I would suggestion this, however, in a day in which most foreign countries have publication within 18 months of the earliest filing date, in many instances, both in software and other areas, one may not even get a first Office action by that point. This is an area in which the owner of the technology will make a decision whether to stick with trade secret protection or to opt the patent mode.

I think an 18-month period is too short sometimes. What we would suggest as a change to that would be that a period of time after the first Office action has been issued, say three to six to nine months there would be publication that would then allow the applicant to see what the prior art looks like and make a determination at that point whether or not to continue on with it.

I would like now to turn briefly to some of the issues that are related in the second theme, that of disclosure to the Patent Office. I've been practicing in this area since at least the early 1980s when one could practice in this area or unless you flip back to the 1960s. I'm not that old.

One, question three posits whether the Patent Office should impose special disclosure standards on software-related inventions. We firmly believe that such a disclosure requirement would be inappropriate as there is no reason for treating software-related inventions differently than other patentable technology. So long as the disclosures meet the requirements of Section 112 and other requirements, we don't believe there should be any other changes.

Question six questions whether the applicants for software-related inventions ought to do a prior art search. Such prior art search, of course, is not required in other areas. We believe it would be inappropriate to require a prior art search. Obviously, myself and other of my colleagues will from time to time do a prior art search for a particular invention but not always. We always have, of course, our great duty of disclosure rules which would take care of any prior art of which the attorney or the inventor is aware is not disclosed.

Questions 7, 8 and 9 I kind of jumbled together and relate to the most effective way to describe software and patent applications. This is something that myself and some of my colleagues in the early 1980s started having to deal with. The issue became, well, do we include codes, do we not

UNITED STATES PATENT AND TRADEMARK OFFICE
Public Hearing on Patent Protection for Software-Related Inventions
Arlington, Virginia -- February 10 & 11, 1994

include codes; do we use flow charts, are flow charts sufficient.

I've seen a tendency and a change over time. In the very beginning, the early '80s, we always included code because you never know just disclosing flow charts may not be sufficient and you don't want to get caught with a nonenabling patent.

Then we shifted over in the later times to flow charts are sufficient. I see now people flipping back again. I guess the point I'd like to make is that there is no best way. Certain inventions are best described by the code. Certain inventions are best described by flow charts or pseudo code, and certain inventions, such as combinations of hardware and software, are very unclear how they should be described.

The bottom line again is Section 112. Is the description sufficient to meet the requirements of the statute? A related issue to the requirements of requiring that a list patent software -- I'm sorry -- computer software listings be included as a requirement I think would be inappropriate. It is akin to me to requiring that applicants for mechanically related inventions disclose to the Patent Office the detailed blueprint drawings that make up the machine under issue there.

I think that would be improper in that case; it would be proper in this case. In addition, required computer software listings and software-related inventions would prevent those who wish to file an application and get a constructive date of reduction to practice prior to writing the code. I think that would be another problem with that.

There are many other issues and comments we would like to make had we had an unlimited amount of time which, of course, doesn't exist. But we expect our organization, and we are now planning to give many more detailed submissions in the written March details.

We thank you for the opportunity to have spoken to you and wish you very good luck in what I think will be very interesting endeavors. Thank you.

COMMISSIONER LEHMAN: Thank you very much, Mr. Mirabito and thanks to the Boston Patent Law Association. As I recall you testified or the Association testified in the last hearings that we had here on -- I think it was the harmonization hearings. They also came before us.

MR. MIRABITO: That's correct.

COMMISSIONER LEHMAN: Thank you for putting in your work as an Association and for, you know, going through all the trouble to get here with the weather.

Next, I'd like to ask Jonathan Band if he's here to come forward. Mr. Band is an attorney with Morrison & Foerster.

PRESENTATION BY JONATHAN BAND

MORRISON & FOERSTER

MR. BAND: I am Jonathan Band, a partner in the intellectual property group of the Washington, D.C. office of Morrison & Foerster. The views I express here today are my own.

I attended the PTO hearings two weeks ago in San Jose and I would like to share with you three observations based not on the testimony which you heard, but in my conversations with many of the Silicon Valley spectators. This is, if you will, a report from the Peanut Gallery.

First, using Ron Lorings' perceptive classification a small but not insignificantly minority of the audience fell into the software patents are bad category. While the majority fell into the bad software patents are bad category.

By further discussions with the software patents are bad adherence revealed that they were confused and frustrated by the case law and patentability or software-related inventions and that they had no confidence in the ability of the PTO to search the prior art.

This suggests that if the PTO successfully addresses the concerns of the bad software patents are bad people, many of the software patents are bad people will be satisfied as well.

Second, and following from the first point, I detected a strong mandate for serious procedural reforms that would improve the quality of software patents and eliminate submarine patents. The PTO has already announced that it will introduce legislation establishing a 20-year term from filing and reforming the reexamination process. These proposals met with near universal support in San Jose.

There was also strong support for pre-grant publication of applications and reform of the continuation and division practice. The PTO should give these and the many other amendments suggested close consideration. As the PTO reviews these proposals, it should place the interests of the inventing community ahead of those of the Patent Bar, the primary beneficiaries of the current obfuscation and litigation.

Reform of the system to make it simpler and more predictable while eliminating the game playing and the lawsuits would be a lasting legacy of the Clinton Administration in the technological history of our nation.

And speaking of game playing in the Patent Bar, the current hopelessly confusing state of the case law on the patentability of software-related inventions means that the success of the software patent application turns more on the cleverness of the patent lawyer than on the quality of the invention. This, of course, is backwards.

The PTO should establish a commission consisting of programmers, law professors, practitioners and jurists to establish some order in this area.

My third observation on the San Jose hearings is that there's an underlying concern in the inventing community that in the past decade the pendulum may have swung too far from too little intellectual property protection to too much protection.

As Judge Kazinski of the Ninth Circuit has observed, overprotecting intellectual property is as harmful as underprotecting it. Judge Kazinski further notes that creativity is impossible without a rich public domain. For this reason the intellectual properties are full of what Judge Kazinski calls careful balances between what's set aside for the owner and what's left in the public domain for the rest of us.

Because patents and copyrights are monopolies created by the intellectual property laws, regulation of those monopolies is the responsibility primarily of the intellectual property laws and only secondarily of the anti-trust laws.

Given the PTO Commissioner's emerging role as the administration's intellectual property policy advisor, the PTO must be vigilant about maintaining the balance between protection and competition. Thank you for your attention.

COMMISSIONER LEHMAN: Thank you very much for those comments. I really don't have any questions. They simply strike a responsive chord on my own thinking. I thought that was a good description and analysis of our San Jose hearings.

Next, I'd like to call Michael Chakansky. I hope he's here. We're running a little outside of the 20 minutes.

If not, is Paul Heckel here? I did not see him. Well, we're going to have a quick hearing this afternoon.

Leonard Suchyta, from Bellcore, Bell Communications Research, General Attorney there.

PRESENTATION BY LEONARD CHARLES SUCHYTA

BELLCORE, BELL COMMUNICATIONS RESEARCH

MR. SUCHYTA: Good afternoon. My name is Leonard Charles Suchyta. I'm a patent attorney and I'm also the Assistant Vice President and general attorney for the intellectual property managers for Bell Communications Research, Inc., more commonly known as Bellcore.

The views that I will be presenting today are the views of Bellcore. On behalf of Bellcore and myself, we express our sincerest appreciation for the Patent Office permitting us to present our views on this important matter.

A short history of Bellcore. Bellcore is owned by and is a research engineering organization of the seven regional telephone companies which was established in 1984 as a result of the divestiture of what was known as the Bell System.

Bellcore's research activities are in support of the exchange and exchange access telecommunications services offered by these companies and a large part of these activities are the development and the maintenance of software systems utilized in the provision and the administration of the exchange and exchange access telecommunication services.

Revenues for Bellcore are roughly $1 million and they have slightly less than 7,000 employees, most of whom are employed in New Jersey. Software development and maintenance is a significant portion of these activities, in that of the 7,000 employees roughly 3,000 Bellcore employees have this type of function.

More from a perspective point of view, there are roughly 4,500 technical employees at Bellcore with approximately 2,100 actually performing software-related services. The software that Bellcore develops costs in excess of tens of millions of dollars to develop and these are protected both by patents and copyrights as well as by trade secrets.

As a result, Bellcore views patent protections for software as critical to the protection of the investment of Bellcore and its owner companies and the rate payer ultimately. Bellcore, while not offering any detailed testimony on Topic A, would like to set forth for the record that it strongly favors patent protection for software-related inventions. When Bellcore provides its written comments it will certainly provide detailed comments with respect to Topic A.

With respect to Topic B, Bellcore would like to address the specific questions that were raised in the notice of the hearing. First of all, do the patents and the printed publications provide examiners with a sufficient and representative collection of the prior art to assess novelty and obviousness. We believe that patents and the printed publications provide sufficient prior art.

We base this conclusion on the fact that major companies who are actively seeking patent protection utilize patents for the protection and also publish. This includes Bellcore. We believe that publication as well as patent protection is especially true for the computer and the telecommunications industries.

However, we are well aware that prior art collections can always be improved. As a result, Bellcore has agreed that it would voluntarily submit nonproprietary software publications to the Patent Office's library to assist them in their collection for prior art.

The next question that we would like to comment on is, can an accurate measurement of the ordinary level of skill in the art in the field of computer programming be derived from printed publications and issued patents. The answer is yes.

The ordinary level of skill for a software-related invention is the same as that as for any other invention. It makes no difference whether they be software or hardware. There is an assumption that software patents are those inventions conceived by programmers or they're somewhere down at the programming level. This is generally not the case and certainly this is not the case in the case of Bellcore.

The software-related inventions for Bellcore, which we seek to protect by patents, come from software systems designers whose tasks are to conceive and to define the various functions and their interrelationships which can then be combined to comprise the software system. The inventive aspects are generally found with these tasks, not with the detailed coding implementations that are left to other non-highly-technical people.

The third question is: Should the PTO influence a special duty on patent applications for software-related inventions? We believe that the requirements of Rule 56 are sufficient and we do not believe that software-related inventions should be treated any differently from those afforded any other patent application for other technology.

UNITED STATES PATENT AND TRADEMARK OFFICE
Public Hearing on Patent Protection for Software-Related Inventions
Arlington, Virginia – February 10 & 11, 1994

We would, however, be receptive to helping the examiner to identify the areas of search or to comment on those references where the examiner has some difficulty finding their relevance.

The next question is: Do the standards governing novelty and obviousness as applied by the PTO and the federal courts accurately reflect the inventive activity in the field of software design and development? Our answer is yes.

Novelty and obviousness are statutory standards that are equally applicable to software-related inventions as well as to other inventions. The fact that you mentioned hardware or software should not change that statutory standard.

The next question we'd like to address is: Should the PTO require applicants for software-related inventions to conduct a search and include copies of documents? We believe the answer is no.

The applicant for a software-related invention should not be required to undertake any additional obligations other than those set forth in Rule 56 and we believe that Rule 56 adequately sets forth the standard.

The last item we'd like to comment on is the format that software applications should take. Should the filing of source codes be required? Our answer to that is, when we file software-related applications, meeting the requirements of 35 U.S.C. 112 is sometimes very troubling. Also sometimes uncertain and we do not believe that the filing of the source code serves any particular beneficial purpose, the same for the object code.

The patentable methodologies and the techniques of software-related inventions are really best described by some detailed specification that's accompanied by drawings which include flow charts and block diagrams. To require the filing of source code or object code would do little to meet the requirements of Section 112 since the source code and the object code may not even be readily understandable by those skilled in the art or by the patent attorneys who are actually preparing and filing the patent applications.

In fact, the source code and the object code may even serve to obfuscate the patentable subject matter. The obfuscation would especially be true where the amount of the source code or the object code filed is so large as to make it superfluous and/or nonintelligible.

Also the source code or the object code may not be sufficiently annotated to provide any source of information or it just simply may not be directed to the patentable aspects of the invention.

It is our position that the filing of the source code should not be required and, in fact, should not even be permitted because we believe that it will do nothing to facilitate searching and that it is really contrary to some of the other protections that -- I'm sorry.

Also we believe that the filing of the source code may not be appropriate in certain circumstances since it really may disclose the trade secret aspects of subject matter which is not the subject of the patent application. This certainly is not consistent with requirements nor the objectives of the other forms of statutory protection.

Once again, on behalf of Bellcore we thank you for permitting us to be heard on this important matter. And if you have any further questions we would be more than happy to answer them. Thank you very much.

COMMISSIONER LEHMAN: Thank you very much, Mr. Suchyta. We appreciate the time you have put into this and Bellcore has.

I'd like to go back now and see if Michael Chakansky has arrived. Apparently not. And I don't think Mr. Heckel has arrived either. I think we apparently are having some transportation problems up and down the east coast here.

Did Mr. DeAngeli arrive?

(No audible response.)

COMMISSIONER LEHMAN: Then we'll go on to D.C. Toedt. Oh, I'm sorry, Vern Blanchard. I'm sorry, I missed Mr. Blanchard. Sorry.

PRESENTATION BY VERN BLANCHARD

AMERICAN MULTISYSTEMS

MR. BLANCHARD: Good afternoon. According to Mr. Band I probably fall within the software patents, or bad bunch and even on a good day I think bad software patents are bad. So maybe we can take it from there.

I'm CEO and janitor of what's left of American Multisystems. I'm hopefully representative of the smaller companies which generally don't have the opportunity to come speak before you.

COMMISSIONER LEHMAN: That's one reason we went to the Silicon Valley and we had a lot more of the people who felt that software patents were bad out there. So we do know a little bit. They don't tend to have Washington lawyers as much.

MR. BLANCHARD: Well, I think that's maybe why they sent me.

COMMISSIONER LEHMAN: Where are you from?

MR. BLANCHARD: I'm from San Diego.

COMMISSIONER LEHMAN: I see, so you came all the way.

MR. BLANCHARD: Yes, I did.

COMMISSIONER LEHMAN: Thanks.

MR. BLANCHARD: The patent system was enacted to promote the useful sciences. You've heard arguments stating that without the patent process the software industry won't produce and it will ultimately fail. My belief is that until the door for software patents was opened judicially we had a flourishing software industry.

I believe that unless we close that door and get back to where we used to be, the United States will be relegated to a third world status as far as software is concerned. Programmers are not a stupid bunch. When we're faced with endless and expensive litigation and uncertainty, we're just going to migrate to other fields.

And you, by keeping things as they are, will cause the best and the brightest in the software industry to go to other activities and professions. Our innovations will be stillborn. The public loses when that happens. I'll get up on a little high horse here. It probably sounds a little melodramatic, but right now we have the power --

Specifically, you have the power in changing some of the rules that will make or break an entire industry. I believe that software patents must be eliminated. The patents granted over the last decade or so are now being used to attack developers for selling programs that they have independently developed.

We're reaching a point where new companies are going to be barred from the software arena because most programs will require licenses from dozens of patents. I've seen quite a few of them that in my opinion are absurd and were very obvious even at the time they were granted.

By requiring the licenses it's going to make projects unfeasible and I was one of those particular companies. You're going to be inundated with platitudes from both sides of this issue -- hopefully I'll inundate you with a few things that will change your mind -- you'll be told of lofty principles and moral and ethical high grounds.

But the bottom line is, the actions of the PTO affect people. You've heard that software patents are necessary to protect the small company. American Multisystems is one person. That's me. I'm probably typical of many start-up companies. And we'll get into what my story is.

I'm a pretty good programmer. In fact, outside of this room I'll probably tell you I'm a great programmer and lay out a couple other descriptions of how well I can program. In 1991 I was approached by a client who invited me to partake in the American dream. If I could program a bingo program I could taste the good life, which I did. I thought there would be no problem at all. Bingo is a real simple program. It's a child's game, in fact.

Most computer programming classes, this is first year stuff, you design a bingo game or a checkers game or something along those lines, very, very simple. Besides, I had already, as it turned out, just by coincidence, played an electronic bingo game back in the early '80s on some OSI computers, for those of you that remember OSI.

Certainly patent law had nothing to do with my analysis of whether or not I could do the project. I abandoned all my other projects for two years. And what you can read into that is I did it without pay. I saw the opportunity and I went for it.

Ultimately I developed a superior product. My customers liked it. The competition out there respected it. Life was good. And then I was introduced to the patent system. One of my competitors sued me for patent infringement. And irrespective of the fact that I always believed that software was an expression of an idea and covered under the First Amendment -- and we won't get into legal details because I'm sure there are probably many of my colleagues

out here who will take issue with that -- besides that the fact that playing bingo on a computer is not novel, it's not unique. There's nothing inherently brilliant about it.

The program that I created is nothing more than mathematical algorithms. And the fact is, I did nothing ethically or morally wrong and effectively I was put out of business.

The realities of the patent system as it relates to computer software is this --

COMMISSIONER LEHMAN: You need to tell us a little more how that happened. There are only two ways, it seems to me that you would be put out of business. One is that you decided to shut your doors in the face of the patent claims from your competitor or two, that the competitor actually enforced their patent in some way that caused you to go out of business.

MR. BLANCHARD: In fact, that's what happened. That's what I'm getting to. They filed suit for patent infringement. The patent in question covered a hand-held calculator type device and it was broadly written enough to where since I was a competitor they thought they could include my program, which happened to be run on plain vanilla, IBM-clone, off-the-shelf Comp-USA kind of hardware.

The filed for an injunction which, of course -- the problem with the system as it is now is judges are not particularly literate in technical issues. When they see a patent they presume that it's valid, as they should. They're in a position if the PTO says that this is a valid patent, well, of course, it's a valid patent. They're not necessarily schooled in knowing the nuances of whether a particular claim reads on an invention or not.

So initially the small company or the people that are defendants in these actions are behind the eight ball. We must, even though the burden of proof is supposed to be on the Plaintiff showing that their patent is valid, the realities are that judges, when they see a patent, believe that the patent is valid.

Now what the bottom line is, is when small companies are involved in patent litigation you have just about by filing of the suit put most companies out of business. My particular situation was unique. As it turns out, I had some legal schooling. Everything that could possibly have gone right, went right in my case and yet I'm out of business and I'm in debt over $100,000.

The mere filing of a patent infringement suit will kill most small companies.

COMMISSIONER LEHMAN: Does that mean you won the suit?

MR. BLANCHARD: Well, yes, I'm victorious. There was actually -- I'll take that back. We're still in litigation. The state of our suit was that they filed for a preliminary injunction which was granted. We, of course, countered with points that we made stating why she should overturn it, which she ultimately did.

And, again, everything -- in my particular case things went well. I was able to do most of the legal work, saving

UNITED STATES PATENT AND TRADEMARK OFFICE
Public Hearing on Patent Protection for Software-Related Inventions
Arlington, Virginia -- February 10 & 11, 1994

probably hundreds of thousands of dollars. My adversary spent more than $450,000. Now this was just at the very first stage and I was into it thankfully only for $100,000.

We had prior art searches done by the League for Programming Freedom. We found perfect prior art. Everything went right. I had experts in the industry sign on and file -- and I'll make this brief -- on my behalf. We had a judge who after giving a decision that said yes, this infringes and you're restrained actually took the time to learn about patent law and actually realized that she had made a mistake and reversed her decision.

That rarely a happens. I mean, how often have you heard a judge say, I've made a mistake, here's the new ruling. I mean, we even expected her to say, if you don't like it, appeal it. Everything went right in my particular case and yet American Multisystems is not a viable company today.

I copied nothing as far as the code. Very simple. Again, it's a very simple code, playing bingo.

COMMISSIONER LEHMAN: Well, is that because the preliminary injunction was lifted so that you could continue to do business? Why did you go out of business then?

MR. BLANCHARD: The cost. We have $100,000 in legal fees, not including all the time and effort that we were down, patent companies -- or the aggressor in my particular case, of course, went out into my particular industry and waved around the preliminary injunction. Effectively, we no longer can partake in that market.

The realities are, is that happens all the time. By filing suit against the small company -- in fact, I'm sure that there are many patent attorneys here will tell you what a retainer will cost and what just even answering a complaint will cost small companies.

COMMISSIONER LEHMAN: Was your case, your defense, based upon the fact, the response that you did not infringe or was it based on the validity of the plaintiff's patent?

MR. BLANCHARD: Yes, we took it from all those aspects.

COMMISSIONER LEHMAN: And apparently there hasn't been a final judgment, so the judge has not ruled on the patentability claim?

MR. BLANCHARD: No.

COMMISSIONER LEHMAN: On the viability of the patent.

MR. BLANCHARD: At this point we're still --

COMMISSIONER LEHMAN: And is it your view that the patent was -- the basis of the infringement lawsuit was not valid?

MR. BLANCHARD: My opinion is yes, that it was not valid. It was written so broadly that it covered everything from a wristwatch, calculator, computer, laptop.

COMMISSIONER LEHMAN: So it fell back into the second category that Mr. Band described as bad software patents in your view?

MR. BLANCHARD: Yes.

COMMISSIONER LEHMAN: Did you ever think of using the reexamination procedure which would have presumably been a lot less costly way for you to resolve this?

MR. BLANCHARD: Yes. We did consider that. The problem with that is, by reexamining they may very well have had a good patent as to a particular device. But we still did not believe that it would read on our invention. By going and reexamining it and coming back with you, the PTO, saying that it's valid we then have no chance in court.

I'm supposed to stop speaking. But if you have any other questions.

COMMISSIONER LEHMAN: Well, I've kept you going. So if you want to -- if you have a couple more minutes, why don't you continue because I interrupted you unlike some of the other witnesses. But I wanted to flesh out what the main objections and the main points were in your experience.

MR. BLANCHARD: Sure. The problem that's unique, I believe, to software and I've heard some of the other speakers state that software should not be differentiated from other fields. I was able to complete a very complex project because of the programming tools I had available, not because of any technique or patent or anything else that anybody had taught by virtue of the patents.

The innovation in software is because of the tools that we have available to us. We can nearly instantaneously change things, see how they will work. The tools provide the innovation, not the prior coding.

The overall effect if we continue to have software patents, in my opinion hinder, the industry, is that the PTO will obstruct that which you were charged to promote, which was the useful sciences. Computer programmers, we share a program all the time. I invite you to log onto many of the informational services. We help each other. We submit code back and forth. And that's how computer programmers assemble pieces of code, bits of ideas, bits of techniques into finished products.

Where computer software is different from many of the other fields are because of the tools that we have. Our compilers today do things that were unheard of even five years ago, and not because someone had patented any particular technique. It's just the evolution of the software process.

So I would implore you to change the rules as to software patents to eliminate them or at least make it so that we fall into the bad software patents or eliminate the bad software patents.

COMMISSIONER LEHMAN: Thank you very much. Now you could help us a little bit if you would -- since we don't have the time to get into all the details of your case. But I assume since you were in litigation you have memoranda or motions and so on and so forth --

MR. BLANCHARD: Yes.

COMMISSIONER LEHMAN: -- filed in court, maybe even a decision of the judge. It would be really useful to have a

UNITED STATES PATENT AND TRADEMARK OFFICE
Public Hearing on Patent Protection for Software-Related Inventions
Arlington, Virginia -- February 10 & 11, 1994

record to look at as an example, you know, to find out what was really going on there, get to the bottom of your concerns. Obviously to the extent that, in fact, you had a truly valid patent there and you may have, in fact, been infringing that patent. That creates one circumstance.

If in fact your allegations had some merit to them or your defense did, that the initial patent was overly broad, that suggests that it was a bad software patent, bad software patents are bad and maybe that we should have been doing something about that.

But we can't really get to the heart of that until we look at some of the more details of your case. We hear this, certainly this statement, made. We've heard it in the Silicon Valley. We've heard it from you, that there is a real chilling effect going on here. I would like to get to the bottom of that. Is that indeed the case?

And to get some very specific examples of it if people are, in fact, having that problem, so that we can determine whether or not there is a serious problem of widespread scope and then to maybe address if there is how to deal with it or are these just idiosyncratic rare circumstances that every -- and that happens in life.

I mean every once in a while in business sometimes, you know, you get some bad luck. I'm trying to determine whether this is bad luck occasionally or whether there's some systematic pattern of problems here. You can help us with that by supplying what you have.

MR. BLANCHARD: I've got probably five feet of filings. Would you like them all?

COMMISSIONER LEHMAN: Yes, you can send them to Jeff Kushan here and he can stay up until 3 o'clock in the morning for a week, which he will do.

MR. BLANCHARD: Thank you.

COMMISSIONER LEHMAN: And you got his Internet number. Actually, it's in the witness list, I think, or one of the handouts that's out on the table.

Next, is Mr. Heckel here yet?

(No audible response.)

COMMISSIONER LEHMAN: Apparently not. Did Mr. Chakansky come?

(No audible response.)

COMMISSIONER LEHMAN: Mr. DeAngeli?

(No audible response.)

COMMISSIONER LEHMAN: Apparently not. Then I guess we're down to D.C. Toedt of Arnold, White and Durkee from Texas. I think people are having a hard time getting into National Airport now and he wasn't on our list until 4:30, but I don't think we're going to be here until 4:30.

Joseph Hofstader is here, I think.

Well, I don't know quite what to do. I think he was the last witness. So actually we're at the end of witnesses here. Yes, sir?

MR. CURRY: Given that you have some time, would you allow some informal discussion? Just for a couple of minutes.

COMMISSIONER LEHMAN: Well, I would permit you to come forward if you wanted to make a statement for a few minutes since we have time. Let me say this, we have a lot of stuff to do here. We're really busy and really crunched time wise. So it's not like we have all afternoon to -- we have a lot of good things to do with our time if we do adjourn the hearing early. But since we do have a few minutes and since these people didn't come, I'd be happy to let you come forward and make a statement if you'd like. If you'll identify yourself, please.

PRESENTATION BY EDDIE CURRY

IMAGE SOFT, INC.

MR. CURRY: My name is Eddie Curry. I'm from a company called ImageSoft, Inc. based in New York. We're a software publishing company. We are right now are involved in a patent infringement suit which has been suggested that a patent that we're offering is infringing on someone else's patent. I just want to make a couple of brief remarks if I may. I appreciate your allowing me to speak.

I've been in the software publishing business since 1975. I was at a small company in Albuquerque called Mentz. It built the first microcomputer. That's where Microsoft originated. I've spent a lot of time watching the industry develop.

This is my first experience with patent issues. And what I've experienced, briefly, is that in looking at the particular patent in question the patent is incredibly broad, making it very difficult for us to respond in a way that we would like to.

There is virtually no reflection of any consideration of prior art in the patent itself, other than some oblique references to some existing patents, which are pretty far afield from the material that's covered in the patent itself. But there is a considerable body of prior art which we've been able to document.

The dilemma is the following. It's pretty obvious from listening to the comments that have bee made here, it's pretty obvious in what I've read and what I've learned, that the reexamination process is a fundamentally flawed process from the perspective of someone like ourselves.

We have spent to date about $120,000 just arguing over the venue in which this case is going to be heard and we still don't have a venue decision. We filed an action in Federal Court in New York.

We would like to use the reexamination process because we are confident that if we, in fact, could have a fair and equitable hearing of the facts that it would be very difficult for this patent to stand.

I have spoken in the last 30 days to about six law firms in New York City, all of whom specialize in intellectual property, to a man, every firm, or to a firm every firm has

UNITED STATES PATENT AND TRADEMARK OFFICE
Public Hearing on Patent Protection for Software-Related Inventions
Arlington, Virginia -- February 10 & 11, 1994

suggested strongly that we do not avail ourselves of the reexamination process because they have little faith and belief in it, because they believe it accrues largely to the benefit of the patent holder, that it will afford an opportunity for the patent holder to extend or otherwise modify the coverage of the patent in ways that may not have been anticipated at the time the patent was filed, but certainly wouldn't accrue to our benefit or may not.

And more importantly, if we invoke that process, we are then operating in a substantial handicap if that process produces a result that is not in our favor in terms of litigation as we would go forward.

Now I represent at the moment about 15 different authors of software products. Our business is to take small companies such as the one you heard about here. We specialize in development tools. It's a fairly high technology end of the business.

I think the problem here is that we ought to be able to appeal to the Patent Office, we ought to be able to appeal to the reexamination process, we ought to have confidence that we would have a fair and equitable hearing and if the facts bear out that we have, in fact, infringed then we'll suffer the consequences.

My suggestion is that at a minimum the Patent Office ought to recognize the fact that it probably has issued some patents that were overly broad, that probably in retrospect ought to be reexamined, ought to be critically reexamined. They ought to broaden the opportunities for people such as ourselves to participate in that process so that we don't have to be at arm's length in terms of making submissions and then waiting in the wings to find out what the conclusions are going to be; and that that process ought to work and be fair and equitable.

My guess is that if we poll the people in this room we'd find out that they would agree this is not a process to be used. I would further suspect that if we poll the people sitting up here they, if they're candid, would have to admit, although they probably may choose not to, that it's not a fair and equitable process.

Now I think that at a minimum there ought to be a watershed that says we're going to take into consideration that there are people that right now are suffering from this flawed process and do something to address that where possible.

The other problem we have is, it's not likely that you will do anything in the near term that will help us. So we probably are going to be left to proceed without the reexamination process even though we believe very strongly that we could present a very substantial case that an error has been made.

So you can't plot a curve with only one data point, but we are one data point. We're spending a lot of money for reasons that we don't fully understand. We're convinced we shouldn't be spending this kind of money and we don't have recourse through the Patent Office that we can feel comfortable with. That's really my comment.

COMMISSIONER LEHMAN: Well, thank you. I appreciate those comments. I think those were extremely helpful and useful about perspective. They certainly lend a sense of urgency to our work here to try to get a more responsive system in place as quickly as possible.

Let me just call the witnesses again here. See if anybody's come in the door. I don't think they have. Michael M. DeAngeli. Michael Chakansky. Paul Heckel. D.C. Toedt -- is it Toedt? -- and Joseph Hofstader.

I think what I'm going to do in view of the fact that we're way ahead of the schedule and we did say for people to be here at least 20 minutes in advance, and we have a real backed up schedule. I have a very backed up schedule and lots of prices and problems to deal with.

What I'm going to do is suggest that we recess the hearing until 4:15 and that at that time I ask Mr. Kushan to reconvene the hearing and to chair it and to take testimony from -- if we have any of these people who manage to straggle in and at least give them some testimony since I suspect some of them are trying to get here by plane, and it would be very unfair to have them go through the hell of trying to fly in this weather and then land at National Airport, get all the way here and then not have the hearing.

So I think we at least want to give them that opportunity to put their views on the record here in this forum. If they don't show up by 4:15 then we'll obviously take their testimony in written form, either through the mail or if they want to send it to us on electronic mail through the Internet they can do that.

So with that I'm going to adjourn the hearing until 4:15 and Mr. Kushan will reconvene it for any of the stragglers that there may be.

(Recess.)

MR. KUSHAN: We've reached a consensus. The two speakers that we've identified as being here are going to testify tomorrow morning in our a.m. session.

So unless the other three people, which I should probably read off one last time are here, we will cancel the hearing for the remainder of the day and reconvene in the morning. The three people that weren't identified before Michael DeAngeli, Michael Chakansky, and Paul Heckel. I don't see Paul. Michael DeAngeli is in California.

So we're 0 for 3. That means that we're going to cancel for the rest of the day today and we'll reconvene tomorrow morning at 9:00 a.m., probably until about 12:15. Thank you.

(Whereupon, at 3:20 p.m., the hearing in the above-entitled matter was adjourned, to reconvene on Friday, February 11, 1994 at 9:00 a.m.)

UNITED STATES PATENT AND TRADEMARK OFFICE
Public Hearing on Patent Protection for Software-Related Inventions
Arlington, Virginia -- February 10 & 11, 1994

PROCEEDINGS

MORNING SESSION

COMMISSIONER LEHMAN: Let me just make a couple of opening comments. First let me introduce everyone here, in case you don't know, I'm Bruce Lehman. My title is the Assistant Secretary of Commerce and Commissioner of Patents and Trademarks. And this is Larry Goffney, who is our Assistant Commissioner for Patents designate.

And then we also have Mike Fleming who is one of our SPE supervisory patent examiners. If you have any follow-up or any questions today to this, you can talk to Mike about it, administrative type questions, or any other questions he can help you with.

But the staff person for these hearings if Jeff Kushan. His telephone number is 703-305-9300, he's way out at the far reaches of Northern Virginia, and he's not here today.

I think among the papers somewhere there is this Internet address on there, too. You can certainly find it there.

For those who weren't here, we will have a transcript of this hearing. The transcripts will be available after February 21st this year, and paper copies will be available for $30 and they will be available on the Internet at our FTEP site for free. That site is comments, period, USPTO, period, GOB.

Also, the transcript from our December 20 Federal Register notice will be available about the same FTEP site.

What I would like to do is that we have two witnesses from yesterday who didn't make it. They had problems with airplanes. It started yesterday and so we found ourselves finishing very early yesterday. So we'll start with them. And the first is D.C. Toedt, from Arnold, White and Durkee who comes all the way from Texas.

Shall we just have them -- do you mind sitting in here? And you can turn towards us and use that microphone and talk into it.

PRESENTATION BY MR. D.C. TOEDT

ARNOLD, WHITE AND DURKEE

MR. TOEDT: First off, thank you very much for accommodating the viscidities of travel. I found out a little while ago that the real reason for my trip, which was a federal circuit oral argument this morning, was canceled. So I'm glad this was able to go forward. I appreciate your working it in.

COMMISSIONER LEHMAN: I should say, this is the advantage of a fully user fee funded agency.

(Laughter.)

COMMISSIONER LEHMAN: You've got to be there when your customers are there. The court is not a full user fee.

MR. TOEDT: As Mr. Commissioner indicated my name is D.C. Toedt. As requested in the Federal Register notice of this hearing, let me summarize briefly for the record my affiliation.

I'm a shareholder and chair of the Patent Prosecution Practice Committee at Arnold, White and Durkee, practicing in the firm's Houston office. Much of my firm's practice and my own work relates to the computer industry and to computer software. My remarks today, however, represent my own views and not necessarily those of my firm nor of any of its clients or its other attorneys. My remarks are directed strictly to procedural questions and not to the substantive issues that have come up in these hearings.

For the convenience of the panel, the written version of my remarks includes something of an executive summary beginning on page 2.

Mr. Secretary, you mentioned just now, and in San Jose two weeks ago, your focus on the customers of the PTO, and we're all aware of the Clinton Administration's commitment to reinventing government. It sounds as though you're familiar with the concept of reengineering.

The PTO has made considerable progress lately in improving the quality of examinations, but the challenge faced by the Office is broader than that. The Office should be concerned with doing the right things in today's high technology world, and not just doing things right as that might have been defined years or decades or even centuries ago.

One of the first steps, of course, is figuring out who the customers are and what is it they want. In the broadest terms, the PTO's customers are the people who participate in patent enforcement, by which I mean, not just litigants -- judges, juries, attorneys -- but companies doing license negotiations, design work, deciding whether they can compete with a patent owner, or whether they stay out because they respect the patent rights.

I'd like to address three points today concerning what the PTO can do for those customers. Some of my suggestions frankly even to me seem a little bit off the beaten track. Some might work. Some might need fine-tuning. Some might be wildly impractical upon further thought or maybe in actual practice.

First, the Office should experiment within the existing statutory framework through notice and comment rulemaking, with borrowing some approaches from the Securities and Exchange Commission. In some notable respects the PTO's work is very similar to that of the SEC. A company or an individual does similar things when it applies for a patent and when it issues securities. In each case, it's going to the public and asking, broadly speaking, to give it an asset for use in its business. In effect, it's saying to the public, let's make a deal.

The price the public levies is information in the offering document, whether that's a patent application or a securities prospectus. Both the PTO and the SEC are charged with ensuring that when a company goes to the public seeking such an asset, the public gets what it pays for.

The U.S. securities markets are considered to be the best in the world, so maybe there's some lessons to be had there. And it's interesting because the PTO and the SEC

UNITED STATES PATENT AND TRADEMARK OFFICE
Public Hearing on Patent Protection for Software-Related Inventions
Arlington, Virginia -- February 10 & 11, 1994

take considerably different approaches to their work and to their respective uses of administrative resources.

The SEC does not use a one size fits all philosophy. If your proposed securities offering is a limited one, a low end offering with limited potential impact on the public, you can use short form disclosures, streamlined SEC approval proceedings.

If you're willing to settle for a low end asset, restrictions on the dollar amount of the offering, the amount of solicitation you could do and so forth, you can use a qualification proceeding under Regulation A as recently amended specifically for small business owners, instead of a full blown public offering registration, or you could even be exempt from registration entirely.

Every venture capitalist and every small business pretty much knows it can make a lot more sense for a company to go for such a low end securities offering first, and hold off on a full blown public offering until it clearly makes sense.

The other difference is that the SEC tries a different way of getting the most bang for its buck. It prescribes fairly detailed requirements in advance for a disclosure content and format of an organization, and in some instances certification by outside professional CPAs, for example.

The SEC is very selective about how it uses its investigation and examination resources. It doesn't do merit review of securities offerings at all unless a problem comes up and they have to deal with enforcement proceedings. They save their resources for when they can do the most good for the public.

The SEC's examination of offering documents is usually confined to determining that the documents comply with the extensive formal requirements. If you're in this kind of business, you need to disclose this, this, and this, in such and such order.

Staff can get pretty picky about whether you've complied. But even so, securities offerings are approved with what we patent lawyers would regard as blinding speed.

The Commissioner might have authority under the existing statute to create analogous low end patents for people who want them, like small businesses, for example, that can be obtained quickly and inexpensively without a full blown examination proceeding.

By regulation the Commissioner might require applicants to file applications that conform to specified content and format standards, depending on the argument they're in. And an applicant that wanted to could file a written election to waive certain statutory rights associated with a patent, and reduce the impact of the patent on the public.

The Commissioner could then cause a limited examination to happen. The statute says only that the Commissioner shall cause an examination to be made -- and then issue the patent quickly.

The applicant's written election might include, for example, voluntary acceptance of limitations on statutory rights and remedies, maybe an obligation to prove patentability in any infringement litigation, maybe just a few claims, maybe an independent prior art search.

If the application and the written election documents appear to be in order, issue the patent. Treat the written election as a continuation application. Suspend action on the continuation for some period of time. And if it turns out to be worth it to the patent owner in the long run, the patent owner can ask for a full blown examination to go to a conventional, what would now be a 20-year patent, subject to broadening of reissue limitations and intervening right considerations.

I think many small businesses and large companies would love to have such an option available. One of my colleagues that deals mostly in biotech areas said that she thought many of her clients would be delighted to be able to get some protection up front, and wait until it becomes more clearly advantageous to go through a full blown proceeding.

The Office should try that out on an experimental basis. My written remarks go into a fair amount of more detail about that possibility.

Now, a friend of mine who is in-house at a large company's patent department commented that this sounds uncomfortably like the Japanese system, where an applicant can wait years to request examination and businesses might have to wait that long to know whether a patent got ever issued.

I see a critical difference. In Japan, as I understand it, the applicant's incentive to request examination at the end of the -- I think it's a seven-year period -- is to go from zero protection to full protection. Here the differential is much smaller. The low end patent owner has some protection already. So there's much less upside and much less incentive to try and go for a full blown examination at the end of whatever the waiting period is.

My second suggestion is that we get rid of file ping-pong in examination proceedings. As an attorney, I never know when an Office action is going to hit my in box. It could be years after filing. The examiner never knows when I'm going to respond, if at all. He never knows when I'm going to pick up the phone and call and ask for an interview, he or she.

I sometimes wonder whether, as a result, some attorneys and examiners unconsciously focus more on getting the file off of their desk and onto someone else's desk, than on getting a client's project finished.

Moreover, sometimes it can seem like it's difficult to get meaningful attention from an SPE. The SPEs are busy. They are very busy. They might have a dozen or more assistants to supervise. And every now and then you get the feeling that you're like in a situation where you're buying a car.

You talk to the salesman, and the salesman says, yeah, I think we can do that. But the salesman has to go off to talk to the sales manager in the back room. Sometimes you make the deal, and sometimes the salesman comes back and says, sorry, we can't do that.

UNITED STATES PATENT AND TRADEMARK OFFICE
Public Hearing on Patent Protection for Software-Related Inventions
Arlington, Virginia -- February 10 & 11, 1994

It's not like that in appeals to the board. It's not like that in interferences. And more particularly, it's not like that in trial work. If the judge wants it to, the scheduling order means what it says. If you're on the Eastern District in the rocket docket, in Judge Sam Kent's court in Galveston, you will get your pretrial work done, and you will go to trial on schedule. You get in, you get it done. Everybody gets very focused because that's their one shot.

Let's try doing some patent examinations that way. Let an assistant examiner function like a junior prosecutor in a DA's office. He can try cases under the tutelage of a more experienced attorney, but he's trying the cases. Let a primary examiner be the "judge." Have discovery cutoffs for exchanging prior art. Do whatever claim amendments are desired, whatever evidence of patentability against patentability is desired. Propose filings and conclusions just like examiners do now, just like attorneys do now. And let the primary make the decision, a first and final action.

If the action is adverse, take it up on appeal. Tape record the hearing maybe. It could be just a low key interview. It doesn't' need to be a complete adversarial proceeding. Transcribe it to get a written decision. It could be a lot like a board of appeal, a lot like an interference.

It would make life easier for attorneys, I think. Many examiners would probably enjoy doing administrative trials instead of having work shoved into their in-box. I think the quality of the examination would go up, and the throughput volume might even go up.

Now, my in-house friend said he thought a lot of old-time patent lawyers would be very nervous about this, that a lot of them like the leisurely practice, where you've got three to six months to handle an Office action that comes in.

That is a valid concern, but it is certainly not the driving one.

Mr. Secretary, many practitioners are delighted that the Office is working so hard on the examination process. You have a wonderful opportunity to help improve the role of the PTO in promoting the progress of science and the useful arts.

Thank you very much for the chance to participate.

COMMISSIONER LEHMAN: Thank you very much. I might want to just ask you a question, if you would bear with me for just a second.

First, I would like to say for the record that your testimony was extremely polished and very well delivered. And I know what the reason for that was. You were a student of my colleague Larry Goffney when he taught you at the University of Texas.

So it's a good illustration of, you know, if this is what we get from the student, just think what we will get from the master.

The procedure you were talking about offers sort of a range of options. In a sense, some of the other countries already have this. In Europe some countries have sort of

petty patent systems. The Germans have it. And that's one of the kinds of things that you're talking about, right?

MR. TOEDT: Correct.

COMMISSIONER LEHMAN: The advantage of that specifically for what we're talking about today would be that at least this would enable us to focus the examination resources on the really critical issues and the really critical technology.

It would also have the advantage, then, I assume for the -- if you want to use the term petty patents, whatever you want to use -- it would have the advantage of getting that information out there, at least, in the public domain so that people would know that it was there, would be aware that it was lurking out there.

Presumably they would then be able to prepare, should that -- if they disagreed with the patent claims and the patent applicant decided to go for the full-blown patent, they would be well-positioned then to come in to make certain that the Patent Office had the relevant prior art and so on.

Does that sort of describe the advantages of the system that you just outlined?

MR. TOEDT: Those are among them, yes, sir.

COMMISSIONER LEHMAN: Those are among the advantages. That was the answer to that.

Professor?

COMMISSIONER GOFFNEY: Great presentation. Thank you very much.

(Discussion off the record.)

COMMISSIONER LEHMAN: Next I'd like to call Joseph Hofstader. Joseph Hofstader is basically sitting in for his father, Christian Hofstader.

MR. HOFSTADER: My brother.

COMMISSIONER LEHMAN: Oh, your brother. I didn't think there was anybody your father's age in the League for Programming Freedom. So I was really surprised at that when I was told it was your father. But it's your brother. And he is here to represent the League for Programming Freedom.

PRESENTATION BY JOSEPH HOFSTADER

LEAGUE FOR PROGRAMMING FREEDOM

MR. HOFSTADER: Thank you for giving me the opportunity to testify before you today. The League for Programming Freedom is an organization of software developers opposed to software patents and copyrights on user interfaces.

I would like to use this opportunity to clarify some of the issues that were raised in an earlier round of hearings in San Jose. To evaluate the numerous conflicting arguments that have been made, we must organize them within a systematic framework. Since the patent system is an economic system, economics is the best framework.

UNITED STATES PATENT AND TRADEMARK OFFICE
Public Hearing on Patent Protection for Software-Related Inventions
Arlington, Virginia — February 10 & 11, 1994

What questions need to be answered? What issues should be confronted prior to determining whether software patents should be granted?

The goal of the patent system is to provide science in the useful arts. Whether software should be patentable is therefore a question of whether patents promote innovation and progress in the software industry in the computer sciences. The economic interpretation of this question is whether granting patents on software benefits the economy by making the software industry more efficient.

The League for Programming Freedom asks: Does the transfer of economic resources, which software patents represent, constitute a transfer whereby the resources are going to be employed more productively?

As an example of how the patent system is dependent on economic factors that will vary from one industry to another, I will mention just one factor, the overall size of an industry.

Let's imagine there are 5,000 people employed by the candlemaking industry in the U.S. and that it has been determined based on sound economic principles that the optimal life for a patent in the candlemaking industry is 20 years. Suppose the demand for candles is twice what it actually is. The candle making industry would be almost twice its earlier size, employing close to 10,000 people.

Under a set of economic assumptions reasonable for the candlemaking or software industry, economics would then dictate a cut in the length of patents for the candlemaking industry. Cutting the length of patents by one-half would yield roughly the same incentive to invent, and thus the same rate of progress that existed earlier.

Alternatively, we might consider cutting the length of patents by one quarter. In doing so, we're sending a signal to the candlemaking industry regarding the increase net economic value of improvements in the candlemaking process.

This signal, however, has to be effectively traded off against the increased lack of competition. When the size of an industry increases, the optimal lifetime for patents needs to be shortened. Without knowing various factors relating to the inventive process in the candlemaking industry, the new length for patents is a matter of debate.

It isn't fair to directly compare the software industry to the candlemaking industry. The software is much larger, and it is also much broader. From the example of the candlemaking industry, it should be possible to understand how the traditional 17-year patent grant may in some industries conceivably hurt progress by stifling competition more than it helps progress by encouraging innovation.

The software industry employs some 6 million people. A significant fraction of them develop software. More people are probably engaged in the software development than in all other branches of engineering combined. As a result, in the software industry reinvention has become

commonplace, and software patents seriously harm the competition.

In eliminating software patents, is it going to be possible to legislatively define software? This issue was raised frequently at the San Jose hearings. It is surprising that such an argument can be to justify risking the future efficiency of a $50 billion a year industry.

Since this argument is apparently one of the key arguments in favor of the continued granting of software patents, the League decided to subject it to intense scrutiny.

It is true that many things in this world form part of a continuum. Nonetheless, we are able to legislatively differentiate between them. The post office is able to distinguish between a letter and a letter packet. The FDA is able to distinguish between a cheese spread and a cheese-flavored spread. There is no way to draw a perfect line between drunk and sober, but the law does draw a line, and it works.

On a larger scale, the IRS classifies capital goods into many different categories, to determine depreciation rates, while the Customs Service is able to classify things to apply duties. Considerable financial incentives exist to try to circumvent these classification systems, yet they work. There is little problem with them being circumvented, or with their complexities imposing great financial burdens. The legal system effectively handles disputes over occasional borderline cases.

A legislative definition of software need not embody absolute truth. It need only work effectively and efficiently. Searching for absolute truth makes no more sense than determining the exact definition the IRS should use for wood pulping machinery.

The definition the League proposes is, "Software is composed of an ideal infallible mathematical component whose outputs are ineffective by the components they feed into."

I'm confident that the PTO and the courts would be able to readily distinguish between software and hardware using this definition. The PTO is already skilled at administering a classification system that deals with far more subtle distinctions.

To show that it is possible to legislatively define software patents, the League performed an ambitious experiment. The League examined 2,000 patents issued during a one-week period. We tediously analyzed the details of every software-related patent granted in that week. We found little difficulty existed in identifying software-related patents.

The League then took each software-related patent and analyzed its claim according to a number of different criteria. These criteria were chosen on the basis that their presence could be used as a part of a test to identify software patents that should not be granted. The results of this research clearly showed us that it would be relatively simple to legislatively define and identify software patents.

This is not surprising, given that legislation already exists, that it is able to successfully identify far more nebulous

UNITED STATES PATENT AND TRADEMARK OFFICE
Public Hearing on Patent Protection for Software-Related Inventions
Arlington, Virginia -- February 10 & 11, 1994

concepts than the difference between software and hardware.

At the San Jose hearings, Tom Cronin of Taligent forcefully suggested start up companies require software to attract venture capital. He described Taligent as a recent start up that has succeeded in attracting a large amount of venture capital, and for whom software patents were considered as vital.

He failed to mention Taligent was an IBM-Apple joint venture staffed by transferring surplus personnel from these two companies. Taligent is quite unique when compared to most other startups.

The numerous two-kids-in-a-garage stories demonstrate that successful software ventures require very little capital. It isn't necessary to attract large amounts of capital to produce software, or at least it was not necessary. Defending against patent threats may increase this expense.

All the software companies spawned by the micro-computer revolution gathered sufficient starting capital without any software patents. Microsoft, Oralent, Novelle, Adobe, Systematic, Oracle, and WordPerfect are just a few examples.

The final prepared remark I have deals with why copyright is the most suitable form of intellectual property protection for the software industry. Patents are used in other industries to prevent companies from using, but not paying for, the results of their rivals' research and development. Permitting this would be a serious disincentive against R&D investment.

Unlike every other industry subject to patents, the software industry is unique in that its products are also subject to copyrights. Copyrights ensure that to be commercially successful a company choosing to follow another must spend as much to develop program as the original firm. Indeed, the history of spreadsheets, word processors, and virtually every other software product suggests that it is actually more expensive to follow than to lead.

A product that seeks to displace the market leader can only do so by incorporating new features, thereby making it more expensive to develop the original product.

Copyright is effective because it protects precisely the product that has been developed. It prevents other companies from benefiting by copying your products, while at the same time permitting them to reap the full benefits of anything they develop.

Copyright is efficient because it enables firms to compete on the basis of rival implementations. This competition is vital for the efficient allocation of economic resources. The traditional literal aspects of copyright doctrine is also efficient because it has negligible administrative overhead and presents no uncertainties. A small start up has the knowledge that they control what they create.

Given that copyright law effectively and efficiently achieves the economic aims of the patent system, there is simply no need for software patents.

This concludes the League for Programming Freedom's response to issues raised at the San Jose hearings. I would be happy to take any questions you might have.

COMMISSIONER LEHMAN: First, are you a computer programmer yourself, or are you just delivering Christian's --

MR. HOFSTADER: I'm not a programmer. I've worked for a high-tech firm in their legal department, though.

COMMISSIONER LEHMAN: So you are a lawyer?

MR. HOFSTADER: I'm not a lawyer, no. I'm not a programmer, though, either.

COMMISSIONER LEHMAN: You mentioned that the League had done an analysis of 2,000 computer program patents. Do you have that analysis available that you could share with us?

MR. HOFSTADER: I don't have it with me right now.

COMMISSIONER LEHMAN: Does Christian have it?

MR. HOFSTADER: Yes. What's happening and how I'm here right now is that they were stuck in Boston during the snowstorm. So the speech got faxed to me. The other materials are being sent Federal Express.

COMMISSIONER LEHMAN: I'd be interested in following up on that. We have to proceed on the basis of facts and take a look at these analyses. We might have some of our people -- Mike Fleming and others -- might take a look at it. And we might even want to have some further dialogue with you, or with the League, about that because it gets really into the question of our prior art database and what's going on here.

So I think, rather than just sort of have a statement about the results of this analysis, we'd really like to take a look at it to see if we would come to the same conclusion. If we would, obviously it would have some impact on what we would do.

MR. HOFSTADER: Okay.

COMMISSIONER LEHMAN: So you can pass that back. Thank you very much.

Now we're ready for Mr. Scanlon, Tim Scanlon. Would you identify where you're from?

PRESENTATION BY MR. TIMOTHY SCANLON

ALLEN-BRADLEY COMPANY

MR. SCANLON: Yes. Good morning. I'm with the Allen-Bradley Company. And the views that I'm expressing will be those of the Allen-Bradley Company.

COMMISSIONER LEHMAN: There was an Allen-Bradley witness who was --

MR. SCANLON: That was John J. Horn yesterday, who is our legal patent counsel at our headquarters office in Milwaukee.

COMMISSIONER LEHMAN: Yes. He was here, wasn't he?

UNITED STATES PATENT AND TRADEMARK OFFICE
Public Hearing on Patent Protection for Software-Related Inventions
Arlington, Virginia -- February 10 & 11, 1994

MR. SCANLON: Yes. He still is. He's right there.

COMMISSIONER LEHMAN: Oh, yes.

MR. SCANLON: He may be here for longer than he wants to be here.

COMMISSIONER LEHMAN: He's the guy that gave us the donuts. We have to pay, you know. I didn't realize they were coming from Allen-Bradley.

(Laughter.)

COMMISSIONER LEHMAN: If they're coming from you, it's okay. This is a widely-attended event. We can take a donut. But we can't take a donut from Allen-Bradley.

MR. SCANLON: You'd better save some for your stay in the airport tonight.

COMMISSIONER LEHMAN: I'm from Wisconsin and I'm familiar with that company pretty much. I doubt if they support the Clinton administration too much, but anyway.

(Laughter.)

COMMISSIONER LEHMAN: I'm just joking. Go ahead, please.

COMMISSIONER LEHMAN: Thank you.

MR. SCANLON: Good morning, Commissioner Lehman and other distinguished members of the panel, participants, and attendees.

Thank you for providing this forum to share our views relating to these important issues, and most importantly, thank you for your time.

My name is Timothy Scanlon. I'm representing the Allen-Bradley Company. Allen-Bradley is a world leader in industrial automation and control. We provide a diverse range of hardware and software products and services to enable our customers worldwide to compete in their respective markets.

As Allen-Bradley patent counsel John Horn presented yesterday, there is a fast and furious trend in our industry, like other industries, towards replacing hardware functionality with software. My position with Allen-Bradley is not that of legal counsel, but rather I'm a human interface specialist within a corporate-wide software marketing organization. It's a little bit different slant perspective from the past couple of days, hopefully.

My formal education is in industrial design in human factors. And I've been practicing these disciplines for the past 10-plus years. At Allen-Bradley I work with talented software developers, communication designers, and useability specialists to create new and innovative software user interface solutions.

These software graphical user interface designs enable a broad spectrum of users in the industrial control sector to interact with complex and sophisticated technologies to do what they really want to do, effectively perform work to satisfy their job requirements.

In general, people don't really want to use computers, they just want to get their work done.

So why are the visual aspects of software significant to the Allen-Bradley company and so important to protect? I'd like to address three key areas of significance to help foster an understanding of our position, and encourage appreciation for the impact that this has on our businesses and the businesses that use our software.

But before I address these three areas, I'd like to establish a definition for the visual aspects of our software.

The visual aspects of our software that we'd like to protect are what we call user interface components. These consist of icons, bit maps, and controls, developed specifically for our verticals markets in industry.

These are different from platform standard components, such as common dialogue boxes, et cetera, that are widely used across vertical industries. And we're not advocating protection of commonly and generally -- widely used standards as far as the windows controls and things of that nature.

Now back to the three key areas. The first one is the level of effort involved in establishing a usable graphical user interface. And I'd like to emphasize "usable." What the usability of Allen-Bradley software means to our customers will be area number two. And number three, how the software graphical user interface is an extensive of Allen-Bradley's expertise and knowledge of the industrial control and automation industry.

There are several constraints considered during the design of our graphical user interfaces. Key considerations include the accommodation of a broad spectrum of end users. Allen-Bradley, through extensive research and studies, has identified six types of users for our software products. Each and every software product that we design is designed to accommodate these user profiles.

The six categories of users and their educational backgrounds, just to give you an idea of the challenge, is, at the low end, a maintenance technician who has a high school diploma and maybe a two-year technical school certificate in electronics.

Next would be an operator who has a high school diploma and maybe a two-year technical degree certificate from a technical school.

Third on the way up the scale would be an installer, somebody who installs our equipment, whose educational background is high school, a two-year technical certificate, and possibly an apprenticeship.

Next would be an implementer, somebody who has a two-year certificate, an engineering degree in computer science, perhaps.

The last two on the high end of the scale would be a designer, a system designer, who typically has a two-year certificate, an engineering degree in computer science. And at the top level, a planner who actually plans a facility or a plant who typically would have a Bachelor of Science in Electrical Engineering, and possibly has completed a graduate level education program.

UNITED STATES PATENT AND TRADEMARK OFFICE
Public Hearing on Patent Protection for Software-Related Inventions
Arlington, Virginia -- February 10 & 11, 1994

The reason that I walked through these and gave these brief profiles was to illustrate the challenges that we face when designing graphical user interfaces. We have to accommodate a broad range of users in every product that we design, and we consider these.

In addition, all of our GUIs are designed to facilitate translation into seven languages, namely, English, French, German, Russian, Japanese, Spanish, and Italian. Special considerations are made to ensure that user interface components can accommodate expansion due to text screen growth, for instance, following translation.

We also developed symbology to incorporate into our tool buyers and in other areas of our software. And it's carefully designed for global recognition. So we developed several different symbols, and we actually test these. So there's quite a lot of money spent in developing these components.

As you can see, designing the GUI for --

COMMISSIONER LEHMAN: What's your status on the international market in your exports as a percentage of your sales?

MR. SCANLON: Percentage of sales? Boy, I'll tell you, that would be tough for me to quantify, since we've been traditionally a hardware-oriented company and we're now growing into software.

Rather than answering it that way, I'd like to tell you what products we have translated and --

COMMISSIONER LEHMAN: But I assume that a lot of your hardware is exported?

MR. SCANLON: Absolutely.

COMMISSIONER LEHMAN: Allen-Bradley is a big export company.

MR. SCANLON: Yes, we're very heavily --

COMMISSIONER LEHMAN: My impression was, it was like 50 percent or something like that, not that much.

MR. SCANLON: Is that about what it is, John?

MR. HORN: I don't know exactly know the figures, but if I were to take a rough guess, they are probably 20 or 30.

COMMISSIONER LEHMAN: Twenty or thirty? Yes.

MR. SCANLON: We're very heavily entrenched in the European markets and now starting to expand into the Asian markets at a fast rate.

COMMISSIONER LEHMAN: In the area of controls, that's your area, isn't it?

MR. SCANLON: Yes.

COMMISSIONER LEHMAN: My understanding is that there was some proprietary French technology which basically was a software technology, which has sort of a central position in this industry. Is that true?

MR. SCANLON: That would be the graphs set?

MR. HORN: Vision Recognition.

COMMISSIONER LEHMAN: Vision Recognition? Do you use that?

MR. HORN: Oh, yes.

COMMISSIONER LEHMAN: And is that covered under copyright or patents, or trade secrets, and do you license it?

MR. SCANLON: John?

MR. HORN: It is covered under -- there are hardware components and there are software components. So you've got really what yesterday was referred to by one of the witnesses as an embedded microprocessor system.

It runs software, which has been designed in France, and we do have patents on some of the aspects of that software. It happens in that particular case that there isn't that much patent coverage available because a lot of the ideas behind that software, which I think personally would have been patentable, actually were surfaced in academic circles 10 or 15 years ago.

COMMISSIONER LEHMAN: I asked about the French technology here, which you are licensing even though it has limited intellectual property rights protection in this country, I gather. I mean, it doesn't have patent protection. I assume you license it because you want to get access to the proprietary know how that comes along with it. What causes you not just to take it instead of license it?

MR. HORN: Well, when you say we license it, I must add that the software is actually developed by a French subsidiary of the company. We bought it.

COMMISSIONER LEHMAN: Okay. Well, then I guess that's the answer. So this is a company that's now owned by Allen-Bradley?

MR. HORN: Right. And we have a design center in France that continues to improve this software.

COMMISSIONER LEHMAN: I see. So then I guess the question is, are other people licensing it, or are they just taking it?

MR. HORN: My impression is -- and I must say that I'm not an expert on the vision industry -- is that most of it is homegrown stuff developed by the individual vision companies to work with their special hardware. And again, most of these are embedded systems. Most of them have specialized hardware, and then the custom software that goes with that specialized hardware.

COMMISSIONER LEHMAN: One of the reasons that Allen-Bradley is interested in a pretty strong patent protection here is because it would -- now, I'm not saying this -- I think a yes answer is perfectly acceptable -- because it would obviously help them to exploit this technology which they have.

MR. HORN: It would help us to exploit the technology in cases where we have major innovations in which we've made significant major investments. And we feel that those do occur on occasion.

COMMISSIONER LEHMAN: I'm sorry to interrupt you.

UNITED STATES PATENT AND TRADEMARK OFFICE
Public Hearing on Patent Protection for Software-Related Inventions
Arlington, Virginia -- February 10 & 11, 1994

MR. SCANLON: That's quite all right. I'm glad that John's able to --

COMMISSIONER LEHMAN: The great thing about an informal atmosphere and having all day is that we can have this colloquy which is helpful to us to flesh out the issues.

MR. SCANLON: John is based in the legal department in Milwaukee, so he has a broader view into that. So I'm glad he was able to answer your questions.

So as you can see, designing the graphical user interface for software is something that requires a significant investment. And I've only mentioned a few of the scenarios that we have to design for, and some of the constraints that we deal with.

The second key point is what the usability of Allen-Bradley software means to our customers. We have a concept of measuring software usability at various points during the software development process. And many people have probably seen more and more about software usability as it enters the mainstream media and gets broader and broader coverage.

We handle this through the conduct of usability studies in controlled environments, typically usability labs, with carefully selected test subjects that have certain user profiles and experience.

We measure speed: how long it takes for a person to perform a particular task. Accuracy: what's the percentage of error during that performance. Training: how much training is involved to bring the individual up to a certain level of proficiency. Then more of a qualitative rating, which is a level of acceptance for our software.

Usability to our customers is very important, because it means reduced system integration time. That is, taking the hardware of the control system and programming it to communicate in effect the manufacturing process. System integration cost is very high in the control industry, sometimes even as much as the actual hardware cost.

With the new and more usable graphical interfaces that we are developing, we can significantly reduce the integration cost and enable our customers to go online faster. This is an important competitive advantage for Allen-Bradley.

A case in point is a product that we sell that gives programmers the capability to program motion controllers graphically, versus the traditional text-based method. The product is GML, which stands for graphical motion language. Our customers can perform the same tasks with GML, that is programming motion controllers, in 20 percent of the time it used to take them with a reduced percentage of error.

Key point number three is how the software graphical user interface is an extension of Allen-Bradley's expertise and knowledge of the industrial automation and control industry. GML is a good example of this. At Allen-Bradley we've developed and continue to develop graphical user interfaces like GML for areas other than motion control. These areas include vision and bar code systems, logical programming tools, statistical process data gathering and analysis tools, operator interfaces for control in the plant floor, or supervisory control at remote locations. The list goes on.

We're able to create graphical user interface like GML for all of these products because we understand these businesses. We understand how our customers perform work. Consequently we can create GUIs like graphical motion language, that create this domain expertise -- that reflect this domain expertise and translate the productivity tools for end users and customers.

The problem for us is that it is very easy to take something like our graphical user interface concepts that reflect this domain expertise, translate it into a graphical form, and are painstakingly refined to become globally usable and duplicated or create knockoffs.

Given the graphical user interfaces are an important feature of our present and future product offerings, we believe that they are worthy of proper legal protection. It seems to us the existing copyright protection is not fully adequate in view of the utilitarian aspects that are closely linked to our unique industry-specific user interface components.

For our purposes, copyright law concentrates too heavily on the details of expression. We believe that design patents are somewhat appropriate for protecting these graphically oriented technologies, despite their focus on the ornamental aspects.

We would like to encourage the Patent Office to allow design patent protection of graphical user interface components that include icons, bit maps, and controls. So we're kind of going beyond just the icons because there's a lot more there.

We would also encourage the Patent Office to seek any necessary legislative authority to make design patents and/or utility patents effective for the protection of these new and valuable uses for graphical interface components.

It looks like I'm running out of time. I had another idea about the parallel aspects of --

COMMISSIONER LEHMAN: Why don't you tell it to us?

MR. SCANLON: Sitting in the meetings for the past couple of days, as a marketing person who generates market requirements and hands those over to developers, it's very difficult to communicate the features functionality or the behavior of graphical user interfaces.

I see a parallel problem in the traditional medium that is used to submit patent applications. So possibly some lessons could be learned. Typically what we do is we generate market requirements documents there, go to engineering. They respond with a function requirements spec. We are now actually building in prototypes and using some alternative approaches to communicating the behavior, not just the visual aspects of our software.

So there's more behavioral elements associated with that. And those are very important in creating these competitive user interfaces. So there may be something there that could be investigated and used for the future for the U.S. Patent and Trademark Office.

UNITED STATES PATENT AND TRADEMARK OFFICE
Public Hearing on Patent Protection for Software-Related Inventions
Arlington, Virginia -- February 10 & 11, 1994

Allen-Bradley would like to support these endeavors through continued participation in future gatherings such as this. Once again, thank you for your time.

COMMISSIONER LEHMAN: Thank you very much. In the process, we're big users of software technology, of course, ourselves. We're spending a very large sum of money automating the patent system, and it's a big management problem for me. Right now we're in very much a transitional phase, not just because the administration has changed, but because our leadership of that whole operation, the two top people, have retired.

Actually, we have two jobs open. Our director of information systems position for the whole Patent and Trademark Office is open. If anybody has some good candidates, send them our way. We'll pay the top money we can pay in the Federal Government, give them all the benefits we can. And it's interesting work.

But one of the things that we're doing is that we're just now starting our electronic applications system, which involves the creation of graphical interfaces that I personally am quite excited about. We have a pilot program going right now. I think it's going to help us produce much, much better and more usable patent applications because when you actually have to fill out an electronic form, the interface won't let you proceed until it gets all the information. From step one you can't go to step two.

And I think it will help -- and it educates the user all the way along the line. So we're actually in that business ourselves, and it's a very exciting thing. I think you've chosen a very good profession for yourself.

MR. SCANLON: Thank you. It's a lot of fun.

COMMISSIONER LEHMAN: Thanks.

Now I think we're done with yesterday's witnesses. We can start this morning. Again, earlier, about an hour ago -- or more than an hour ago -- I went through and called off people, and I know some of the people here. I'm going to do that again so I can see who's here.

Michael Kurtz of the Oracle Corporation. Has he come?

Daniel Kluth of Schwegman, Lundberg & Woessner.

R. Lewis Gable of Welsh & Katz is here.

Robert Greene Sterne, Sterne, Kessler, Goldstein and Fox.

John E. DeWald, Prudential was here, is still here.

David Clark of Aquilino & Welsh, who is here now, okay.

Allen M. Lo of Finnegan, Henderson, is now here.

Samual Oddi is here.

And David Webber, LNK Corporation.

Bernard Galler. I mentioned that if he's not here, he's not going to be here because of the snow.

Gregory Aharonian was here.

I don't see Bill Fryer here.

We have one, two, three, four, five, six people then. I'm going to start with R. Lewis Gable of Welsh & Katz.

Oh, David Cornwell. I don't have him on my -- is David Cornwell here?

(No audible response.)

COMMISSIONER LEHMAN: Is there anybody who was scheduled to testify that I haven't named who is here?

(No audible response.)

COMMISSIONER LEHMAN: I guess not, thanks.

PRESENTATION BY MR. R. LEWIS GABLE

WELSH & KATZ

MR. GABLE: Mr. Secretary, Professor Goffney, and Mr. Fleming, I'm very pleased to have dug out of my garage this morning and to be here. My name is Lewis Gable. I'm an attorney with the law firm of Welsh & Katz. We're an intellectual property law firm. And our offices are in Chicago, and also one here in Arlington, Virginia.

I have practiced patent law for 30-plus year, specializing in the preparation and prosecution of complex electronic and computer and software-related patent applications.

I started my career in the Patent Office where for approximately two years I examined patents while I was going to law school. I have practiced through the '70s when the entire issue of whether computer patents, computer-related patents, was patentable subject matter under 35 U.S.C. Section 101.

I have talked, and I have written extensively about the 101 issue, some of it with Mr. Fleming on many occasions, which I have enjoyed very much.

I have chaired the Electronic and Computer Law Committee of the American Intellectual Property Law Association.

My comments this morning are strictly for myself, and should not be attributed to Welsh & Katz, or any association, or of course the clients of Welsh & Katz.

I will focus on questions 2 and 6 of topic B. Fundamentally both ask how can the PTO improve the quality of its examination?

Question 2 asks, how can an examiner measure the ordinary skill of art? And question 6, how can the PTO improve its examination of novelty and obviousness?

It's apparent that these questions go right to the very heart of the obvious determinations required by the Supreme Court in their Graham decision.

My point this morning, my focus this morning, is that the experience level of the average patent examiner is low. And that the lack of experience affects the quality of patent examination.

This is true of all arts, but it is particularly true of software-related inventions. And that difficulty quickly rises in that area because of the complexity of the technology and the difficulty really to learn it.

UNITED STATES PATENT AND TRADEMARK OFFICE
Public Hearing on Patent Protection for Software-Related Inventions
Arlington, Virginia -- February 10 & 11, 1994

The positive aspect of this problem is that there is perhaps some rather effective solutions. I do not want my comments this morning to be interpreted that the people employed by the Patent Office are unqualified. My point is that it's very difficult to become an efficient, effective, competent patent examiner within the tenure that many patent examiners serve in the Office.

The average years of experience has dropped significantly since I joined the profession perhaps about 30 years ago. When I joined the Patent Office, my division -- at that time there were no groups or art units -- was comprised mostly of experienced primary examiners. Many of them had 10, 20, even 30 years of experience.

As a novice non-primary examiner, all of my work had to be supervised. And my primary examiner was John Burns. He had two examiners besides myself to train. He spent a lot of time with me, and if I made a mistake in an office action that I was about ready to issue, he told me about it. If I had missed a reference, he had the uncanny ability to go right over to the shoe, and pick that reference out, and say, this is where such and such a feature is shown.

He gained that experience because he had been in that art unit, or that group, that limited number of sub-classes for a very long time. He supervised it. He had supervised the examiners that had examined in that area. And he knew, literally in detail, all the references at issue. And that's a great help in examining.

Then the ratio of inexperienced, non-primary examiners to primary examiners was very low. However, today that ratio literally has been turned upside down. Any time I now receive a patent office action, one of the first things I do is to turn to the last page, and see whether the examiner that signed was a primary or non-primary examiner. And that gives me a good idea of how good this action is going to be.

I rarely have a primary examiner examine my applications. When I go in to have an interview with the examiners in the Office, one of the things I do is I walk up and down past the Office of the examiner, and I count the number of examiners or non-primary examiners, and the number of primary examiners. Often that ratio may be 9 or 10 to 1.

That ratio tells me something about the supervision that the non-primary examiners who will receive from the SPE in that particular art unit.

One patent that I had examined I think illustrates the difference between experienced and inexperienced examiners. I had prepared and filed a very complex application involving the application of artificial intelligence to setting up a printing press.

The application had 100 pages. There were at least 25 pages of flow diagram. The initial Patent Office action came back with but a single rejection, and that was that the specification was inadequate. There was no prior art rejection, no references cited. And so it was time for me to have an interview with the examiner.

And I found out that the examiner that I had gotten had six months of experience, and that the application had come into this art unit, this group, and all the more experienced examiners really didn't want to take the time to examine it. So it ended up literally with the least experienced examiner in the group.

I went to the supervisor, the group director. And he appointed a more experienced, a senior examiner, to help her. And the Office action that I got back was a very fine Office action. The references that were cited were even better than some of them of which I was aware of.

COMMISSIONER LEHMAN: You're obviously very familiar with our Office. You've worked in it. You've really worked very closely with it. And one of the things that concerns me about, that I'm picking up on that is a real problem -- and it's not just in the Group 2300, but I think because of the pressures on Group 2300 it probably has a bigger effect on it -- and that is our performance evaluation system in the Patent Office basically is based on numbers. It's pushing the papers out. You know, how many first actions do you issue? How many patents are issued? And so on and so forth.

I can see why in that situation that you've just described the more senior people see this, and there's sort of a pecking order. They want to get the papers out. They want to get that higher performance rating. And they get a bonus if they get a higher performance rating.

So naturally, the low person on the totem pole is going to get stuck with the cases obviously that are going to be harder to move out. So in a sense, I think our system -- my impression is that we may well have a system that pushes these harder cases down the totem pole to the person that doesn't have the seniority because those are the cases that take longer.

Do you have a sense that that may be the case? Do you think that that evaluation system that we have, that performance system, needs to be looked at?

MR. GABLE: I think you understand the system quite well. My impression is that experienced examiners maybe at the 12, 13, 14 level may have as many what we call bogey, or to make per week, maybe four, five, maybe six actions per week. And if you get, say, a very complex, lengthy patent application, there is no way that you can approach that and get five or six of them out in a week.

So at least where you have complexity and length of cases, typically like you have in 2300 or 2600, there has to be something done to permit people to achieve -- examiners to achieve, meet their goals, and yet be realistic in terms of the time that a particular patent application may be examined.

It gives me great pause -- and I'm going off of my talk a little bit here -- that when you get to the higher levels in terms of examiners, that they may have only eight hours to examine a very complex examination, much like the one I put in. And in that eight hours, you have to read 100 pages, maybe review 40 claims. Then you go to your shoes where you keep your prior art, search that, come back,

- 46 -

UNITED STATES PATENT AND TRADEMARK OFFICE
Public Hearing on Patent Protection for Software-Related Inventions
Arlington, Virginia -- February 10 & 11, 1994

evaluate that, make the critical comparisons that you do in patentability between what is taught and what is not taught. And then, does that rise to the level of unobviousness?

And then you write up a report that conveys all of these determinations. You do this in eight hours, and it becomes an Herculean if not an almost impossible task.

COMMISSIONER LEHMAN: I don't think we can underestimate the importance of this problem. This is our fourth day of testimony where people are saying that we're issuing patents when we haven't caught all the prior art. And I think you're pinpointing one of the reasons that that takes place.

Even though it wasn't part of your prepared statement, I think this little colloquy and dialogue in terms of identifying some major issues is very important.

MR. GABLE: It's hard to set limits on doing a good job. It depends -- it's so particular to a given application and also to a given technology.

COMMISSIONER GOFFNEY: I'd like to ask one question about the quality level that you find in the more experienced examiners. Is that manifested in 103 rejections? Has that been your experience?

MR. GABLE: Yes. My particular complaint is that with the younger examiners the art that is cited, the patents that are cited, many have very little relevance to the invention that you're claimed. I come away and I think many of my colleagues come away, with the idea, was the invention understood? How could someone cite this reference back?

I'm not talking about the situation where we disagree, where we're hassling and bargaining with each other with regard to the questions, is this sufficiently different, so that it will be obvious and you can allow this claim? The question is, is this reference, or are these sets of references really pertinent or even in the same ball park?

And it's not surprising, particularly with young examiners, you come into a particular area of the technology, and you try to learn it. I would say the first six months, maybe a year, is a real struggle, particularly in the very complex technologies. And you could have a EE degree or you could have a computer science degree, and you will not know the details of the technology, of the software, of the hardware, that may be involved in what you're searching.

So it's just a struggle until you know that. You learn this. It's surprising. If you've been there two, three, four, five, ten years, you know, you've read, you've examined yourself all these references so that the problem of searching is much easier.

If I know maybe -- literally you get to know a couple of thousand patents. And so, when you see this in an application in front of you, you have probably a very good idea of where the basic references are, you know where the various features are. And so you can short-cut a good part of the process by just going and picking up maybe five, ten references. And the examination moves on.

Otherwise, if good references are not cited, you're spinning your wheels. You have to respond and point out that this has very little relevance to the invention.

Typically what I've had to do is say, well, look at these references over here. These are really much more pertinent, and try to move the prosecution on so that we can get to the issues of 103 and 102 and maybe 112, first and second paragraphs, and really deal with what is the substance of what an examination should be about.

The difficulty with the younger examiner is that we don't really get to the issues. And as I said, I'm not criticizing the examiner. I mean, these people are well trained, they have good degrees. They just have not been there long enough to absorb and know the technology thoroughly.

COMMISSIONER GOFFNEY: Now, just one further question. I can see how that might be the case with the experience with the technology. But I'm curious about the legal rationale that you might get from the examiners.

MR. GABLE: Of course, most of it is in terms of what the art -- I mean, the fundamental question of obviousness depends upon a critical evaluation of the references. And of course, then you define the difference.

If you don't have good art to begin with in your rejection, regardless of whether you say it's obvious or not -- in other words, your legal conclusion -- it has no basis. And you may write that down very nicely on the Office action, but it makes no sense to the person reading it trying to respond to it.

One of the other things you mentioned was some of the legal determinations that you make. Particularly in the 2300 area, one of the most difficult ones is a 101 determination. There are perhaps maybe 40 to 50 relevant decisions. I think it's easy to say, and I think Mike would confirm this, that there are no bright lines. It is an extremely complex decision.

I find particularly with the younger examiners that, when they give a 101 rejection, they really have not done it within the confines or in accordance with the guidelines the Patent Office sets out.

That is not because of any lack of training on the part of the Office, because I know Mike is involved in extensive programs on 101 issues within and without the Office. But it's a problem of just, having dealt with these very complex issues over a sufficiently long time to absorb and to know very intimately maybe 10 or 15 cases, and to apply, and to know how to apply them to the claims and the facts. It's tough.

When the ratio of non-primary to primary examiners is high, it's difficult to adequately supervise all the novice examiners. Actions may come out, and I think they have, where the SPE has to supervise 10 or more non-primary examiners. There is literally no way that the SPE in a particular art unit can take a look at the work product, the Office actions, that come across his or her desk, and to really have a good feel for whether it represents a quality examination.

UNITED STATES PATENT AND TRADEMARK OFFICE
Public Hearing on Patent Protection for Software-Related Inventions
Arlington, Virginia -- February 10 & 11, 1994

The Ps and Qs may be well stated, but the underlying very complex decisions, which depend upon a grasp of what is disclosed in the application and a grasp of what is disclosed in the technology, may or may not be apparent until maybe you've spent a couple of hours. And simply the SPEs now do not have a couple of hours for office action for each of their nine or ten non-primaries.

My personal observations -- and a lot of what I've said so far are personal -- are pretty much confirmed by some of the personnel figures that have been provided by PTO, focusing on the computer group 2300. Right now there are approximately 160 examiners. Of that total, 130 examiners, or over 80 percent, are non-primary examiners; 89 examiners of that total, or over 55 percent, have less than two years experience.

Appreciate that, if you don't have a primary authority, you cannot issue yourself an office action or issue a patent. So your Office action has to be supervised by an SPE. So what you're looking at is the ratio of SPEs to the number of non-primaries. And the arithmetic is fairly simple. There are approximately on average 2,300 10 non-primary examiners for each SPE. In some art units, there are as many as 14 non-primary examiners for one SPE.

The significance of this, as I've implied, is somewhat discouraging and disturbing. I believe it's impossible for a single SPE to review the work output of 10 and perhaps 14 non-primary examiners. These numbers also indicate that there has been a massive examiner drain, particularly at the two or three level. I think when you say there's 55 percent with less than two years experience, you can see that seems to be a place when a lot of people are leaving.

After two or three years, the Patent Office pays these non-primaries approximately $32,000 to $35,000. And it's a fact of life that firms and corporations can exceed that pay significantly.

The problem is not so much with the primary or more experienced examiners, because it seems that to some degree the pay does catch up in later years, but the problem is that most examiners don't wait around much past two or three years to get to the higher salaries.

Thus the cycle continues. An examiner comes to the PTO, is trained for two or three years, and then he or she leaves.

Mr. Secretary, I heard your comments at the AIPLA and the IPLA and I was very impressed with your efforts to reach out to the examiner to make the work conditions and the work support there better. I certainly would encourage you to continue that. But I think you also have to look at the pay schedules, particularly for young examiners.

I appreciated this time to come and talk with you this morning.

COMMISSIONER LEHMAN: Thank you very much, Mr. Gable. I really thought that was very -- a little different perspective than some of the other witnesses whose statements were very valuable. But I think you hit on some

very practical issues that we were aware were there, but I think you put them in really sharp relief, and helped me a lot, and I'm sure Commissioner Goffney to put them in sharp relief. And we'll go back and redouble our efforts to work on it.

MR. GABLE: Thank you.

COMMISSIONER LEHMAN: Thank you.

Next, Mr. John DeWald from the Prudential Insurance Company of America.

I should add that if people have written statements, that we would appreciate it if you'll make sure that Mike Fleming gets them, it will help us a lot to make sure that we have the best kind of transcript that we can have of these proceedings.

PRESENTATION BY MR. JOHN E. DeWALD

THE PRUDENTIAL INSURANCE COMPANY OF AMERICA

MR. DeWALD: Good morning. My name is John DeWald. I'm an Assistant General Counsel at The Prudential Insurance Company of America, and I'm responsible for its intellectual property matters.

My remarks this morning will focus on the impact of software-related inventions on The Prudential as a large insurance and financial services company. I believe our experience in this regard is representative of the industry as a whole.

In San Jose, my colleague and client Charlie Morgan confronted the panel of a software patent infringement charge against his Prudential business unit under a patent that essentially claims a method of doing business. A computer system is used in that product to estimate tax contribution limits, forecast premiums, and the like for health benefits using a 501(c)(9) trust.

That charge is a specific example of a general issue I'd like to discuss today. For several years there have been practitioners advising in trade journals, such as the National Underwriter and Insurance Trade Weekly, and elsewhere, that you could virtually lock in for 17 years the exclusive rights to market a new product or service by patenting the computer system created to support it.

Those who know the insurance industry and have no special self-interest would probably agree that most such efforts should fail for inability to prove novelty or nonobviousness, or as for claiming a mere method of doing business, which is non-statutory subject matter.

But the patent confronted by Charlie Morgan illustrates graphically that many an insurance or financial product, even one based squarely on the Internal Revenue code, can be patented if the applicant simply embeds it within a computer system.

This is relatively easy to do because in fact everybody already uses computers to crunch the large numbers involved with any insurance product or financial instrument.

UNITED STATES PATENT AND TRADEMARK OFFICE
Public Hearing on Patent Protection for Software-Related Inventions
Arlington, Virginia -- February 10 & 11, 1994

In theory, defending against such a claim should be a straightforward matter. But in reality, the risks and costs of responding are so extensive that economics alone often dictates that many such claims be settled rather than defended, even where the accused infringer is advised by counsel that the patent is invalid.

The presumption of validity in favor of the patent-holder, the so-called patentee advantage, creates economic risks far out of proportion to the intrinsic merit of the patent. This is because insurance by its very nature involves contractual obligations and risks for large numbers of policyholders and beneficiaries, and these numbers can easily run into the millions.

Further, to the average business person who must decide whether or not to deal with an insurance company, the patent itself appears to give an impartial government stamp of approval to the patentee's allegations. Even the informed business person with competent legal advice does not want to become involved in any insurer's complex, possibly costly, patent disputes, let alone be drawn into a lawsuit.

This has a chilling effect on the market. If customers decide not to purchase a product, the market freezes, and the business can die. And all of this can happen before the insurer has even a reasonable opportunity to obtain an adjudication on the patent.

Even if an alleged infringer wants to contest the merits of the patent claim, the long delays involved, the burden to identify, locate, and produce a compelling array of prior art, plus the cost of counsel, let alone the huge potential cost of litigation, becomes a daunting and expensive alternative, even beyond the expenses typically associated with patent litigation.

This raises the nuisance value of such claims, so patentees and their advisers expect huge sums in settlement. Because of all this, the patentee gets much more than the right to sue. Given the right circumstances, the patent holder gets in effect a lottery ticket.

And with this result comes the social cost of diverting the insurer's resources away from actually doing business, the possible withdrawal of products from the market, hurting individuals as well as companies. And it could also mean an increase in the cost of products to consumers to cover added legal costs.

For mutuals like Prudential Insurance, it could also mean a diversion of revenues which otherwise could have gone to the policyholders as dividends. And again, all this cost comes without any corresponding value added to the economy or technological benefit.

Accordingly, I'm responding to the first six questions on Topic B as follows:

First, patents and printed publications do not provide examiners with sufficient representative collection of prior art to assess the novelty or obviousness of software-related inventions, particularly in the insurance and financial area. For example, many program products constitute

prior art by virtue of being on sale, or the subject of public use.

It's been traditional not to publish these methods embodied in the packages. So the public is unaware of the nature of -- and unable to search -- this type of prior art. The collection of prior art must be drastically improved. I endorse in principle the establishment of the machine-readable database now being organized by the Software Patent Institute. That project should be enthusiastically supported.

But also, much of the internal programming which companies did in this area has been treated as, and considered a trade secret, and not patented at all.

Finally, to the extent appropriate, that database should also include policy filings from state insurance departments or other regulatory agencies.

Two, for the same reasons, an accurate measurement of the ordinary skill in computer programming, particularly in insurance and financial services, cannot be derived from printed publications and issued patents alone. New products or variations on old existing ones are constantly being developed by the industry in response to market demands, changing economic conditions, or changes in the law.

Internal computer programs at these companies are modified accordingly on a continuous basis.

In view of this situation, the PTO should impose a special duty on patent applicants for software-related inventions, particularly in the insurance and financial services field, to disclose information relevant to the invention.

Applicants should not be rewarded, and everyone else penalized, for the proverbial empty head and clean heart.

As a practical matter, the manner of implementing standards of novelty and obviousness is returning results that do not accurately reflect software inventive activities. We appreciate and applaud the efforts that the Commissioner has made in this matter. But so far to date what's happened is that applying a competent standard to an incompetent database has yielded a deficient result.

Perhaps most importantly, implementing on a computer a process technique, system, or method of doing business which is well known but for the use of the software should not be considered novel and nonobvious unless implementing the well known process on a computer results in a novel and nonobvious process. Generally this will not be the case.

To do otherwise merely invites speculators to gain the system --

COMMISSIONER LEHMAN: Can I interrupt you and ask for Mike who is here, what kind of guidance can you give on that at the moment to our examiners, if any?

MR. FLEMING: Presently we are applying the same standard as in any computer arts. Unfortunately, we are having to find the particular features that are being claimed to apply an obvious standard. And if that happens to be a

UNITED STATES PATENT AND TRADEMARK OFFICE
Public Hearing on Patent Protection for Software-Related Inventions
Arlington, Virginia — February 10 & 11, 1994

business practice, we have to find that business practice in order to apply a 103. And that's been very difficult.

COMMISSIONER LEHMAN: Especially since business practices aren't to be found in our patent shoes very much.

MR. FLEMING: Right. Nor do we have -- sometimes understand what the business practices are since we're trained as technology-types and not business -- in the insurance. And we have a large variety of fields that these come into.

COMMISSIONER LEHMAN: It reminds me -- as a lawyer, one of the most frustrating things that can ever happen to you sometime is when you know exactly what the law is and then you a very inexperienced adversary who may have not -- and then they come up with all kinds of totally off-the-wall ideas that everyone who really is an expert knows are off-the-wall.

Then when you actually try to explain this to a court, or whatever, a judge who may be similarly inexperience, well, judge this is something everybody knows -- he may actually -- it sometimes is very difficult to actually define and explain and elaborate on what may to those who do it every day seem to be obvious.

And I have a feeling that in the software area, now that we've opened up this Pandora's box a little bit and where people realize, hey, you can patent a lot of stuff, we're getting people coming in with things that are really quite bizarre patent applications, and the system just isn't used to or able to deal with this.

I see you're shaking your head yes that you agree with it, and I gather that's a problem that Prudential is having.

MR. DeWALD: Exactly, Commissioner. Yes.

To treat the matter otherwise merely invites speculators to gain in the system by sandwiching software into products and services that are already well known. In effect, large blocks of insurance products unjustifiably become sitting targets.

There should be enough flexibility in the patent system to reward the truly innovative software inventor without allowing a host of free riders to cash in on the system without making a contribution to it.

For 6.A, until the database deficiency has been rectified, the PTO should require patent applicants to conduct diligent search of prior art before filing and to distinguish claimed software inventions from the resulting references. In many instances, the applicant may be able to identify technology that PTO would be unable to uncover.

I realize this may impose on software applicants a burden not imposed on others. But nevertheless, given the importance of this technology and the curable problems inherent in its present treatment, this temporary burden is justified and in the public interest.

6.B, the PTO should require software patent applicants to prove their inventions overall are distinct over the prior art. If the only difference between the claimed invention and the prior art is implementation on a computer, then the claimed invention is not patentable unless the computer implementation is nonobvious over the preexisting implementation.

Anything less allows software soldiers of fortune to bootstrap the patent system without adding value to the product, the economy, or improving our technical body of knowledge.

6.C, as in the case of requirement applicants search, the PTO should be permitted at least temporarily to distinguish software-related inventions by setting a standard less than prima facia to establish that such an invention is not novel, or is obvious.

With the tremendous leverage afforded to the patentee in the huge private and social costs in challenging the presumption of validity, substance, not form, should prevail, especially where there is not yet developed an adequate database.

The closed nature of the examination process should be revisited. After initial approval there ought to be publication for opposition. And that opposition should allow for a meaningful internal adversarial process. Challengers should have a right to rebut the patentee's response.

A form which allows for the reasonable determination of contested facts without the need to resort to multi-million dollar litigation will enhance the integrity of both the system and issued patents, discourage frivolous applications, and hopefully eliminate some of the roadblocks along the information superhighway we hear so much about these days.

Thank you very much for you attention and for the opportunity to make these remarks today.

COMMISSIONER LEHMAN: Thank you very much, Mr. DeWald.

Our next witness is David Clark. You can come up right now -- or hold off. I want to take about a three-minute stretch break, and then we'll be right back. But don't go away too far. We'll be right back.

(Recess.)

COMMISSIONER LEHMAN: Shall we proceed? David Clark, Aquilino and Welsh. By the way, we have three more witnesses after Mr. Clark. I would think we would probably be able to finish up by about 20 minutes after the hour, certainly by 12:30, even if we ask a lot of questions.

PRESENTATION BY DAVID L. CLARK

AQUILINO & WELSH, P.C.

MR. CLARK: Mr. Commissioner, members of the panel, my name is David Clark. I was an examiner in Group 2300 for 10 years from 1983 to 1993. When I left the Patent Office, I was a supervisor in the group.

I'm currently an intellectual property attorney with the law firm of Aquilino & Welsh. I figure I have about one year per minute to cover here. I've been thinking about this process for quite a while, so I'll try to jam it all together.

When I became a supervisor -- I guess I'm living proof of Lou's statistics -- I had 11 people in my art unit. I did not have any primary examiners, and seven of the people that I was in charge of had less than a year of experience.

The technology that we worked with in the art unit was database technology, which is very often Ph.D. level work, and the legal issues that we did confront in the database technology were often the first impression as far as legal issues go.

I relay this story because it's typical of the group at this point, as was told to you by Lou earlier. And I believe it directs attention to the key problem in the group, which is retention. I think that many of the issues being discussed by these hearings can be addressed at least partly by solving the problem of retention.

For many people with computer backgrounds, the Patent Office is not considered a career path, but rather just a stepping stone. The high turnover places great stress on the senior personnel. And the costs of constantly training new people is extremely high.

Over the years, the resources of the group have literally been drained as a result of this. This has created a vicious cycle of eroded resources and high turnover, which I think are very closely related.

I've heard a lot of talk about hiring during these hearings. I don't think hiring alone will solve the problems of retention, because the group currently hires many capable people. But the years of training necessary for developing the skills of -- nuances -- understand nuances of the law, the technology, and how the law applies to the technology, cannot be hired.

The key resource of Group 2300 is people. People who have developed the skills of effectively analyzing and expressing the technical and legal issues of these very complex technologies. It's my contention that all resources should be directed towards improving these skills and maintaining these skills within the Office once they've been attained.

I think the problem of retention can be addressed by focusing on two things, providing tools which will lead to an effective examination and satisfaction among the examining corps, as well as proper recognition for the people in the groups that improve the Office and perform a good job.

And perhaps more importantly, I think Group 2300 has to realize that they must compete with the career alternatives available to the examining staff. That is, the group must consider itself a competitor for these people's services.

First I'd like to discuss tools. The two fundamental tools of examining are time and efficient access of information. The time to examine an application in Group 2300 has remained constant over at least the last decade that I'm aware of. Even though the technology has accelerated at a much faster pace than what was going on 10 years ago. I think this has led to an increased dissatisfaction among the examining staff with respect to what is attainable within that time period.

I would recommend, as you alluded to earlier, a very strong analysis of the time constraints imposed on the examining staff, as well as the incentives created by the present system. And this should include a review, at least where possible, of similar activities on the outside.

The second tool is efficient access of information. And this can either be in the form of physical tools used by an individual, or the exchange of information among people. In either case, the ideal is to be able to immediately access -- and I would put forth without searching for it -- relevant art.

And then the process of examination should be just merely review of that art, rather than -- the current process of searching, I would say, characterizes out of control. You're often lucky if you can find ballpark art in many instances for cases.

And I think that if the information is already organized before they go to access it, this will lead to a much greater sense of satisfaction with the job.

COMMISSIONER LEHMAN: How would we do that? What do we need to do to organize it better? Is it still the classification system?

MR. CLARK: Yes. That's actually my next couple of topics here.

The Office should immediately implement in Group 2300 a dynamic, ongoing classification of the information that's coming in and being developed. The first step is to create a structure which supports this effort and then to provide the time necessary to update and maintain the system.

In this rapidly developing technology, the classification really needs to be a lock-step with the developments as they are coming out, instead of the typical process of every couple of years undergoing a reclassification.

This will reduce the frustration presently experienced among the examining staff, which I think will -- it's my belief it will lead to more retention. And I think that the further that the Office is away from these ideals, the more problems it will have with retention.

The Office should also implement existing technologies which encourage and facilitate the flow of information both between examiners and between examiners and outside information-gatherers. Each art area should be encouraged and supported in forming a network entity for exchanging information on an ongoing basis. Information services within the PTO should serve the examiners' goals in developing these tools.

As a way to further facilitate the flow of information among examiners, I would recommend developing discussion groups for technology areas. And these should be supported by the system, the incentives in place, and management.

I can attest to the value of these because I was involved in two discussion groups in the database and graphics processing area when I was in the Office. These are extremely valuable for developing resources, exchanging

UNITED STATES PATENT AND TRADEMARK OFFICE
Public Hearing on Patent Protection for Software-Related Inventions
Arlington, Virginia -- February 10 & 11, 1994

ideas with respect to the technology being examined in particular cases, and also discussing the legal issues that surround these cases.

I think that these discussions often lead to a much greater consistency in the examination process. And it can be tied to retention because it reduces the isolation of the examiner and it puts a team concept into the process.

COMMISSIONER LEHMAN: Now, that sort of thing, though, requires -- again, given how we evaluate people.

MR. CLARK: Right.

COMMISSIONER LEHMAN: They don't get any credit for discussion groups. So that really goes again to the criteria that we use for judging performance. Right now you can get the wrong paper out the door and you get as much credit for it as if you get the right paper out the door.

MR. CLARK: That's right. In fact, the discussion groups which we had were all supported -- well, we were not given time by management to do these. It was a grassroots type effort.

There should also be a technology liaison between each discussion group and industry and the bar for bringing in people and receiving information relevant to that area.

I'd like to make a final comment on tool development. I think that the attitude which should pervade this process should be one of empowering the examiners to define the tools that they need for their job. And this should be supported by management so that they can define what their future is like in the Office.

I have to admit that this concept was given to me by somebody in industry because I don't think I had the mind set for it coming out of the patent office.

The second area is recognition, both in monetary form and in nonmonetary form. An example of -- I know somebody who recently left the Office who had been in the Office approximately three or four years. Their take-home pay doubled when they left the Office. And they expect increases in salary of $15,000 to $20,000 over the next year.

I think that the gap needs to be closed to some extent, and maybe it's not possible to close it all the way. But with whatever is left, as far as a gap between the outside and the PTO, the Office is going to have to very aggressively compete in the other areas.

Then with nonmonetary recognition, I think the system needs to be realigned to effectively recognize the groups of people that work together to attain the goals of the Office.

COMMISSIONER LEHMAN: Is it your view that the -- Mr. Gable mentioned that we have a pay problem, particularly at that GS -- at that sort of early middle level -- or do you think we have a problem at every level? Do you think that if you spend 20 years at the Patent Office and you get to be a GS-15 and you get a bonus, that even that isn't enough?

MR. CLARK: I think somebody who has made that decision, at least at this point, has signed on to whatever salary -- I think, as far as retention goes, early on they look

at the salary that they have, the salary they could get for very similar type of work.

COMMISSIONER LEHMAN: So you really agree with him that the real problem is more in that, say, in the two to five year, two to ten year category?

MR. CLARK: Yes. I could see the upper GS levels being relevant in terms of long-term growth within the Office, that somebody with career alternatives who is being lured away from the Office could look down the line and say, well, GS-15 -- you know, that economic analysis that the GS-15 makes this, and where will I be in the same timeframe that it would take me to attain a GS-15 level?

COMMISSIONER LEHMAN: Of course, it's my impression that in terms of a non-lawyer examiner, that the options for the really large six-figure-plus incomes are somewhat limited. I mean, at that point we're fairly competitive. But if you have the law degree, as you do -- you went to law school and became a lawyer -- then we really become very noncompetitive, almost at every stage. And it's extremely hard to close that gap.

But with the at least non-lawyer examiner, my sense of it is that within the overall context of the government's pay scale that at least theoretically we could close the gap.

MR. CLARK: Right. Yes, I think the compensation for attorneys within the Office, that's a very sensitive subject. But I think that that possibly could be -- it happened indirectly with me. I was given certain cases because of my legal skills, which in my case I stayed in the Office longer as a result of that.

I think that that's what I was talking about earlier, where maybe there are alternatives to salary, even after closing the gap.

COMMISSIONER LEHMAN: You found the work itself to be more interesting and stimulating when you've got some legal challenges that made it worth staying there.

MR. CLARK: Right.

COMMISSIONER LEHMAN: One of the concerns I have that I'm picking up, not at these hearings of course, but in my discussions with Patent Office employees, is that there is a real cultural bias in certain areas in the patent corps against lawyers. It's kind of like when you go to law school, you join another group. Did you experience that at all?

MR. CLARK: I think that depends. I don't think there's an overall bias, but I know -- and I did not personally experience that. I think that's a tribute to my supervisors.

COMMISSIONER GOFFNEY: I'm curious as to when you went to law school. Could you give us a little background as to when you went to law school and finished?

MR. CLARK: '86 to '90.

COMMISSIONER GOFFNEY: I mean, during your tenure. Did you come here and go to law school while you were an examiner, and when did that happen? After the first year? Second year?

UNITED STATES PATENT AND TRADEMARK OFFICE
Public Hearing on Patent Protection for Software-Related Inventions
Arlington, Virginia -- February 10 & 11, 1994

MR. CLARK: Well, I was in the Office. I joined in '83, and for the first year and a half I just focused on examining and reading books, actually, that I had gathered over my undergraduate years. And then I went and attained my master's degree for the next two years, from '84 to '86. Then from '86 to '90 I attended law school.

During that time, I went through the partial and full sig programs.

COMMISSIONER GOFFNEY: So it was about three years after you attained your law degree that you went out to industry, or went out to practice?

MR. CLARK: Right.

COMMISSIONER GOFFNEY: Thank you.

COMMISSIONER LEHMAN: What was your undergraduate degree in?

MR. CLARK: Computer engineering, which was a very good degree for what the technology is in Group 2300.

I guess just to summarize it, I think it's -- in order for this problem to be resolved, I think the group is going to have to be competitive, and really look into maximizing its advantages, especially in the upgrading of the examination, tools for the examiner, to provide a better environment.

And I think this will break this current cycle of the eroded resources and poor retention, and hopefully start a new cycle of much better resources, higher retention, which will be to a more experienced staff. And I think a better treatment of the legal and technical issues that are creating problems in the public domain.

COMMISSIONER LEHMAN: Well, I really appreciate your -- again, like Mr. Gable's testimony, I think you really focused on some very important practical issues. We might even want to have you back informally for some discussions about it. Maybe we can get a little discussion group going of people like you who have left the Office, and if we can get to the bottom of why they do.

MR. CLARK: I'd love to participate.

COMMISSIONER LEHMAN: Great. Thank you very much.

MR. CLARK: Thank you.

COMMISSIONER LEHMAN: Professor Galler has arrived, I assume. Great. I think we're not quite ready yet, though. We're running way behind because we thought we had all the time in the world.

Our next witness is Allen M. Lo, a student associate at Finnegan, Henderson, Farabow, Garrett & Dunner.

PRESENTATION BY MR. ALLEN M. LO

FINNEGAN, HENDERSON, FARABOW GARRETT & DUNNER

MR. LO: Good morning, Mr. Commissioner. My name is Allen Lo. I'm also another example of a casualty from Group 2300. I worked as an examiner in Group 2300 for about two and a half years, examining patent applications involving computer control systems, computer-aided

product manufacturing, and error correction and detection systems.

Last March I left the PTO to work for the law firm of Finnegan, Henderson, Farabow, Garrett & Dunner, where I currently prosecute and write patent applications, much of which involves software-related inventions. I currently attend the Georgetown University Law Center as a third-year evening student.

Today I'm speaking on my own behalf. The views that I express today are my own and not the views of the firm or its clients.

Mr. Commissioner, I'd like to address two different matters this morning. First I'd like to speak about the group's policy regarding the patentability of claims drawn to software stored on a disk. Second, I'd like to supplement the comments that Dave Clark made about what the PTO can do to improve the quality of examination based on my own experience.

Beginning with the first issue, it's been the policy of Group 2300 that claims drawn to software stored on a disk are per se unpatentable. During the examination of an application involving a software related invention, examiners in Group 2300 place claims into one of two groups: implemented and nonimplemented computer software.

Implemented computer software generally refers to computer software that's claimed as being executed on a computer, which Group 2300 treats as being patentable, subject, of course, to the novelty and nonobviousness requirements. For example, a claim reciting a general purpose computer running a novel and nonobvious computer program is treated as being a new machine, and thus would be allowed by Group 2300.

In contrast, nonimplemented computer software refers to computer software that is not executed on a computer. In other words, simply a static program.

Claims reciting nonimplemented computer software may be directed either to the computer program itself, such as a computer program comprising followed by either source code or means plus function language, or to software that's stored on a disk, such as a computer-readable medium, storing a computer program comprising, followed by source code or means plus function language.

Group 2300 views these claims, the nonimplemented computer software, as per se unpatentable.

I'd like to focus my comments on one particular type of nonimplemented computer software, and that is claims reciting a disk that store a computer program claimed in terms of means for performing a function, say a function -- means for performing function A, means for performing function B, et cetera.

Examiners in Group 2300 are trained to reject this type of claim under 35 U.S.C. Sections 101, 102, 103, 112 first paragraph, and 112 second paragraph. These rejections can be simplified, and I would generally classify them into three different categories.

UNITED STATES PATENT AND TRADEMARK OFFICE
Public Hearing on Patent Protection for Software-Related Inventions
Arlington, Virginia -- February 10 & 11, 1994

First, these kind of claims are rejected under 35 U.S.C. Section 101 as being directed to printed matter. The second category, the claim is rejected under 35 U.S.C. Sections 101, 102, and 103 over a prior art disk by effectively reading out any specific recitations in the claims directed to the computer program, and then concluding that either the claims are anticipated by a prior art disk, or that storing any type of data on a disk would have been obvious.

The third category of rejections are under 35 U.S.C. Section 112 first and second paragraphs, because the disk itself is unable to perform the recited functions, but requires a computer to actually perform the functions, and therefore is either indefinite, or the specification doesn't disclose how a disk can perform the functions.

I believe that these type of rejections are either unsupportable under the case law, or can be easily drafted to avoid these kind of rejections.

First, with regard to the printed matter rejections, these type of claims do not attempt to claim the mere arrangement of words, which is really what the printed matter rejection is all about, such as the program code itself. But rather, these type of claims specifically are directed to the functionality that is provided by the computer program. And thus the claim really doesn't contain printed matter.

However, even if the computer program could be analogized to printed matter, the case law does provide an exception to the printed matter rule, which is that if there is a functional relationship between the printed matter and the medium that the printed matter is stored on, then those claims are not considered printed matter -- printed matter rejections are not applicable to those types of claims.

In the case of a computer program stored on a disk, the computer program really transforms the disk into new disk kind of the same way that a computer program transforms a general purpose computer into a new machine.

With respect to the rejections over a prior art disk, it's simply improper for the PTO to ignore any limitations in the claim, particularly in this case where the computer program is claimed in means plus function language.

And finally, with respect to rejections based on the disk being unable to provide the claimed functions, the claim can be drafted to be more specifically and particularly claimed if actual function performed by the disk. For example, the claim could be drafted differently, and rather than being claimed as a disk storing a computer program comprising means for performing a function, means for performing a function, it could be claimed as a disk storing a computer program comprising a means for instructing a processor to perform the function, means for instructing a processor to perform another function.

So in this way it actually is claiming what it actually does, which is really to instruct a processor. And I think that can avoid those types of rejections.

It should be noted that the claiming of software on a disk is not simply a trivial exercise in claim drafting. Patentees have an interest in obtaining claims drawn to software stored on a disk.

By disallowing these types of claims, patentees must obtain patents with claims drawn to software that is run on a computer. When patentee seeks to enforce this type of patent, manufacturers and sellers of infringing software would not be liable for direct infringement, but rather it would be the users of the software that would be liable for direct infringement by virtue of the fact that they're running the software, because that's what the claims really recite.

Manufacturers and sellers of infringing software would not be liable for direct infringement, but instead they would only be liable to the patentee under some cumbersome theory of contributory infringement, or inducement infringement, requiring the patentee to prove additional elements, including knowledge and intent.

Whether or not the PTO changes its policy toward nonimplemented computer software, I think it's important that the PTO at least publish in the official gazette clear guidelines and rules defining the types of software claims which they PTO considers to be acceptable.

I believe that a lot of these guidelines are not published. And so a lot of this information I have is only as having been an examiner in the group.

Turning to the matter of improving the quality of examination, I'd like to make the following observations and suggestions.

First, as others have suggested, examiners in Group 2300 need to receive more legal and technical training. Many of the examiners who attend law school eventually end up leaving the PTO to accept more lucrative positions in private practice, resulting in fewer and fewer examiners with legal training in the PTO.

I would recommend at least more in-house legal courses that teach basic legal skills, such as legal research and writing, be offered to those examiners who don't attend law school.

Further, examiners should be invited and encouraged to attend meetings and lectures that relate to software patenting, for example, such as today's hearings. Yesterday I attended, and I didn't see any patent examiners. I don't believe that they were actually notified of the hearings. And I think attendance at these kinds of things would be helpful to examiners, at least so that they can understand the big picture and appreciate the issues that they are actually facing during examination.

Further, more technical courses need to be offered to increase the level of technical understanding within the group. It is awfully difficult for an examiner to appreciate the advantages of an invention when they don't really understand what it is.

And as Dave Clark pointed out earlier, the training of examiners is undermined if the PTO is unable to retain its examiners. My experience has been that examiners leave

UNITED STATES PATENT AND TRADEMARK OFFICE
Public Hearing on Patent Protection for Software-Related Inventions
Arlington, Virginia -- February 10 & 11, 1994

the PTO for various reasons. Certainly many examiners are lured from the PTO by the higher salaries that are offered by patent law firms. This problem could be alleviated somewhat by raising salaries in groups with high turnover rates, such as Group 2300.

However, I believe that some examiners, myself included, leave the PTO because they feel the examining function is no longer stimulating or challenging. Finding solutions for retaining these types of people may be difficult, but I believe that, for example, the Examiner Enrichment Program which you mentioned yesterday is a definite step in the right direction.

Finally, there is natural tension between the count system and having a high quality of examination, as you mentioned. I think the count system is something that is necessary. I think you had mentioned reevaluating the number of hours, perhaps, that the examiners should spend on a particular case. I think that would be helpful.

Some of the suggestions that Dave made earlier about having group meetings and that kind of thing, and how that doesn't really count towards an examiner's performance, can -- those types of meetings can be counted by the fact that PTO oftentimes does offer write-off time. So time that people spend in these types of meetings, they're not really held accountable to produce additional cases.

I'd like to thank you for allowing me this opportunity to testify, and I can answer any questions you may have.

COMMISSIONER LEHMAN: Thank you very much. I don't think I have a need at this point, but I think that was very helpful. And it's very helpful, the perspective of people like you who have been in the corps, who are young attorneys or attorneys-to-be, because you're exactly the kind of people we need to know what's going on with. Thank you very much.

Our next witness is Professor Samual Oddi of the Northern Illinois University College of Law.

PRESENTATION BY SAMUAL ODDI

NORTHERN ILLINOIS UNIVERSITY COLLEGE OF LAW

MR. ODDI: My name is Samual Oddi. I'm Professor of Law at the Northern Illinois University College of Law in DeKalb, Illinois.

My comments are premised on research I have done into the area of the economic impact that intellectual property has in various spheres. I started this research because of my interest in the international patent system and its impact on the economic development of Third World countries. That study is published in the Duke Law Journal.

Then, due to my economic research into that, I came upon a number of economic theories which I thought had more specific applicability, if you would, to the United States and developed countries.

I then published an article in the American University Law Review entitled "Invention Protection in the 21st Century Beyond Obviousness" where I proposed a revolutionary patent which provided an enhanced degree of protection

for those very rare revolutionary inventions which I will define in a moment.

Most pertinent to these hearings is an article that was published very recently, late last year, in the Nebraska Law Review entitled "On Uneasier Case for Copyright Than for Patent Protection for Computer Programs."

COMMISSIONER LEHMAN: An Uneasier Case?

MR. ODDI: On Uneasier -- rather ungrammatical, but that's the title which is based upon a previous use of the "uneasier" in the copyright context.

I have heard this morning a couple of comments which I think are very typical of what's happening in this field today. There is a League for Programming Freedom and perhaps a league for insurance company freedom. We love intellectual property, as long as our ox isn't gored. And there are costs. Indeed, there are costs. They may be spurious lawsuits. They may be lack of access.

Intellectual property is always the context of access versus incentive. I want to talk about the positive aspect of it this morning, about the incentives.

The question I'd like to address is whether the present regime of intellectual property provides adequate incentives for the creation of software-related inventions in general, and for what I call revolutionary software-related inventions in particular.

Now, incentives are fundamental to our intellectual property system. The instrumentalist intent of Article I, Section 8, Clause 8 of the Constitution is clear: To promote the progress of science and useful arts. This was not a novel concept even 200 years ago when our Constitution was framed. It can be traced back to at least the Venetian patent statute of 1474, which states -- and the language is rather interesting and I'll quote it for you.

"Now, if provision were made for works and devices discovered by men of great genius apt to invent and discover ingenious devices so that others who may see them could not build them and take the inventor's honor away, more men would then by their genius would discover and would build devices of great utility and benefit to our commonwealth."

Again, this idea of the incentive being provided. The underlying assumption of providing the patent incentive of exclusivity for the creation of inventions is that in the absence of such an incentive and inadequate number of inventions would be provided. This would be to the detriment of society.

Now, there are costs associated with that. We are willing to suffer the indignity of the patent, the copyright monopoly, in order to achieve these inventions. However, as all of us know, many inventions would still be created, even if there were no patent system.

After all the aphorism, necessity is the mother of invention, still rings true. The market will induce many inventions with such factors as lead time, learning curve advantage, market recognition, among others, often being sufficient incentives.

Thus we can distinguish patent-induced inventions, that is, those which are actually induced by the availability of a patent, from market-induced inventions, which do not rely upon this patent system for their creation. The market drives them.

Economists tell us that if patents were limited to those of the market-induced variety, the result would be a net benefit to society. The problem is that the patent system protects all inventions. It boils down to a question of whether society should pay for something that it would otherwise get for nothing. So we built in costs because we inherently protect all types of inventions.

Now, the Supreme Court recognized this in Graham versus John Deere in the context of discussing the standard for invention. And I quote: "The inherent problem was to develop some means of weeding out those inventions which would not be disclosed or devised but for the inducement of the patent."

The requirement, however, that an invention not be obvious to one skilled in the art is at best a fickle tool for weeding. There are of course many inventions that would satisfy, and do satisfy, the nonobvious requirement, which are induced by the market rather than the patent system. These tend to be inventions which are of a high benefit/cost ratio variety.

That is, those which are in the product line of the enterprise, and which fit into existing product lines which you need to develop for competitive purpose, or else you're going to be out of business whether or not you're going to patent it.

Now, in my view, the important category inventions that rely upon the patent system for their creation are revolutionary inventions. These inventions, as defined by Professor F.H. Chair, who is an economist at Harvard, are those that revolutionize production or consumption. These are the industry-creating and job-creating inventions.

Examples will include telephones, geography, black and white television, transistor, and there are many, many others. The revolutionary inventions tend to require the patent system for inducement because of their uncertain benefit/cost ratio. They do not lend themselves to a bottom-line type of analysis because of the uncertainty involved in even creating a viable invention.

There's a final class of patent-inducing inventions. These are the detailed inventions that companies will typically use in a defensive manner to carve out some small area, and they tend not to be very important because there is competition. So they are not extremely costly.

Now, if revolutionary inventions are the important category, how does the present patent system deal with them? In my view, it deals with them poorly. And indeed, discriminates against them with respect to requirements of patent law. One, the statutory subject matter requirement, and two, the utility requirement.

Because revolutionary inventions tend to be at the cutting edge of knowledge and very close to discoveries of scientific principles or laws of nature, they may tend to run afoul of Section 101 definition of statutory subject matter.

In addition, as such inventions tend to be at an early stage of development where full utility has not been fully determined, they may have difficulty in complying with the utility requirement as rather rigidly defined in Brennar versus Manson.

Now, statutory subject matter has plagued software inventions, as all of you know. Benson and Flute are still lurking out there somewhere, although narrowly interpreted by the Court of Appeals for the Federal Circuit, and also the Patent and Trademark Office.

The utility requirement may also present some problems for these cutting edge software inventions. On the other hand, market-induced inventions have little trouble satisfying statutory subject matter in utility requirements. The only filtering aspect is the nonobvious standard. And as you also know, secondary consideration, such as commercial success, may even open up the filter with respect to many market-induced, because the market loves these. They were needed in the first place.

Now, let me change gears a bit and talk just a moment about copyrights. It is clear that literary and artistic works tend to require the inducement of copyright -- novels, poetry, musical compositions. To a lesser extent, factual work, such as compilations that require the expenditure of sweat of the brow, may need some inducement.

But, the category of works requiring the least incentive would seem to be utilitarian works that provide a function outside of expression.

I would suggest three dimensional lamp bases, for example. And of particular relevance here, computer programs. It seemed quite clear that there was a tremendous market incentive to create, for example, application programs. This symbiotic relationship between hardware and software drives development in both directions.

Now, if I can be permitted to generalization, present copyright law provides excessive incentives for the creation of software in general. There is a low substantive standard, originality, for protection. The scope of protection might be quite broad, and is inherently ambiguous. Little information is conveyed when programs are published in object form. And the cost of acquisition is negligible.

Now, notable examples of excess protection in the copyright sphere would include Welan, the Lotus case, lingering linguistic charm of look and feel. The Second Circuit case of Computer Associate versus Altay at least attempts to provide a filtering form of analysis to eliminate some functional features of utilitarian programs.

However, there are inherent difficulties in attempting to use a literary form of copyright infringement analysis in the context of a utilitarian work. Nonetheless, does the copyright system, even as presently interpreted, provide an adequate system of protection for what may be called revolutionary software?

UNITED STATES PATENT AND TRADEMARK OFFICE
Public Hearing on Patent Protection for Software-Related Inventions
Arlington, Virginia — February 10 & 11, 1994

It seems clear to me that reasonable business people would not rely on copyright alone for the protection of revolutionary developments. The important aspects of such developments would reside in the ideas contained therein, which would be subject to strong attack under even the most generous and ambiguous literary forms of analysis.

What then about trade secrets? Trade secrets, particularly in combination with copyright, provide a relatively strong regime of protection for programs. However, with respect to revolutionary software, once the idea has been conveyed publicly, there is no misappropriation, and competitors would be free to use these basic ideas, which indeed make the software revolutionary.

Finally, a word about suigenerous protection. There's been a lot said about that, a lot published about providing a suigenerous protection for computer software. This may or may not be a good idea. Such a system may solve certain problems, but will create others.

In any event, with respect to revolutionary software, it does not provide an adequate solution. None of the proposals I have seen have the temerity to suggest the protection of ideas.

Now, my general conclusion is that the current regime of intellectual property -- let me state my general conclusion once more. My general conclusion that the current regime of intellectual property inadequately protects revolutionary software invention.

What then would I recommend? As a minimalist position, I would urge the Patent and Trademark Office to stay the course. The law with respect to the patentability of software-related inventions seems to be advancing in a desirable manner under the benign leadership of the Court of Appeals for the Federal Circuit in its application by the PTO.

It would be nice to have Benson and Flute overruled legislatively. To the extent that statutory subject matter would include, as indicated in the Shakovardy decision, "anything under the sun made by man."

It would also seem desirable to have Deere clarified as to the definition of a process so that it was made clear that there is no transformational requirement.

Also, it may be helpful, if this comes into issue, to look at the definition of utility again. The Manson standard, in my view, is far too narrow. It impacts adversely on revolutionary types of invention.

In closing, I'd like to say a few words about the economic importance of revolutionary inventions, and in particular revolutionary software inventions. The United States is the current recognized leader in software development. Nonetheless, in my view, it will not retain that leadership if development is concentrated in the creation of new game programs or further adaptations of application programs.

The future lies in those revolutionary inventions that will change how we do business, consume, communicate, whatever. This may be with reference to the information superhighway, interactive media, data compression, and more importantly, for uses that haven't even been thought about at this time.

Along this line, it should be noted that Americans are probably the most creative individuals in the world. Look at the number of Nobel prizes awarded to Americans. Look at the number of revolutionary inventions created here, even though they may be commercialized elsewhere.

In addition, Americans are noted for their entrepreneurship. Small businesses create the vast majority of the jobs in this country today. The downsizing of major corporations is unfortunate, but it is a reality.

It is also known that entrepreneurs are willing to risk capital in the development of inventions that do not have a bottom line driven benefits/cost ratio. It is this risk-taking of the entrepreneur, when coupled with the creativity of the individual, that is likely to produce revolutionary inventions.

This is particularly pertinent to the software industry, which still tends to be a cottage industry and requires relatively little capital investment -- only access to a computer, a creative mind, and an entrepreneurial experience. We should build upon our leadership in the software area and exploit the creativity and entrepreneurship of those already working in this field and those who will enter this field.

Thus, I would urge that the policies be adopted so that an adequate system of protection for revolutionary inventions, particularly in the software field, can be maintained and implemented.

Thank you.

COMMISSIONER LEHMAN: Thank you very much, Professor Oddi. I was all set to ask you a question that I think you sort of answered at the very end. But when you talked about the incentive of the patent system and really focused on the incentive of the patent system as a means of inducing invention.

We, not only in this forum -- and in this forum we heard it, but definitely in San Jose and here and other places -- the patent system also is a mechanism for inducing investment as well. I gather that -- as I said, I think at the end you sort of clarified that, but you can tell me whether I'm right or not in terms of my interpretation of your analysis -- and that is that you indicated that actually investment in run-of-the-mill -- that the present system actually encourages investment in the run-of-the-mill technology as opposed to the really innovative breakthrough technology. So that actually an analysis which really focuses on innovation, and a system which focuses on innovation, are still the preferred system.

MR. ODDI: Yes. Let me clarify. When I talk about inducing, I'm talking at all stages, not at the creation stage, which is what I primarily focused on today. In my article I go in and talk about at the innovation stage -- commercialization stage -- economists like to call it innovation when it goes into production. It's actually commercialized.

UNITED STATES PATENT AND TRADEMARK OFFICE
Public Hearing on Patent Protection for Software-Related Inventions
Arlington, Virginia -- February 10 & 11, 1994

Yes, those would be induced, too, because certainly the basic idea has to be implemented. And we need incentives all the way throughout the development.

COMMISSIONER LEHMAN: We also heard in San Jose quite a bit of criticism of the way we implement Section 101, and that we're really spending too much time on very artificial determinations. And I think to some degree that was an underlay of some of Mr. Lo's comments, too, working day to day on this, in fact to the point where he was in a sense almost offering suggestions as to how we might further refine these, to some degree, semantic distinctions simply so they'll create fewer problems.

And I gather that that's something that you think really does need review.

MR. ODDI: I certainly do. So I think Section 101 should not be a filter for inventions. And it was mentioned here earlier, the methods of doing business -- well, in my view, that is an arbitrary categorization based upon 19th century formalistic jurisprudence, which today we know that the United States is a great service industry. And I think there's a great deal of creativity in the service industry.

And certainly if somebody comes up with a revolutionary invention in the field of how you do business in the insurance, or whatever business, I think our society benefits at the margin from having that invention, rather than having people invest in that so that we will have it, because it will be a more efficient way of doing business. We will have value added, and I think that's important to our economic development.

COMMISSIONER LEHMAN: Well, actually in San Jose I think one of the things that came out, quite apart from whether or not inventions get -- applications are rejected inappropriately on these grounds, which would be your thrust -- that the mere fact that we spend so much time worrying about it takes away from the -- focuses our attention on the wrong issue, which is really nonobviousness --

MR. ODDI: Yes, I know that.

COMMISSIONER LEHMAN: -- as opposed to, you know, trying to fit this square peg in the round hole.

MR. ODDI: My only comment on that, that I think the nonobvious standard ought to be a rigorous high standard because it is the only mechanism that we have for filtering out these costly inventions, which the market would otherwise create.

COMMISSIONER LEHMAN: Well, I think that really goes to the core of what you're talking about too. I got the impression there's a fair amount of satisfaction with the direction of the Court of Appeals for the Federal Circuit on that. That would not necessarily be my view of --

MR. ODDI: With a caveat about secondary considerations and other -- because that tends to show you that the market really was a factor in the creation of it. I'd like to see a more objective evaluation of the nonobvious issue based upon the prior art, rather than what happens post hoc.

COMMISSIONER LEHMAN: I really want to thank you for coming all the way out here. I hope you're not snowed in forever.

MR. ODDI: I hope not.

COMMISSIONER LEHMAN: You're used to it, though, in Illinois.

MR. ODDI: Right. Thank you very much.

COMMISSIONER LEHMAN: Next, actually, because we've dilly-dallied around, we've supplied time for Bernard Galler of the University of Michigan Software Patent Institute to get here. So if Professor Galler would come forward?

MR. GALLER: Yes. One plane canceled, one late. The taxi drivers couldn't find the place. But I got here.

COMMISSIONER LEHMAN: Great. The Federal Government is closed today.

MR. GALLER: I heard that it was closed, but I had confidence that you would continue with these hearings.

(Laughter.)

PRESENTATION BY BERNARD GALLER

UNIVERSITY OF MICHIGAN SOFTWARE PATENT INSTITUTE

MR. GALLER: I'll introduce myself. I'm Bernie Galler, Professor of Computer Science at the University of Michigan, and former president of the ACM. But I'm here today as the founder and chairman of the Software Patent Institute in Ann Arbor, Michigan. And I'm speaking here as Software Patent Institute representative.

The history of inventions in the software area is not recorded well. There are a few formal journals, such as the Annals of the History of Computing, and some textbooks. But the prior art that is needed by the PTO is not available in many of the forms that more mature fields support.

For example, in the fields of chemistry or physics, in addition to a large number of patents available to the PTO, most researchers' results are published in a relatively few journals.

This is not the case in the software community. Not only are the results and inventions not published in formal journals most of the time, they usually described if at all, primarily in informal conference reports or newsletters. Add to that the almost complete lack of issued patents before 1981 in this field, and it is clear why PTO examiners have a difficult time finding prior art, even when previous work that is relevant is well-known in the field.

There are some repositories of program code, but it's very difficult to extract, or abstract, the innovative and nonobvious algorithms and ideas that are detailed there.

What is needed is not the detailed code, but some level of description of what is in that code. Unless the author carefully documents the developing algorithm, the control flow and the data structures, it's very difficult to discover these concepts to understand the underlying process.

UNITED STATES PATENT AND TRADEMARK OFFICE
Public Hearing on Patent Protection for Software-Related Inventions
Arlington, Virginia -- February 10 & 11, 1994

It is well known, however, that programmers are usually too interested in moving on to the next task to take the time to document the last one.

It isn't difficult to understand why software results are so often not published in formal journals. Most of the work in this emerging field has been done outside academia, since software is almost always immediately applicable to the solution of problems that already exist in industry.

Of course, there is theoretical work in computer science and compute engineering. But the explosion of computing in our society has led to a corresponding explosion in software techniques in advance of the theory. And in the rush to exploit these techniques, relatively little effort has been devoted to disseminating these results and techniques widely.

In fact, even when this kind of information is not regarded as a trade secret, many companies are not particularly anxious to have it made widely available.

During the years before 1980, there was much confusion as to the kind of protection that might be available, if any, for software inventions. And there was little incentive for programmers to try to publish their work. Much of the communication that did go on occurred at thematic conferences and workshops. The reports of such conferences constitute a very valuable source of prior art, but they are not readily available to the PTO.

Thus, the PTO has found it difficult to identify the relevant sources for prior art, or to collect that prior art into a usable database for the purpose of evaluating patent applications.

What are the relevant sources for prior art in the software area? I already mentioned our conference and workshop proceedings from both general and specialized conferences. These are usually sponsored by professional societies such as the ACM and the IEEE, and special interest groups, the sigs, or societies. And the sigs publish newsletters also, often containing nuggets describing new ideas and techniques which eventually prove to be important prior art.

Universities such as Michigan and UCLA have for many years offered short courses lasting one or two weeks in which leading edge research results are presented, disclosing new ideas, concepts, and techniques. The notes which are distributed to attendees contain valuable descriptions of such work and in time prove to be important prior art publicly disclosed.

Manuals for commercial systems and applications often contain important descriptions of the techniques these systems and applications embody, and are a valuable source of prior art. Such sources would not be readily available to PTO examiners unless the PTO would have the funding to build an extensive library with appropriate indexing for that purpose.

A number of software vendors publish internal reports and/or research journals, which are made available to their customers, and are thus publicly disclosed. These reports and journals and other materials used for the education and training of customers often describe innovative ideas and techniques which could be used as prior art if they were available to the PTO examiners.

Government sponsored research is often documented in reports generated by the principal investigators and published by the sponsoring government agencies. While these are public documents, it's not easy to know where to look for them. They often contain the earliest reports of significant research and applications in the software area.

Another source of material can be found in books published on various subjects in computer science and computer engineering. These include textbooks for the more advanced courses, and research publications from academic institutions.

It is not always easy to find the kinds of prior art that examiners need in such books. But if they were on-line instead of only in printed form, it would be much easier to discover which books contain material relevant to a particular claimed invention.

Finally, corporate defense of disclosure publications can be important sources of relevant prior art. A company that wants to make sure that a competitor does not obtain a patent covering a process or technique that is essential to its own business might publish a description of that process or technique to have it publicly disclosed without taking the additional step of applying for a patent. And there are well-known examples of this.

On the other hand, that company may not be particularly anxious to advertise its discovery or use of that process or technique, so the publication would not be very widely disseminated. There are also well-known examples of that.

If indeed a patent is later issued for that process or technique, the company can point to the disclosed art during litigation, but that is a very late stage in the cycle.

Companies that rely on defense of disclosure should be encouraged to deposit their published disclosures in a database available to the PTO so the controversial patent most likely will not be granted at all.

Well, the Software Patent Institute is a nonprofit institution dedicated to providing information to the public, to assisting the PTO and others by providing technical support in the form of educational and training programs, and to providing access to information and retrieval sources.

The primary goal of the Software Patent Institute is to provide the best available information as to prior art in the software field for utilization by the public and the PTO.

We applaud the efforts by Dr. Dobb's journal of Miller Friedman publications to make its articles available on CD ROM. And the efforts of Ziff/Davis Publications to put a number of recent computer-related publications on CD ROM, as well as the efforts by the IEEE and the ACM to make available abstractive computer science articles.

We also applaud the efforts of those who are working to identify, collect, and distribute copies of the patents they consider software-related, especially since many of the

UNITED STATES PATENT AND TRADEMARK OFFICE
Public Hearing on Patent Protection for Software-Related Inventions
Arlington, Virginia -- February 10 & 11, 1994

patents that have been identified come from a large number of PTO classes. These efforts are valuable contributions to the overall effort to document the history of software technology, and to make the results available in online form.

The Software Patent Institute, for its part, is tracking these efforts carefully so that our collection supplements rather than duplicates these other efforts. To track the history of an exploding industry with rapidly developing technology is a massive undertaking that will require significant efforts by a number of organizations. We are committed to being one of them.

The Software Patent Institute also provides an educational resource from which the PTO and the public can obtain an enhanced understanding of the nature of software, of software engineering, and of the history of the discipline and its relationship to the patent process.

Several lectures have already been given to the examiners of the PTO on aspects of software history and techniques. And several more are scheduled during the next few weeks and the coming months. We will have a professor from Carnegie Mellon there next week, and a professor from Michigan there the week after that, lecturing to the examiners. And we hope to continue that.

We plan to offer our first one-day session on related topics to patent professionals and the general public sometime this spring.

Although there is a current debate on the overall desirability of having software patents, the Software Patent Institute has deliberately taken no position on that question. We recognize that the patent system is in place, and working, but that there is currently a problem regarding software-related patents. We are dedicated to helping alleviate that problem independent of longer-range considerations that must eventually be resolved.

The Software Patent Institute has asked people throughout the software industry, government, and academia, to contribute descriptions of software techniques and processes to the Software Patent Institute database. These descriptions form the content of the SPI database, and have now been made available for computer-aided searching by the PTO, and by members of the Software Patent Institute. Access by the general public will follow shortly.

The SPI database already contains many examples of each of the kinds of relevant prior art outlined above, and it is growing rapidly.

Our recommendation to this panel is to issue a strong recognition and endorsement of this kind of activity by the Software Patent Institute and by others, and to encourage the PTO to take advantage of the services of the Software Patent Institute as much as possible.

We strongly believe that the PTO can and will do a better job than it has if it has the right tools and the right information.

I thank you for being able to talk to you, and I certainly would answer questions.

COMMISSIONER LEHMAN: Thank you very much, Professor Galler.

One of the issues that came up earlier today was the whole question of the classification system that we have right now, that it very rapidly gets out of date. And this makes it very difficult for examiners even to take advantage of the information that's already in our patent files.

Obviously you're struggling with that, working with that, as you try to organize this new database. Maybe you could expand on that, about, do we have a problem? What's the nature of the problem? And maybe you have some suggestions about it.

MR. GALLER: Well, for the time being we're providing full text search with whatever words the patent examiners know about.

What's really needed down the line, though, is a thesaurus kind of help, which says, if you're looking with this term, you really ought to be looking for those, also, and here are some additional suggestions. Here are some related articles or entries that you may not have thought about, but they might be close to what you want.

There are an awful lot of database techniques that are well-known here which we certainly will start to use once we have a process that is working and bringing in the revenue that we need to keep going.

But is this kind of -- well, two things. One is, the database service can provide such help. Here are some suggestions for what you want to do.

The other thing is, as we give these lectures and other people give lectures, and the examiners become more technology-knowledgeable, they themselves will expand their knowledge of how to search. What are the relevant terms? What are the relevant things they ought to be knowing about?

The classification that the PTO has doesn't help. You know, from the computer science point of view, it's not a very good classification. But it exists. And we can hope to help map it into more coherent, technology-based classifications. And we certainly plan to do that.

COMMISSIONER LEHMAN: Thank you very much. We look forward to cooperating with you and working with you.

MR. GALLER: Thank you.

COMMISSIONER GOFFNEY: Bernie, Jerry Goldberg, who is the director of Group 2300, certainly endorses your activity, as do we. He wasn't here, wasn't able to get here today, but he has told me a lot about your work, and it's certainly appreciated.

MR. GALLER: Well, he's been very helpful to us in helping us understand the problems of the Patent Office, absolutely.

COMMISSIONER GOFFNEY: Thank you.

COMMISSIONER LEHMAN: Thank you very much.

We're getting there. Finally, unless Professor Fryer has arrived -- he hasn't. I know him personally, and I don't see him.

Then finally, we're at Gregory Aharonian, who has waited very patiently for two days now. He was also in San Jose.

PRESENTATION BY GREGORY AHARONIAN

SOURCE TRANSLATION AND OPTIMIZATION

MR. AHARONIAN: Before I address the topic -- I'll mainly be speaking about software prior art -- there were three kind of little tidbits that came out of other discussions I thought I'd share with everyone.

About a year ago, a group either with the German Patent Office or the European Patent Office did a study of the maintenance fee renewal process for German patents. In Germany I guess they're done every year as opposed to being done every three or four years, as in the U.S. So that from an economic analysis point of view, yearly data is very easy to analyze.

They found that for the computer software industry -- no, for the computer industry as a whole, that the average length of the patent was about six or seven years before they effectively stopped renewing the patent. So these talks about lowering the patent life, I mean you could go down as far as about seven years. And if you actually look at renewal rates, it would have absolutely no impact.

It's a little known study, but it's one that probably should be circulated more widely.

The second thing that was also talked about is, there are a growing number of investment funds in New York City that are pooling money to find people with patents so they can go chase lawsuits and stuff. So that all these problems we're talking about are going to get a lot worse because there's going to be a lot more floating around to play these games. Especially in the field of software, there's a definite window of time before it gets really messy with the monies being thrown into this stuff.

And the third is a patent I just came across out of Microsoft that -- I had seen something in there that I had never seen before. In the preamble to the specification, they said that part of the patent specification contained copyrighted material. And there was a warning in there of some sort.

It was the first time I've actually seen anything copyrighted inside of a patent. And I'm wondering if this is going to be a whole new family of hybrid copyright patent things that are going to confuse everyone to death.

COMMISSIONER GOFFNEY: Did that happen to be code that was in there?

MR. AHARONIAN: I didn't look. I was just examining something over at the Public Search Room, and the first page had this paragraph that I Xeroxed because it was just something I'd never seen before.

PARTICIPANT: For clarification, it's a notice that says that, for purposes -- that you can copy this patent application or patent, once it issues, for any purpose you want related to the patent application. But you can't -- all other copyright rights are reserved. And it's a common practice by practitioners.

MR. AHARONIAN: I'd never seen it before, and I thought it was kind of interesting. A couple of us were chuckling.

I'm here to talk about software prior art, and I happen to know a little bit about the subject.

Software prior art comes up in six areas of activities. In the information disclosure document, when the applicant files a document, during the patent examination when the examiner is dealing with issues of novelty and obviousness, during reexaminations when somebody is going to challenge it, infringement lawsuits, and the circuit court decisions.

Each of these need to have access to what's been done in the field before. Actually, in terms of economic activities, which dwarfs all software prior art activities, there's just some general software technology trends for reuse, well, they have actually the same question: What is out there that exists that can be used?

For many years now, at least eight years now, I've been maintaining a very large -- the largest software prior art reuse database in the country. I have information over 15,000 computer programs coming out in government, corporate, and university facilities, 5,000 patents, and over 100,000 abstracts to articles in the field.

This is in a sense an active collection. Each of the items are items that I've actively sought out to include in my database and examined either in depth or just briefly to look at them.

I'm located in the Boston area, and in this modern era I'm located on the Internet.

One of the things I do is that every year or two years I publish a directory of -- what I call the Government Source Code Directory -- since a lot of the public domain software, a lot of the university software, even a lot of corporate software is actually funded under government contract, except for obviously corporate commercial software.

The current directory has the titles to about 10,000 programs. It's actually a pretty good guide to both what is state-of-the-art, what is historical, how to classify software. It's just such a large body of information that there is a lot you can do with it.

I run a business of helping companies get at the software, helping them reuse it in their business practices, helping them examine the technology inside of it, things of that nature. It's a very rich source material. This country spends about $50 billion a year developing this stuff. And there are a lot of good programmers working here, so that there's a tremendous wealth of technology available.

I also, in recent years, as software patenting has become active, and I tend to share a lot in the information I have, I've started up something called Internet Patent News Service, where each week I mail out over the Internet the titles and numbers to the most recent patents and the most

UNITED STATES PATENT AND TRADEMARK OFFICE
Public Hearing on Patent Protection for Software-Related Inventions
Arlington, Virginia -- February 10 & 11, 1994

recent gazette that happens to hit the Boston Public Library where I do a lot of my research.

I have about 1,000 subscribers around the world, many of which are actually rebroadcast sites, gopher sites where they collect the information and make it available -- 880 of the subscribers get the news service, where I, for example, announce the PTO hearings and other such things. Nine hundred or so are electronic, most of which are software. There is a tremendous demand on the Internet for software patenting information. These people would kill for almost anything.

I have all types of people, government agencies, people in 35 states, 28 countries, corporations, universities, and one of the Texas patent depositories got tired of getting their data so late down there they just figured they'd get it through me.

This is a map that was collected by one of the Internet node maintainers of traffic flow over the Internet. And it's kind of a pretty picture which I like showing to people. But it also kind of shows both the sites where a lot of software activity is going on in the U.S., where I track a lot of the software. That does come out, where a lot of the software prior art is being made, and where actually a lot of my Patent News Service subscribers are.

It's all pretty much the same thing. And not surprisingly, there are heavy concentrations in New York, Boston, and Washington on the East Coast, obviously. And then up on the West Coast, it's the Bay Area, Silicon Valley, and down in LA, San Diego. There's a decent movement in Texas and somewhere in the Midwest. But for the most part, it's regionalized into the five big tech cities of the country that are up there.

Where do you find software prior art? Well, the sources I find out when I'm traveling around the country are in these seven categories: technical reports, both government, corporate, and academic; journal articles; conference proceedings; theses and books -- and universities theses are probably one of the most richest sources of software prior art, in a timely sense; commercial products; Internet files; bulletin board systems, which are in many cases not part of the Internet formally but tend to store growing mounts of information; and in software patents.

Each of those sources of information have a legacy of history behind the organizations involved with them. And you have to learn about them to learn how to search through them.

What types of software prior art do I search for? Well, obviously, source code is the most obvious one to look for, since that is the best description of a program.

Then there are object libraries and executables. There are flow charts and state charts. There are pseudo-code which you see in a lot of journal articles. There are patent claims. Obvious things, obvious description of those software.

Then there are some things that kind of border on the software field, the SPICE and VHDL circuit description languages, and with the growing convergence of hardware and software, they too become prior art of a sort that have

to be searched for, even though to most people concerned searching for software prior art, they would not look in such sources.

Then spreadsheets and numerical data also can be considered software as a form.

Now, when I think of software prior art -- and what follows is a series of slides that I'm going to give you a tour of where I hang out most of my life. When I think of software prior arts, I think of dusty, grungy old basements. That's where most of this type of literature can be found. You have to look for it. But this is where you're going to find it a lot of times -- dark basements, with endless stacks of materials that you have to search through one by one.

Most of this stuff is not on computer databases at all. The only way you're going to really find any of this stuff is to pull out these volumes one by one and flip through them. It's a very tedious, lengthy process. It's the only way it really can be done.

This happens to be a collection of books dealing purely with software. So in some cases, the information is fairly compact. These I think are programming language books in a variety of languages. I think those green books up top are all the ADA books.

In some cases, the information is tightly concentrated, and it does make the search easier.

In other cases, for example, the bookcases you see in the background, are for the subject matters of physics and engineering. Normally you wouldn't consider searching through such stacks for software, especially since they're really not in software. But there is a growing amount of software prior art in such subjects. Physicists do a lot of cutting edge software development that does qualify as prior art. And when you deal with stacks like that, the books are very scattered in there and it takes a long time to go through them all.

Another source is journals. This is a series of journals. And most of the journals up there come from one of the leading societies, the ACM. I think the third and fourth rows up there are mostly the ACM journals.

But there are a variety of other journals in related fields to software that all have to be searched through, all coming out every month, all potentially sources of prior art. And each journal has a family of editors and reviewers behind it, associations behind it. There are certain styles of software in there. Knowing that is very important to tracking software prior art.

The journals you just saw up there were one current month's work for all the journal from like A to Z. There are tremendous numbers of them. These are all the back journals. In this case, for those familiar with searching for such stuff, the IEEE has the previous journals around. They just use lots of different colors for their journal covers, and you can usually identify which section of the library deals with them. But in each case you have to flip through each one of these volumes to find stuff.

UNITED STATES PATENT AND TRADEMARK OFFICE
Public Hearing on Patent Protection for Software-Related Inventions
Arlington, Virginia -- February 10 & 11, 1994

Then there are collections of technical reports. And these tend to be even more unorganized and scattered about. But even there, there is structure to how they are kept. If you'll see, in the middle you'll see some white journals with a colorful band across them. Those happen to belong to the Electric Power Research Institute, and they actually do some software development which they've had patents on. So you have to search through all of them.

Next to them are some orange journals which are characteristic of the Japanese Atomic Energy Research Institute. And again, they have software. In that case, it's even more difficult to search for that stuff because their reports tend to be all in Japanese except for an English abstract in source code and usually FORTRAN or something. And you know, I can read FORTRAN, but I'm still trying to learn to read Japanese.

But again, it's there and it's something that has to be dealt with.

These are again even older technical reports. These are so old that they've lost most of their colors. The orange ones are the NASA reports, and NASA tends to have bright orange and dull blue covers. The middle ones are from a European defense group, AGARD, that has a lot of software prior art.

Endless number of these in these libraries all over the country, that require one to go through them.

In some cases, the volumes of reports are so great that no library could contain them all, and you reduce them down with microfiche. This happens to be one subsection of a collection of microfiche for NASA technical reports.

Again, you have to go through each one of these one by one, stick them into the microfiche reader, and examine them to see if they have prior art, flow charts, whatever. It's not a fun process, and I've got a fair number of cuts on my fingers over the years from going through these things.

Again, here are more cabinets of microfiche. And in the background you see microform, which is a different type of film, with its set of printers. And it's just endless volumes of these things.

One of the richest sources of software prior art are university theses, because they tend to let their students do things that are as wacky as wacky can be, mainly because students are there to learn how to do wacky things as opposed to doing anything really meaningful. So a lot of the ideas -- I mean, something like Compton's patents I initially laughed at it because I've seen theses in the '80s that did all types of things with CD ROMs, because back then they were first coming out. And some student said, hey, there's a new CD ROM, let me try doing something educational with it.

Unfortunately most thesis information is not on any database, and it's very hard to find short of actually going to each university and flipping through these reports one by one. It can be a pain.

And finally, there is in the academic community, even in the corporate research community, the preprint system where

people tend to distribute copies of their reports before they're published, or in many cases they don't even get published, they just pass them out anyway.

These things are very unorganized, and you tend to find them in stacks on carts. I think this is actually an IBM library in the Boston area I happened to be floating through. Searching that stuff is a pain.

Now, increasingly computers are making an impact on the library world. This is the main reference section for one such library. But in terms of prior art, most of the really interesting stuff predates most databases so that, while such computer systems will help in the future, they really won't help in the past.

Of course, I complain about a lot of the places I hang out. But this happens to be out the window of one of the MIT libraries, and during the summer it's a very pretty view. So it is somewhat relaxing sometimes in doing my prior art searches.

Now, in San Jose -- and once again I'd like to reiterate it out here -- recent developments in the hardware design world are really blurring the distinctions between hardware and software. And I'll disagree with some of the others who say that there are such distinctions. While this will have an impact on patenting issues and procedures, it has a great impact on software prior art because it opens up tremendous sections of hardware research over the past 20 years as potential software prior art.

There exists programs that allow me to scan in circuits what anyone would consider to be a pure piece of hardware, and turn them into a software algorithm. That means that in building a software prior art database you have to include all of the hardware prior art that exists out there because nowadays it can be turned into software.

And based on some counts I've made, there's at least twice as much hardware prior art as there is software prior art, so it basically triples the size of such an effort.

This is just a little article on a company in Germany that combined case tools, which is basically software engineering, with their hardware design tools, so that within one environment for the most part the engineer doesn't even care what the end result will be, hardware or software. He's just worrying about processes and algorithms and devices and things like that. At the end he pushes a button to get out a chip or a computer program. So that this issue of prior art is becoming more complicated even as we're holding these hearings.

Building prior art databases is not for amateurs. I mean, over the past ten years at least eight government efforts have tried to do similar things, and they all have failed for a variety of reasons. It's a very complicated process. There are at least 10 different knowledge classification schemes I've had to learn over the years, Library of Congress, IEEE has one, ACM has one, I have two, the Patent Office has one, there's the Dewey decimal system.

When you're going through all these sources of information out there, each one classifies its stuff differently. And to do these searches effectively and cost-

UNITED STATES PATENT AND TRADEMARK OFFICE
Public Hearing on Patent Protection for Software-Related Inventions
Arlington, Virginia -- February 10 & 11, 1994

efficiently, you have to know each one. It's a tremendous amount of information.

There have been suggestions that the Internet could be a substitute. I'm very skeptical. I think that doing prior art searches and requests over the Internet has actually caused more problems than it will solve.

In recent months a variety of different people have actually asked me how much it would cost to build a truly useful software prior art database. My guess is, based on what I've been doing over the past eight years, is that you need a minimum of $10 million, plus $2 million a year as maintenance.

Now, that might seem a lot, but remember, this is to track a $50 billion a year development process. And out of that, $10 million is fairly minor. But given the vast amount of literature that already exists out there, you're going to need a very rapid development effort to catch up with all of that, plus future development efforts to do so into the future.

With the databases I already have in my knowledge, I could reject about a quarter of all existing software patents. So I would think that there is indeed a problem. And most people have recognized that.

As a kind of incentive to the Patent Office, if they're considering actually building such databases, the software prior art database would have even greater benefits to the U.S. software development community. And you could score a fair number of brownie points by helping them out at the same time.

The last slide illustrates some of the problems we're now facing with software patents. This is from the January 4th, 1994 Official Gazette. And it's a patent from IBM for choosing items off of a menu.

Now, the Official Gazette includes the first claim and a diagram of the best mode embodiment. And it is inconceivable to me that in 1994 the best mode embodiment of a menu selection system is what appears in the Gazette and what appears in the patent. I haven't examined this patent in detail, but I suspect what we see there reflects what's in the rest of it.

Those type of menu selection systems date back to the '60s. And the fact that something was issued with such diagrams makes me kind of nervous that the problem is even worse than we think it is.

But like I said, you flip open recent Gazettes, and you'll see patents in there that are truly questionable.

That's it.

COMMISSIONER LEHMAN: Thank you very much, Mr. Aharonian.

Well, I think we did pretty well today for a snowy day. We actually got all but a handful of people that were supposed to testify, and we got a couple more from yesterday. And I want to thank everybody for coming through the snow.

As I indicated, this hearing transcript will be made available after February 21st. But we're happy to accept more supplemental information, either written information that

can be sent directly to us, or information that can be sent to Jeff Kushan on the Internet.

We're always open to information at any time, even two, three years from now if you -- you know, reelect President Clinton, we'll be available for information even then, and then maybe President Gore, and then maybe President Hillary Clinton. By then we'll have the prior art database completely resolved, that problem.

So anyway, thank you very much, and have a good day.

(Whereupon, the hearing in the above-entitled matter was adjourned.)

Due to the inclement weather, a number of speakers were unable to attend or provide oral remarks. Prepared remarks from these individuals has been included in the transcripts in response to their request.

PREPARED REMARKS FROM ROBERT GREENE STERNE

Thank you, Mr. Commissioner.

My name is Robert Greene Sterne and I am testifying on behalf of myself. I want to focus on five specific issues which I believe need to be explored further in order to round out the record in these hearings. These five areas deal with the preparation and prosecution of computer related patent applications.

While my views are my own, they are based on the experience of the ten members of my firm who prepare and prosecute patent applications in the computer area. The experience base that is being drawn upon encompasses literally hundreds of original US cases. I mention this because you need to know the perspective from where my views come.

First, I want to address whether program listings or flowcharts or pseudocode or other specific types of disclosure should be required in the patent application for the software aspects of the invention? It is tempting both for practioners and the Office to have very specific disclosure requirements concerning software. But my view is that it would be a mistake to establish specific disclosure requirements. Our experience is that there is no agreement among experienced patent attorneys or among software inventors concerning what is the optimal disclosure strategy. Moreover, as the technology races forward, the disclosure strategies change based on our experience. The patent system is very robust since it, unlike a sui generis system, can adapt to rapidly developing technology in emerging areas. I understand that to reduce printing costs and database costs the Patent Office would like to limit certain types of listings, and that many people believe that more higher level forms of representation of the invention are more effective in explaining the critical functionality and architecture and operation of the software invention. I agree with these sentiments, but believe that the system is better served by maintaining the flexibility of allowing the applicant to decide the best way of discloses the invention in the patent application.

To amplify on this point, let me say a few things about the technology that will support my view. First, I agree with the

UNITED STATES PATENT AND TRADEMARK OFFICE
Public Hearing on Patent Protection for Software-Related Inventions
Arlington, Virginia -- February 10 & 11, 1994

opinion that machine code, such as object code, does not aid in enabling one skilled in the art to make and use the invention. But I believe that source code combined with adequate accompanying description is often sufficient to satisfy the disclosure requirements under Section 112. This is particularly true with computer programs written in higher level computer programming languages, such as Pascal and ADA. As the computer programming arts progresses, computer programs will be just as easy to read by humans as english text. In fact, it is the objective of such computer programming languages to be human readable. Thus, it would be wrong for the Office to adopt rules which would prohibit the submission of source code.

Second, as an attorney in private practice, I am very sensitive to deadlines and budgets, and I applaud the Patent Office's efforts in the area of enlightened management, management by objective, and total quality control. These are all good and encourage Examiners to utilize their time in the examination process in the most optimal way. However, I am quite concerned that the very complexity of these state of the art software inventions by necessity require more time for examination that is being allocated by the Office. Examiners in these areas of technologies should be careful supervised, and their performance measured, like all other examiners. However, the Office must make sure that it is allowing them the time that they need to do a quality examination job that the patent system and the public requires.

Third, I applaud the efforts being made to hire examiners with significant educational and work experience in software technology. This expertise is absolutely essential for the Examination process, and the patent system is very well served by the Office raising the technical competence of the Examining corp in the software area as soon as possible. Similarly, applicants for the patent agents exam who have significant computer science backgrounds should qualify to sit for the exam. Computer science in this day and age should be considered to be a sufficient technical expertise to qualify to take the patent agents exam. But I agree with the sentiment expressed by some that there is a broad range of technical training in computer hardware and software from degrees from different educational institutions. Consequently, both in terms of hiring examiners and qualifying applicants for the agents exam the Office must carefully examine the educational qualifications of the individuals involved so that qualified-people are let into the system and people without sufficient training are excluded. By necessity, this will require line drawing, but like many areas of patent law the ability to distinguish the shades of gray is the strength of the system. In other words, neither the approach of excluding all computer science people nor the policy of letting all computer science people in should be taken.

Fourth, our experience in prosecuting applications on state of the art software related inventions is that the Examination process in the real emerging areas of technology is effectively being delayed pending these hearings and the political uncertainty over patents on this technology. Mr. Commissioner, you should be aware that we are encountering situations in prosecution where applications, in our opinion, are not being allowed because the Examining Corp is afraid of the political ramifications associated with possible adverse publicity to the Office if applications in these technical areas are issued. This delay and uncertainty hurts the patent system and American innovation. These political forces should be removed from the examining process and the focus should be on examination and not on a fear that the anti-software patent forces will raise a great hue and cry over the issuance of a particular patent in an emerging area of technology. Now, I don't want to be misunderstood on this point. In no way am I arguing that a patent should be issued on an invention that is too broad based on the prior art or is non-statutory based on a liberal interpretation of Section 101. But I am deadset against any type of delay that is being caused by fear of issuance of patent applications on patentable inventions merely because they involve state of the art software technology.

My fifth and final point concerns your database. As other speakers have stated, one of the great benefits to the public of patent protection for software related inventions is that such inventions, which in the past have been maintained as trade secrets, will be disclosed to the public so that others will not have to reinvent the wheel. This will be of great benefit to the software industry. As an aside, the software industry in this regard is 180 degrees from what happens in another emerging area of technology, biotech, where the tradition is to publish or perish and inventors oftentimes lose their patent rights here or abroad though premature publication of their inventions in the technical literature. The biotechnology area clearly shows the benefit of rapid disclosure of technology in that competing researchers are allowed to rapidly build on the work of others and not recreate the same inventions.

Turning to the database problem involving the examination of software related inventions, my view is that this database problem is not different that the problems encounter by the Office in other areas of emerging technology, such as biotech. It is critical that the Patent Office take all reasonable steps to create the most robust database possible in these emerging areas of technology, and to provide efficient and economical access to this database to members of the public both in Washington and in remote locations. The electronics superhighway being pushed by this administration could form the backbone for this remote access. The patent office should squarely embrace initiatives for building the most comprehensive database possible and for opening it up for ready access by members of the public. I know that this in practice is a tali order and one that could be very expensive. However, the benefits of providing a comprehensive database appear to outweigh the cost.

Thank you for this opportunity.

PREPARED REMARKS FROM MR. DANIEL J. KLUTH
TESTIMONY OF DANIEL J. KLUTH
AT THE PUBLIC HEARINGS BY THE
U.S. DEPARTMENT OF COMMERCE
PATENT & TRADEMARK OFFICE ON

UNITED STATES PATENT AND TRADEMARK OFFICE
Public Hearing on Patent Protection for Software-Related Inventions
Arlington, Virginia -- February 10 & 11, 1994

PATENT PROTECTION FOR SOFTWARE-RELATED INVENTIONS

February 11, 1994 Marriot Crystal Forum, Arlington, VA.

Good morning ladies and gentlemen. My name is Daniel J. Kluth and I am a patent attorney with Schwegman, Lundberg & Woessner, P.A. of Minneapolis, Minnesota. I am the chair of the Software Protection Committee of the Minnesota Intellectual Property Law Association and I am the Chair of the Government Relations Committee of the Minnesota Software Association. Although I am the chair of these two Committees, I must point out that my remarks today do not have the complete endorsement of these organizations. I have polled many of the members of these two organizations and, specifically, the Software Protection Committee, and I will try to convey the impressions I received.

The USPTO has been kind enough to allow me some extra time today to address both Topic B (Standards and Practices used in Examination of Patent Applications for Software Related Inventions) and Topic C (Significance of and Protection for Visual Aspects of Software Related Inventions). Thus, I will speak on both topics.

First, Topic B. In reviewing the testimony given in the San Jose hearing last month, many concerns were voiced about the quality of the examination process and the issuance of seemingly overbroad and invalid software patents. I won't belabor that point. I would like to point out, however, that I believe establishing new rules in the CFR or new or special procedures in the MPEP for software inventions would be wrong. Software patent applicants should stand on the same footing as any other technology groups or classes. I do not believe there is any basis in the current statutes which would allow special burdens to be placed on software applicants. The first insurmountable barrier would be how to decide if a patent application is a "software" patent.

Because there already has been so much comment in this area, I thought I would focus on questions 7-12 of Topic B. This set of questions deals with the problem of effectively and meaningfully disclosing software-related inventions.

A patent application must teach one skilled in the art how to make and use the invention (enablement) and the best mode in which an invention may be practiced. Failure to disclose the invention and teach the best mode robs the public of its part of the bargain in the patent system.

In many instances, the application is filed with a source code appendix in accordance with 37 CFR Section 1.96, either in paper form or on microfiche. This is one of the few rules promulgated by the USPTO which provides special consideration to a technology class: namely software.

As an aside, I would like to point out that a lot of the testimony presented in January and yesterday was directed to areas outside of the control of the USPTO. Many comments, if acted upon, would require changes to statutes and in one or two extreme cases, an amendment to the Constitution. But improving the quality of examination of software patents is very much in the sphere of authority of the Patent Office and in some cases, can be done without rule changes. Simple refinements in procedure and using existing statutes and rules will suffice. This is particularly true in the area of disclosures. The source code appendix has proven in many instances to be a burden on the USPTO and does not appear to provide the applicant with a better patent application. I suggest that we eliminate Rule 96 and place the burden on the applicant to do a better job in explaining the software operation in the body of the specification.

Many patent applicants provide the source code in a patent application as a "backstop" to their application to satisfy both the best mode and the enablement requirements. I will first discuss enablement. Applicants hope that they can overcome an enablement rejection from the USPTO on their software patent application by relying on the source code to overcome the rejection. This reliance actually works against the public interest in permitting lax disclosures or poorly written disclosures in the body of the specification. By eliminating Rule 96, the applicants would be forced to do a better job of describing their invention.

In many cases, Rule 96 encourages this poor practice. In many cases, the source code appendix does not teach the public anything unless an expert is hired to decode, decompile or flow chart the appendix. Unfortunately, Rule 96 has become a de facto standard. By itself, eliminating Rule 96 would return the earlier practice of submitting source code listings in the body of the specification. This practice was a terrible burden on the public and the USPTO in creating many jumbo patent applications. But this practice should never have been allowed to flourish since it violates the requirements under 35 USC Section 112 which requires that the applicant describe the invention in clear and concise terms. Patent applications filed with the source code embodiment in the specification should be rejected as not being concise and the rules allowing substitute specifications be invoked to clean up the application. This procedure would be still useful in the case of rush-filed applications, especially if the U.S. adopts a first-to-file system. Applicants who file source code listings [only if necessary] in the body of the specification would be required to follow up with a concise substitute specification.

Source code listings are also submitted to satisfy the best mode requirement. But best mode is an objective standard which can rarely be tested in the USPTO examination process. This determination is made during litigation and is assisted by the discovery practice to determine the inventor's state of mind and to determine if the best mode was suppressed or concealed. In all other technology areas for patents, the best mode for practicing the invention is a comparison of the specification to information obtained during discovery. Software patents should be treated the same as other technology areas and the specification should stand alone without reliance on a source code appendix. Allowing for and even encouraging the submission of source code listings also hurts the public by discouraging

UNITED STATES PATENT AND TRADEMARK OFFICE
Public Hearing on Patent Protection for Software-Related Inventions
Arlington, Virginia -- February 10 & 11, 1994

some applicants from filing software patent applications for fear of losing trade secret protection for the non-patentable aspects of the software disclosed in the source code appendix. In short, source code listings are similar to the submission of a model of the invention which is no longer required or even allowed. Eliminating Rule 96 is consistent with my position that no special burdens or rules be carved out for software-related technology or patent applications.

Once the source code is gone, how best to describe software? Question 9 asks the question in effect "Should the PTO require a standardized disclosure format for software patent applications?"

Patent applicants already are granted a broad range of disclosure options in all other technology classes. Requiring a standard submission format would place a heavy burden on the application since different software is best described in different ways. In many cases, high level pseudo-code is more descriptive than flow charts. State diagrams are often better for sequential operation descriptions. All these forms should still be allowed.

It is true that many players in the software industry have complained about the readability of the patent applications. But the existing drawing requirements in the CFR require that the claimed invention be shown in a drawing (with some limited exceptions). This rule should be used by examiners to improve the disclosures and allow the submission of drawings taken from the description in the specification..

Another existing rule which is used very little in my experience is the discretionary authority of Examiners to require that the Abstract and the Summary of the Invention sections of the patent application be amended to reflect the allowed claims. The use of this tool by the Patent Office may work to improve the readability of many software patents thereby diffusing much unfounded criticism of overbroad software patents in the software industry. And now I would like to address my remarks to Topic C: The Significance of and Protection for Visual Aspects of Software- Related Inventions.

I will not go into a lengthy history of the development of this issue, but I have followed the topic with great interest ever since the first icon design patents issued to Xerox Corporation in June of 1988. In August of 1988, Steven Lundberg and I published an article in the Computer Lawyer entitled "Design Patents: A New Form of Intellectual Property Protection for Computer Software", which was later republished in the JPOS. This article and the ensuing interest in the matter resulted in a single letter being written to the Commissioner of Patents and Trademarks opposing this form of protection. I learned through an FOIA request that other letters were also received, but they were all supportive. This led to a chain of events in which the pending Xerox design patent applications were rejected under 35 USC Section 171 and that those rejections led to the Patent Office Board of Patent Appeals and Interferences decision In re Strijland and other decisions.

The strict holding in the Strijland decision was that the Xerox design patent applications as originally filed did not show an article of manufacture and, hence, were deficient. The later amendments to the application to describe the icons for use on a computer screen were rejected as new matter by the Board.

The Strijland decision went beyond the holding to suggest that if Xerox had shown a three-dimensional article of manufacture on which the icon was displayed, this would be proper subject matter under 35 USC Section 171 and the article of manufacture was then a programmed computer screen display.

To date, the Patent Office has not issued any comments on the Strijland decision or the other related cases. The Patent Office is instead suspending all prosecution of these cases even if they comply with the Strijland requirements.

My position is that the Strijland decision was correct in stating that the application as originally filed did not disclose an article of manufacture if you adopt their position that the word ICON is not limited to the computer field. If an application for an icon or a screen display properly describes the article of manufacture in the title or description as being software for a programmed computer screen display, I believe this is enough to pass muster under 35 USC Section 171.

This leads me to my second point which is that the Board misconstrued what is the article of manufacture. I contend that the article of manufacture is the software, not the programmed screen display. This is consistent with the test for infringement for a design patent which as stated in the Supreme Court case of Gorham v. White reads:

"If in the eye of the ordinary observer, giving such attention as a purchaser usually gives, two designs are substantially the same, if the resemblance is such as to deceive such an observer, inducing him to purchase one supposing it to be the other, the first one patented is infringed by the other".

So, like in the trademark infringement test, inducement of an ordinary purchaser is key.

The point is that an ordinary purchaser of software would not be induced to purchase one computer thinking it to be another. The purchaser would confuse the software. This clarity of definition of the article of manufacture harmonizes the infringement test with the other issue in the Strijland decision: namely - the dicta which required future cases to show a three-dimensional computer screen adorned by the icon. This is not necessary since the article of manufacture, the software, defies a three-dimensional drawing.

The drawing requirements of 37 CFR are not rigid in their requirement of a three-dimensional object and the statute, 35 USC Section 171, does not require it. The Patent Office has not required it in type font design patents, game board design patents and watch faces, to name a few. To require three-dimensional drawings for icon or screen display design patent application is setting an extra burden for these cases which is unjustified.

UNITED STATES PATENT AND TRADEMARK OFFICE
Public Hearing on Patent Protection for Software-Related Inventions
Arlington, Virginia -- February 10 & 11, 1994

In summary, I believe that the holding in the Strijland
decision can be satisfied by describing the icon designs as
for display on a screen display of a programmed computer.
I do not believe the dicta of the Strijland decision need be
followed since three- dimensional drawings are not
required, and I believe that the article of manufacture is the
software.

Finally, I have detected very little concern in the software
industry for the issuance of design patents for screen
displays. 35 USC Section 171 should not be used as a
gatekeeper in this regard since the requirements of novelty
and non-obviousness under 35 USC Sections 102 and 103
will ferret out designs that are not worthy of protection.
Thank you,

Daniel J. Kluth

UNITED STATES PATENT AND TRADEMARK OFFICE
Public Hearing on Patent Protection for Software-Related Inventions
Arlington, Virginia — February 10 & 11, 1994

Index to Participant Testimony

SOFTWARE CLASSIFICATION SYSTEM OF THE UNITED STATES PATENT AND TRADEMARK OFFICE

CLASS 364 ELECTRICAL COMPUTERS AND DATA PROCESSING SYSTEMS

130	DATA PROCESSING CONTROL SYSTEMS, METHODS OR APPARATUS
131	.Plural processors
132	..Master-slave
133	..Parallel
134	...Shared memory
135	..Hybrid types (analog, digital)
136	..Including sequence or logic processor
137	.Cascade control
138	.Supervisory control
139	..Of analog controllers
140	.Sequential or selective
141	..State of condition or parameter (e.g., on/off)
142	...Position responsive
143	...Time responsive (duration)
144	....With display
145	....Clock-calendar (e.g., time of day)
146	..Operator interface (e.g., display with controls)
147	...Specific programming (e.g., relay or ladder logic)
148	.Optimization or adaptive control
149	..With model
150	...Comparison with model (e.g., model reference)
151	..With adjustment of model (e.g., update)
152	.Specific criteria of system performance
153	...Constraints or limits (e.g., max/min)
154	....Variable
155	....Bidirectional (e.g., oscillatory)
156	....Economic (e.g., cost)
157	...Gain (e.g., tuning)
158	..With perturbation
159	...Test signal
160	..Plural modes
161	...Proportional-integral (P-I)
162	...Proportional-integral-derivative (P-I-D)
163	...Proportional-derivative (P-D)
164	..Feed-forward (e.g., predictive)
165	...Combined with feedback
166	..Rate control
167.01	.Digital positioning (other than machine tool)
172	.Plural variables
173	..Ratio
174	..Positional (e.g., velocity, acceleration)
175	...Positional with nonpositional
176	.Specific compensation or stabilization feature
177	..Lag (e.g., deadtime)
178	.Sampled data system
179	..Variable rate
180	.Multiple modes (e.g., digital/analog)

181	..Manual/automatic
182	..Fine/coarse
183	.With specific error signal generation (e.g., up/down counter)
184	.With protection or reliability feature
185	..Warning or alarm
186	..Self-test
187	..Backup/standby
188	.With operator control interface (e.g., control/display console)
189	..Keyboard
190	..Positional (e.g., joystick)
191	.With preparation of program
192	..Editing/modifying
193	..Playback
194	.With specific algorithm
400	APPLICATIONS
401	.Business practice and management
402	..Operations research
403	..Inventory
404	...With cash register
405	..Cash register
406	..Accounting
407	..Reservations
408	.Finance (e.g., securities, commodities)
409	Government activities (e.g., voting, law enforcement)
410	.Games and amusements
411	..Scoring
412	..Wagering
413.01	.Life sciences
413.02	..Patient monitoring or diagnostics
413.03	...Vital signs (e.g., respiration, temperature, blood pressure, pulse)
413.04	....Physiological conditioning system
413.05	...Wave or rhythm
413.06	....Electrocardiogram
413.07	...Blood
413.08	....Blood cell analysis
413.09	....Blood chemistry (e.g., oxygen level)
413.1	...Cellular composition or activity
413.11	...Body chemistry (e.g., urine analysis)
413.12	...Fertility cycle
413.13	...Medical imaging
413.14	...Computed tomography using X-ray
413.15	....Particular data acquisition technique
413.16	....Particular projection data set creation technique
413.17	.....Weighting factors
413.18	.....Interpolated or extrapolated data
413.19	....Particular image reconstruction technique
413.2	.....Fourier transformation
413.21	.....Convolution or back projection
413.22	....Image display

364-2

CLASS 364   ELECTRICAL COMPUTERS AND DATA PROCESSING SYSTEMS

DECEMBER 1993

	APPLICATIONS	426.02	...Antiskid/antilock
	.Life sciences	426.03	...Antispin
	..Medical imaging	426.04	...Road vehicle speed control
413.23	...Subtraction radiography using X-ray	426.05	...Railway vehicle speed control
413.24	...Including gamma camera system	427	..With indication or control of take-off
413.25	...Using ultrasound	428	..With indication or control of landing
413.26	..Radiation detection or treatment	429	...I.L.S. or radar guidance
413.27	..For control of bodily function (e.g., muscle stimulation)	430	...Profile of descent
413.28	..Dental	431.01	..With indication or control of power plant (e.g., performance)
413.29	..Diet	431.02	...Gas turbine, compressor
413.3	..Survival in hostile environment	431.03	...Internal-combustion engine
413.31	...Diving decompression analysis	431.04	....Digital or programmed data processor
419.01	.Linguistics	431.05	.....Air/fuel ratio, injection, optimization
419.02	..Translation machine		
419.03	...With particular input/output device (e.g., optical scanner, voice synthesizer, etc.)	431.06	......Exhaust gas recirculation (EGR)
		431.07	.....Speed, acceleration, deceleration
		431.08	.....Vibration, roughness, knock
419.04	...Based on phrases, clauses, or idioms	431.09	.....Engine stop, fuel shutoff
419.05	...For partial translation	431.1	.....Starting, warmup
419.06	...Punctuation	431.11	.....Backup, interrupt, reset, or test
419.07	...Storage and retrieval of data	431.12	.....Specific memory or interfacing device
419.08	..Natural language (e.g., parsing, grammatical rules, etc.)	432	..With indication or control to maintain fixed position
419.09	..Ideographic or non-roman character generators	433	..With indication or control of altitude/depth or rate of ascent or descent
419.1	.Word processing		
419.11	..Dictionary	434	..With indication or control of vehicle attitude
419.12	...Spell check		
419.13	...Text searching	435	...Angle of attack
419.14	..Replacement for characters or words	436	..Traffic analysis or control of surface vehicle
419.15	..Input of abbreviated word forms (i.e., short form, speed typing, etc.)	437	...With determination of traffic density
		438	...With determination of traffic speed
419.16	..Multilingual	439	..Traffic analysis or control of aircraft
419.17	..Editing (i.e., deletion, insertion, blocking, hyphenation, or punctuation)	440	...With speed control or order
		441	...With course diversion
419.18	..Footnotes	442	..With indication of fuel consumption rate or economy of usage
419.19	.Document indexing or retrieval		
419.2	.Measuring or testing human emotions or responses	443	.Navigation
		444	..Determination of course or distance from present position to destination
420	.Earth sciences (e.g., weather)		
421	..Seismology	445	...Great circle route
422	..Well logging	446	..Determination of E.T.A.
423	.Military applications	447	..Determination of along-track or cross-track deviations
424.01	.Vehicle guidance, operation, or indication		
		448	..Employing way point navigation
424.02	..Automatic route guidance system	449	..Employing position-determining equipment
424.03	..Vehicle maintenance or diagnostic		
424.04	...With data recording device	450	...Using dead-reckoning apparatus
424.05	..Vehicle accessory control	451	...Using R-O (D.M.E. and path) or Tacan equipment
424.06	..Flight condition indicating system		
424.07	..Construction or agricultural vehicle type (e.g., crane, forklift)	452	...Using Loran or Shoran or Decca equipment
424.1	..Control of transmission		
425	.Engineering of vehicles	453	...Using inertial sensor
426.01	.With indication or control of braking acceleration or deceleration		

CLASS 364　ELECTRICAL COMPUTERS AND DATA PROCESSING SYSTEMS

	APPLICATIONS
	.Navigation
	..Employing position-determining equipment
	...Using inertial sensor
454	....With correction by noninertial sensor
455	...Using star tracker
456	...With radar or optical ground scanner
457	..With indicated course correction (compass deviation)
458	..Determining range without range measurement
459	..Space orbits or paths
460	.Relative location
461	..Collision avoidance
462	..Course to intercept
463	.Determining balance or center of gravity (e.g., load distribution of vehicle)
464.01	..For cost/price
464.02	..Postage meter system
464.03	...Including mailed item weight
464.04	..Utility usage
465	..Fluid
466	..Weight
467	..Distance or time (e.g., taximeters)
468	.Product manufacturing
469	..Continuous material processing
470	...Textiles
471	...Paper products
472	...Metals
473	...Glass, plastic, and rubber
474.01	..Machining
474.02	...With particular tool or tool operation
474.03	....Tracing or duplicating
474.04	....Electrical discharge machining (EDM)
474.05	....3-D sculpturing using nontracing prototype sensor
474.06	....Grinding
474.07	....Bending (e.g., press brake)
474.08	....Laser
474.09	...Of elongated material (e.g., timber, veneer, web)
474.1	...Portable (e.g., hand-held)
474.11	...Supervisory control (e.g., plural tools or plural processors)
474.12	...Having particular control of a motor parameter
474.13	...Material usage optimization
474.14	...Multiple mode (e.g., rough-finish, coarse-fine)
474.15	...Adaptive (optimizing) system
474.16	...Performance monitoring
474.17	....Condition of tool or workpiece (e.g., tolerance, tool wear)
474.18	.....Offsetting
474.19	....Protective or diagnostic feature
474.2	.....Tool/workpiece interference prevention

474.21	...Tool selection/change
474.22	...With operator interface feature
474.23	....Specific programming format (e.g., macro)
474.24	....Including CAD, CAM, or CIM technique
474.25	....Preset pattern
474.26	....Machining path display
474.27	...Prompting technique
474.28	...Digital positioning technique
474.29	....For curve or contour
474.3	....Including velocity or acceleration control
474.31	....Interpolation
474.32	....Specified tool feed path at entry or withdrawal
474.33	.....Repeated machining passes
474.34	....Alignment of tool or workpiece (e.g., origin or path return)
474.35	....Positional compensation or modification
474.36	...Coordinate transformation technique
474.37	...With particular measuring device (e.g., probe)
476	.Pressing or molding
477	.Heating, sintering, or melting
478	.Article handling or distribution
479	.Dispensing
480	.Electrical/electronic engineering
481	..Measuring or testing
482	...Impedance
483	...Voltage, current, or power
484	...Frequency
485	....Frequency spectrum
486	...Pulse
487	...Waveform
488	..Design and analysis
489	..Circuits
490	....Integrated
491	.....Layout
492	..Power generation or distribution
493	...Economic dispatching
494	...Turbine or generator control
495	...With model
496	.Chemical and engineering sciences
497	..Chemical analysis
498	...Spectrum analysis (composition)
499	...Chemical property
500	..Chemical process control
501	...Distillation
502	...Physical mixing or separation
503	...Kilns
505	.Mechanical and civil engineering
506	..Measuring or testing
507	...Flaw or defect
508	....Stress, strain, or vibration
509	....Fluid
510	.....Fluid flow
511	...Power
512	...Structural design

364-4

CLASS 364   ELECTRICAL COMPUTERS AND DATA PROCESSING SYSTEMS

DECEMBER 1993

	APPLICATIONS
514	.Communication engineering (e.g., pictorial and pulse communication)
516	..Object detection or tracking
517	...Signal evaluation (target or noise)
524	.Physics
525	..Optics or photography
526	...Color analysis
527	..Atomic or nuclear physics
550	MEASURING, TESTING, OR MONITORING
551.01	.Measuring and evaluating (e.g., performance)
551.02	..Of machine tool
552	..Quality control determinations
553	..Transfer function evaluation
554	..Statistical data (e.g., stochastic variable)
555	..Particle count, distribution, size
556	.For basic measurements
557	..Temperature
558	..Pressure or density
559	..Orientation
560	..Dimension
561	...Distance
562	....Length or height
563	....Width or thickness
564	...Area or volume
565	..Rate of change of dimension (e.g., speed)
566	..Acceleration and further derivatives
567	..Weight
568	...Basis weight
569	..Time or time intervals
570	.Operations performed
571.01	..Calibration or compensation
571.02	...Having mathematical operation on initial measurement data
571.03	....Including environmental factors (e.g., temperature)
571.04	....Including predetermined stored data
571.05	....Using difference involving initial measurement data
571.06	....Using analog calculating elements
571.07	...By table look-up
571.08	...Using operator provided data
572	..Filtering
573	..Linearization
574	..Noise reduction
575	..Averaging
576	..Fourier analysis
577	..Interpolation/extrapolation
578	..Simulation or modeling
579	..With control of testing or measuring apparatus
580	..Programmed testing conditions
581	..Weighting
582	..Normalization
600	ELECTRIC HYBRID COMPUTER
601	.Plural complete computers
602	.Specialized function performed
603	..Evaluation of trigonometric functions

604	..Correlation, convolution, or transformation
605	..Integration or differentiation
606	..Multiplication or division
607	..Function generation
608	...Piece-wise linear synthesis
700	ELECTRIC DIGITAL CALCULATING COMPUTER
701	.Pulse repetition rate
702	..Digital differential analyzer
703	..Multiplication or division
704	.Plural complete computers
705.01	.Combined with diverse art device
705.02	..Checkbook
705.03	..Writing instruments (e.g., pen)
705.04	..Tape recorder
705.05	..Communication device (e.g., telephone, radio, television)
705.06	..Business device (e.g., billing, memorandum)
705.07	..Horological device
705.08	...Calendar
706	.Programmable calculator
707	.With power saving feature
708.1	.With specialized housing or casing
709.01	.With specialized input
709.02	..Having supplemental environment related input
709.03	...Cooking
709.04	...Business
709.05	..For security
709.06	..Input verification
709.07	..Fraction input
709.08	..Flexible input
709.09	..Including specific computing system interconnection
709.1	..Modular or overlay
709.11	..Including specific nonkeyboard type information entry
709.12	..Including specific keyboard type information entry
709.13	...Nonmechanical key actuation
709.14	...User definable key
709.15	...Plural function key
709.16	...Key sequencing (i.e., sequence defines function)
710.01	.With specialized output
710.02	..Having supplemental environment related output
710.03	...Teaching
710.04	...Business
710.05	..Output verification
710.06	..Blanking
711	...Zero suppression
710.07	..Prompting
710.08	..Selective output
710.09	..Sequential output
710.1	..Using particular format
710.11	..Symbol accompanying output
710.12	..Audio
710.13	..Printer

CLASS 364 ELECTRICAL COMPUTERS AND DATA PROCESSING SYSTEMS

DECEMBER 1993

364-6

CLASS 364   ELECTRICAL COMPUTERS AND DATA PROCESSING SYSTEMS

DECEMBER 1993

●●●●●●●●●●●●●●●●●●●●●●●●●●●●●●●●●

DIGESTS - ELECTRONIC INDEX TERMS

●●●●●●●●●●●●●●●●●●●●●●●●●●●●●●●●●

CLASS 364   ELECTRICAL COMPUTERS AND DATA PROCESSING SYSTEMS

> NOTE: DIGEST 1 includes all the patents formerly found in Class 364, Electrical Computer and Data Processing Systems, subclass 200. The indented terms below, formerly corresponding to subclasses 221-286.6, are useable for searching DIGEST 1 on the APS Messenger system using the /CCLS field, the class number (364) and the term number found in parentheses at the end of each term. A search in this area should be indicated on the file wrapper by using the format: 364/term number. Paper copies of all patents searchable using this system are found as one numerically-ordered set labeled DIGEST 1. At the time of issue, the examiner may assign DIGEST 1 terms to the patent by entering the appropriate term number on the blue slip as a cross-reference. However, when this is done, a cross-reference must also be placed in DIGEST 1. Definitions of the terms can be found in the definition of Class 364 as subclass definitions in term-number order. Terms whose titles contain an (*) are complete only for patents issued since 1980.

APPLICATIONS
.Control systems (221)
..Adaptive (221.1)
..Model/simulator (221.2)
..Learning/trainable (221.3)
..Sampled data/signal processing (221.4)
..Time sharing/multiplexing
..Multiple mode (221.6)
..Testing/monitoring (221.7)
..Signal/function generation (221.8)
.Process control (221.9)
.Machine control (222)
.Environment (222.1)
.Communication/data transmission (222.2)
..Telephone exchange (222.3)
.Traffic/vehicular (222.4)
.Security (222.5)
.Material/article handling (222.6)
..Conveyor system (222.7)
..Dispensing system (222.8)
.File maintenance (222.81)
..Insertion/deletion/updating (222.82)
..Sorting/merging (222.9)
.Scientific (223)
..Aeronautics/space (223.1)
..Biology (223.3)
..Chemistry (223.4)
..Civil engineering (223.6)
..Electrical/electronic engineering (223.7)
..Earth science (223.8)

...Seismology (223.9)
..Mathematics (224)
...Statistics (224.1)
...Data analysis (224.2)
...Random number generation (224.21) *
...Other specific mathematics application (224.3)
..Mechanical engineering (224.4)
..Medical (224.5)
...Patient monitoring (224.6)
..Physics (224.7)
...Optics (224.8)
...Nuclear (224.9)
..Other specific scientific application (224.91)
.Business (225)
..Accounting (225.1)
..Banking (225.2)
..Document analysis (225.3)
..Document retrieval (225.4)
...Film (microfilm, microfiche, slide) (225.5)
..Document or display preparation/word processing (225.6)
...Justification/hyphenation (225.7)
...Editing (225.8)
...Typesetting (225.9)
...Photocomposing (226)
...Other specific display preparation (226.1)
..Education (226.2)
..Inventory control (226.3)
..Language translation (226.4)
..Library (226.6)
..Manufacturing/industry (226.7)
..Public utility (226.8)
...Electric power (226.9)
..Reservation (227)
..Sports/amusement (227.1)
..Stock market (227.2)
..Other specific business application (227.3)
.Other application (227.4)
SYSTEM ARCHITECTURE
.Plural processors with different internal structures (228)
.Shared memory (228.1)
.Virtual processor/machine (228.2)
.Plural (redundant) central processors (228.3)
.Central processor combined with terminal processor (228.4)
.Central processor combined with interface processor (228.5)
.Central processor combined with coprocessor (228.6) *
.Multiple instruction multiple data (MIMD) (228.7) *
..Loosely coupled MIMD (228.8) *

364-8

CLASS 364   ELECTRICAL COMPUTERS AND DATA PROCESSING SYSTEMS

DECEMBER 1993

SYSTEM ARCHITECTURE
.Multiple instruction multiple data
  (MIMD) (228.7) •
..Tightly coupled MIMD (228.9) •
.Multiprocessor interconnection (229)
..Direct (229.1)
..Parallel (common bus) (229.2)
..Loop (229.3)
..Reconfigurable (229.4)
..Tree structure (229.41) •
..Other specific multiprocessor
   interconnection (229.5)
.Multiprocessor/Processor control (230)
..Priority assignment (230.1)
..Interrupt handling (230.2)
..Task assignment (230.3)
..Supervisory (master/slave) (230.4)
..Other specific multiprocessor control
   (230.5)
.Other specific multiprocessor system
  (230.6)
.Mini/Micro/Personal computer (231)
..Portable (231.1)
...Hand-held/Carried on person (231.2)
...Other portable computer (231.3)
..Other specific mini/micro/personal
   computer (231.31) •
.Timeshared (231.4)
..Peripheral devices (231.5)
..Plural programs (Multiprogrammed)
   (231.6)
..Other specific timeshare (231.7)
.Pipelined (231.8)
.Parallel array/Single instruction
  multiple data (SIMD) (231.9)
.Orthogonal (232)
.Virtual (232.1)
.Adaptive (232.2)
.Vector processor (232.21) •
.Data flow (232.22) •
.Reduced instruction set computer (RISC)
  (232.23) •
.Simulator/Emulator (232.3)
.Hybrid (Analog-Digital) (232.4)
.Electro-optical (232.5)
.Magnetic bubble (232.6)
.Modular (232.7)
.Integrated circuit/Chip/Microprocessor
  (232.8)
.Multiple mode (232.9)
.Mixed/Technologies (232.91)
.Other system architecture (232.93)
INPUT/OUTPUT DEVICES
.Keyboard/Switch (234)
..Data (234.1)
..Function (234.2)
..Program select (234.3)
..Other specific keyboard/switch (234.4)
.Printer (235)
..Bar (235.1)

..Chain/Belt (235.2)
..Disc/Drum (235.3)
..Matrix/Dot (235.4)
..Single character (235.5)
..Multiple character (235.6)
..Other specific printer (235.7)
.Typewriter (236)
.Drum storage (236.1)
.Disc storage (236.2)
.Tape storage (236.3)
..Magnetic (236.4)
..Paper (236.5)
..Cartridge/cassette (236.6)
..Other specific tape storage (236.7)
.Mouse (236.8) •
.Card reader/punch(237)•
.Pen/Pointer (237.1)
.Display (237.2)
..Cathode-ray tube (CRT) (237.3)
..Lights (237.4)
..Other specific display (237.5)
.Character recognizer/generator (237.6)
.Plotter (237.7)
.Analog/Analog-digital converter (237.8)
..Voice (237.81) •
.Scanning (237.82) •
..Optical character (237.83) •
..Magnetic character (237.84) •
..Bar code (237.85) •
.Other input/output device (237.9)
INTERFACING OR COMMUNICATION TECHNIQUE
.Multiplex (238)
.Central switch (238.1)
.Input/Output interface switch (I/O
  exchange) (238.2)
.Input/Output controller (238.3)
.Memory controller (238.4)
.Line adapter/Modem (238.5)
.Buffer structure (238.6)
..Shift register (238.7)
..Recirculating (238.8)
..Other specific buffer structure
   (238.9)
.Buffer/Interface function (239)
..Rate control (239.1)
..Serial/Parallel conversion (239.2)
..Formatting/Alignment (239.3)
..Program/Data control/look ahead
   (239.4)
..Alternate load/unload (239.5)
..Simultaneous load/unload (239.51) •
..Buffer full/empty (239.6)
..With input/output buffer (239.7)
..Other specific buffer function (239.8)
.Other interfacing (239.9)
.Bus (240) •
..Common/parallel (240.1)
..Plural (240.2) •

INTERFACING OR COMMUNICATION TECHNIQUE
.Bus (240) •
..Variable width/speed (240.3) •
..Decentralized control (240.4) •
..Controller (240.5) •
..Optical (240.6) •
..Switching (240.7) •
.Protocols (240.8) •
..Answer back/acknowledge (240.9) •
.Direct polling (241)
.Loop polling (241.1)
.Priority interrupt (241.2)
..Fixed (241.3)
..Variable (241.4)
..Multilevel (241.5)
..Other priority interrupt (241.6)
.Mailbox (241.7) •
.Token passing (241.8) •
.Port/channel (241.9) •
.Time controlled interrupt (242)
.Condition/Mode controlled interrupt
   (242.1)
.Queued/Tabled interrupt (242.2)
.Direct access/DMA (242.3)
..DMA control/operation (242.31) •
...Multimode (242.32) •
...Plural (242.33) •
...Other DMA control/operation (242.34)
   •
.Real time (242.4)
.Arbitration (242.6) •
..Fixed priority (242.7) •
..Variable/dynamic priority (242.8) •
..Multilevel (242.9) •
..Memory (242.91) •
..Bus (242.92) •
..Other arbitration (242.93) •
.Networking (242.94) •
..Local area network (LAN) (242.95) •
..Other networking (242.96) •
.Other communication technique (242.5)
STORAGE SYSTEM
.Plural memory configuration (243)
..Plural main memories (243.1)
..Main memory with external bulk store
   (243.2)
..Data store with program store (243.3)
..Fast and slow (243.4)
...Cache (243.41) •
....Instruction (243.42) •
...Bypass (243.43) •
...Plural (243.44) •
....Multilevel (243.45) •
..Main memory with Input/Output store
   (243.5)
.With multiplex access (243.6)
.Other specific plural memory
   configuration (243.7)
.Single memory configuration (244)

..Compound type (244.1)
..Logic-in-memory cell type (244.2)
..Queue/stack (244.3)
..Recirculating (244.4)
..Shifting (244.5)
..Read-Only-Memory (ROM)/Microprogram
   (244.6)
..Multiport (244.8) •
..PLA/PAL (244.9) •
..Other specific single memory
   configuration (244.7)
.Storage reconfiguration (245)
..Variable length (245.1)
..Relocatable (245.2)
..Defective storage substitution (245.3)
..Expansion (245.31) •
..Other Specific storage configuration
   (245.4)
.Storage dedication (245.5)
..To input/output device (245.6)
..To processor (245.7)
..To user (245.8)
..Other specific storage dedication
   (245.9)
.Storage assignment (246)
..Priority resolution between memories
   (246.1)
...Swapping (246.11) •
....Least recently used (246.12) •
....Most recently used (246.13) •
..Priority resolution within single
   memory (246.2)
.Mapped/Partitioned/Segmented (246.3)
..Interleaved (246.4)
..Other specific storage assignment
   (246.5)
.Storage protection (246.6)
..Comparison of boundary addresses
   (246.7)
..Locked/unlocked (246.8)
..Other specific storage protection
   (246.9)
.Refresh (246.91) •
.Register (247) •
..Accumulator (247.1) •
..Address (247.2) •
..Condition code/flag/status (247.3) •
..Data (247.4) •
..Index (247.5) •
..Instruction (247.6) •
..Stack pointer (247.7) •
..Other specific register (247.8) •
.Other specific storage system (246.92)
STORAGE ELEMENTS
.Drum (248)
.Disk (248.1)
.Tape (248.2)
.Core (248.3)
.Thin film (248.4)

364-10

CLASS 364   ELECTRICAL COMPUTERS AND DATA PROCESSING SYSTEMS

DECEMBER 1993

STORAGE ELEMENTS
.Bubble (248.5)
.Delay line (248.6)
.CRT storage tube (248.7)
.Cryogenic (248.8)
.Semiconductor (249)
..Charge coupled type (249.1)
..Integrated circuit (249.2)
..Other specific semiconductor storage
    (249.3)
.Optical (249.4)
..Hologram (249.5)
..Other specific optical storage (249.6)
.Capacitive (249.7)
.Other specific storage element (249.8)
STORAGE ACCESSING/ADDRESSING
.Sequential (251)
..Unit increment/decrement (251.1)
..Nonunit increment/decrement (251.2)
..Counter controlled (251.3)
..Timer controlled (251.4)
..Chained (251.5)
..Tree structure (251.6)
..Other specific sequential
    accessing/addressing (251.7)
.Random (252)
..Shortest distance (252.1)
..Other specific random
    accessing/addressing (252.2)
.Key/Partial (252.3)
..Key (252.4)
..Masking (252.5)
..Word byte/Field (252.6)
..Other specific key/partial
    accessing/addressing (252.7)
.Associative (253)
..Matching data (253.1)
..User (253.2)
..Other specific associative
    accessing/addressing (253.3)
.Group (254)
..Multiple instruction per word (254.1)
..Multiple location per access (254.2)
..Block/Page (254.3)
..Chip/Module (254.4)
..Queue/Stack (254.5)
..Linked (254.6)
..Other specific group
    accessing/addressing (254.7)
.Multiple mode (254.8)
.Variable length (254.9)
.Substituted (255)
.Address modification (255.1)
..Indexing (255.2)
..Prefixing (255.3)
..Bit insertion (255.4)
..Base and Segment/tag and set (255.5)
..Table look-up (255.7)
..Other specific address modification
    (255.8)

.Complementary (256)
..Digit (256.1)
..Other specific complementary
    accessing/addressing (256.2)
.Virtual (256.3)
..Table look-up (256.4)
..Converted (256.5)
..Other specific virtual
    accessing/addressing (256.6)
.Other specific storage
    accessing/addressing (256.8)
OPERATIONAL CONTROL
.Arithmetical (258)
..Add/Subtract (258.1)
..Multiply (258.2)
..Divide (258.3)
..Other specific arithmetical operation
    (258.4)
.Logical (259)
..AND/OR/Other (259.1) *
..Compare (259.2)
..Sense (259.3)
..Special character detection (259.4)
..Shift (259.5)
..Masking (259.7)
..Bit manipulation (259.8)
..Decoding (259.9) *
..Other specific logical operational
    control (259.6)
.Data transfer (260)
..External (260.1)
..Internal (260.2)
..Other specific data transfer (260.3)
.Transform (260.4)
..Invert (260.5)
..Compress/Expand (260.6)
..Pack/Unpack (260.7)
..Set/Reset (260.8)
..Encryption/decryption (260.81) *
..Other specific transform operation
    (260.9)
.Modify (261)
..Command (261.1)
..Other specific modify operation
    (261.2)
.Branching (261.3)
..Unconditional (261.4)
..Conditional (261.5)
..Trap (261.6)
..Look ahead (261.7)
..Timed (261.8)
..Other specific branching operation
    (261.9)
.Repeating (262)
..Iterated function (262.1)
..Error detection (262.2)
..Other specific repeating operation
    (262.3)
.Instruction sequence (262.4)

CLASS 364 ELECTRICAL COMPUTERS AND DATA PROCESSING SYSTEMS

OPERATIONAL CONTROL
.Instruction sequence (262.4)
..Chaining/Linking (262.5)
..Fixed (Hardwired) (262.6)
..Macro instructions (262.7)
..Micro instructions (262.8)
..Variable width (262.81) *
..Other specific instruction sequence
  operation (262.9)
.Instruction Execution Overlap (263)
.Instruction Lookahead (Prefetch)
  (263.1)
.Instruction Interrupt (Internal)
  (263.2)
.Other specific operational control
  (263.3)
PERFORMANCE MONITORING
.Anticipate/Monitor (264)
..Internal/Condition code (264.1)
..External criteria (264.2)
..Simulated (264.3)
..Statistical (264.4)
..With control response (264.5)
..Status/Busy/Idle (264.6)
..Other specific performance
  anticipation/monitoring (264.7)
.Error detection (265)
..Data transmission (265.1)
..Data encoding/decoding (265.2)
..Storage/Addressing (265.3)
..Arithmetic/Logic (265.4)
..Input/Output (265.5)
..Execution/Sequencing control (265.6)
..Monitoring/Error circuitry (266)
..Of synchronization error (266.1)
..Intermittent/Transient error (266.2)
..By parity/validity check (266.3)
..By comparison with expected result
  (266.4)
..With automatic error recovery (266.5)
..Other specific error detection (266.6)
.By Diagnostic/Tracing routine (267)
..Scheduled/Periodic (267.1)
..Real time (267.2)
..With repeated operation (267.3)
..Program controlled (267.4)
..Operator controlled (267.5)
..Hardware controlled (267.6)
..With fault isolation (267.7)
..Watchdog timer (267.9) *
..Debugging (267.91) *
.Other specific diagnostic/tracing
  routine (267.8)
.Alternate/Backup (268)
..Concurrent (Realtime) (268.1)
..Periodic (268.2)
..Redundant element (268.3)
...Arithmetic/Logic unit (268.4)
...Memory/Sector (268.5)

...Input/Output (268.6)
...Channel (268.7)
...Other specific redundant element
  (268.8)
..Fault tolerant (268.9) *
..Synchronization of systems/elements
  (269)
..with majority vote for output (269.1)
..With substitution for faulty element
  (269.2)
..Other specific alternate/backup
  (269.3)
.Other specific performance monitoring
  (269.4)
TIMING OF PROCESSING SYSTEM
.Interval/Clock generation (270)
..Fixed (270.1)
..Variable (270.2)
..Multiple (270.3)
..Other specific time interval
  generation (270.4)
.Asynchronous time control (270.5)
..Between processor and input/output
  (270.6)
..Between processors (270.7)
..Within processor (270.8)
..Other specific asynchronous time
  control (270.9)
.Synchronous time control (271)
..Of external device (271.1)
..Of plural processors (271.2)
..Of plural programs (271.3)
..Other specific synchronous time
  control (271.4)
.Time delay (271.5)
.Cycle control (271.6)
..Cycle steal (271.7)
..Other specific cycle control (271.8)
.Other specific timing (271.9)
POWER SYSTEM CONTROL
.Sequenced/Programmable (273)
.Reduction (273.1)
.On demand (273.2)
.Partial (273.3)
.Failure (273.4)
.Other specific power system control
  (273.5)
ARTIFICIAL INTELLIGENCE
.Artificial intelligence (AI) (274) *
..Software (274.1) *
...Expert system (274.2) *
....Knowledge base (274.3) *
.....Model bases (274.4) *
.....Rule based (274.5) *
......Fuzzy logic (274.6) *
....Rule interpreter/inference engine
  (274.7) *
....Other specific expert system
  (274.71) *
...Natural language (274.8) *

CLASS 364   ELECTRICAL COMPUTERS AND DATA PROCESSING SYSTEMS

DECEMBER 1993

ARTIFICIAL INTELLIGENCE
.Artificial intelligence (AI) (274) *
..Software (274.1) *
...Neural net (274.9) *
...Specific programming language (275) *
...Application (275.1) *
....Control (275.2) *
.....Manufacturing/robotic (275.3) *
.....Vehicle control/navigation (275.4)
     *
....Debugging/Diagnostic (275.5) *
....Design/CAD/CAE (275.6) *
....Diagnosis/Medical (275.7) *
....Instruction (275.8) *
....Interpretation/speech/pattern
     recognition (275.9) *
....Monitoring (276) *
....Planning (276.1) *
....Prediction/weather (276.2) *
....Repair (276.3) *
....Other specific application (276.4) *
..Hardware (276.5) *
...Neural net (276.6) *
...Single processor (276.7) *
...Plural processors (276.8) *
...Specific memory technique (276.9) *
.Other artificial intelligence (277) *
SYSTEM MANAGEMENT (SOFTWARE)
.Operating system (280) *
..Assembler/disassembler (280.1) *
..Booting/initialization (280.2) *
...Restart (280.3) *
..Compiler/translator (280.4) *
...Optimizing (280.5) *
..Distributed (280.6) *
..Editor (280.7) *
..Interrupt handler (280.8) *
..Kernel/BIOS (280.9) *
..Memory reclamation/garbage collection
     (281.1) *
..Process (task) management (281.3) *
...Concurrent (281.4) *
...Dead lock/Synchronization (281.5) *
...Load balancing (281)
....Resource allocation (281.6) *
...Multitasking (281.7) *
...Scheduling (281.8) *
..System reconfiguration after fault
     (281.9) *
..Test and set (282) *
.Data base (282.1) *
..Allocation/deallocation (282.2) *
..Directory structure (282.3) *
..Distributed (282.4) *
..File organization (283.1) *
..Hierarchical (283.2) *
..Interactive (283.3) *

..Relational (283.4) *
.Communication (284) *
..Buffering (284.1) *
..Input/output (284.2) *
..Message sending (284.3) *
..Network communication (284.4) *
.Reliability (285) *
..Backup procedures (285.1) *
..Checkpoint/restart (285.2) *
..Fault tolerance (285.3) *
..Verification (285.4) *
.Program management (286) *
..Prompting (286.1) *
...Menu driven (286.2) *
..Window/split screen (286.3) *
..Security (286.4) *
...Access/authentication (286.5) *
...Copy protection (286.6) *

DIG 2   GENERAL PURPOSE PROGRAMMABLE DIGITAL
        COMPUTER SYSTEMS

NOTE: DIGEST 2 includes all the
patents formerly found in Class
364. Electrical Computer and
Data Processing Systems.
subclass 900. The indented terms
below, formerly corresponding to
subclasses 916-978.3, are useable
for searching DIGEST 2 on the APS
Messenger system using the /CCLS
field, the class number (364) and
the term number found in parentheses
at the end of each term. A search
in this area should be indicated on
the file wrapper by using the format:
364/term number. Paper copies of
all patents searchable using this
system are found as one numerically-
ordered set labeled DIGEST 2.
At the time of issue, the examiner
may assign DIGEST 2 terms to the
patent by entering the appropriate
term number on the blue slip as a
cross-reference. However, when this
is done, a cross-reference must
also be placed in DIGEST 2.
Definitions of the terms can be
found in the definition of Class
364 as subclass definitions in
term-number order. Terms whose
titles contain an (*) are complete
only for patents issued since 1980.

APPLICATIONS
.Adaptive (916)
..Bionic (916.1)
..Learning/Trainable (916.2)
..Model/Simulator (916.3)
..Other specific adaptive application
     (916.4)
.Amusement/Sport (916.5)
.Article manufacturing (917)
..Assembly/test (917.1)

CLASS 364 ELECTRICAL COMPUTERS AND DATA PROCESSING SYSTEMS

DECEMBER 1993

APPLICATIONS
.Article manufacturing (917)
..Assembly/test (917.1)
...Successive stations or operations
      (917.2)
..Pattern scaling/design (917.3)
..Other specific article manufacturing
      (917.4)
.Article/Material handling (917.5)
..Conveying (917.6)
..Dispensing (917.7)
..Storage (917.8)
..Other specific article/material
      handling (917.9)
.CAD/CAM (917.96) *
.Commerce/Business (918)
..Accounting/billing (918.1)
..Banking (918.2)
..Credit (918.3)
..Inventory (918.4)
..Point of sale
...Vending (918.51) *
..Postage meter (918.52) *
..Reservations (918.6)
..Stock market (918.8)
..Other specific commerce/business
      application (918.9)
.Communications/Data transmission system
      (919)
..Facsimile (919.1)
..Radio/TV (919.2)
..Via satellite (919.3)
..Telephone (919.4)
..Other specific communications
      application (919.5)
.Data collection/Recording (920)
.Education (920.1)
.Engineering (920.2)
.Environment (920.3)
.Image processing (920.7) *
..Three dimensional (920.8) *
.Language translation (920.4)
.Law/Law enforcement (920.5)
.Library (920.6)
.Machine control (921)
..Textile/loom (921.1)
..Tool (921.2)
..Other specific machine control
      application (921.3)
.Manufacturing process (921.4)
..Chemical (921.5)
..Petroleum (921.6)
..Other specific manufacturing process
      (921.7)
.Measure/Test/Monitor (921.8)
..With controlled response (921.9)
..Statistical (921.91)
.Medical (922)
..Accounting (922.1)
..Diagnostic (922.2)
..Monitoring (922.3)
..Other specific medical application
      (922.4)

.Military (922.5)
.Mining (922.6)
.Music (922.7)
.Navigation (922.8)
.Public utility (923)
..Electric power (923.1)
..Meter reading (923.2)
..Other specific public utility
      application (923.3)
.Radar/Sonar (923.4)
.Scientific (924)
..Astronomy (924.1)
..Biology (924.2)
..Chemistry (924.3)
..Physics/Nuclear (924.4)
..Seismology (924.5)
..Other specific scientific application
      (924.6)
.Vehicle/Transportation (925)
..Air/Space (925.1)
..Land (925.2)
..Other specific vehicle/transportation
      application (925.3)
.Other specific application (925.4)
GENERIC DEVICE
.Analog input/output (926)
.Arithmetic/logic structure (923.5) *
..Parallel (923.6) *
..Bit slice (923.71) *
..Bit map (923.81) *
.Buffer structure (926.1)
..Multiple register buffer (926.2)
..Plural buffers (926.3)
..Recirculating (926.4)
..Shift register (926.5)
..Other specific buffer structure
      (926.6)
.Character generator (926.7)
.Character recognizer (926.8)
.Chip topography (925.5) *
.Chip - integrated circuit (927.8)
.Chip - Micro single chip computer
      (925.6) *
.Controller (926.9)
..Bus (926.91) *
..Memory (926.92) *
..Input/output (926.93) *
.Desk top/hand-held (927)
.Digitizer, coordinate (927.1)
.Display (927.2)
..Color/intensity (927.3)
..CRT/TV (927.4) *
..Digital display/lights (927.5)
..With pen/pointer (927.6)
..Cursor (927.61) *
..Scrolling (927.62) *
..Window (927.63) *
...Overlapping (927.631) *
...Sizing (927.632) *
..Touch sensitive (927.64) *
..Update (927.66) *
..Bit map (927.67) *

364-14

CLASS 364   ELECTRICAL COMPUTERS AND DATA PROCESSING SYSTEMS

DECEMBER 1993

GENERIC DEVICE
.Display (927.2)
..Other specific display (927.7)
.Emulator (927.81) •
.Firmware (927.82) •
.Housing, special (927.83) •
.Interface (927.92) •
..Bus (927.93) •
..Channel (927.94) •
..Port (927.95) •
..Network (927.96) •
..Memory (927.97) •
..Processor (927.98) •
..Input/output (927.99) •
..Line adapter/modem (929)
.Keyboard/switch (928)
..Data (928.1)
..Function (928.2)
..Program select (928.3)
..Test/monitor (928.4)
..Keystroke decoder (928.6) •
..Other specific keyboard/switch device
   (928.5)
.Matrix/switching array (929.1)
.Modular (929.2)
.Mouse (929.12) •
.Plotter/graphical (929.3)
.Plugboard/card/overlay (929.4)
..Motherboard/Backplane (929.5)
..Special application (929.61) •
..Other specific plugboard/card/overlay
   device (929.71) •
.Printer (930)
..Bar (930.1)
..Chain/belt (930.2)
..Disc/drum (930.3)
..Dot matrix (930.4)
..Ink jet (930.41) •
..Laser (930.42) •
..Multiple character (930.5)
..Single character (930.6)
..Other specific printer (930.7)
.Processor type/mode (931)
..Array processing (931.01) •
...Cellular array (931.02) •
...SIMD (931.03) •
..Bit/Byte processor (931.1)
..Data flow (931.11) •
..Electro-optical (931.2)
..Hybrid (analog-digital) (931.3)
..Plural/multiprocessor (931.4)
...Parallel processing (931.41) •
...Multiple instruction multiple data
   (MIMD) (931.42) •
...Distributed processing (931.43) •
...Master/slave (931.44) •
...Redundant (931.45) •
...Shared memory (931.46) •
...Dedicated memory (931.47) •
...Synchronization (931.48) •
...Coprocessing (931.49) •
...Vector processing (931.51) •

...Scalar processing (931.52) •
..Reduced instruction set computer
   (RISC) (931.55) •
..Other specific processing type/mode
   (931.5)
.Reader/punch (932)
..Card (932.1)
..Cartridge/cassette (932.2)
..Film (932.3)
..Magnetic (932.4)
..Paper (932.5)
..Tape (932.6)
..Optical character (932.61) •
..Scanner (932.62) •
..Other specific reader/punch (932.7)
.Receiver/transmitter (932.8)
.Register (933)
..Accumulator (933.1)
..Address/Program counter (933.2)
..Data (933.3)
..Index (933.4)
..Instruction (933.5)
..Stack pointer (933.6)
..Condition code (933.61) •
..Status (933.62) •
..Other specific register (933.7)
.Simulator (933.8)
.Terminal (933.9)
.Time interval generator (clock) (934)
..Fixed (934.1)
..Multiple rates (934.2)
..Variable rates (934.3)
..Disable (934.51) •
..Expanding/stretching (934.61) •
..Frequency control (934.71) •
..Other specific time interval generator
   (934.4)
.Transmission medium (935)
..Electromagnetic (935.1)
..Line/link (935.2)
...Bidirectional (935.3)
...Bus (935.4)
....Arbitration (935.41) •
....Driver (935.42) •
....Decentralized control (935.43) •
....Input/output (935.44) •
....Construction (935.45) •
.....Plural (935.46) •
.....Variable width (935.47) •
.....Extension (935.48) •
.....Segmented (935.49) •
.....Ring (935.51) •
......Logical (935.52) •
......Physical (935.53) •
....Optical (935.54) •
....Other specific bus medium (935.55) •
...Coax (935.5)
...With separate data and control
   (935.6)
...Other specific line/link (935.7)
.Typewriter/TTY (936)

GENERIC DEVICE
.Other specific generic device (936.1)
GENERIC OPERATION
.Arbitration (937.01) *
.Arithmetical (937.1)
..Addition/subtraction (937.2)
..Division (937.3)
..Multiplication (937.4)
..Statistics (937.5)
..Trigonometry (937.6)
..Vector (937.7)
..Other specific arithmetical operation
    (937.8)
.Branching (938)
..Conditional (938.1)
..Lookahead (938.2)
..Unconditional (938.3)
..Other specific branching operation
    (938.4)
.Buffer function (939)
..Alternate load/unload (939.1)
..Formatting (939.2)
..With Input/Output device (939.3)
..Rate control (939.4)
..Serial/parallel conversion (939.5)
..Status checks (939.6)
..Simultaneous load/unload (939.81) *
..Other specific buffer function
    operation (939.7)
.Communication, interdevice (940)
..Accessing/Polling (940.1)
...Common bus (940.2)
...Concatenated/chained (940.3)
...Direct (940.4)
...Loop (940.5)
...Address/name table (940.71) *
...Token (940.8) *
...Mailbox (940.9) *
...Semaphore (940.91) *
...Tree/network (940.92) *
...Other specific accessing/polling
    operation (940.6)
..Interconnection (940.61) *
...Local area network (LAN) (940.62) *
...Ring (940.63) *
...Nodal network (940.64) *
...Star coupled (940.65) *
...Systolic array (940.66) *
...Hypercube (940.67) *
...Other specific interconnection
    (940.68) *
..Interrupt (941)
...Condition controlled (941.1)
...Fixed priority (941.2)
...Multiple level priority (941.3)
...Queued/table (941.4)
...Time controlled (941.5)
...Variable priority (941.6)
...Lockout (941.8) *
...Snapshot (941.9) *
...Daisy chained (941.91) *

...Other specific interrupt operation
    (941.7)
...Protocol/handshaking (940.81) *
....Answer-back/status (937)
..Multiplexed (942)
...Time division (942.03) *
...Between memories (942.04) *
...Between processors (942.05) *
...Between devices (942.06) *
...Between processes (942.07) *
...Packet switching (942.08) *
...Timeshared/Timeslot/Session (942.1)
..Other specific communication
    interdevice operation (942.2)
.Control, interdevice (942.3)
..Master/slave (942.4)
..Task assignment/Scheduling (942.5)
...Self-configuration (942.51)
..Other specific interdevice control
    operation (942.6)
.Counting (942.7)
.Data flow (942.79) *
.Decoding (942.8)
.Error/fault detection/prevention
    (943.9)
..Alternate/backup (943.91)
...Concurrent operation (943.92)
...With element substitution (944)
...Periodic operation (944.1)
...Redundant elements (944.2)
...Other specific alternate/backup
    operation (944.3)
..Arithmetic/logic (944.4)
.Data encode/decode (944.5)
..Execution sequence control (944.6)
..Fault tolerant/reconfigurable (944.61)
    *
.Input/output (944.7)
.Intermittent/transient errors (944.8)
.Monitor/error circuitry (944.9)
.Noise (944.91) *
.Storage addressing (944.92) *
.With automatic recovery (945)
...Repeated operations (945.1)
...Other specific automatic recovery
    operation (945.2)
.Data save (945.3)
..With fault isolation (945.4)
.Operator controlled (945.5)
.Parity/validity (945.6)
.Program controlled (945.7)
.Skew correction (945.8)
.Synchronization (945.9)
..Verification (946)
..Other specific error/fault
    detection/prevention operation
    (946.1)
.Instruction/program (946.2)
..Chained/linked (946.3)
..Hardwired (946.4)
.Macro (946.5)

364-16

CLASS 364 ELECTRICAL COMPUTERS AND DATA PROCESSING SYSTEMS

DECEMBER 1993

GENERIC OPERATION
.Instruction/program (946.2)
..Micro (946.6)
..Modify (946.7)
..Repeat (946.8)
..Other specific instruction/program
   operation (946.9)
.Logical (947)
..AND/OR/other logic (947.1)
..Compare (947.2)
..Invert (947.3)
..Mask (947.4)
..Sense special identifiers (947.5)
..Shift/rotate (947.6)
..Other specific logical operation
   (947.7)
.Lookahead/prefetch (948)
.Multimode (948.1)
.Multi-tasking (948.11) *
.Overlapping/Simultaneous/Concurrent
   operations (948.3)
..Simultaneous read/write (948.31) *
..Plural process (948.32) *
..External device (948.33)
.Pipeline (948.34) *
.Power control (948.4)
..Failure (948.5)
..On demand (948.6)
..Partial (948.7)
..Reduction (948.8)
..Sequenced (948.9)
..Other specific power control operation
   (948.91)
.Programmable (949)
..Micro program (949.1)
..Other specific programmable operation
   (949.2)
.Real time (949.3)
.Reconfigurable (949.4)
.Routing (949.91) *
..Static (949.92) *
..Dynamic (949.93) *
..Optimizing (949.94) *
.Sampled data (949.5) *
..Security (918.7)
..Encryption/Decryption (949.71)
..Copy protection (949.81) *
..Other specific security measure
   (949.96) *
.Stochastic process (949.6)
.Time control (950)
..Asynchronous (950.1)
..Cycle control/steal (950.2)
..Synchronous (950.3)
..Time delay (950.4)
..External cycle (950.61) *
..Other specific time control operation
   (950.5)
.Transfer register to register (951)
.Transform (951.1)
..Complement (951.2)

..Compress/expand (951.3)
..Other specific transform operation
   (951.4)
.Variable length (951.5) *
.Zero supression (951.6) *
SPECIFIC STORAGE ELEMENT
.Dynamic (952)
..Disc (952.1)
..Drum (952.2)
..Film/fiche (952.3)
..Optical (952.31) *
..Tape (952.4)
...Cartridge/cassette (952.5)
...Magnetic (952.6)
...Paper (952.7)
...Other specific dynamic tape element
    (952.8)
..Other specific dynamic storage element
   (952.9)
.Static (953)
..Bubble (953.1)
..Capacitor (953.2)
..Card (953.3)
..Core (953.4)
..CRT storage tube (953.5)
..Cryogenic (953.6)
..Delay line (953.7)
..Hologram (953.8)
..Semiconductor (954)
...Charge coupled (954.1)
...Integrated circuit (954.2)
...Other specific static semiconductor
    storage element (954.3)
..Thin film (954.4)
..Other specific static storage element
   (954.5)
STORAGE ACCESSING/ADDRESSING
.Address modification (955)
..Base and segment/tag and set (955.1)
..Bit insertion (955.2)
..Indexing (955.3)
..Prefixing (955.4)
..Table look-up (955.5)
..Other specific address modification
   (955.6)
.Associative (956)
..Matching data (956.1)
..User (956.2)
..Other specific associative storage
   accessing (956.3)
.Complementary (956.4)
..Digit (956.5)
..Other specific complementary storage
   accessing (956.6)
.Group (957)
..Block/page (957.1)
...Replacement (957.8) *
...Prefetch (957.9) *
..Chip/module (957.2)
..Linked (957.3)
..Multiple instruction per word (957.4)

CLASS 364　ELECTRICAL COMPUTERS AND DATA PROCESSING SYSTEMS

DECEMBER 1993

STORAGE ACCESSING/ADDRESSING
.Group (957)
..Multiple location per access (957.5)
..Queue/stack (957.6)
..Other specific group
    accessing/addressing (957.7)
.Key/partial (958)
..Key (958.1)
..Masking (958.2)
..Word/byte field (958.3)
..Other specific key/partial accessing
    (958.4)
.Multiple mode (958.5)
.Multiplex (959)
.Random (959.1)
..Shortest distance (959.2)
..Track/sector identification (959.3)
..Other specific random accessing
    (959.4)
.Sequential (960)
..Chained (960.1)
..Counter controlled (960.2)
..Nonunit increment/decrement (960.3)
..Timer controlled (960.4)
..Tree structured (960.5)
..Unit increment/decrement (960.6)
..Other specific sequential accessing
    (960.7)
.Substituted (961)
..Address transparency (961.4) *
.Variable length (961.1)
.Virtual (961.2)
.Other specific storage-
    accessing/addressing (961.3)
STORAGE MANAGEMENT
.File maintenance/operation (962)
..Insert/Delete/Update (962.1)
..Merge/collate (962.2)
..Sort (962.3)
..Other specific file
    maintenance/operation (962.4)
.Information retrieval (963)
..By content (963.1)
..By location (963.2)
..By table lookup/linking (963.3)
..Of film/document (963.4)
..Other specific information retrieval
    (963.5)
.Plural memory configuration (964)
..Data store and program store (964.1)
..Fast store and slow store (964.2)
...Bypass (964.21) *
...Instruction (964.22) *
...Data (964.23) *
...Instruction prefetch (964.24) *
...Address (964.25) *
...Pipeline (964.26) *
...Common/shared (964.27) °
...Parallel (964.28) *
...Variable length (964.29) *
...Dual ported (964.31) *

...Plural (964.32) *
...Interleaved (964.33) *
...Update (964.34) *
....Store through (964.341) *
....Nonstore through (964.342) *
...Multilevel (964.343) *
..Main memory and external bulk store
    (964.3)
..Main memory and I/O local store
    (964.4)
..Main memory and intermediate store
    (964.5)
..With memory to memory transfer (964.6)
..Plural main memories (964.7)
.Refresh (964.9) *
.Self-clocking record sensing (964.8)
.Single memory configuration (965)
..Compound type (965.1)
..Logic in memory (965.2)
..With memory to memory transfer (965.3)
..Multiported (965.9) *
..Queued/stacked (965.4)
..Read only/micro program (965.5)
..Recirculating (965.6)
..Shifting (965.7)
..PROM/EPROM/EEPROM (965.76) *
..PLA/PAL (965.77) *
..Volatile (965.78) *
..Nonvolatile (965.79) *
..Other specific memory management
    (965.8)
.Specific storage encoding/decoding
    technique (966)
.Storage assignment (966.1)
..Hierarchical (966.2)
..Interleaved/interlaced (966.3)
..Mapped/partitioned (966.4)
..Redun:... information (966.5)
.Resolution between memories (966.6)
.Resolution within single memory
    (966.7)
...Other specific storage assignment
    (966.8)
.Storage dedication (967)
..Input/output device (967.1)
..User (967.2)
..Resource allocation (967.4) *
...Free storage allocation (967.5) *
..Other specific storage dedication
    (967.3)
.Storage medium controller (968)
.Storage medium preparation (968.1)
..Key to card/tape/disc (968.2)
..Other specific storage medium
    preparation (968.3)
.Storage protection (969)
..Comparison of boundary address(es)
    (969.1)
..Locked/unlocked (removable) (969.2)
.Unauthorized access (969.4) *

364-18

CLASS 364   ELECTRICAL COMPUTERS AND DATA PROCESSING SYSTEMS

DECEMBER 1993

STORAGE MANAGEMENT
.Storage protection (969)
..Other specific storage protection
    (969.3)
.Storage reconfiguration (970)
..Defective storage substitution (970.1)
..Expansion (970.5) •
..Relocatable (970.2)
..Variable length (970.3)
..Other specific storage reconfiguration
    (970.4)
.Storage status (971)
.Other specific storage management
    (971.1)
PROGRAMMING SYSTEMS
.Artificial intelligence (972) •
..Natural language interface (972.1) •
..Expert system (972.2) •
...Rule based (972.3) •
..Neural network (972.4) •
.Compiler (973) •
.Data base system (974) •
..Model (974.1) •
...Network (974.2) •
...Hierarchical (974.3) •
...Relational (974.4) •
...Entity attribute (974.5) ∘
..Query (974.6) •
..Distributed (974.7) •
.Dictionary (975) •
.Document or display preparation (943)
..Insertion/deletion/correction (943.1)
..Justification/hyphenation (943.2)
..Photocomposing (943.3)
..Typesetting (943.4)
..Spelling check (943.41) •
..Synonym (943.42) •
..Word processing (943.43) •
..Text processor/formatter (943.44) •
..Other specific document or display
    preparation operation (943.5)
.Downloading/uploading (975.1) •
.Initialization/bootstrap program
    (975.2) •
.Kernal (975.4) •
.Load balancing (975.5) •
.Operating system (976) •
..Host (976.1) •
..Guest (976.2) •
..Plural (976.3) •
..Recovery (976.4) •
.Operator prompting/guidance (948.2)
..Menu driven (948.21) •
..User friendly (948.22) •
.Petri net (976.5) •
.Programming language (977) ∘
..Graphic (977.1) •
..Nonprocedural (977.2) •
..Dialogue (977.3) •
.State machine (977.5) •

.Virtual (978) •
..Machine (978.1) •
..Operating system (978.2) •
..Terminal (978.3) •

APPENDIXES

596

CLASS 395 INFORMATION PROCESSING SYSTEM ORGANIZATION

395-1

DECEMBER 1993

CLASS 395   INFORMATION PROCESSING SYSTEM ORGANIZATION

DECEMBER 1993

	ARTIFICIAL INTELLIGENCE	126	...Lighting/shading
	.Robot control	127	...Space transformation
81	..Combined with knowledge processing (e.g., natural language system)	128	..Adjusting resolution or level of detail
82	..Plural controlled devices or plural nonvision controlling devices	129	..Surface detail/characteristic
83	...Plural robots	130	...Texture
84	...Plural processors	131	...Color
85	..Specific enhancing or modifying techniques (e.g., adaptive control)	132	...Intensity
86	...Coordinate transformation	133	..Object processing
87	...Interpolation	134	...Clipping
88	...Programmed data (e.g., path) modified by sensed data	135	...Merge/overlay
89	...Compensation or calibration	136	...Affine
90	...Collision prevention	137	...Rotation
91	...Overload prevention	138	...Translation
92	...Based on user input	139	...Scaling
93	..With particular sensor	140	..Generating graphs
94	...Vision sensor (e.g., camera, photocell, etc.)	141	..Generating shapes
95	..With control of force	142	...Curves
96	..With control of robot torque	143	...Lines
97	..Using particular manipulator orientation computations (e.g., vector/matrix calculations)	144	..Text
98	..Using Jacobian computations	145	...Document
99	..With particular operator interface (e.g., teaching box, digitizer, tablet, pendant, dummy arm)	146	....Edit document
		147	....With graphics
		148	....Format control
		149	....Form filling
100	DATA PRESENTATION/COMPUTER GRAPHICS (E.G., IMAGE, GRAPHICS, TEXT)	150	.Font (i.e., character generation)
101	.Static presentation processing (e.g., for printers)	151	...Changing particular character
102	..Size or scale control	152	..Animation
103	..Plotters	153	.Plural simultaneous presentations
104	..Plural marking means	154	..Multimedia
105	..Position or velocity determined	155	.Operator interface (interactive)
106	..Specific to image source	156	...Menu
107	..Flying dot (e.g., laser beam)	157	..Window
108	..Dot matrix array (e.g., printheads)	158	...Priority
109	..Attribute control	159	.Icon
110	..Character or font	160	.Hierarchical
111	..Details of medium positioning (e.g., movement to or from presentation location of medium)	161	..For specific applications
112	..Emulation or plural modes	162	.Computer display processing hardware
113	..Data corruption, power interruption, or print prevention	163	..Plural processors
114	..With communications (e.g., data compression, data expansion, plural devices)	164	..Memory
		165	...Reconfigurable memory
		166	..Addressing
115	..With memory	200	TRANSMISSION OF INFORMATION AMONG MULTIPLE COMPUTER SYSTEMS
116	...Page or frame memory	250	BUFFERING FUNCTIONS
117	..Details of image placement or content	275	I/O PROCESSING
118	.Presentation processing	325	SYSTEM INTERCONNECTIONS
119	..Three-dimension	375	INSTRUCTION PROCESSING
120	...Solid modelling	400	STORAGE ADDRESS FORMATION
121	...Hidden line/surface determining	425	STORAGE ACCESSING AND CONTROL
122	....Z buffer (depth buffer)	500	COMPATIBILITY, SIMULATION, OR EMULATION OF SYSTEM COMPONENTS
123	...Tessellation	550	TIMING
124	...Voxel	575	RELIABILITY
125	...Mapping image onto surface of 3D object	600	DATABASE OR FILE MANGEMENT SYSTEM
		650	PROCESSING (TASK) MANAGEMENT
		700	SYSTEM UTILITIES
		725	ACCESS CONTROL PROCESSING
		750	POWER CONTROL
		775	INTERNAL CONTROL

CLASS 395   INFORMATION PROCESSING SYSTEM ORGANIZATION

800	PROCESSING ARCHITECTURE
	••••••••••••••••••••••••••••••
	CROSS-REFERENCE ART COLLECTIONS
	••••••••••••••••••••••••••••••
900	FUZZY LOGIC
901	SPECIAL ROBOT STRUCTURAL ELEMENTS
902	APPLICATIONS USING AI WITH DETAILS OF THE AI SYSTEM
903	.Control
904	..Manufacturing or machines (e.g., agricultural machinery, machine tools, robots)
905	..Vehicle or aerospace
906	..Process plants
907	...Power plants
908	..Electronic or computer (internal or network) circuits
909	..Communication
910	..Elevators
911	.Nonmedical diagnostics
912	..Manufacturing or machines (e.g., agricultural machinery, machine tools, robots)
913	..Vehicle or aerospace
914	..Process plants
915	...Power plants
916	.Electronic or computer (internal or network) circuits
917	..Communications
918	..Elevators
919	.Designing, planning, programming, CAD, CASE
920	..Simulation
921	..Layout (e.g., circuit, construction)
922	..Computer program préparation
923	..Construction
924	.Medical
925	.Business
926	..Time management
927	.Education or instruction
928	.Earth sciences
929	..Geological (e.g., seismology)
930	..Environment
931	...Weather
932	.Mathematics, science, or engineering
933	.Law, law enforcement, or government
934	.Information retrieval or information management

APPENDIX C

LETTER OF THOMAS JEFFERSON TO ISAAC MCPHERSON DATED AUGUST 13, 1813

To Mr. Isaac McPherson.

Monticello, August 13, 1813

Sir,—Your letter of August 3d asking information on the subject of Mr. Oliver Evans' exclusive right to the use of what he calls his Elevators, Conveyers, and Hopper-boys, has been duly received. My wish to see new inventions encouraged, and old ones brought again into useful notice, has made me regret the circumstances which have followed the expiration of his first patent. I did not expect the retrospection which has been given to the reviving law. For although the second proviso seemed not so clear as it ought to have been, yet it appeared susceptible of a just construction; and the retrospective one being contrary to natural right, it was understood to be a rule of law that where the words of a statute admit of two constructions, the one just and the other unjust, the former is to be given them. The first proviso takes care of those who had lawfully used Evans' improvements under the first patent; the second was meant for those who had lawfully erected and used them after that patent expired, declaring they "should not be liable to damages therefor." These words may indeed be restrained to uses already past, but as there is parity of reason for those to come, there should be parity of law. Every man should be protected in his lawful acts, and be certain that no *ex post facto* law shall punish or endamage him for them. But he is endamaged, if forbidden to use a machine lawfully erected, at considerable expense, unless he will pay a new and unexpected price for it. The proviso says that he who erected and used lawfully should not be liable to pay damages. But if the proviso had been omitted, would not the law, construed by natural equity, have said the same thing. In truth both provisos are useless. And shall useless provisos, inserted *pro majori cautela* only, authorize inferences against justice? The sentiment that *ex post facto* laws are against natural right, is so strong in the United States, that few, if any, of the State constitutions have failed to proscribe them. The federal constitution indeed interdicts them in criminal cases only; but they are equally unjust in civil as in criminal cases, and the omission of a caution which would have been right, does not justify the doing what is wrong. Nor ought it to be presumed that the legislature meant to use a phrase in an unjustifiable sense, if by rules of construction it can be ever strained to what is just. The law books abound with similar instances of the care the judges take of the public integrity. Laws, moreover, abridging the natural right of the citizen, should be restrained by rigorous constructions within their narrowest limits.

Your letter, however, points to a much broader question, whether what have received from Mr. Evans the new and proper name of Elevators, are of his invention. Because, if they are not, his patent gives him no right to obstruct others in the use of what they possessed before. I assume it is a Lemma, that it is the invention of the machine itself, which is to give a patent right, and not the application of it to any particular purpose, of which it is susceptible. If one person invents a knife convenient for pointing our pens, another cannot have a patent right for the same knife to point our pencils. A compass was invented for navigating the sea; another could not have a patent right for using it to survey land. A machine for threshing *wheat* has been invented in Scotland; a second person cannot get a patent right for the same machine to thresh *oats,* a third *rye,* a fourth *peas,* a fifth *clover,* &c. A string of buckets is invented and used for raising water, ore &c., can a second have a patent right to the same machine for raising wheat, a third oats, a fourth rye, a fifth peas, &c? The question then whether such a string of buckets was invented first by Oliver Evans, is a mere question of fact in mathematical history. Now, turning to such books only as I happen to possess, I find abundant proof that this simple machinery has been in use from time immemorial. Doctor Shaw, who visited Egypt and the Barbary coast in the years 1727-8-9, in the margin of his map of Egypt, gives us the figure of what he calls a Persian wheel, which is a string of round cups or buckets hanging on a pulley, over which they revolved, bringing up water from a well and delivering it into a trough above. He found this used at Cairo, in a well 264 feet deep, which the inhabitants believe to have been the work of the patriarch Joseph. Shaw's travels, 341, Oxford edition of 1738 in folio, and the Universal History, I. 416, speaking of the manner of watering the higher lands in Egypt, says, "formerly they made use of Archimedes's screw, thence named the Egyptian pump, but they now generally use wheels (wallowers) which carry a rope or chain of earthen pots holding about seven or eight quarts apiece, and draw the water from the canals. There are besides a vast number of wells in Egypt, from which the water is drawn in the same manner to water the gardens and fruit trees; so that it is no exaggeration to say, that there are in Egypt above 200,000 oxen daily employed in this labor." Shaw's name of Persian wheel has been since given more particularly to a wheel with buckets, either fixed or suspended on pins, at its periphery. Mortimer's husbandry, I. 18, Duhamel III. II., Ferguson's Mechanic's plate, XIII; but his figure, and the verbal description of the Universal History, prove that the string of buckets is meant under that name. His figure differs from Evans' construction in the circumstances of the buckets being round, and strung through their bottom on a chain. But it is the principle, to wit, a string of buckets, which constitutes the invention, not the form of the buckets, round, square, or hexagon; nor the manner of attaching them, nor the material of the connecting band, whether chain, rope, or leather. Vitruvius, L. x. c. 9, describes this machinery as a windlass, on which is a chain descending to the water, with vessels of copper attached to it; the windlass being turned, the chain moving on it will raise the vessel, which in passing over the windlass will empty the water they have brought up into a reservoir. And Perrault, in his edition of Vitruvius, Paris, 1684, fol. plates 61, 62, gives us three forms of these water elevators, in one of which the buckets are square, as Mr. Evans' are. Bossut, Histoire des Mathematiques, i. 86, says, "the drum wheel, the wheel with buckets and the *Chapelets,* are hydraulic machines which come to us from the ancients. But we are ignorant of the time when they began to be put into use." The *Chapelets* are the revolving bands of the buckets which Shaw calls the Persian wheel, the moderns a chain-pump, and Mr. Evans elevators. The next of my books in which I find these elevators is Wolf's Cours de Mathematiques, i. 370, and plate 1, Paris 1747, 8vo; here are two forms. In one of them the buckets are square, attached to two chains, passing over a cylinder or wallower at top, and under another at bottom, by which they are made to revolve. It is a nearly exact representation of Evans' Elevators. But a more exact one is to be seen in Desagulier's Experimental Philosophy, ii. plate 34; in the Encyclopedie de Diderot et D'Alembert, 8vo edition of Lansanne, 1st volume of plates in the four subscribed Hydraulique. Norie, is one where round eastern pots are tied by their collars between two endless ropes suspended on a revolving lantern or wallower. This is said to have been used for raising ore out of a mine. In a book which I do not possess, L'Architecture Hidraulique de Belidor, the 2d volume of which is said [De la Lande's continuation of Montuclas' Historie de Mathematiques, iii. 711] to contain a detail of all the pumps, ancient and modern, hydraulic machines, fountains, wells, &c, I have no doubt this Perisan wheel, chain pump, chapelets, elevators, by whichever name you choose to call it, will be found in various forms. The last book I have to quote for it is Prony's Architecture Hydraulique i., Avertissement vii., and §§ 648, 649, 650. In the latter of which passages he observes that the first idea which occurs for raising water is to lift it in a bucket by hand. When the water lies too deep to be reached by hand, the bucket is suspended by a chain and let down over a pulley or windlass. If it be desired to raise a continued stream of water, the simplest means which offers itself to the mind is to attach to an endless chain or cord a number of pots or buckets, so disposed that, the chain being suspended on a lanthorn or wallower above, and plunged in water below, the buckets may descend and ascend alternately, filling themselves at bottom and emptying at a certain height above, so as to give a constant stream. Some years before the date of Mr. Evans' patent, a Mr. Martin of Caroline county in this State, constructed a drill-plough, in which he used the band of buckets for elevating the grain from the box into the funnel, which let them down into the furrow. He had bands with different sets of buckets adapted to the size of peas, of turnip seed, &c. I have used this machine for sowing Benni seed also, and propose to have a band of buckets for drilling Indian Corn, and another for wheat. Is it possible that in doing this I shall infringe Mr. Evans' patent? That I can be debarred of any use to which I might have applied my drill, when I bought it, by a patent issued after I bought it?

These verbal descriptions, applying so exactly to Mr. Evans' elevators, and the drawings exhibited to the eye, flash conviction both on reason and the senses that there is nothing new in these elevators but their being strung together on a strap of leather. If this strap of leather be an invention, entitling the inventor to a patent right, it can only extend to the strap, and the use of the string of buckets must remain free to be connected by chains, ropes, a strap of hempen girthing, or any other substance except leather. But, indeed, Mr. Martin had before used the strap of leather.

The screw of Archimedes is as ancient, at least, as the age of that mathematician, who died more than 2,000 years ago. Diodorus Siculus speaks of it, L. i., p. 21, and L. v., p. 217, of Stevens' edition of 1559, folio; and Vitruvius, xii. The cutting of its spiral worm into sections for conveying flour or grain, seems to have been an invention of Mr. Evans, and to be a fair subject of a patent right. But it cannot take away from others the use of Archimedes' screw with its perpetual spiral, for any purposes of which it is susceptible.

The hopper-boy is an useful machine, and so far as I know, original.

It has been pretended by some, (and in England especially,) that inventors have a natural and exclusive right to their inventions, and not merely for their own lives, but inheritable to their heirs. But while it is a moot question whether the origin of any kind of property is derived from nature at all, it would be singular to admit a natural and even an hereditary right to inventors. It is agreed by those who have seriously considered the subject, that no individual has, of natural right, a separate property in an acre of land, for instance. By an universal law, indeed, whatever, whether fixed or movable, belongs to all men equally and in common, is the property for the moment of him who occupies it; but when he relinquishes the occupation, the property goes with it. Stable ownership is the gift of social law, and is given late in the progress of society. It would be curious then, if an idea, the fugitive fermentation of an individual brain, could, of natural right, be claimed in exclusive and stable property. If nature has made any one thing less susceptible than all others of exclusive property, it is the action of the thinking power called an idea, which an individual may exclusively possess as long as he keeps it to himself; but the moment it is divulged, it forces itself into the possession of every one, and the receiver cannot dispossess himself of it. Its peculiar character, too, is that no one possesses the less, because every other possesses the whole of it. He who receives an idea from me, receives instruction himself without lessening mine; as he who lights his taper at mine, receives light without darkening me. That ideas should freely spread from one to another over the globe, for the moral and mutual instruction of man, and improvement of his condition, seems to have been peculiarly and benevolently designed by nature, when she made them, like fire, expansible over all space, without lessening their density in any point, and like the air in which we breathe, move, and have our physical being, incapable of confinement or exclusive appropriation. Inventions then cannot, in nature, be a subject of property. Society may give an exclusive right to the profits arising from them, as an encouragement to men to pursue ideas which may produce utility, but this may or may not be done, according to the will and convenience of the society, without claim or complaint from any body. Accordingly, it is a fact, as far as I am informed, that England was, until we copied her, the only country on earth which ever, by a general law, gave a legal right to the exclusive use of an idea. In some other countries it is sometimes done, in a great case, and by a special and personal act, but, generally speaking, other nations have thought that these monopolies produce more embarrassment than advantage to society; and it may be observed that the nations which refuse monopolies of invention, are as fruitful as England in new and useful devices.

Considering the exclusive right to invention as given not of natural right, but for the benefit of society, I know well the difficulty of drawing a line between the things which are worth to the public the embarrassment of an exclusive patent, and those which are not. As a member of the patent board for several years, while the law authorized a board to grant or refuse patents, I saw with what slow progress a system of general rules could be matured. Some, however, were established by that board. One of these was, that a machine of which we were possessed, might be applied by every man to any use of which it is susceptible, and that this right ought not to be taken from him and given to a monopolist, because the first perhaps had occasion so to apply it. Thus a screw for crushing plaster might be employed for crushing corn-cobs. And a chain-pump for raising water might be used for raising wheat: this being merely a change of application. Another rule was that a change of material should not give title to a patent. As the making a ploughshare of cast rather than of wrought iron; a comb of iron instead of horn or of ivory, or the connecting buckets by a band of leather rather than of hemp or iron. A third was that a mere change of form should give no right to a patent, as a high-quartered shoe instead of a low one; a round hat instead of a three-square; or a square bucket instead of a round one. But for this rule, all the changes of fashion in dress would have been under the tax of patentees. These were among the rules which the uniform decisions of the board had already established, and under each of them Mr. Evans' patent would have been refused. First, because it was a mere change of application of the chain-pump, from raising water to raise wheat. Secondly, because the using a leathern instead of a hempen band, was a mere change of material; and thirdly, square buckets instead of round, are only a change of form, and the ancient forms, too, appear to have been indifferently square or round. But there were still abundance of cases which could not be brought under rule, until they should have presented themselves under all their aspects; and these investigations occupying more time of the members of the board than they could spare from higher duties, the whole was turned over to the judiciary, to be matured into a system, under which every one might know when his actions were safe and lawful. Instead of refusing a patent in the first instance, as the board was authorized to do, the patent in the first instance, as the board was authorized to do, the patent now issues of course, subject to be declared void on such principles as should be established by the courts of law. This business, however, is but little analogous to their course of reading, since we might in vain turn over all the lubberly volumes of the law to find a single ray which would lighten the path of the mechanic or the mathematician. It is more within the information of a board of academical professors, and a previous refusal of patent would better guard our citizens against harassment by law-suits. But

England had given it to her judges, and the usual predominancy of her examples carried it to ours.

It happened that I had myself a mill built in the interval between Mr. Evans' first and second patents. I was living in Washington, and left the construction to the mill-wright. I did not even know he had erected elevators, conveyers and hopper-boys until I learnt it by an application from Mr. Evans' agent for the patent price. Although I had no idea he had a right to it by law, (for no judicial decision had then been given,) yet I did not hesitate to remit to Mr. Evans the old and moderate patent price, which was what he then asked, from a wish to encourage even the useful revival of ancient inventions. But I then expressed my opinion of the law in a letter, either to Mr. Evans or to his agent.

I have thus, Sir, at your request, given you the facts and ideas which occur to me on this subject. I have done it without reserve, although I have not the pleasure of knowing you personally. In thus frankly committing myself to you, I trust you will feel it as a point of honor and candor, to make no use of my letter which might bring disquietude on myself. And particularly, I should be unwilling to be brought into any difference with Mr. Evans, whom, however, I believe too reasonable to take offence at an honest difference of opinion. I esteem him much, and sincerely wish him wealth and honor. I deem him a valuable citizen, of uncommon ingenuity and usefulness. And had I not esteemed still more the establishment of sound principles, I should now have been silent. If any of the matter I have offered can promote that object, I have no objection to its being so used; if it offers nothing new, it will of course not be used at all. I have gone with some minuteness into the mathematical history of the elevator, because it belongs to a branch of science in which, as I have before observed, it is not incumbent on lawyers to be learned; and it is possible, therefore, that some of the proofs I have quoted may have escaped on their former arguments. On the law of the subject I should not have touched, because more familiar to those who have already discussed it; but I wished to state my own view of it merely in justification of myself, my name and approbation being subscribed to the act. With these explanations, accept the assurance of my respect.

TABLE OF CASES

INDEX